Zits

UNDIVIDED INATTENTION

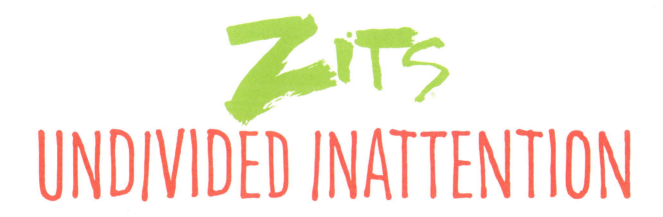

ALSO BY JERRY SCOTT AND JIM BORGMAN

Zits: Sketchbook 1
Growth Spurt: Zits Sketchbook 2
Don't Roll Your Eyes at Me, Young Man!: Zits Sketchbook 3
Are We an "Us"?: Zits Sketchbook 4
Zits Unzipped: Zits Sketchbook 5
Busted!: Zits Sketchbook 6
Road Trip: Zits Sketchbook 7
Teenage Tales: Zits Sketchbook No. 8
Thrashed: Zits Sketchbook No. 9
Pimp My Lunch: Zits Sketchbook No. 10
Are We Out of the Driveway Yet?: Zits Sketchbook No. 11
Rude, Crude, and Tattooed: Zits Sketchbook No. 12
Jeremy and Mom
Pierced
Lust and Other Uses for Spare Hormones
Jeremy & Dad
You're Making That Face Again
Drive!
Triple Shot, Double Pump, No Whip Zits
Zits en Concert
Peace, Love, and Wi-Fi
Zits Apocalypse
Extra Cheesy Zits
Dance Like Everybody's Watching!
Not Sparking Joy
Screentime

TREASURIES

Humongous Zits
Big Honkin' Zits
Zits: Supersized
Random Zits
Crack of Noon
Alternative Zits
My Bad
Sunday Brunch
What Was That All About?: 20 Years of Strips and Stories

GIFT BOOK

A Zits Guide to Living with Your Teenager

ZITS®

UNDIVIDED INATTENTION

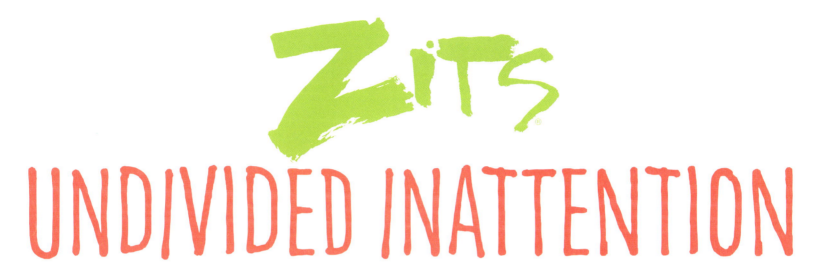

A ZITS® Treasury by Jerry Scott and Jim Borgman

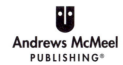

Andrews McMeel
PUBLISHING®

To Frances—Read this one slowly. You're all caught up.

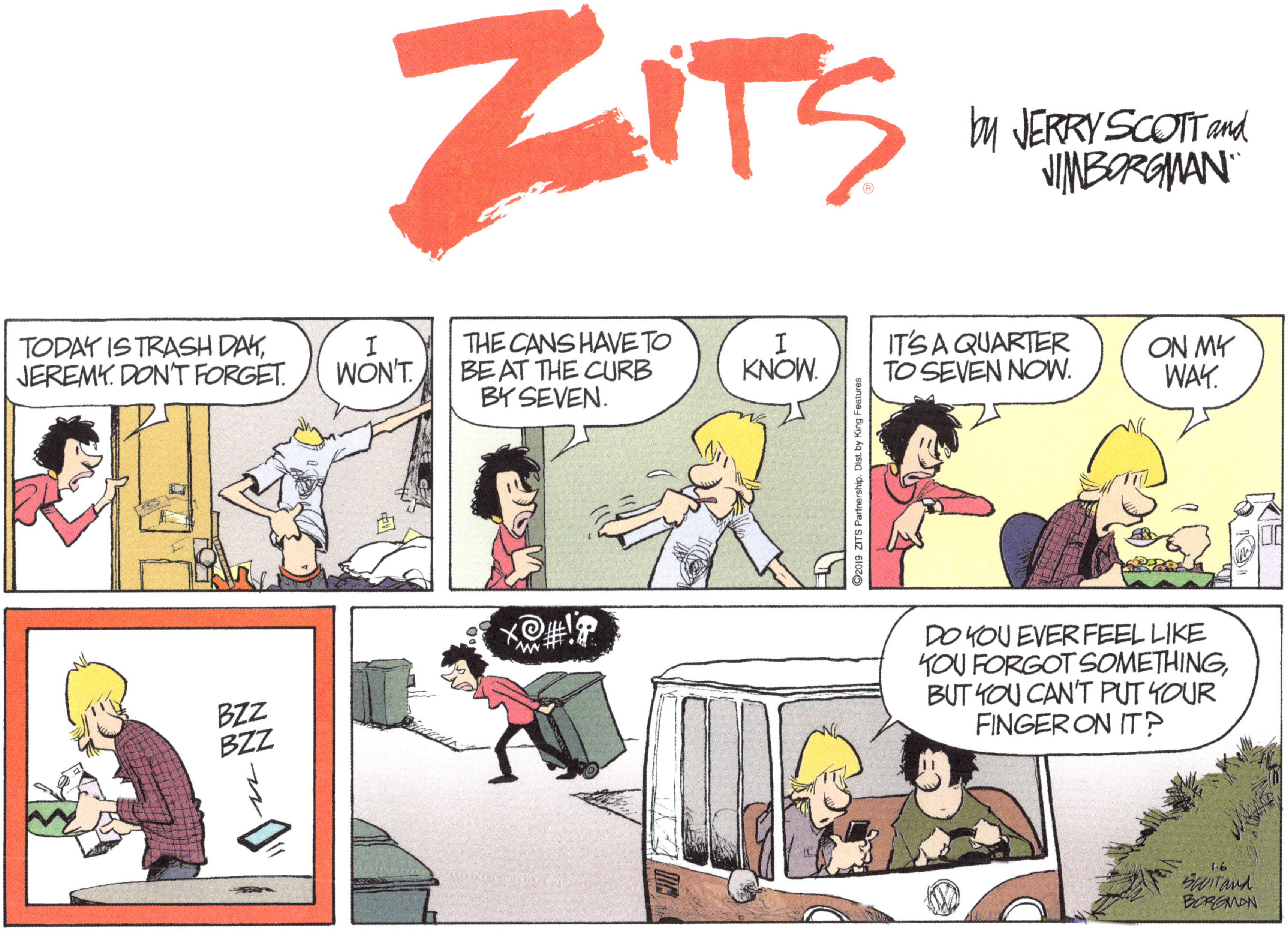
ZITS®
by JERRY SCOTT and JIM BORGMAN
TODAY IS TRASH DAY, JEREMY. DON'T FORGET.
I WON'T.
THE CANS HAVE TO BE AT THE CURB BY SEVEN.
I KNOW.
©2019 ZITS Partnership. Dist. by King Features
IT'S A QUARTER TO SEVEN NOW.
ON MY WAY.
BZZ BZZ
DO YOU EVER FEEL LIKE YOU FORGOT SOMETHING, BUT YOU CAN'T PUT YOUR FINGER ON IT?
1·6
SCOTT and BORGMAN

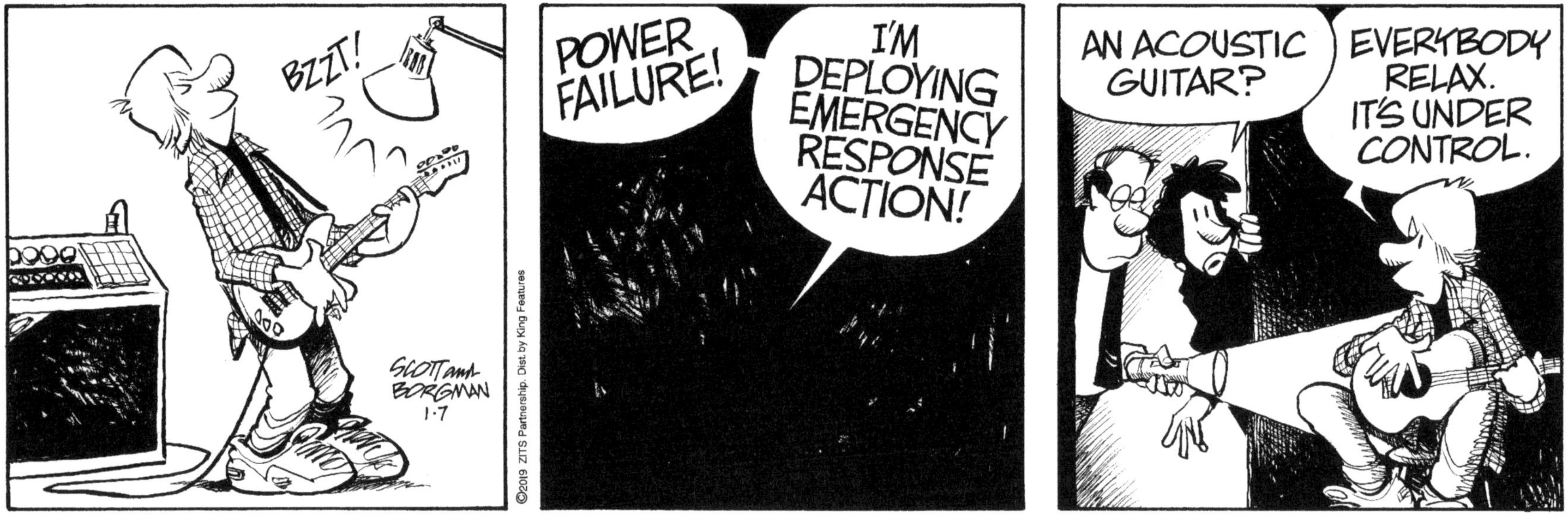
BZZT!
SCOTT and BORGMAN 1·7
©2019 ZITS Partnership. Dist. by King Features
POWER FAILURE!
I'M DEPLOYING EMERGENCY RESPONSE ACTION!
AN ACOUSTIC GUITAR?
EVERYBODY RELAX. IT'S UNDER CONTROL.

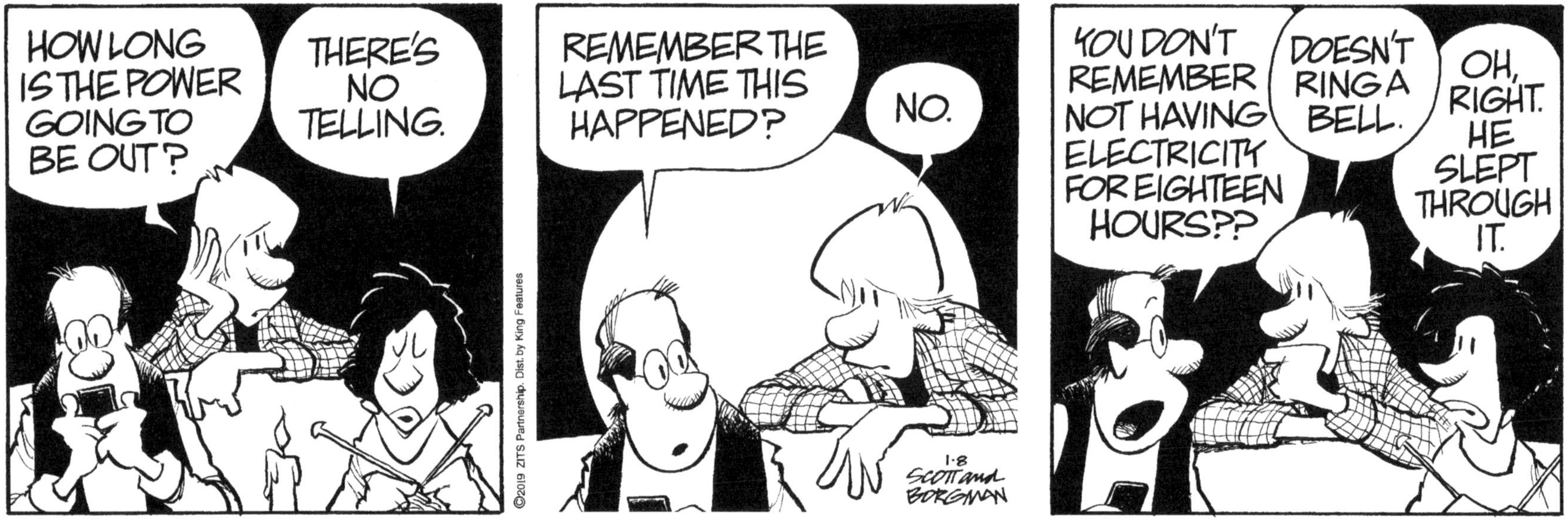
HOW LONG IS THE POWER GOING TO BE OUT?
THERE'S NO TELLING.
©2019 ZITS Partnership. Dist. by King Features
REMEMBER THE LAST TIME THIS HAPPENED?
NO.
1·8 SCOTT and BORGMAN
YOU DON'T REMEMBER NOT HAVING ELECTRICITY FOR EIGHTEEN HOURS??
DOESN'T RING A BELL.
OH, RIGHT. HE SLEPT THROUGH IT.

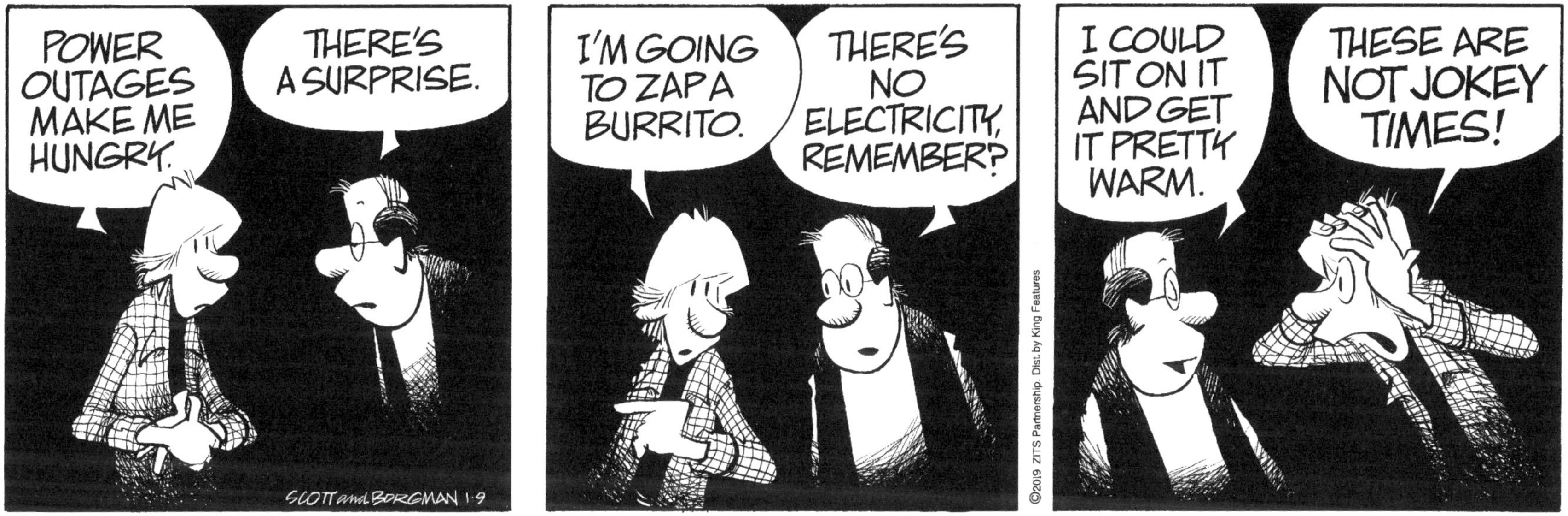
POWER OUTAGES MAKE ME HUNGRY.
THERE'S A SURPRISE.
SCOTT and BORGMAN 1·9
I'M GOING TO ZAP A BURRITO.
THERE'S NO ELECTRICITY, REMEMBER?
©2019 ZITS Partnership. Dist. by King Features
I COULD SIT ON IT AND GET IT PRETTY WARM.
THESE ARE NOT JOKEY TIMES!

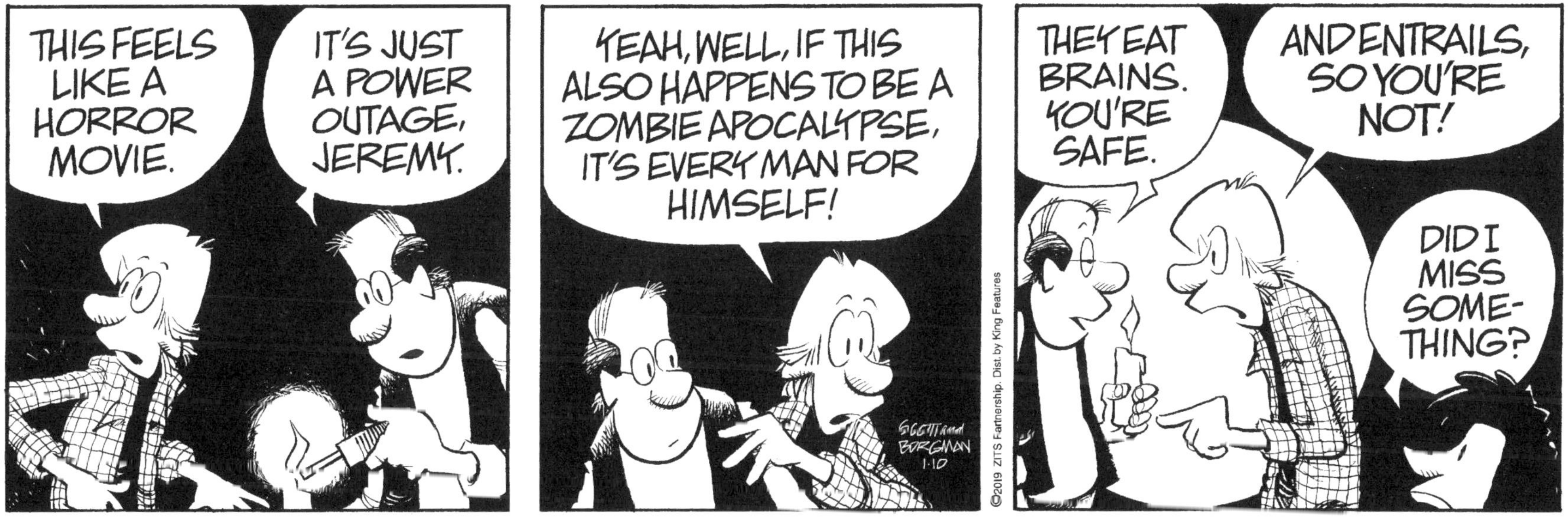
THIS FEELS LIKE A HORROR MOVIE.
IT'S JUST A POWER OUTAGE, JEREMY.
YEAH, WELL, IF THIS ALSO HAPPENS TO BE A ZOMBIE APOCALYPSE, IT'S EVERY MAN FOR HIMSELF!
SCOTT and BORGMAN 1·10
©2019 ZITS Partnership. Dist. by King Features
THEY EAT BRAINS. YOU'RE SAFE.
AND ENTRAILS, SO YOU'RE NOT!
DID I MISS SOME-THING?

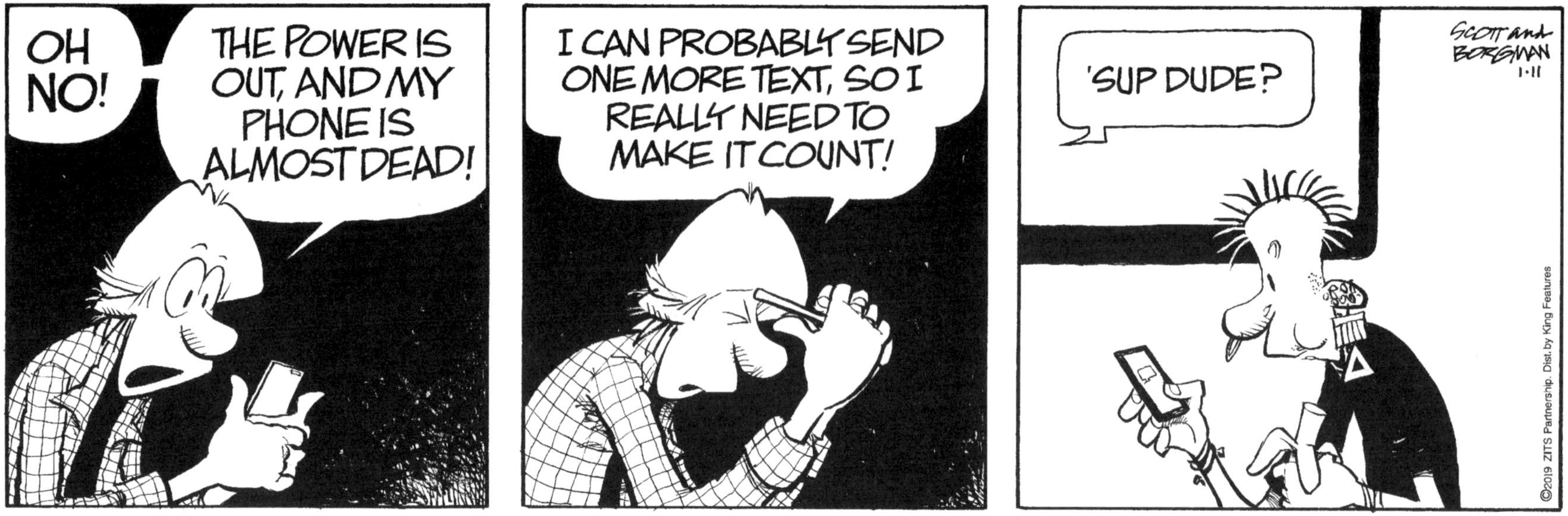
OH NO!
THE POWER IS OUT, AND MY PHONE IS ALMOST DEAD!
I CAN PROBABLY SEND ONE MORE TEXT, SO I REALLY NEED TO MAKE IT COUNT!
'SUP DUDE?
SCOTT AND BORGMAN 1·11
©2019 ZITS Partnership. Dist. by King Features

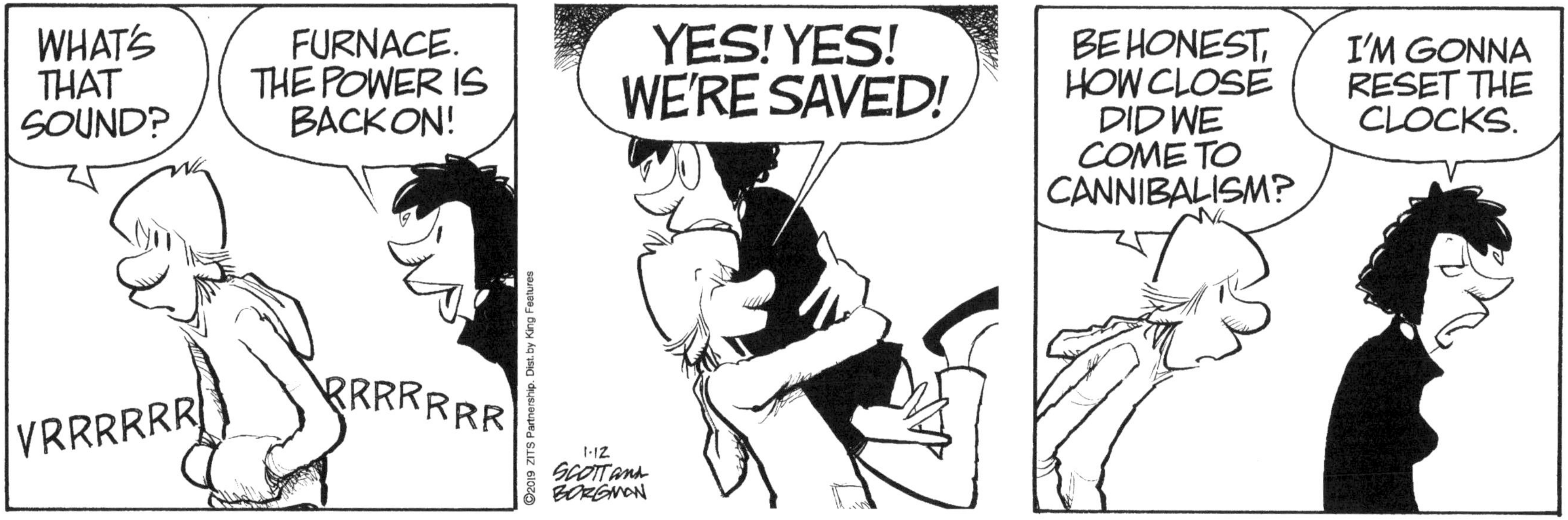
WHAT'S THAT SOUND?
FURNACE. THE POWER IS BACK ON!
VRRRRRRRRRRRRRRR
©2019 ZITS Partnership. Dist. by King Features
1·12 SCOTT AND BORGMAN
YES! YES! WE'RE SAVED!
BE HONEST, HOW CLOSE DID WE COME TO CANNIBALISM?
I'M GONNA RESET THE CLOCKS.

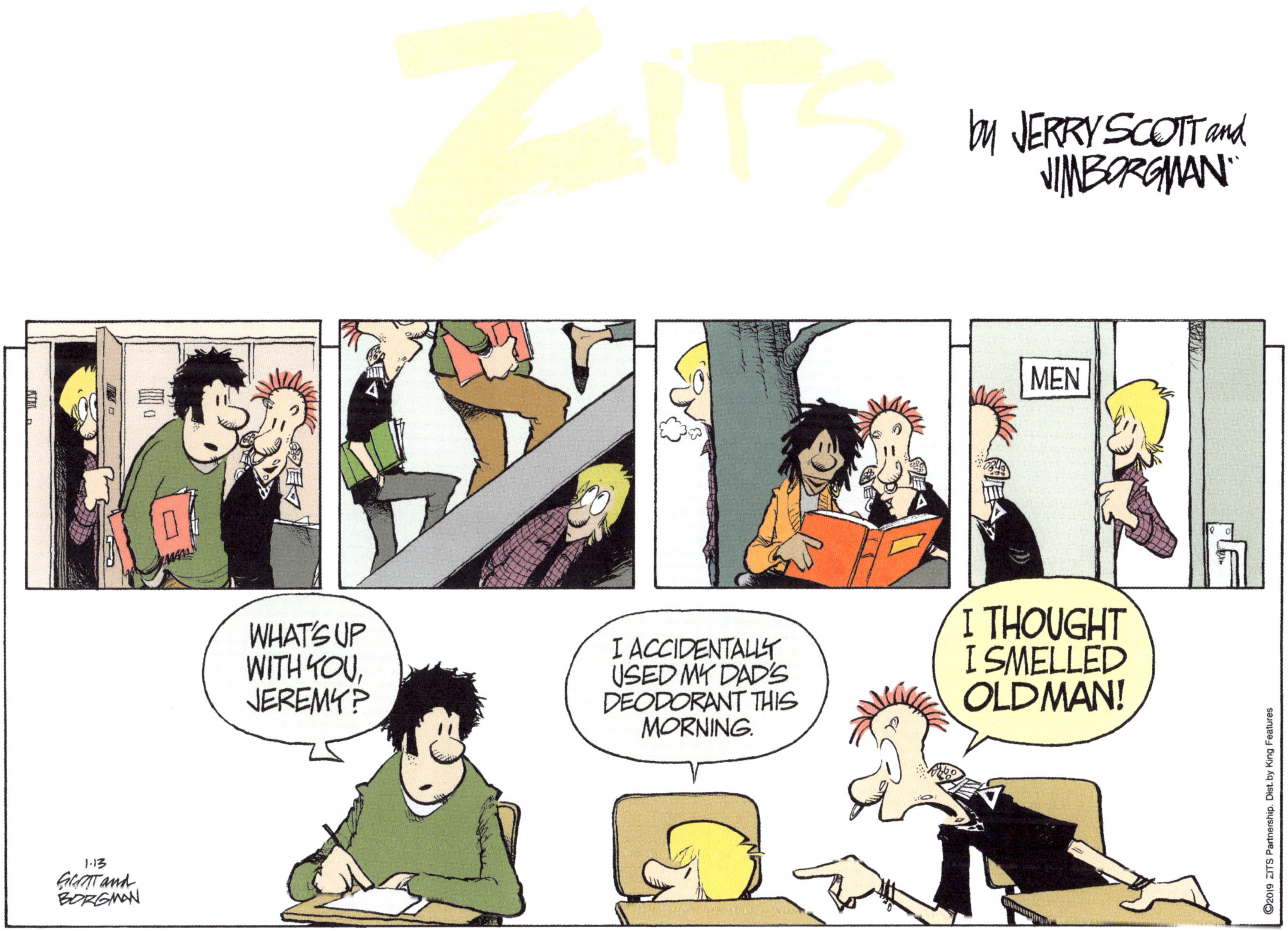

ZITS
by JERRY SCOTT and JIM BORGMAN
MEN
WHAT'S UP WITH YOU, JEREMY?
I ACCIDENTALLY USED MY DAD'S DEODORANT THIS MORNING.
I THOUGHT I SMELLED OLD MAN!
1-13 SCOTT and BORGMAN
©2019 ZITS Partnership. Dist. by King Features

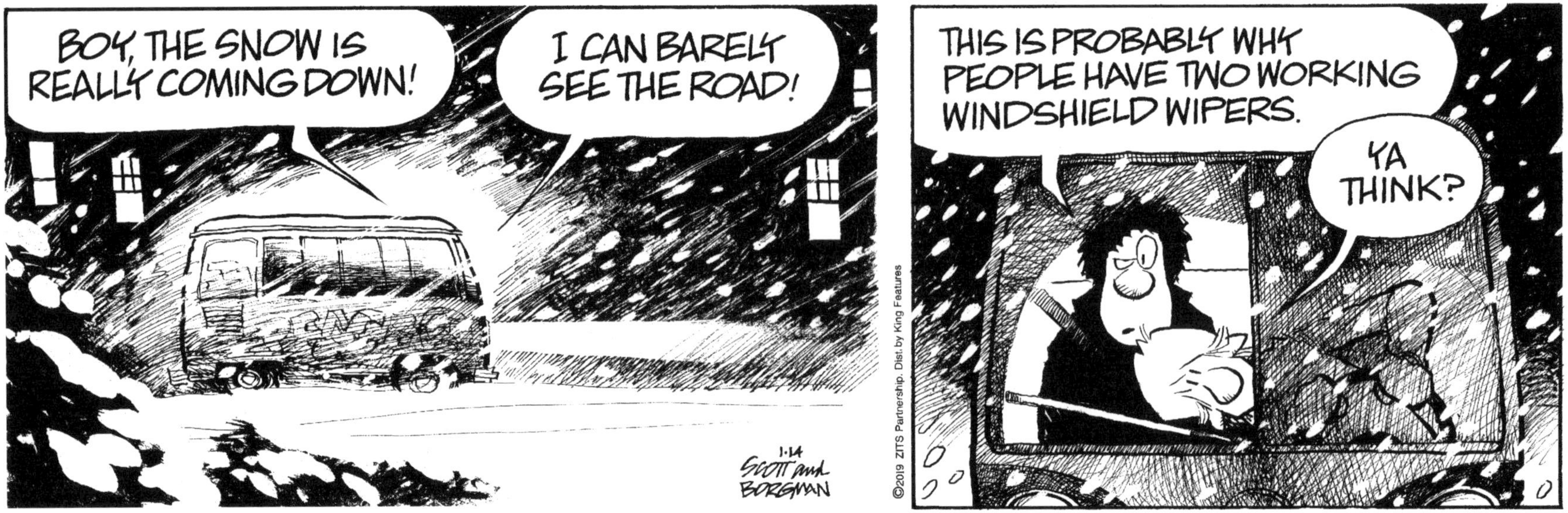
BOY, THE SNOW IS REALLY COMING DOWN!
I CAN BARELY SEE THE ROAD!
1·14 SCOTT and BORGMAN
©2019 ZITS Partnership. Dist. by King Features
THIS IS PROBABLY WHY PEOPLE HAVE TWO WORKING WINDSHIELD WIPERS.
YA THINK?

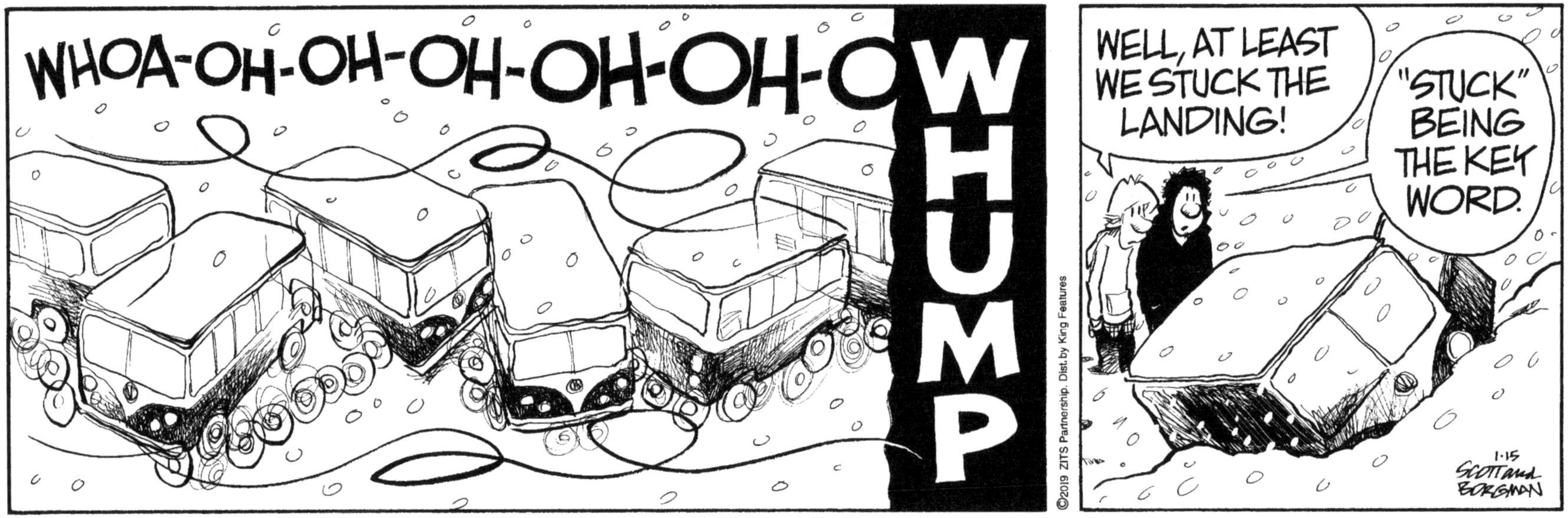
WHOA-OH-OH-OH-OH-OH-O
WHUMP
©2019 ZITS Partnership. Dist. by King Features
WELL, AT LEAST WE STUCK THE LANDING!
"STUCK" BEING THE KEY WORD.
1·15 SCOTT and BORGMAN

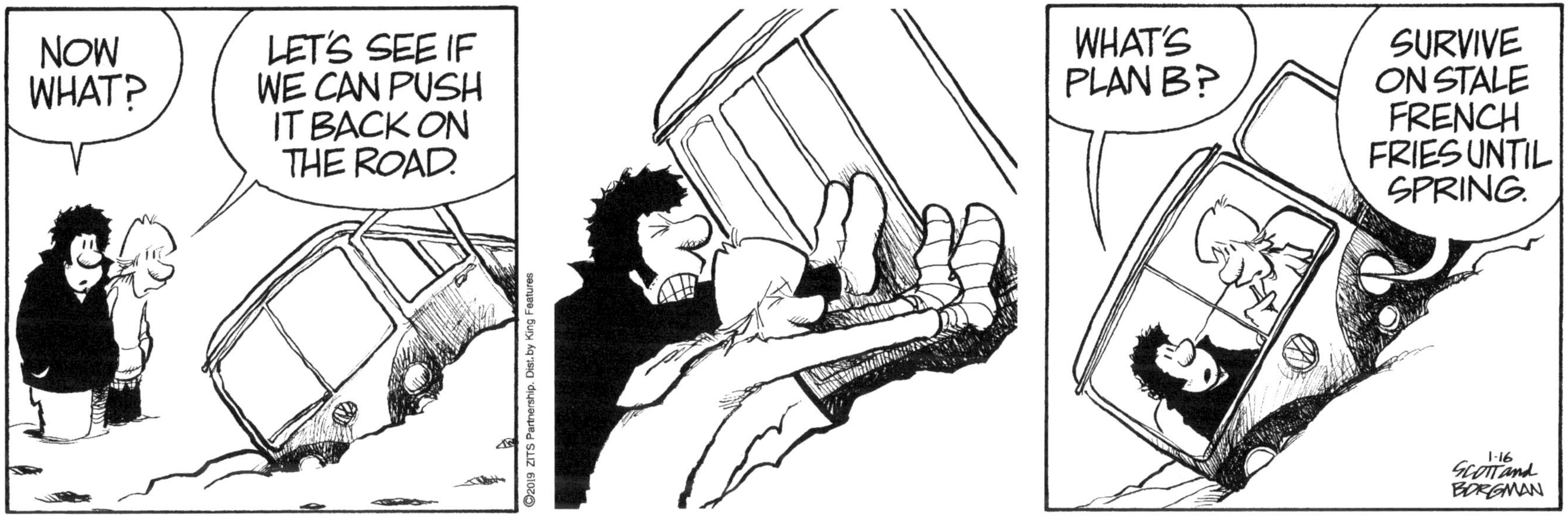
NOW WHAT?
LET'S SEE IF WE CAN PUSH IT BACK ON THE ROAD.
WHAT'S PLAN B?
SURVIVE ON STALE FRENCH FRIES UNTIL SPRING.
1-16 SCOTT and BORGMAN
©2019 ZITS Partnership. Dist. by King Features

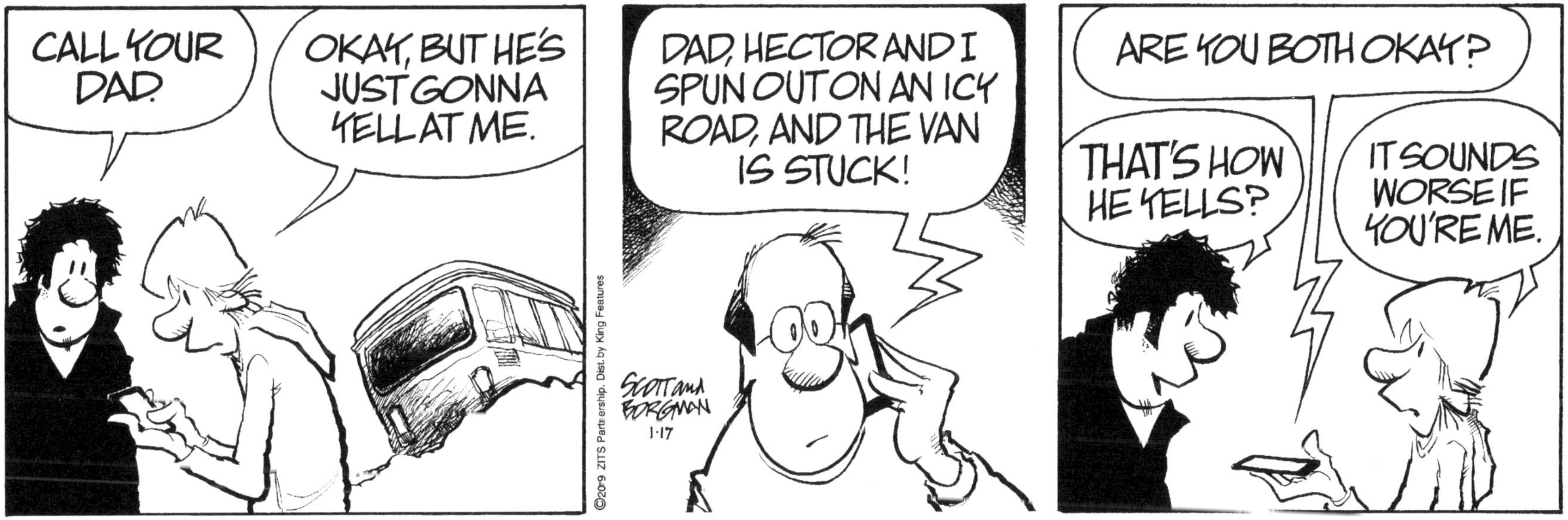
CALL YOUR DAD.
OKAY, BUT HE'S JUST GONNA YELL AT ME.
©2019 ZITS Partnership. Dist. by King Features
SCOTT and BORGMAN 1-17
DAD, HECTOR AND I SPUN OUT ON AN ICY ROAD, AND THE VAN IS STUCK!
ARE YOU BOTH OKAY?
THAT'S HOW HE YELLS?
IT SOUNDS WORSE IF YOU'RE ME.

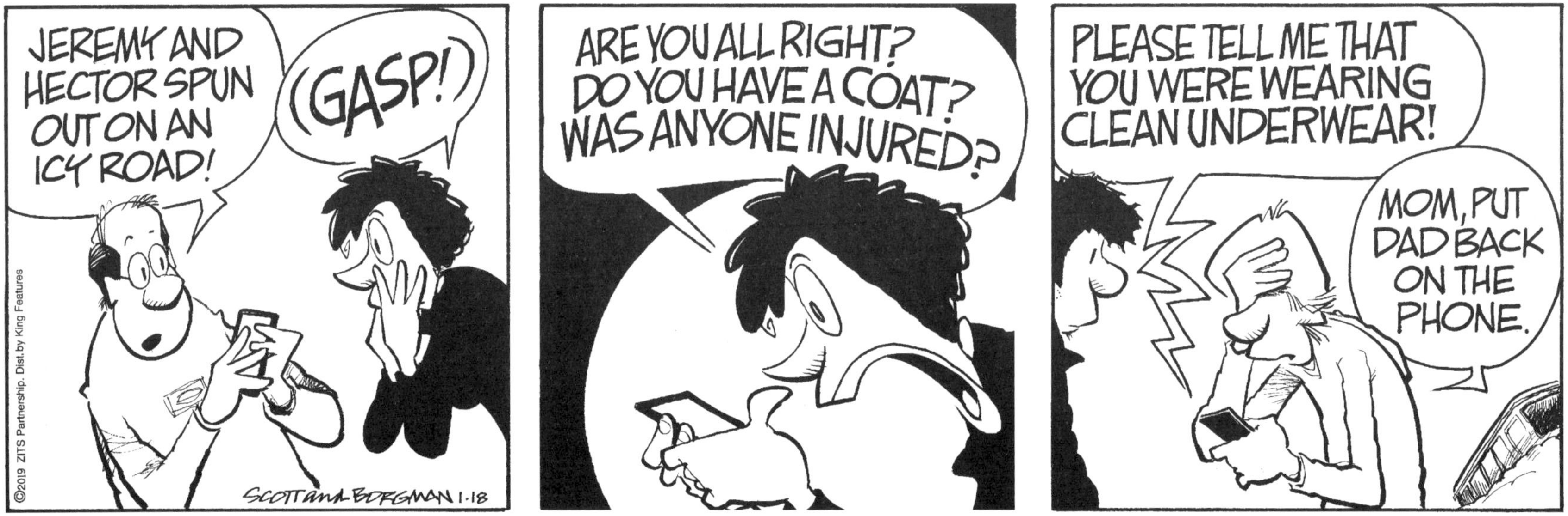
JEREMY AND HECTOR SPUN OUT ON AN ICY ROAD!
(GASP!)
ARE YOU ALL RIGHT? DO YOU HAVE A COAT? WAS ANYONE INJURED?
PLEASE TELL ME THAT YOU WERE WEARING CLEAN UNDERWEAR!
MOM, PUT DAD BACK ON THE PHONE.
©2019 ZITS Partnership. Dist. by King Features
SCOTT and BORGMAN 1.18

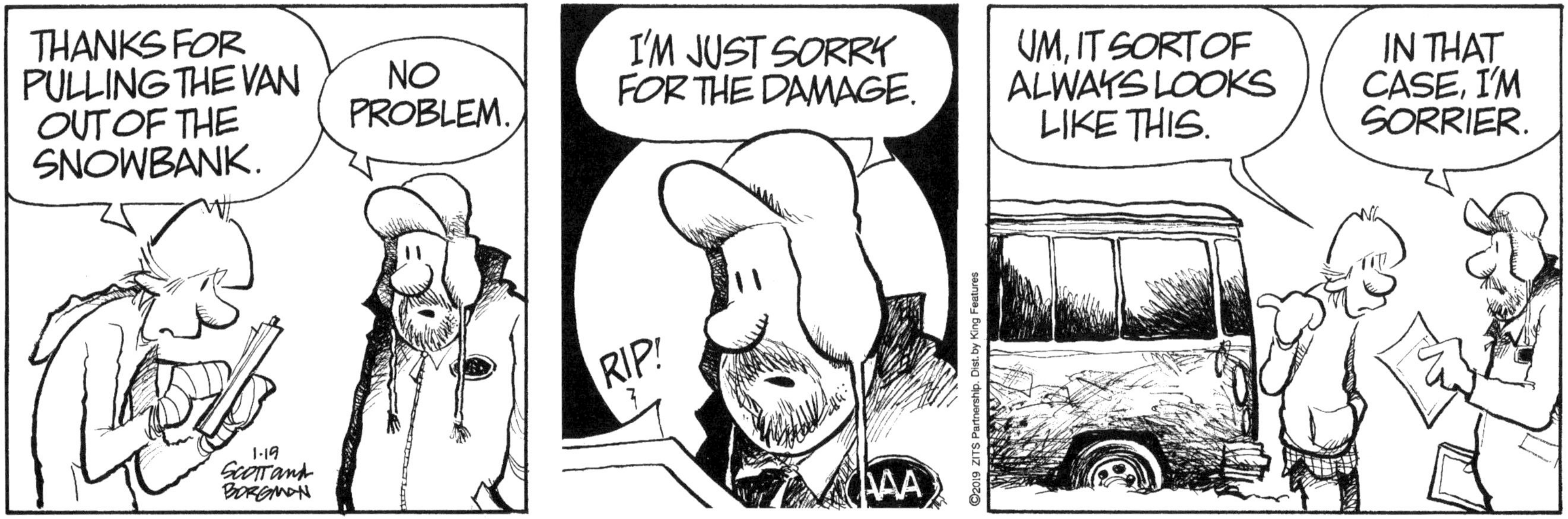
THANKS FOR PULLING THE VAN OUT OF THE SNOWBANK.
NO PROBLEM.
1.19 SCOTT and BORGMAN
I'M JUST SORRY FOR THE DAMAGE.
RIP!
AAA
UM, IT SORT OF ALWAYS LOOKS LIKE THIS.
IN THAT CASE, I'M SORRIER.
©2019 ZITS Partnership. Dist. by King Features

ZITS®

by JERRY SCOTT and JIM BORGMAN

1-20
SCOTT and BORGMAN
©2009 ZITS Partnership. Dist. by King Features
WE NEED A CLOSER PARKING SPACE.
PLUS, JANUARY SUCKS.

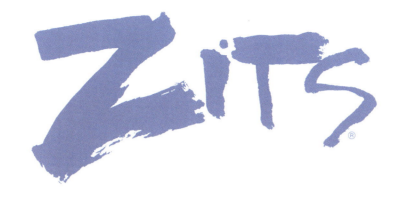

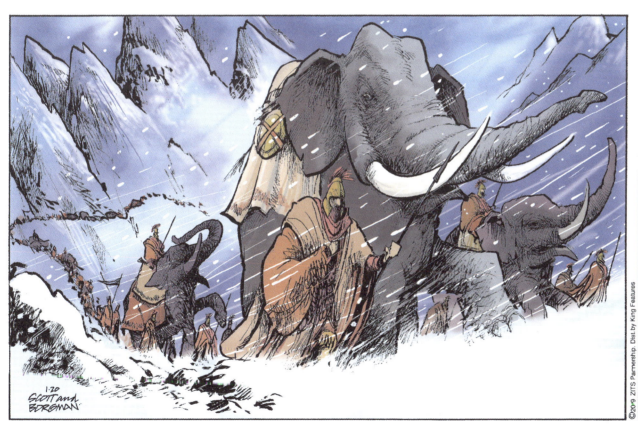

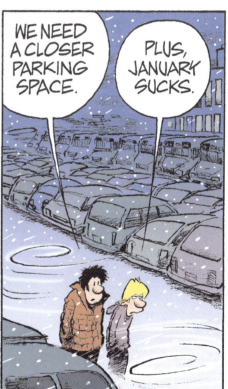

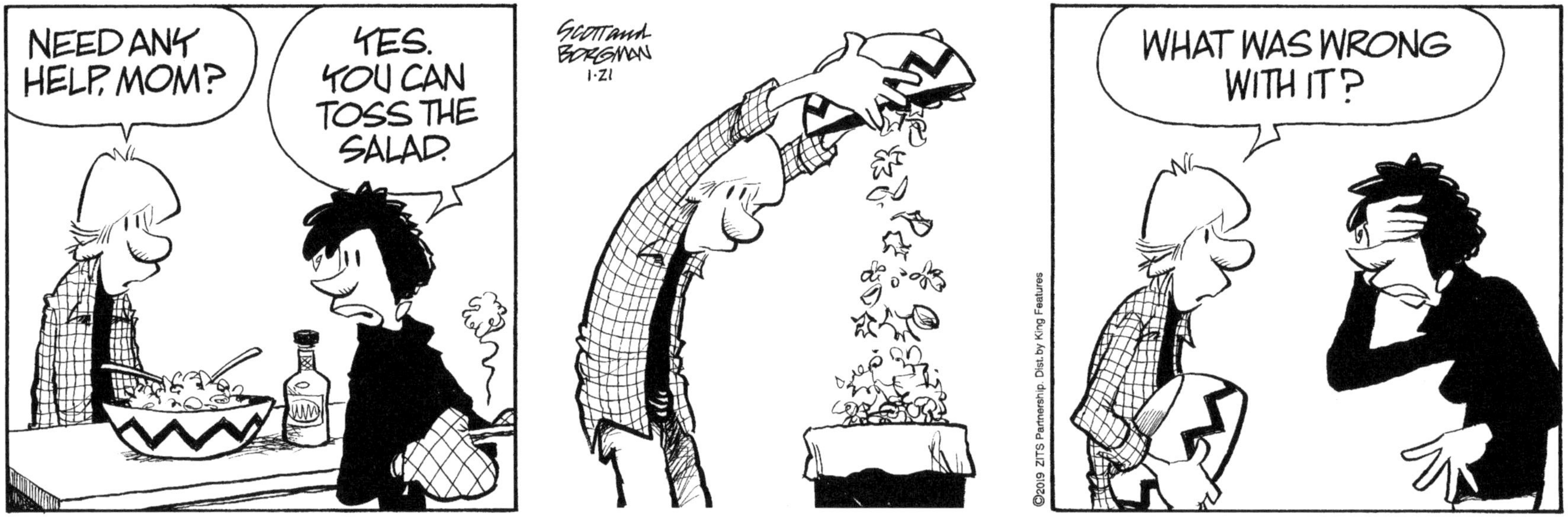
NEED ANY HELP, MOM?
YES. YOU CAN TOSS THE SALAD.
SCOTT and BORGMAN 1·21
WHAT WAS WRONG WITH IT?
©2019 ZITS Partnership. Dist. by King Features

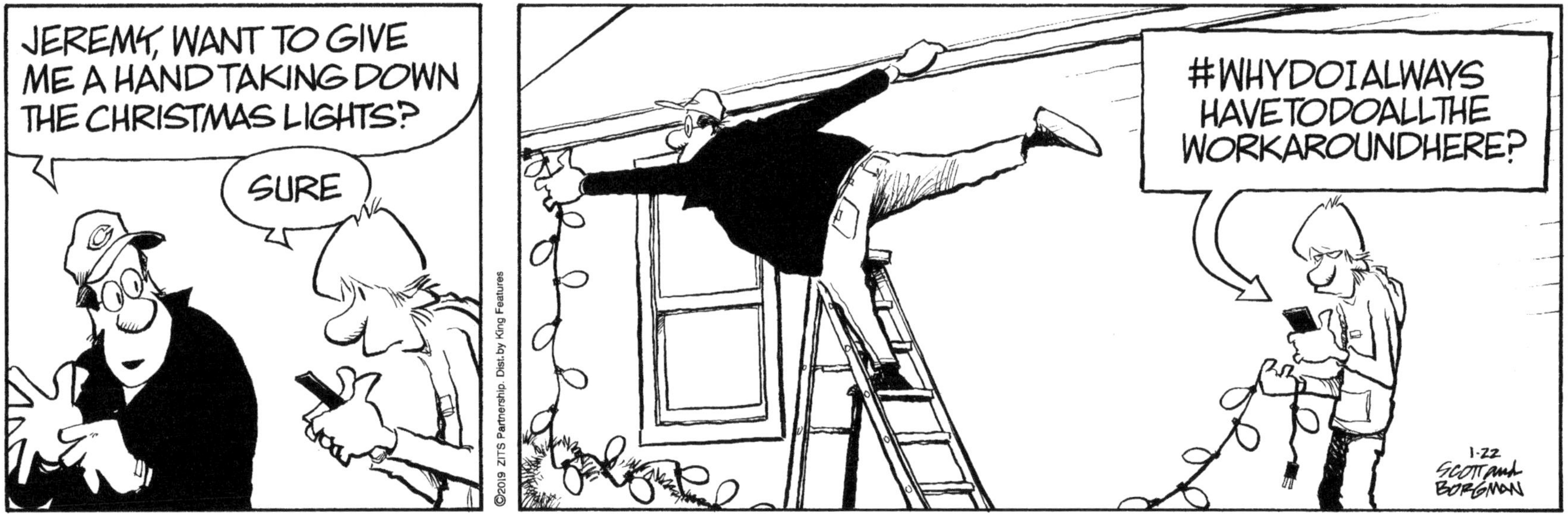
JEREMY, WANT TO GIVE ME A HAND TAKING DOWN THE CHRISTMAS LIGHTS?
SURE
©2019 ZITS Partnership. Dist. by King Features
#WHYDOIALWAYS HAVETODOALLTHE WORKAROUNDHERE?
1·22 SCOTT and BORGMAN

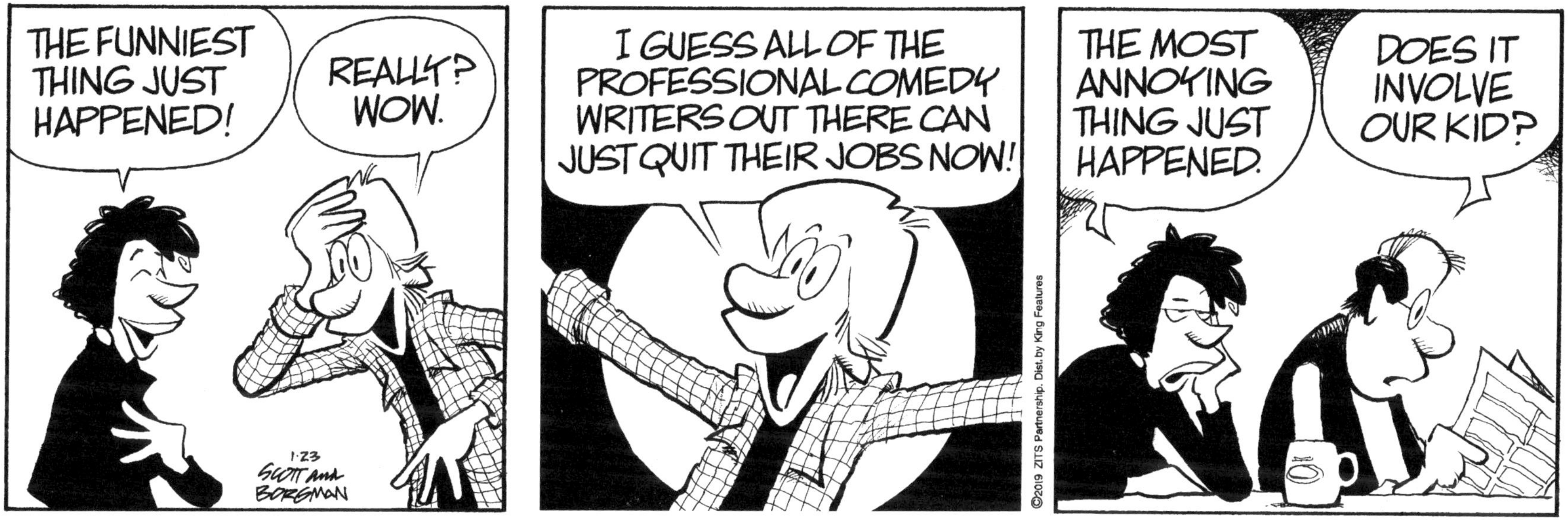
THE FUNNIEST THING JUST HAPPENED!
REALLY? WOW.
I GUESS ALL OF THE PROFESSIONAL COMEDY WRITERS OUT THERE CAN JUST QUIT THEIR JOBS NOW!
THE MOST ANNOYING THING JUST HAPPENED.
DOES IT INVOLVE OUR KID?
1·23 SCOTT and BORGMAN
©2019 ZITS Partnership. Dist. by King Features

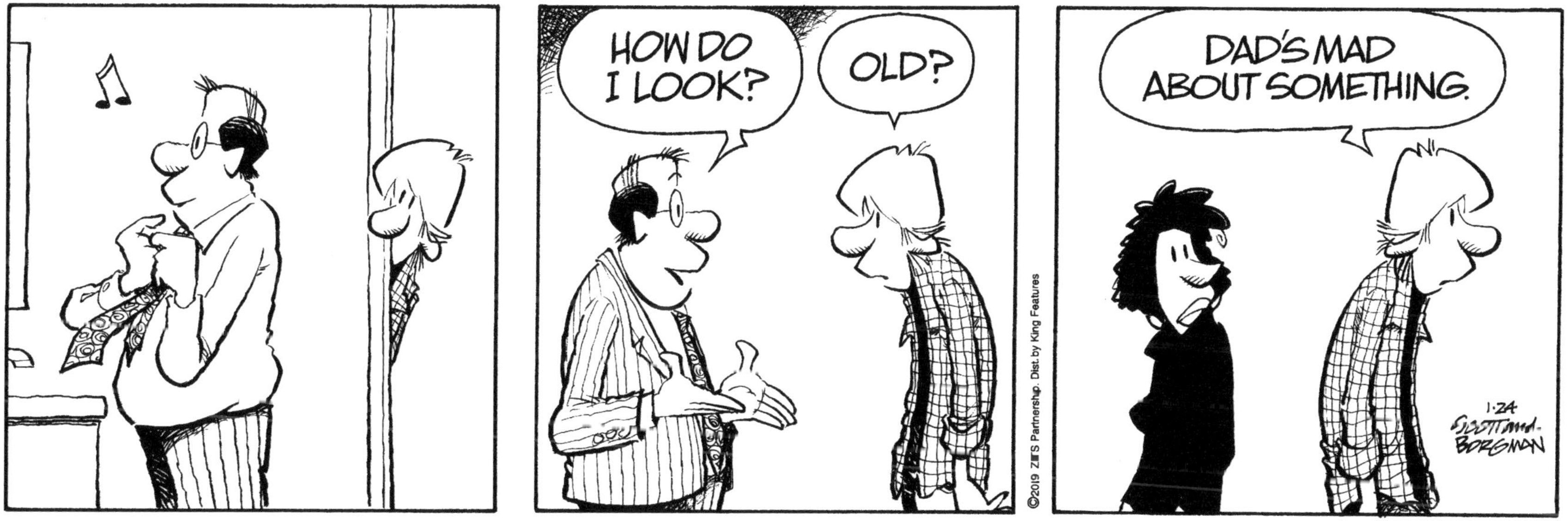
HOW DO I LOOK?
OLD?
DAD'S MAD ABOUT SOMETHING.
1·24 SCOTT and BORGMAN
©2019 ZITS Partnership. Dist. by King Features

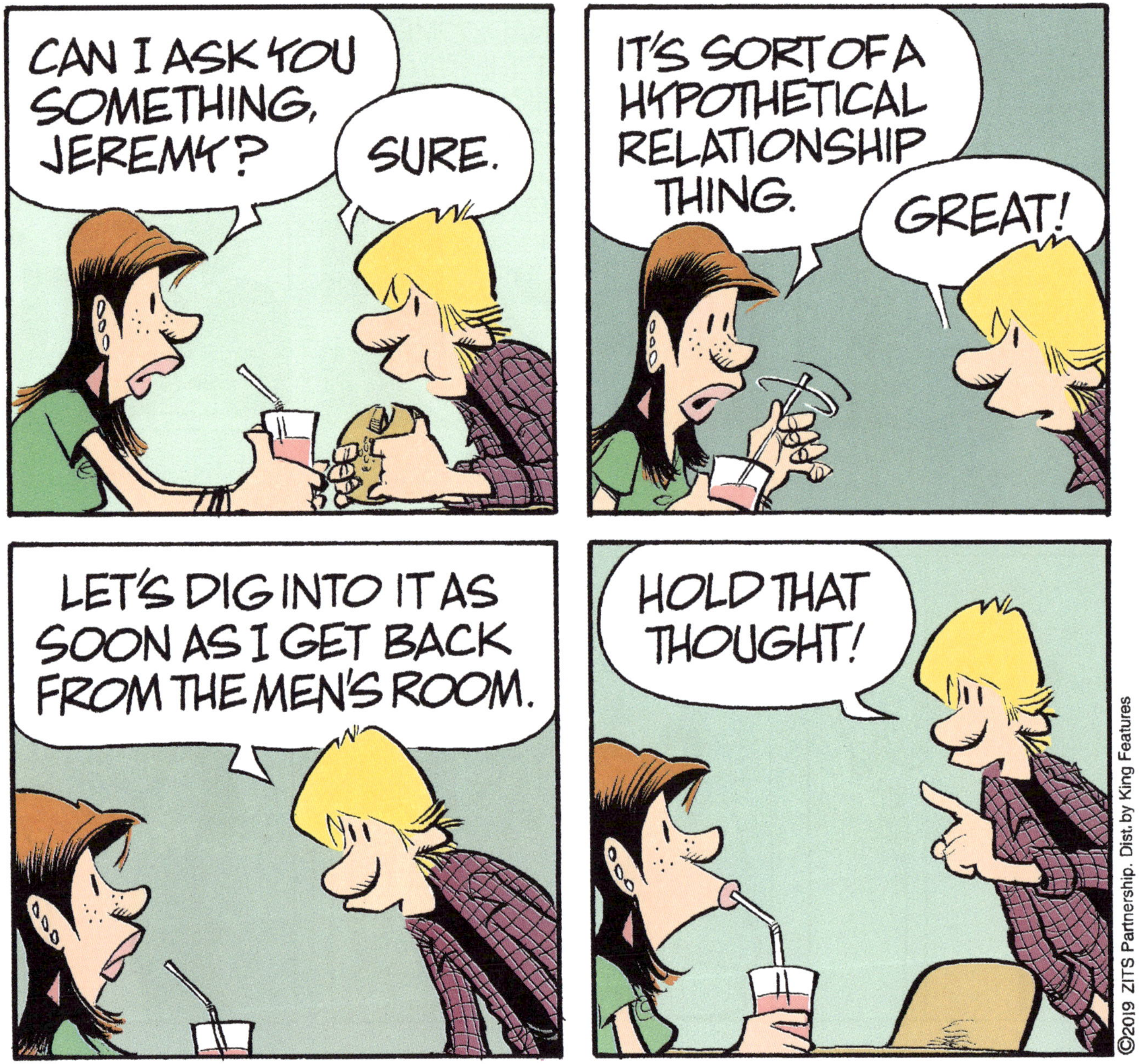
CAN I ASK YOU SOMETHING, JEREMY?
SURE.
IT'S SORT OF A HYPOTHETICAL RELATIONSHIP THING.
GREAT!
LET'S DIG INTO IT AS SOON AS I GET BACK FROM THE MEN'S ROOM.
HOLD THAT THOUGHT!
©2019 ZITS Partnership. Dist. by King Features

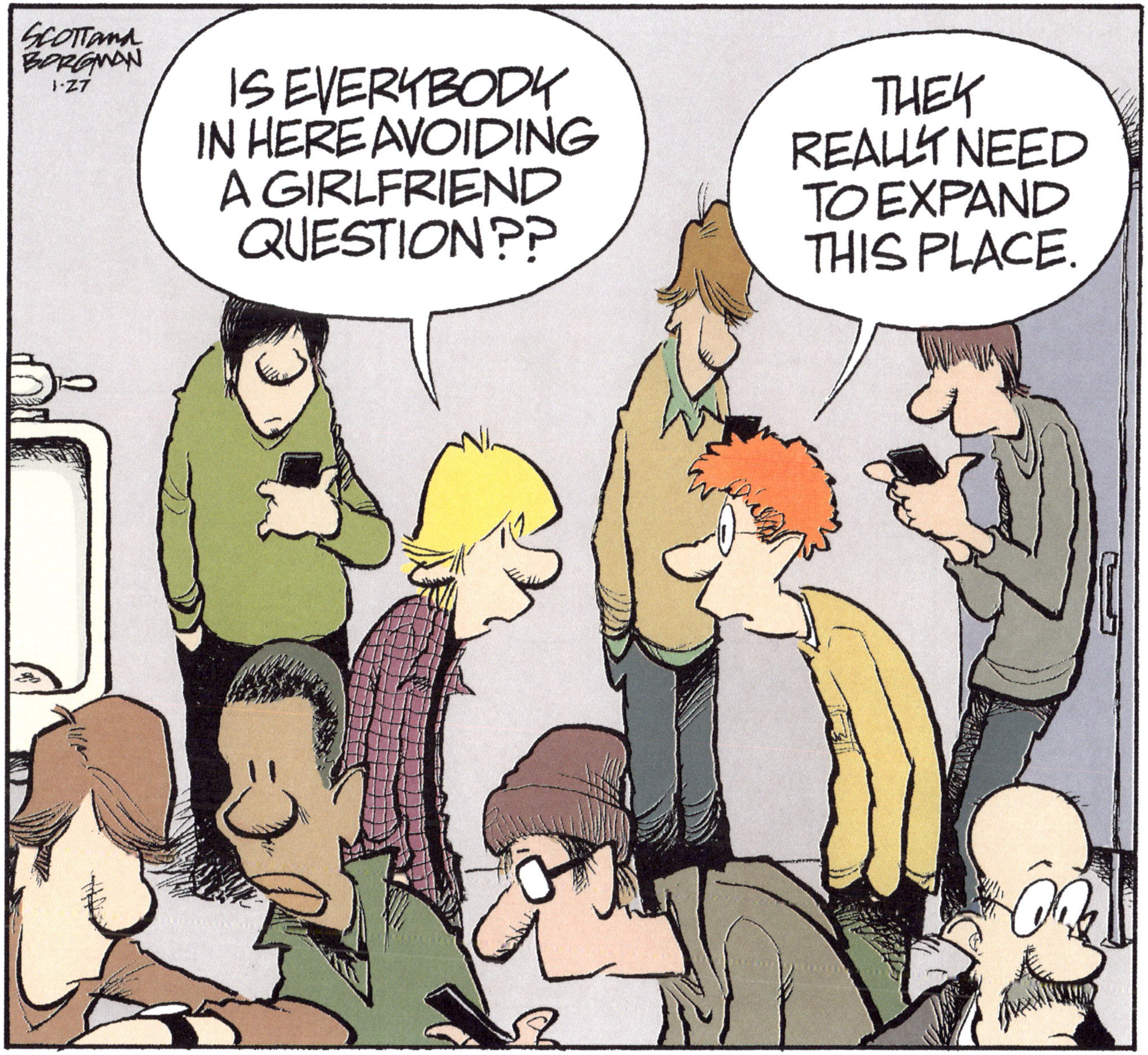
SCOTT and BORGMAN 1-27
IS EVERYBODY IN HERE AVOIDING A GIRLFRIEND QUESTION??
THEY REALLY NEED TO EXPAND THIS PLACE.

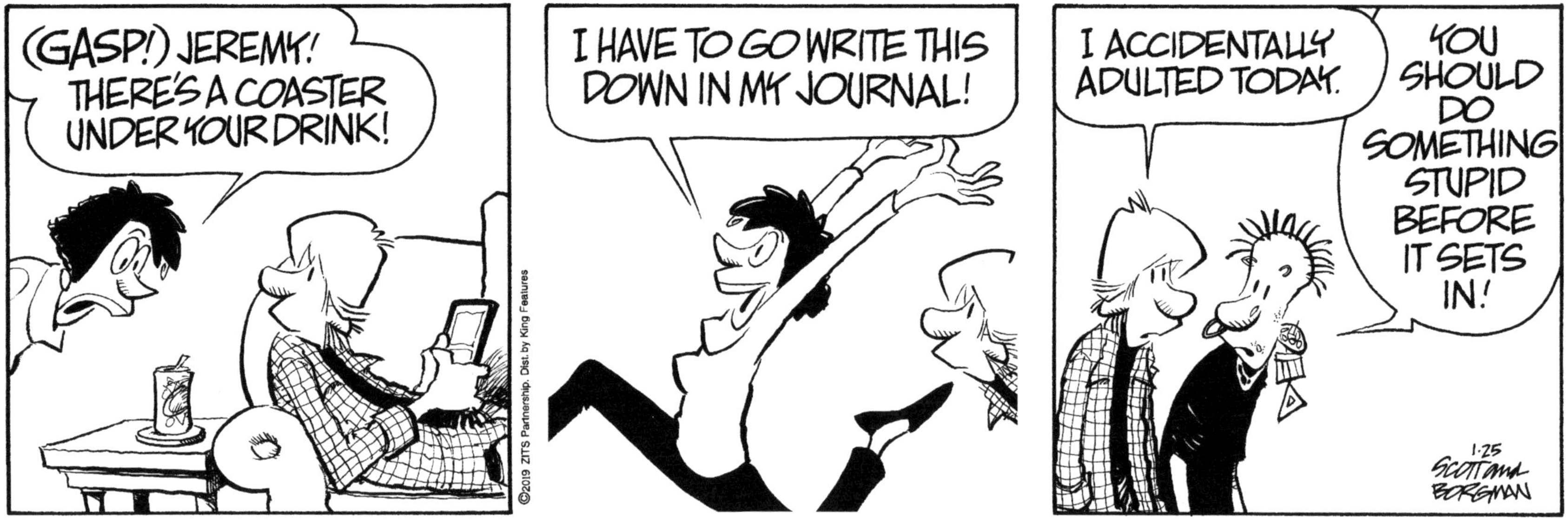
(GASP!) JEREMY! THERE'S A COASTER UNDER YOUR DRINK!
I HAVE TO GO WRITE THIS DOWN IN MY JOURNAL!
I ACCIDENTALLY ADULTED TODAY.
YOU SHOULD DO SOMETHING STUPID BEFORE IT SETS IN!
1·25 SCOTT and BORGMAN
©2019 ZITS Partnership. Dist. by King Features

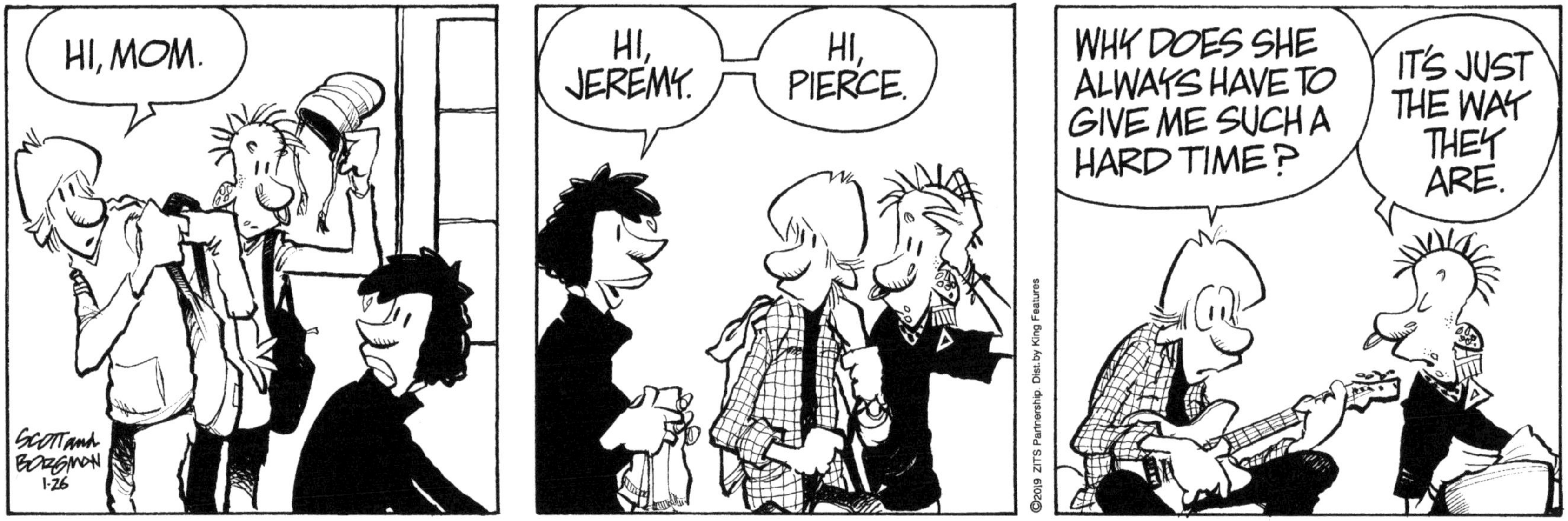
HI, MOM.
SCOTT and BORGMAN 1·26
HI, JEREMY.
HI, PIERCE.
WHY DOES SHE ALWAYS HAVE TO GIVE ME SUCH A HARD TIME?
IT'S JUST THE WAY THEY ARE.
©2019 ZITS Partnership. Dist. by King Features

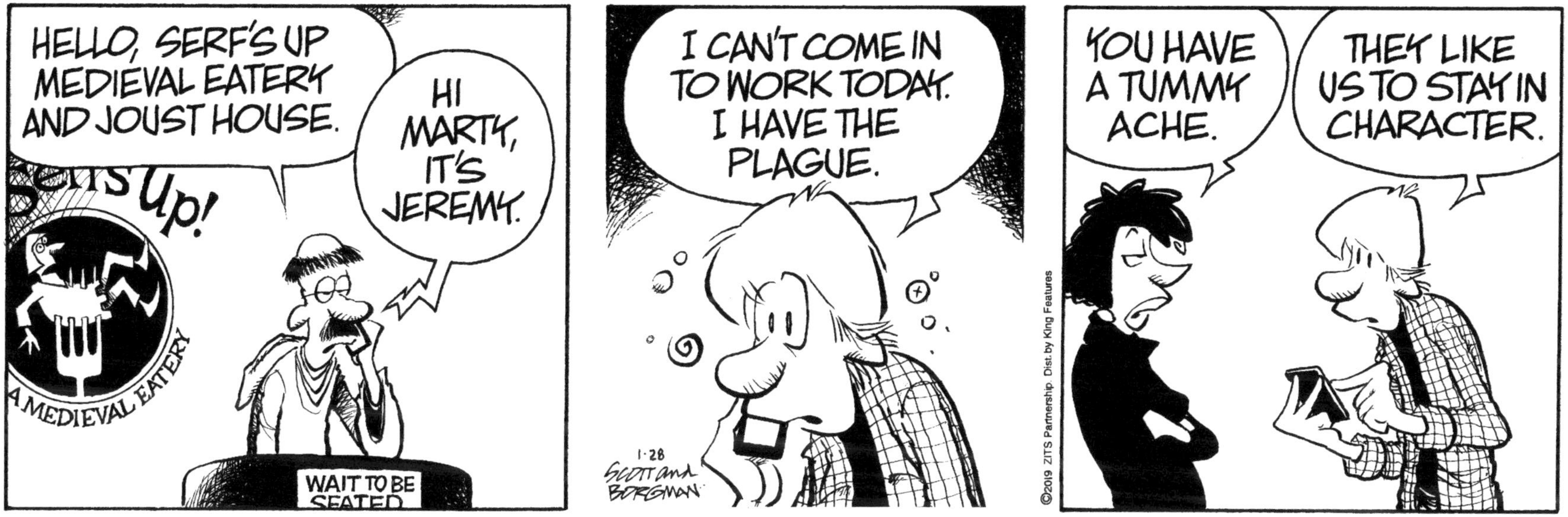
HELLO, SERF'S UP MEDIEVAL EATERY AND JOUST HOUSE.
HI MARTY, IT'S JEREMY.
A MEDIEVAL EATERY
WAIT TO BE SEATED
I CAN'T COME IN TO WORK TODAY. I HAVE THE PLAGUE.
1·28 SCOTT and BORGMAN
YOU HAVE A TUMMY ACHE.
THEY LIKE US TO STAY IN CHARACTER.
©2019 ZITS Partnership. Dist. by King Features

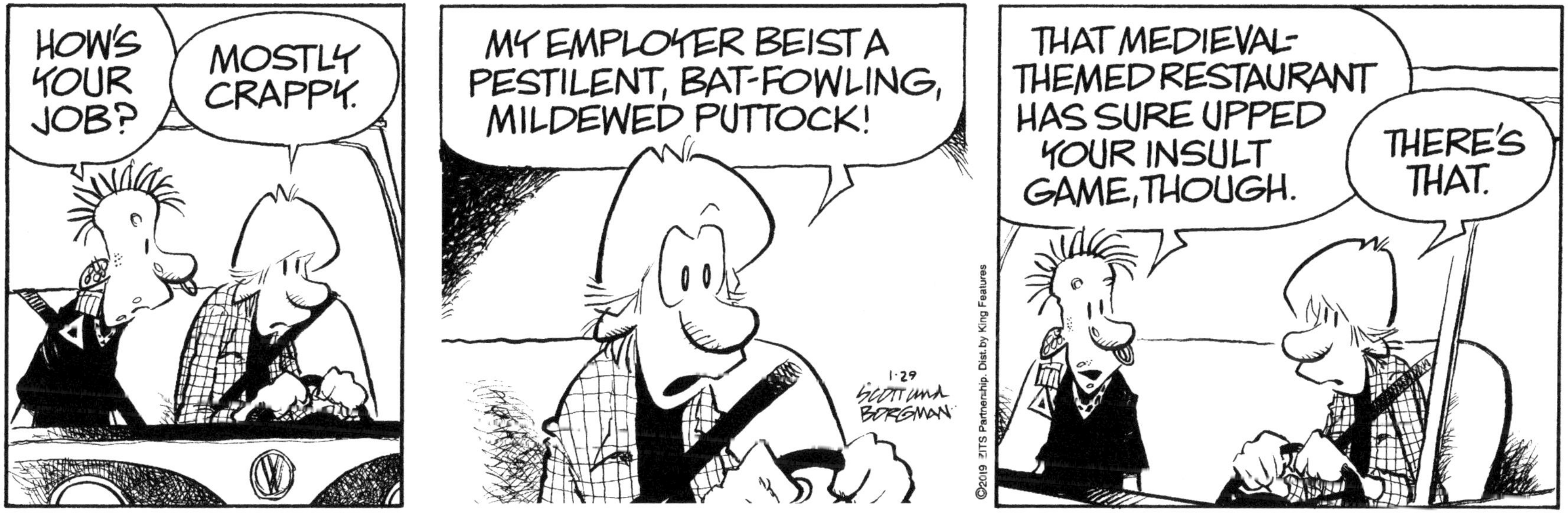
HOW'S YOUR JOB?
MOSTLY CRAPPY.
MY EMPLOYER BEIST A PESTILENT, BAT-FOWLING, MILDEWED PUTTOCK!
1·29 SCOTT and BORGMAN
THAT MEDIEVAL-THEMED RESTAURANT HAS SURE UPPED YOUR INSULT GAME, THOUGH.
THERE'S THAT.
©2019 ZITS Partnership. Dist. by King Features

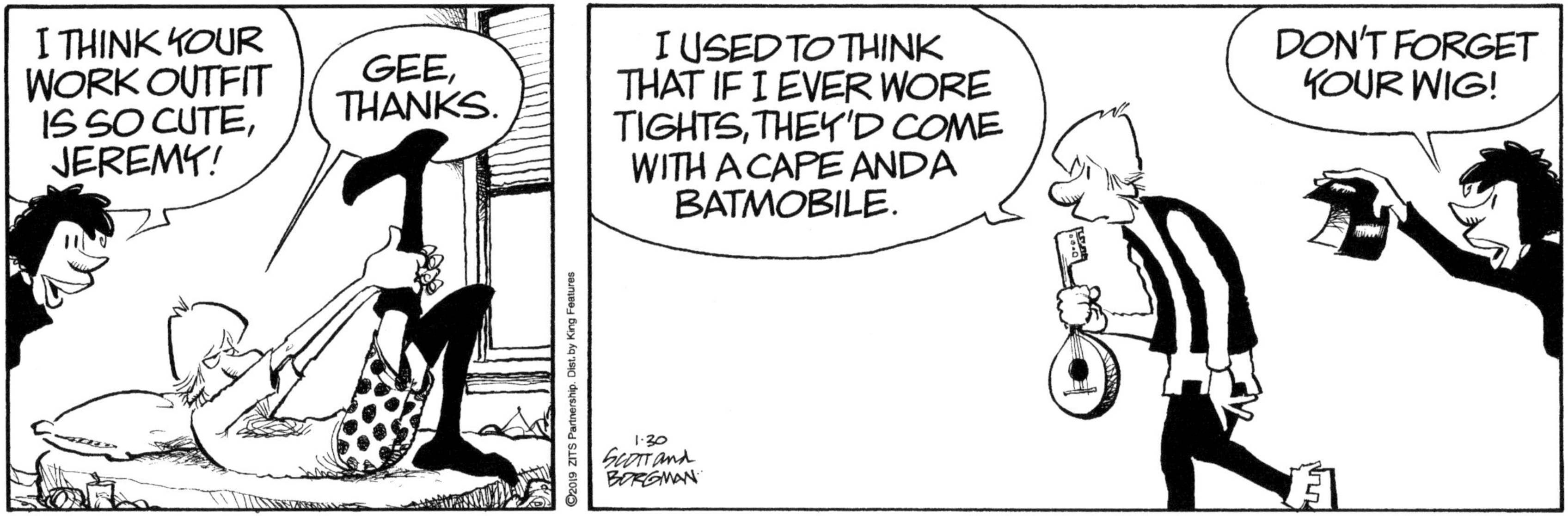
I THINK YOUR WORK OUTFIT IS SO CUTE, JEREMY!
GEE, THANKS.
I USED TO THINK THAT IF I EVER WORE TIGHTS, THEY'D COME WITH A CAPE AND A BATMOBILE.
DON'T FORGET YOUR WIG!
©2019 ZITS Partnership. Dist. by King Features
1·30 SCOTT and BORGMAN

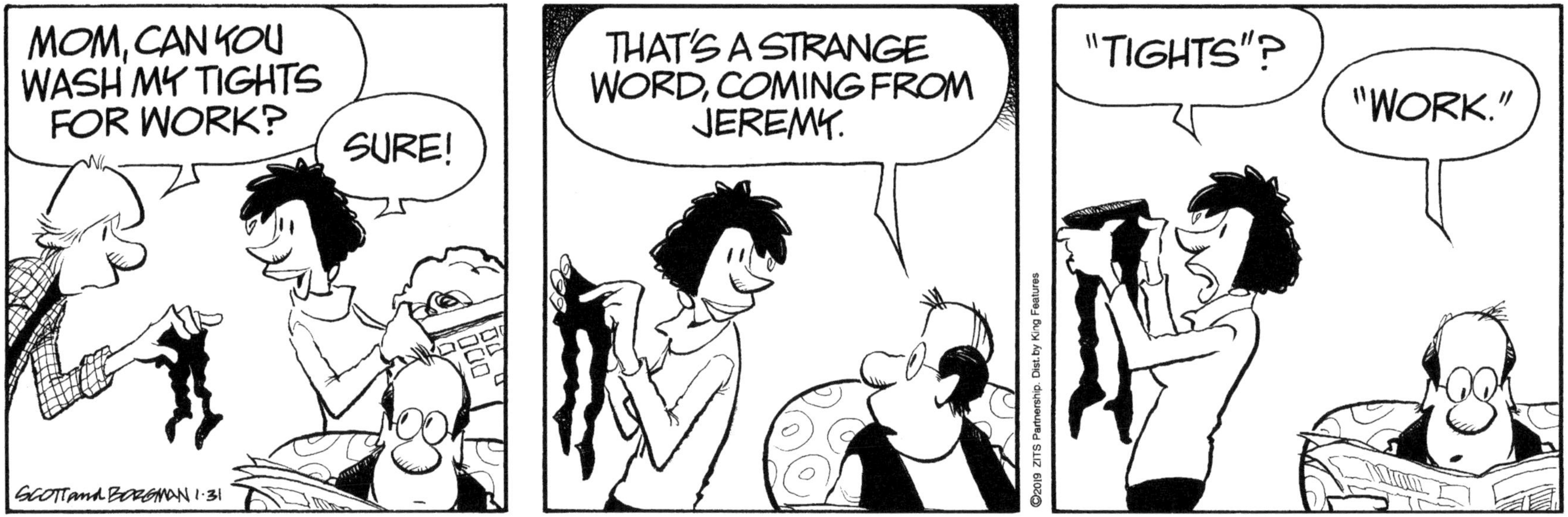
MOM, CAN YOU WASH MY TIGHTS FOR WORK?
SURE!
SCOTT and BORGMAN 1·31
THAT'S A STRANGE WORD, COMING FROM JEREMY.
"TIGHTS"?
"WORK."
©2019 ZITS Partnership. Dist. by King Features

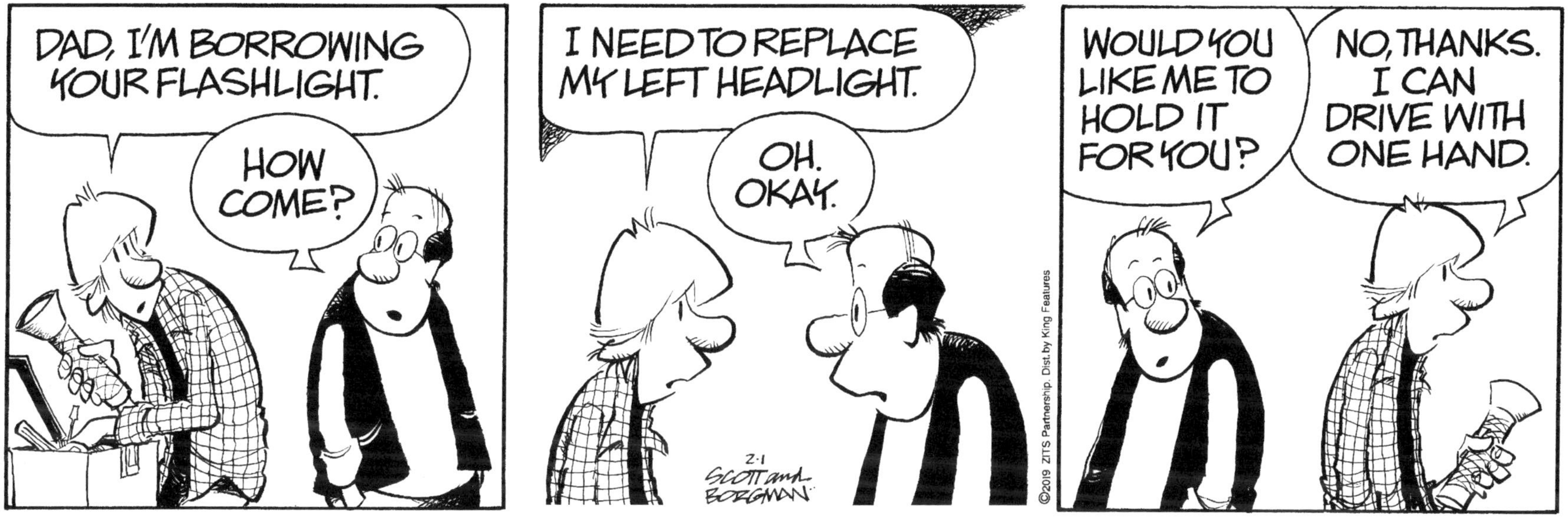
DAD, I'M BORROWING YOUR FLASHLIGHT.
HOW COME?
I NEED TO REPLACE MY LEFT HEADLIGHT.
OH. OKAY.
2-1 SCOTT and BORGMAN
©2019 ZITS Partnership. Dist. by King Features
WOULD YOU LIKE ME TO HOLD IT FOR YOU?
NO, THANKS. I CAN DRIVE WITH ONE HAND.

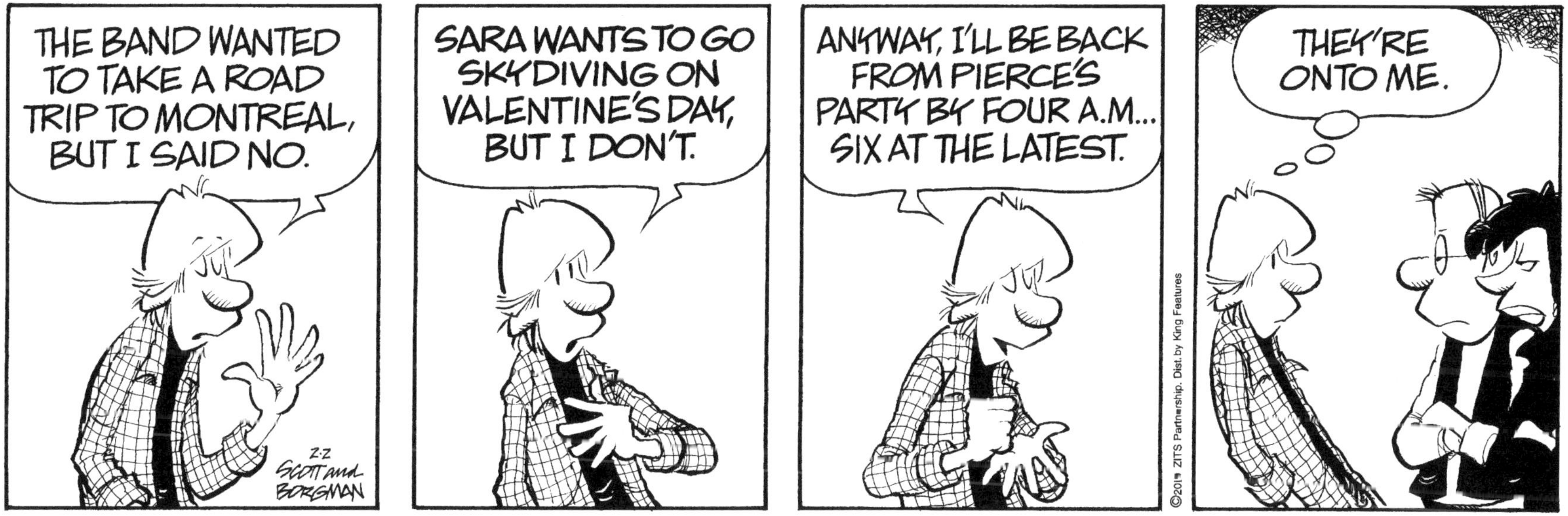
THE BAND WANTED TO TAKE A ROAD TRIP TO MONTREAL, BUT I SAID NO.
2-2 SCOTT and BORGMAN
SARA WANTS TO GO SKYDIVING ON VALENTINE'S DAY, BUT I DON'T.
ANYWAY, I'LL BE BACK FROM PIERCE'S PARTY BY FOUR A.M... SIX AT THE LATEST.
©2019 ZITS Partnership. Dist. by King Features
THEY'RE ONTO ME.

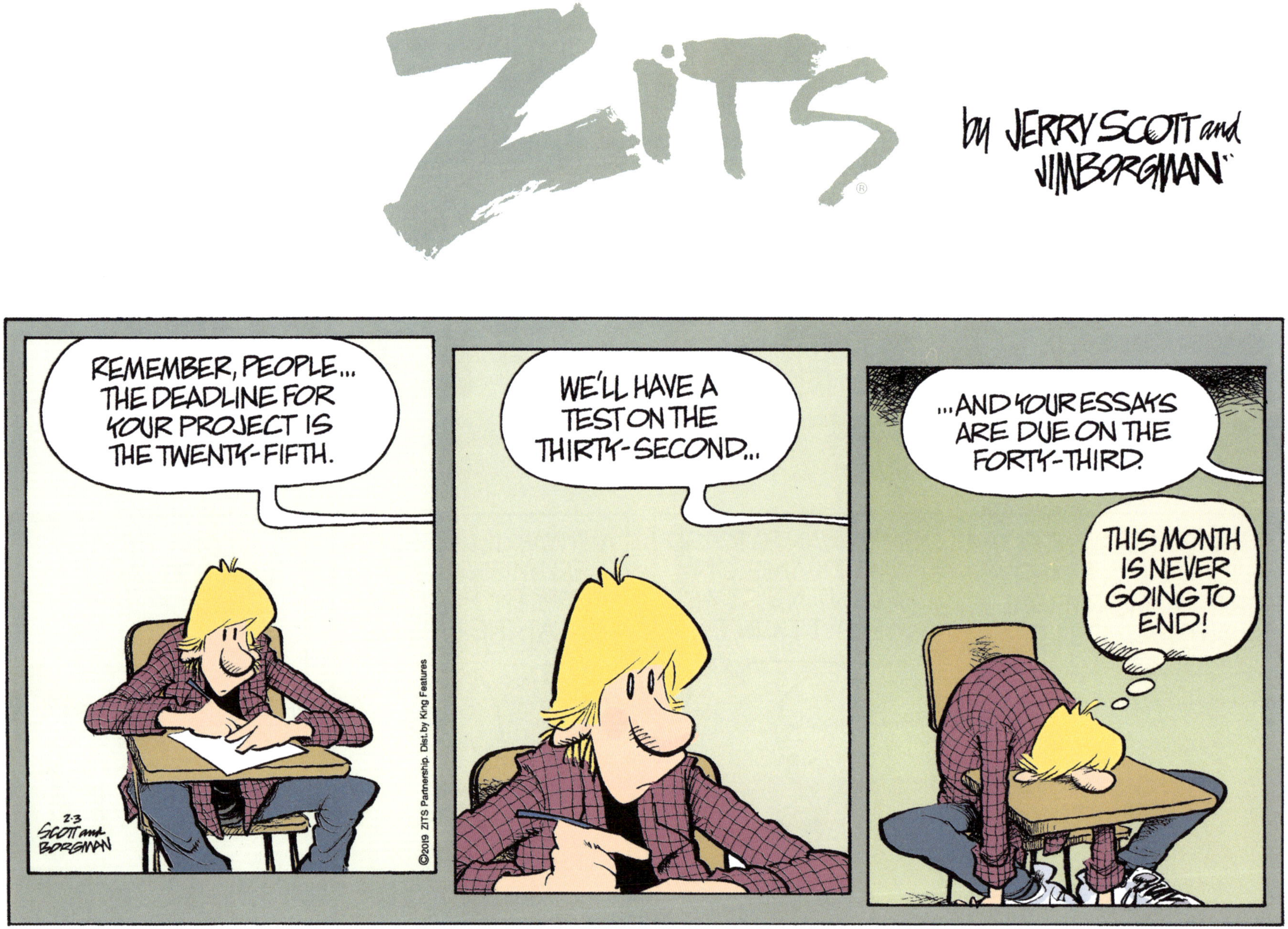
ZITS®
by JERRY SCOTT and JIM BORGMAN
REMEMBER, PEOPLE... THE DEADLINE FOR YOUR PROJECT IS THE TWENTY-FIFTH.
2-3 SCOTT and BORGMAN
©2019 ZITS Partnership. Dist. by King Features
WE'LL HAVE A TEST ON THE THIRTY-SECOND...
...AND YOUR ESSAYS ARE DUE ON THE FORTY-THIRD.
THIS MONTH IS NEVER GOING TO END!

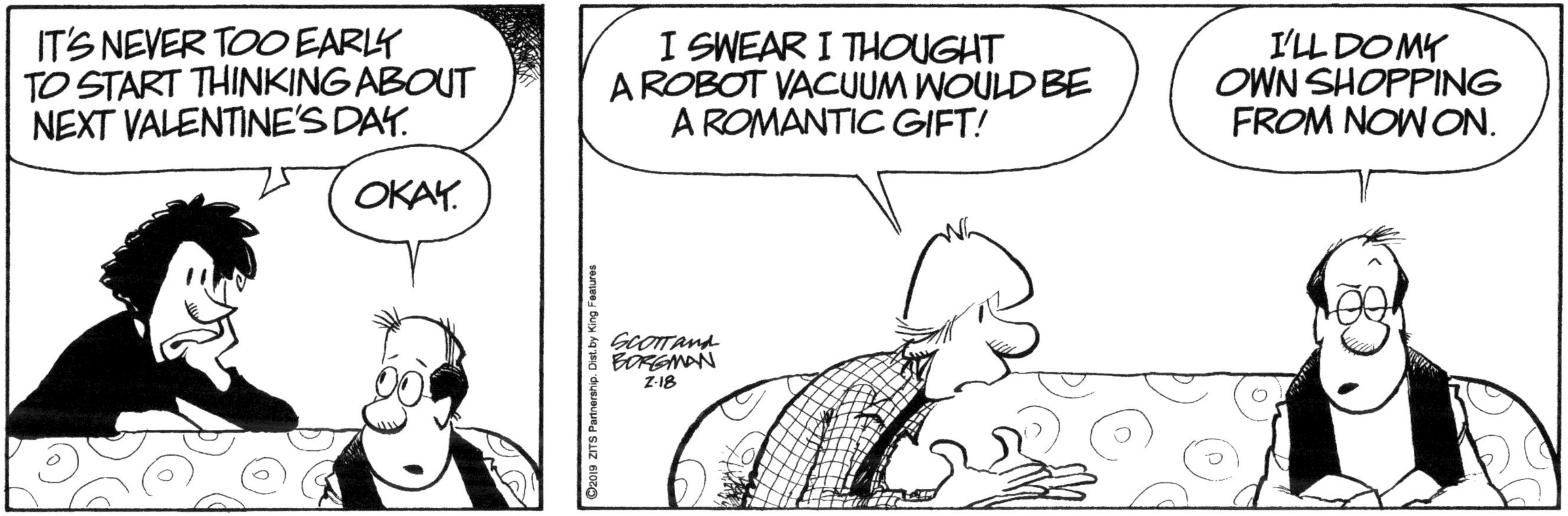
IT'S NEVER TOO EARLY TO START THINKING ABOUT NEXT VALENTINE'S DAY.
OKAY.
©2019 ZITS Partnership. Dist. by King Features
SCOTT and BORGMAN 2-18
I SWEAR I THOUGHT A ROBOT VACUUM WOULD BE A ROMANTIC GIFT!
I'LL DO MY OWN SHOPPING FROM NOW ON.

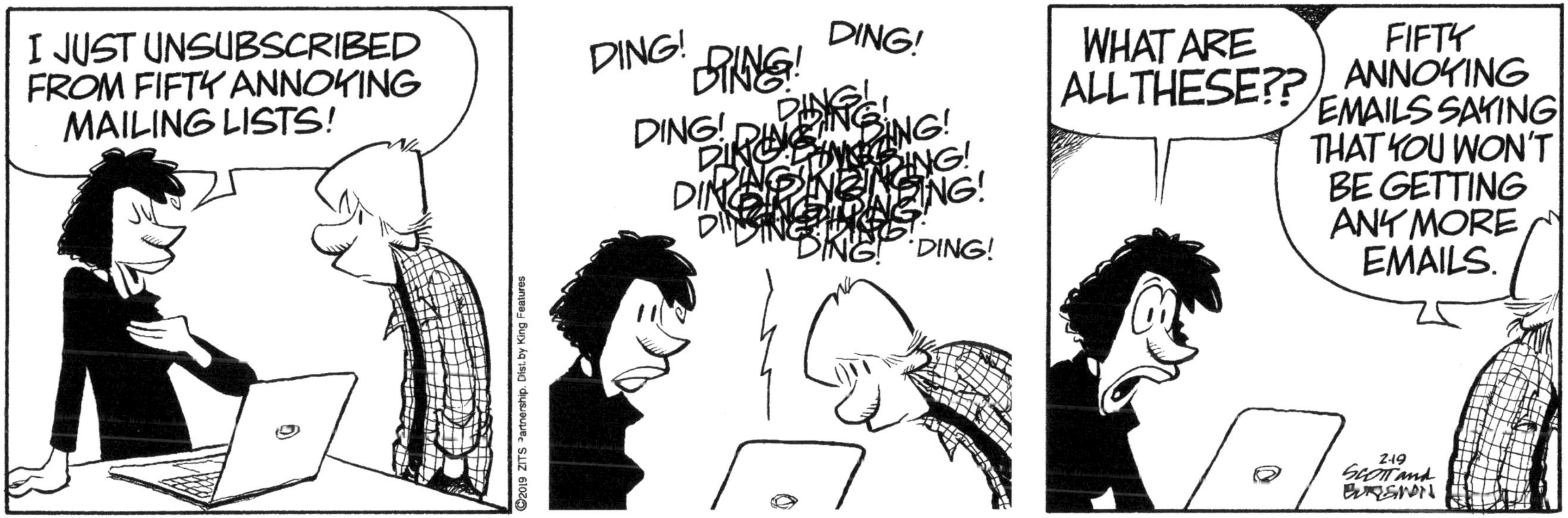
I JUST UNSUBSCRIBED FROM FIFTY ANNOYING MAILING LISTS!
©2019 ZITS Partnership. Dist. by King Features
DING! DING! DING! DING! DING! DING! DING! DING! DING! DING!
WHAT ARE ALL THESE??
FIFTY ANNOYING EMAILS SAYING THAT YOU WON'T BE GETTING ANY MORE EMAILS.
2-19 SCOTT and BORGMAN

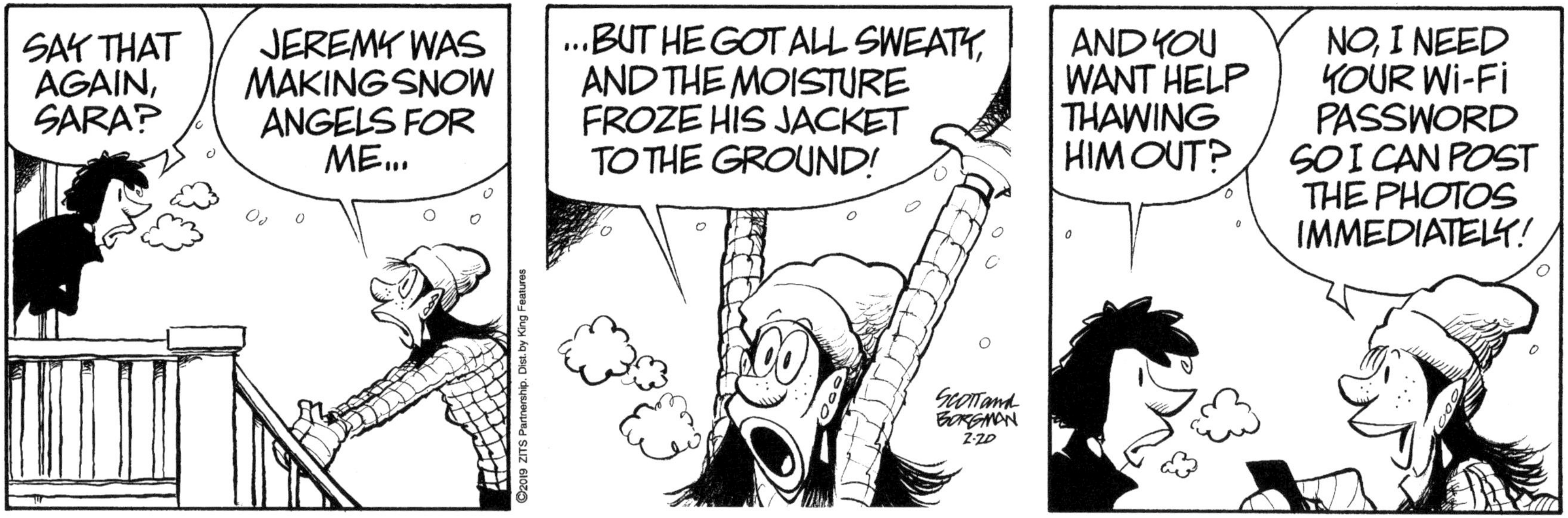
SAY THAT AGAIN, SARA?
JEREMY WAS MAKING SNOW ANGELS FOR ME...
©2019 ZITS Partnership. Dist. by King Features
...BUT HE GOT ALL SWEATY, AND THE MOISTURE FROZE HIS JACKET TO THE GROUND!
SCOTT and BORGMAN 2·20
AND YOU WANT HELP THAWING HIM OUT?
NO, I NEED YOUR Wi-Fi PASSWORD SO I CAN POST THE PHOTOS IMMEDIATELY!

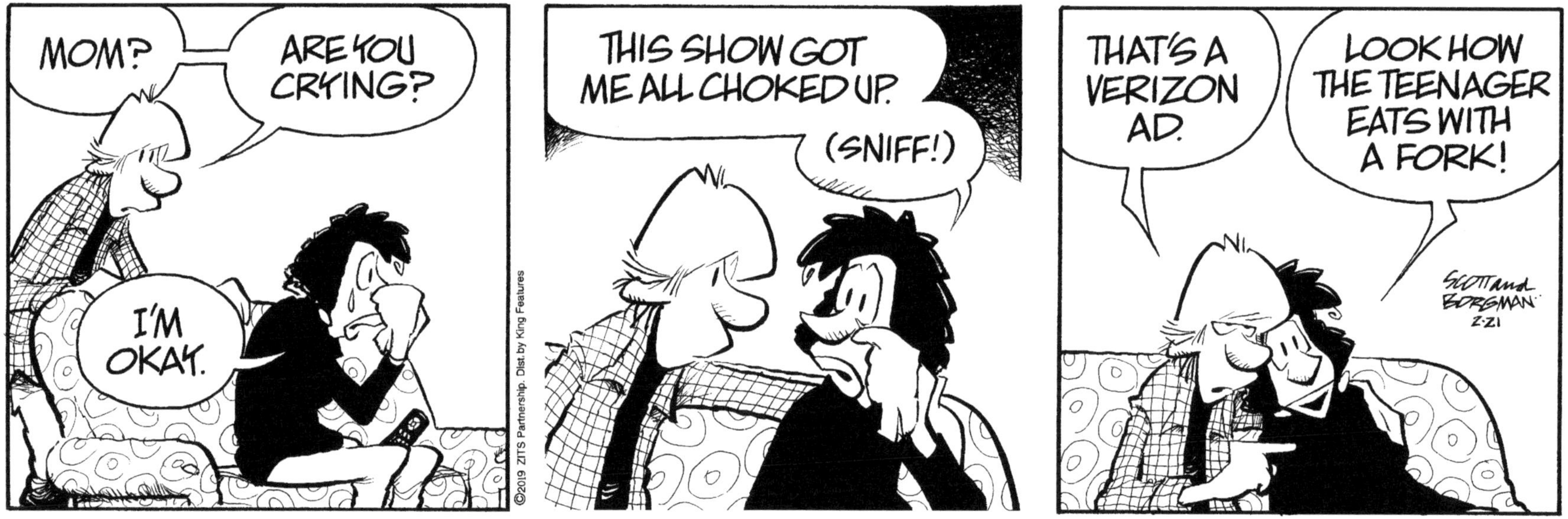
MOM?
ARE YOU CRYING?
I'M OKAY.
©2019 ZITS Partnership. Dist. by King Features
THIS SHOW GOT ME ALL CHOKED UP.
(SNIFF!)
THAT'S A VERIZON AD.
LOOK HOW THE TEENAGER EATS WITH A FORK!
SCOTT and BORGMAN 2·21

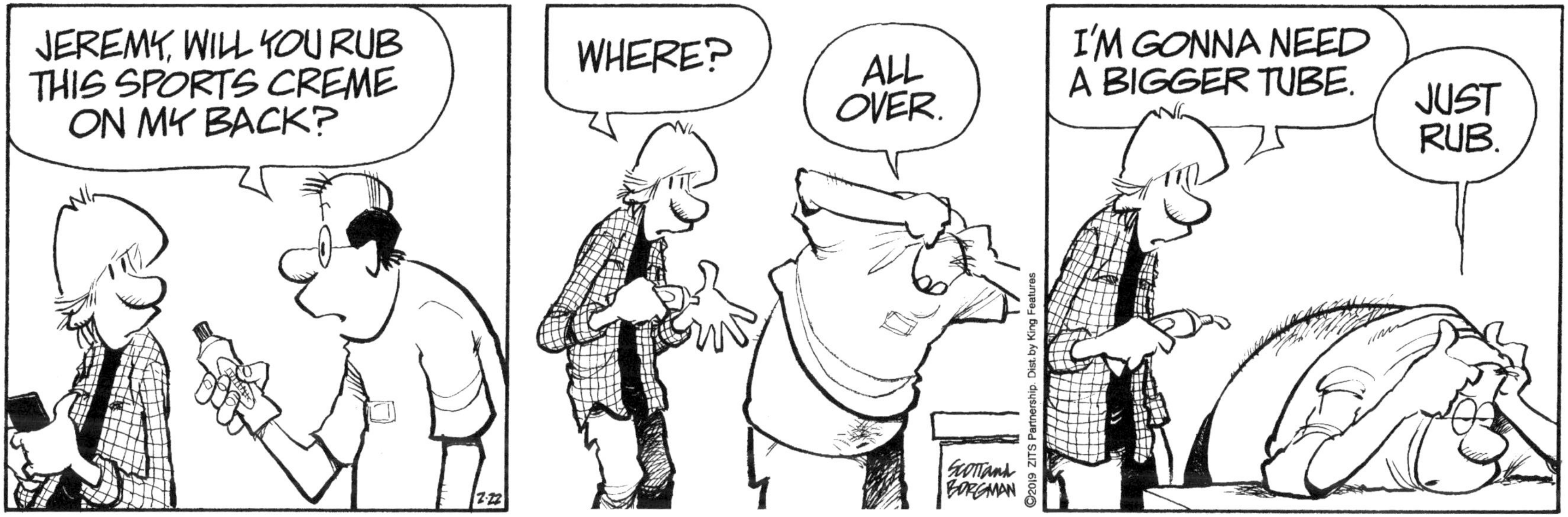
JEREMY, WILL YOU RUB THIS SPORTS CREME ON MY BACK?
2·22
WHERE?
ALL OVER.
SCOTT AND BORGMAN
©2019 ZITS Partnership. Dist. by King Features
I'M GONNA NEED A BIGGER TUBE.
JUST RUB.

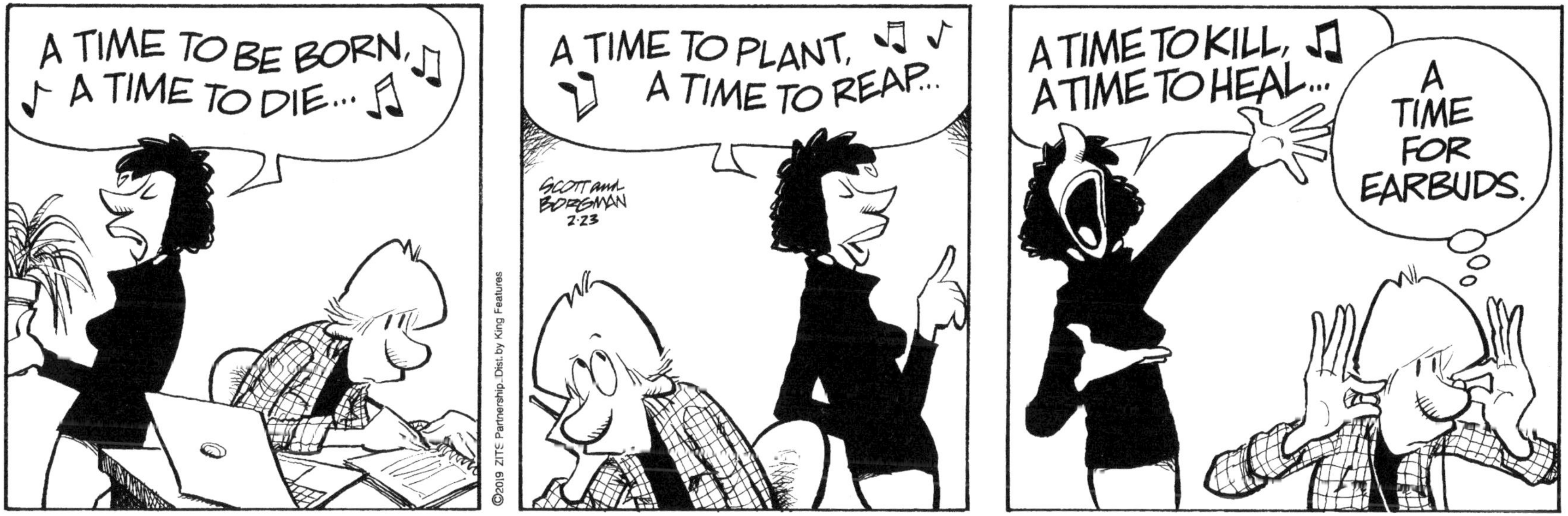
A TIME TO BE BORN, A TIME TO DIE...
©2019 ZITS Partnership. Dist. by King Features
SCOTT AND BORGMAN 2·23
A TIME TO PLANT, A TIME TO REAP...
A TIME TO KILL, A TIME TO HEAL...
A TIME FOR EARBUDS.

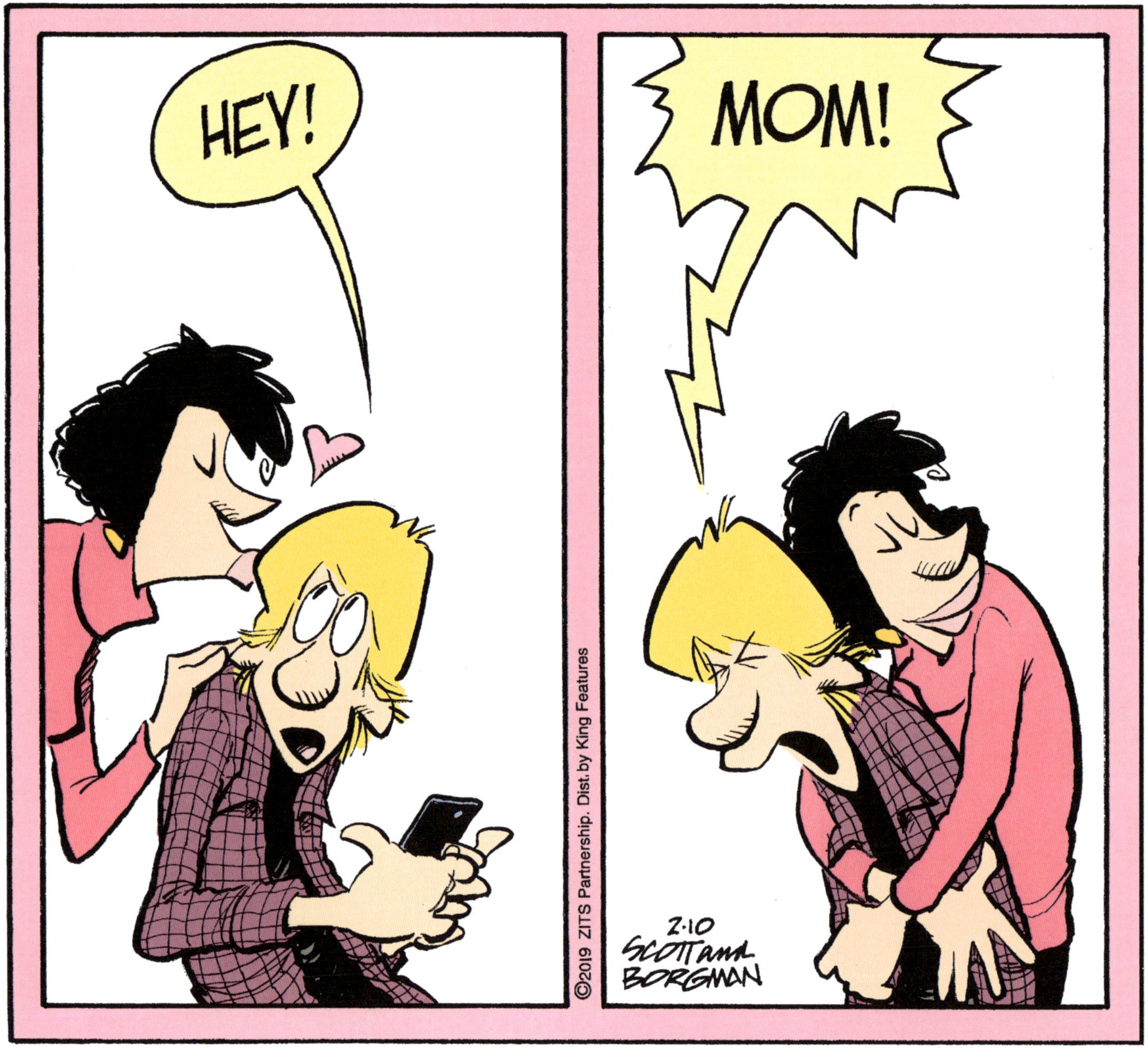
HEY!
MOM!
©2019 ZITS Partnership. Dist. by King Features
2·10
SCOTT and BORGMAN

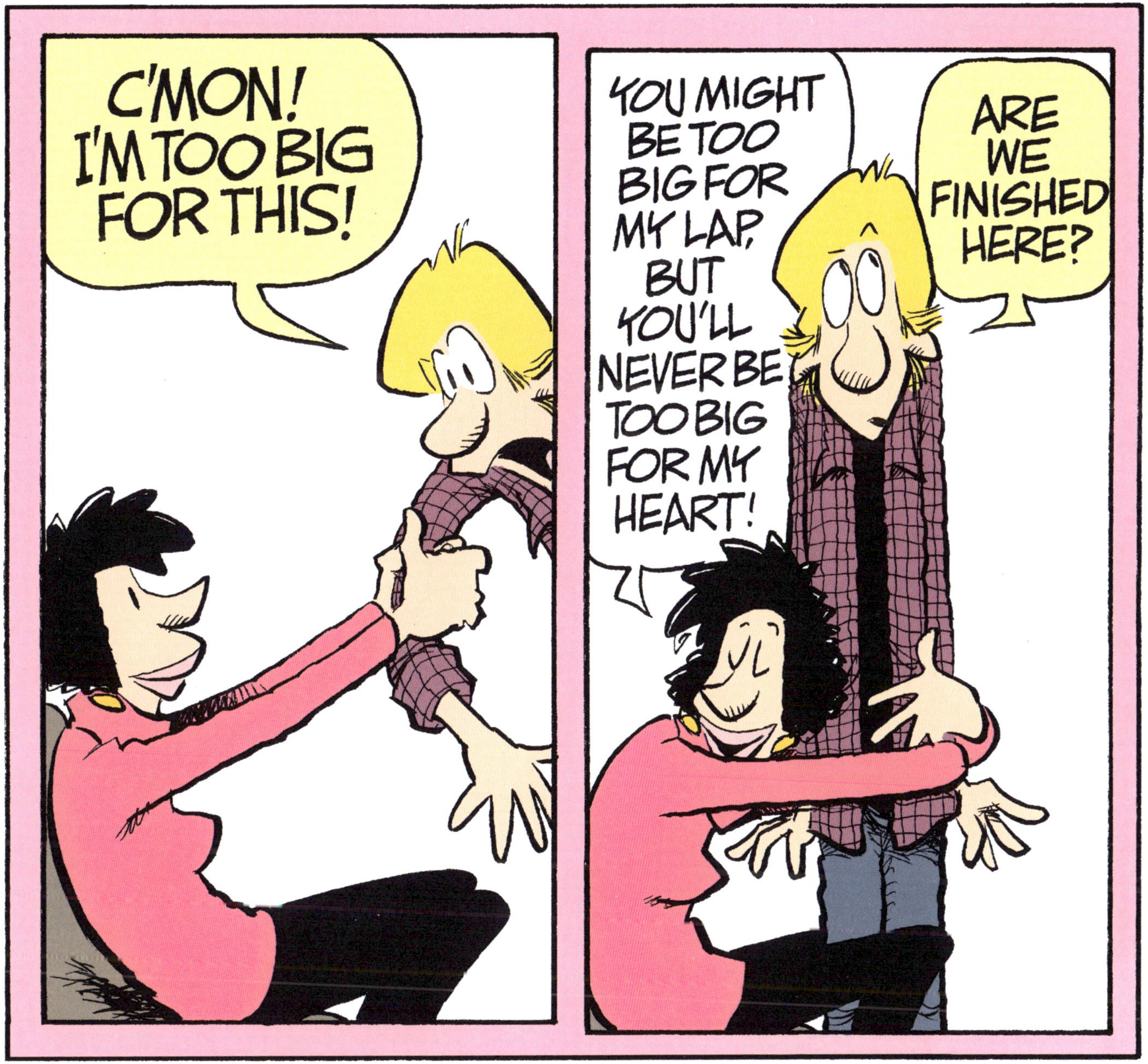
C'MON! I'M TOO BIG FOR THIS!
YOU MIGHT BE TOO BIG FOR MY LAP, BUT YOU'LL NEVER BE TOO BIG FOR MY HEART!
ARE WE FINISHED HERE?

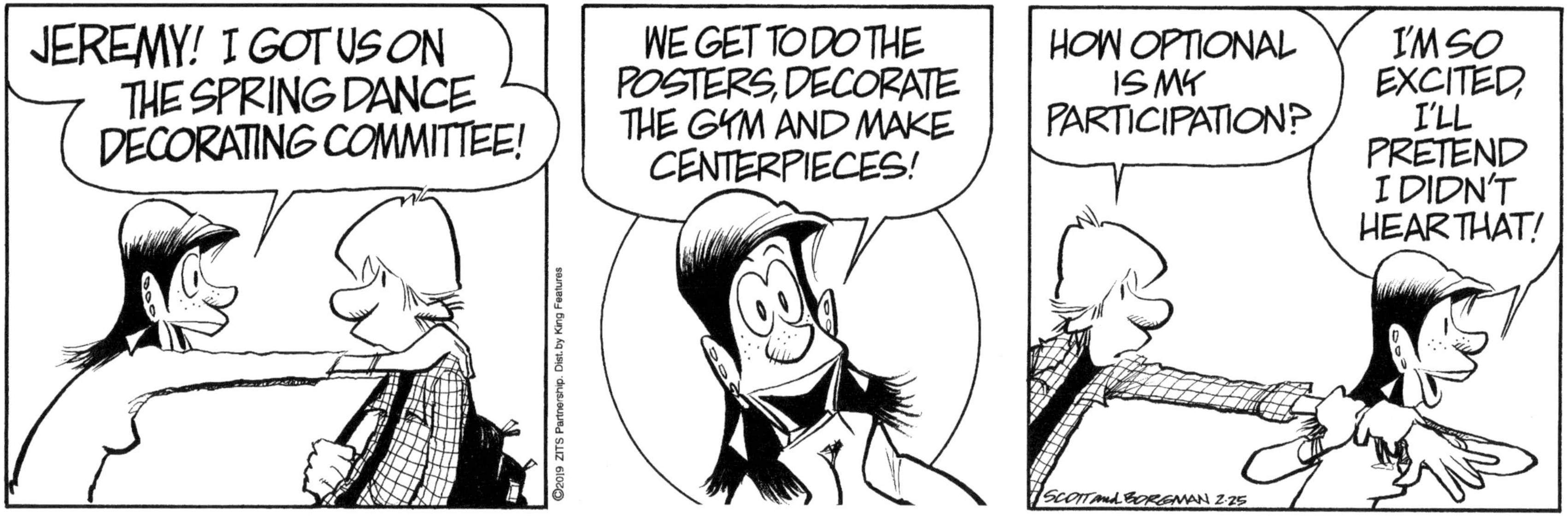
JEREMY! I GOT US ON THE SPRING DANCE DECORATING COMMITTEE!
WE GET TO DO THE POSTERS, DECORATE THE GYM AND MAKE CENTERPIECES!
HOW OPTIONAL IS MY PARTICIPATION?
I'M SO EXCITED, I'LL PRETEND I DIDN'T HEAR THAT!
SCOTT and BORGMAN 2·25
©2019 ZITS Partnership. Dist. by King Features

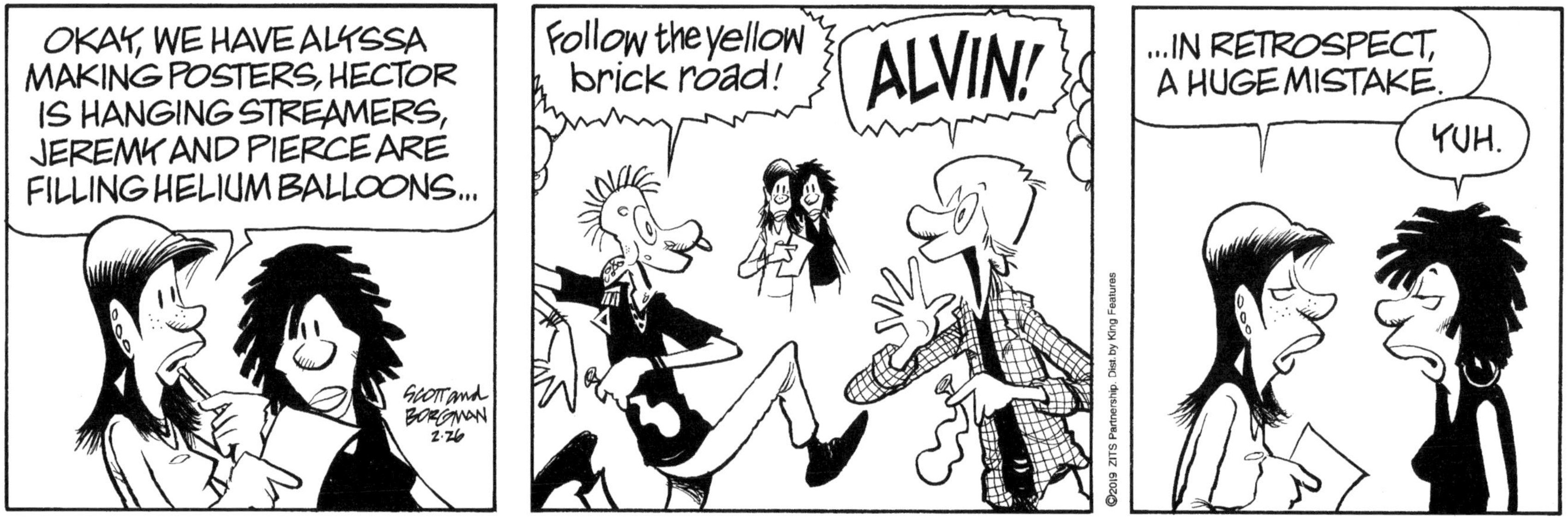
OKAY, WE HAVE ALYSSA MAKING POSTERS, HECTOR IS HANGING STREAMERS, JEREMY AND PIERCE ARE FILLING HELIUM BALLOONS...
SCOTT and BORGMAN 2·26
Follow the yellow brick road!
ALVIN!
...IN RETROSPECT, A HUGE MISTAKE.
YUH.
©2019 ZITS Partnership. Dist. by King Features

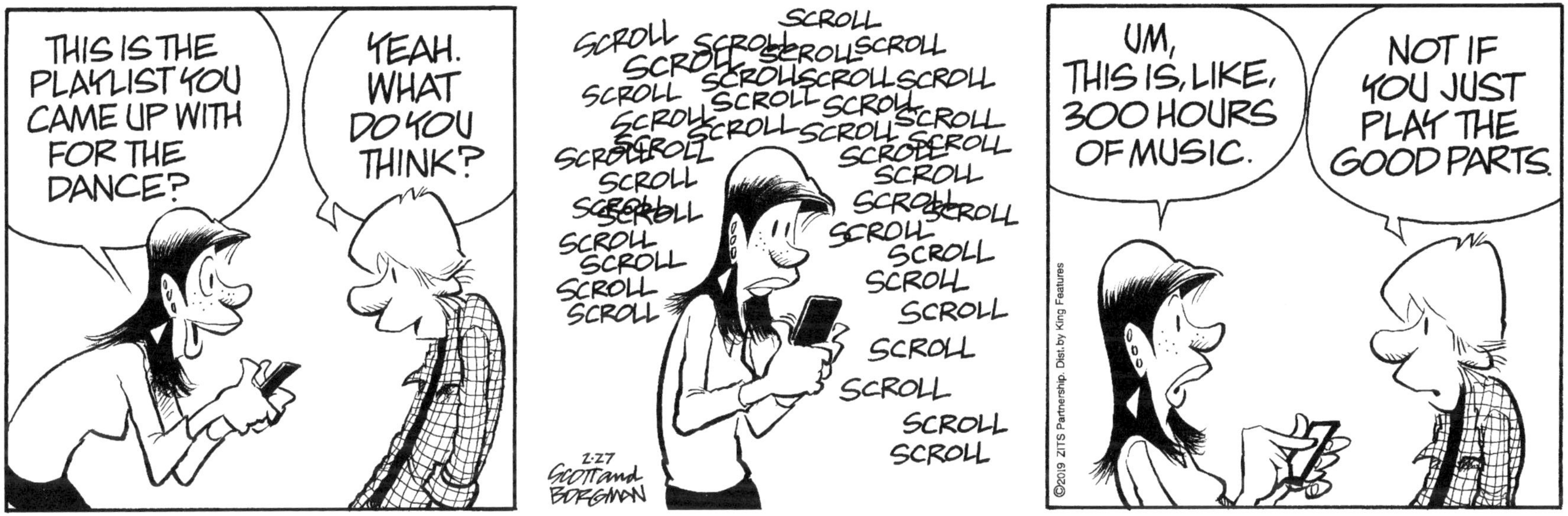
THIS IS THE PLAYLIST YOU CAME UP WITH FOR THE DANCE?
YEAH. WHAT DO YOU THINK?
SCROLL SCROLL SCROLL SCROLL SCROLL SCROLL SCROLL SCROLL
2-27 SCOTT and BORGMAN
UM, THIS IS, LIKE, 300 HOURS OF MUSIC.
NOT IF YOU JUST PLAY THE GOOD PARTS.

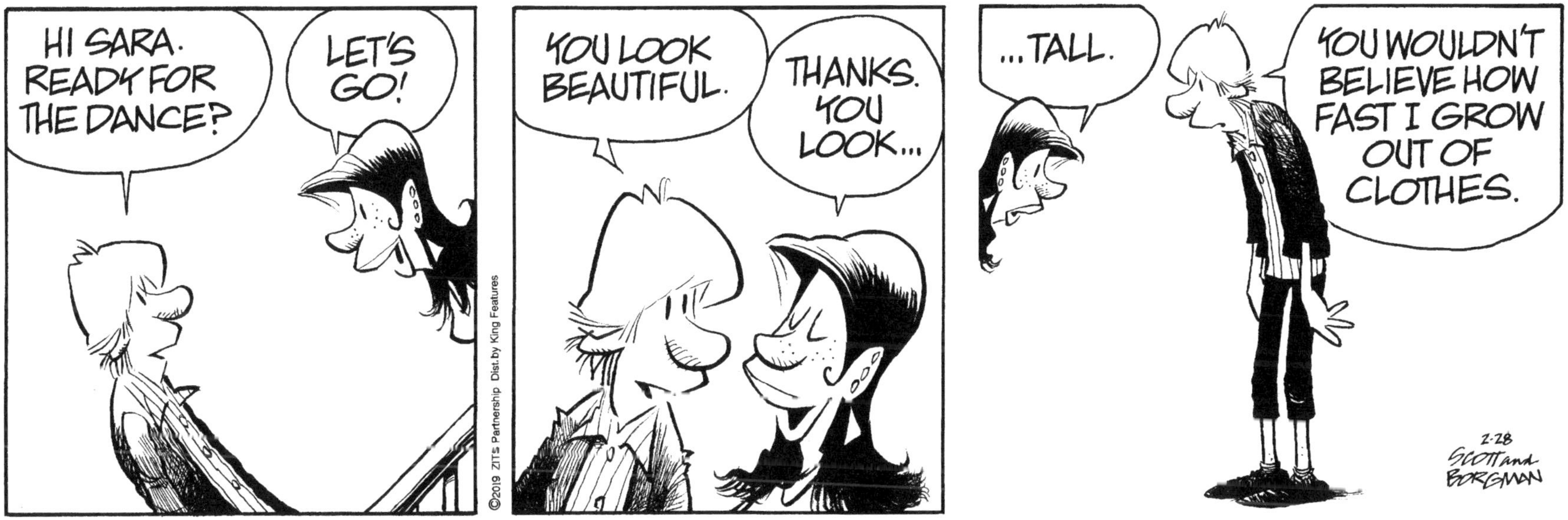
HI SARA. READY FOR THE DANCE?
LET'S GO!
YOU LOOK BEAUTIFUL.
THANKS. YOU LOOK...
...TALL.
YOU WOULDN'T BELIEVE HOW FAST I GROW OUT OF CLOTHES.
2-28 SCOTT and BORGMAN

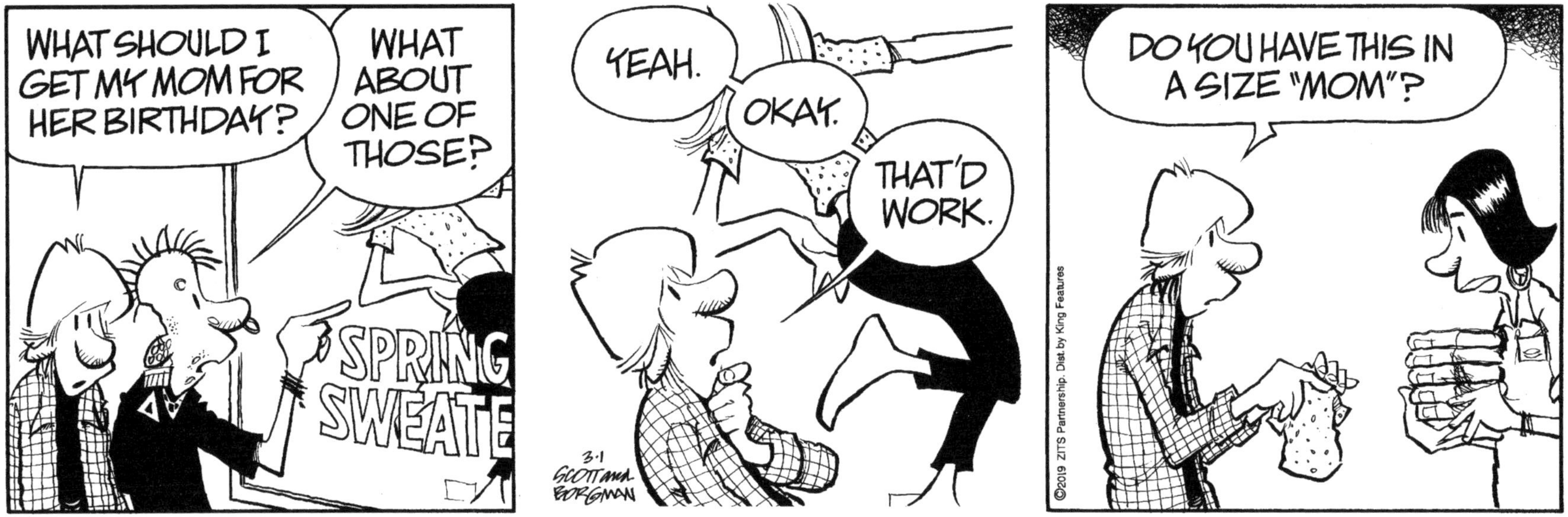
WHAT SHOULD I GET MY MOM FOR HER BIRTHDAY?
WHAT ABOUT ONE OF THOSE?
SPRING SWEATE
YEAH.
OKAY.
THAT'D WORK.
3·1 SCOTT and BORGMAN
DO YOU HAVE THIS IN A SIZE "MOM"?
©2019 ZITS Partnership. Dist. by King Features

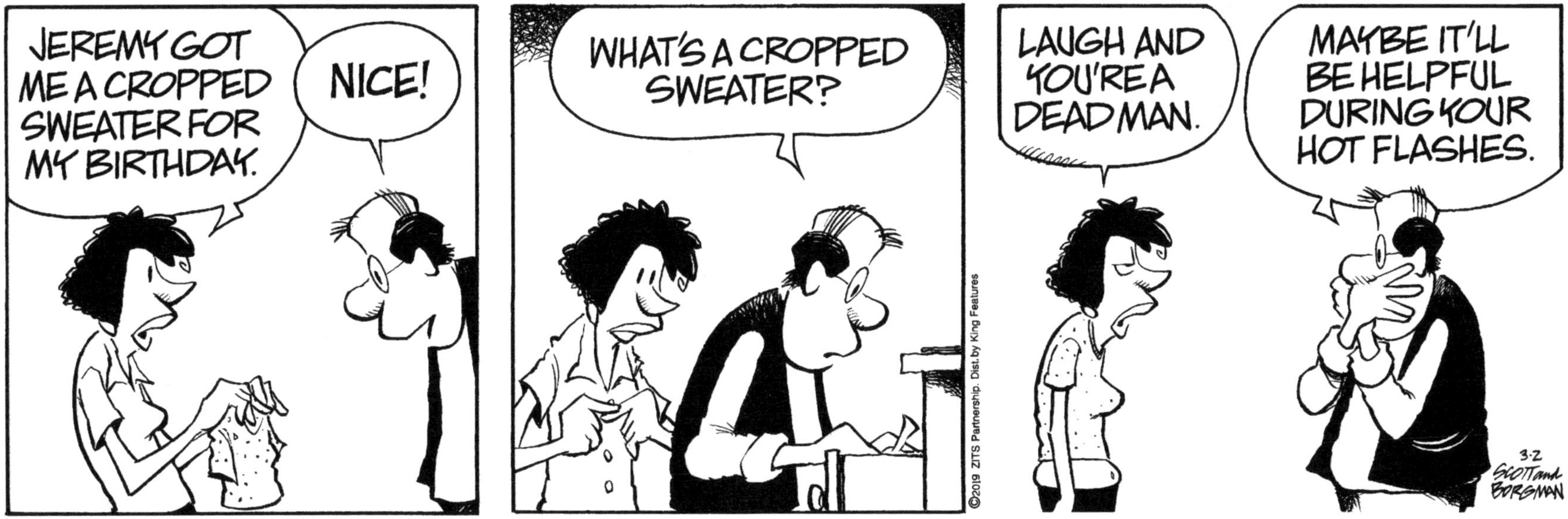
JEREMY GOT ME A CROPPED SWEATER FOR MY BIRTHDAY.
NICE!
WHAT'S A CROPPED SWEATER?
©2019 ZITS Partnership. Dist. by King Features
LAUGH AND YOU'RE A DEAD MAN.
MAYBE IT'LL BE HELPFUL DURING YOUR HOT FLASHES.
3·2 SCOTT and BORGMAN

ZITS

by JERRY SCOTT and JIM BORGMAN

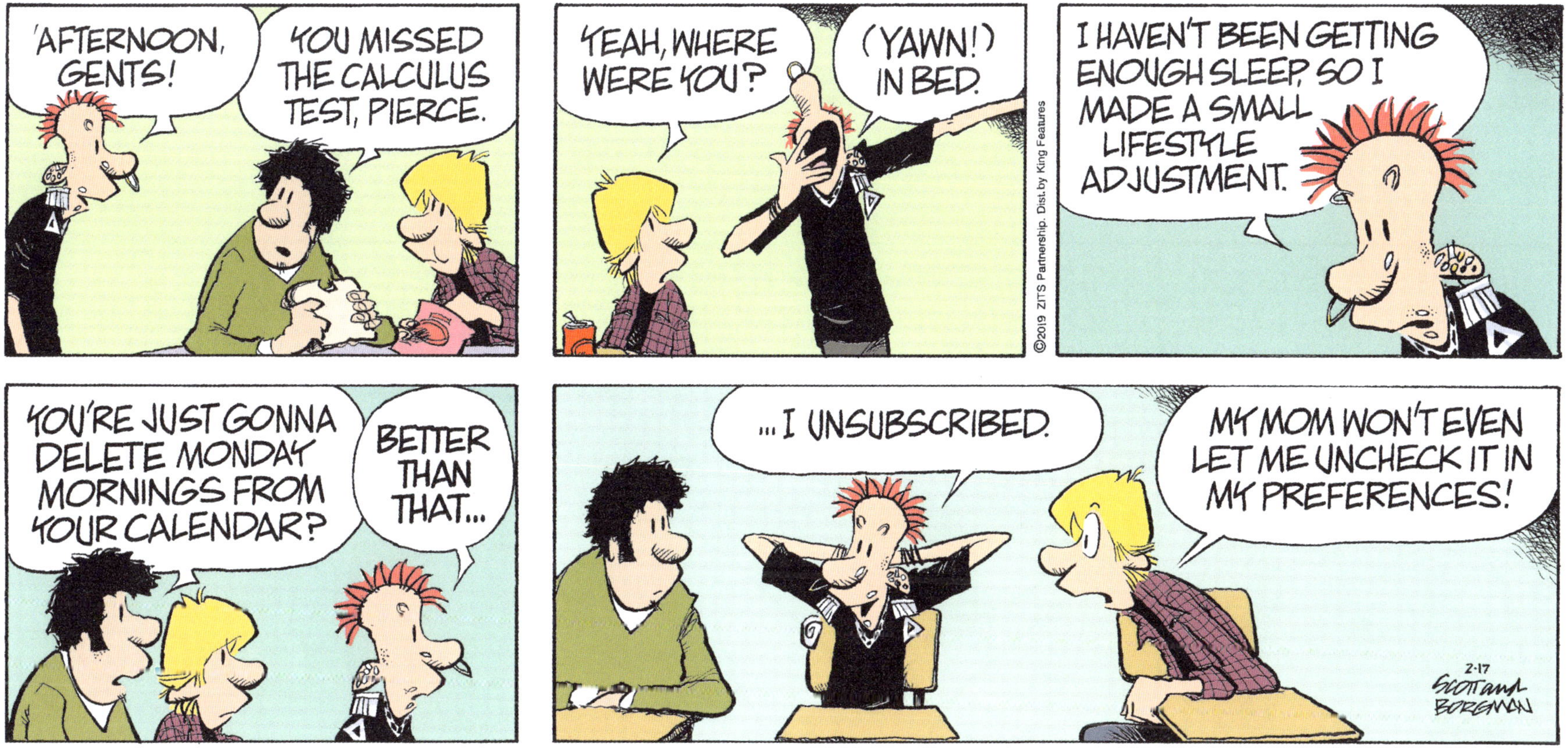
'AFTERNOON, GENTS!
YOU MISSED THE CALCULUS TEST, PIERCE.
YEAH, WHERE WERE YOU?
(YAWN!) IN BED.
©2019 ZITS Partnership. Dist. by King Features
I HAVEN'T BEEN GETTING ENOUGH SLEEP, SO I MADE A SMALL LIFESTYLE ADJUSTMENT.
YOU'RE JUST GONNA DELETE MONDAY MORNINGS FROM YOUR CALENDAR?
BETTER THAN THAT...
...I UNSUBSCRIBED.
MY MOM WON'T EVEN LET ME UNCHECK IT IN MY PREFERENCES!
2-17
SCOTT and BORGMAN

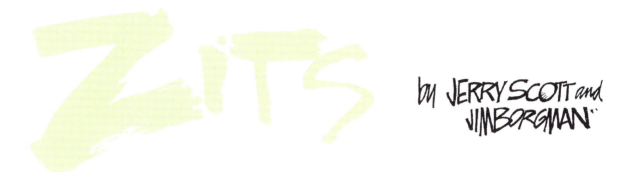

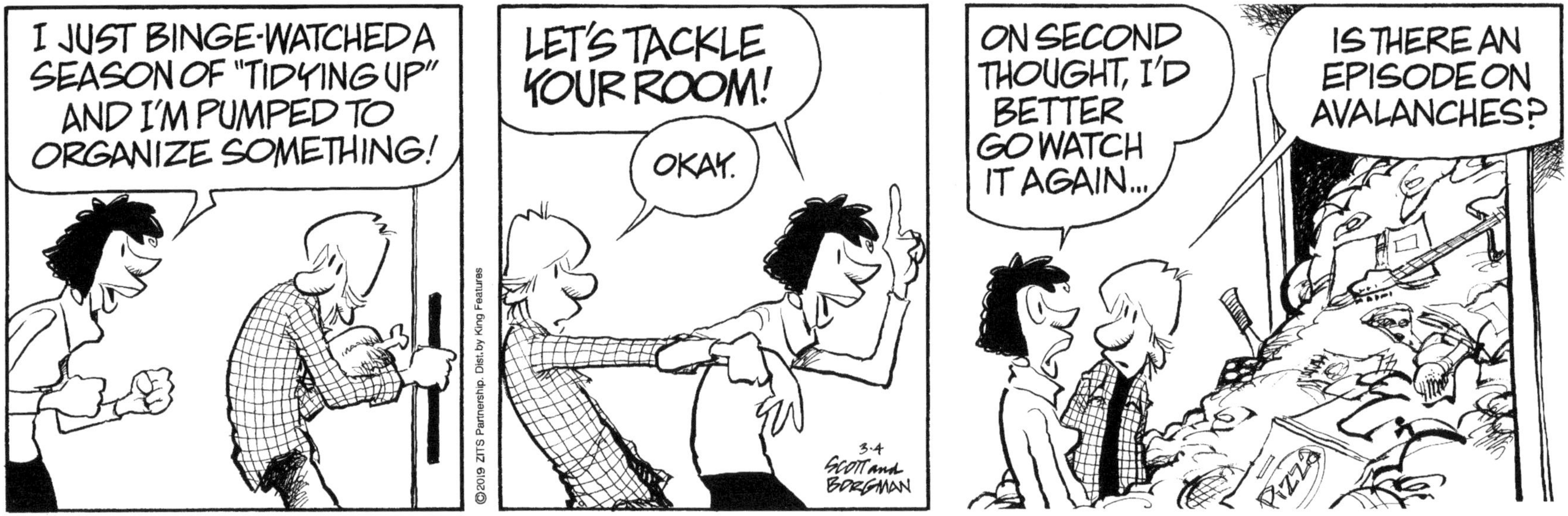
I JUST BINGE-WATCHED A SEASON OF "TIDYING UP" AND I'M PUMPED TO ORGANIZE SOMETHING!
LET'S TACKLE YOUR ROOM!
OKAY.
ON SECOND THOUGHT, I'D BETTER GO WATCH IT AGAIN...
IS THERE AN EPISODE ON AVALANCHES?
PIZZA
3·4
SCOTT and BORGMAN
©2019 ZITS Partnership. Dist.by King Features

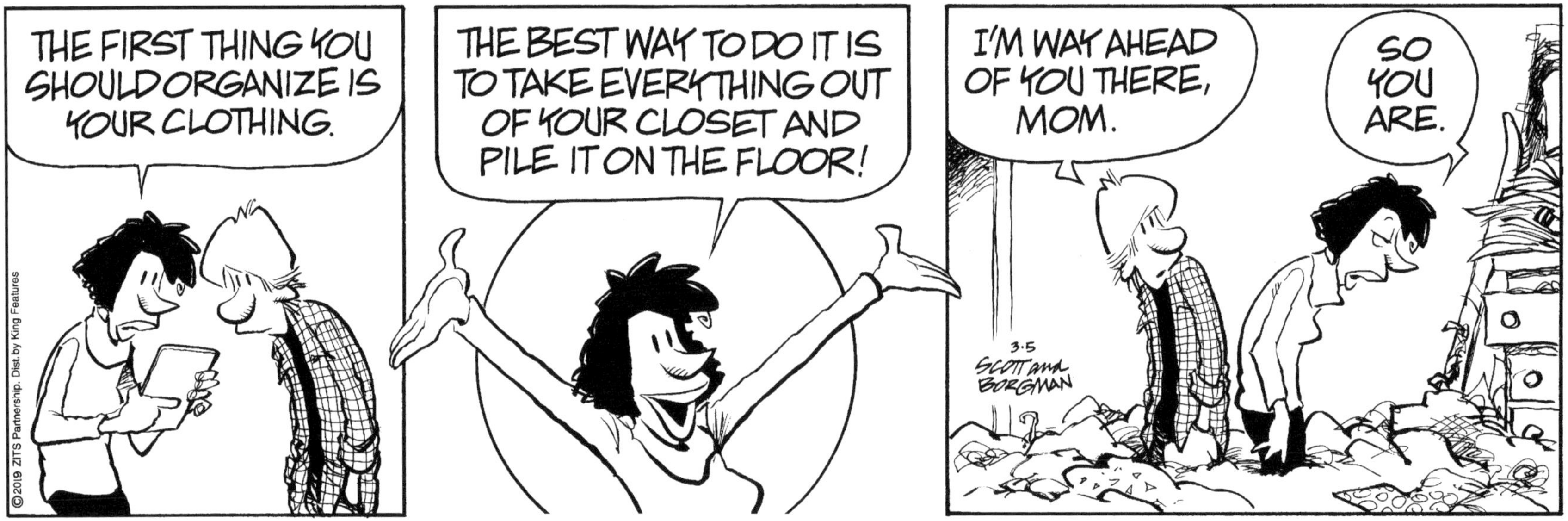
THE FIRST THING YOU SHOULD ORGANIZE IS YOUR CLOTHING.
THE BEST WAY TO DO IT IS TO TAKE EVERYTHING OUT OF YOUR CLOSET AND PILE IT ON THE FLOOR!
I'M WAY AHEAD OF YOU THERE, MOM.
SO YOU ARE.
3·5
SCOTT and BORGMAN
©2019 ZITS Partnership. Dist.by King Features

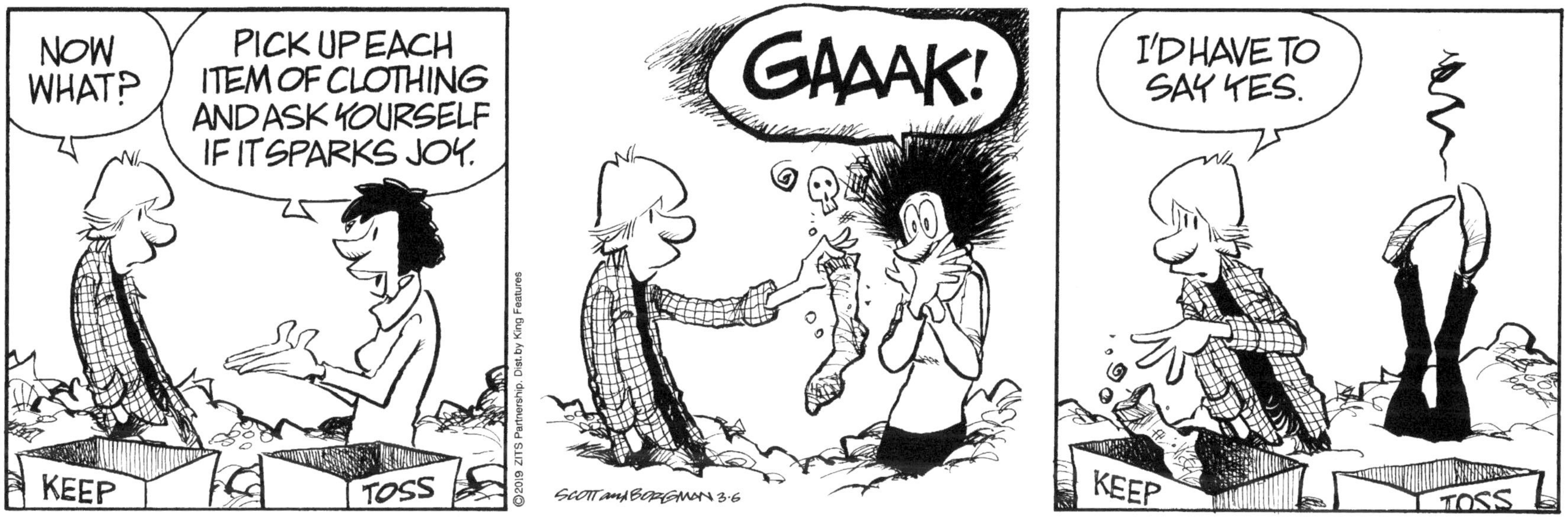
NOW WHAT?
PICK UP EACH ITEM OF CLOTHING AND ASK YOURSELF IF IT SPARKS JOY.
KEEP
TOSS
©2019 ZITS Partnership. Dist. by King Features
GAAAK!
SCOTT and BORGMAN 3·6
I'D HAVE TO SAY YES.
KEEP
TOSS

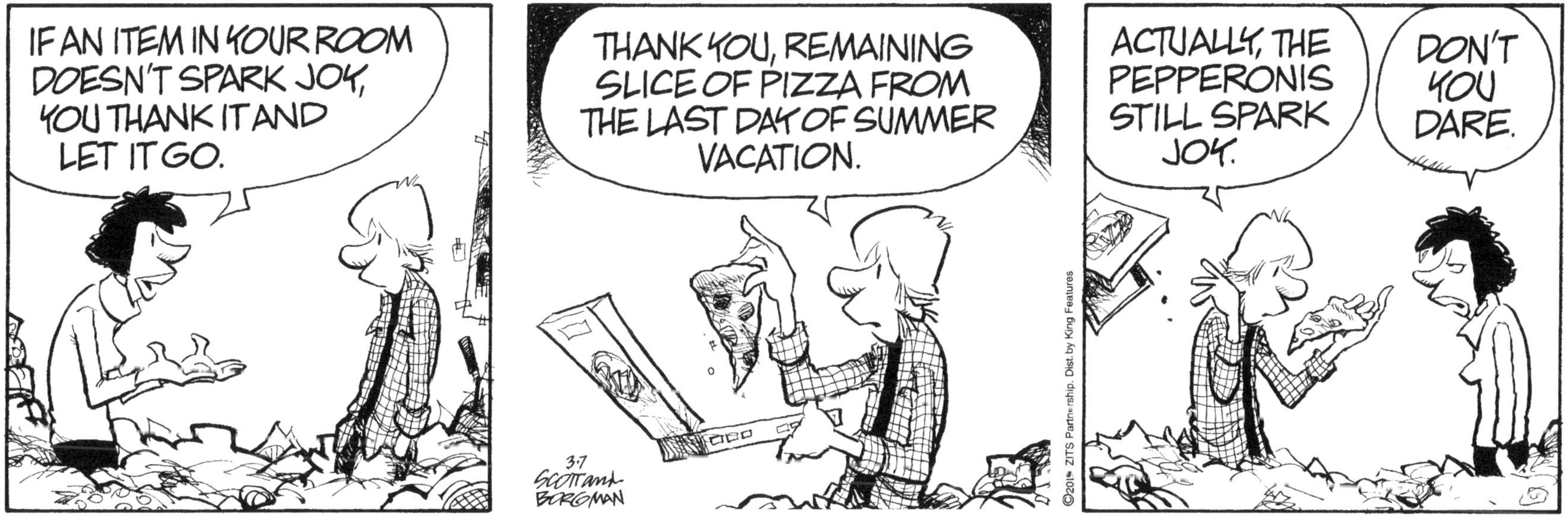
IF AN ITEM IN YOUR ROOM DOESN'T SPARK JOY, YOU THANK IT AND LET IT GO.
THANK YOU, REMAINING SLICE OF PIZZA FROM THE LAST DAY OF SUMMER VACATION.
3·7 SCOTT and BORGMAN
ACTUALLY, THE PEPPERONIS STILL SPARK JOY.
DON'T YOU DARE.

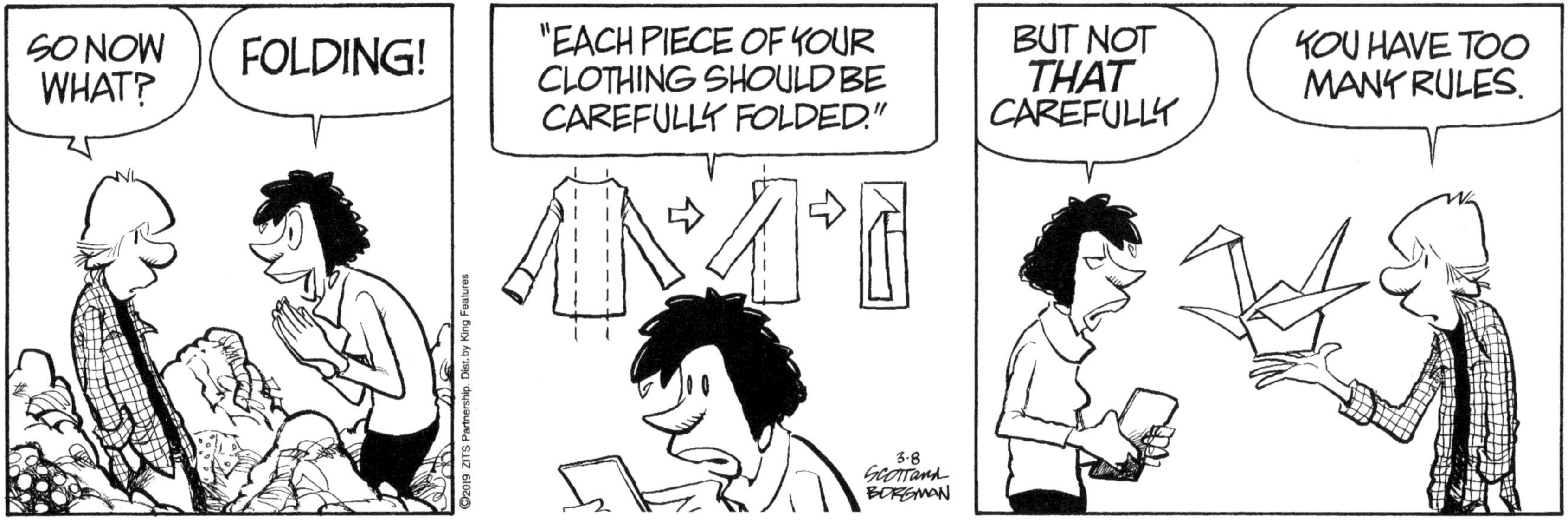
SO NOW WHAT?
FOLDING!
©2019 ZITS Partnership. Dist. by King Features
"EACH PIECE OF YOUR CLOTHING SHOULD BE CAREFULLY FOLDED."
3·8 SCOTT and BORGMAN
BUT NOT *THAT* CAREFULLY
YOU HAVE TOO MANY RULES.

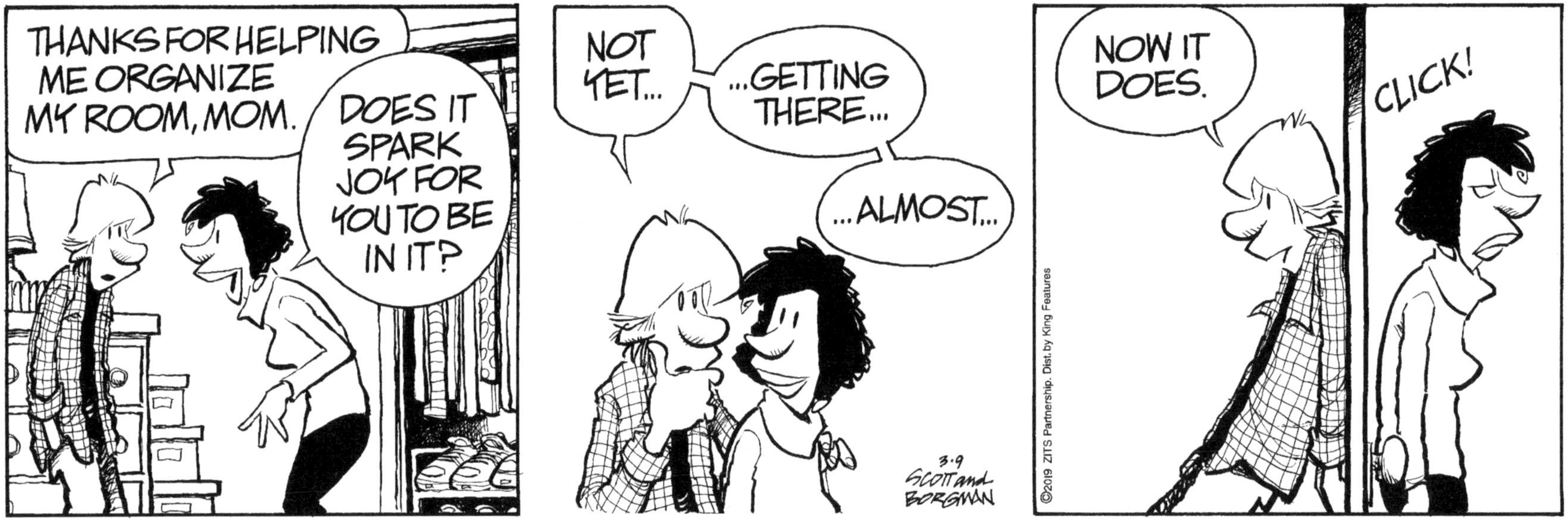
THANKS FOR HELPING ME ORGANIZE MY ROOM, MOM.
DOES IT SPARK JOY FOR YOU TO BE IN IT?
NOT YET...
...GETTING THERE...
...ALMOST...
3·9 SCOTT and BORGMAN
©2019 ZITS Partnership. Dist. by King Features
NOW IT DOES.
CLICK!

ZITS

by JERRY SCOTT and JIM BORGMAN

FINALLY FOUND A PARKING SPACE. HEADING TO THE RESTAURANT NOW. ♥
BE SURE TO PUT MONEY IN THE METER.
I DID.
TAP TAP TAP
©2019 ZITS Partnership. Dist. by King Features
SCOTT and BORGMAN 3·10
TAP TAP TAP TAP
FORGOT TO MENTION THAT WE'RE LOW ON TOILET PAPER AT HOME.
OK
TAP TAP TAP TAP TAP TAP TAP TAP TAP TAP TAP
TAP TAP TAP TAP TAP TAP TAP TAP TAP
WHAT TOOK YOU SO LONG?

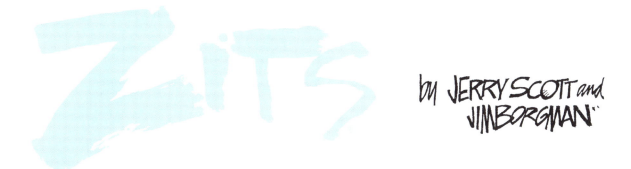

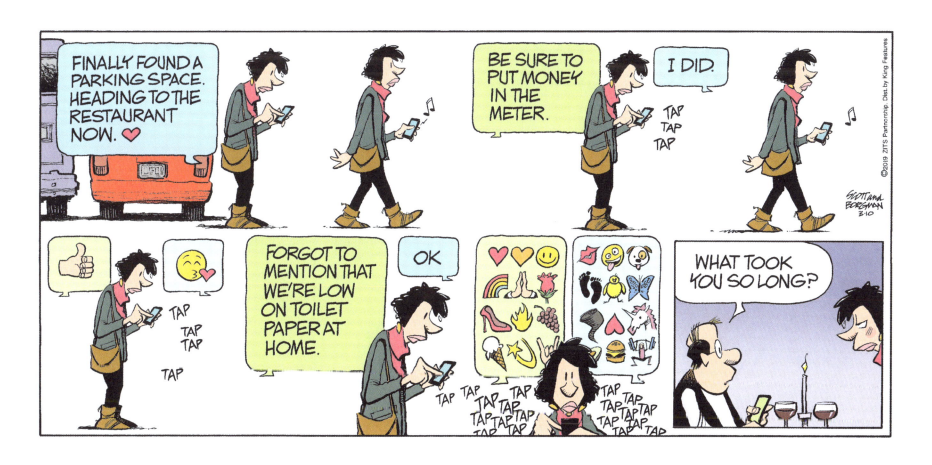

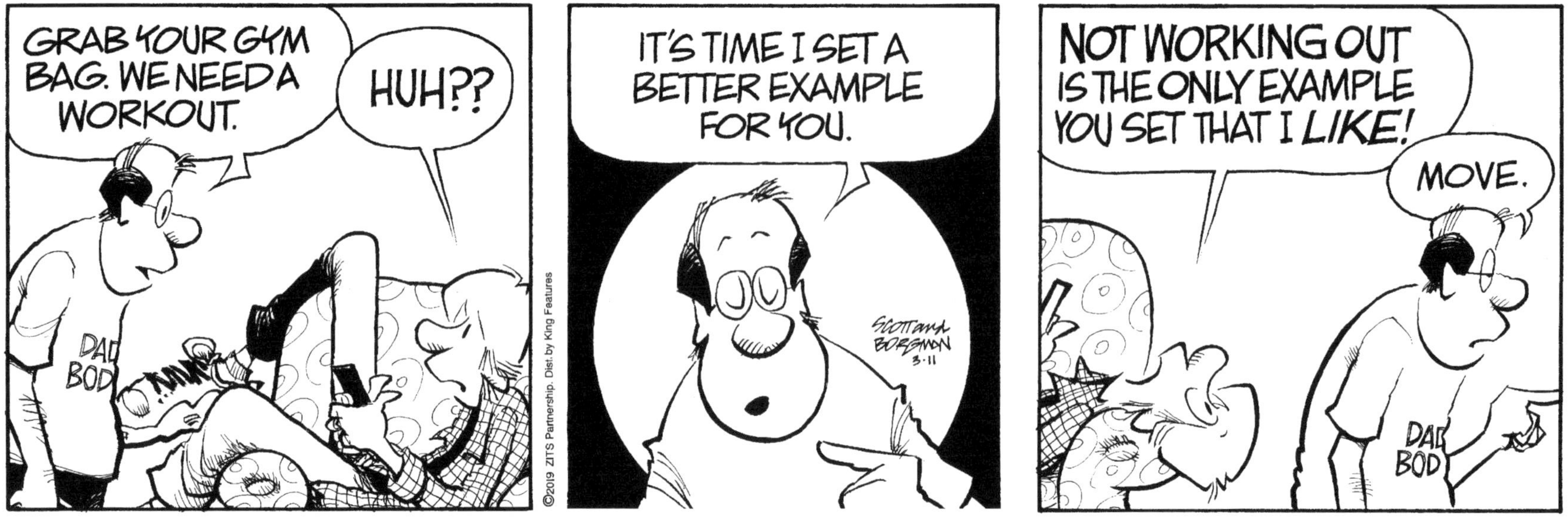
GRAB YOUR GYM BAG. WE NEED A WORKOUT.
HUH??
DAD BOD
©2019 ZITS Partnership. Dist. by King Features
IT'S TIME I SET A BETTER EXAMPLE FOR YOU.
SCOTT and BORGMAN 3-11
NOT WORKING OUT IS THE ONLY EXAMPLE YOU SET THAT I *LIKE*!
MOVE.
DAD BOD

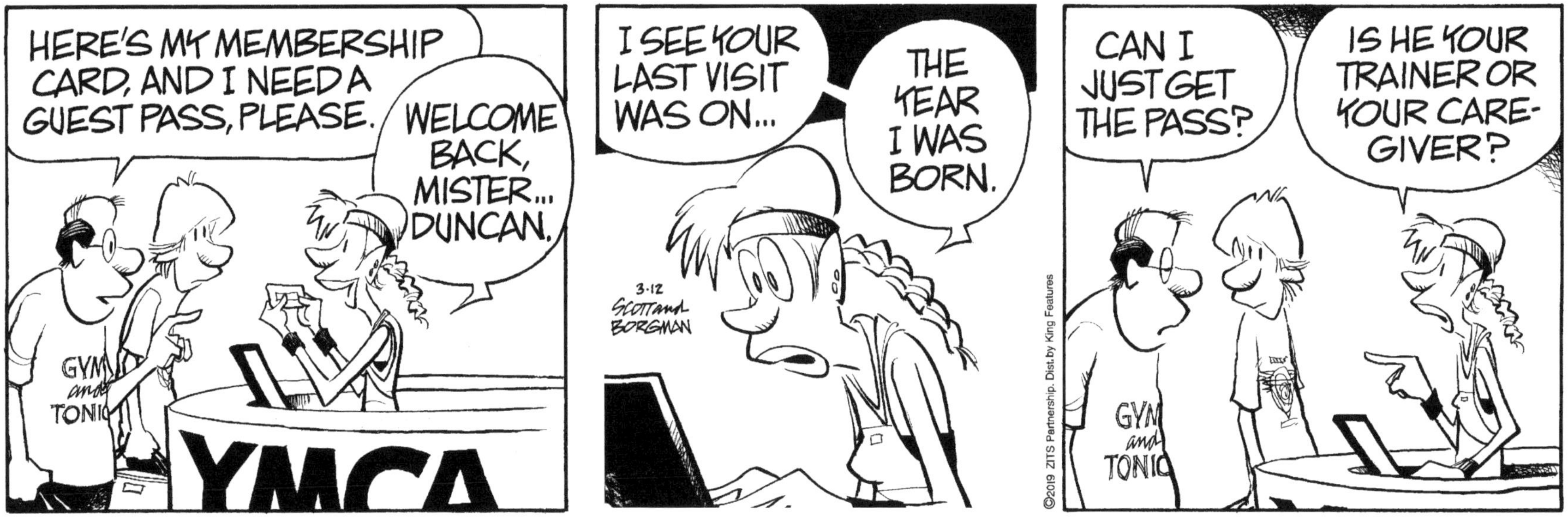
HERE'S MY MEMBERSHIP CARD, AND I NEED A GUEST PASS, PLEASE.
WELCOME BACK, MISTER... DUNCAN.
GYM and TONIC
YMCA
I SEE YOUR LAST VISIT WAS ON...
THE YEAR I WAS BORN.
3-12 SCOTT and BORGMAN
©2019 ZITS Partnership. Dist. by King Features
CAN I JUST GET THE PASS?
IS HE YOUR TRAINER OR YOUR CARE-GIVER?
GYM and TONIC

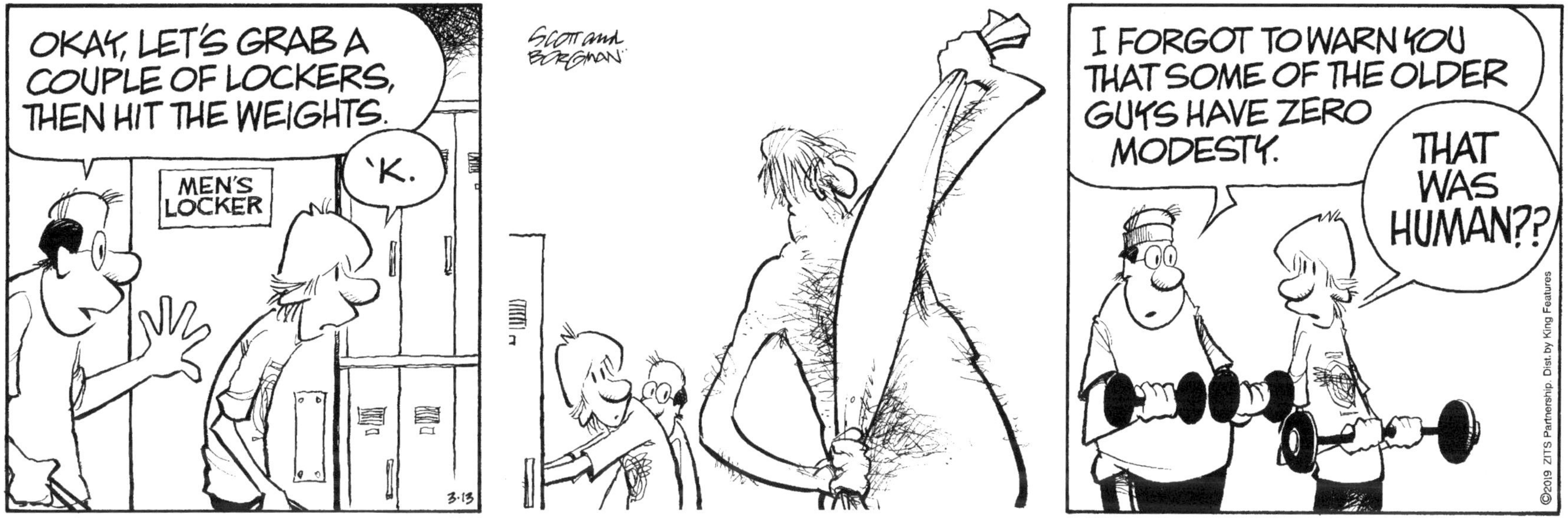
OKAY, LET'S GRAB A COUPLE OF LOCKERS, THEN HIT THE WEIGHTS.
MEN'S LOCKER
'K.
3·13
SCOTT and BORGMAN
I FORGOT TO WARN YOU THAT SOME OF THE OLDER GUYS HAVE ZERO MODESTY.
THAT WAS HUMAN??
©2019 ZITS Partnership. Dist. by King Features

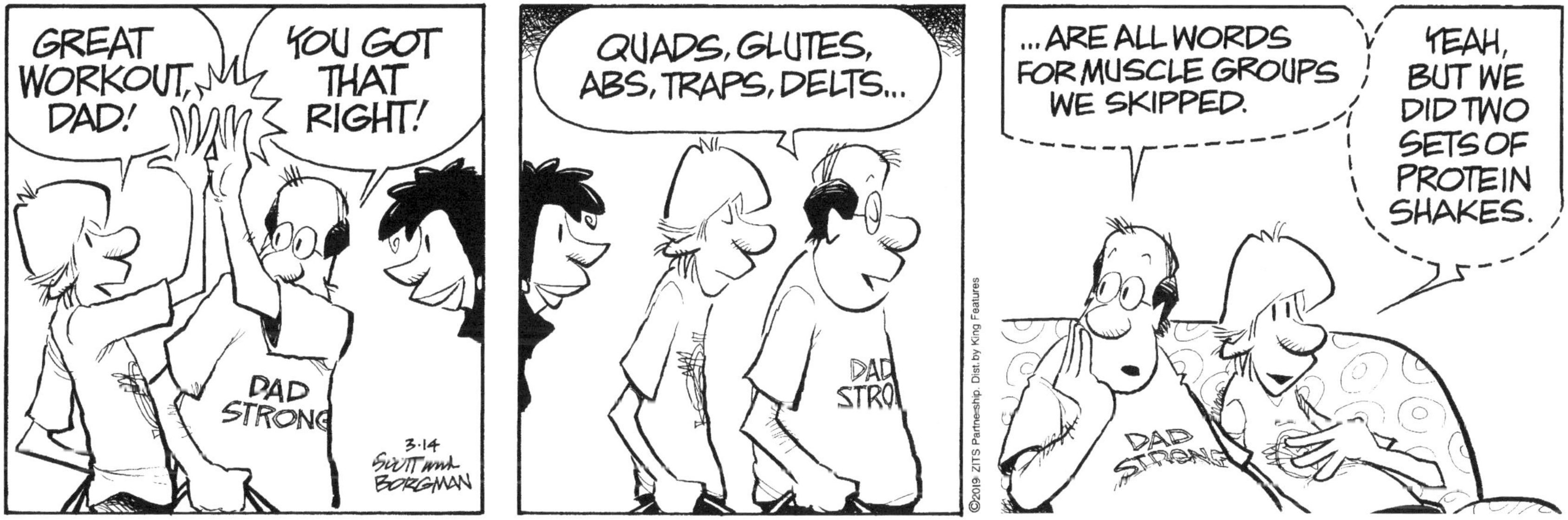
GREAT WORKOUT, DAD!
YOU GOT THAT RIGHT!
DAD STRONG
3·14
SCOTT and BORGMAN
QUADS, GLUTES, ABS, TRAPS, DELTS...
©2019 ZITS Partnership. Dist. by King Features
...ARE ALL WORDS FOR MUSCLE GROUPS WE SKIPPED.
YEAH, BUT WE DID TWO SETS OF PROTEIN SHAKES.

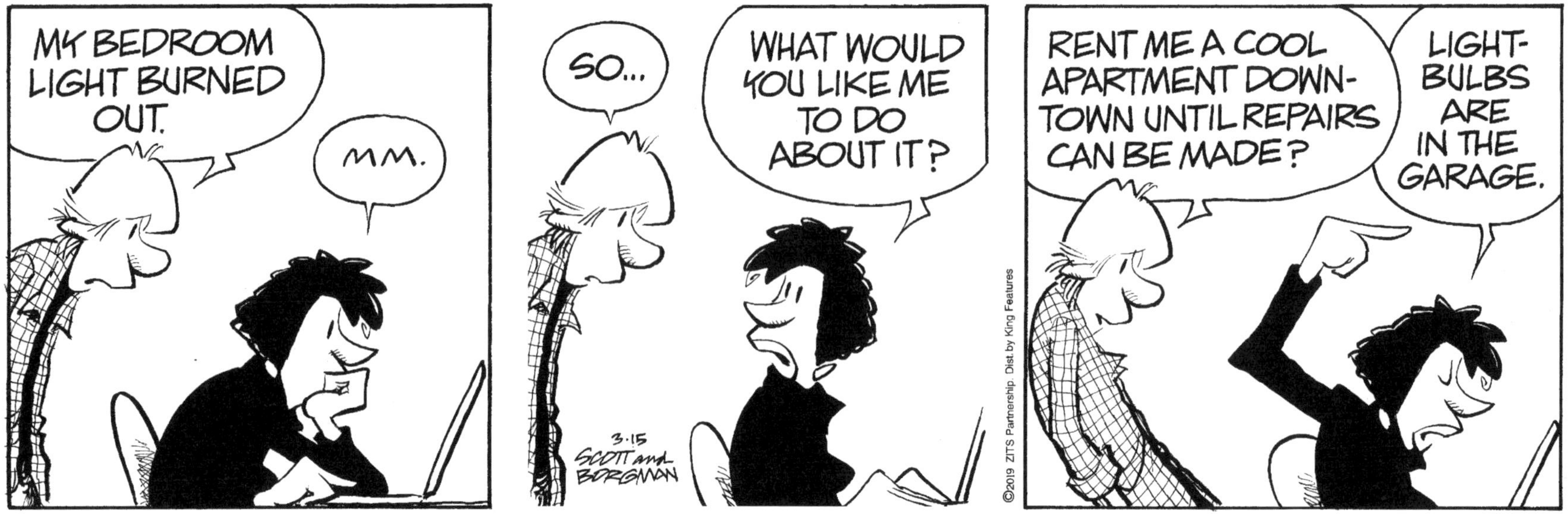
MY BEDROOM LIGHT BURNED OUT.
MM.
SO...
WHAT WOULD YOU LIKE ME TO DO ABOUT IT?
3·15 SCOTT AND BORGMAN
RENT ME A COOL APARTMENT DOWNTOWN UNTIL REPAIRS CAN BE MADE?
LIGHTBULBS ARE IN THE GARAGE.
©2019 ZITS Partnership. Dist. by King Features

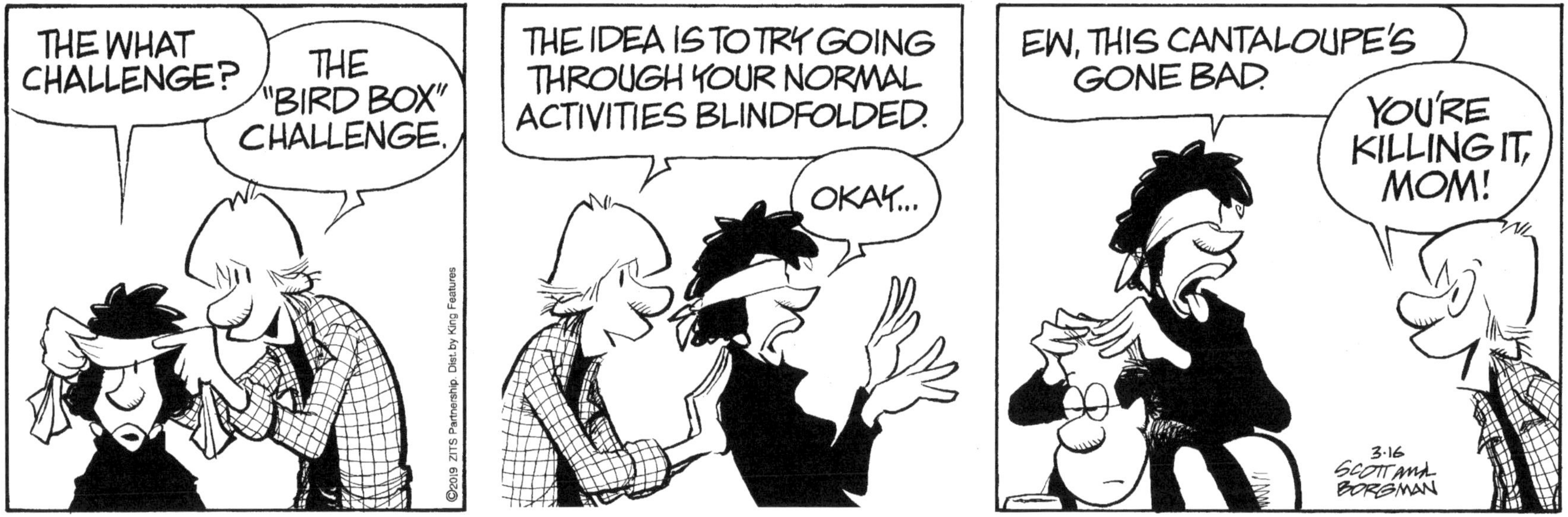
THE WHAT CHALLENGE?
THE "BIRD BOX" CHALLENGE.
©2019 ZITS Partnership. Dist. by King Features
THE IDEA IS TO TRY GOING THROUGH YOUR NORMAL ACTIVITIES BLINDFOLDED.
OKAY...
EW, THIS CANTALOUPE'S GONE BAD.
YOU'RE KILLING IT, MOM!
3·16 SCOTT AND BORGMAN

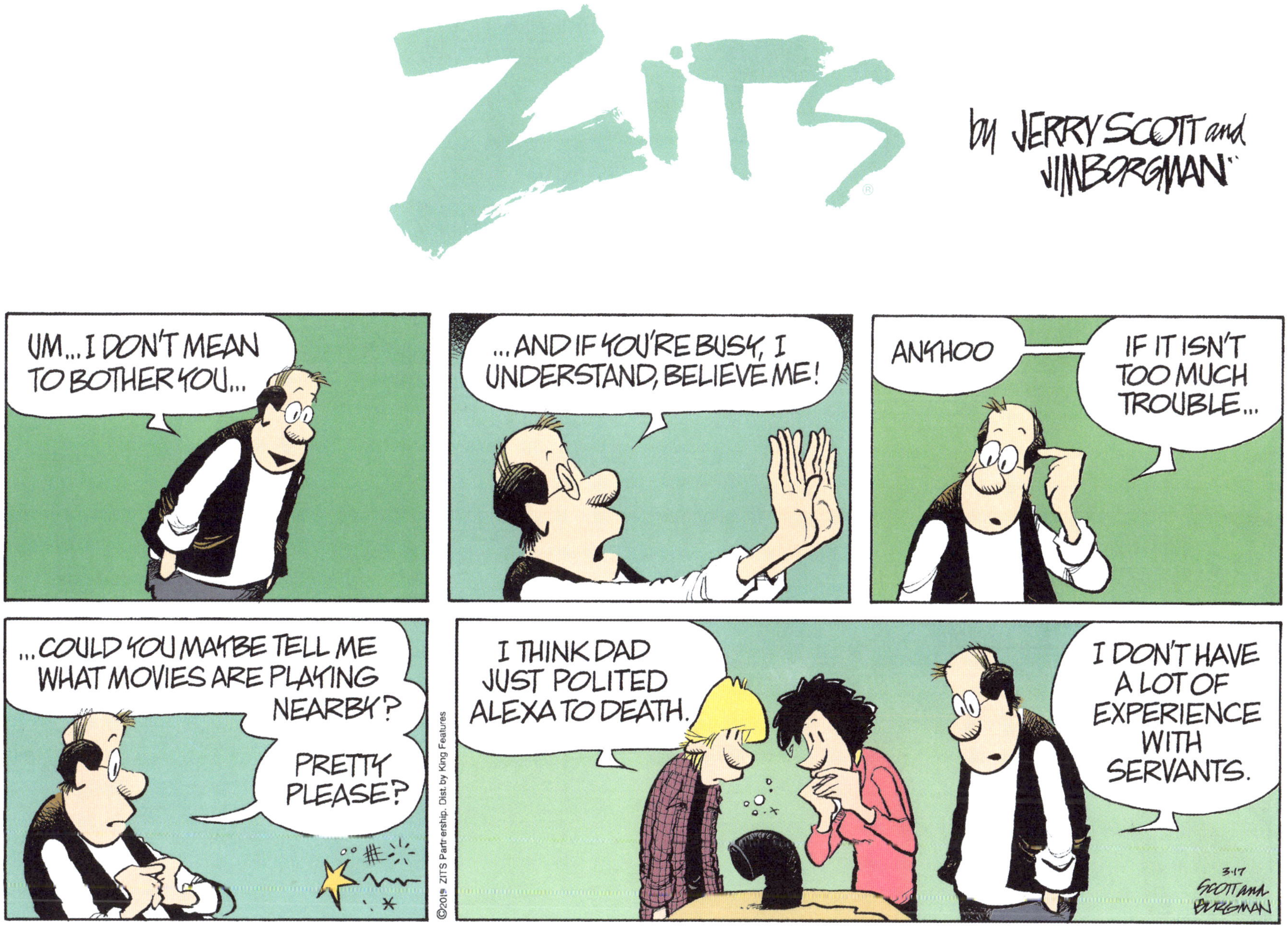
ZITS
by JERRY SCOTT and JIM BORGMAN
UM... I DON'T MEAN TO BOTHER YOU...
...AND IF YOU'RE BUSY, I UNDERSTAND, BELIEVE ME!
ANYHOO
IF IT ISN'T TOO MUCH TROUBLE...
...COULD YOU MAYBE TELL ME WHAT MOVIES ARE PLAYING NEARBY?
PRETTY PLEASE?
©2019 ZITS Partnership. Dist. by King Features
I THINK DAD JUST POLITED ALEXA TO DEATH.
I DON'T HAVE A LOT OF EXPERIENCE WITH SERVANTS.
3-17
SCOTT AND BORGMAN

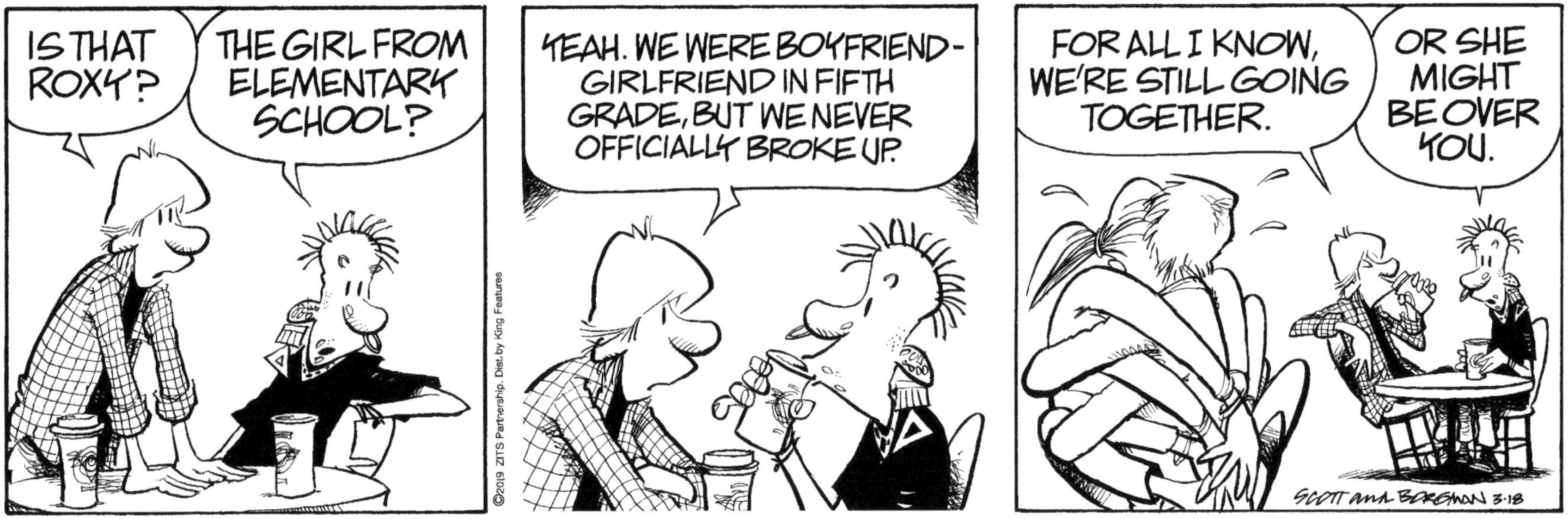
IS THAT ROXY?
THE GIRL FROM ELEMENTARY SCHOOL?
YEAH. WE WERE BOYFRIEND-GIRLFRIEND IN FIFTH GRADE, BUT WE NEVER OFFICIALLY BROKE UP.
FOR ALL I KNOW, WE'RE STILL GOING TOGETHER.
OR SHE MIGHT BE OVER YOU.
©2019 ZITS Partnership. Dist. by King Features
SCOTT and BORGMAN 3·18

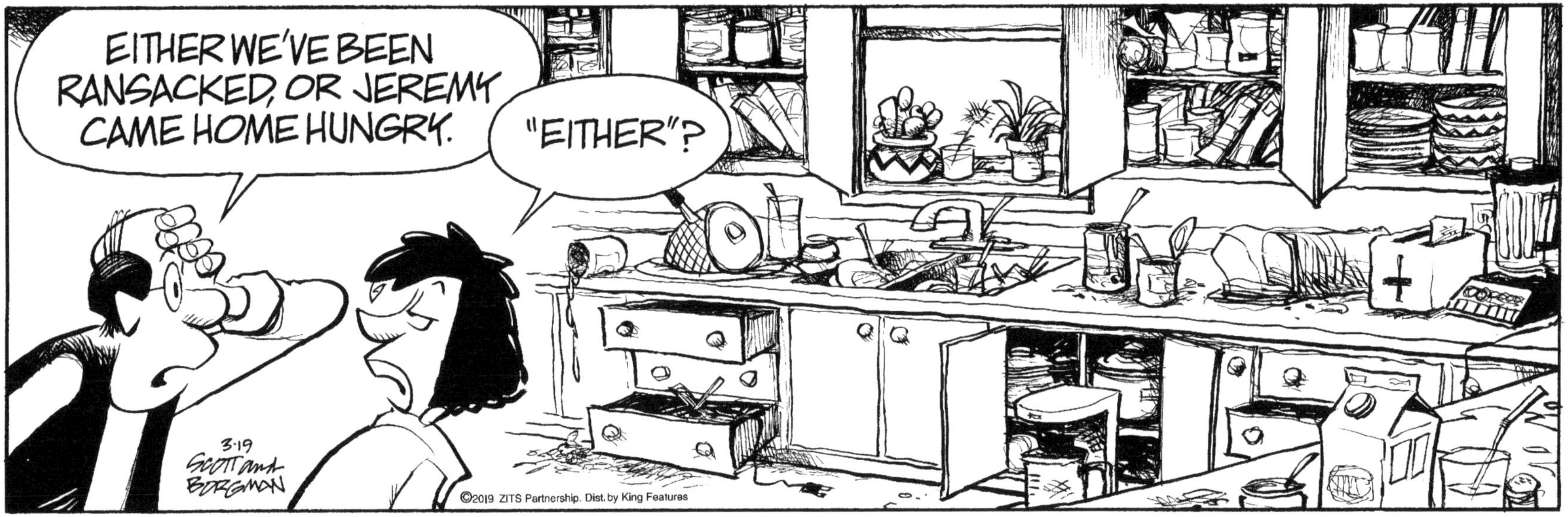
EITHER WE'VE BEEN RANSACKED, OR JEREMY CAME HOME HUNGRY.
"EITHER"?
3·19 SCOTT and BORGMAN
©2019 ZITS Partnership. Dist. by King Features

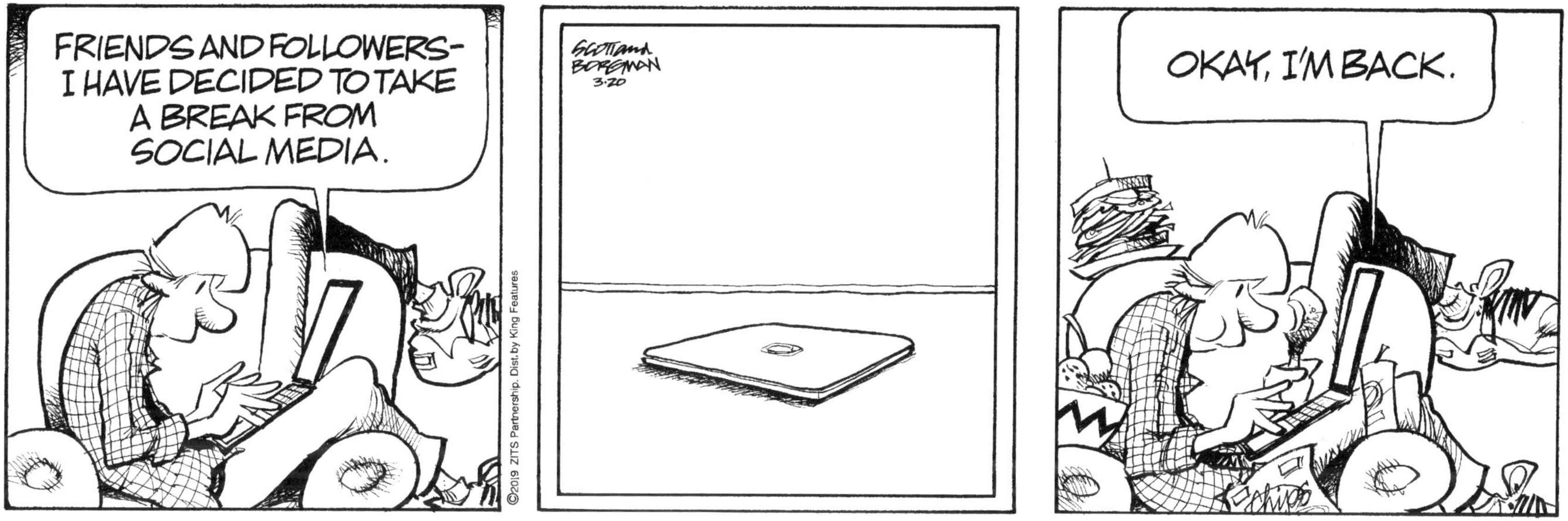
FRIENDS AND FOLLOWERS- I HAVE DECIDED TO TAKE A BREAK FROM SOCIAL MEDIA.
©2019 ZITS Partnership. Dist. by King Features
3-20
OKAY, I'M BACK.
CHIPS

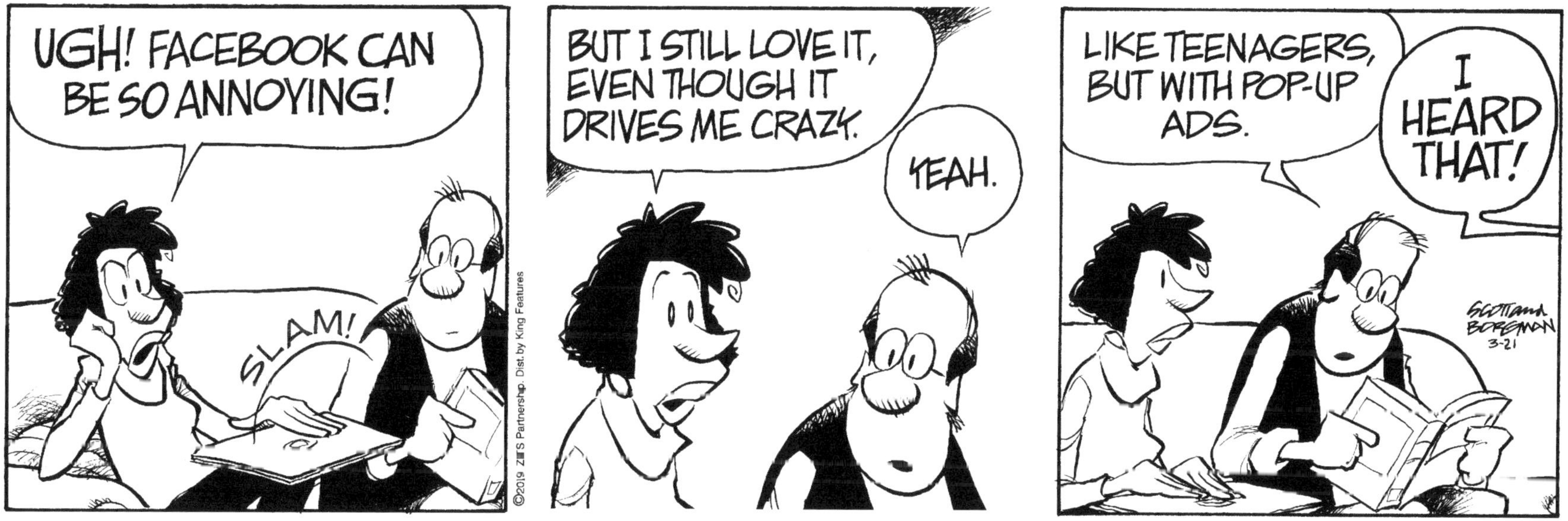
UGH! FACEBOOK CAN BE SO ANNOYING!
SLAM!
©2019 ZITS Partnership. Dist. by King Features
BUT I STILL LOVE IT, EVEN THOUGH IT DRIVES ME CRAZY.
YEAH.
LIKE TEENAGERS, BUT WITH POP-UP ADS.
I HEARD THAT!
3-21

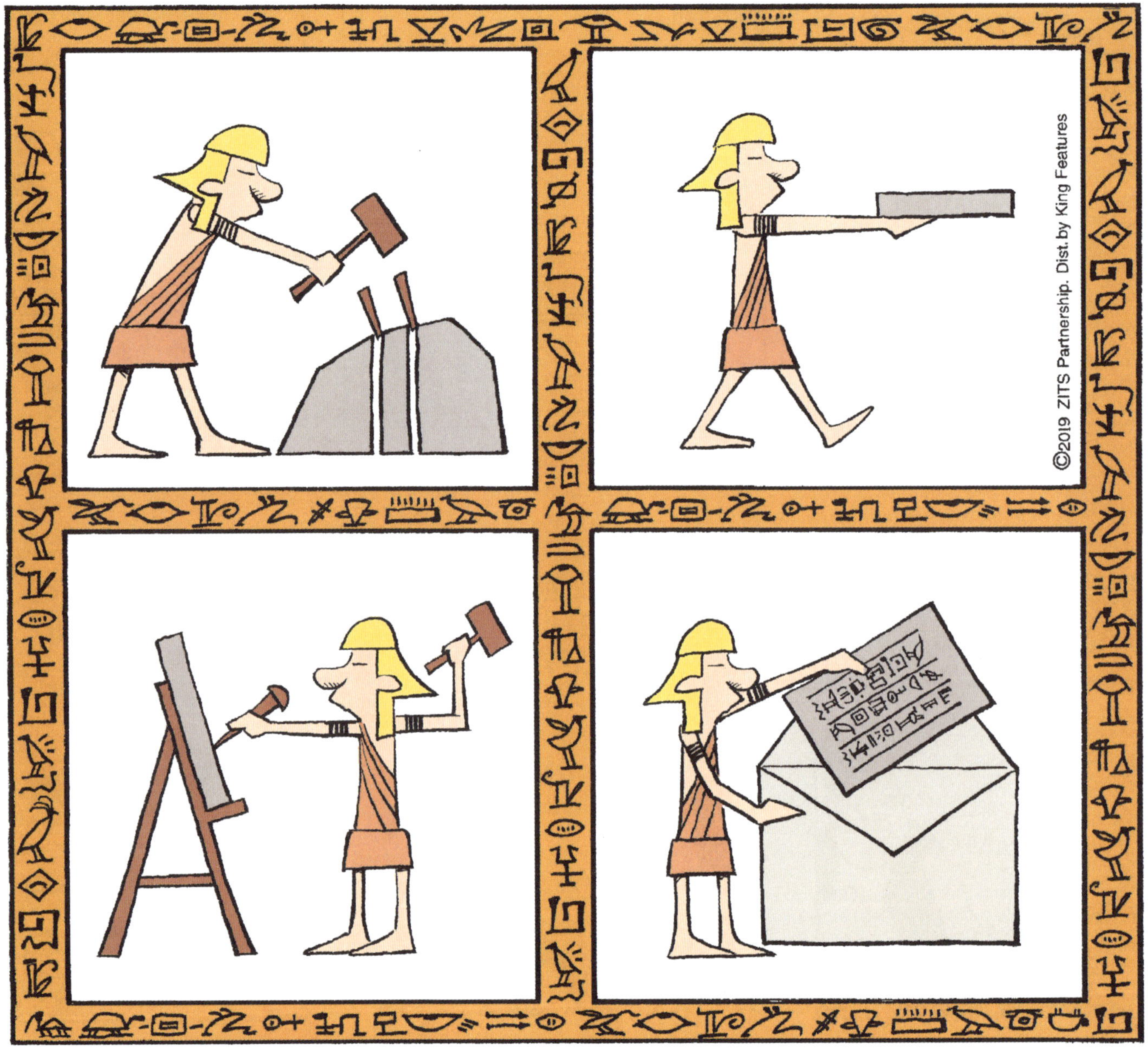
©2019 ZITS Partnership. Dist.by King Features

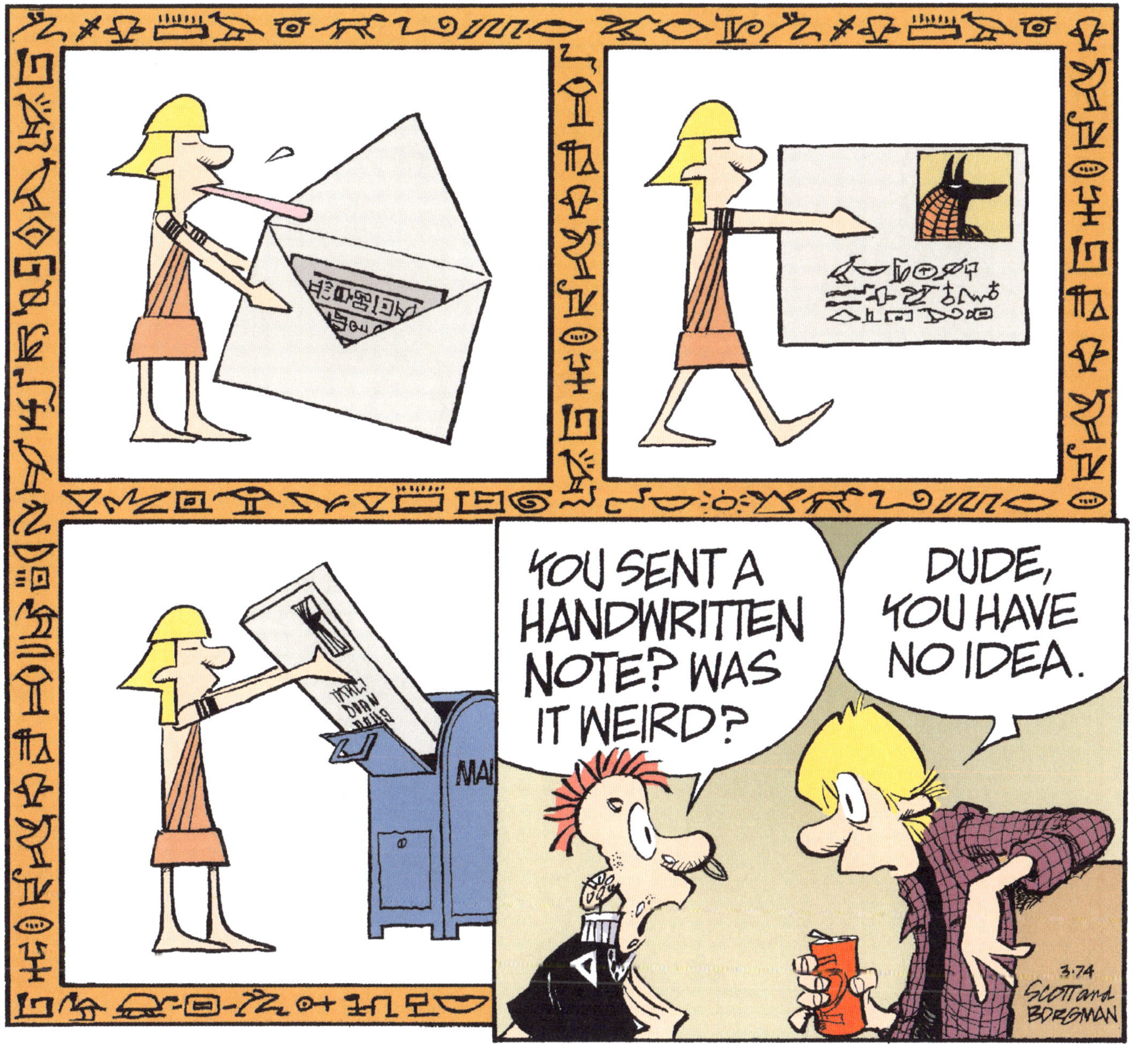
YOU SENT A HANDWRITTEN NOTE? WAS IT WEIRD?
DUDE, YOU HAVE NO IDEA.
3-74
SCOTT and BORGMAN

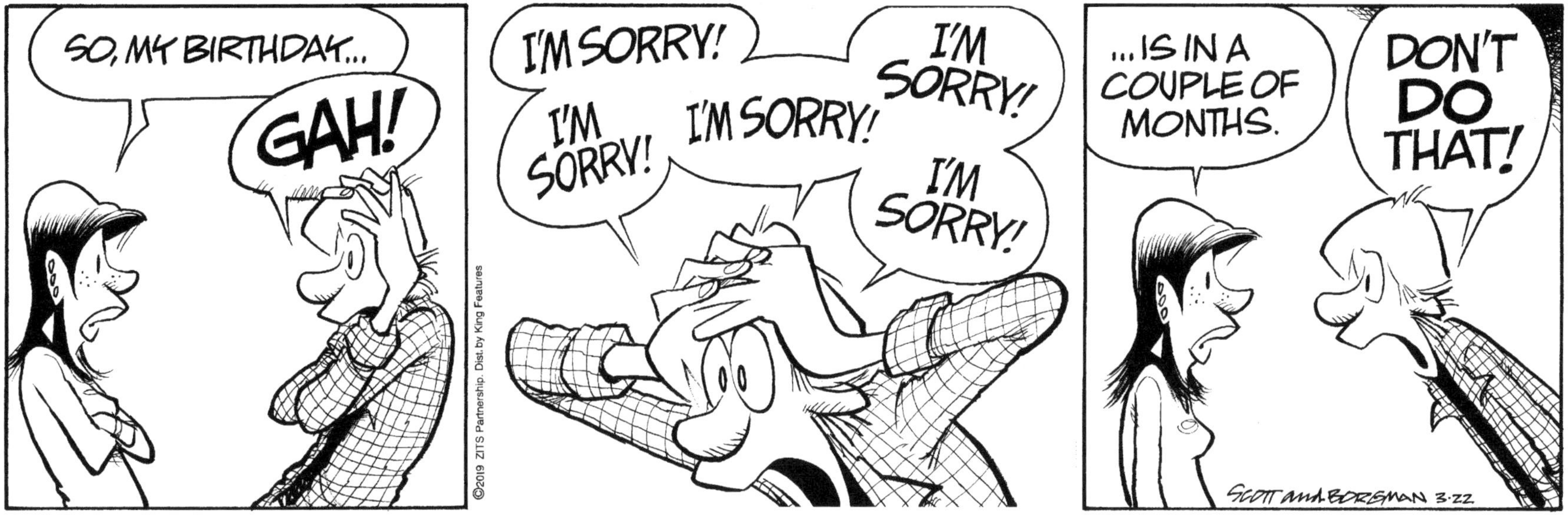
SO, MY BIRTHDAY...
GAH!
©2019 ZITS Partnership. Dist. by King Features
I'M SORRY!
I'M SORRY!
I'M SORRY!
I'M SORRY!
I'M SORRY!
...IS IN A COUPLE OF MONTHS.
DON'T DO THAT!
SCOTT AND BORGMAN 3·22

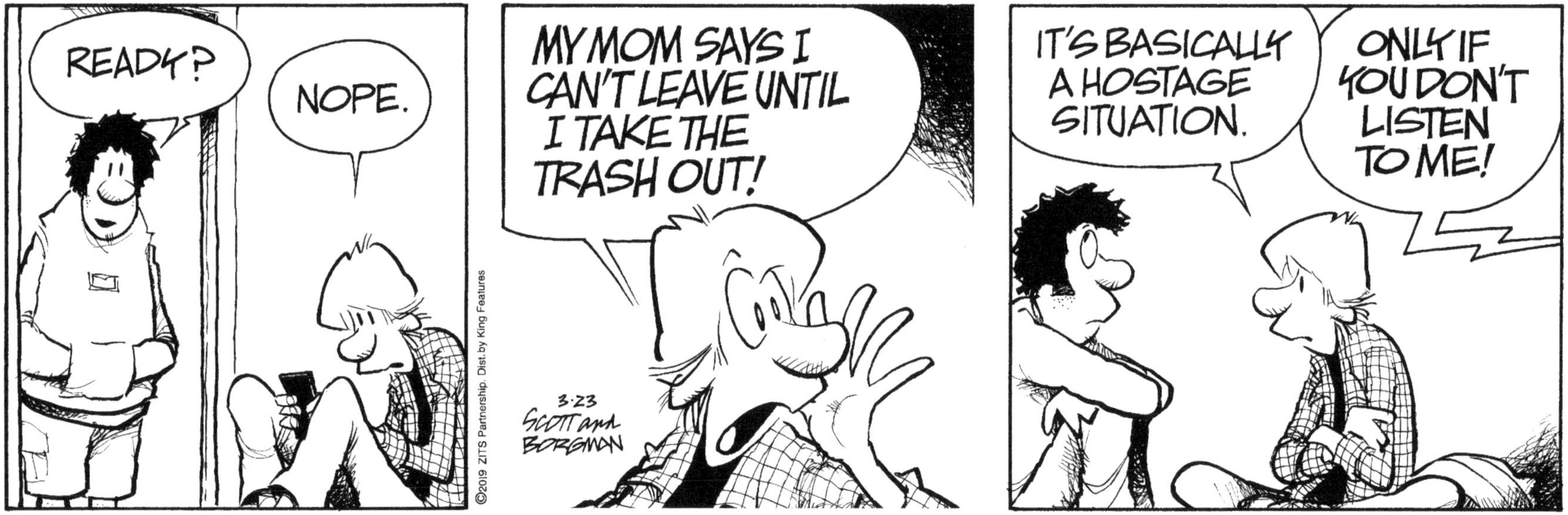
READY?
NOPE.
©2019 ZITS Partnership. Dist. by King Features
MY MOM SAYS I CAN'T LEAVE UNTIL I TAKE THE TRASH OUT!
3·23 SCOTT AND BORGMAN
IT'S BASICALLY A HOSTAGE SITUATION.
ONLY IF YOU DON'T LISTEN TO ME!

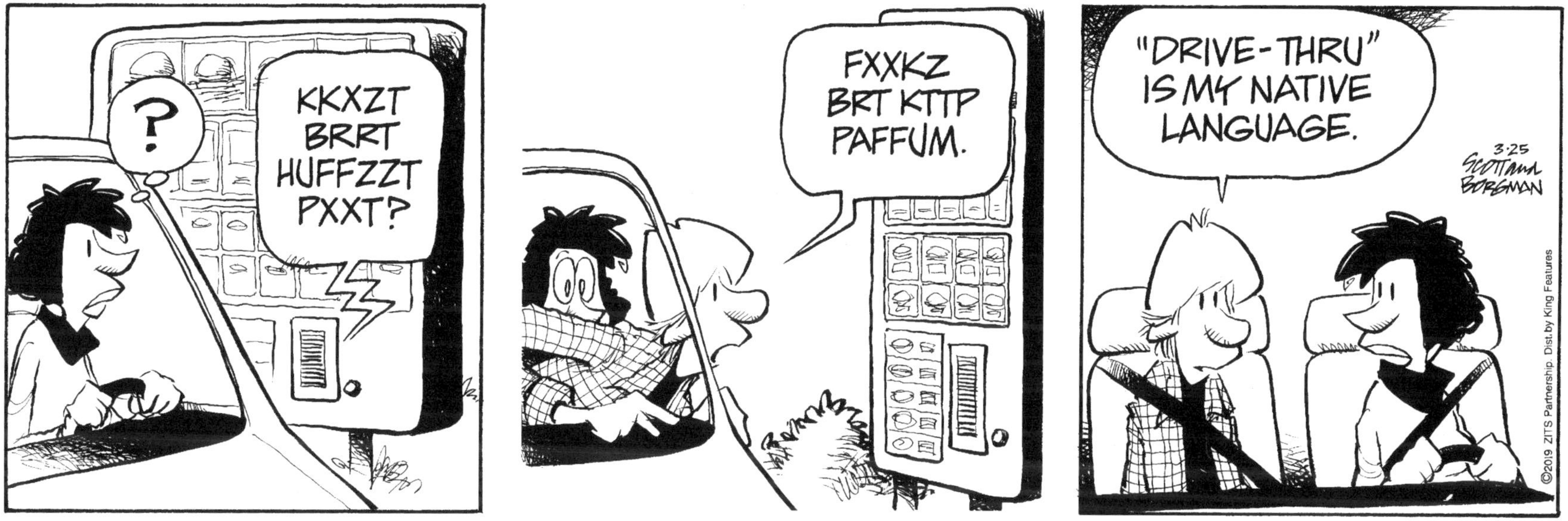
?
KKXZT BRRT HUFFZZT PXXT?
FXXKZ BRT KTTP PAFFUM.
"DRIVE-THRU" IS MY NATIVE LANGUAGE.
3·25
SCOTT and BORGMAN
©2019 ZITS Partnership. Dist. by King Features

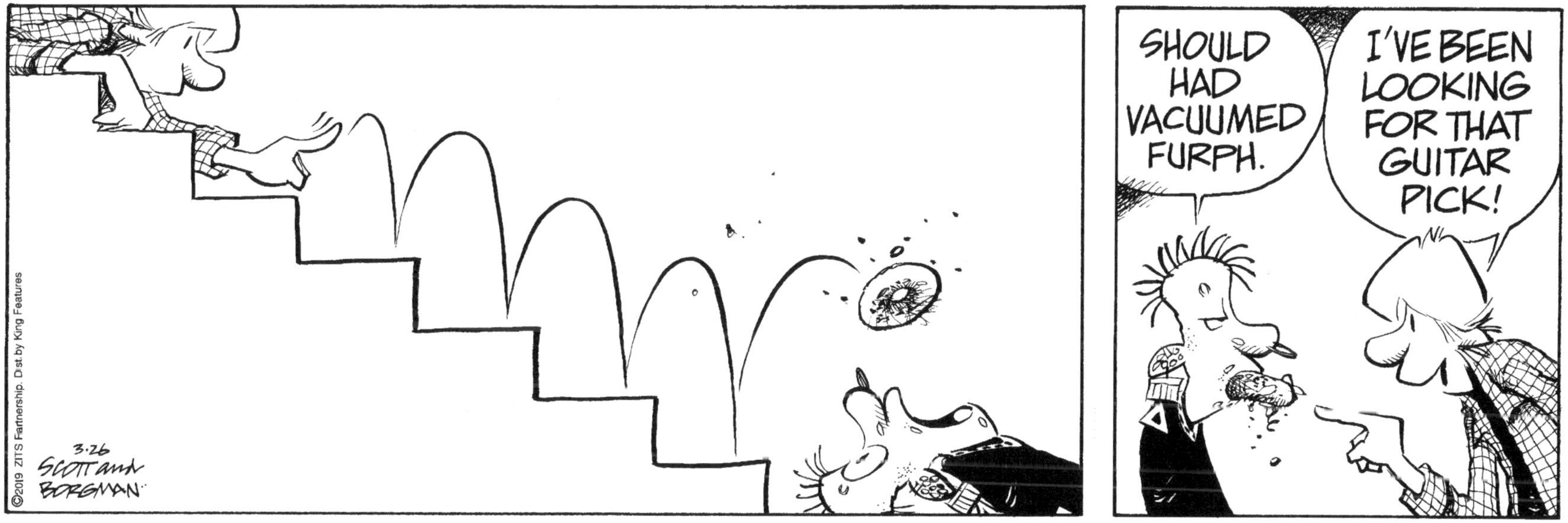
©2019 ZITS Partnership. Dist. by King Features
3·26
SCOTT and BORGMAN
SHOULD HAD VACUUMED FURPH.
I'VE BEEN LOOKING FOR THAT GUITAR PICK!

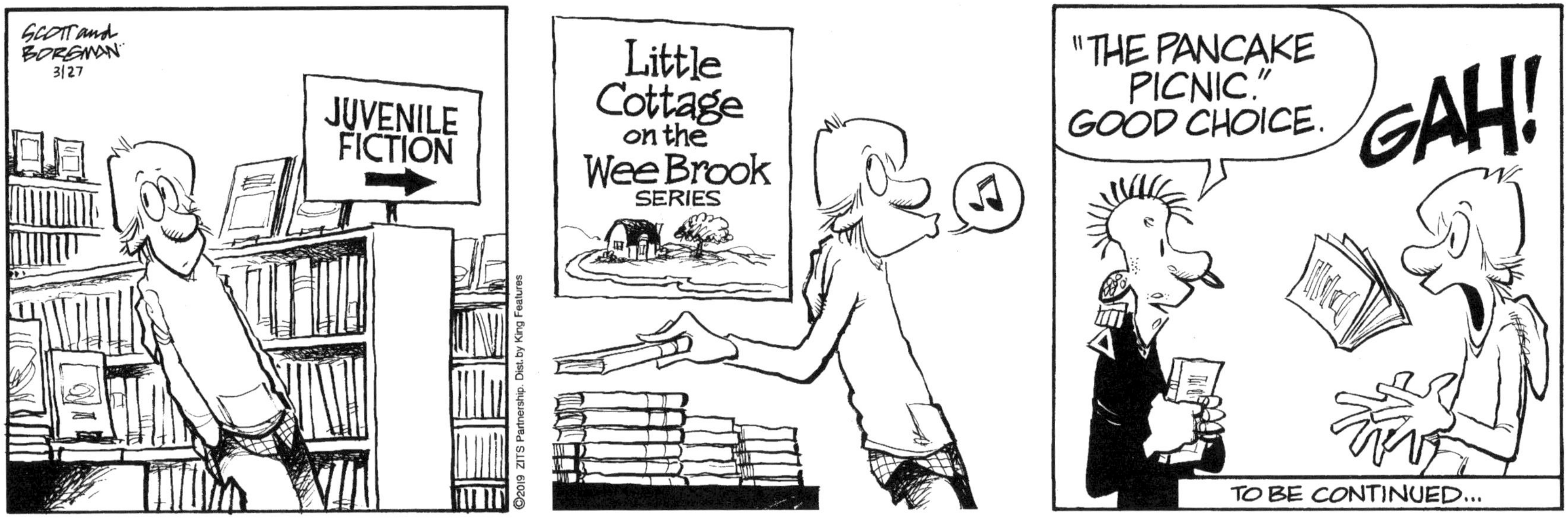
SCOTT and BORGMAN 3/27
JUVENILE FICTION
©2019 ZITS Partnership. Dist. by King Features
Little Cottage on the Wee Brook SERIES
"THE PANCAKE PICNIC." GOOD CHOICE.
GAH!
TO BE CONTINUED...

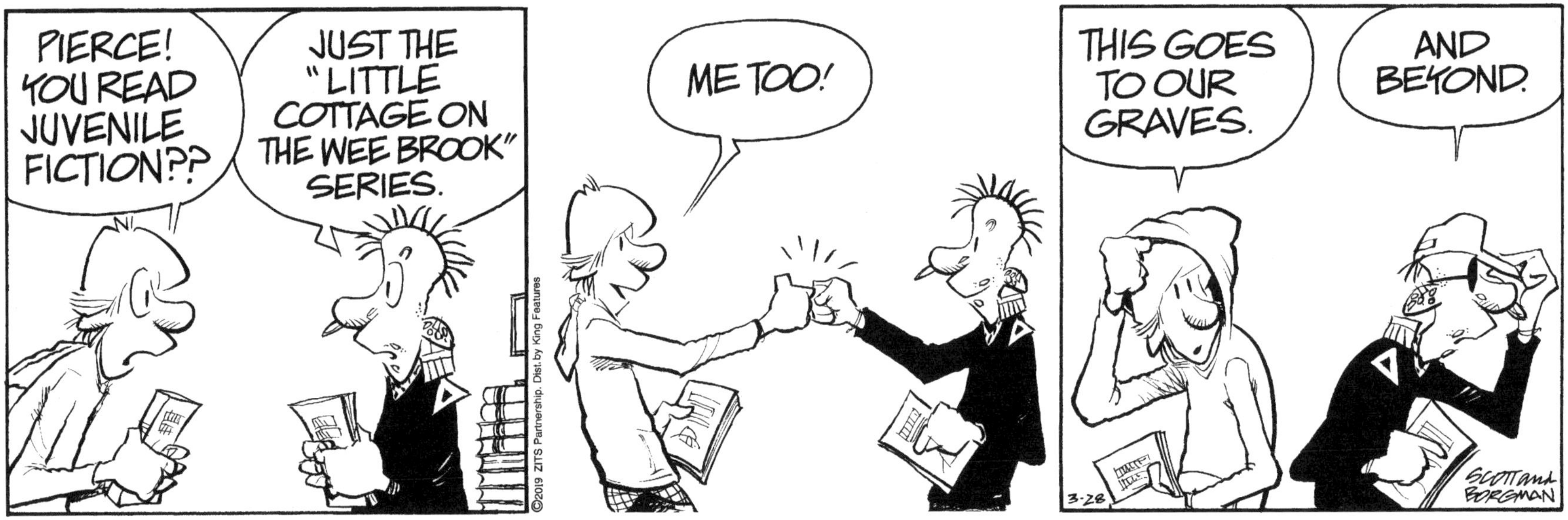
PIERCE! YOU READ JUVENILE FICTION??
JUST THE "LITTLE COTTAGE ON THE WEE BROOK" SERIES.
©2019 ZITS Partnership. Dist. by King Features
ME TOO!
THIS GOES TO OUR GRAVES.
AND BEYOND.
3-28
SCOTT and BORGMAN

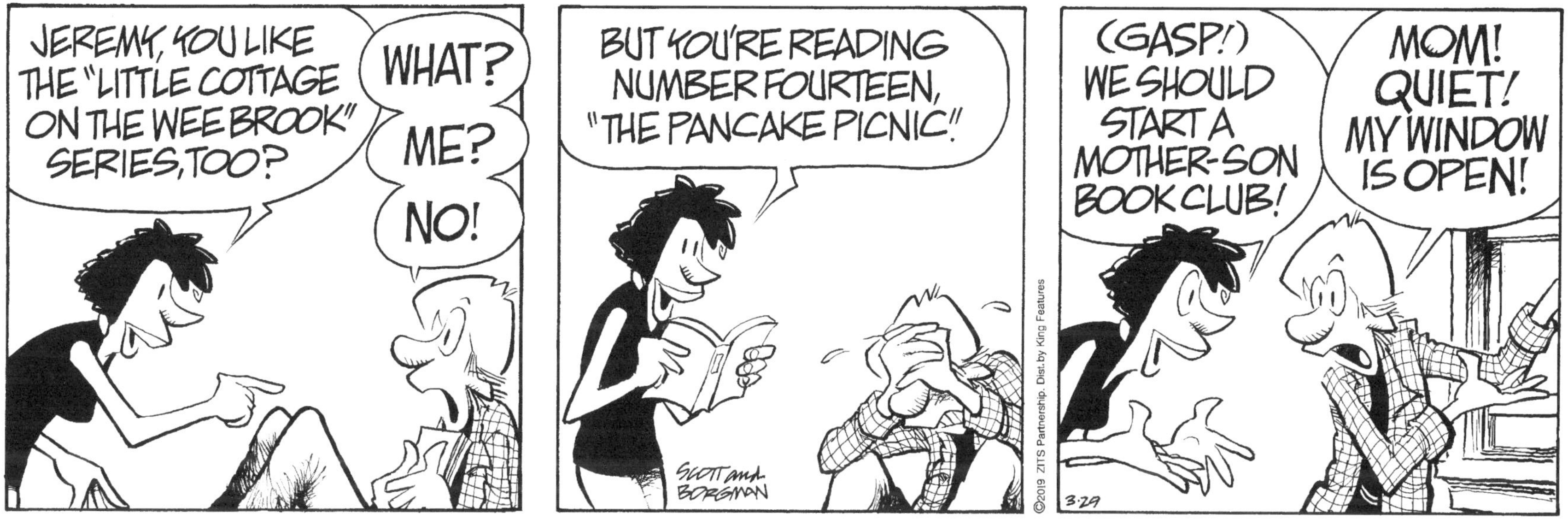
JEREMY, YOU LIKE THE "LITTLE COTTAGE ON THE WEE BROOK" SERIES, TOO?
WHAT?
ME?
NO!
BUT YOU'RE READING NUMBER FOURTEEN, "THE PANCAKE PICNIC!"
SCOTT AND BORGMAN
©2019 ZITS Partnership. Dist. by King Features
(GASP!) WE SHOULD START A MOTHER-SON BOOK CLUB!
MOM! QUIET! MY WINDOW IS OPEN!
3-29

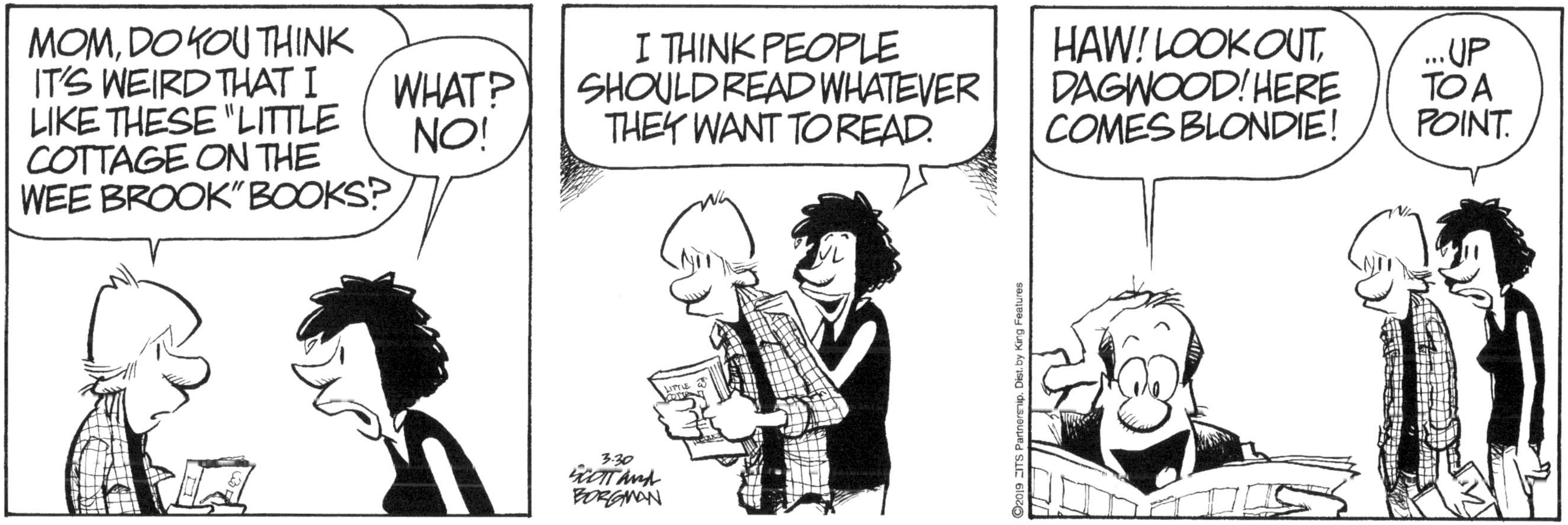
MOM, DO YOU THINK IT'S WEIRD THAT I LIKE THESE "LITTLE COTTAGE ON THE WEE BROOK" BOOKS?
WHAT? NO!
I THINK PEOPLE SHOULD READ WHATEVER THEY WANT TO READ.
3-30
SCOTT AND BORGMAN
©2019 ZITS Partnership. Dist. by King Features
HAW! LOOK OUT, DAGWOOD! HERE COMES BLONDIE!
...UP TO A POINT.

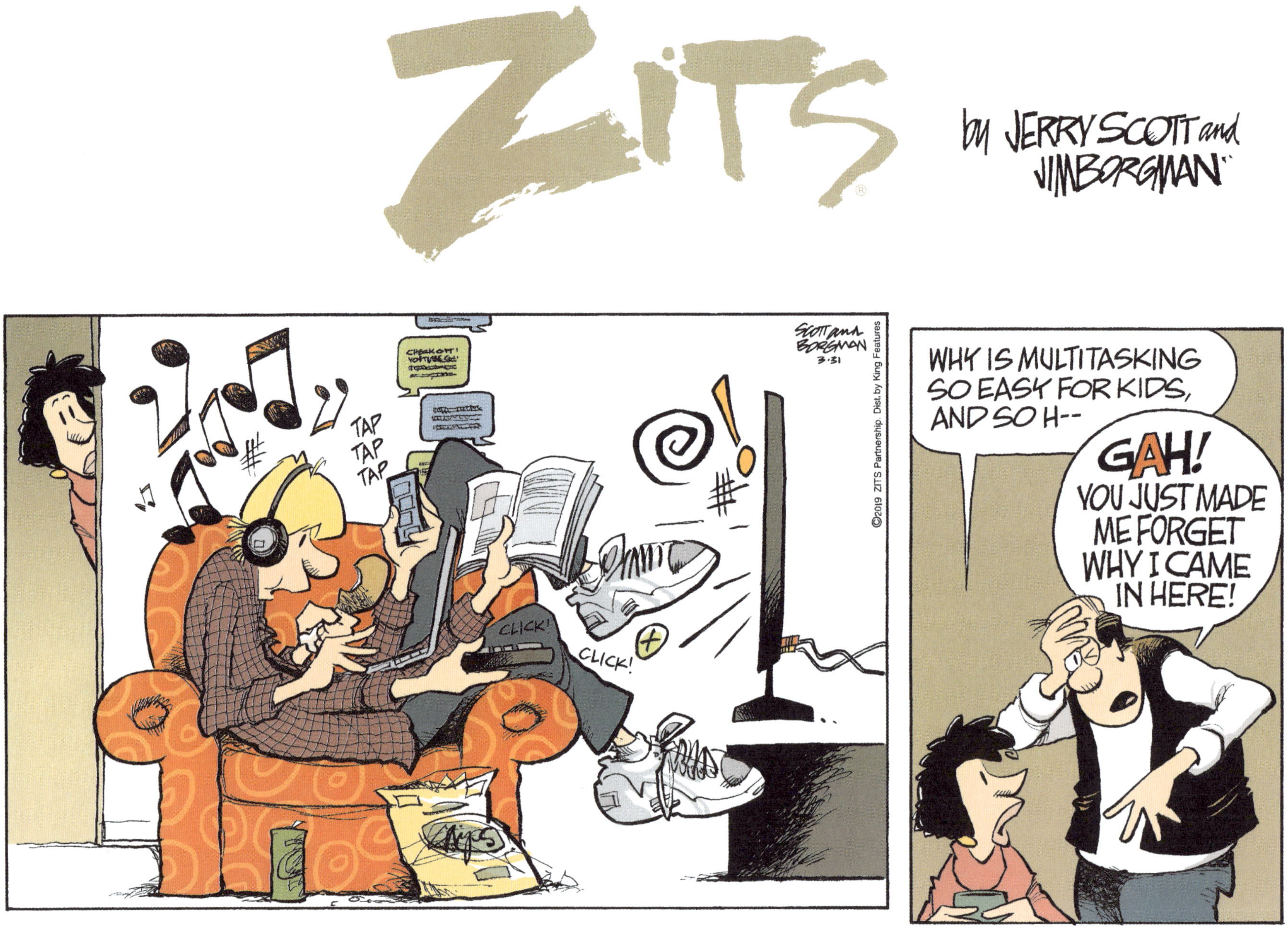
ZITS
by JERRY SCOTT and JIM BORGMAN
SCOTT and BORGMAN 3.31
©2019 ZITS Partnership. Dist. by King Features
TAP TAP TAP
CLICK!
CLICK!
WHY IS MULTITASKING SO EASY FOR KIDS, AND SO H--
GAH! YOU JUST MADE ME FORGET WHY I CAME IN HERE!

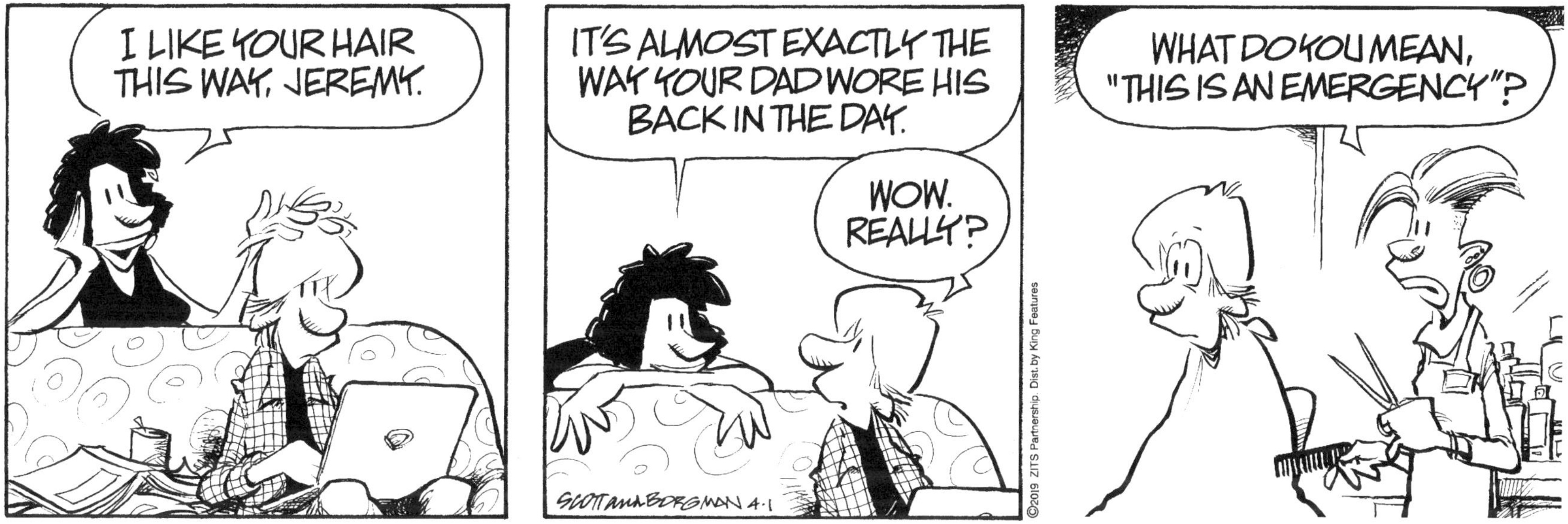
I LIKE YOUR HAIR THIS WAY, JEREMY.
IT'S ALMOST EXACTLY THE WAY YOUR DAD WORE HIS BACK IN THE DAY.
WOW. REALLY?
SCOTT AND BORGMAN 4-1
©2019 ZITS Partnership. Dist. by King Features
WHAT DO YOU MEAN, "THIS IS AN EMERGENCY"?

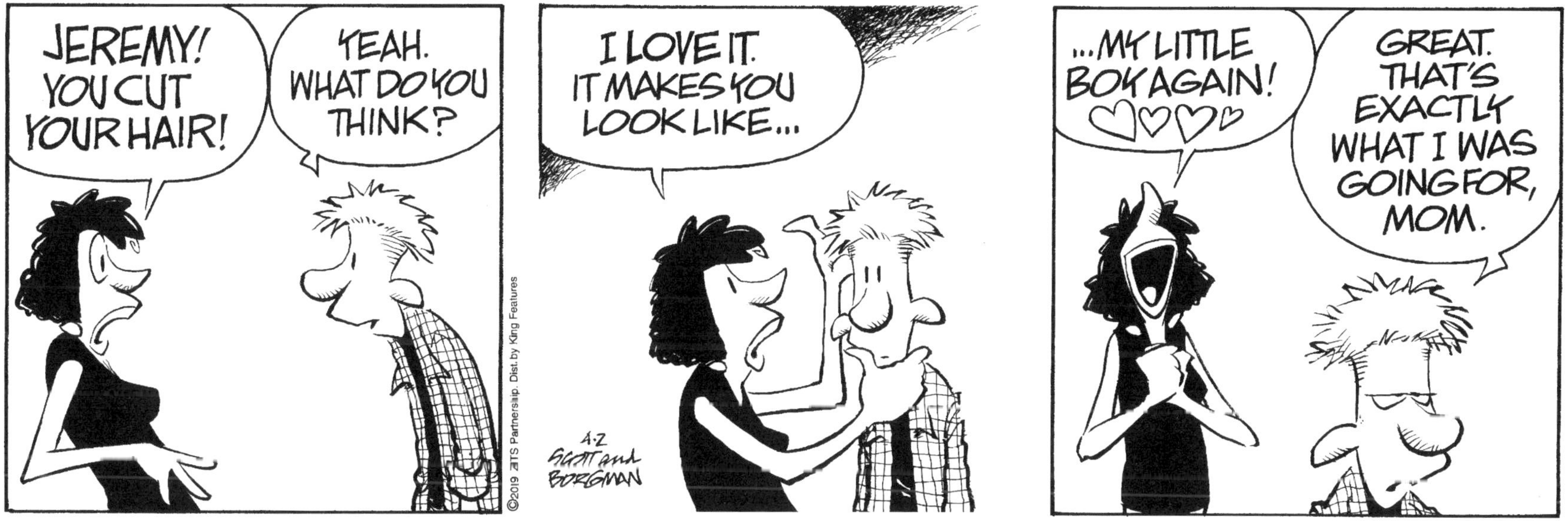
JEREMY! YOU CUT YOUR HAIR!
YEAH. WHAT DO YOU THINK?
©2019 ZITS Partnership. Dist. by King Features
I LOVE IT. IT MAKES YOU LOOK LIKE...
4-2 SCOTT AND BORGMAN
...MY LITTLE BOY AGAIN!
GREAT. THAT'S EXACTLY WHAT I WAS GOING FOR, MOM.

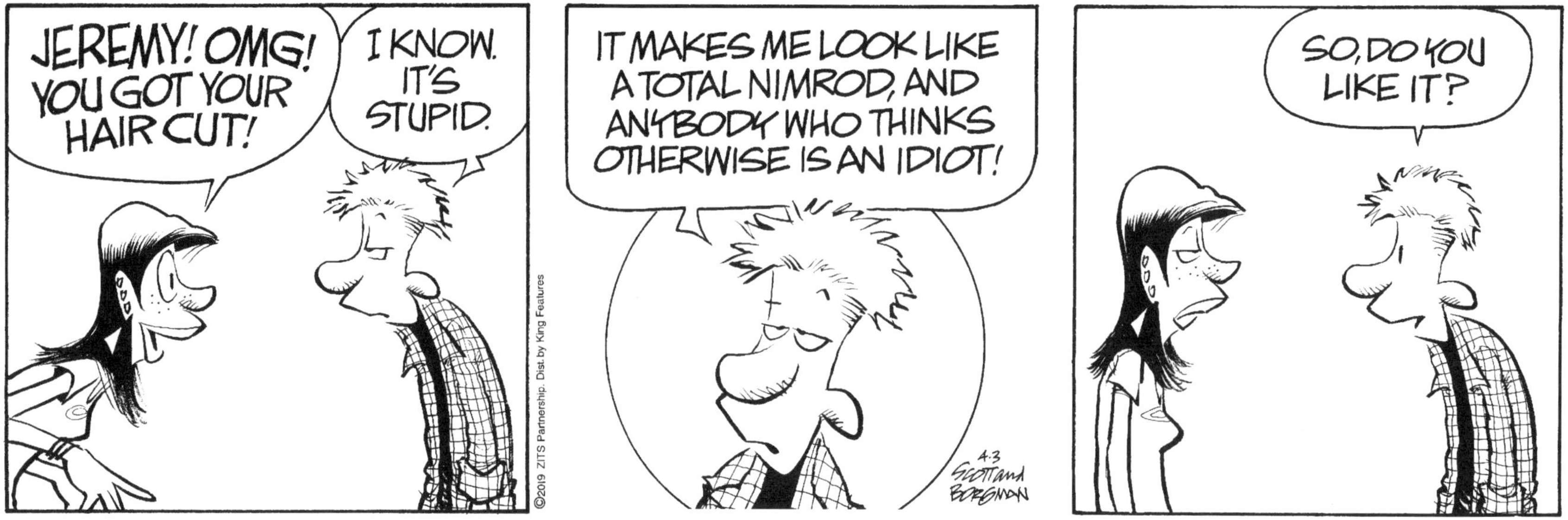
JEREMY! OMG! YOU GOT YOUR HAIR CUT!
I KNOW. IT'S STUPID.
©2019 ZITS Partnership. Dist. by King Features
IT MAKES ME LOOK LIKE A TOTAL NIMROD, AND ANYBODY WHO THINKS OTHERWISE IS AN IDIOT!
4·3 SCOTT and BORGMAN
SO, DO YOU LIKE IT?

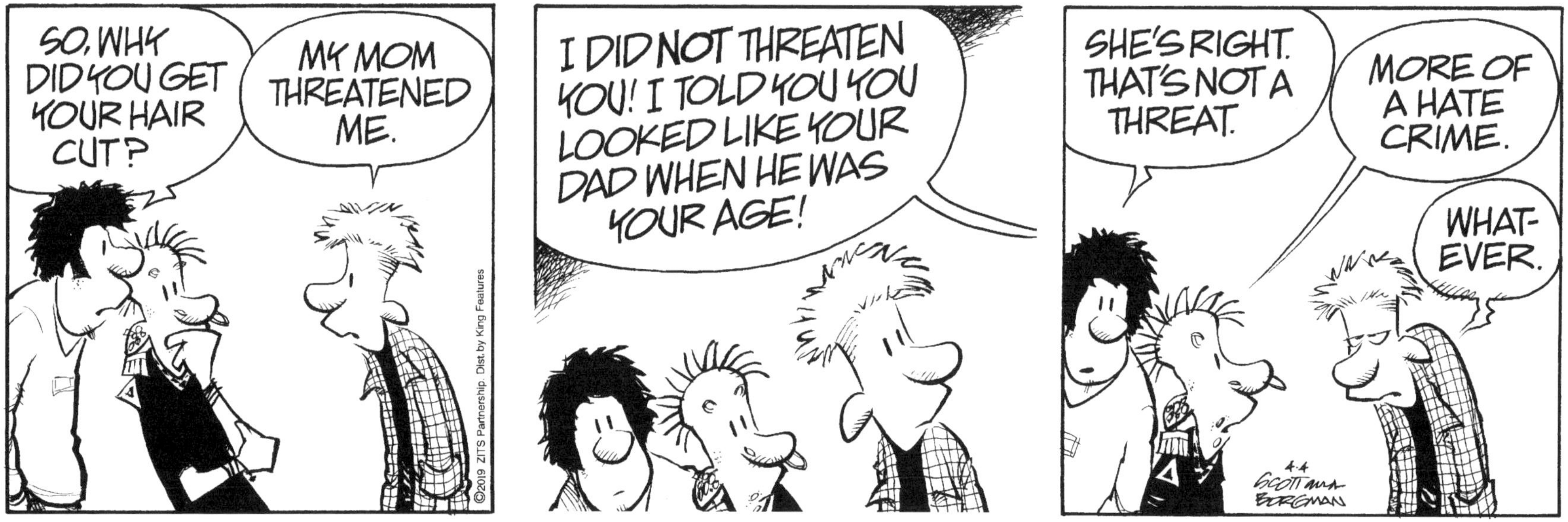
SO, WHY DID YOU GET YOUR HAIR CUT?
MY MOM THREATENED ME.
©2019 ZITS Partnership. Dist. by King Features
I DID NOT THREATEN YOU! I TOLD YOU YOU LOOKED LIKE YOUR DAD WHEN HE WAS YOUR AGE!
SHE'S RIGHT. THAT'S NOT A THREAT.
MORE OF A HATE CRIME.
WHATEVER.
4·4 SCOTT and BORGMAN

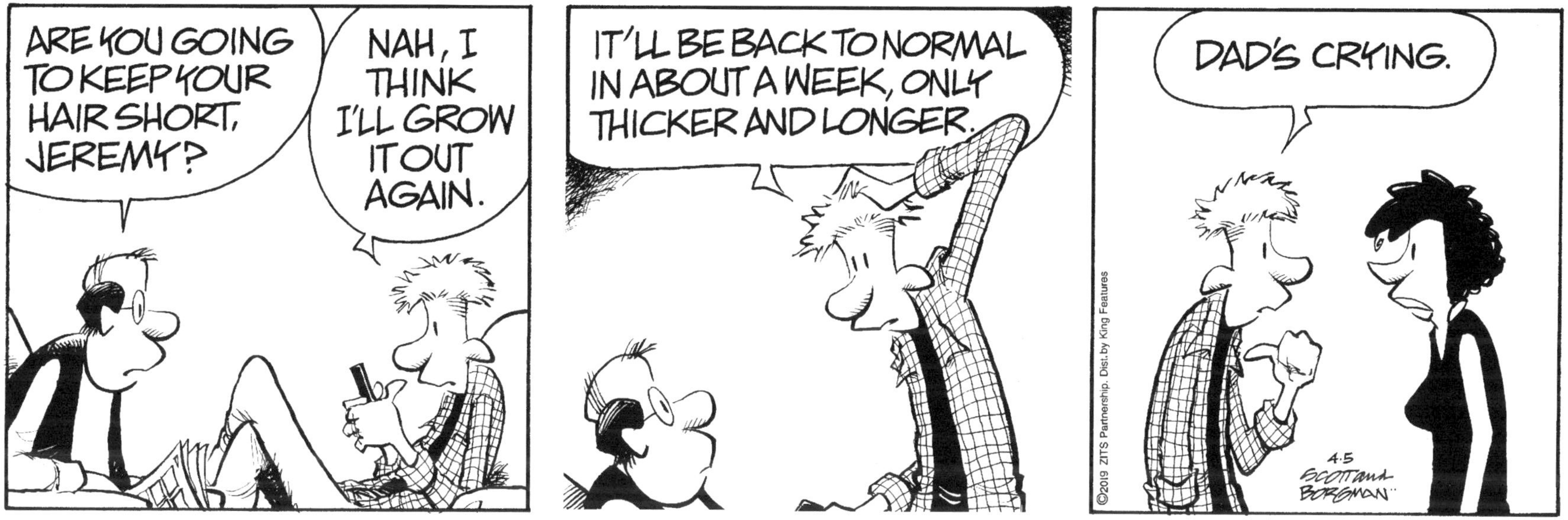
ARE YOU GOING TO KEEP YOUR HAIR SHORT, JEREMY?
NAH, I THINK I'LL GROW IT OUT AGAIN.
IT'LL BE BACK TO NORMAL IN ABOUT A WEEK, ONLY THICKER AND LONGER.
DAD'S CRYING.
©2019 ZITS Partnership. Dist. by King Features
4·5 SCOTT and BORGMAN

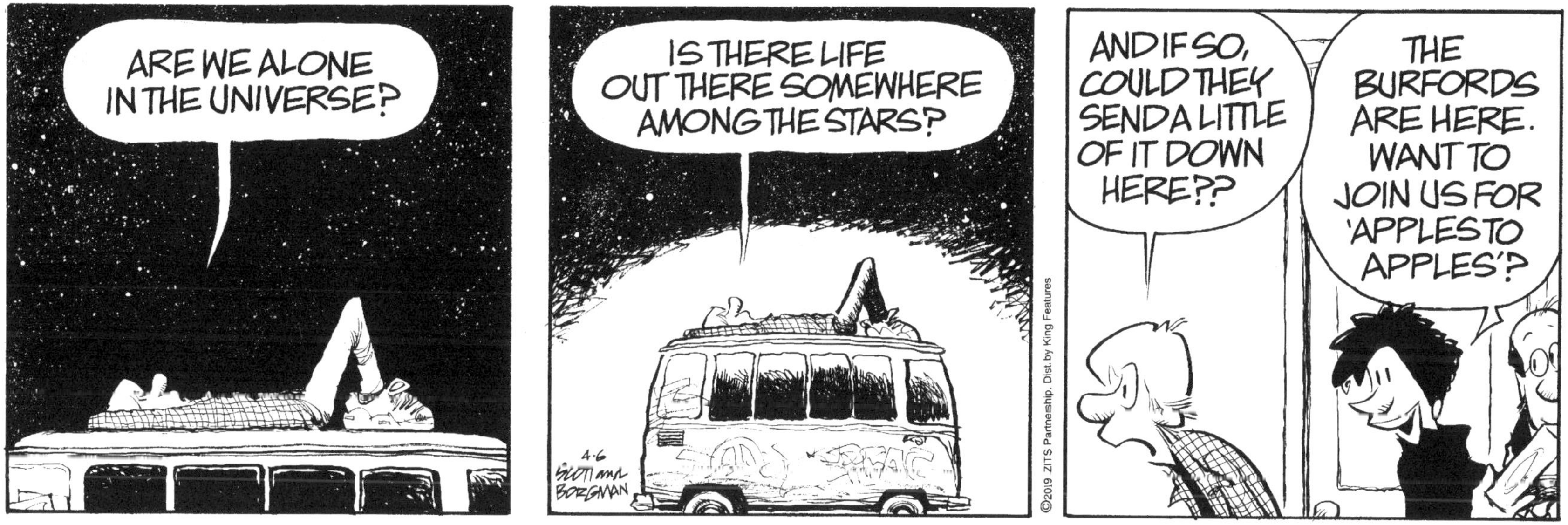
ARE WE ALONE IN THE UNIVERSE?
IS THERE LIFE OUT THERE SOMEWHERE AMONG THE STARS?
4·6 SCOTT and BORGMAN
©2019 ZITS Partnership. Dist. by King Features
AND IF SO, COULD THEY SEND A LITTLE OF IT DOWN HERE??
THE BURFORDS ARE HERE. WANT TO JOIN US FOR 'APPLES TO APPLES'?

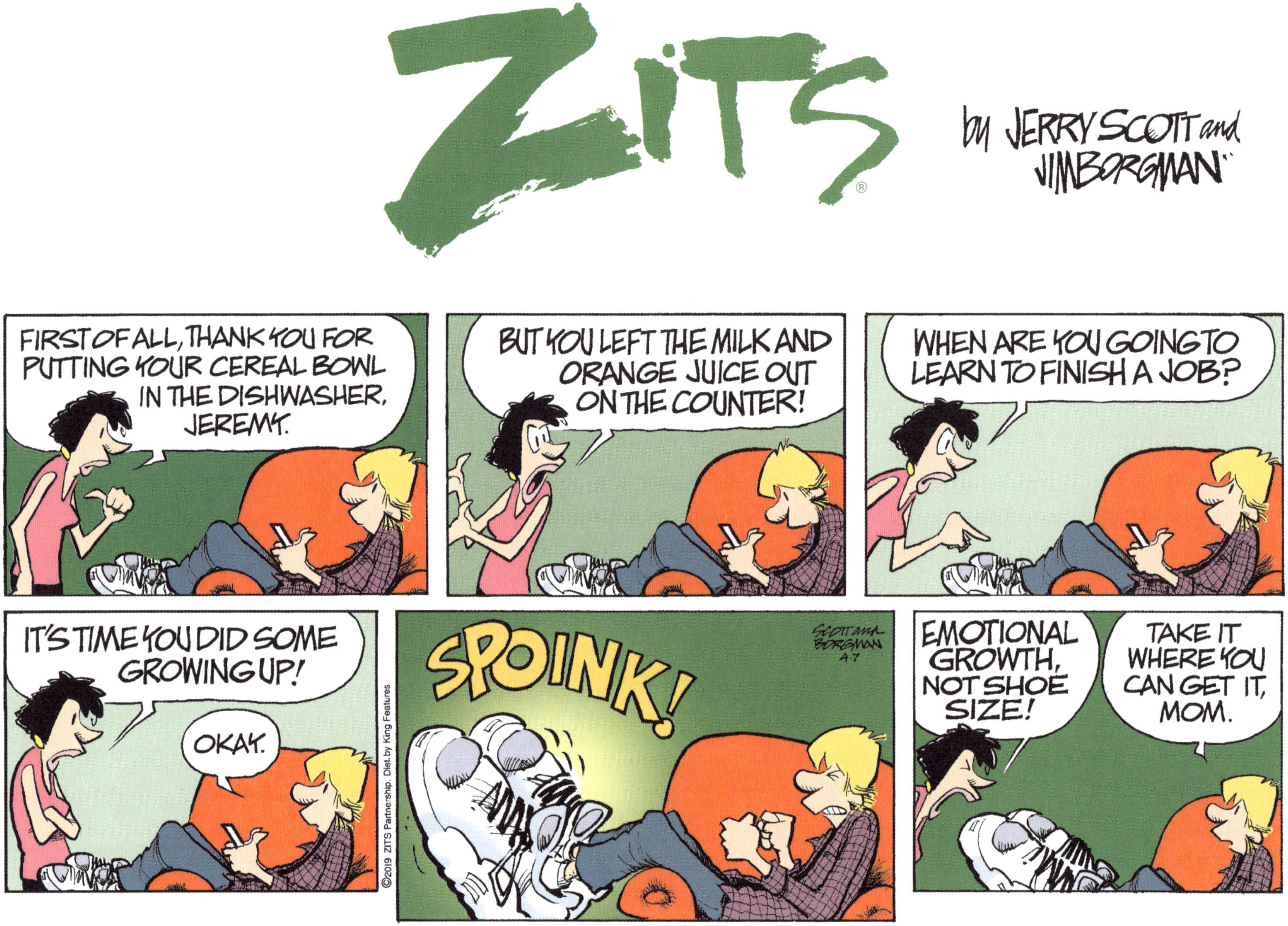
ZITS®
by JERRY SCOTT and JIM BORGMAN
FIRST OF ALL, THANK YOU FOR PUTTING YOUR CEREAL BOWL IN THE DISHWASHER, JEREMY.
BUT YOU LEFT THE MILK AND ORANGE JUICE OUT ON THE COUNTER!
WHEN ARE YOU GOING TO LEARN TO FINISH A JOB?
IT'S TIME YOU DID SOME GROWING UP!
OKAY.
©2019 ZITS Partnership. Dist. by King Features
SPOINK!
SCOTT AND BORGMAN 4-7
EMOTIONAL GROWTH, NOT SHOE SIZE!
TAKE IT WHERE YOU CAN GET IT, MOM.

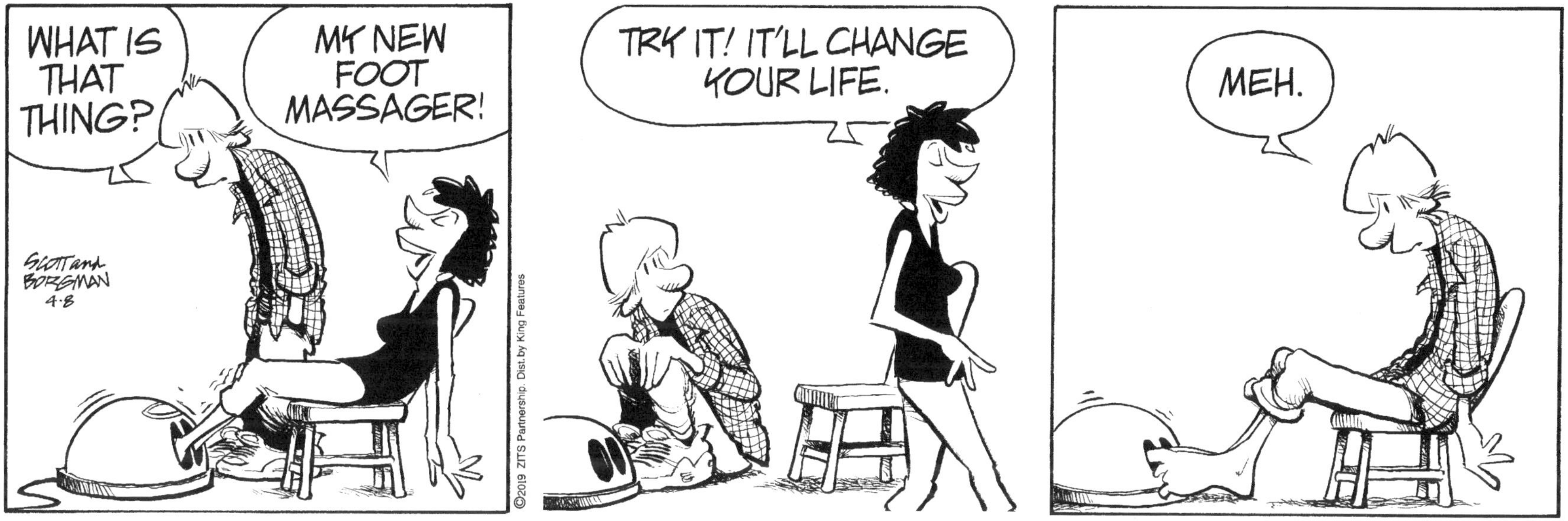
WHAT IS THAT THING?
MY NEW FOOT MASSAGER!
SCOTT and BORGMAN 4·8
©2019 ZITS Partnership. Dist. by King Features
TRY IT! IT'LL CHANGE YOUR LIFE.
MEH.

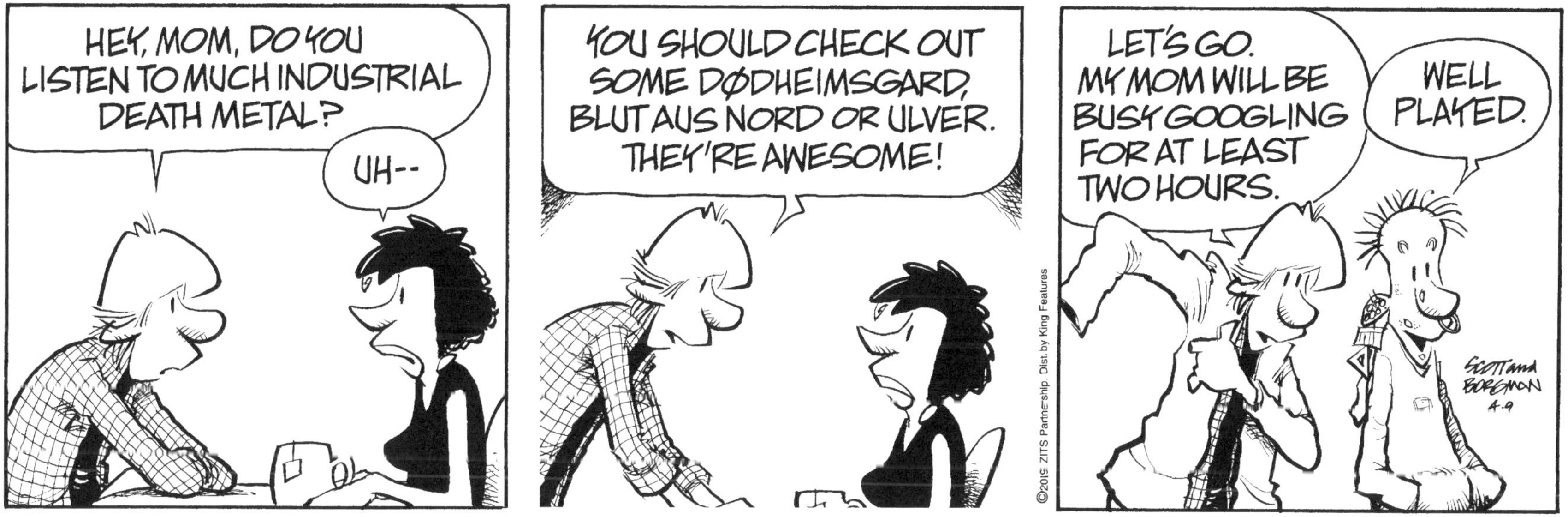
HEY, MOM, DO YOU LISTEN TO MUCH INDUSTRIAL DEATH METAL?
UH--
YOU SHOULD CHECK OUT SOME DØDHEIMSGARD, BLUT AUS NORD OR ULVER. THEY'RE AWESOME!
©2019 ZITS Partnership. Dist. by King Features
LET'S GO. MY MOM WILL BE BUSY GOOGLING FOR AT LEAST TWO HOURS.
WELL PLAYED.
SCOTT and BORGMAN 4·9

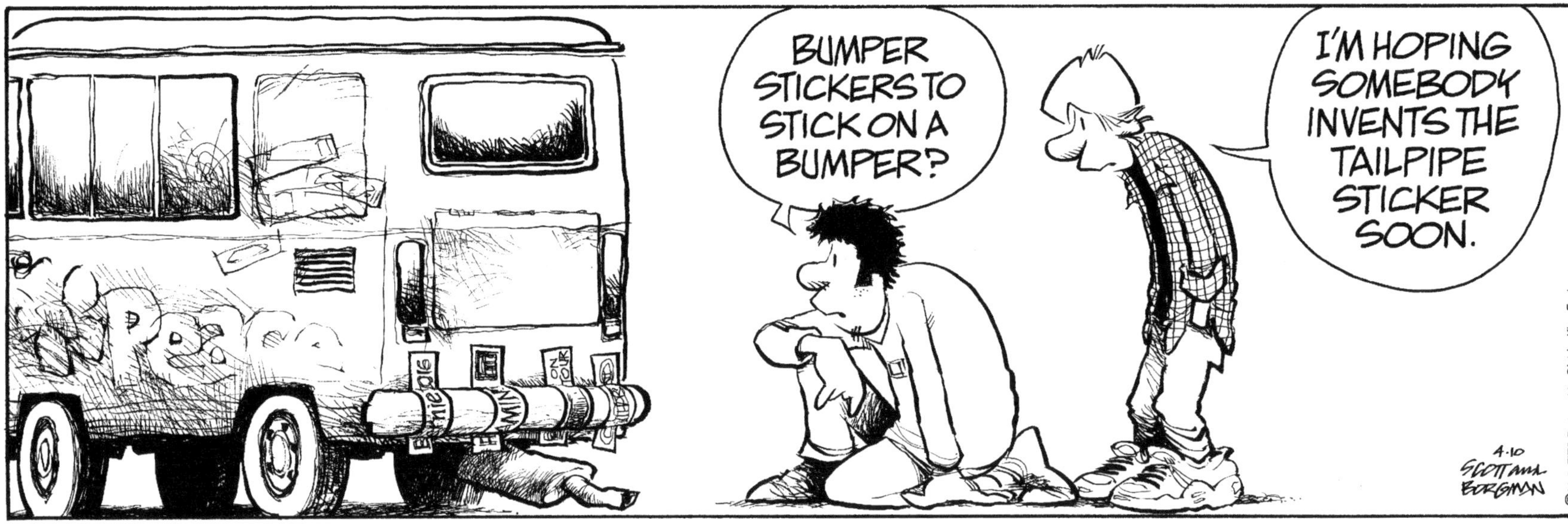
BUMPER STICKERS TO STICK ON A BUMPER?
I'M HOPING SOMEBODY INVENTS THE TAILPIPE STICKER SOON.
4·10
SCOTT and BORGMAN
©2019 ZITS Partnership. Dist. by King Features

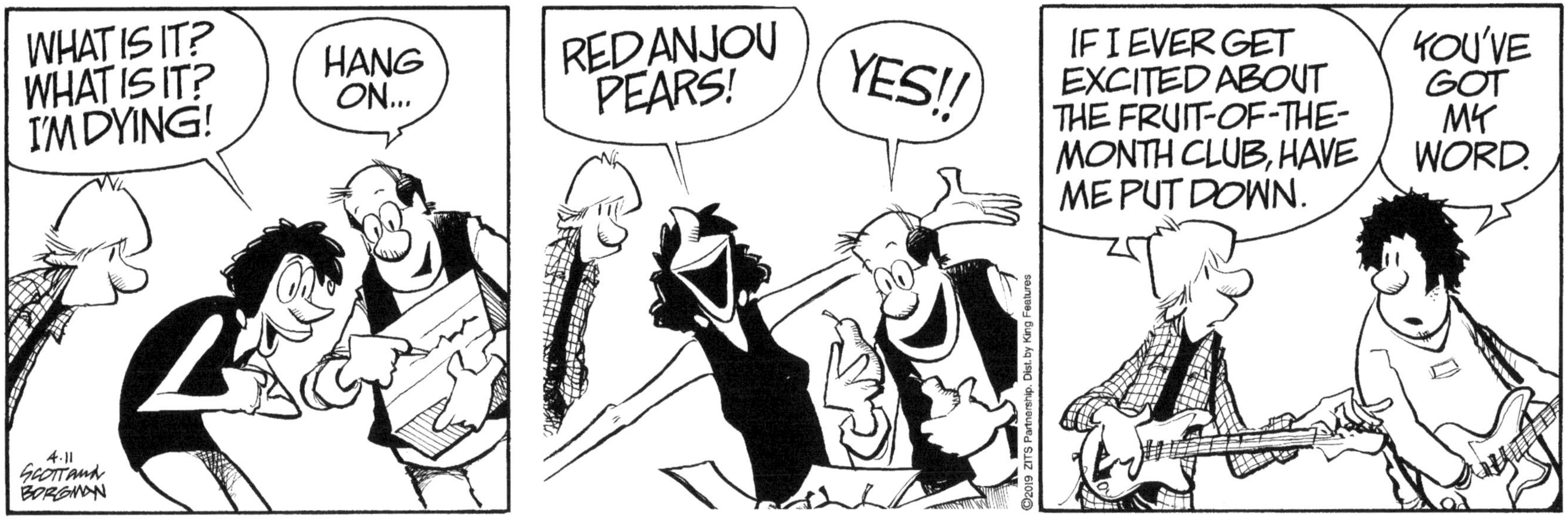
WHAT IS IT? WHAT IS IT? I'M DYING!
HANG ON...
4·11
SCOTT and BORGMAN
RED ANJOU PEARS!
YES!!
©2019 ZITS Partnership. Dist. by King Features
IF I EVER GET EXCITED ABOUT THE FRUIT-OF-THE-MONTH CLUB, HAVE ME PUT DOWN.
YOU'VE GOT MY WORD.

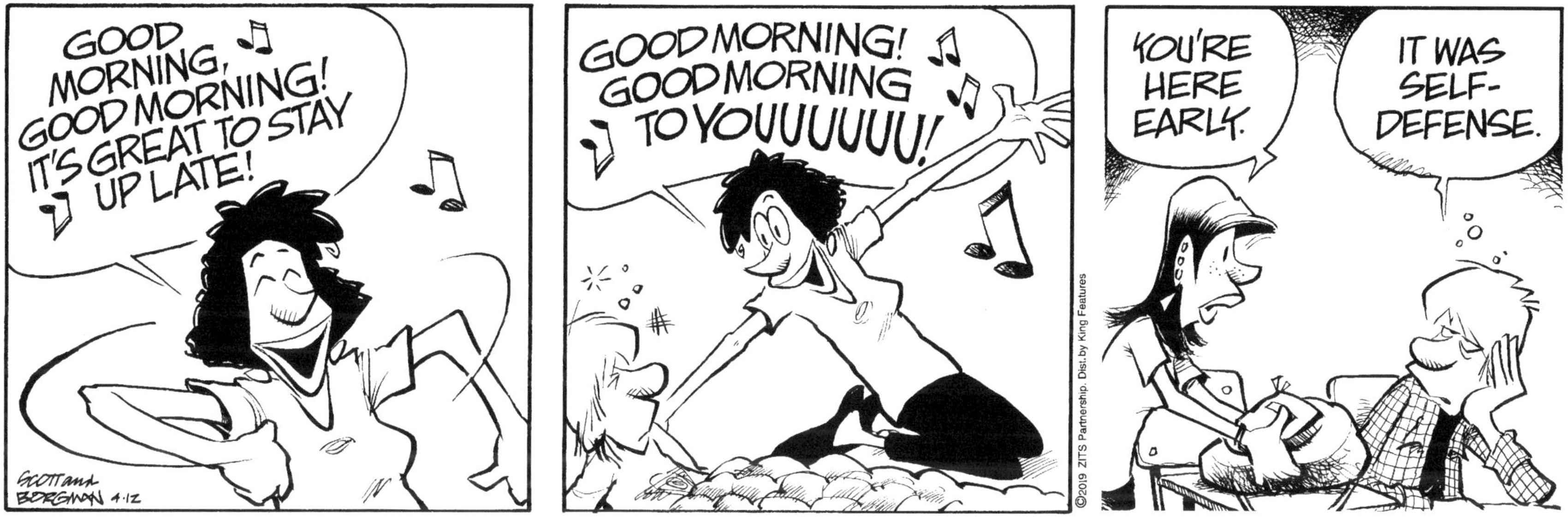
GOOD MORNING, GOOD MORNING! IT'S GREAT TO STAY UP LATE!
SCOTT and BORGMAN 4.12
GOOD MORNING! GOOD MORNING TO YOUUUUUU!
©2019 ZITS Partnership. Dist. by King Features
YOU'RE HERE EARLY.
IT WAS SELF-DEFENSE.

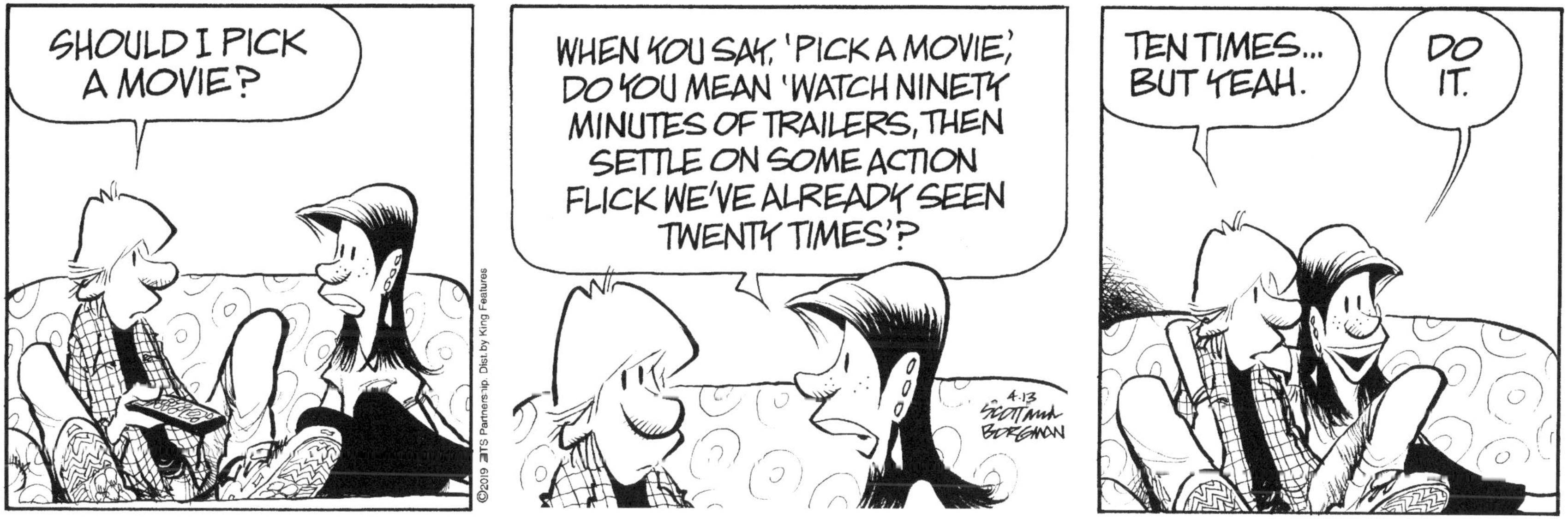
SHOULD I PICK A MOVIE?
©2019 ZITS Partnership. Dist. by King Features
WHEN YOU SAY, 'PICK A MOVIE,' DO YOU MEAN 'WATCH NINETY MINUTES OF TRAILERS, THEN SETTLE ON SOME ACTION FLICK WE'VE ALREADY SEEN TWENTY TIMES'?
4.13 SCOTT and BORGMAN
TEN TIMES... BUT YEAH.
DO IT.

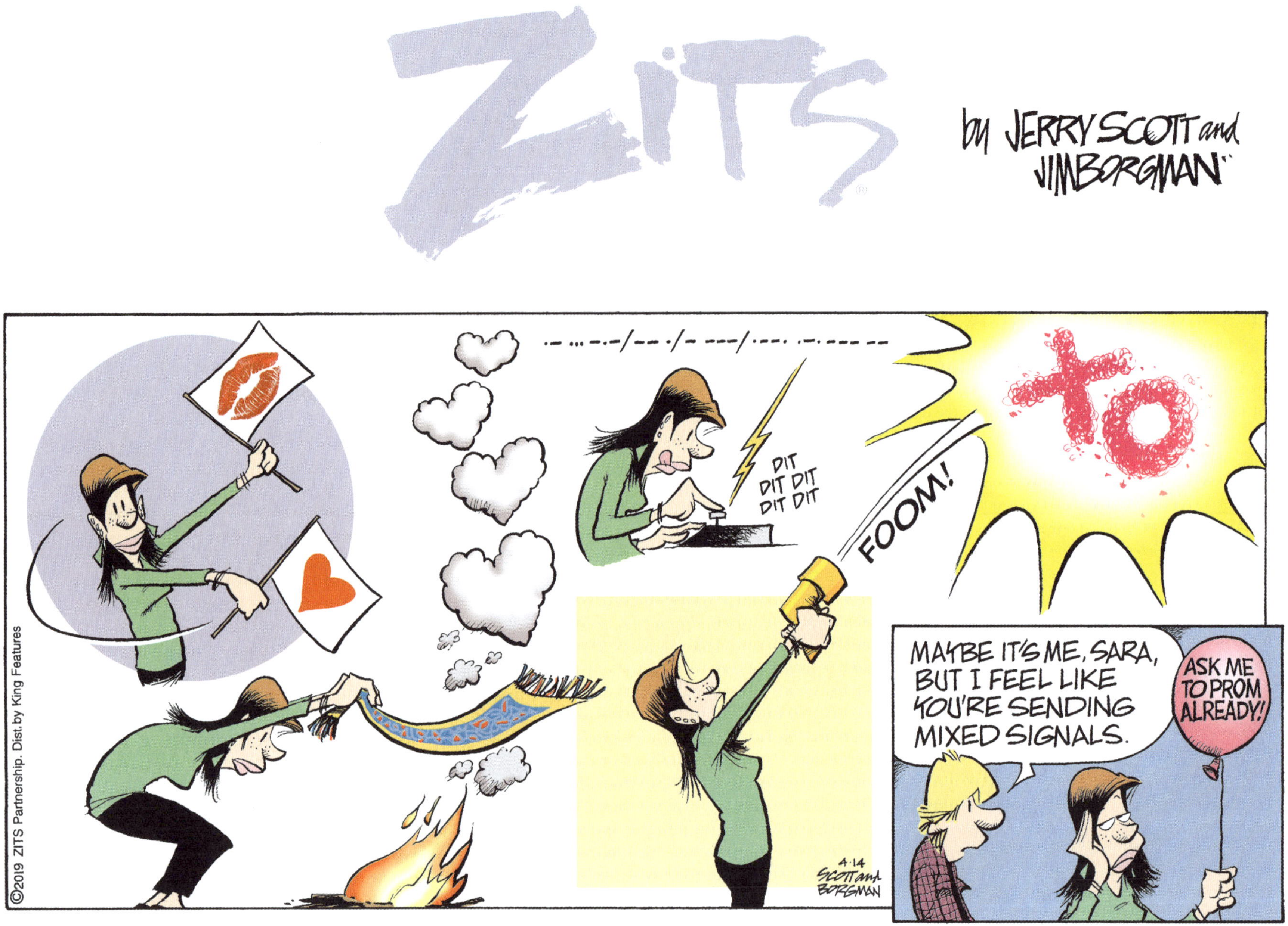
ZITS
by JERRY SCOTT and JIM BORGMAN
DIT DIT DIT DIT DIT
FOOM!
XO
MAYBE IT'S ME, SARA, BUT I FEEL LIKE YOU'RE SENDING MIXED SIGNALS.
ASK ME TO PROM ALREADY!
4·14 SCOTT and BORGMAN

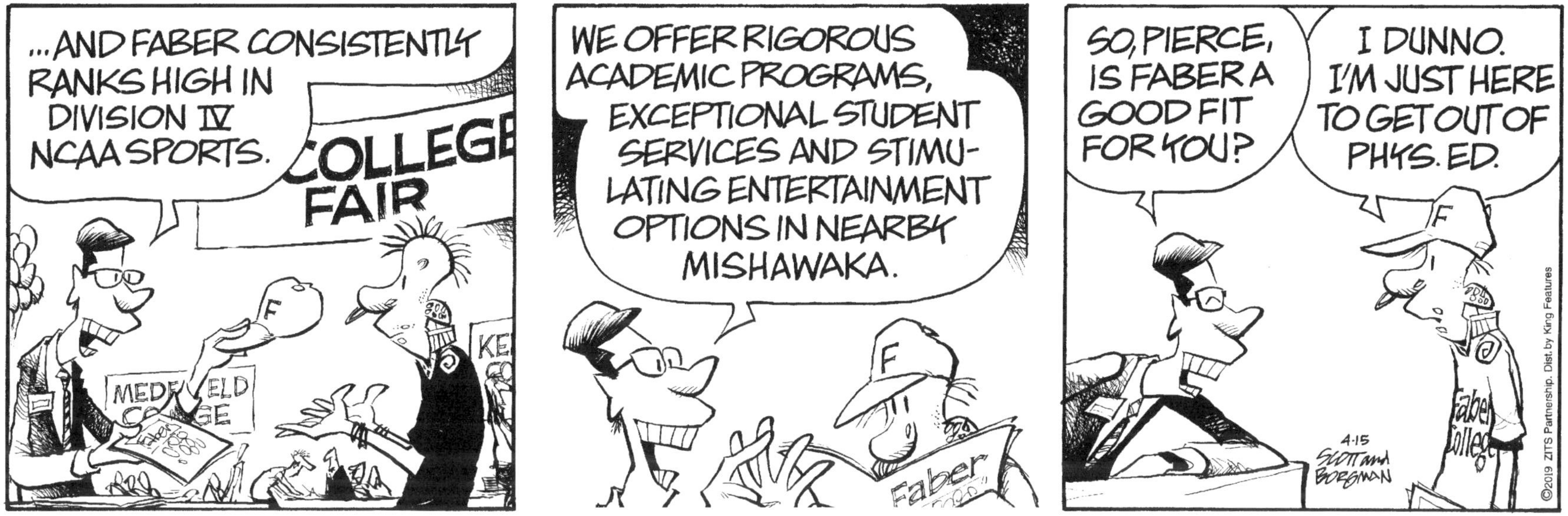
...AND FABER CONSISTENTLY RANKS HIGH IN DIVISION IV NCAA SPORTS.
COLLEGE FAIR
WE OFFER RIGOROUS ACADEMIC PROGRAMS, EXCEPTIONAL STUDENT SERVICES AND STIMU-LATING ENTERTAINMENT OPTIONS IN NEARBY MISHAWAKA.
Faber
SO, PIERCE, IS FABER A GOOD FIT FOR YOU?
I DUNNO. I'M JUST HERE TO GET OUT OF PHYS. ED.
4-15 SCOTT AND BORGMAN
©2019 ZITS Partnership. Dist. by King Features

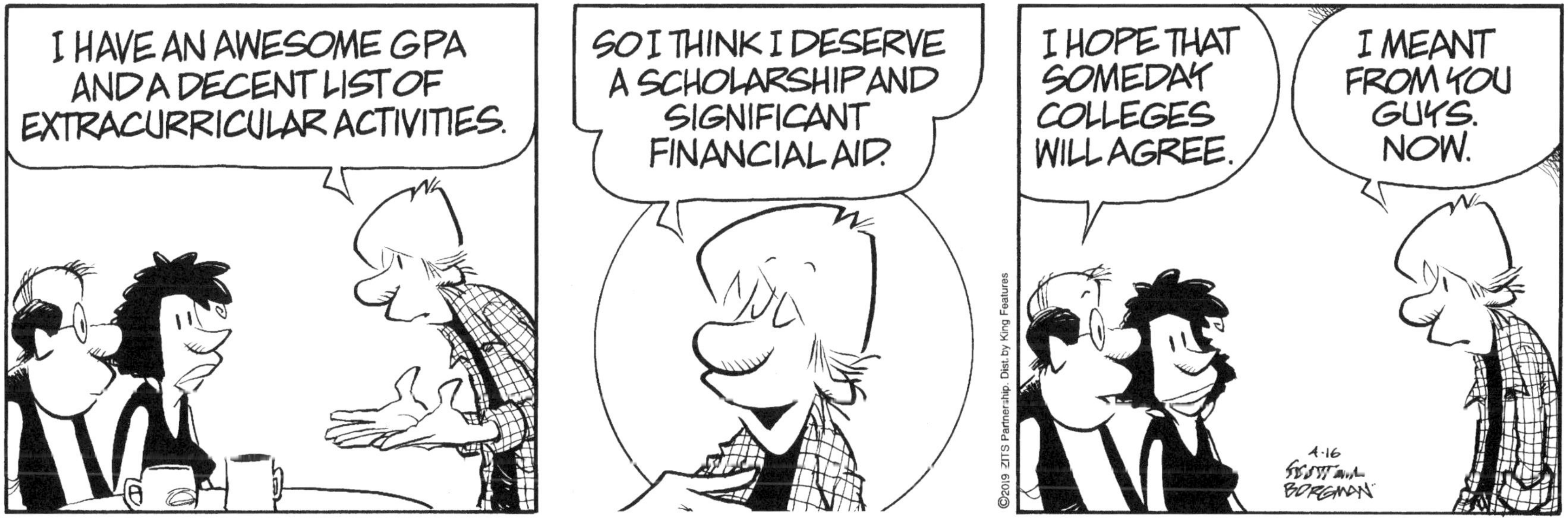
I HAVE AN AWESOME GPA AND A DECENT LIST OF EXTRACURRICULAR ACTIVITIES.
SO I THINK I DESERVE A SCHOLARSHIP AND SIGNIFICANT FINANCIAL AID.
I HOPE THAT SOMEDAY COLLEGES WILL AGREE.
I MEANT FROM YOU GUYS. NOW.
4-16 SCOTT AND BORGMAN
©2019 ZITS Partnership. Dist. by King Features

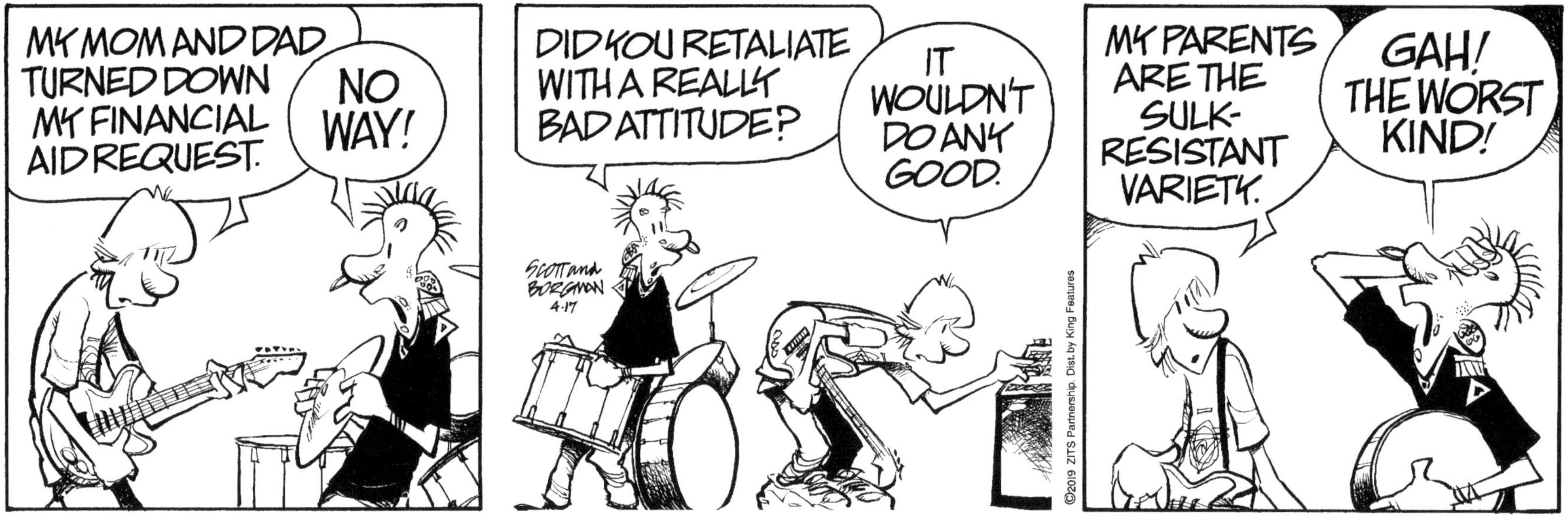
MY MOM AND DAD TURNED DOWN MY FINANCIAL AID REQUEST.
NO WAY!
SCOTT and BORGMAN 4·17
DID YOU RETALIATE WITH A REALLY BAD ATTITUDE?
IT WOULDN'T DO ANY GOOD.
MY PARENTS ARE THE SULK-RESISTANT VARIETY.
GAH! THE WORST KIND!
©2019 ZITS Partnership. Dist. by King Features

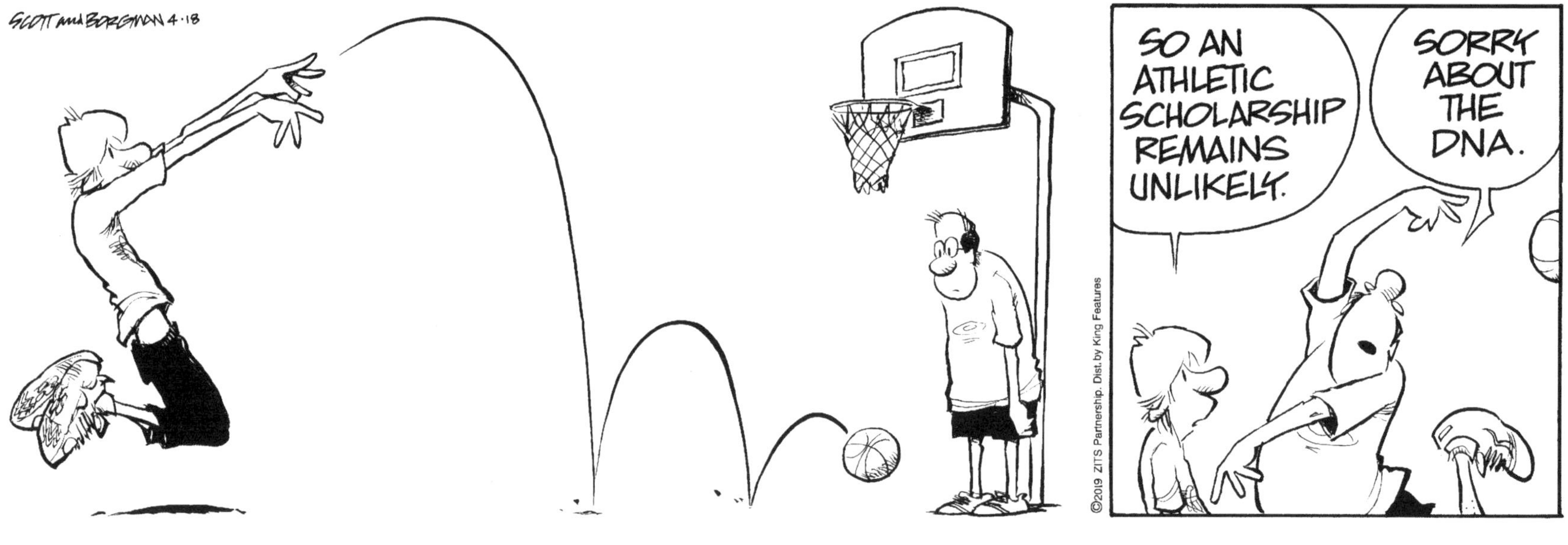
SCOTT and BORGMAN 4·18
SO AN ATHLETIC SCHOLARSHIP REMAINS UNLIKELY.
SORRY ABOUT THE DNA.
©2019 ZITS Partnership. Dist. by King Features

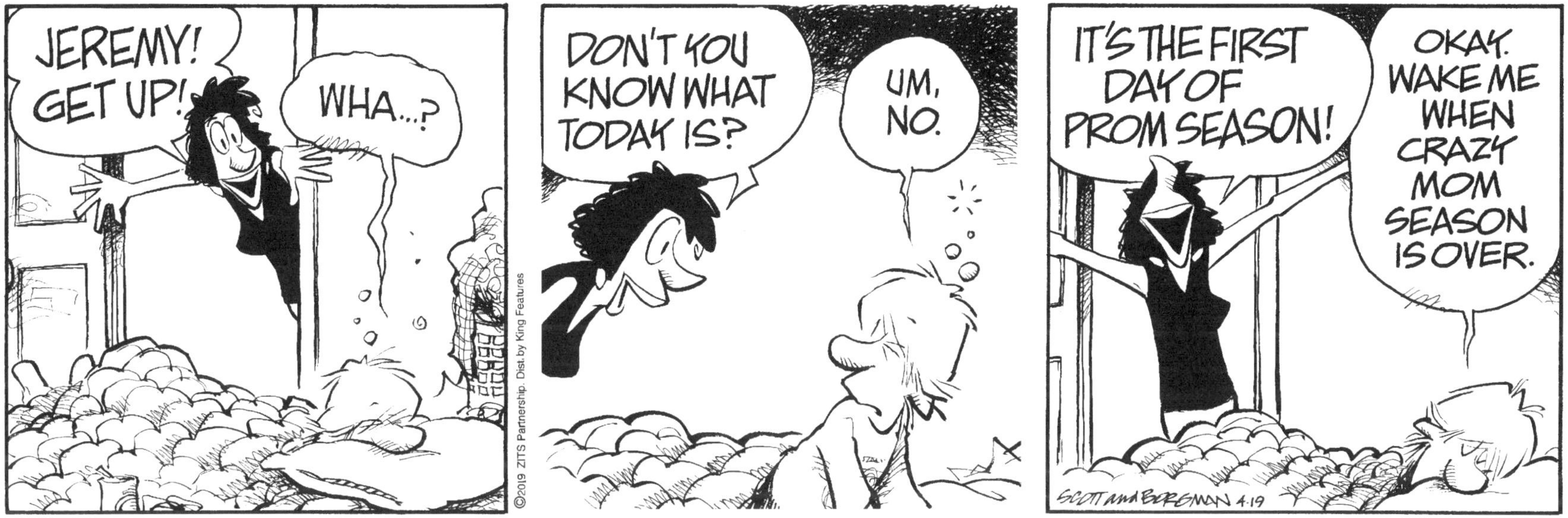
JEREMY! GET UP!
WHA...?
©2019 ZITS Partnership. Dist. by King Features
DON'T YOU KNOW WHAT TODAY IS?
UM, NO.
IT'S THE FIRST DAY OF PROM SEASON!
OKAY. WAKE ME WHEN CRAZY MOM SEASON IS OVER.
SCOTT AND BORGMAN 4.19

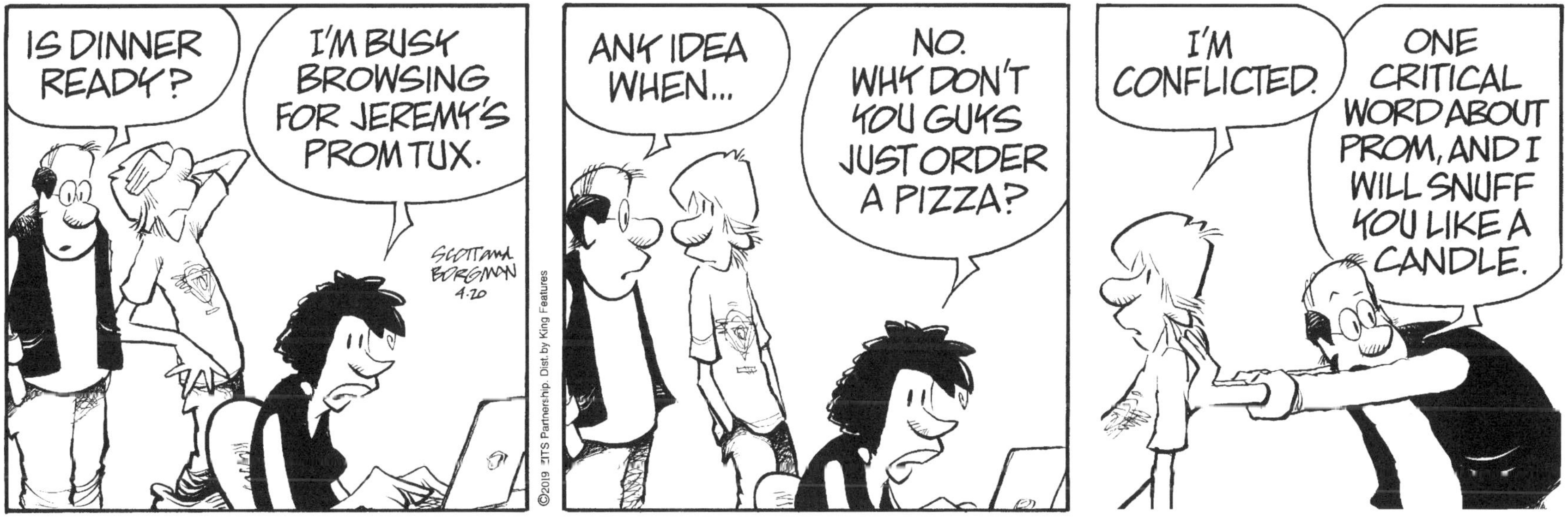
IS DINNER READY?
I'M BUSY BROWSING FOR JEREMY'S PROM TUX.
SCOTT AND BORGMAN 4.20
©2019 ZITS Partnership. Dist. by King Features
ANY IDEA WHEN...
NO. WHY DON'T YOU GUYS JUST ORDER A PIZZA?
I'M CONFLICTED.
ONE CRITICAL WORD ABOUT PROM, AND I WILL SNUFF YOU LIKE A CANDLE.

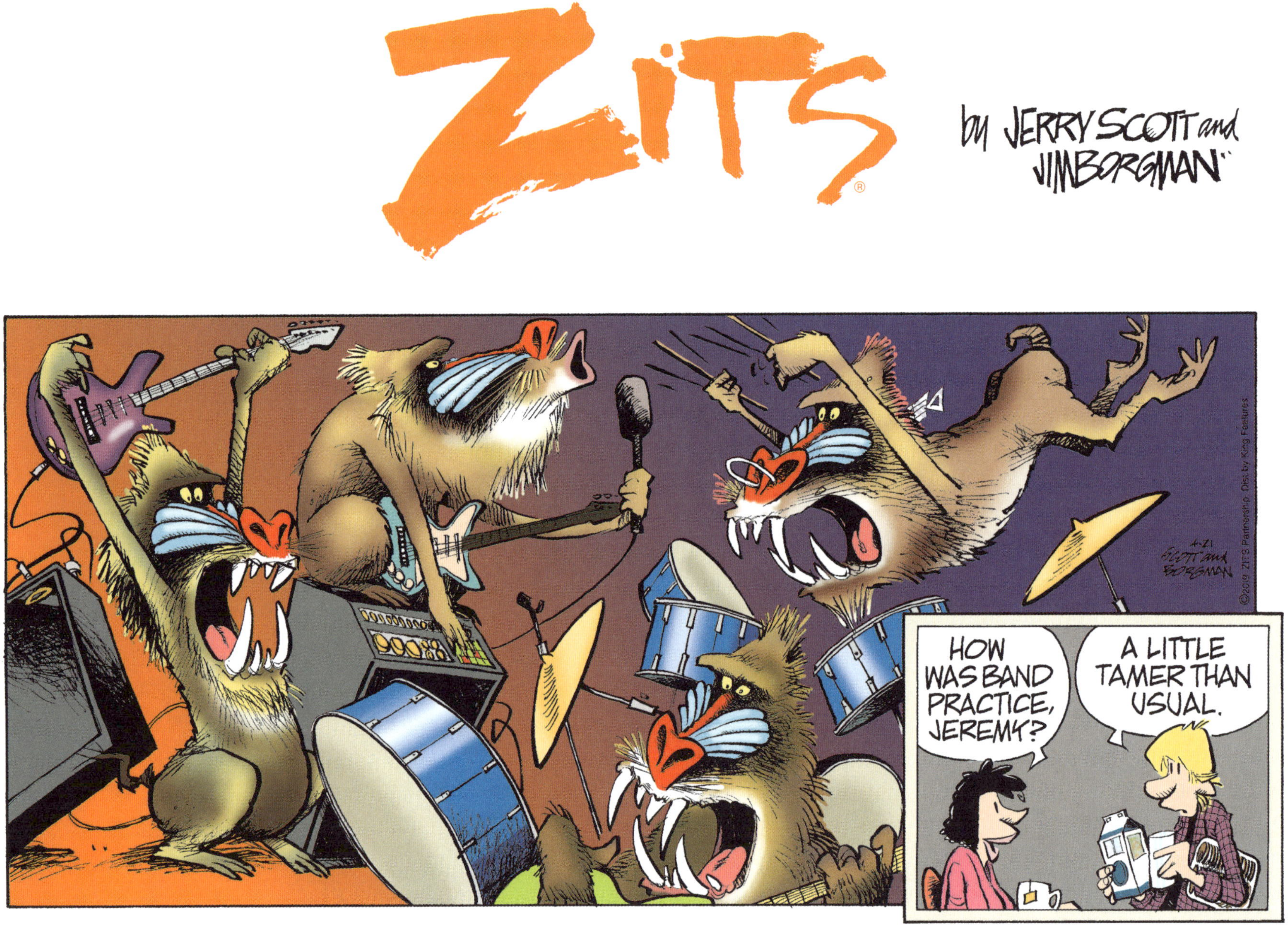
ZITS
by JERRY SCOTT and JIM BORGMAN
©2019 ZITS Partnership Dist. by King Features
HOW WAS BAND PRACTICE, JEREMY?
A LITTLE TAMER THAN USUAL.

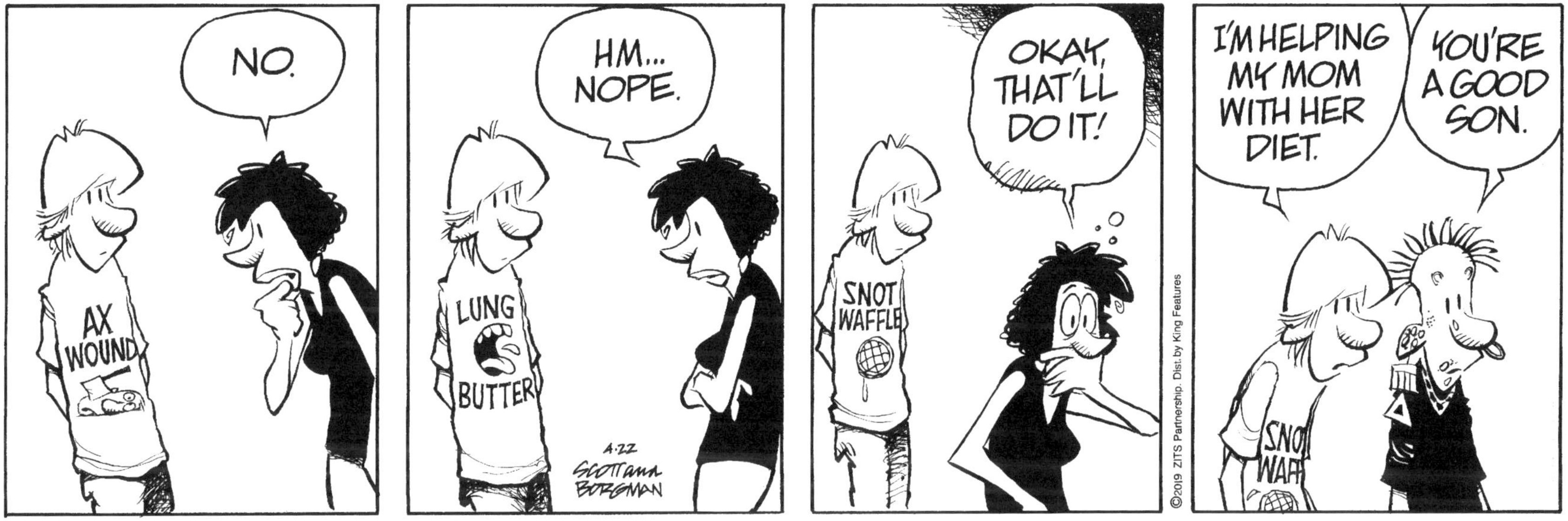
NO.
AX WOUND
HM... NOPE.
LUNG BUTTER
4·22
SCOTT and BORGMAN
OKAY, THAT'LL DO IT!
SNOT WAFFLE
©2019 ZITS Partnership. Dist. by King Features
I'M HELPING MY MOM WITH HER DIET.
YOU'RE A GOOD SON.

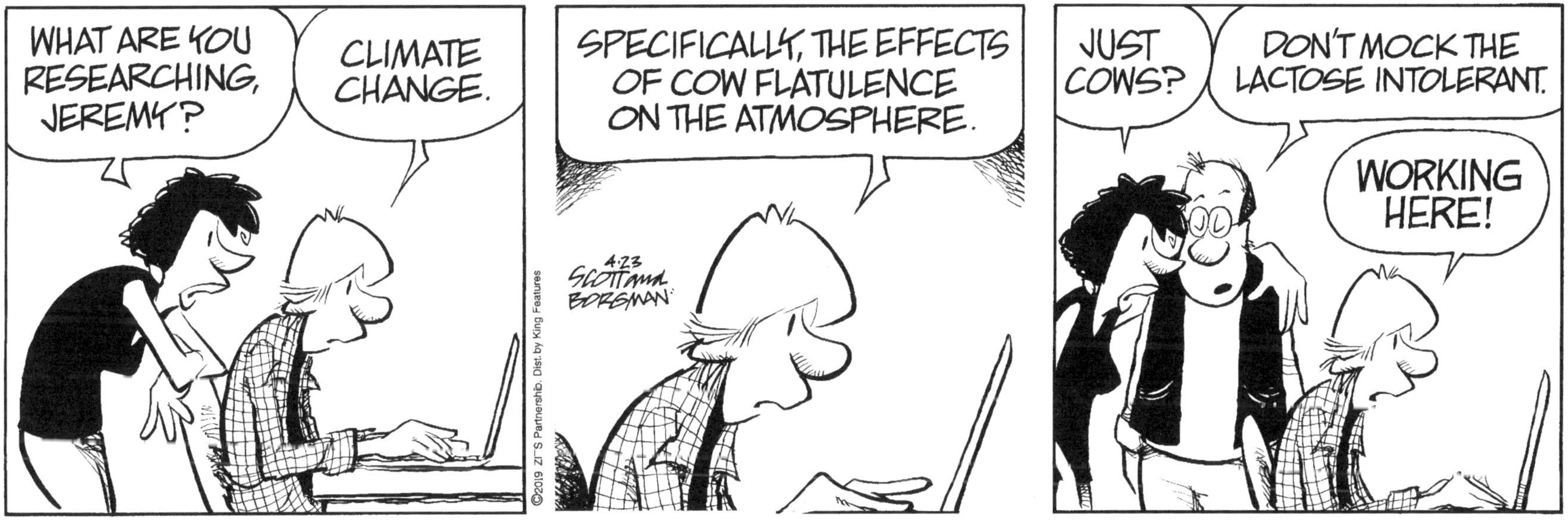
WHAT ARE YOU RESEARCHING, JEREMY?
CLIMATE CHANGE.
©2019 ZITS Partnership. Dist. by King Features
4·23
SCOTT and BORGMAN
SPECIFICALLY, THE EFFECTS OF COW FLATULENCE ON THE ATMOSPHERE.
JUST COWS?
DON'T MOCK THE LACTOSE INTOLERANT.
WORKING HERE!

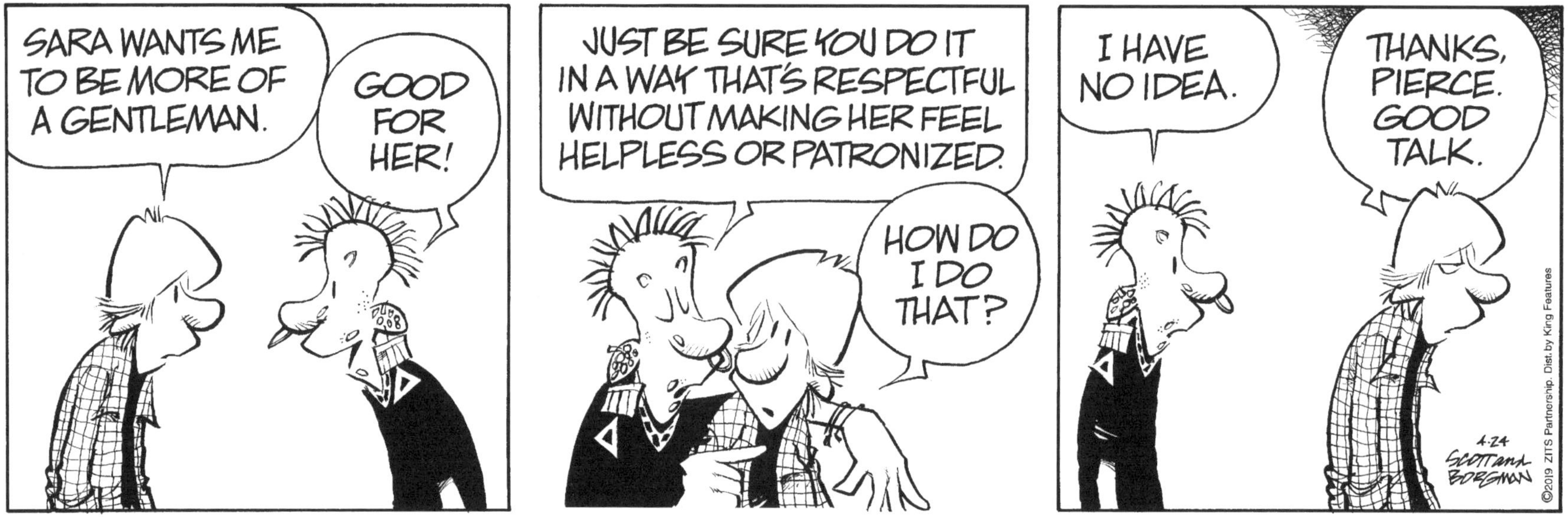
SARA WANTS ME TO BE MORE OF A GENTLEMAN.
GOOD FOR HER!
JUST BE SURE YOU DO IT IN A WAY THAT'S RESPECTFUL WITHOUT MAKING HER FEEL HELPLESS OR PATRONIZED.
HOW DO I DO THAT?
I HAVE NO IDEA.
THANKS, PIERCE. GOOD TALK.
4-24
©2019 ZITS Partnership. Dist. by King Features

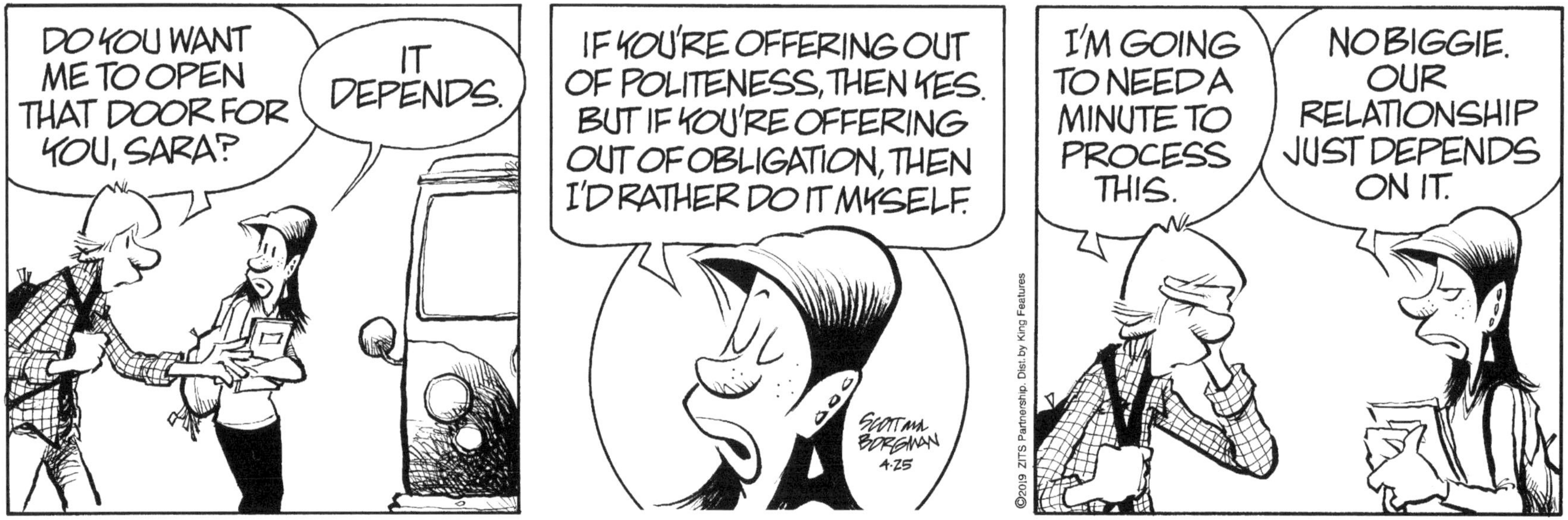
DO YOU WANT ME TO OPEN THAT DOOR FOR YOU, SARA?
IT DEPENDS.
IF YOU'RE OFFERING OUT OF POLITENESS, THEN YES. BUT IF YOU'RE OFFERING OUT OF OBLIGATION, THEN I'D RATHER DO IT MYSELF.
4-25
©2019 ZITS Partnership. Dist. by King Features
I'M GOING TO NEED A MINUTE TO PROCESS THIS.
NO BIGGIE. OUR RELATIONSHIP JUST DEPENDS ON IT.

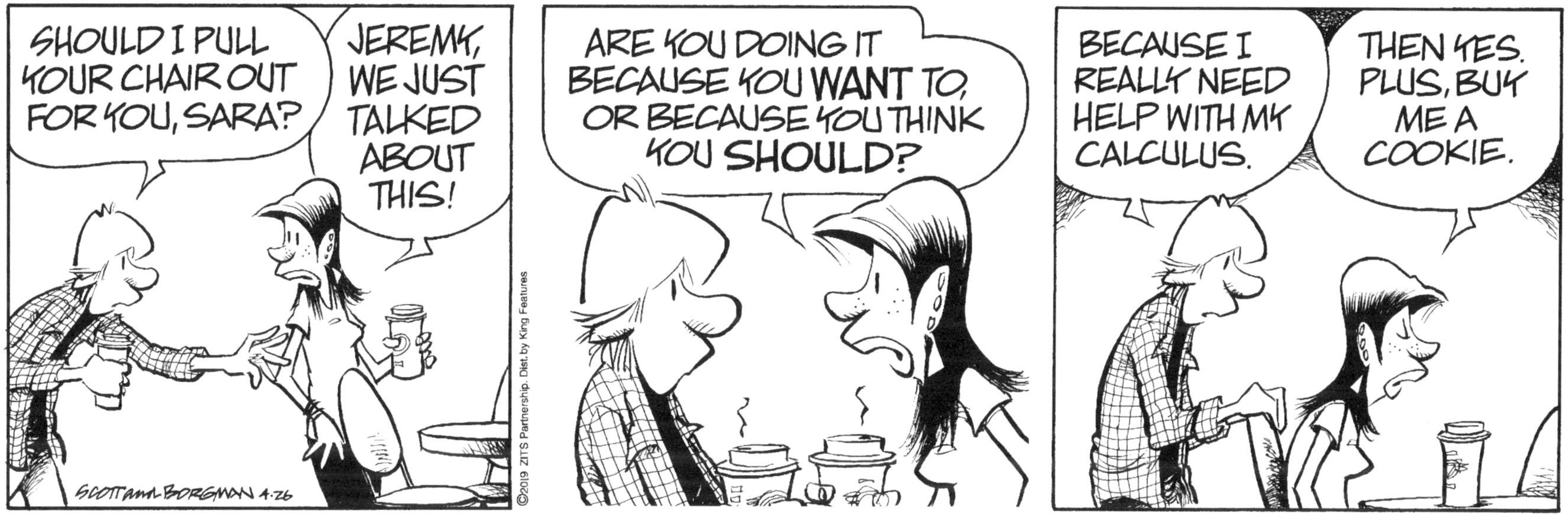
SHOULD I PULL YOUR CHAIR OUT FOR YOU, SARA?
JEREMY, WE JUST TALKED ABOUT THIS!
SCOTT and BORGMAN 4·26
©2019 ZITS Partnership. Dist. by King Features
ARE YOU DOING IT BECAUSE YOU **WANT** TO, OR BECAUSE YOU THINK YOU **SHOULD**?
BECAUSE I REALLY NEED HELP WITH MY CALCULUS.
THEN YES. PLUS, BUY ME A COOKIE.

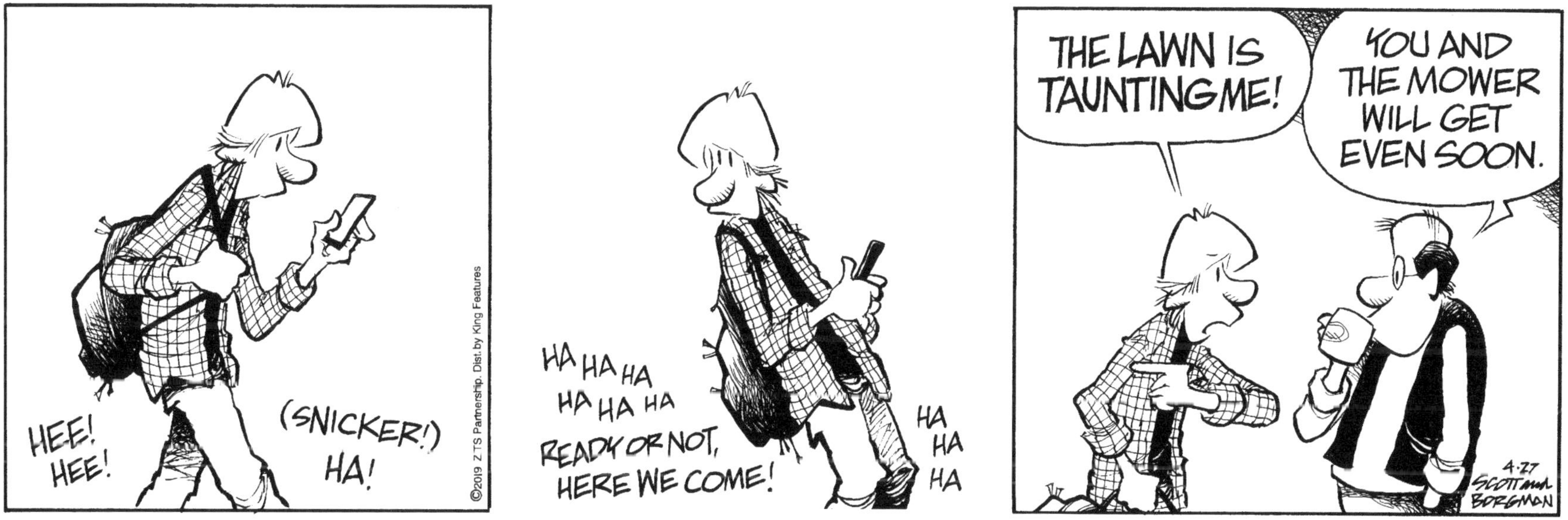
HEE! HEE!
(SNICKER!) HA!
©2019 ZITS Partnership. Dist. by King Features
HA HA HA HA HA HA
READY OR NOT, HERE WE COME!
HA HA HA
THE LAWN IS **TAUNTING** ME!
YOU AND THE MOWER WILL GET EVEN SOON.
4·27 SCOTT and BORGMAN

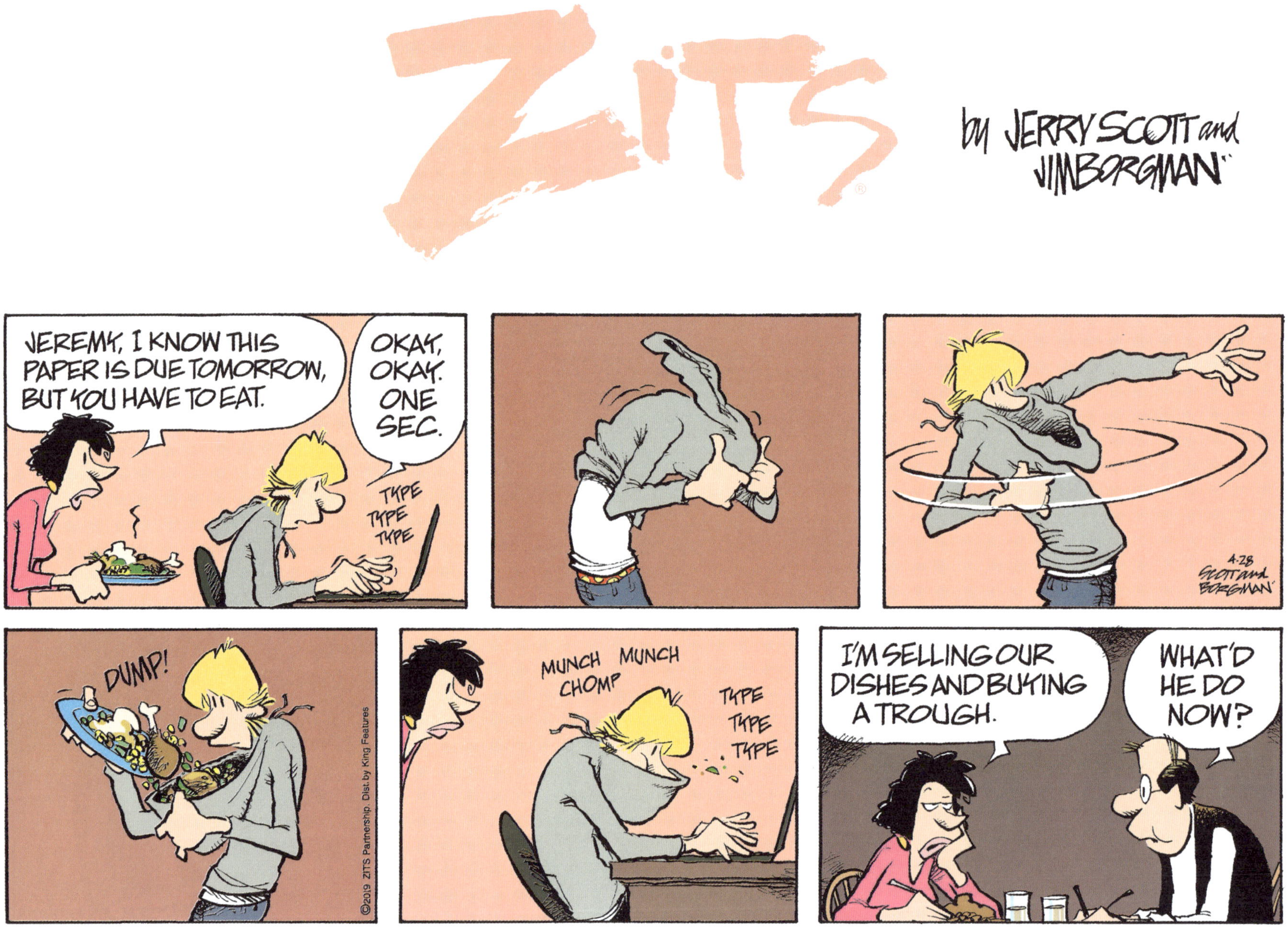
ZITS
by JERRY SCOTT and JIM BORGMAN
JEREMY, I KNOW THIS PAPER IS DUE TOMORROW, BUT YOU HAVE TO EAT.
OKAY, OKAY. ONE SEC.
TYPE TYPE TYPE
4-28 SCOTT and BORGMAN
DUMP!
©2019 ZITS Partnership. Dist. by King Features
MUNCH MUNCH CHOMP
TYPE TYPE TYPE
I'M SELLING OUR DISHES AND BUYING A TROUGH.
WHAT'D HE DO NOW?

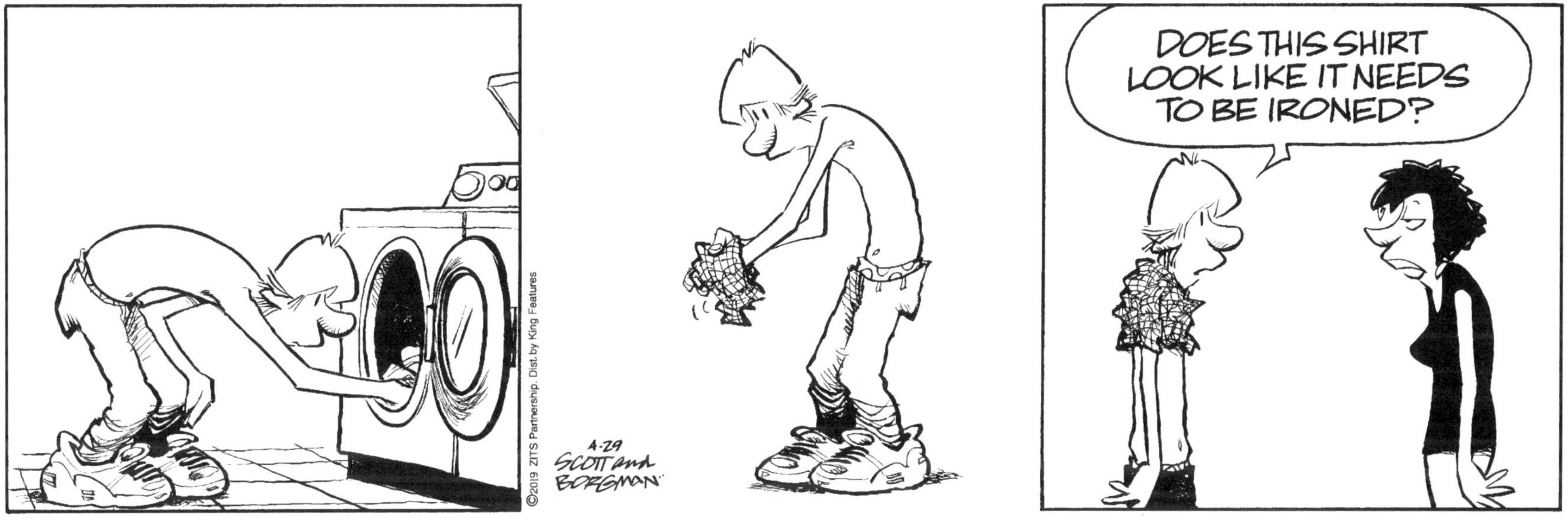
©2019 ZITS Partnership. Dist. by King Features
4-29
SCOTT and BORGMAN
DOES THIS SHIRT LOOK LIKE IT NEEDS TO BE IRONED?

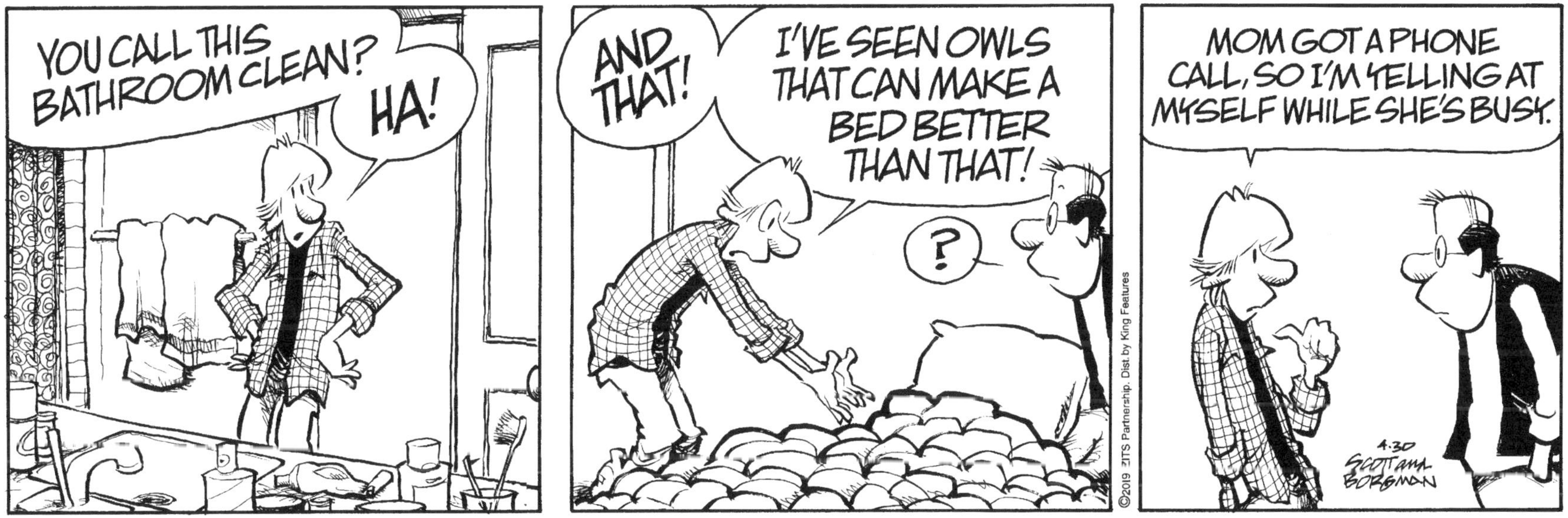
YOU CALL THIS BATHROOM CLEAN?
HA!
AND THAT!
I'VE SEEN OWLS THAT CAN MAKE A BED BETTER THAN THAT!
?
©2019 ZITS Partnership. Dist. by King Features
MOM GOT A PHONE CALL, SO I'M YELLING AT MYSELF WHILE SHE'S BUSY.
4-30
SCOTT and BORGMAN

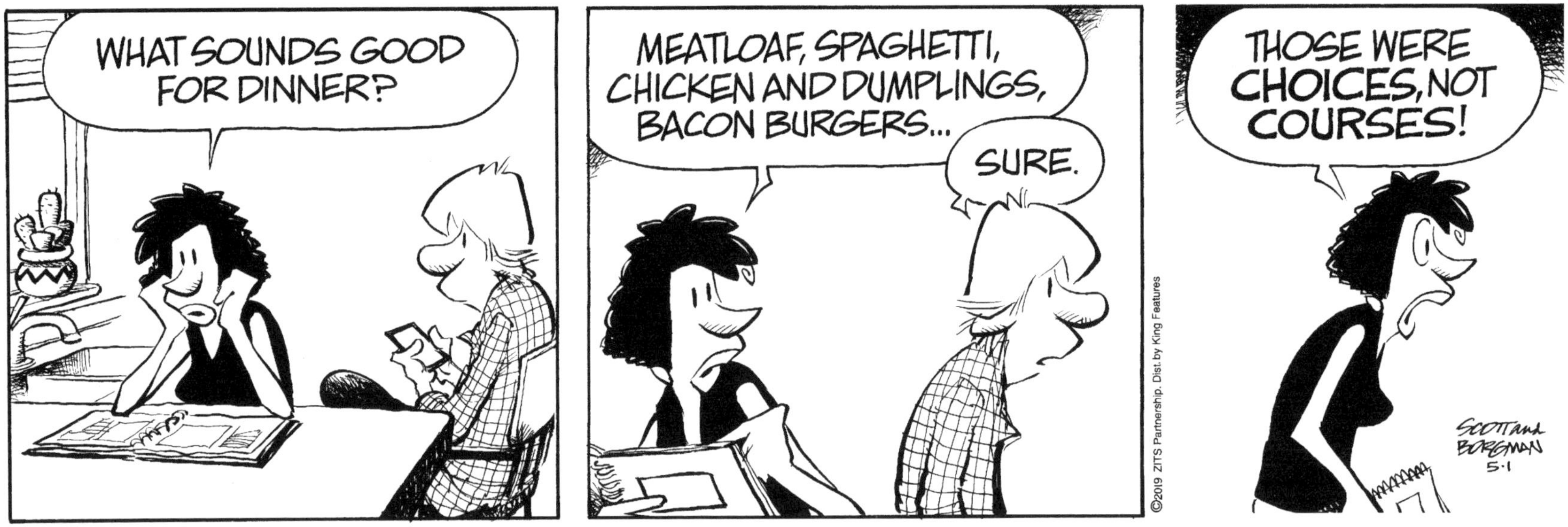
WHAT SOUNDS GOOD FOR DINNER?
MEATLOAF, SPAGHETTI, CHICKEN AND DUMPLINGS, BACON BURGERS...
SURE.
THOSE WERE CHOICES, NOT COURSES!
SCOTT and BORGMAN 5·1
©2019 ZITS Partnership. Dist. by King Features

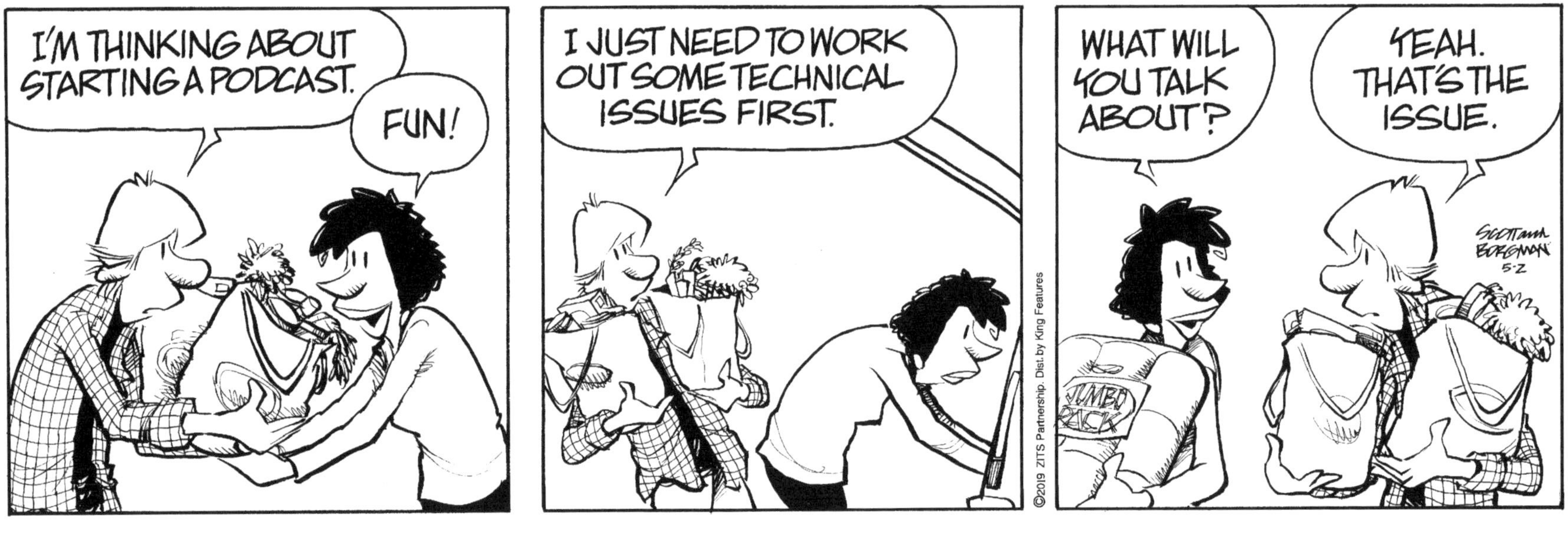
I'M THINKING ABOUT STARTING A PODCAST.
FUN!
I JUST NEED TO WORK OUT SOME TECHNICAL ISSUES FIRST.
WHAT WILL YOU TALK ABOUT?
YEAH. THAT'S THE ISSUE.
JUMBO PACK
SCOTT and BORGMAN 5·2
©2019 ZITS Partnership. Dist. by King Features

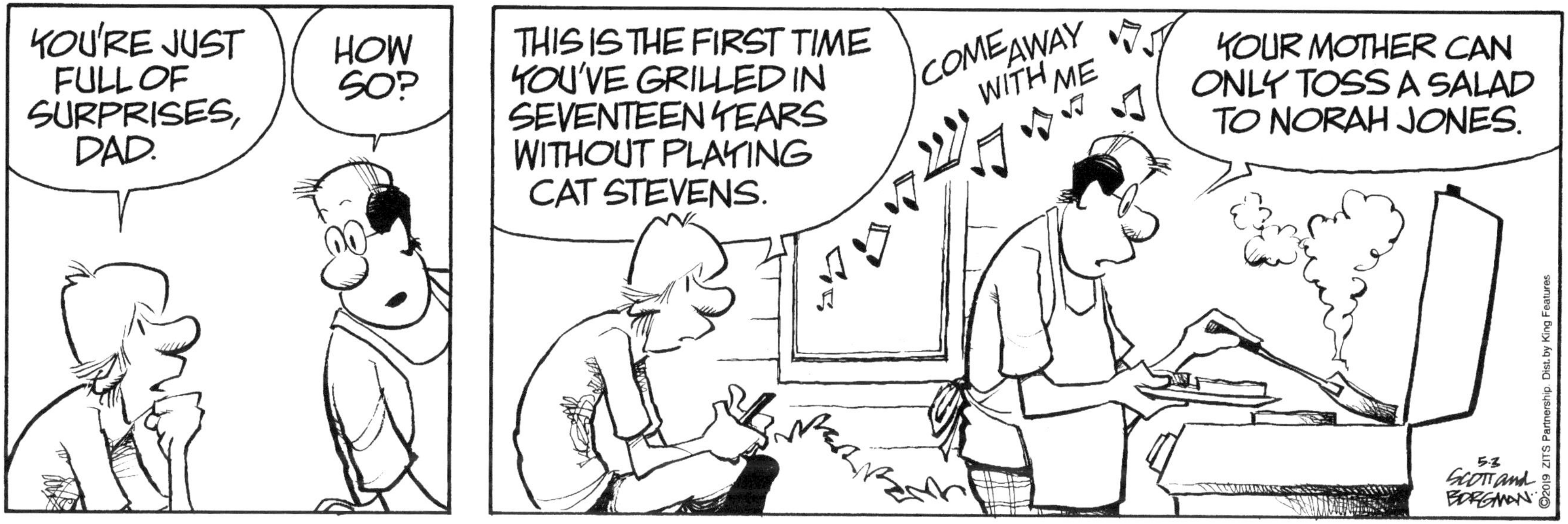
YOU'RE JUST FULL OF SURPRISES, DAD.
HOW SO?
THIS IS THE FIRST TIME YOU'VE GRILLED IN SEVENTEEN YEARS WITHOUT PLAYING CAT STEVENS.
COME AWAY WITH ME
YOUR MOTHER CAN ONLY TOSS A SALAD TO NORAH JONES.
5-3
SCOTT and BORGMAN
©2019 ZITS Partnership. Dist. by King Features

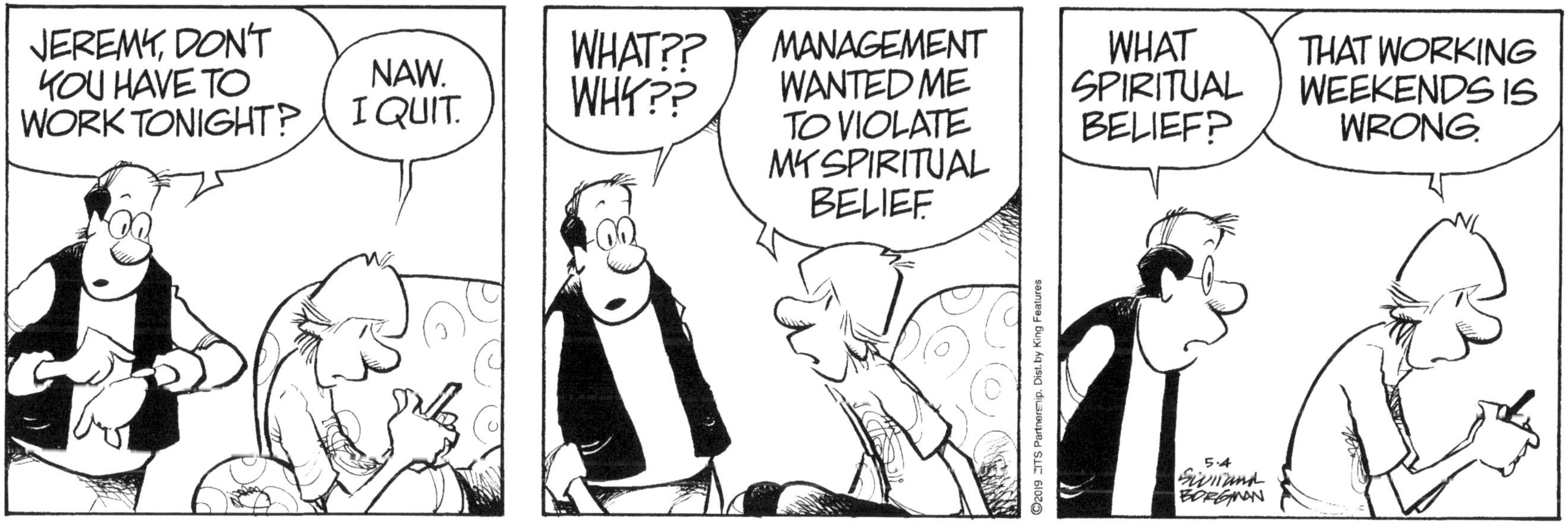
JEREMY, DON'T YOU HAVE TO WORK TONIGHT?
NAW. I QUIT.
WHAT?? WHY??
MANAGEMENT WANTED ME TO VIOLATE MY SPIRITUAL BELIEF.
©2019 ZITS Partnership. Dist. by King Features
WHAT SPIRITUAL BELIEF?
THAT WORKING WEEKENDS IS WRONG.
5-4
SCOTT and BORGMAN

ZITS

by JERRY SCOTT and JIM BORGMAN

TONITE ONLY!
SCOTT and BORGMAN 5-5
©2019 ZITS Partnership. Dist. by King Features
EXACTLY HOW CLASSIC IS THE CLASSIC ROCK THESE GUYS PLAY?
Z

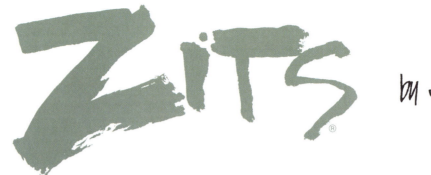

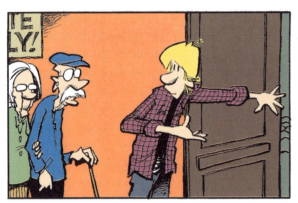

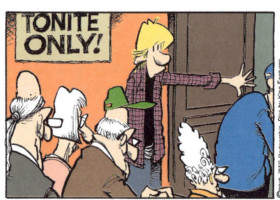

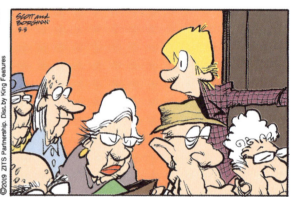

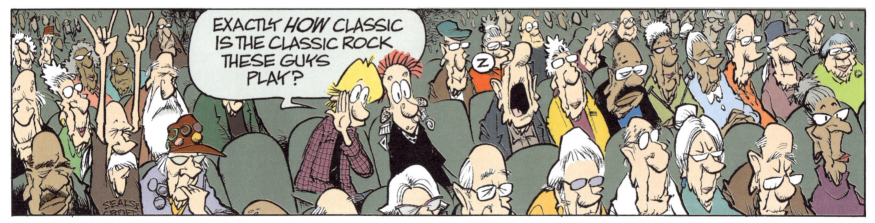

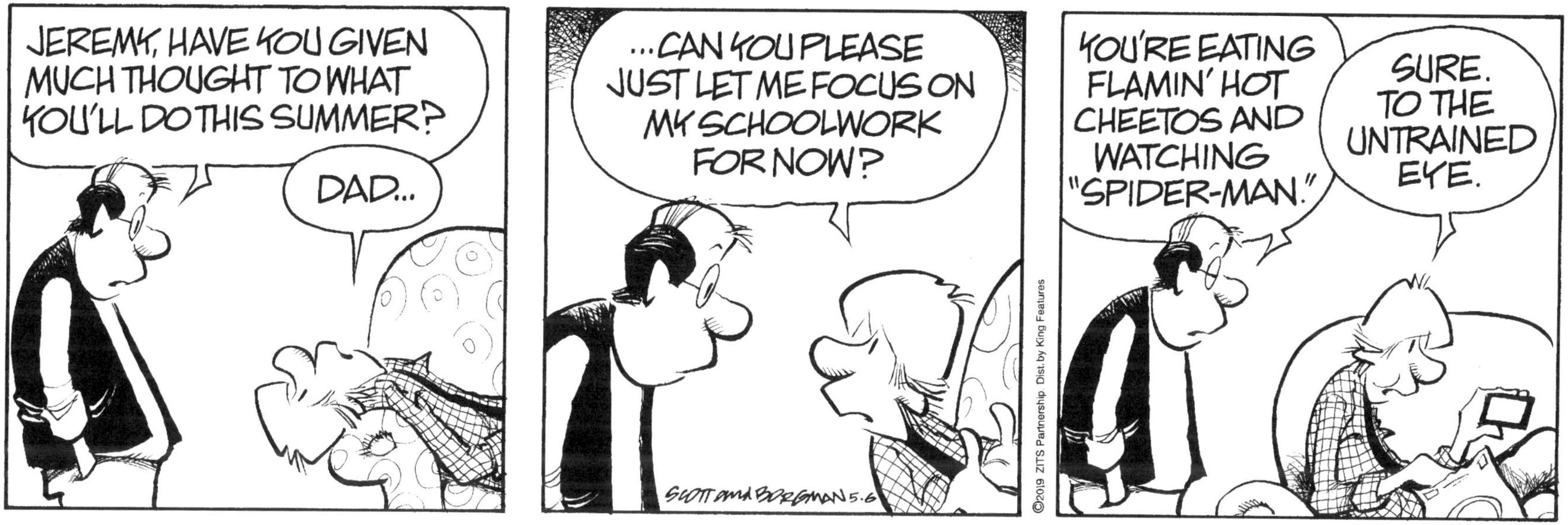
JEREMY, HAVE YOU GIVEN MUCH THOUGHT TO WHAT YOU'LL DO THIS SUMMER?
DAD...
...CAN YOU PLEASE JUST LET ME FOCUS ON MY SCHOOLWORK FOR NOW?
SCOTT and BORGMAN 5.6
©2019 ZITS Partnership. Dist. by King Features
YOU'RE EATING FLAMIN' HOT CHEETOS AND WATCHING "SPIDER-MAN."
SURE. TO THE UNTRAINED EYE.

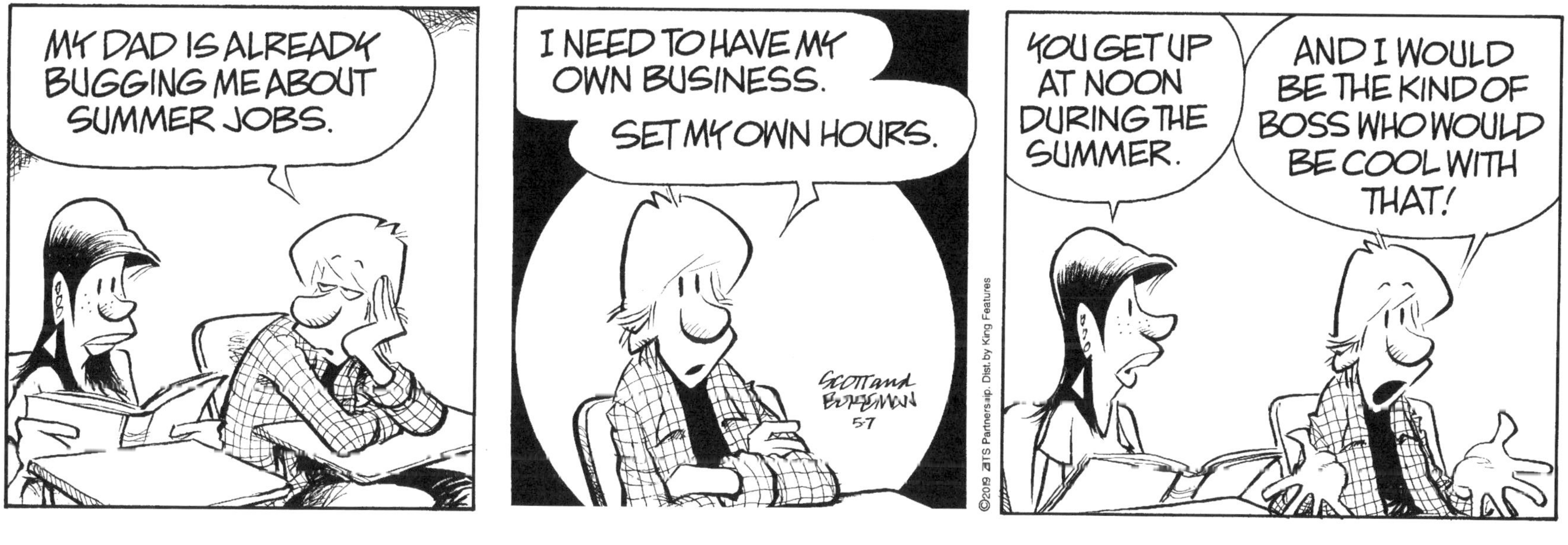
MY DAD IS ALREADY BUGGING ME ABOUT SUMMER JOBS.
I NEED TO HAVE MY OWN BUSINESS.
SET MY OWN HOURS.
SCOTT and BORGMAN 5-7
©2019 ZITS Partnership. Dist. by King Features
YOU GET UP AT NOON DURING THE SUMMER.
AND I WOULD BE THE KIND OF BOSS WHO WOULD BE COOL WITH THAT!

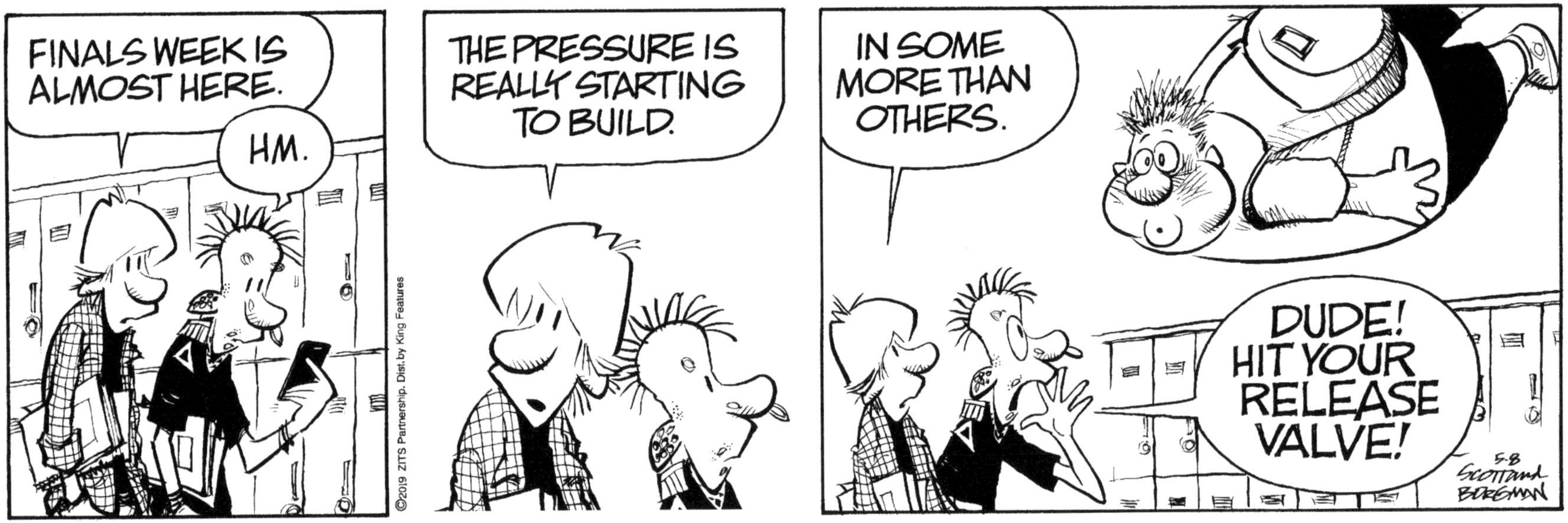
FINALS WEEK IS ALMOST HERE.
HM.
©2019 ZITS Partnership. Dist. by King Features
THE PRESSURE IS REALLY STARTING TO BUILD.
IN SOME MORE THAN OTHERS.
DUDE! HIT YOUR RELEASE VALVE!
5-8
SCOTT and BORGMAN

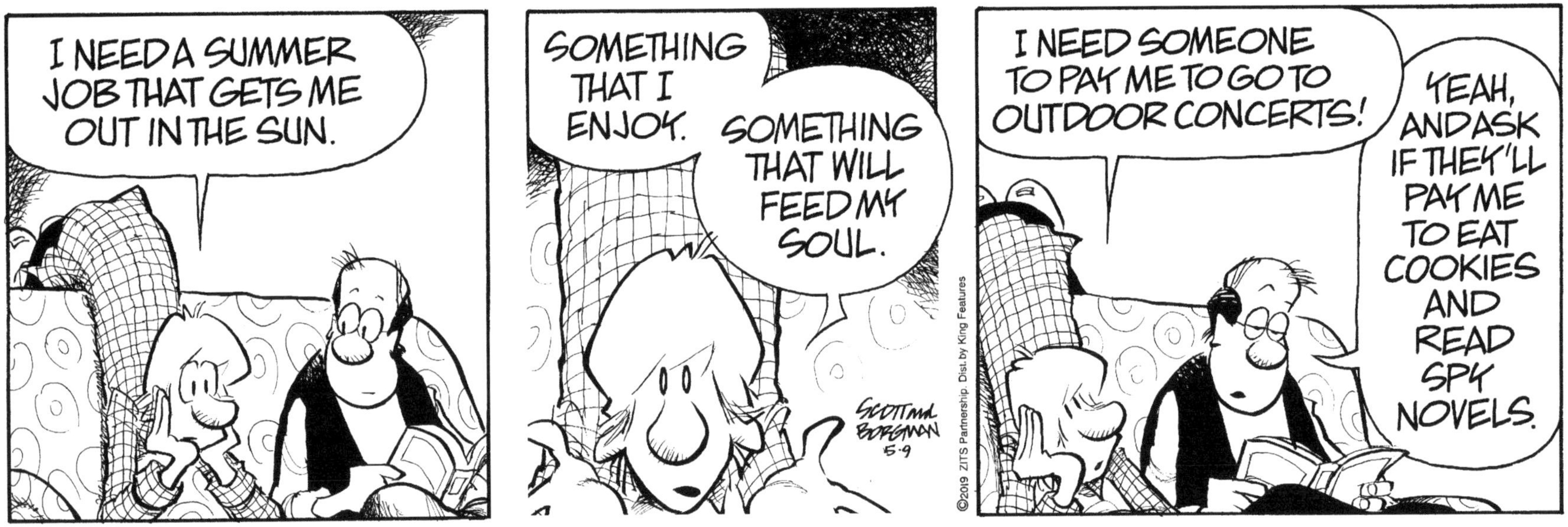
I NEED A SUMMER JOB THAT GETS ME OUT IN THE SUN.
SOMETHING THAT I ENJOY.
SOMETHING THAT WILL FEED MY SOUL.
SCOTT and BORGMAN
5-9
©2019 ZITS Partnership. Dist. by King Features
I NEED SOMEONE TO PAY ME TO GO TO OUTDOOR CONCERTS!
YEAH, AND ASK IF THEY'LL PAY ME TO EAT COOKIES AND READ SPY NOVELS.

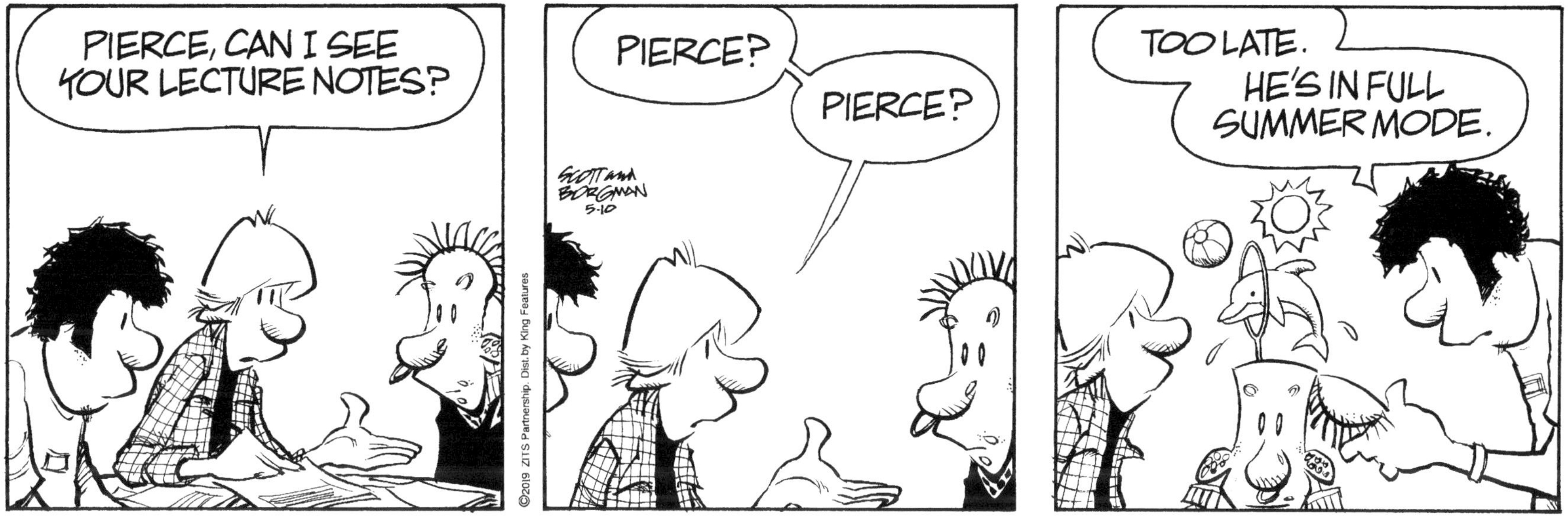
PIERCE, CAN I SEE YOUR LECTURE NOTES?
PIERCE?
PIERCE?
TOO LATE.
HE'S IN FULL SUMMER MODE.
©2019 ZITS Partnership. Dist. by King Features

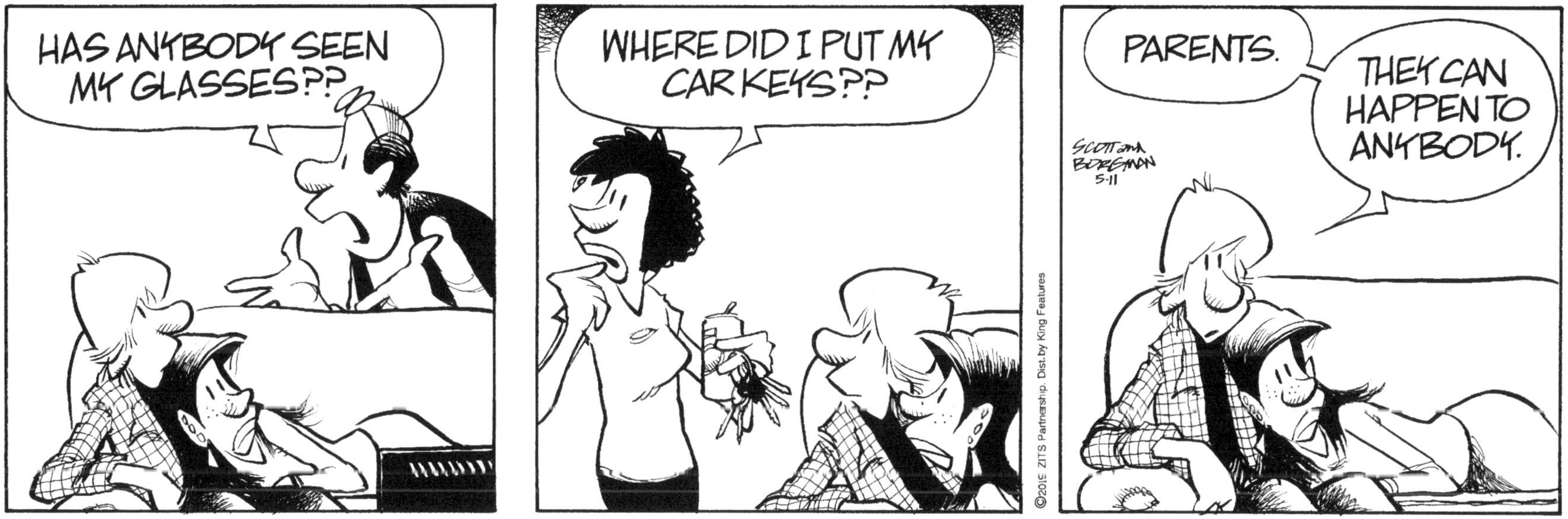
HAS ANYBODY SEEN MY GLASSES??
WHERE DID I PUT MY CAR KEYS??
PARENTS.
THEY CAN HAPPEN TO ANYBODY.
©2019 ZITS Partnership. Dist. by King Features

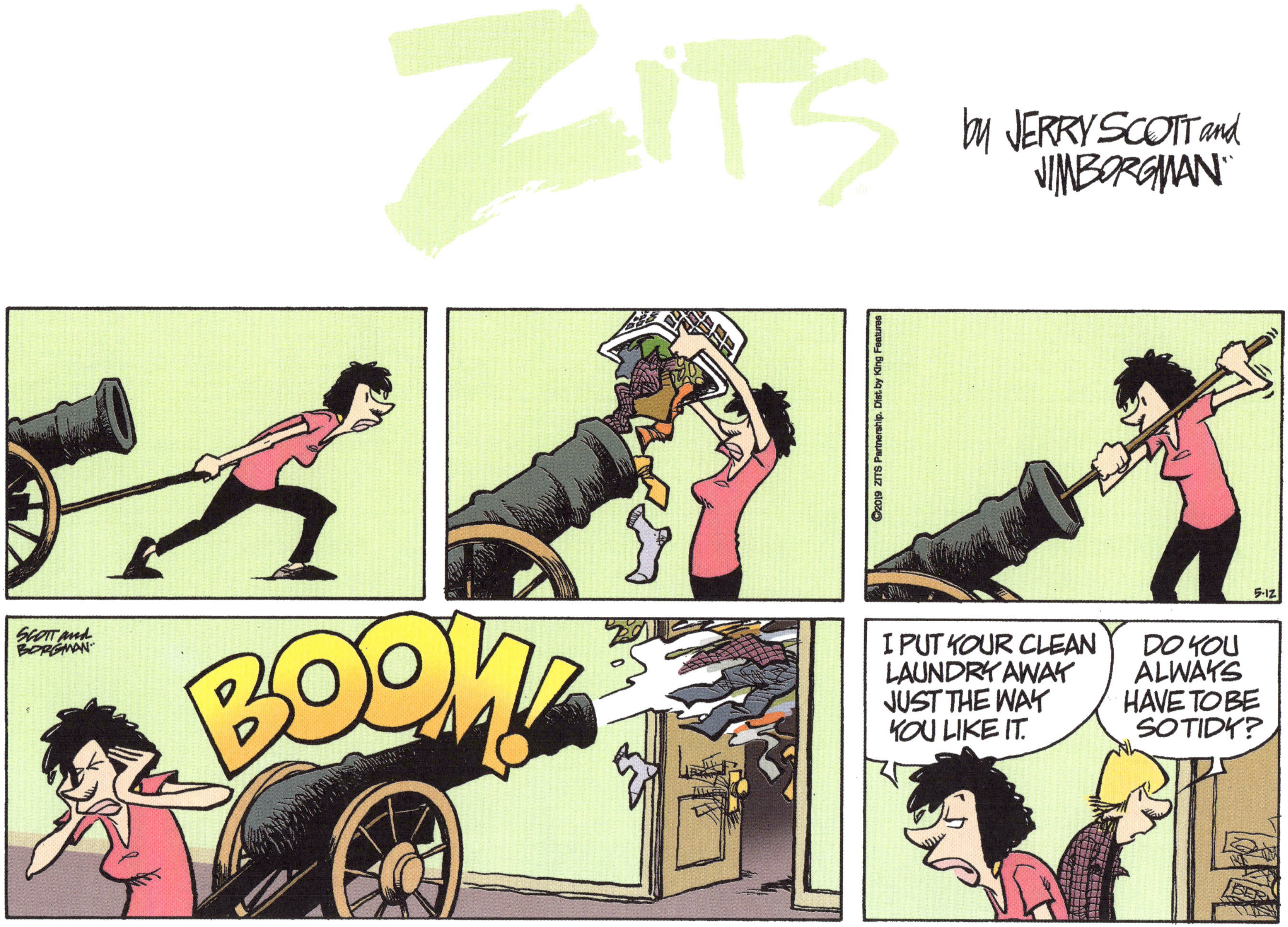

ZITS
by JERRY SCOTT and JIM BORGMAN
©2019 ZITS Partnership. Dist. by King Features
5-12
SCOTT and BORGMAN
BOOM!
I PUT YOUR CLEAN LAUNDRY AWAY JUST THE WAY YOU LIKE IT.
DO YOU ALWAYS HAVE TO BE SO TIDY?

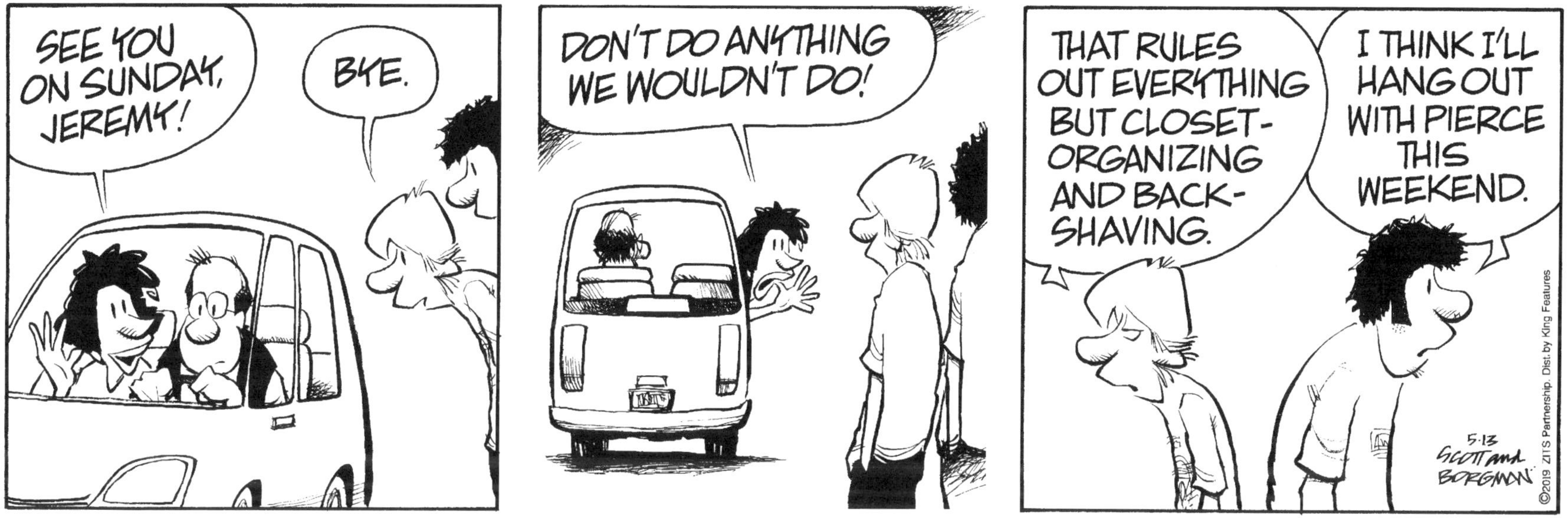
SEE YOU ON SUNDAY, JEREMY!
BYE.
DON'T DO ANYTHING WE WOULDN'T DO!
THAT RULES OUT EVERYTHING BUT CLOSET-ORGANIZING AND BACK-SHAVING.
I THINK I'LL HANG OUT WITH PIERCE THIS WEEKEND.
5.13 SCOTT and BORGMAN
©2019 ZITS Partnership. Dist. by King Features

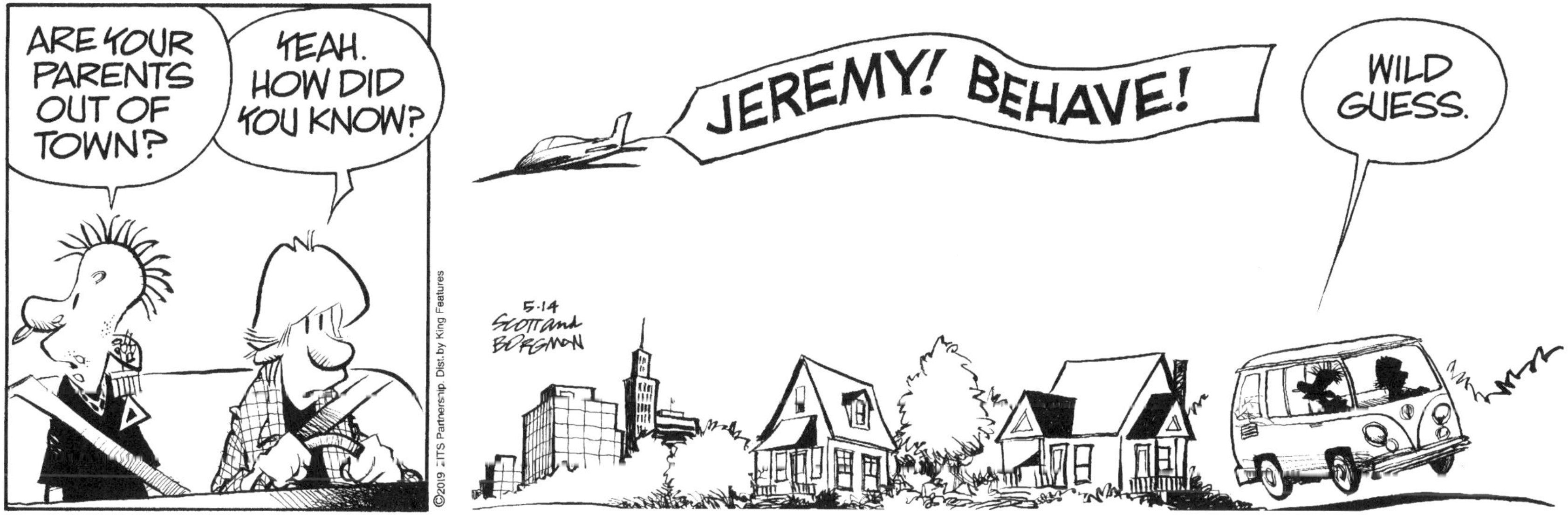
ARE YOUR PARENTS OUT OF TOWN?
YEAH. HOW DID YOU KNOW?
©2019 ZITS Partnership. Dist. by King Features
JEREMY! BEHAVE!
WILD GUESS.
5.14 SCOTT and BORGMAN

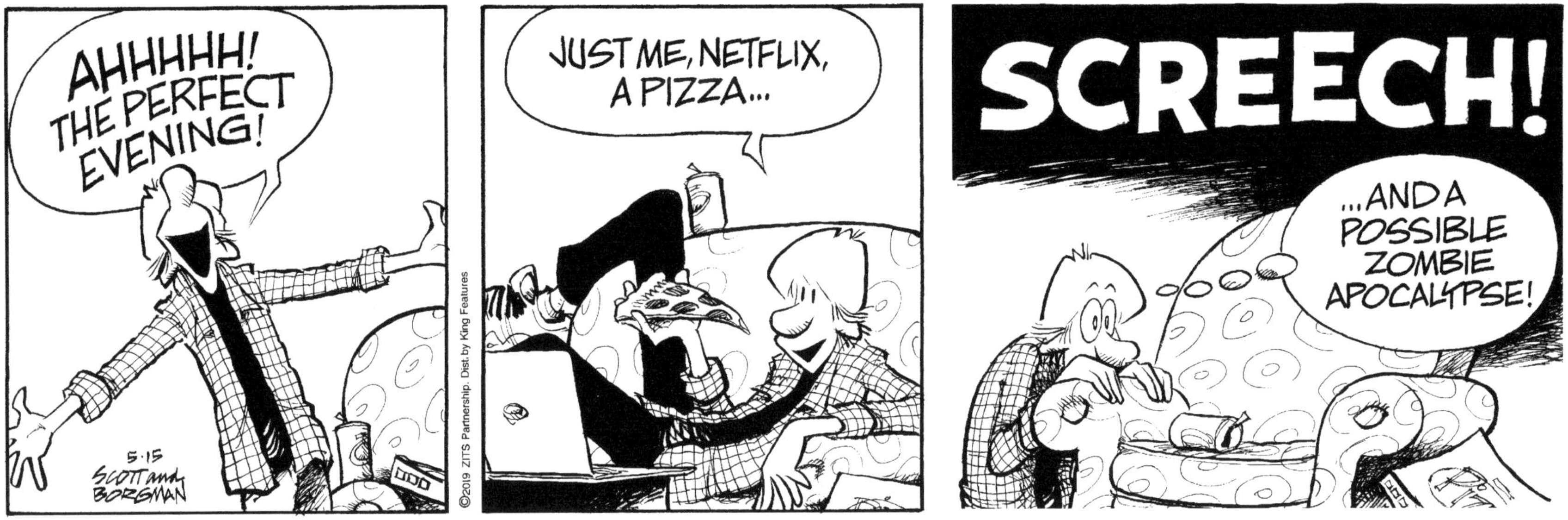
AHHHHH! THE PERFECT EVENING!
5·15
SCOTT and BORGMAN
©2019 ZITS Partnership. Dist. by King Features
JUST ME, NETFLIX, A PIZZA...
SCREECH!
...AND A POSSIBLE ZOMBIE APOCALYPSE!

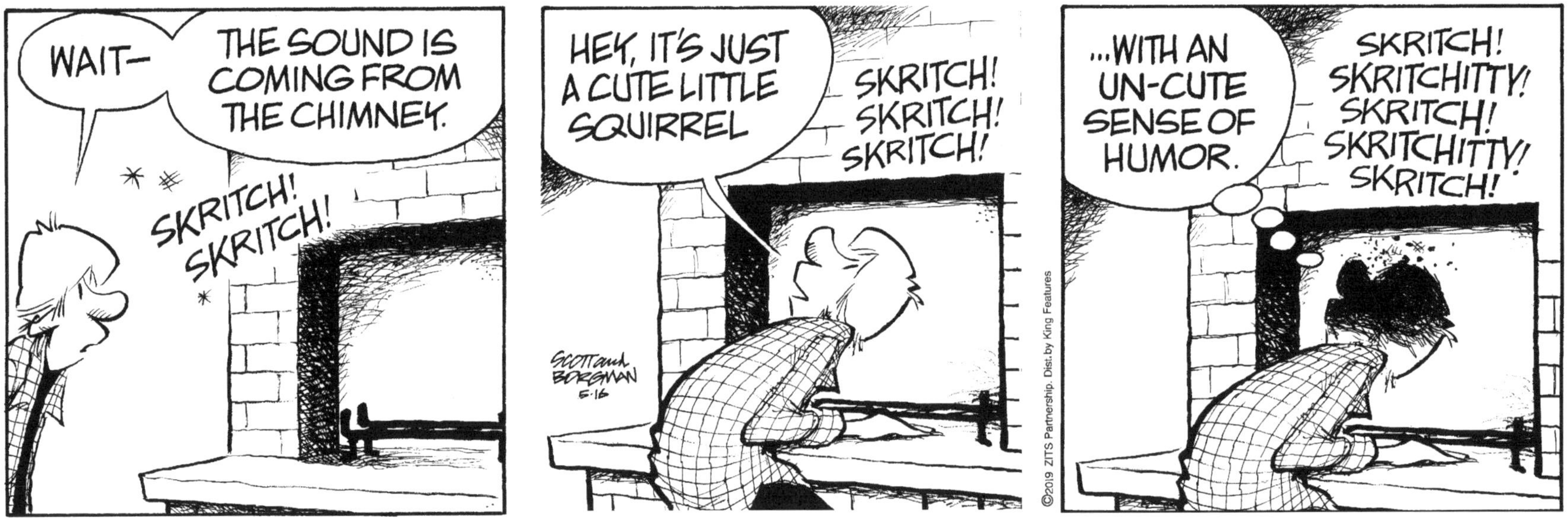
WAIT—
THE SOUND IS COMING FROM THE CHIMNEY.
SKRITCH! SKRITCH!
HEY, IT'S JUST A CUTE LITTLE SQUIRREL
SKRITCH! SKRITCH! SKRITCH!
SCOTT and BORGMAN 5·16
©2019 ZITS Partnership. Dist. by King Features
...WITH AN UN-CUTE SENSE OF HUMOR.
SKRITCH! SKRITCHITTY! SKRITCH! SKRITCHITTY! SKRITCH!

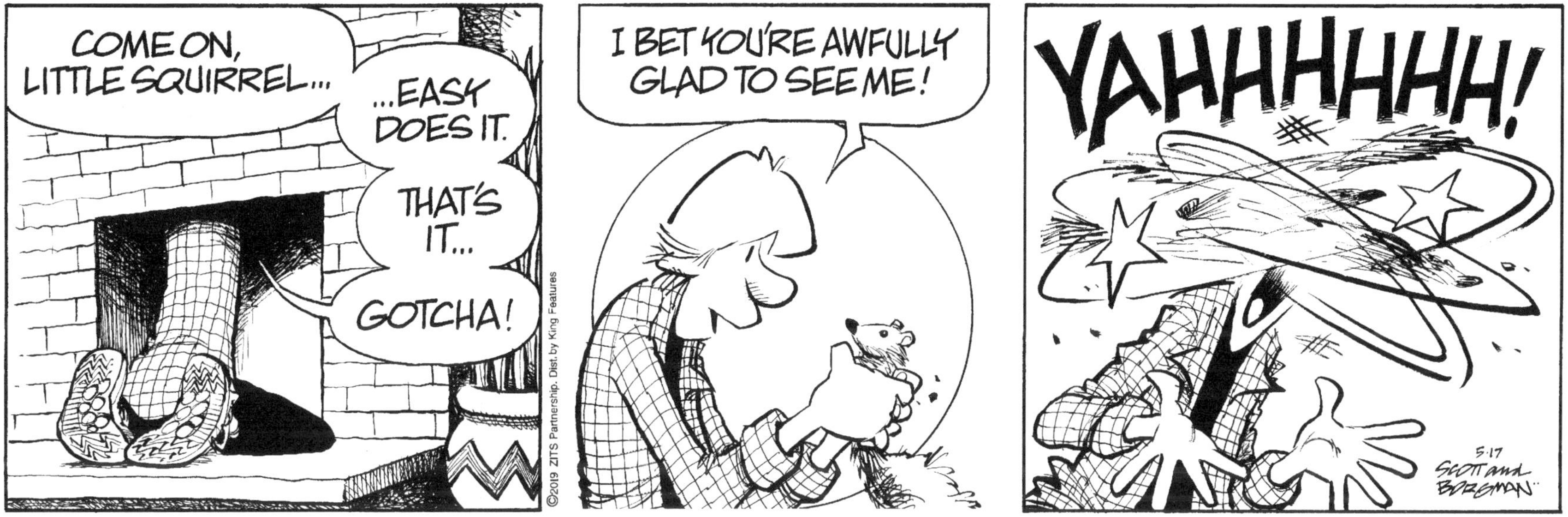
COME ON, LITTLE SQUIRREL...
...EASY DOES IT.
THAT'S IT...
GOTCHA!
©2019 ZITS Partnership. Dist. by King Features
I BET YOU'RE AWFULLY GLAD TO SEE ME!
YAHHHHHH!
5·17 SCOTT and BORGMAN

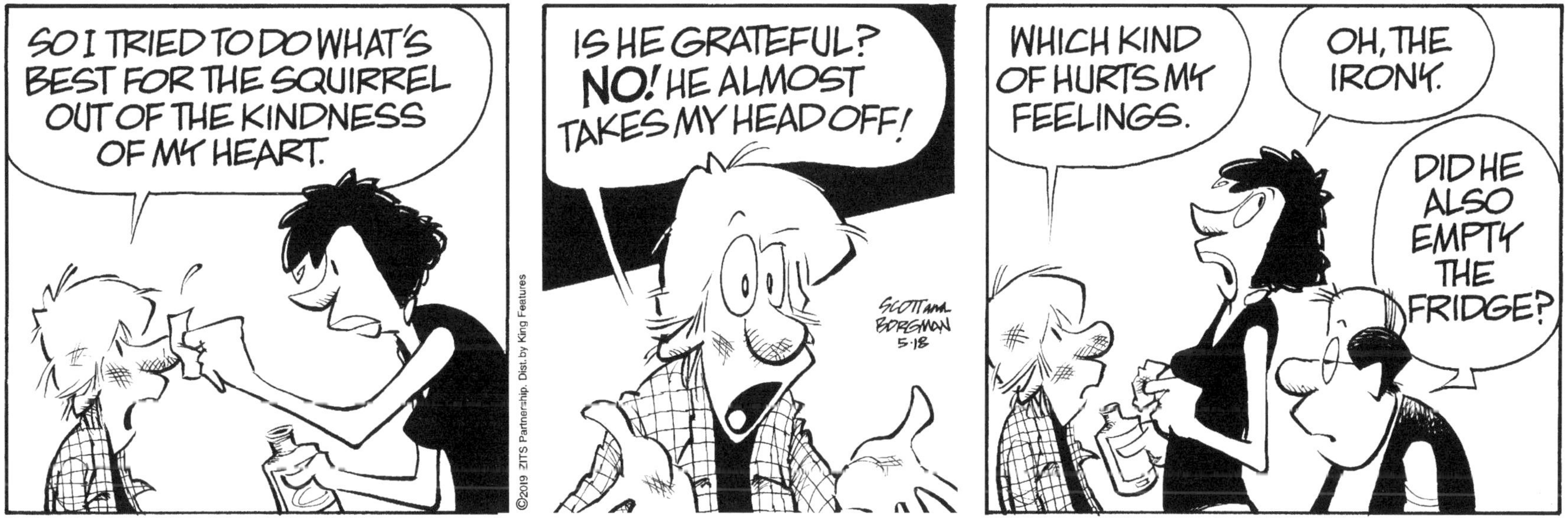
SO I TRIED TO DO WHAT'S BEST FOR THE SQUIRREL OUT OF THE KINDNESS OF MY HEART.
©2019 ZITS Partnership. Dist. by King Features
IS HE GRATEFUL? **NO!** HE ALMOST TAKES MY HEAD OFF!
SCOTT and BORGMAN 5·18
WHICH KIND OF HURTS MY FEELINGS.
OH, THE IRONY.
DID HE ALSO EMPTY THE FRIDGE?

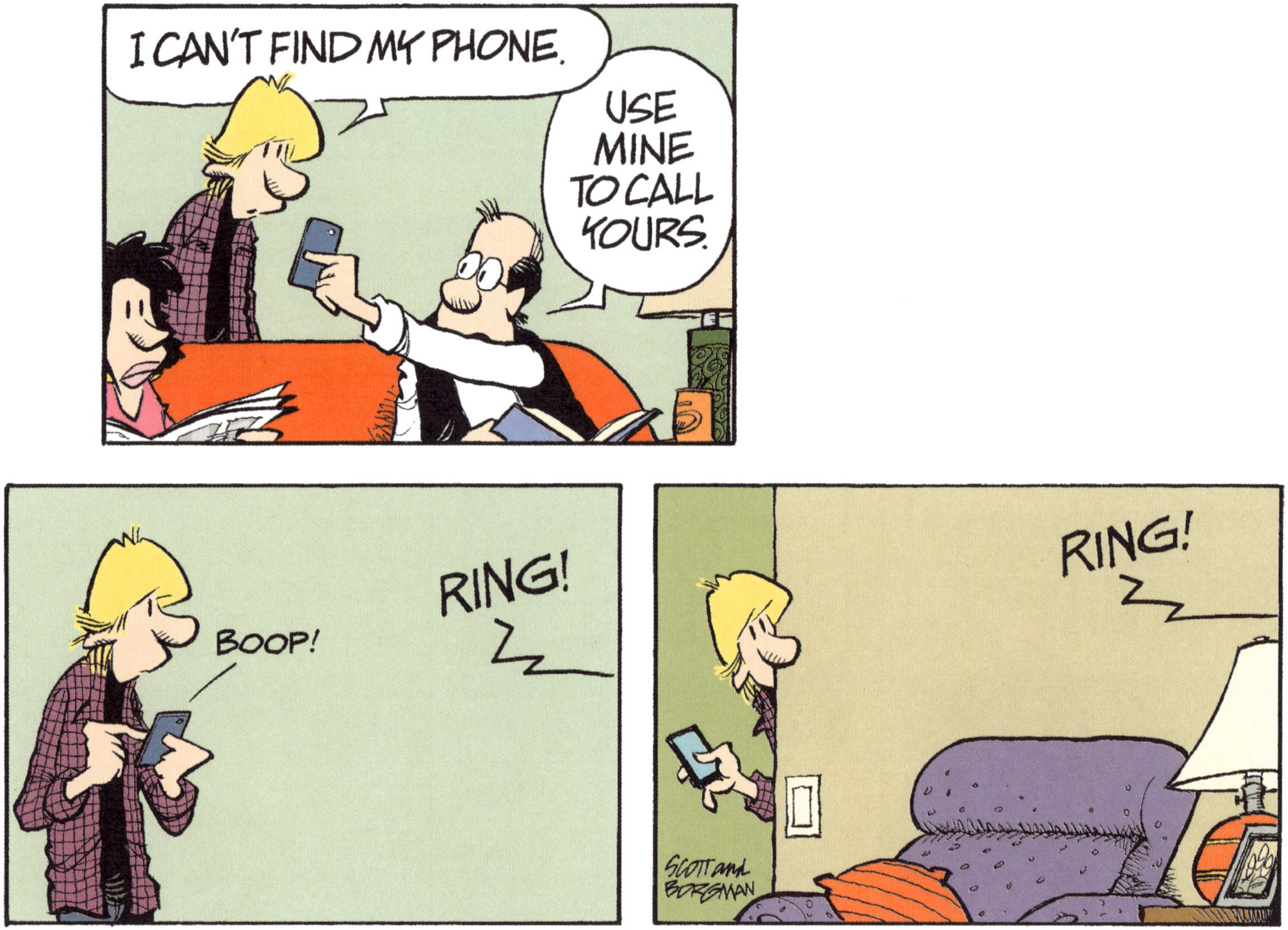
I CAN'T FIND MY PHONE.
USE MINE TO CALL YOURS.
BOOP!
RING!
RING!
SCOTT and BORGMAN

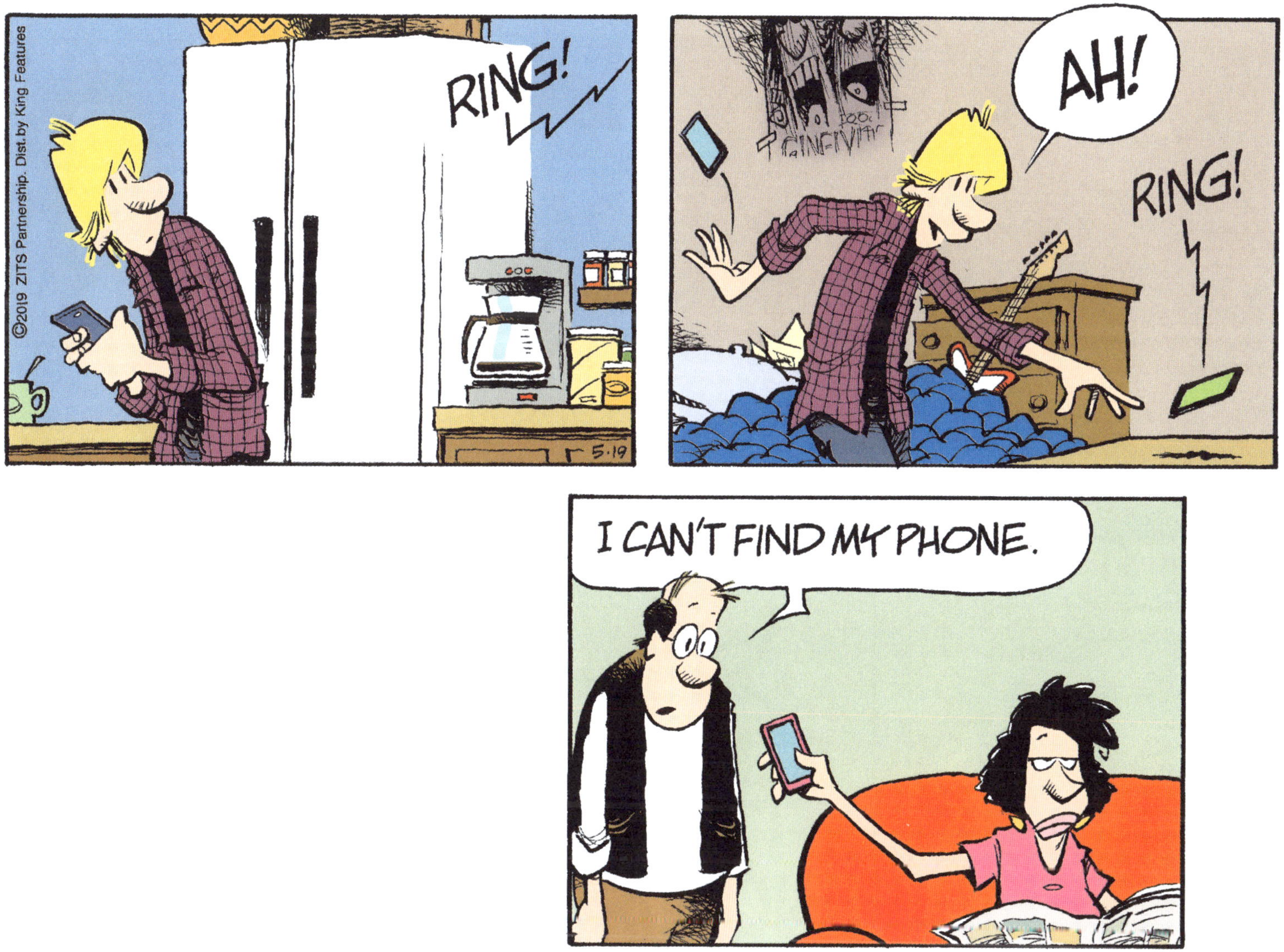
©2019 ZITS Partnership. Dist. by King Features
RING!
5·19
AH!
RING!
I CAN'T FIND MY PHONE.

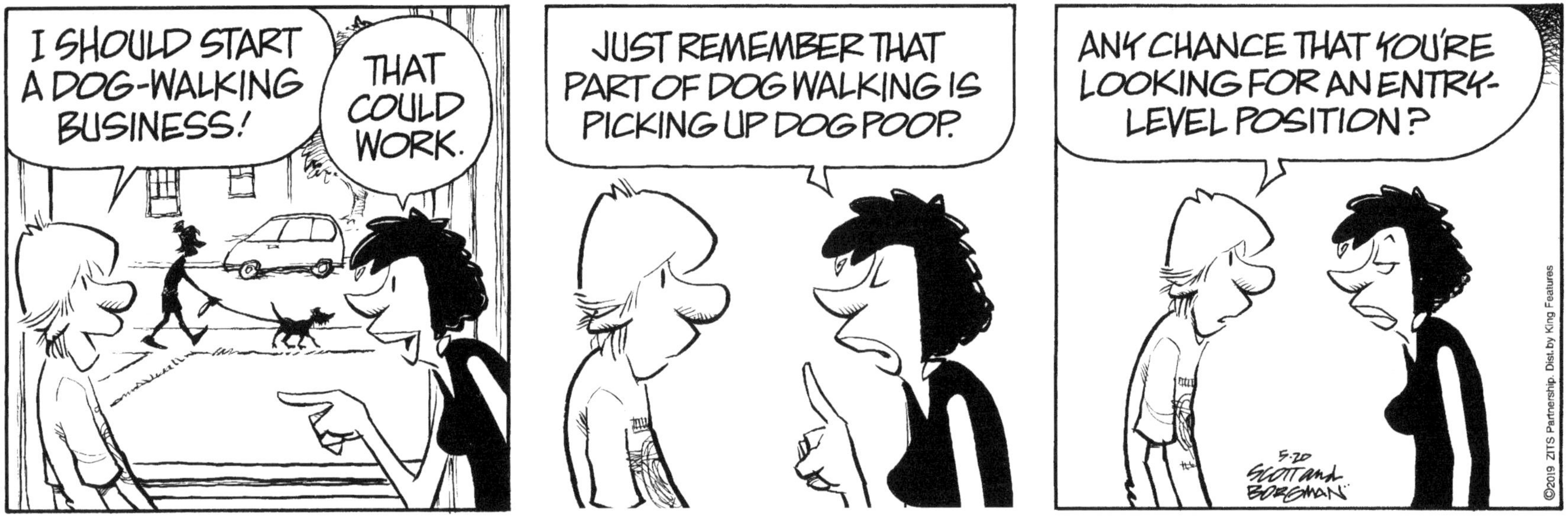
I SHOULD START A DOG-WALKING BUSINESS!
THAT COULD WORK.
JUST REMEMBER THAT PART OF DOG WALKING IS PICKING UP DOG POOP.
ANY CHANCE THAT YOU'RE LOOKING FOR AN ENTRY-LEVEL POSITION?
5-20 SCOTT AND BORGMAN
©2019 ZITS Partnership. Dist. by King Features

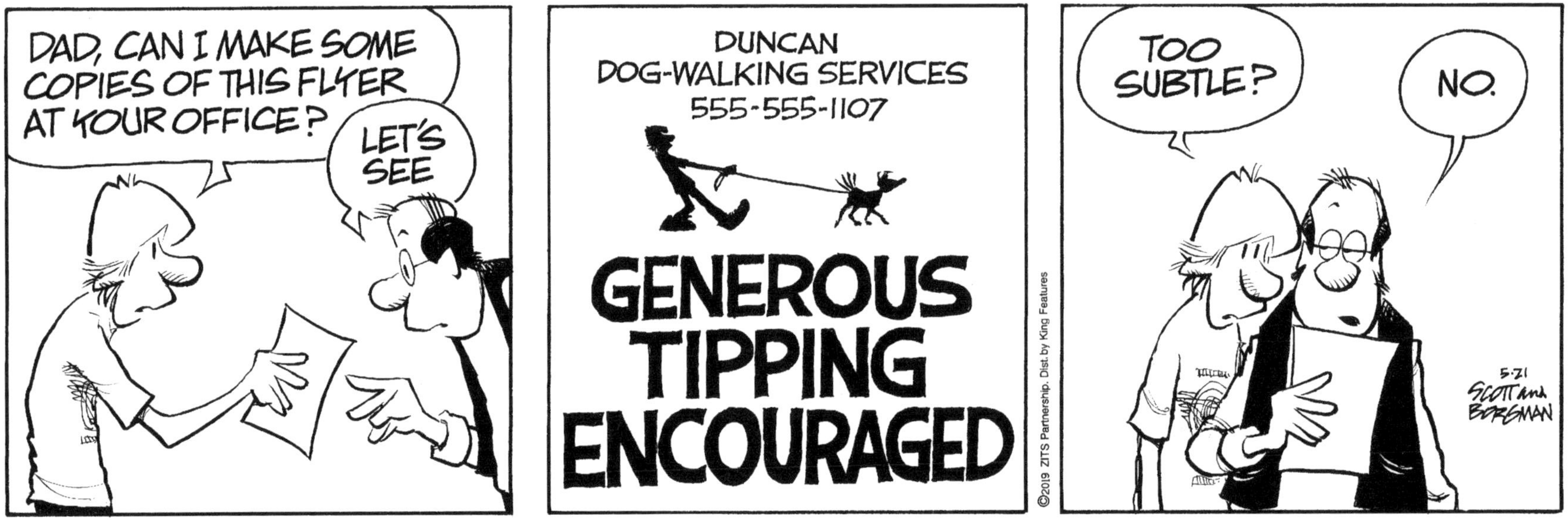
DAD, CAN I MAKE SOME COPIES OF THIS FLYER AT YOUR OFFICE?
LET'S SEE
DUNCAN DOG-WALKING SERVICES
555-555-1107
GENEROUS TIPPING ENCOURAGED
©2019 ZITS Partnership. Dist. by King Features
TOO SUBTLE?
NO.
5-21 SCOTT AND BORGMAN

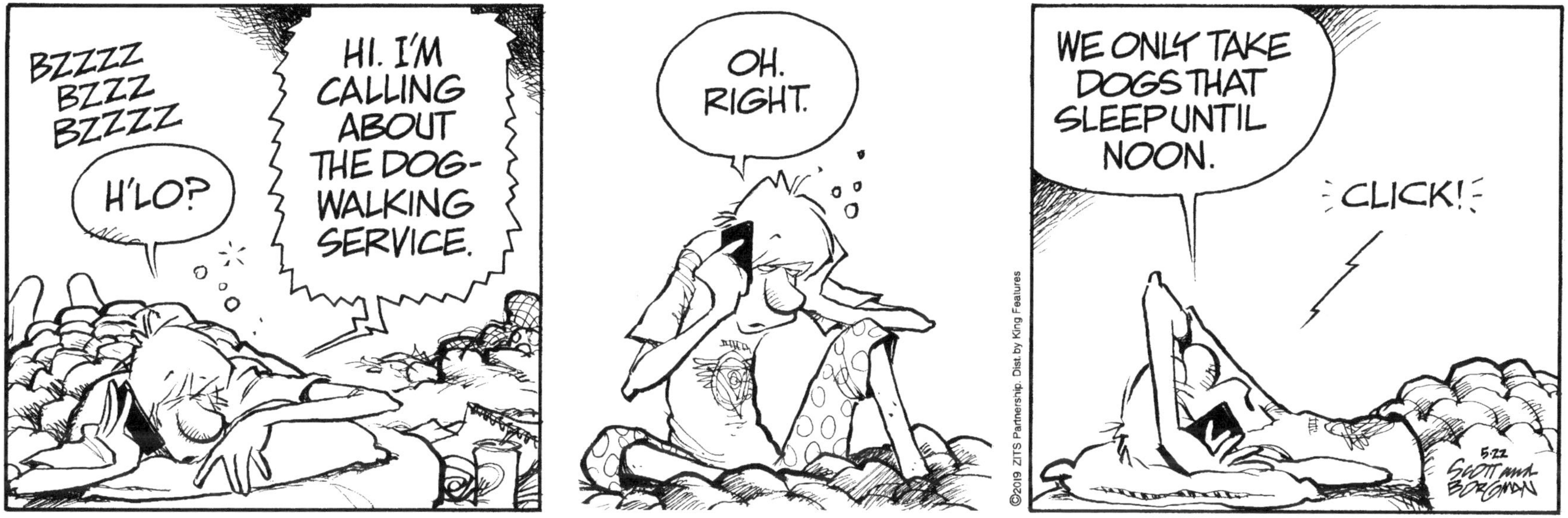
BZZZZ BZZZ BZZZZ
H'LO?
HI. I'M CALLING ABOUT THE DOG-WALKING SERVICE.
OH. RIGHT.
©2019 ZITS Partnership. Dist. by King Features
WE ONLY TAKE DOGS THAT SLEEP UNTIL NOON.
CLICK!
5-22
SCOTT and BORGMAN

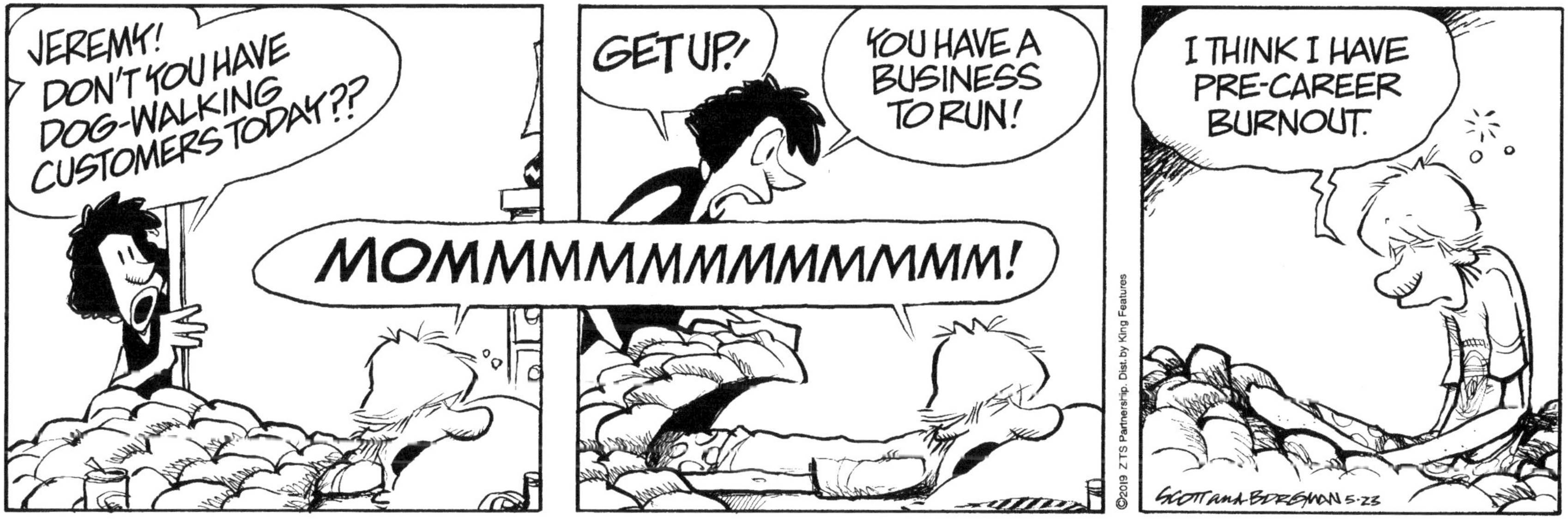
JEREMY! DON'T YOU HAVE DOG-WALKING CUSTOMERS TODAY??
MOMMMMMMMMMMMM!
GET UP!
YOU HAVE A BUSINESS TO RUN!
©2019 ZITS Partnership. Dist. by King Features
I THINK I HAVE PRE-CAREER BURNOUT.
SCOTT and BORGMAN 5-23

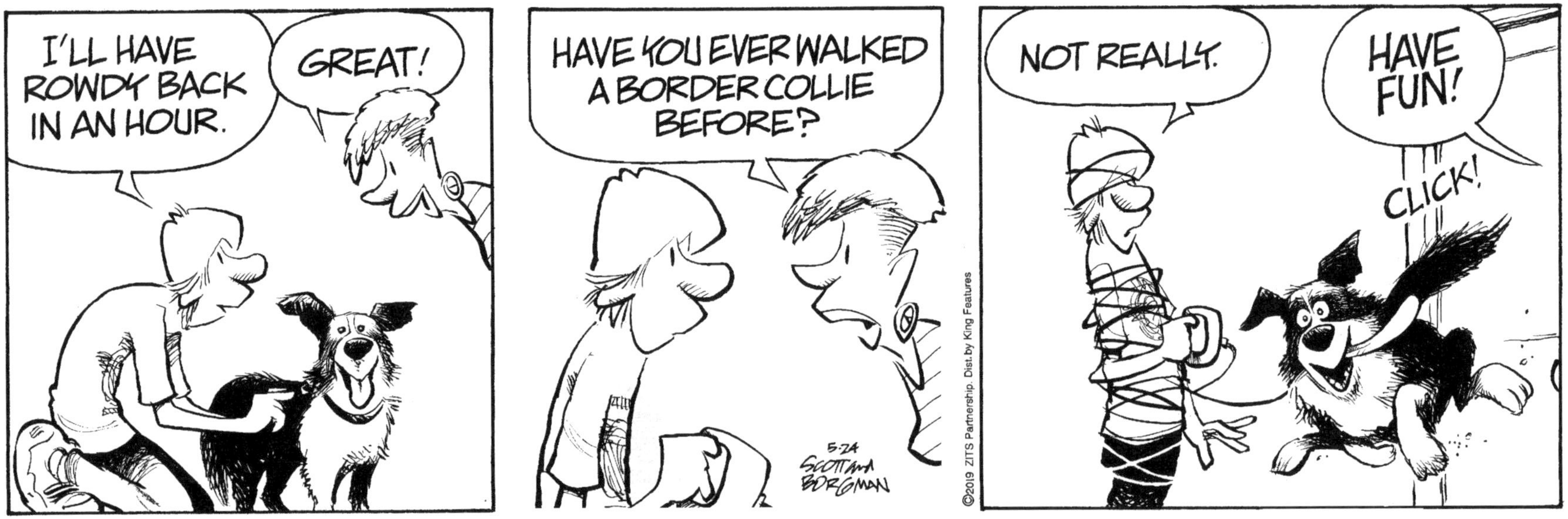
I'LL HAVE ROWDY BACK IN AN HOUR.
GREAT!
HAVE YOU EVER WALKED A BORDER COLLIE BEFORE?
5·24 SCOTT and BORGMAN
©2019 ZITS Partnership. Dist. by King Features
NOT REALLY.
HAVE FUN!
CLICK!

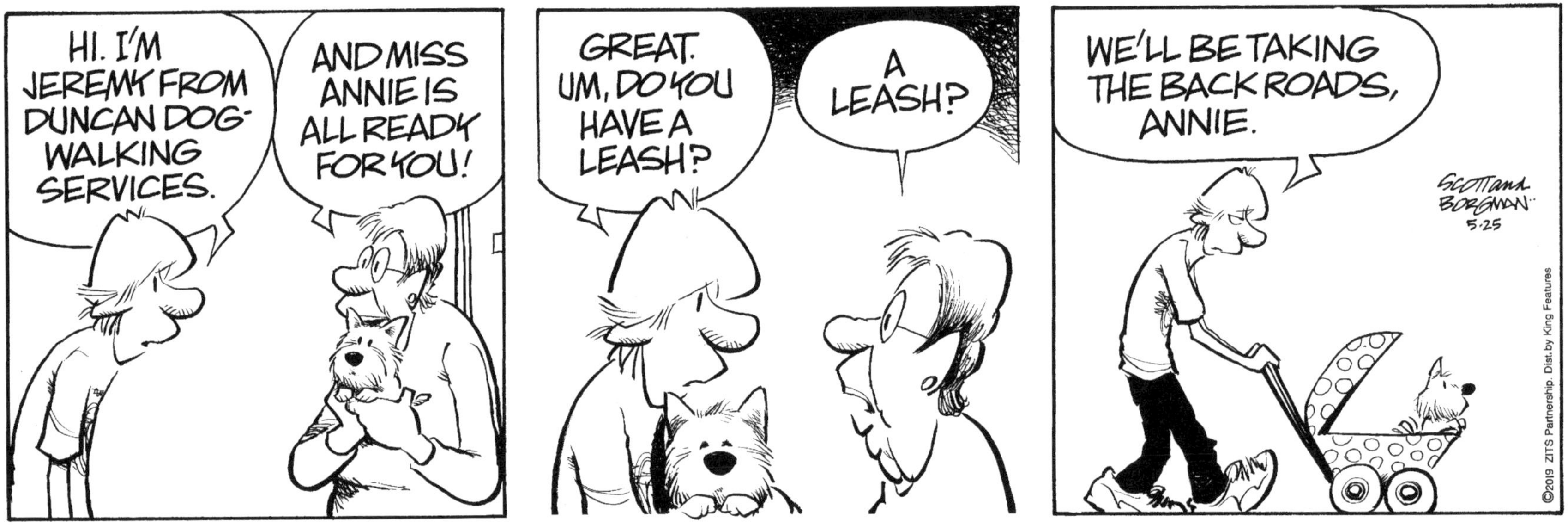
HI. I'M JEREMY FROM DUNCAN DOG-WALKING SERVICES.
AND MISS ANNIE IS ALL READY FOR YOU!
GREAT. UM, DO YOU HAVE A LEASH?
A LEASH?
WE'LL BE TAKING THE BACK ROADS, ANNIE.
SCOTT and BORGMAN 5·25
©2019 ZITS Partnership. Dist. by King Features

ZITS®

by JERRY SCOTT and JIM BORGMAN

5-26 SCOTT and BORGMAN
SLURP!
©2019 ZITS Partnership. Dist. by King Features
YOU KNOW, SOME OF THE THINGS YOU DO DRIVE ME CRAZY, TOO.

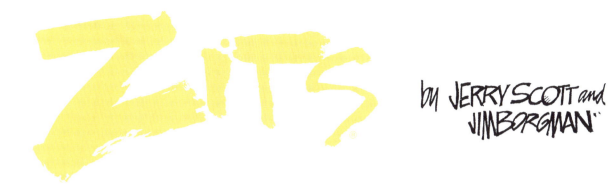

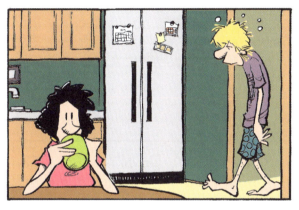

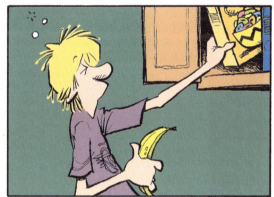

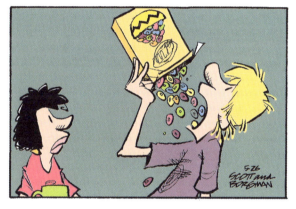

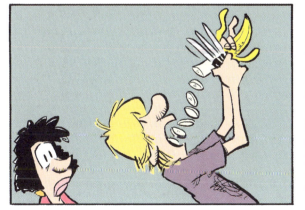

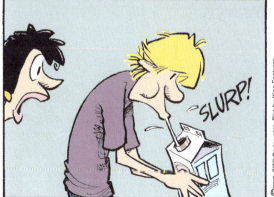

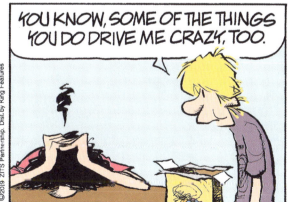

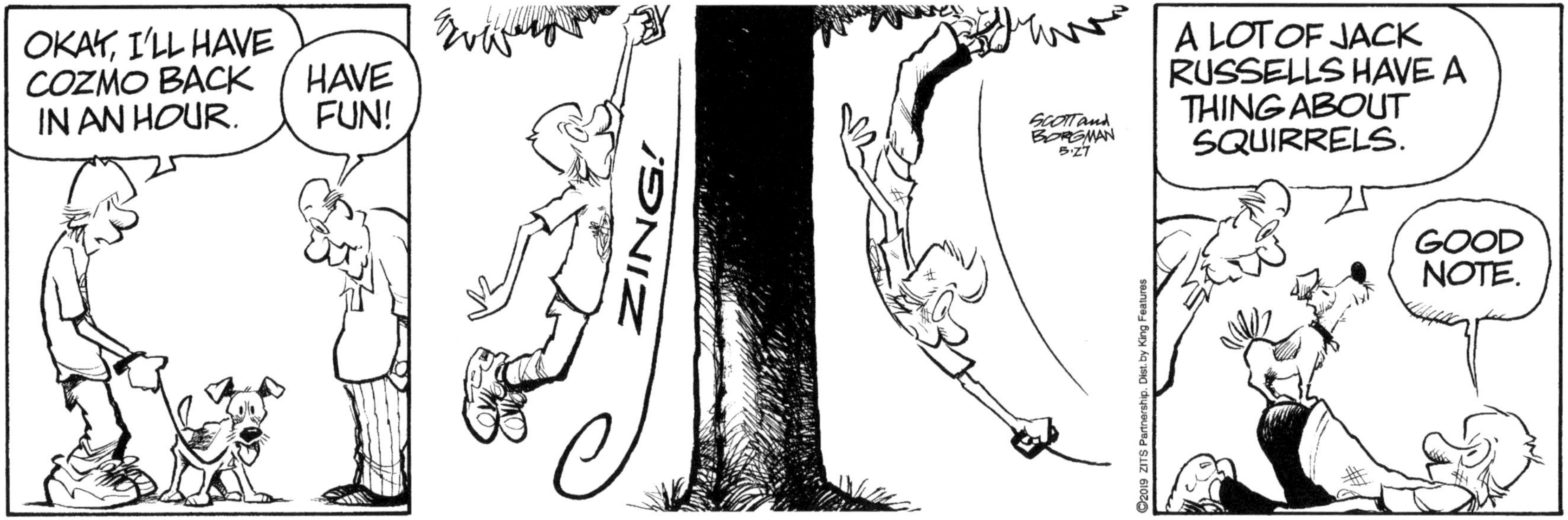
OKAY, I'LL HAVE COZMO BACK IN AN HOUR.
HAVE FUN!
ZING!
SCOTT and BORGMAN 5.27
A LOT OF JACK RUSSELLS HAVE A THING ABOUT SQUIRRELS.
GOOD NOTE.
©2019 ZITS Partnership. Dist. by King Features

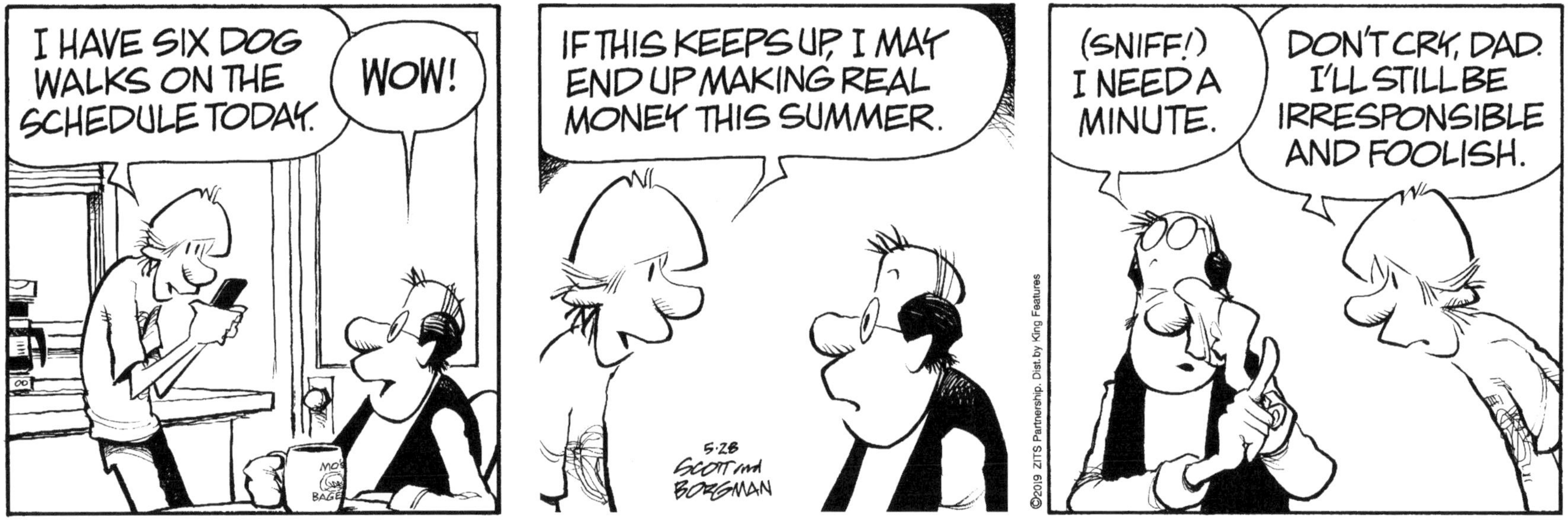
I HAVE SIX DOG WALKS ON THE SCHEDULE TODAY.
WOW!
IF THIS KEEPS UP, I MAY END UP MAKING REAL MONEY THIS SUMMER.
5.28 SCOTT and BORGMAN
©2019 ZITS Partnership. Dist. by King Features
(SNIFF!) I NEED A MINUTE.
DON'T CRY, DAD. I'LL STILL BE IRRESPONSIBLE AND FOOLISH.

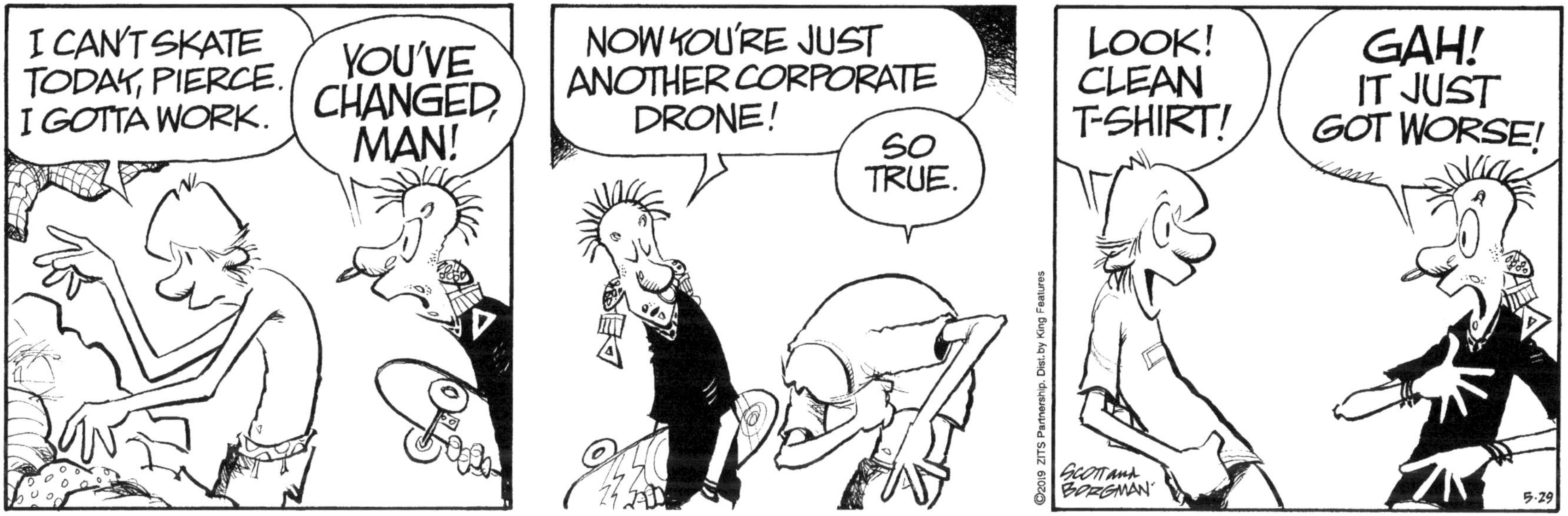
I CAN'T SKATE TODAY, PIERCE. I GOTTA WORK.
YOU'VE CHANGED, MAN!
NOW YOU'RE JUST ANOTHER CORPORATE DRONE!
SO TRUE.
LOOK! CLEAN T-SHIRT!
GAH! IT JUST GOT WORSE!
©2019 ZITS Partnership. Dist. by King Features
SCOTT AND BORGMAN
5·29

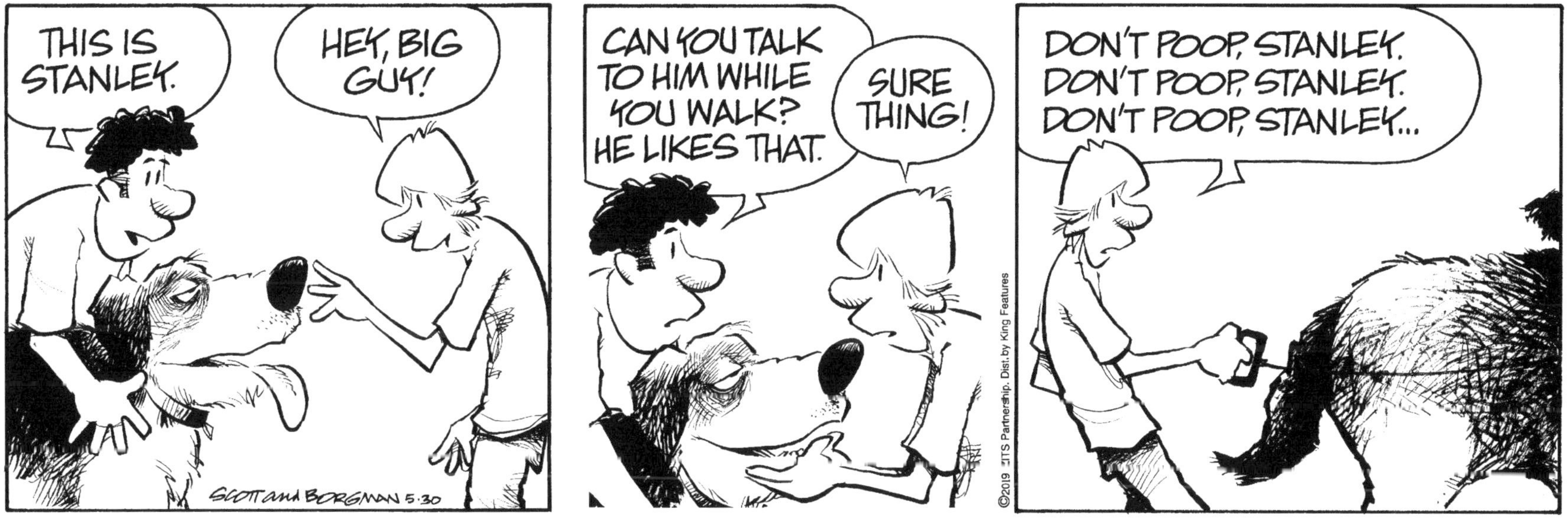
THIS IS STANLEY.
HEY, BIG GUY!
SCOTT AND BORGMAN 5·30
CAN YOU TALK TO HIM WHILE YOU WALK? HE LIKES THAT.
SURE THING!
©2019 ZITS Partnership. Dist. by King Features
DON'T POOP, STANLEY. DON'T POOP, STANLEY. DON'T POOP, STANLEY...

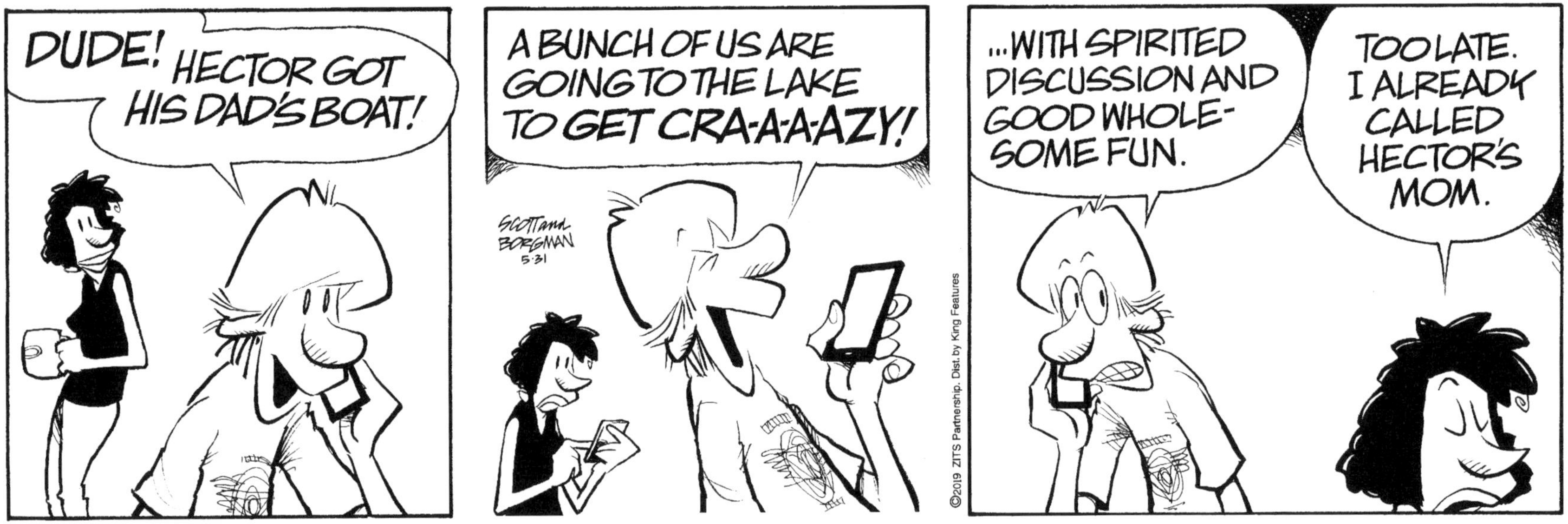
DUDE! HECTOR GOT HIS DAD'S BOAT!
A BUNCH OF US ARE GOING TO THE LAKE TO GET CRA-A-A-AZY!
SCOTT and BORGMAN 5·31
©2019 ZITS Partnership. Dist. by King Features
...WITH SPIRITED DISCUSSION AND GOOD WHOLE-SOME FUN.
TOO LATE. I ALREADY CALLED HECTOR'S MOM.

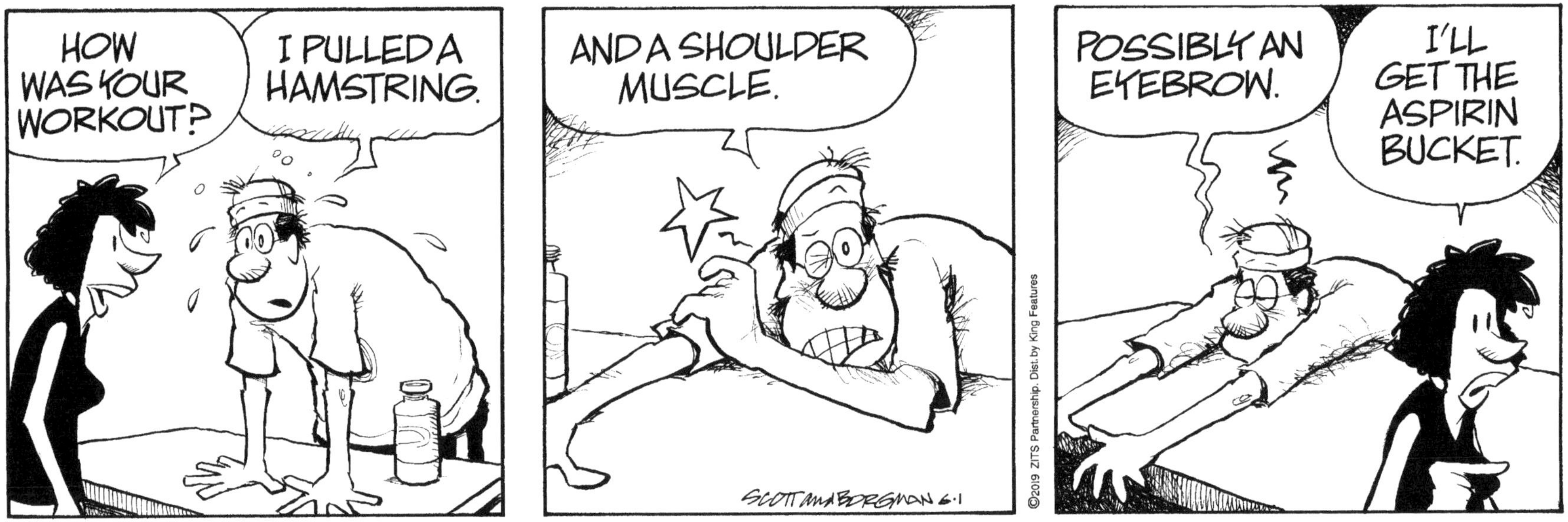
HOW WAS YOUR WORKOUT?
I PULLED A HAMSTRING.
AND A SHOULDER MUSCLE.
SCOTT and BORGMAN 6·1
©2019 ZITS Partnership. Dist. by King Features
POSSIBLY AN EYEBROW.
I'LL GET THE ASPIRIN BUCKET.

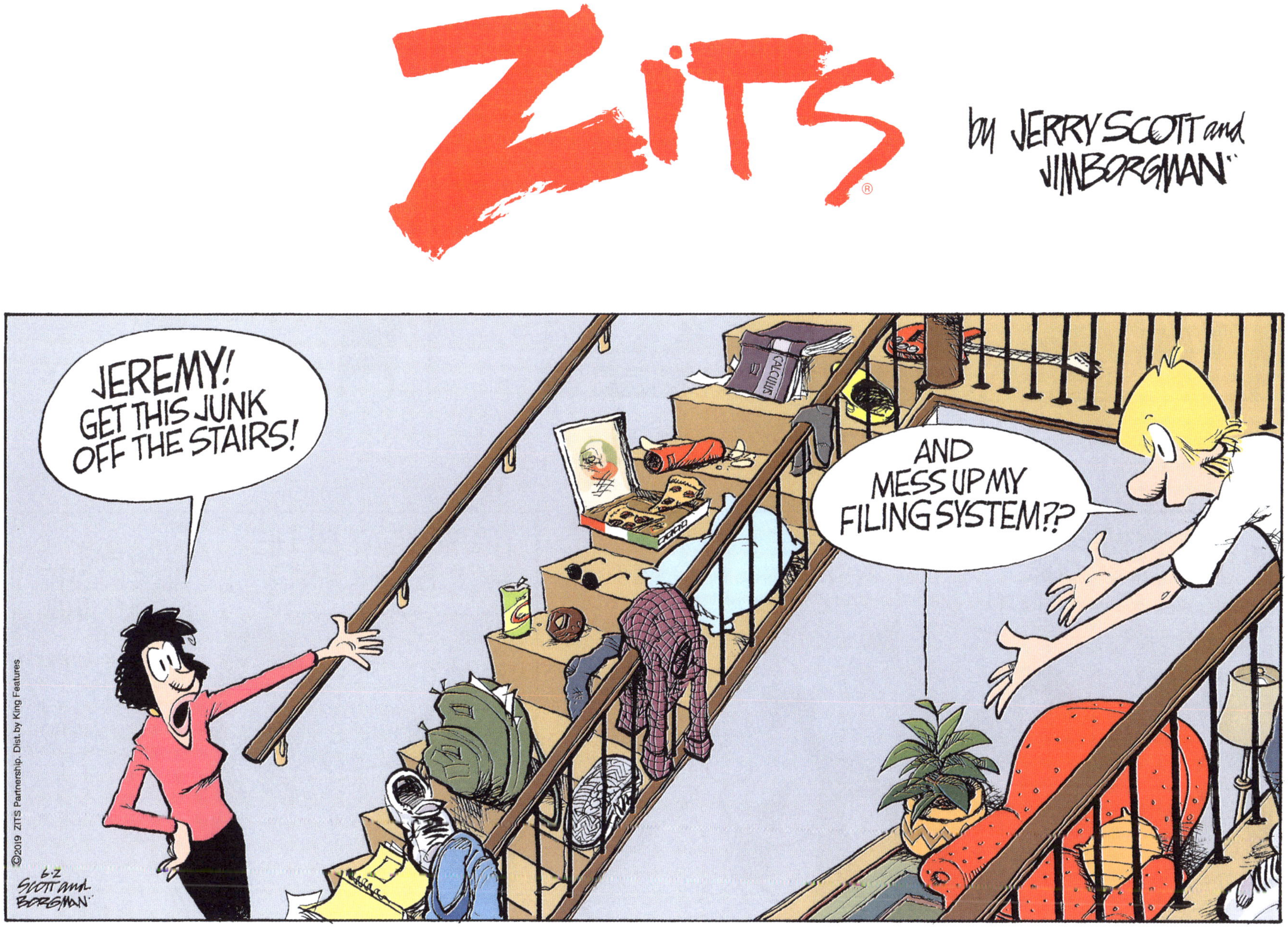
ZITS®
by JERRY SCOTT and JIM BORGMAN
JEREMY! GET THIS JUNK OFF THE STAIRS!
AND MESS UP MY FILING SYSTEM?!?
CALCULUS
©2019 ZITS Partnership. Dist. by King Features
6-2 SCOTT and BORGMAN

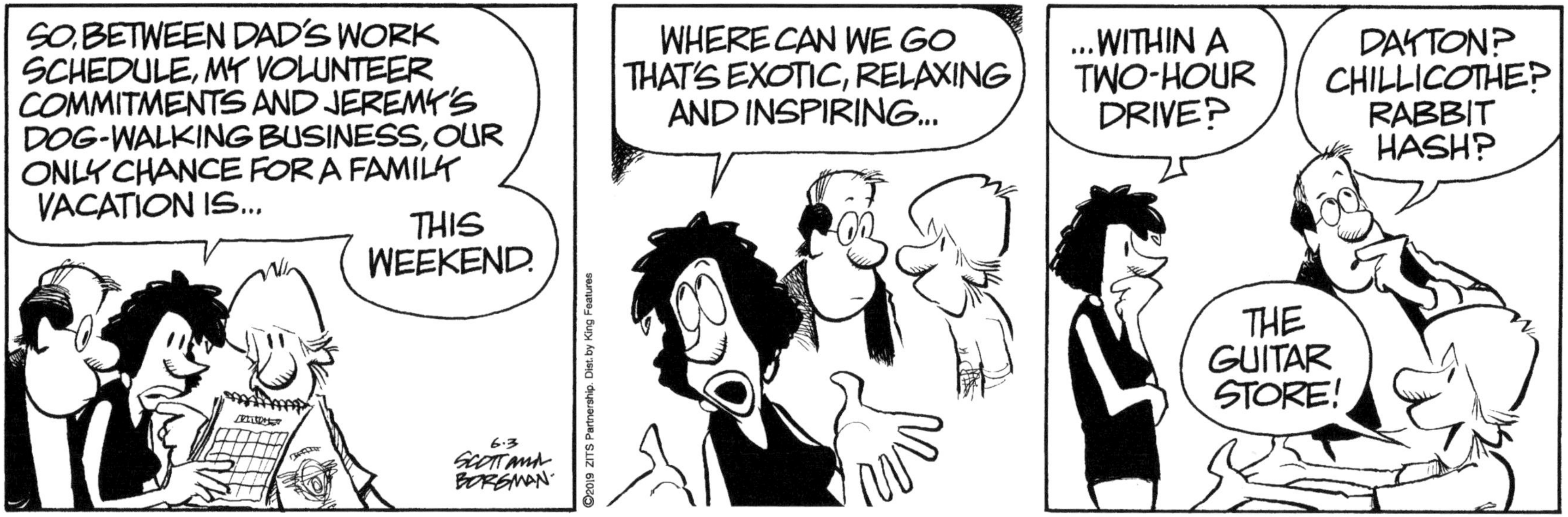
SO, BETWEEN DAD'S WORK SCHEDULE, MY VOLUNTEER COMMITMENTS AND JEREMY'S DOG-WALKING BUSINESS, OUR ONLY CHANCE FOR A FAMILY VACATION IS...
THIS WEEKEND.
6·3
SCOTT and BORGMAN
©2019 ZITS Partnership. Dist. by King Features
WHERE CAN WE GO THAT'S EXOTIC, RELAXING AND INSPIRING...
...WITHIN A TWO-HOUR DRIVE?
DAYTON? CHILLICOTHE? RABBIT HASH?
THE GUITAR STORE!

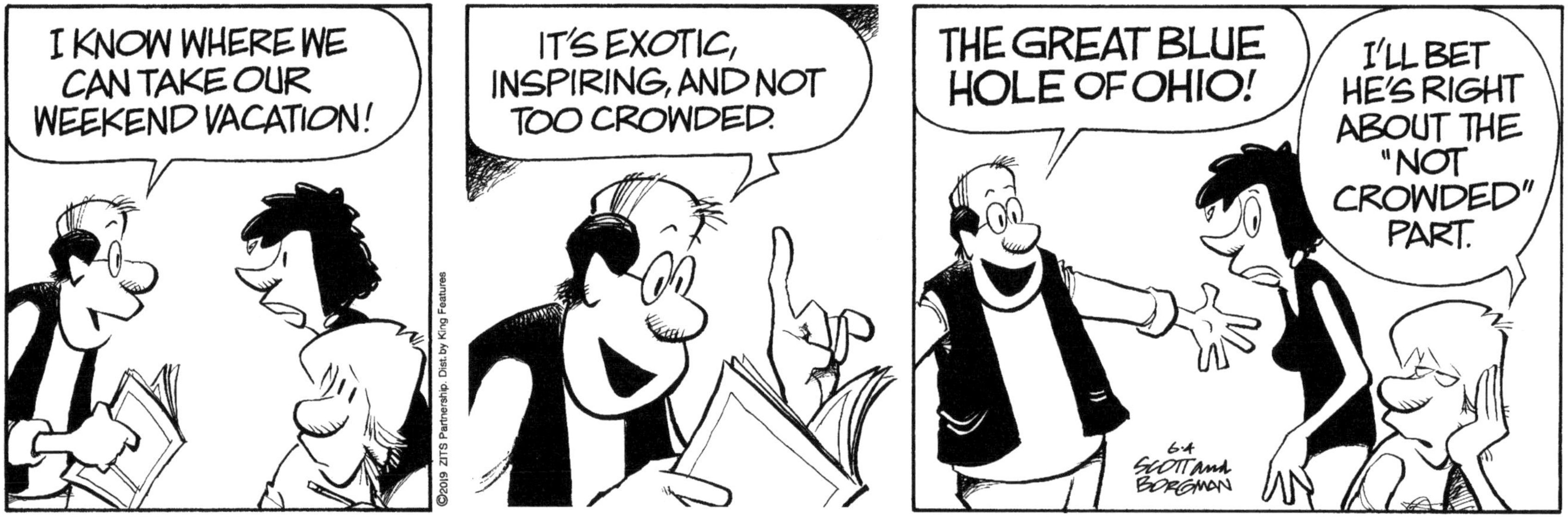
I KNOW WHERE WE CAN TAKE OUR WEEKEND VACATION!
©2019 ZITS Partnership. Dist. by King Features
IT'S EXOTIC, INSPIRING, AND NOT TOO CROWDED.
THE GREAT BLUE HOLE OF OHIO!
I'LL BET HE'S RIGHT ABOUT THE "NOT CROWDED" PART.
6·4
SCOTT and BORGMAN

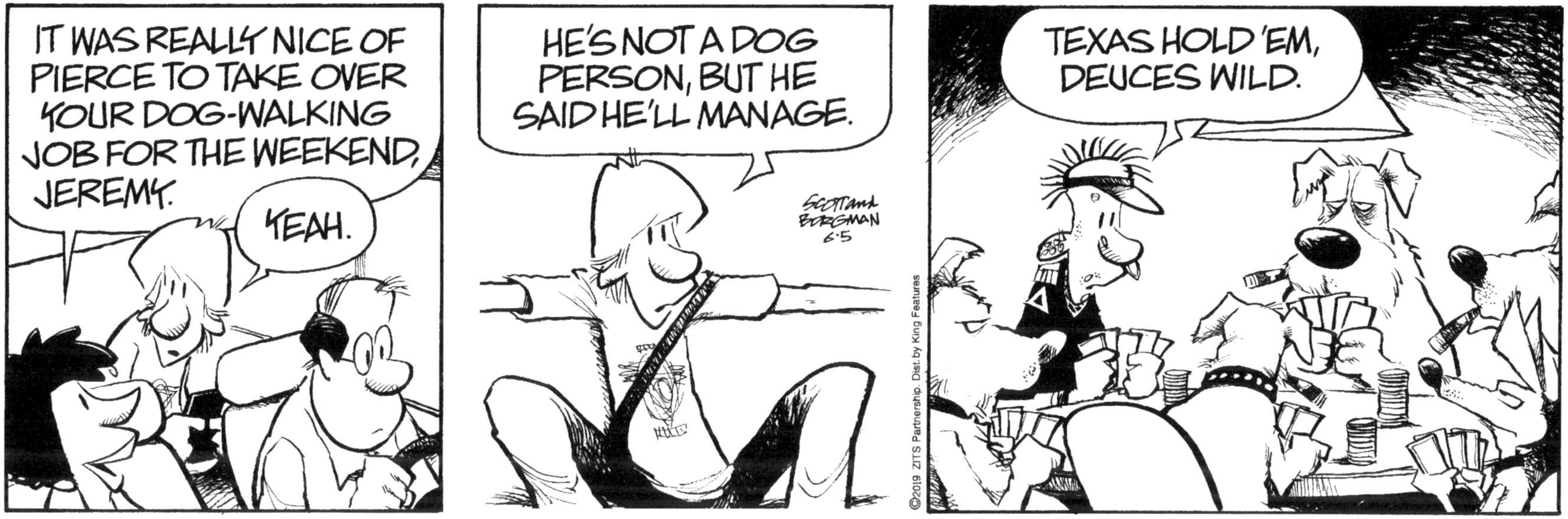
IT WAS REALLY NICE OF PIERCE TO TAKE OVER YOUR DOG-WALKING JOB FOR THE WEEKEND, JEREMY.
YEAH.
HE'S NOT A DOG PERSON, BUT HE SAID HE'LL MANAGE.
SCOTT and BORGMAN 6·5
©2019 ZITS Partnership. Dist.by King Features
TEXAS HOLD 'EM, DEUCES WILD.

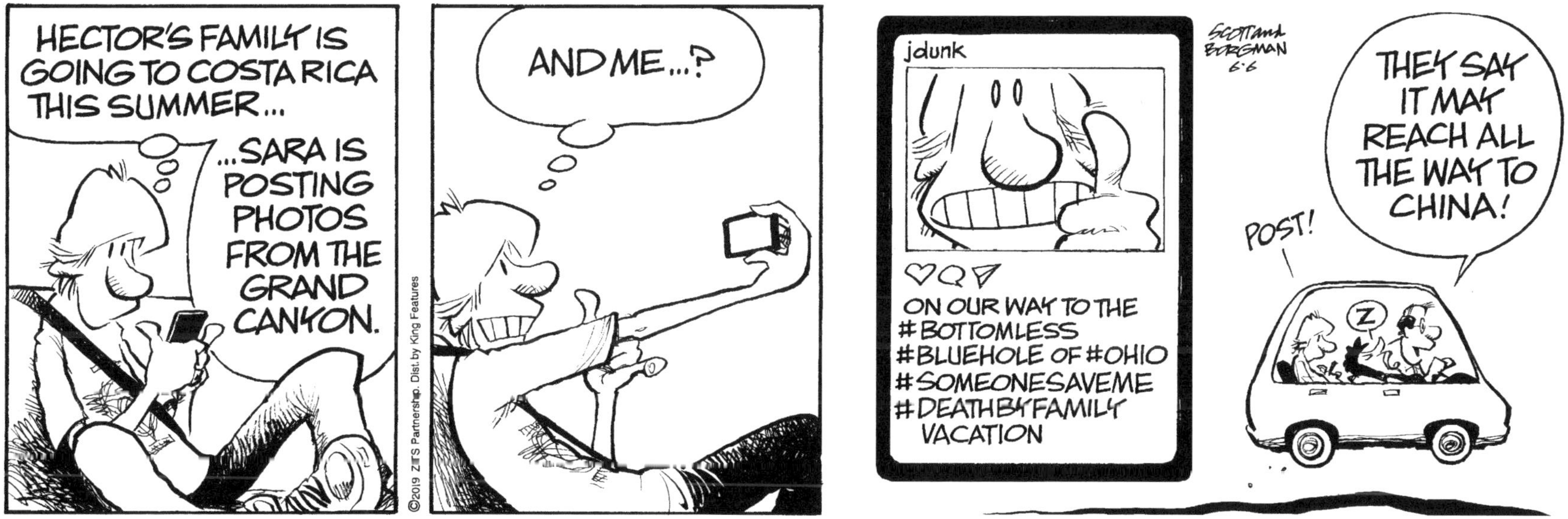
HECTOR'S FAMILY IS GOING TO COSTA RICA THIS SUMMER...
...SARA IS POSTING PHOTOS FROM THE GRAND CANYON.
©2019 ZITS Partnership. Dist.by King Features
AND ME...?
jdunk
ON OUR WAY TO THE #BOTTOMLESS #BLUEHOLE OF #OHIO #SOMEONESAVEME #DEATHBYFAMILY VACATION
SCOTT and BORGMAN 6·6
THEY SAY IT MAY REACH ALL THE WAY TO CHINA!
POST!
Z

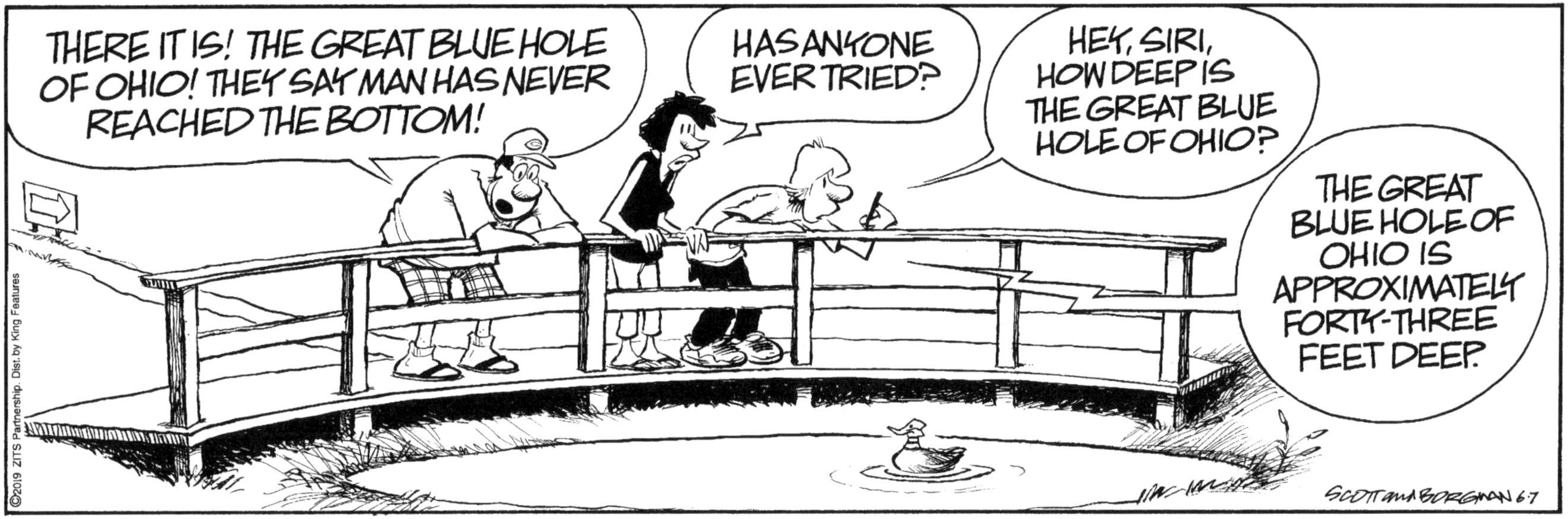
THERE IT IS! THE GREAT BLUE HOLE OF OHIO! THEY SAY MAN HAS NEVER REACHED THE BOTTOM!
HAS ANYONE EVER TRIED?
HEY, SIRI, HOW DEEP IS THE GREAT BLUE HOLE OF OHIO?
THE GREAT BLUE HOLE OF OHIO IS APPROXIMATELY FORTY-THREE FEET DEEP.
©2019 ZITS Partnership. Dist. by King Features
SCOTT and BORGMAN 6·7

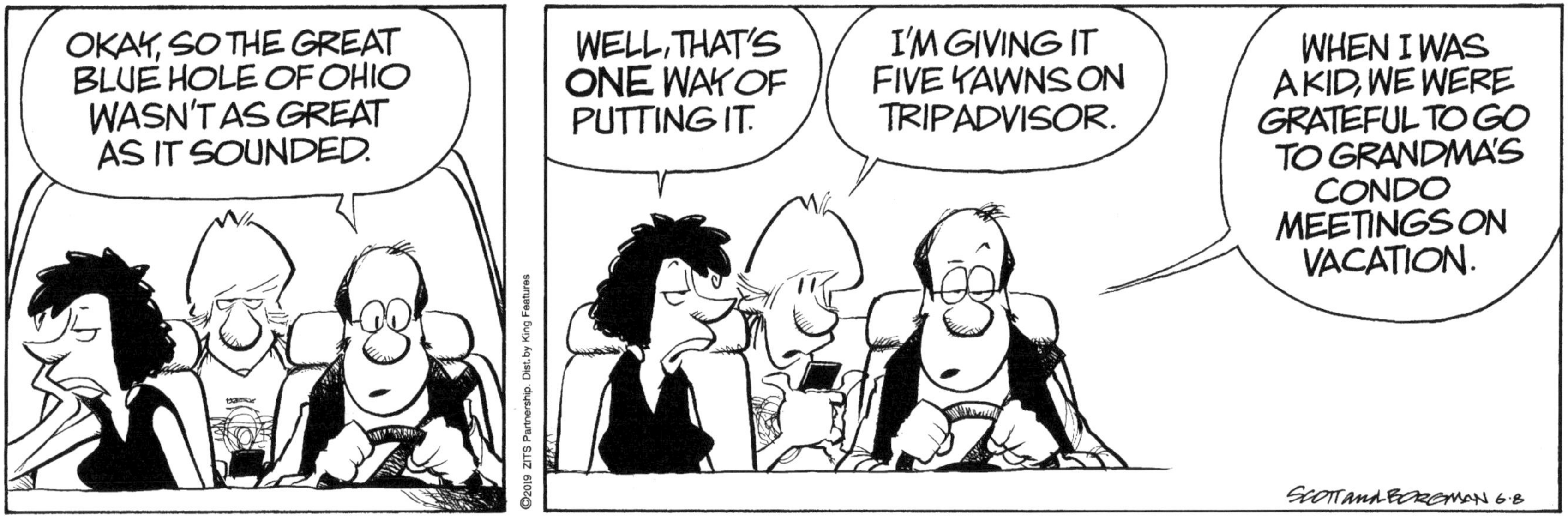
OKAY, SO THE GREAT BLUE HOLE OF OHIO WASN'T AS GREAT AS IT SOUNDED.
©2019 ZITS Partnership. Dist. by King Features
WELL, THAT'S **ONE** WAY OF PUTTING IT.
I'M GIVING IT FIVE YAWNS ON TRIPADVISOR.
WHEN I WAS A KID, WE WERE GRATEFUL TO GO TO GRANDMA'S CONDO MEETINGS ON VACATION.
SCOTT and BORGMAN 6·8

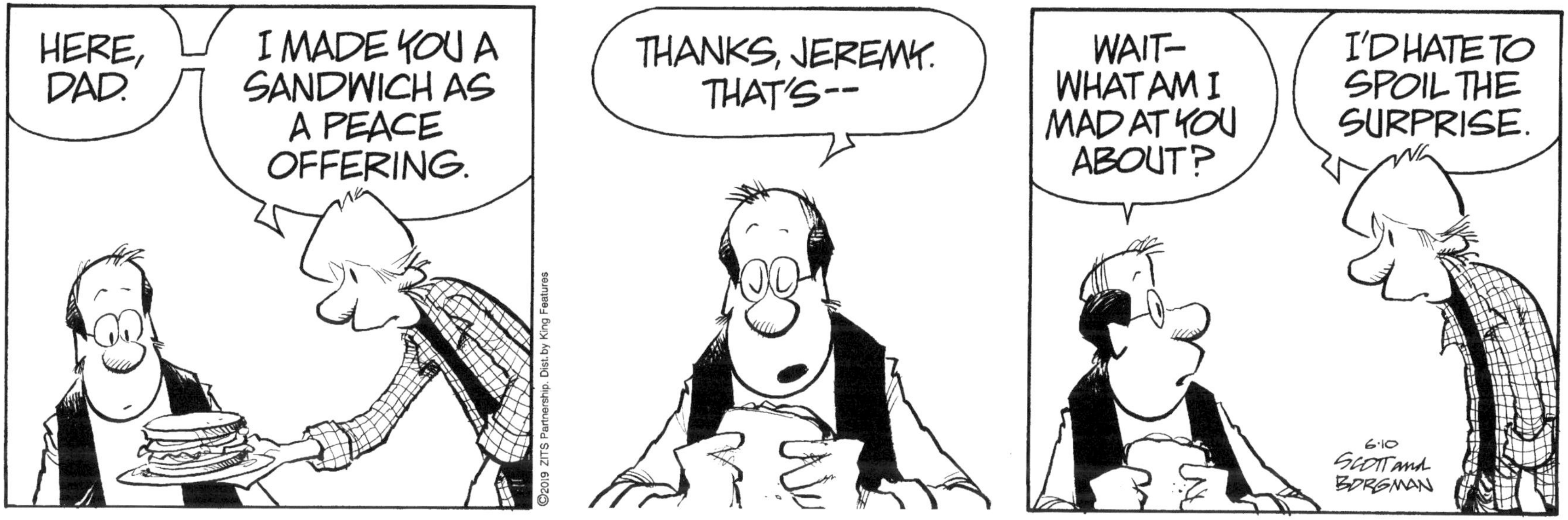
HERE, DAD.
I MADE YOU A SANDWICH AS A PEACE OFFERING.
©2019 ZITS Partnership. Dist.by King Features
THANKS, JEREMY. THAT'S--
WAIT- WHAT AM I MAD AT YOU ABOUT?
I'D HATE TO SPOIL THE SURPRISE.
6·10
SCOTT and BORGMAN

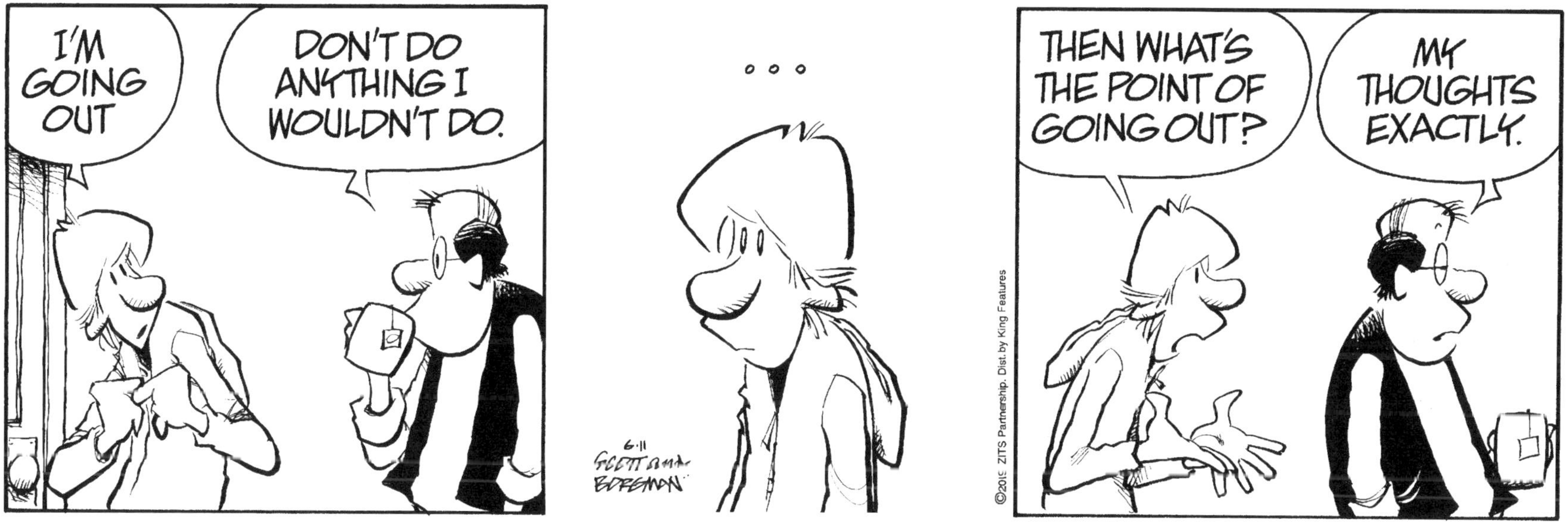
I'M GOING OUT
DON'T DO ANYTHING I WOULDN'T DO.
. . .
6·11
SCOTT and BORGMAN
©2019 ZITS Partnership. Dist.by King Features
THEN WHAT'S THE POINT OF GOING OUT?
MY THOUGHTS EXACTLY.

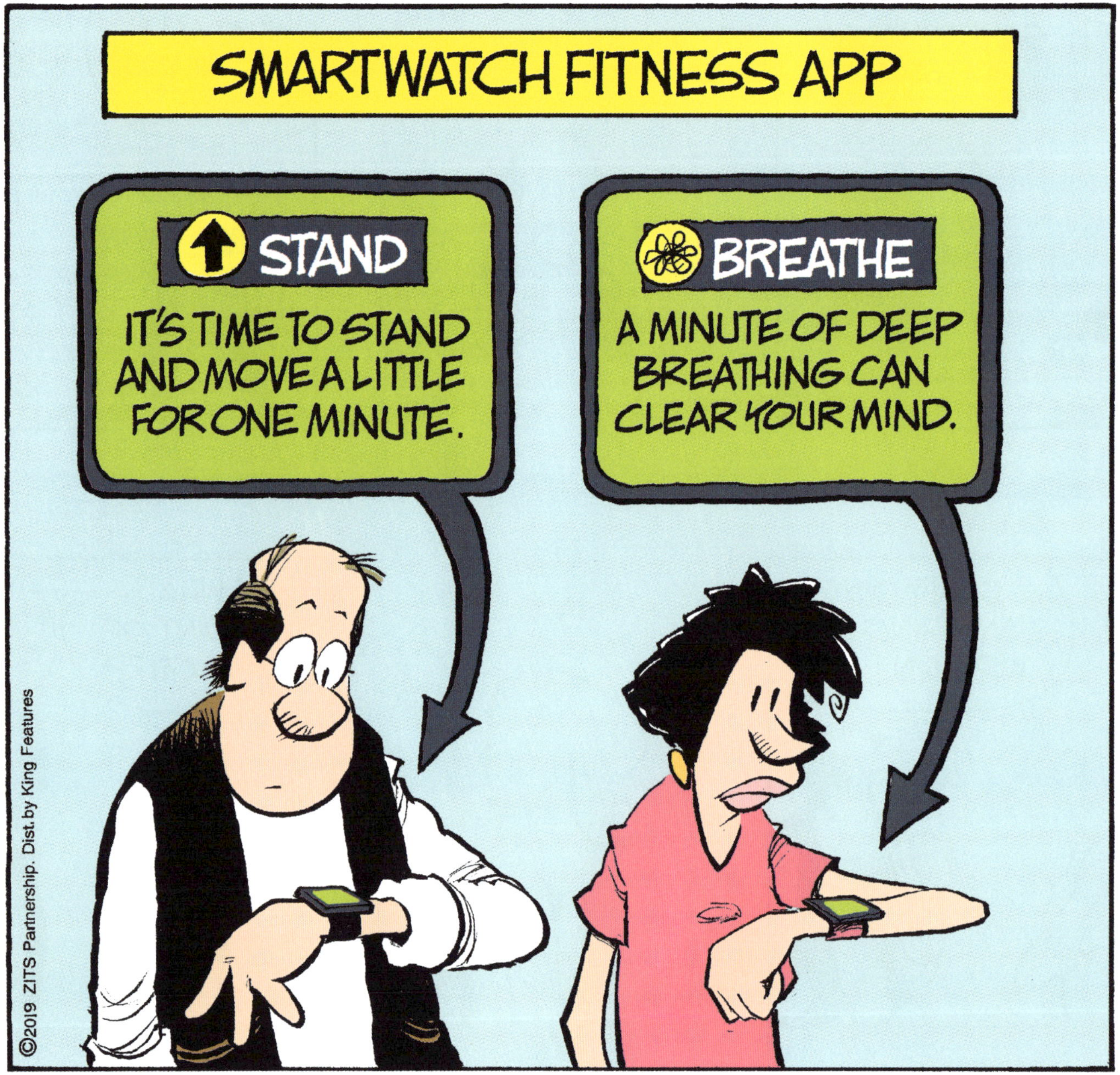
SMARTWATCH FITNESS APP
STAND
IT'S TIME TO STAND AND MOVE A LITTLE FOR ONE MINUTE.
BREATHE
A MINUTE OF DEEP BREATHING CAN CLEAR YOUR MIND.
©2019 ZITS Partnership. Dist. by King Features

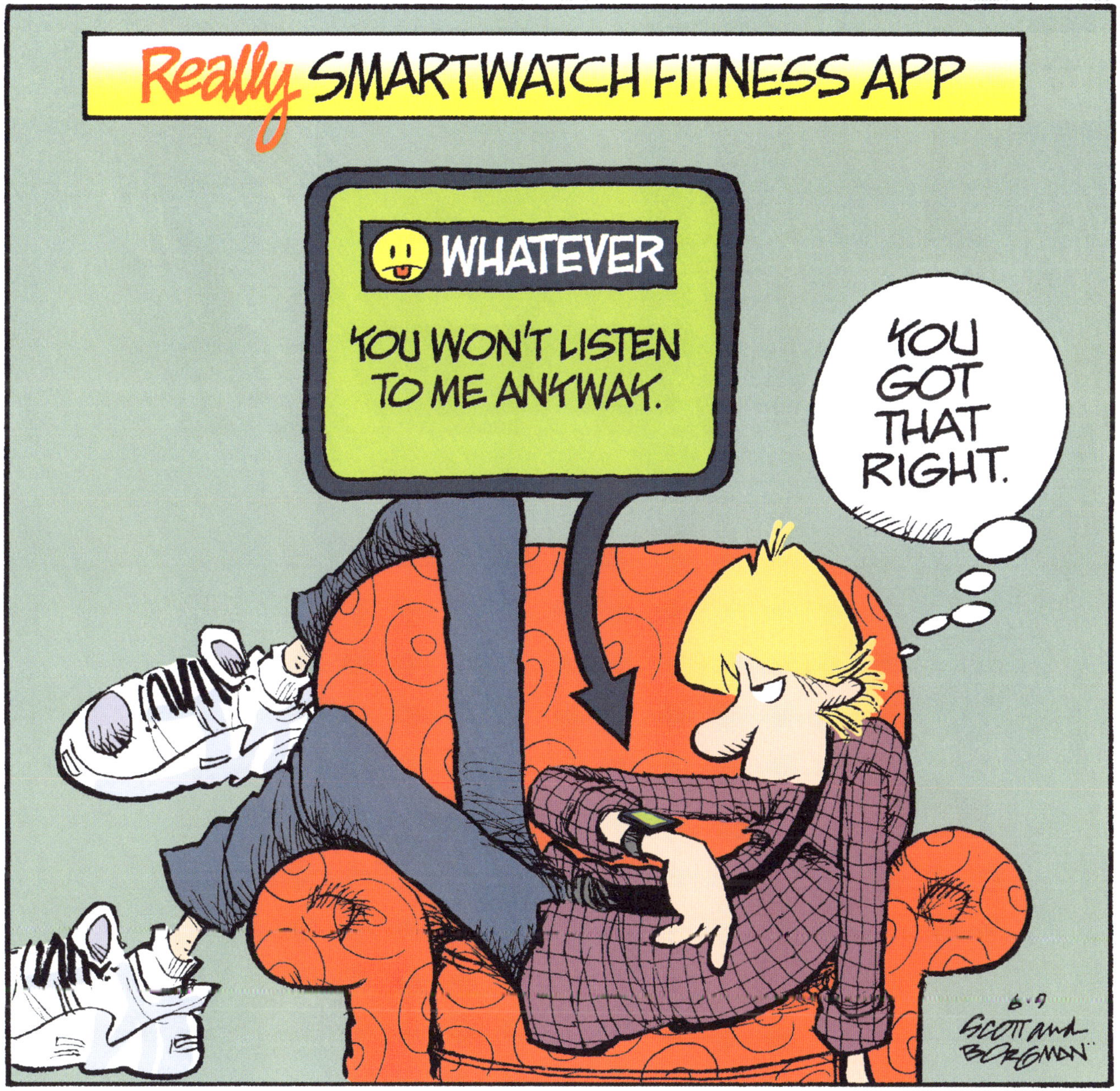
Really SMARTWATCH FITNESS APP
WHATEVER
YOU WON'T LISTEN TO ME ANYWAY.
YOU GOT THAT RIGHT.
6-9
SCOTT and BORGMAN

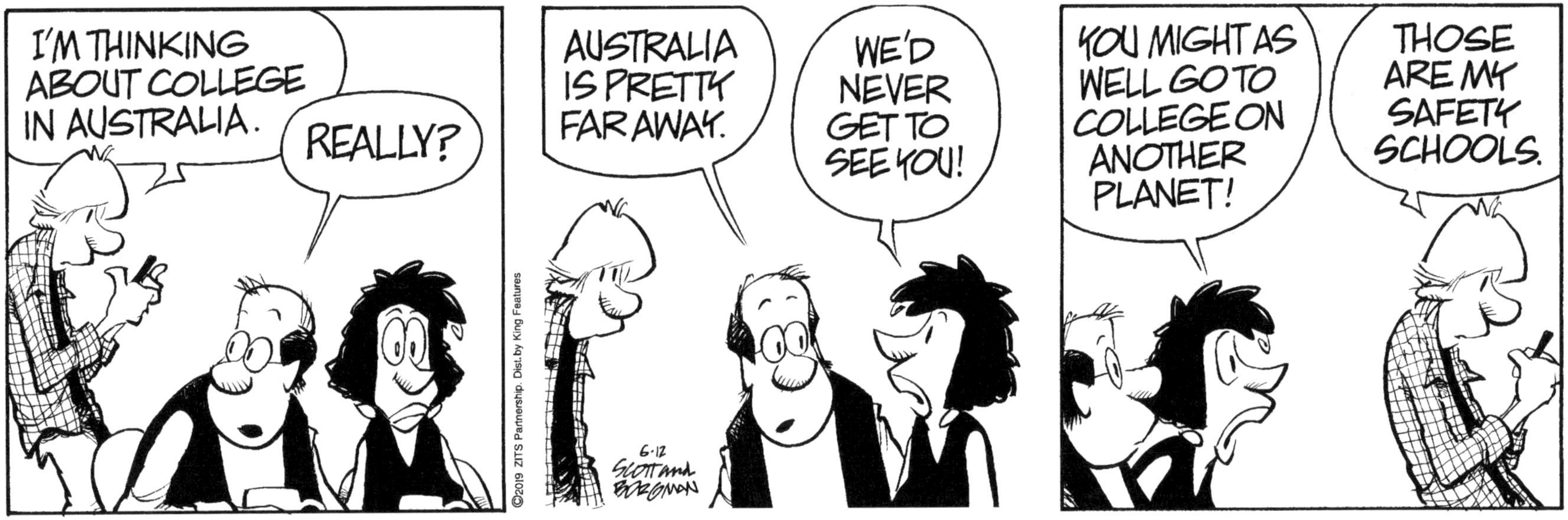
I'M THINKING ABOUT COLLEGE IN AUSTRALIA.
REALLY?
©2019 ZITS Partnership. Dist. by King Features
AUSTRALIA IS PRETTY FAR AWAY.
WE'D NEVER GET TO SEE YOU!
6·12 SCOTT AND BORGMAN
YOU MIGHT AS WELL GO TO COLLEGE ON ANOTHER PLANET!
THOSE ARE MY SAFETY SCHOOLS.

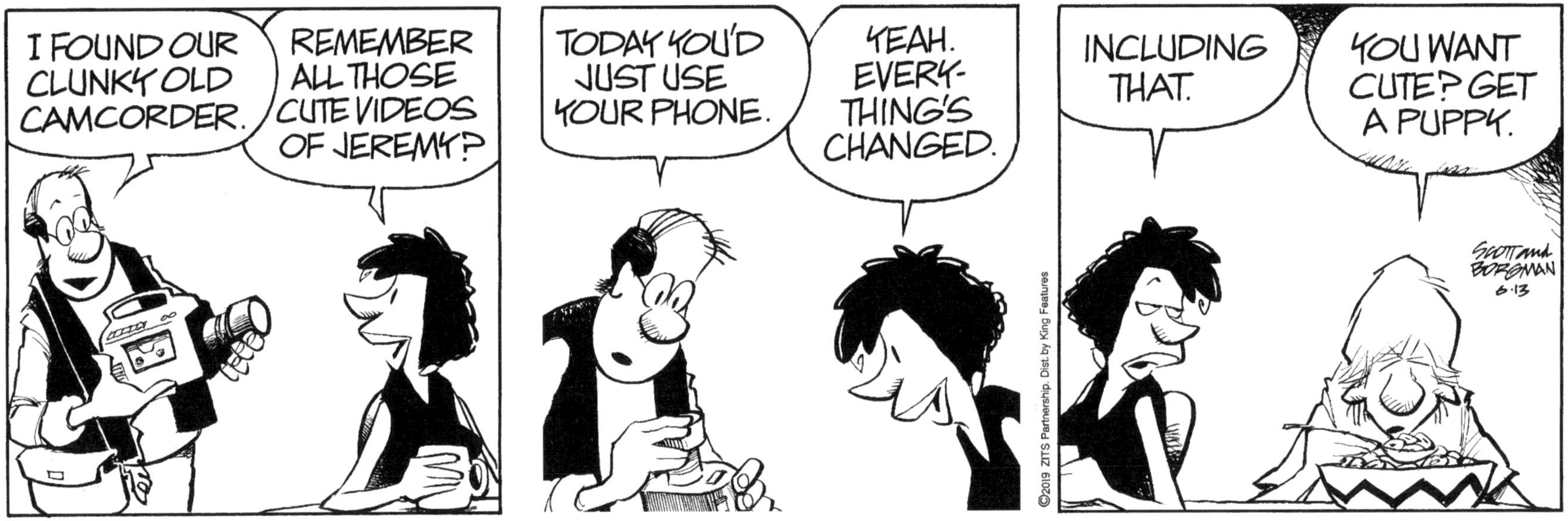
I FOUND OUR CLUNKY OLD CAMCORDER.
REMEMBER ALL THOSE CUTE VIDEOS OF JEREMY?
TODAY YOU'D JUST USE YOUR PHONE.
YEAH. EVERYTHING'S CHANGED.
©2019 ZITS Partnership. Dist. by King Features
INCLUDING THAT.
YOU WANT CUTE? GET A PUPPY.
SCOTT AND BORGMAN 6·13

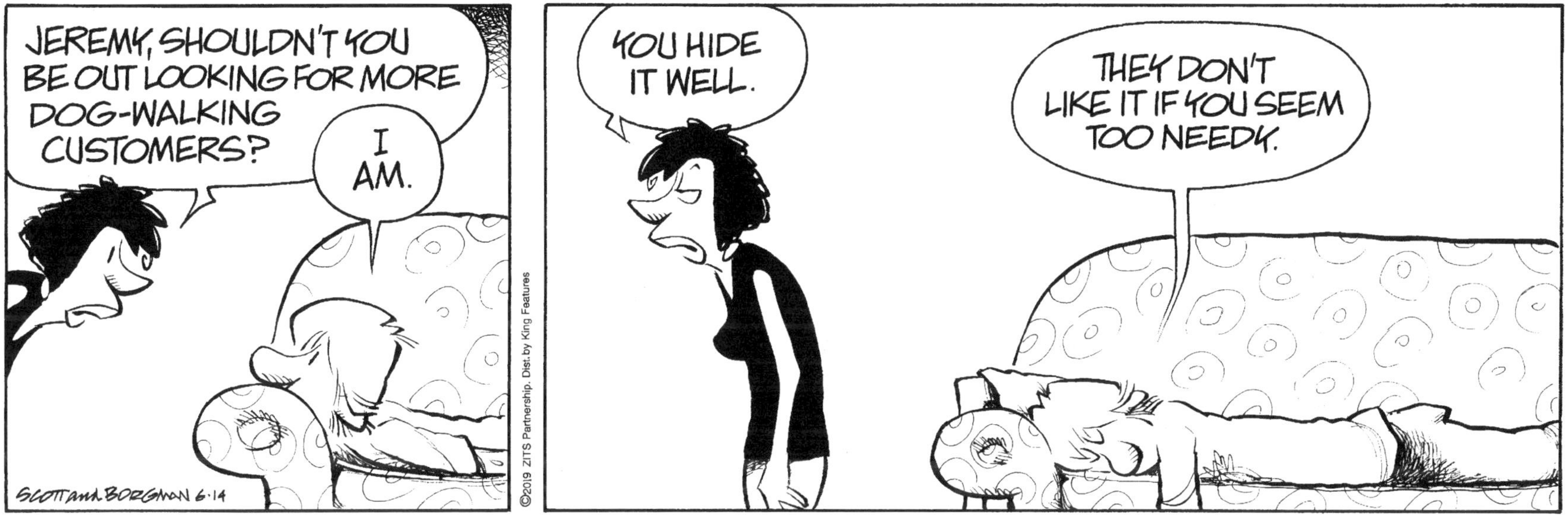
JEREMY, SHOULDN'T YOU BE OUT LOOKING FOR MORE DOG-WALKING CUSTOMERS?
I AM.
YOU HIDE IT WELL.
THEY DON'T LIKE IT IF YOU SEEM TOO NEEDY.
SCOTT and BORGMAN 6·14
©2019 ZITS Partnership. Dist. by King Features

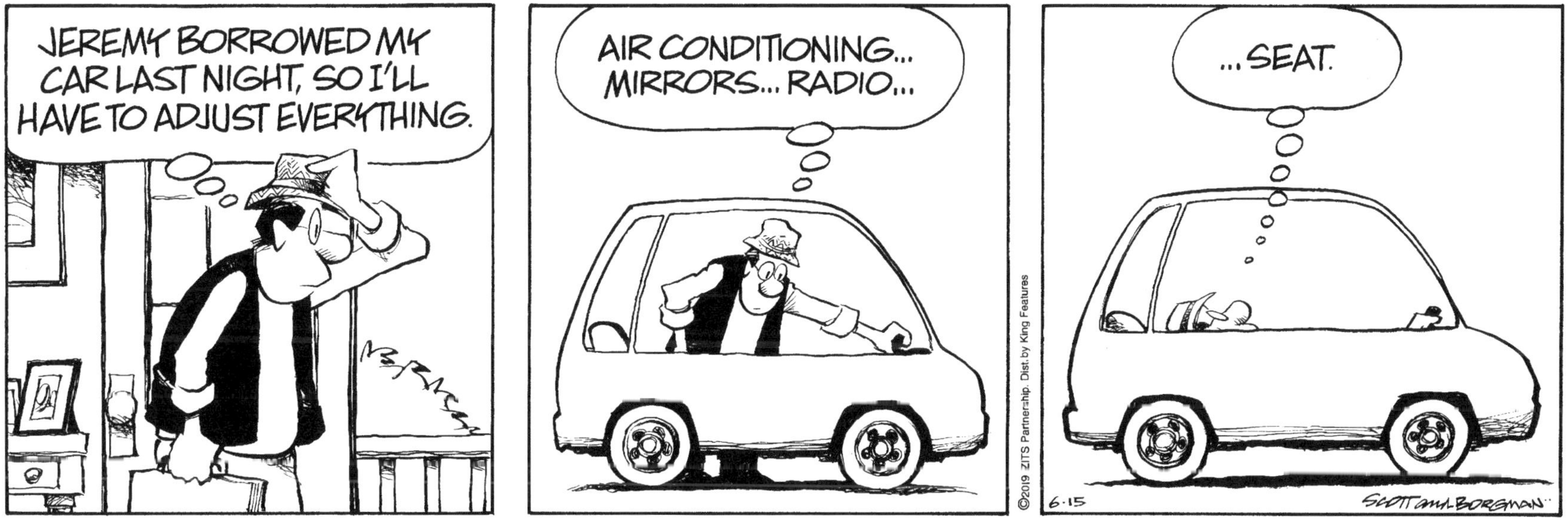
JEREMY BORROWED MY CAR LAST NIGHT, SO I'LL HAVE TO ADJUST EVERYTHING.
AIR CONDITIONING... MIRRORS... RADIO...
...SEAT.
©2019 ZITS Partnership. Dist. by King Features
6·15
SCOTT and BORGMAN

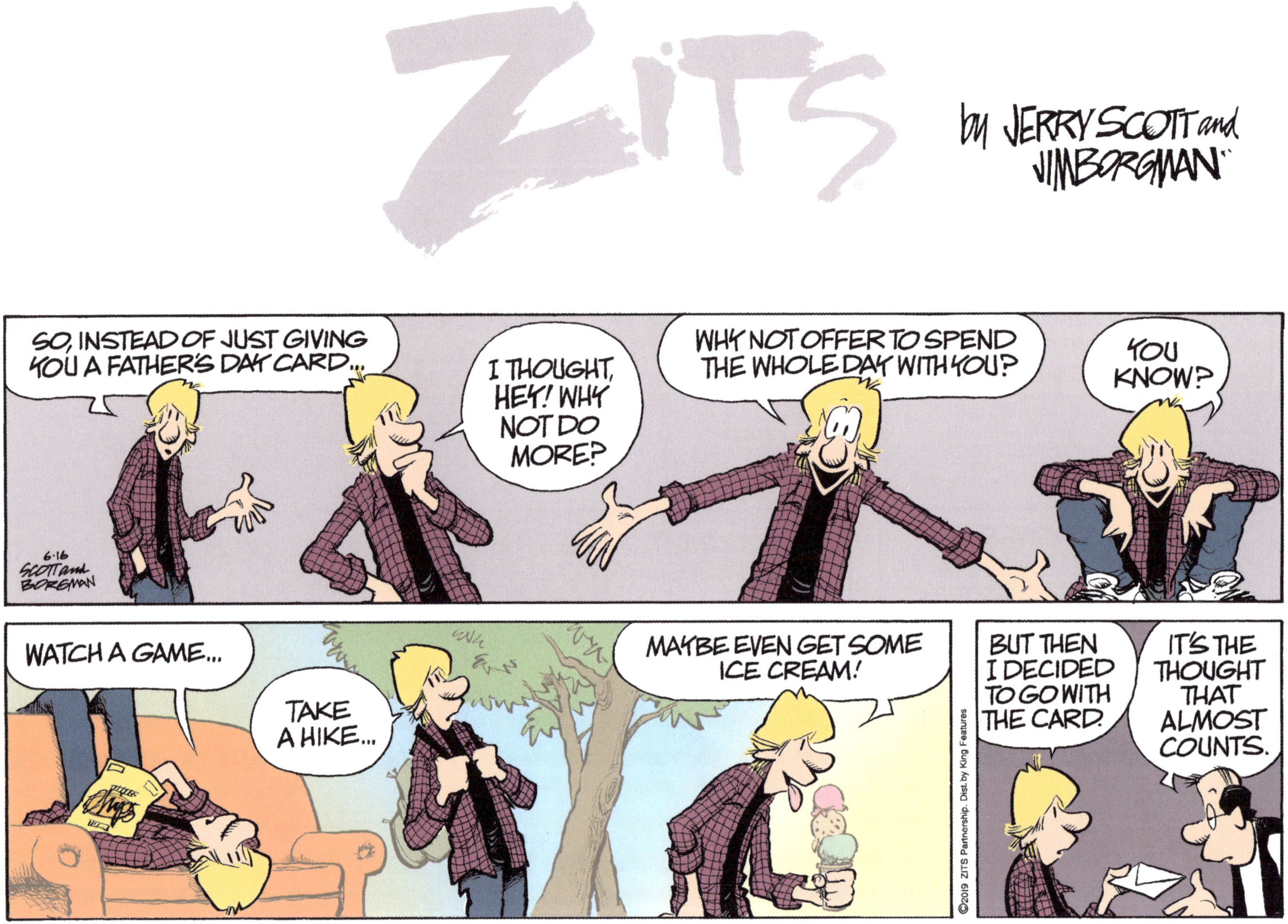
ZITS
by JERRY SCOTT and JIM BORGMAN
SO, INSTEAD OF JUST GIVING YOU A FATHER'S DAY CARD...
I THOUGHT, HEY! WHY NOT DO MORE?
WHY NOT OFFER TO SPEND THE WHOLE DAY WITH YOU?
YOU KNOW?
6-16 SCOTT and BORGMAN
WATCH A GAME...
TAKE A HIKE...
MAYBE EVEN GET SOME ICE CREAM!
©2019 ZITS Partnership. Dist. by King Features
BUT THEN I DECIDED TO GO WITH THE CARD.
IT'S THE THOUGHT THAT ALMOST COUNTS.

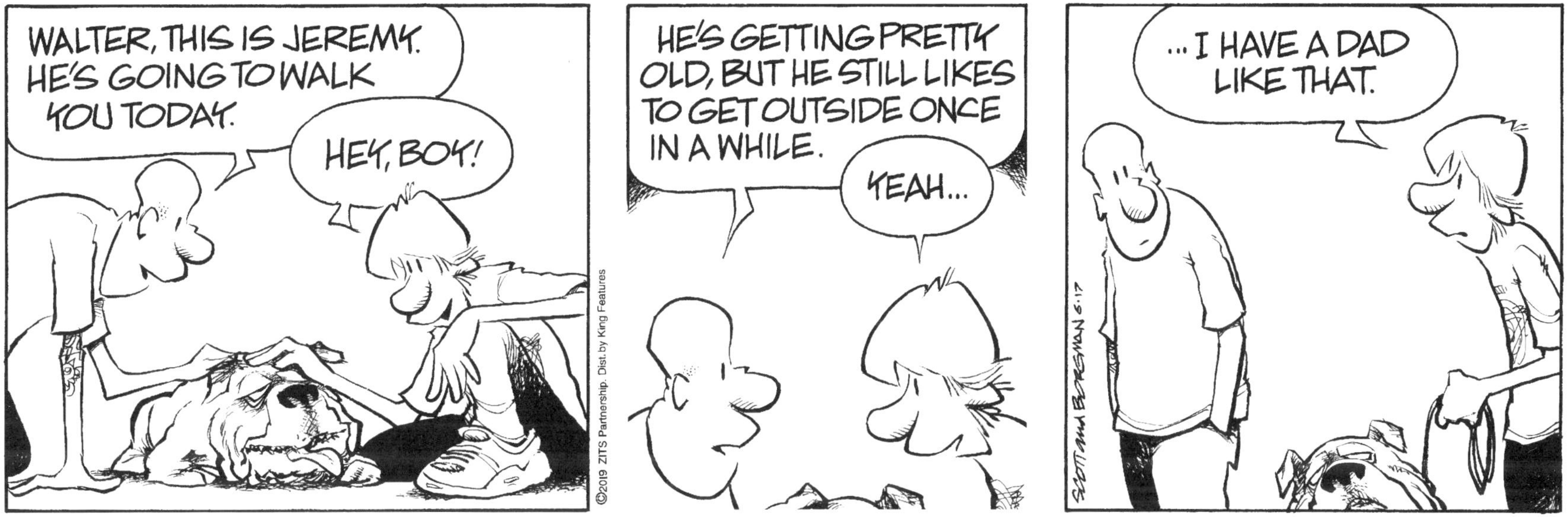
WALTER, THIS IS JEREMY. HE'S GOING TO WALK YOU TODAY.
HEY, BOY!
©2019 ZITS Partnership. Dist. by King Features
HE'S GETTING PRETTY OLD, BUT HE STILL LIKES TO GET OUTSIDE ONCE IN A WHILE.
YEAH...
...I HAVE A DAD LIKE THAT.

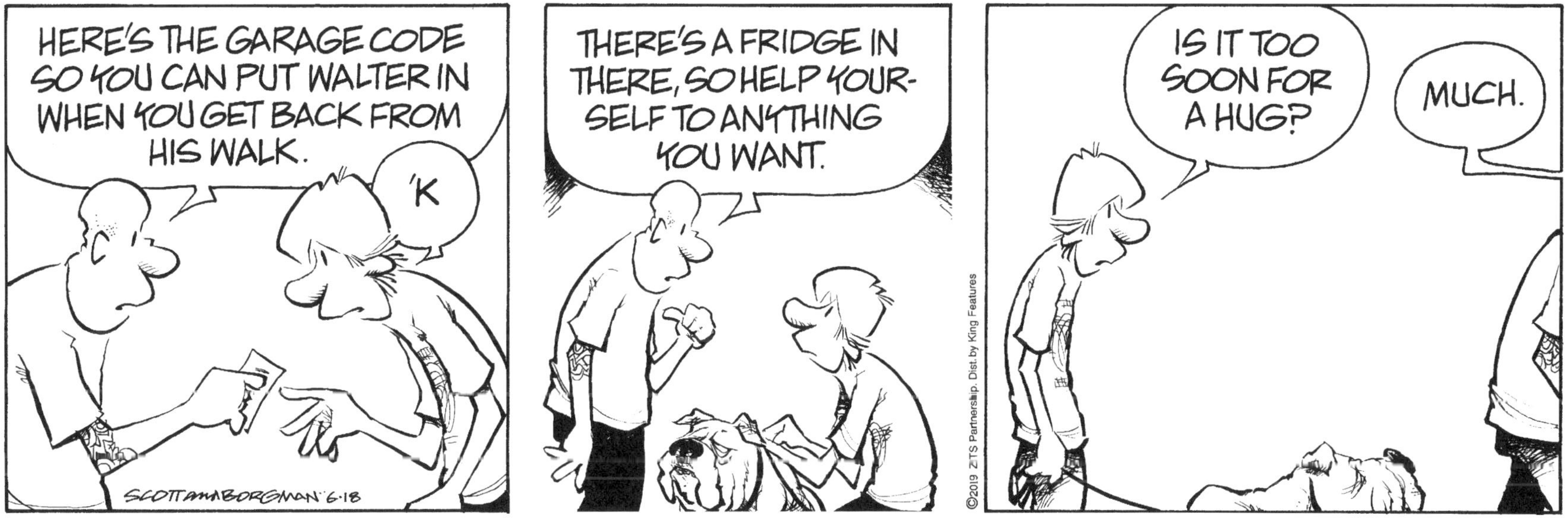
HERE'S THE GARAGE CODE SO YOU CAN PUT WALTER IN WHEN YOU GET BACK FROM HIS WALK.
'K
THERE'S A FRIDGE IN THERE, SO HELP YOURSELF TO ANYTHING YOU WANT.
©2019 ZITS Partnership. Dist. by King Features
IS IT TOO SOON FOR A HUG?
MUCH.

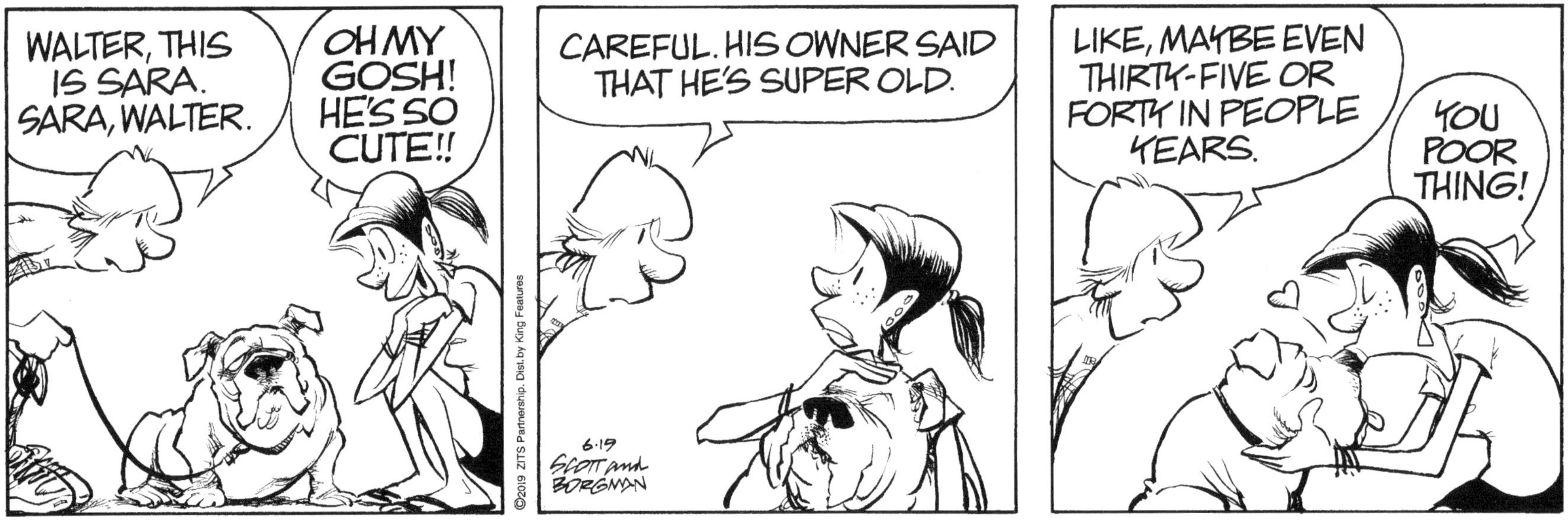
WALTER, THIS IS SARA. SARA, WALTER.
OH MY GOSH! HE'S SO CUTE!!
CAREFUL. HIS OWNER SAID THAT HE'S SUPER OLD.
LIKE, MAYBE EVEN THIRTY-FIVE OR FORTY IN PEOPLE YEARS.
YOU POOR THING!
©2019 ZITS Partnership. Dist. by King Features
6·19 SCOTT and BORGMAN

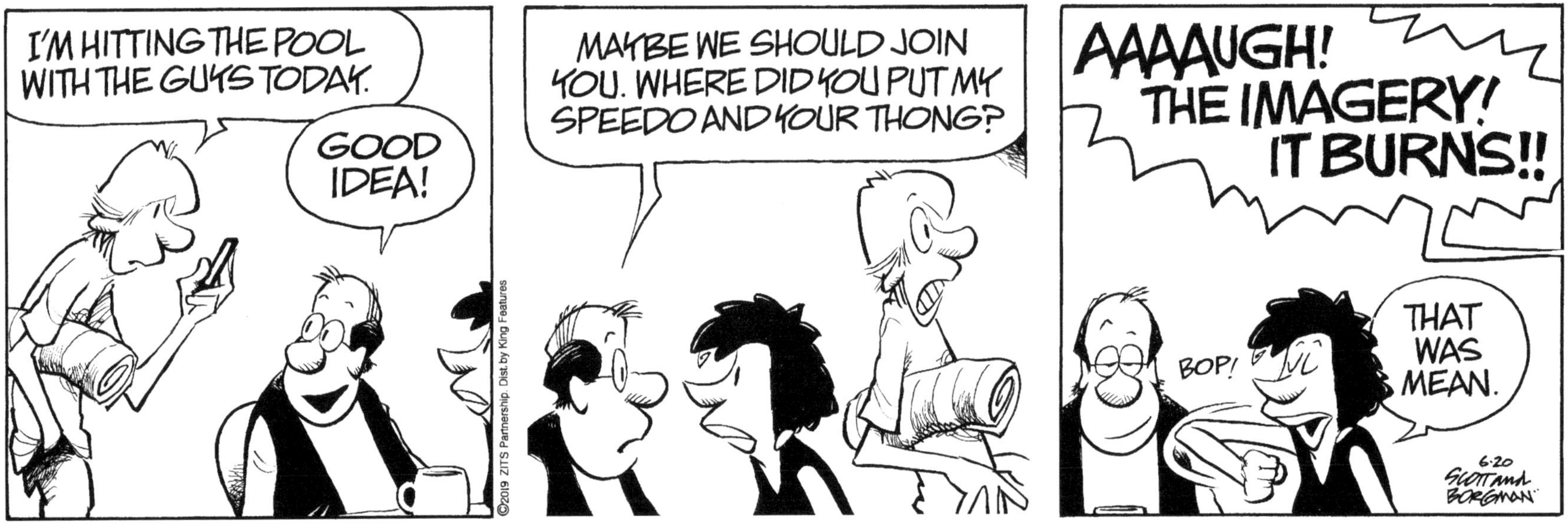
I'M HITTING THE POOL WITH THE GUYS TODAY.
GOOD IDEA!
MAYBE WE SHOULD JOIN YOU. WHERE DID YOU PUT MY SPEEDO AND YOUR THONG?
AAAAUGH! THE IMAGERY! IT BURNS!!
BOP!
THAT WAS MEAN.
©2019 ZITS Partnership. Dist. by King Features
6·20 SCOTT and BORGMAN

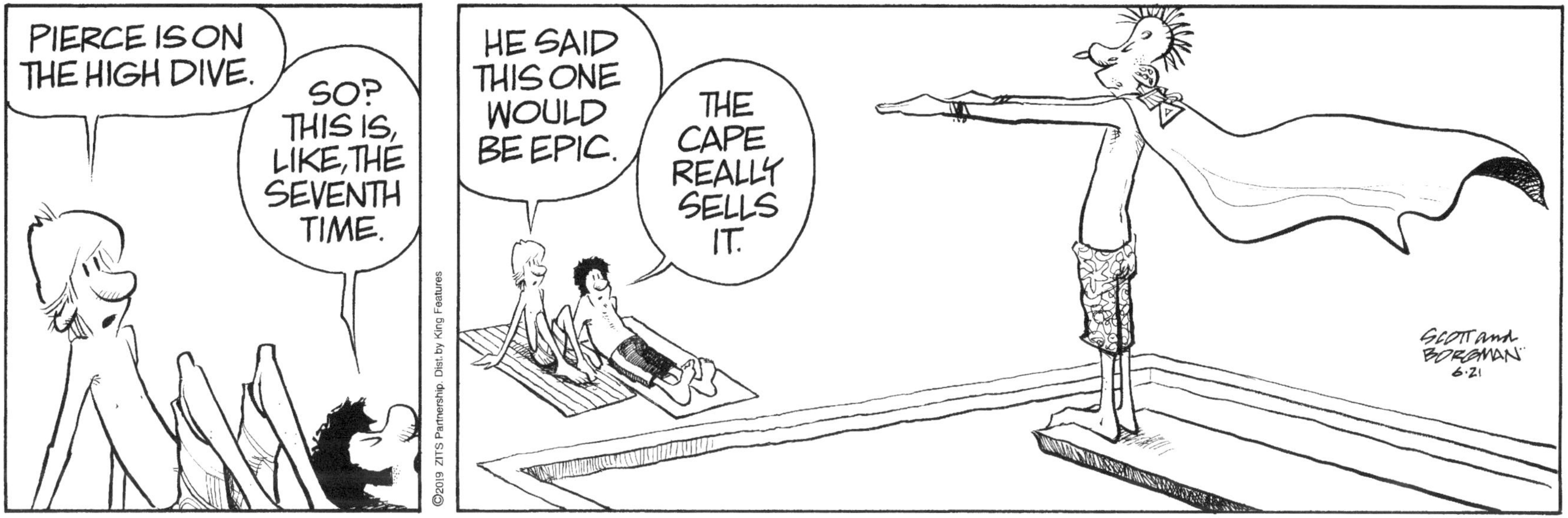
PIERCE IS ON THE HIGH DIVE.
SO? THIS IS, LIKE, THE SEVENTH TIME.
©2019 ZITS Partnership. Dist. by King Features
HE SAID THIS ONE WOULD BE EPIC.
THE CAPE REALLY SELLS IT.
SCOTT and BORGMAN 6·21

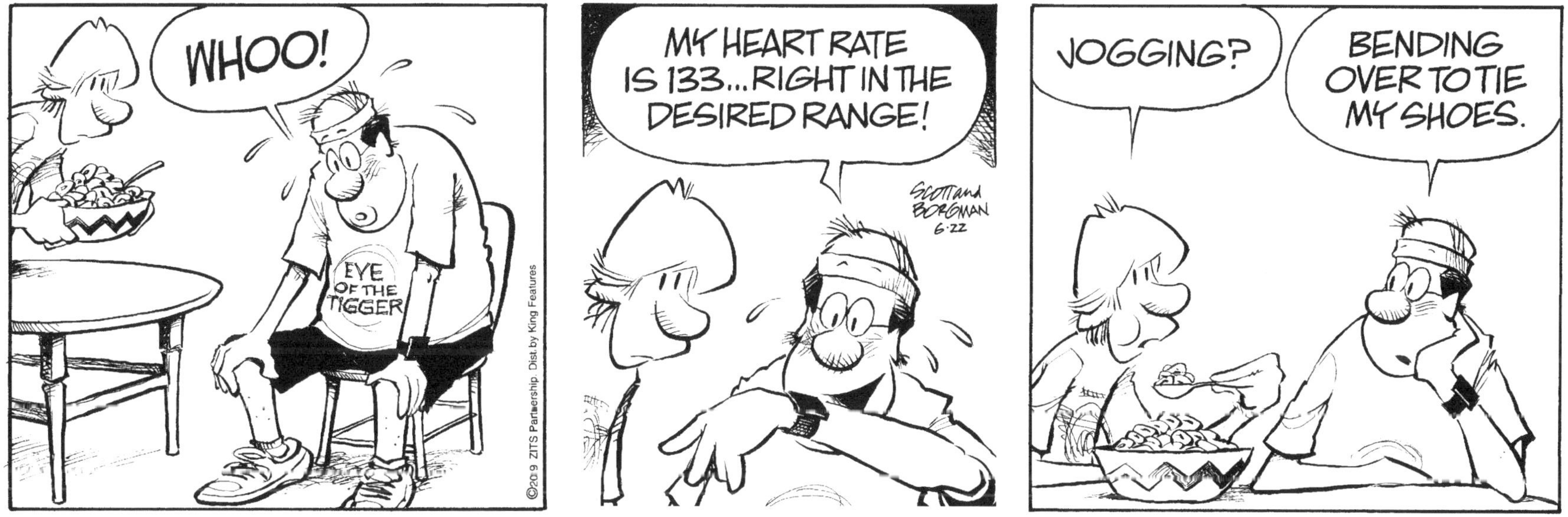
WHOO!
EYE OF THE TIGGER
©2019 ZITS Partnership. Dist. by King Features
MY HEART RATE IS 133... RIGHT IN THE DESIRED RANGE!
SCOTT and BORGMAN 6·22
JOGGING?
BENDING OVER TO TIE MY SHOES.

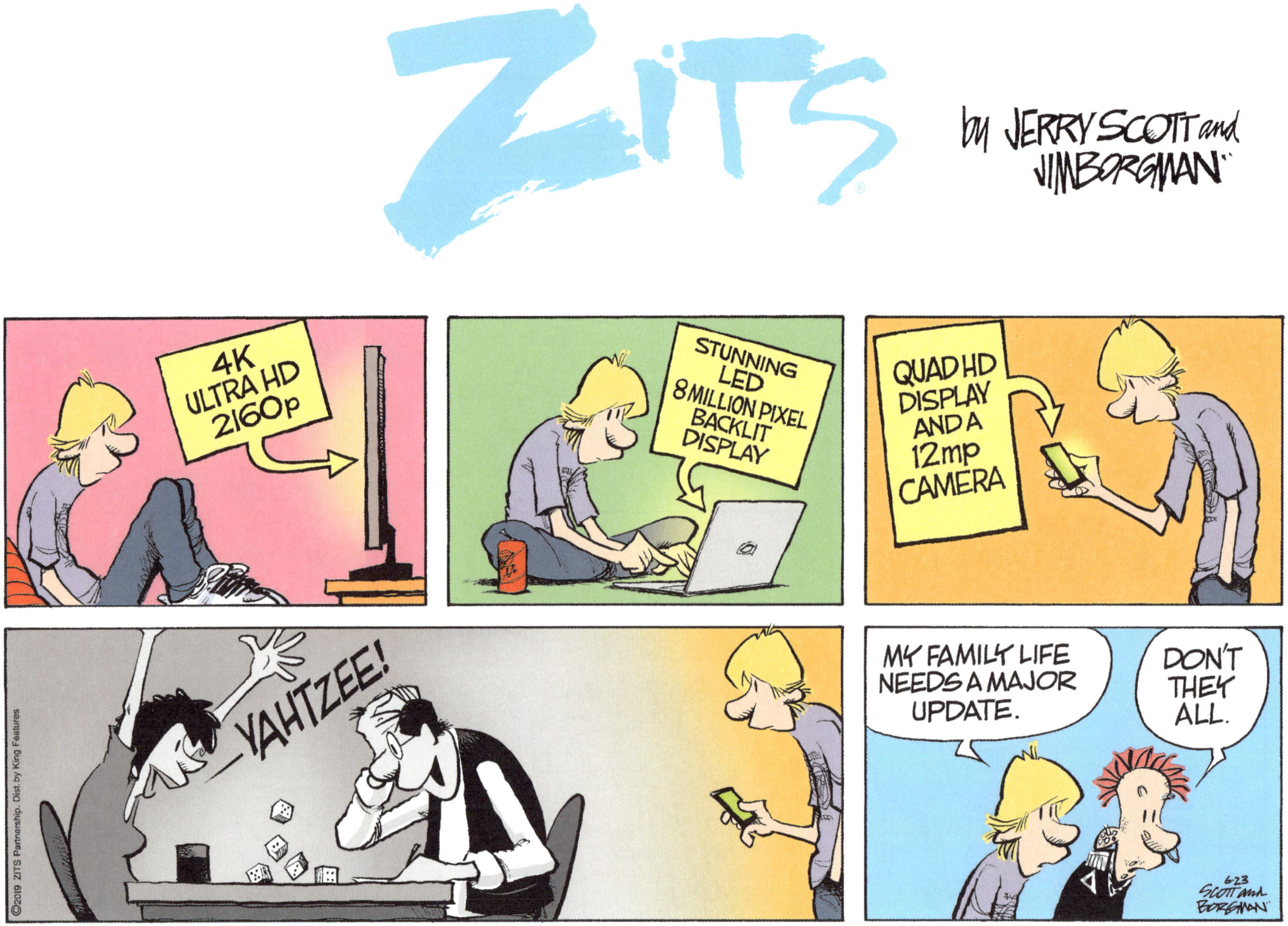
ZITS
by JERRY SCOTT and JIM BORGMAN
4K ULTRA HD 2160p
STUNNING LED 8 MILLION PIXEL BACKLIT DISPLAY
QUAD HD DISPLAY AND A 12mp CAMERA
YAHTZEE!
©2019 ZITS Partnership. Dist. by King Features
MY FAMILY LIFE NEEDS A MAJOR UPDATE.
DON'T THEY ALL.
6-23 SCOTT and BORGMAN

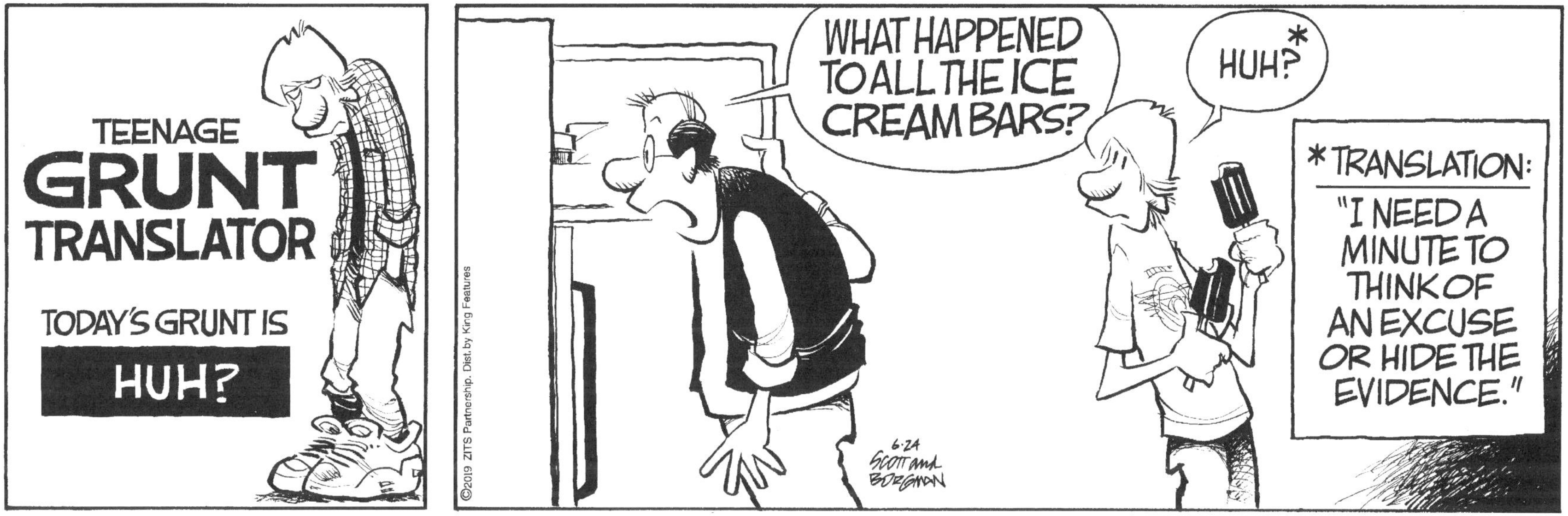
TEENAGE
GRUNT
TRANSLATOR
TODAY'S GRUNT IS
HUH?
©2019 ZITS Partnership. Dist. by King Features
WHAT HAPPENED TO ALL THE ICE CREAM BARS?
HUH?*
*TRANSLATION:
"I NEED A MINUTE TO THINK OF AN EXCUSE OR HIDE THE EVIDENCE."
6.24 SCOTT and BORGMAN

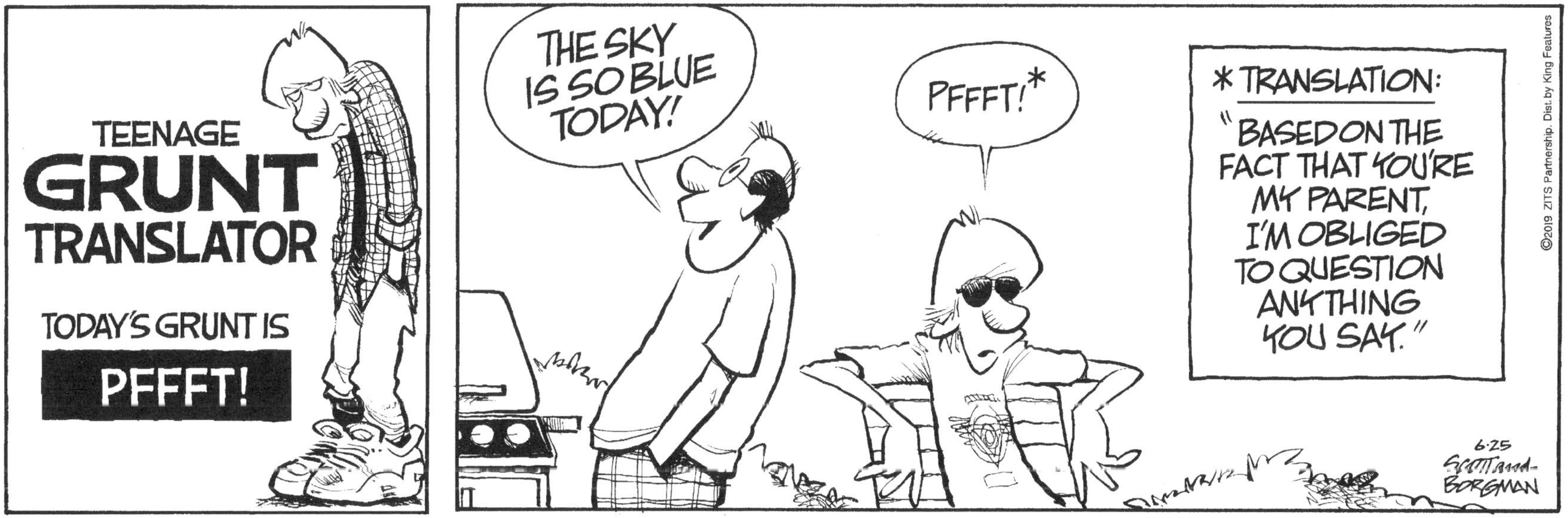
TEENAGE
GRUNT
TRANSLATOR
TODAY'S GRUNT IS
PFFFT!
THE SKY IS SO BLUE TODAY!
PFFFT!*
*TRANSLATION:
"BASED ON THE FACT THAT YOU'RE MY PARENT, I'M OBLIGED TO QUESTION ANYTHING YOU SAY."
©2019 ZITS Partnership. Dist. by King Features
6.25 SCOTT and BORGMAN

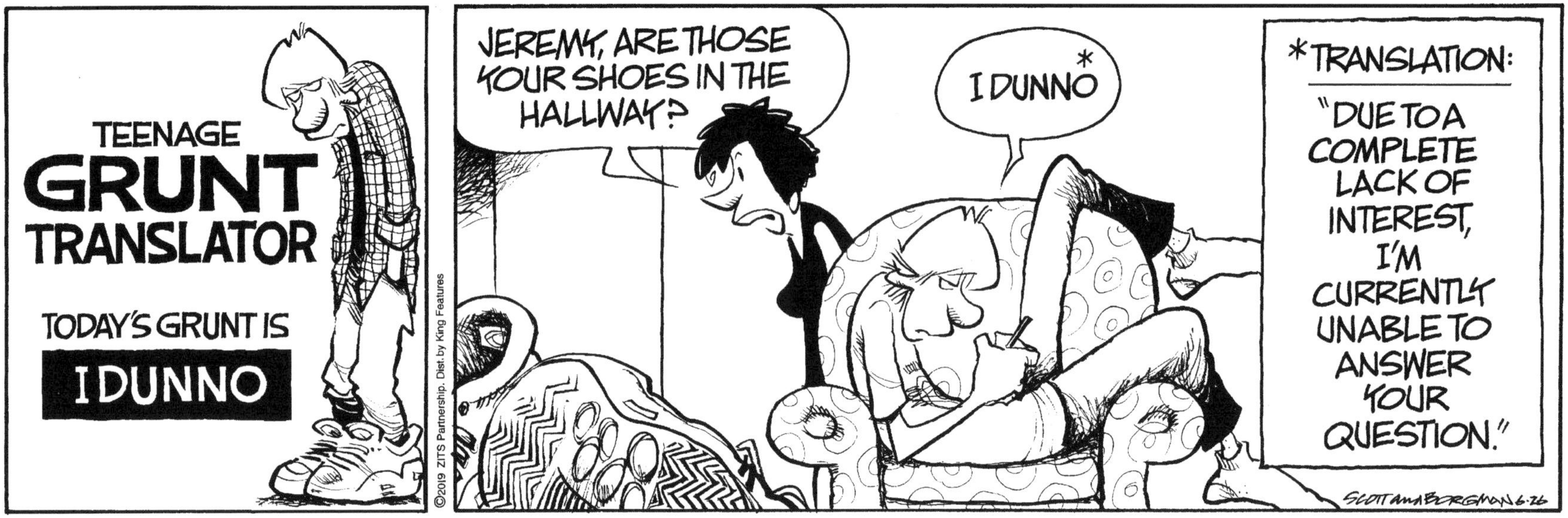
TEENAGE
GRUNT
TRANSLATOR
TODAY'S GRUNT IS
I DUNNO
©2019 ZITS Partnership. Dist. by King Features
JEREMY, ARE THOSE YOUR SHOES IN THE HALLWAY?
I DUNNO*
*TRANSLATION:
"DUE TO A COMPLETE LACK OF INTEREST, I'M CURRENTLY UNABLE TO ANSWER YOUR QUESTION."
SCOTT AND BORGMAN 6-26

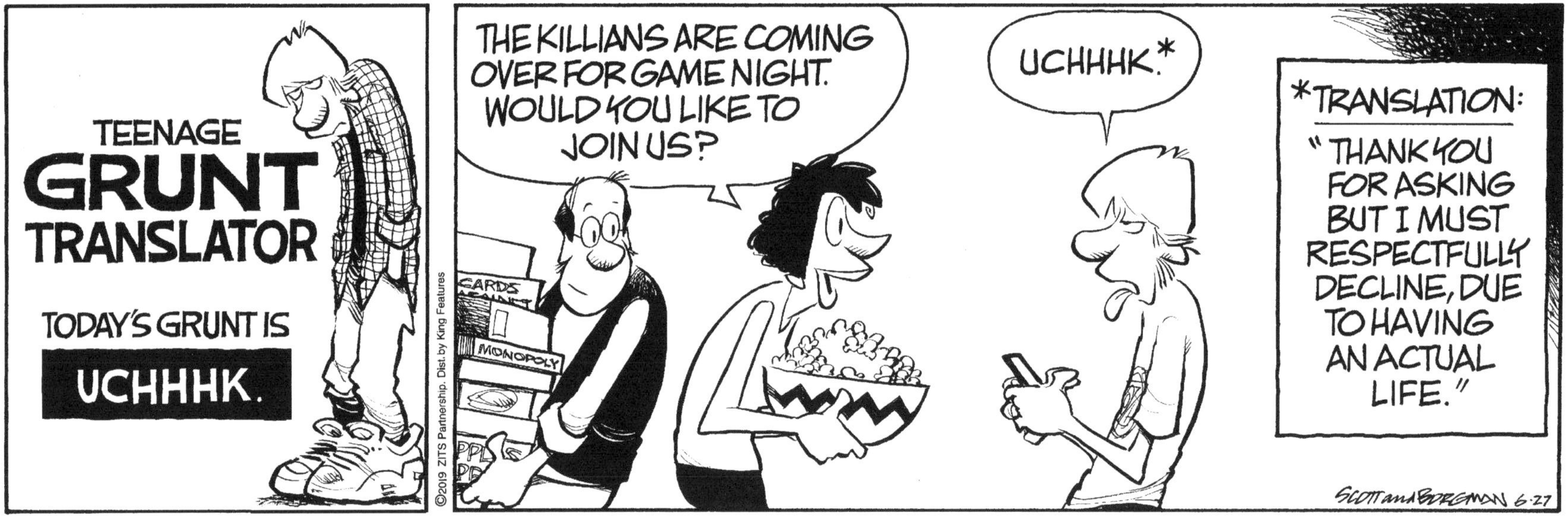
TEENAGE
GRUNT
TRANSLATOR
TODAY'S GRUNT IS
UCHHHK.
©2019 ZITS Partnership. Dist. by King Features
THE KILLIANS ARE COMING OVER FOR GAME NIGHT. WOULD YOU LIKE TO JOIN US?
UCHHHK.*
CARDS
MONOPOLY
*TRANSLATION:
"THANK YOU FOR ASKING BUT I MUST RESPECTFULLY DECLINE, DUE TO HAVING AN ACTUAL LIFE."
SCOTT AND BORGMAN 6-27

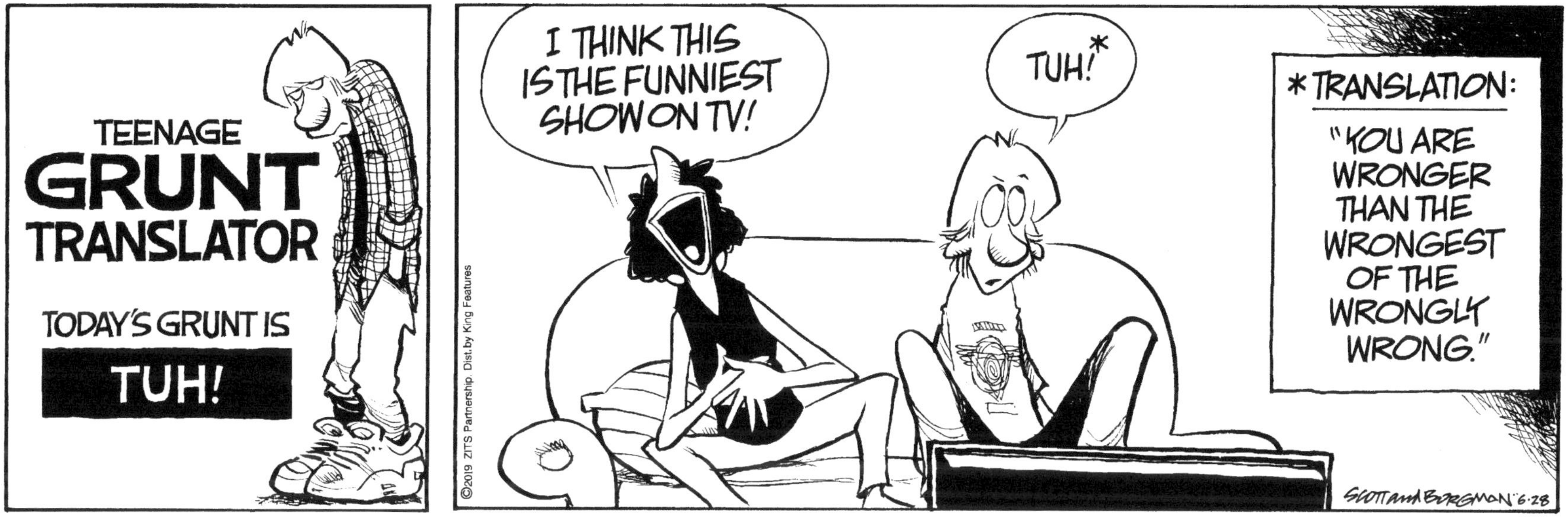
TEENAGE
GRUNT
TRANSLATOR
TODAY'S GRUNT IS
TUH!
I THINK THIS IS THE FUNNIEST SHOW ON TV!
TUH!*
*TRANSLATION:
"YOU ARE WRONGER THAN THE WRONGEST OF THE WRONGLY WRONG."
©2019 ZITS Partnership. Dist. by King Features
SCOTT and BORGMAN 6·28

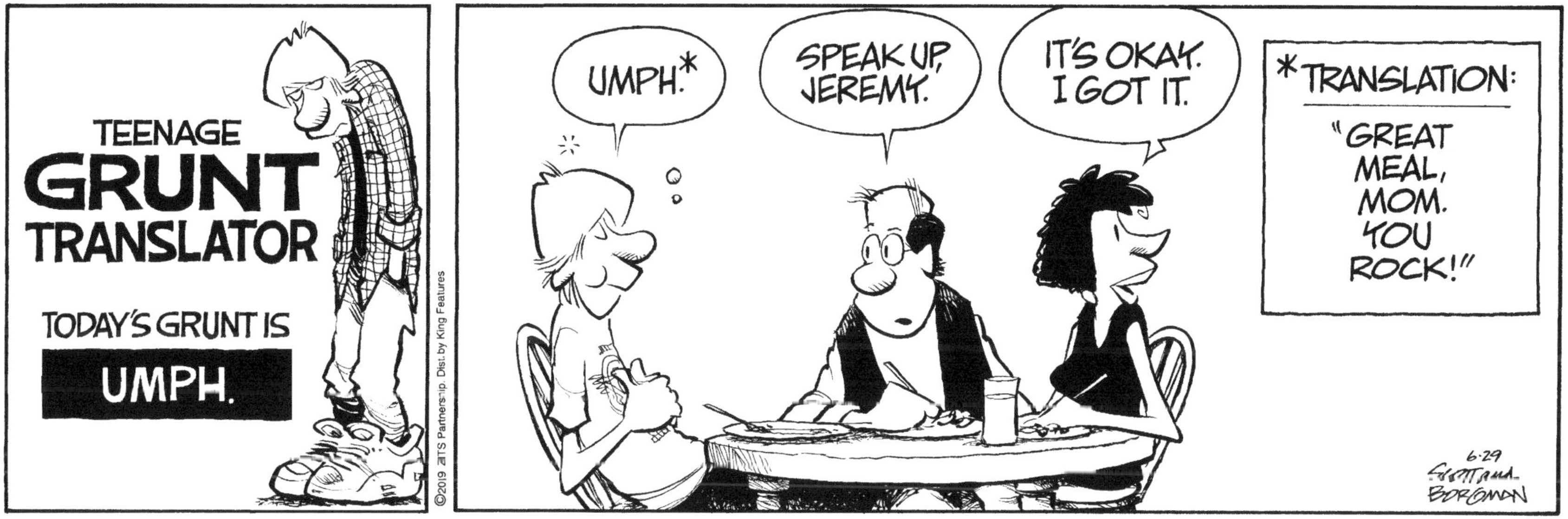
TEENAGE
GRUNT
TRANSLATOR
TODAY'S GRUNT IS
UMPH.
UMPH.*
SPEAK UP, JEREMY.
IT'S OKAY. I GOT IT.
*TRANSLATION:
"GREAT MEAL, MOM. YOU ROCK!"
©2019 ZITS Partnership. Dist. by King Features
6·29 SCOTT and BORGMAN

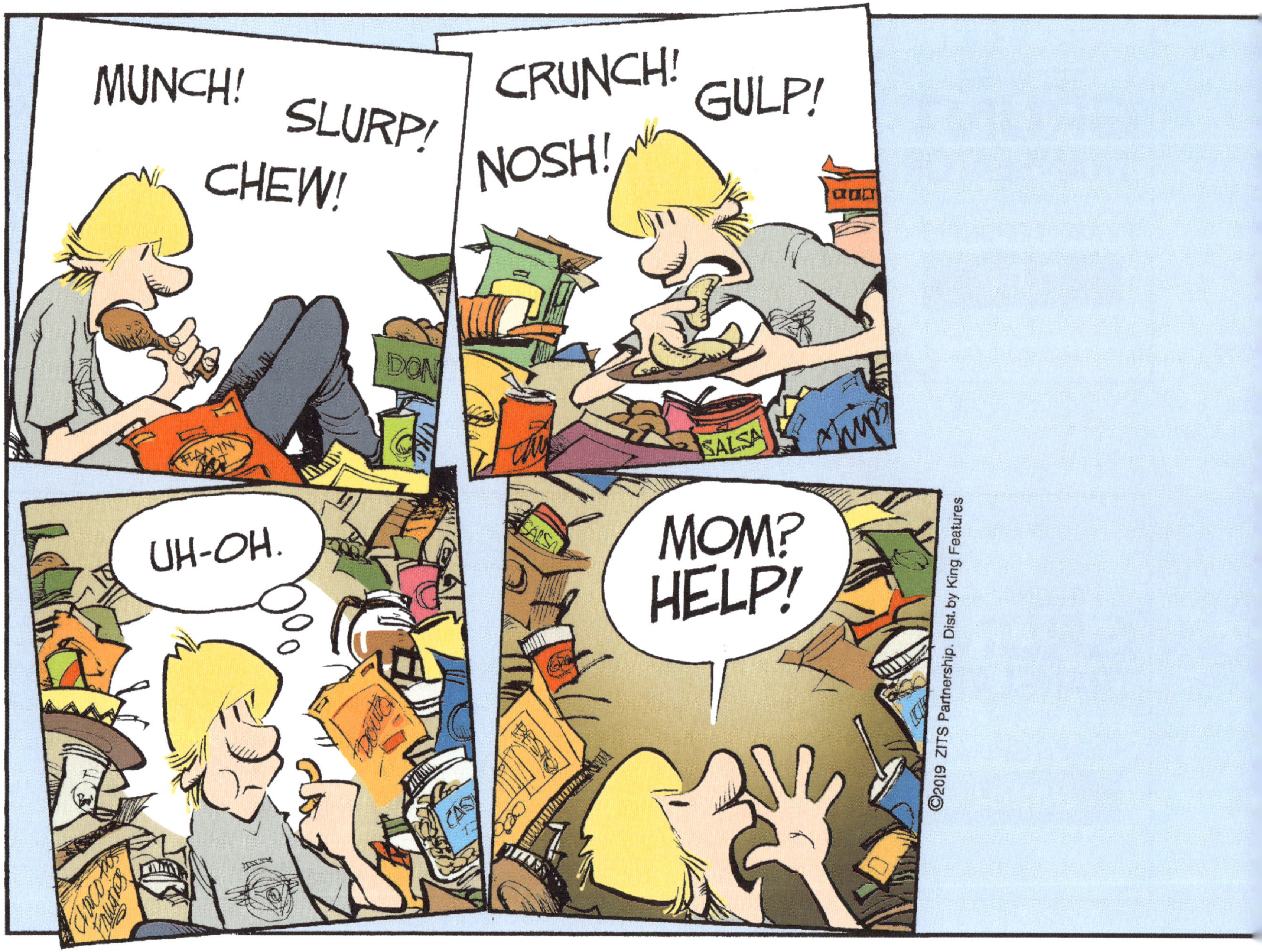
MUNCH!
SLURP!
CHEW!
CRUNCH!
GULP!
NOSH!
SALSA
UH-OH.
MOM? HELP!
©2019 ZITS Partnership. Dist. by King Features

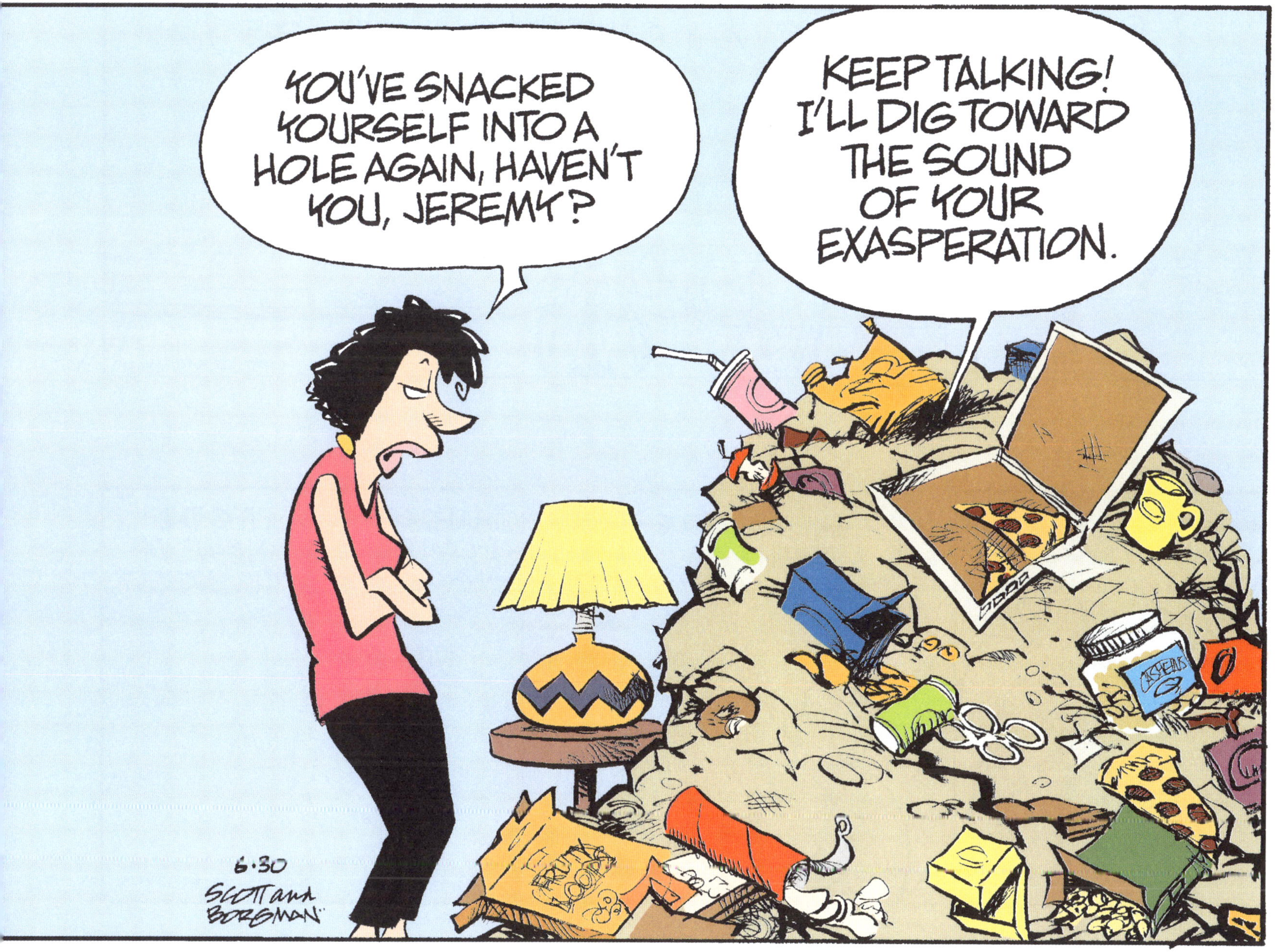
YOU'VE SNACKED YOURSELF INTO A HOLE AGAIN, HAVEN'T YOU, JEREMY?
KEEP TALKING! I'LL DIG TOWARD THE SOUND OF YOUR EXASPERATION.
6.30
SCOTT AND BORGMAN

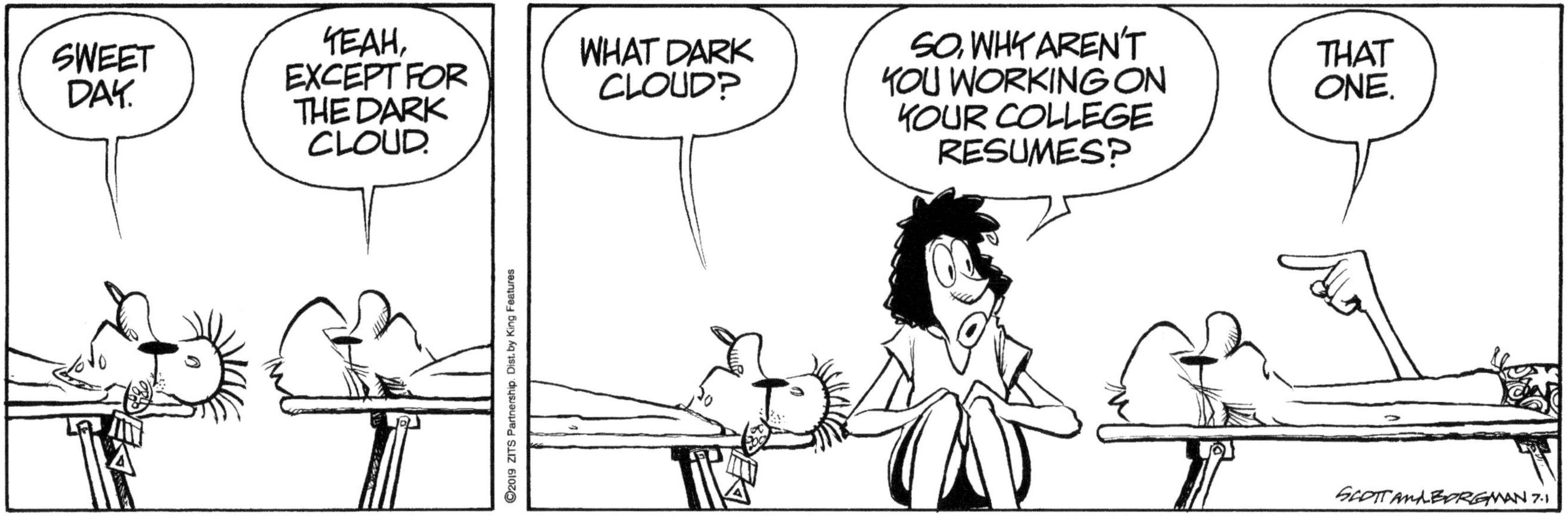
SWEET DAY.
YEAH, EXCEPT FOR THE DARK CLOUD.
©2019 ZITS Partnership. Dist. by King Features
WHAT DARK CLOUD?
SO, WHY AREN'T YOU WORKING ON YOUR COLLEGE RESUMES?
THAT ONE.
SCOTT AND BORGMAN 7·1

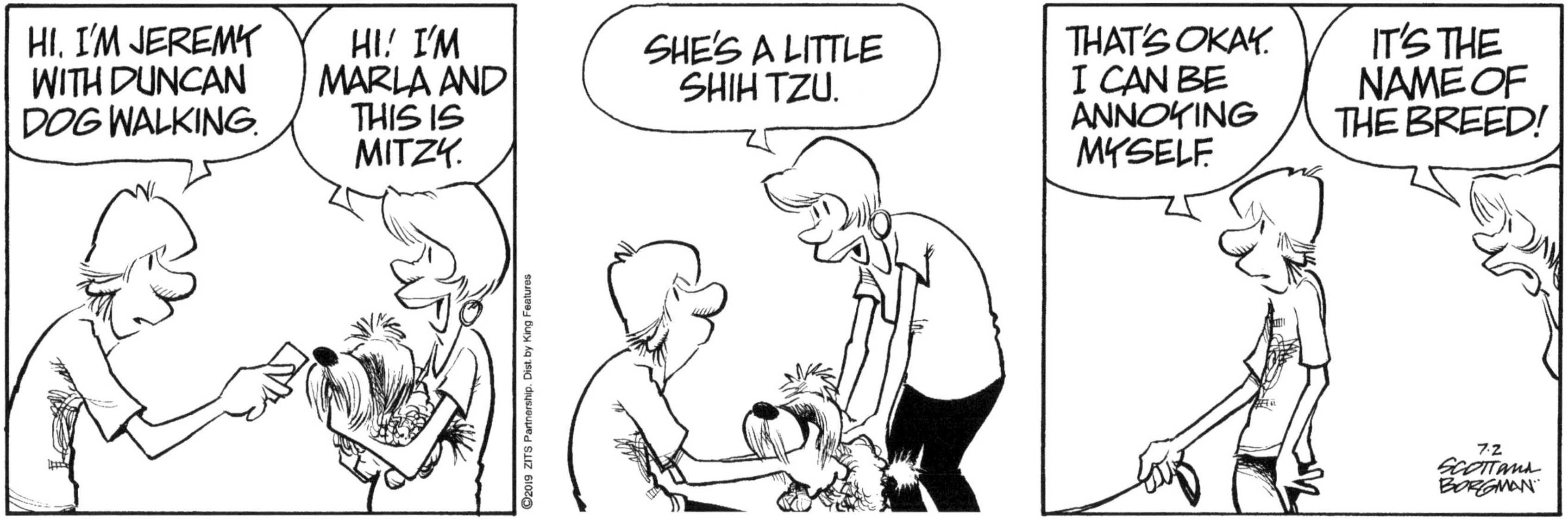
HI. I'M JEREMY WITH DUNCAN DOG WALKING.
HI! I'M MARLA AND THIS IS MITZY.
©2019 ZITS Partnership. Dist. by King Features
SHE'S A LITTLE SHIH TZU.
THAT'S OKAY. I CAN BE ANNOYING MYSELF.
IT'S THE NAME OF THE BREED!
7·2 SCOTT AND BORGMAN

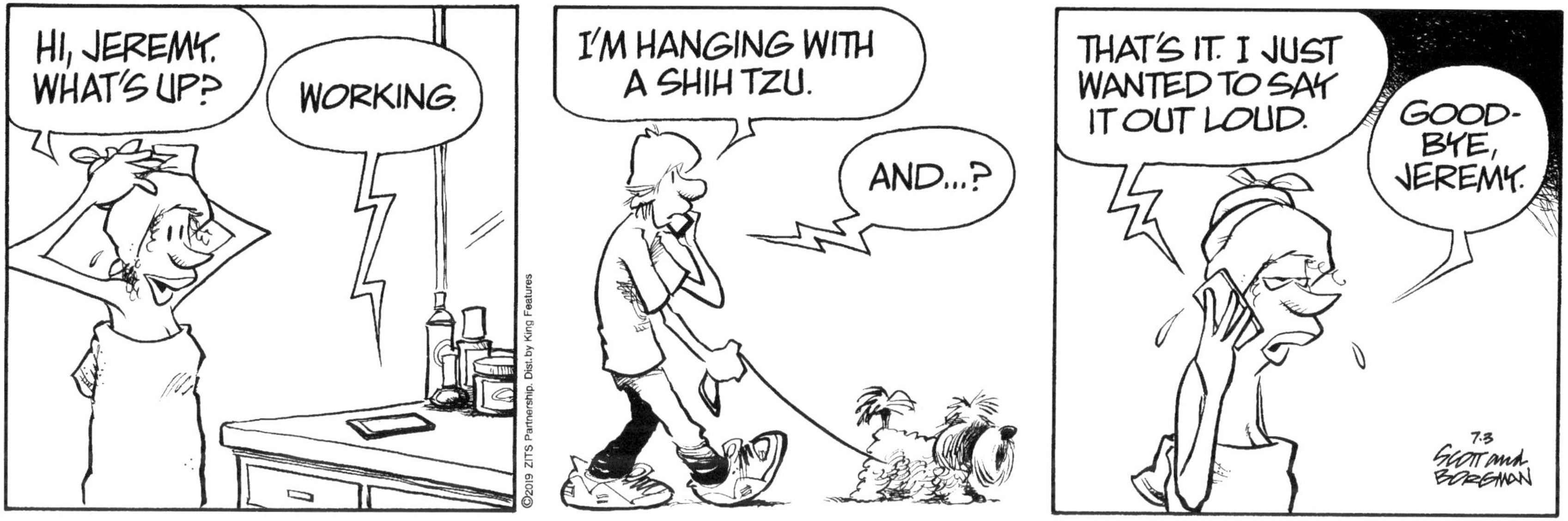
HI, JEREMY. WHAT'S UP?
WORKING.
I'M HANGING WITH A SHIH TZU.
AND...?
THAT'S IT. I JUST WANTED TO SAY IT OUT LOUD.
GOOD-BYE, JEREMY.
©2019 ZITS Partnership. Dist. by King Features
7.3
SCOTT and BORGMAN

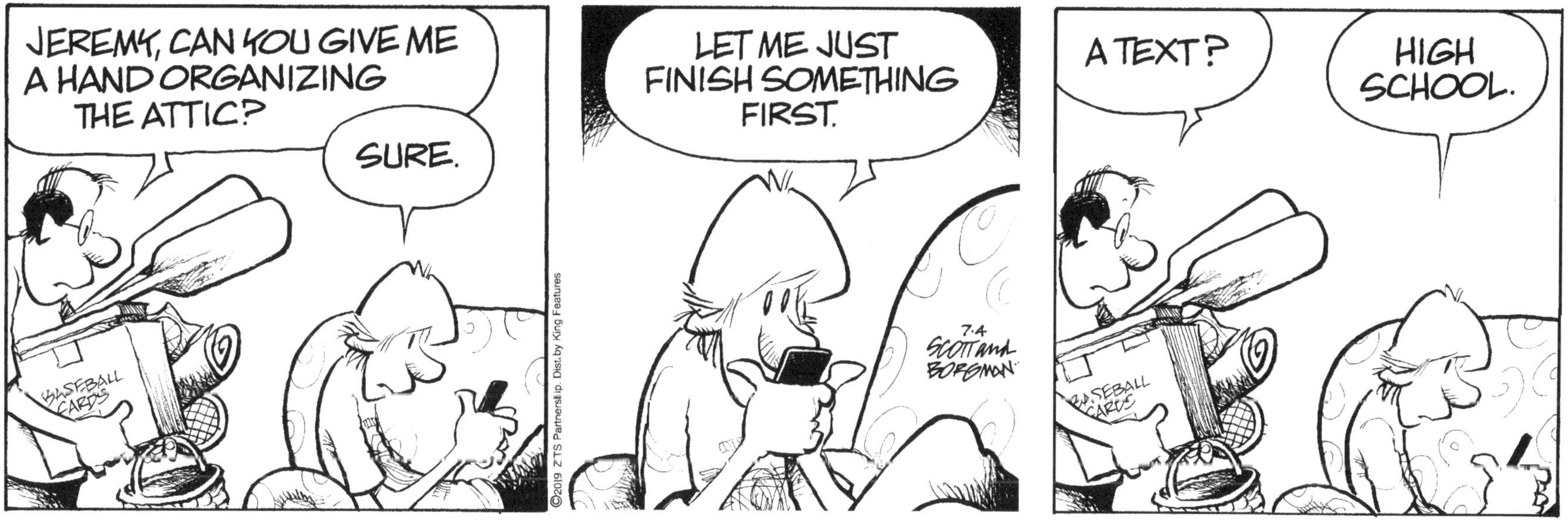
JEREMY, CAN YOU GIVE ME A HAND ORGANIZING THE ATTIC?
SURE.
BASEBALL CARDS
LET ME JUST FINISH SOMETHING FIRST.
©2019 ZITS Partnership. Dist. by King Features
7.4
SCOTT and BORGMAN
A TEXT?
HIGH SCHOOL.

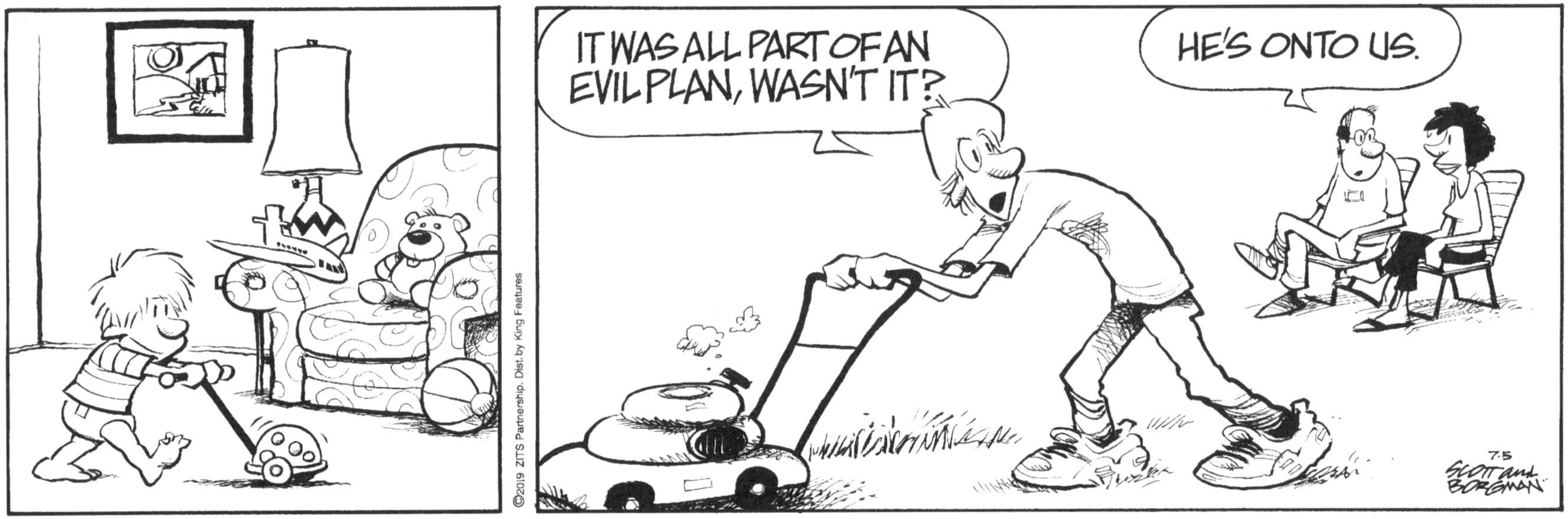
IT WAS ALL PART OF AN EVIL PLAN, WASN'T IT?
HE'S ONTO US.
©2019 ZITS Partnership. Dist. by King Features
7·5
SCOTT and BORGMAN

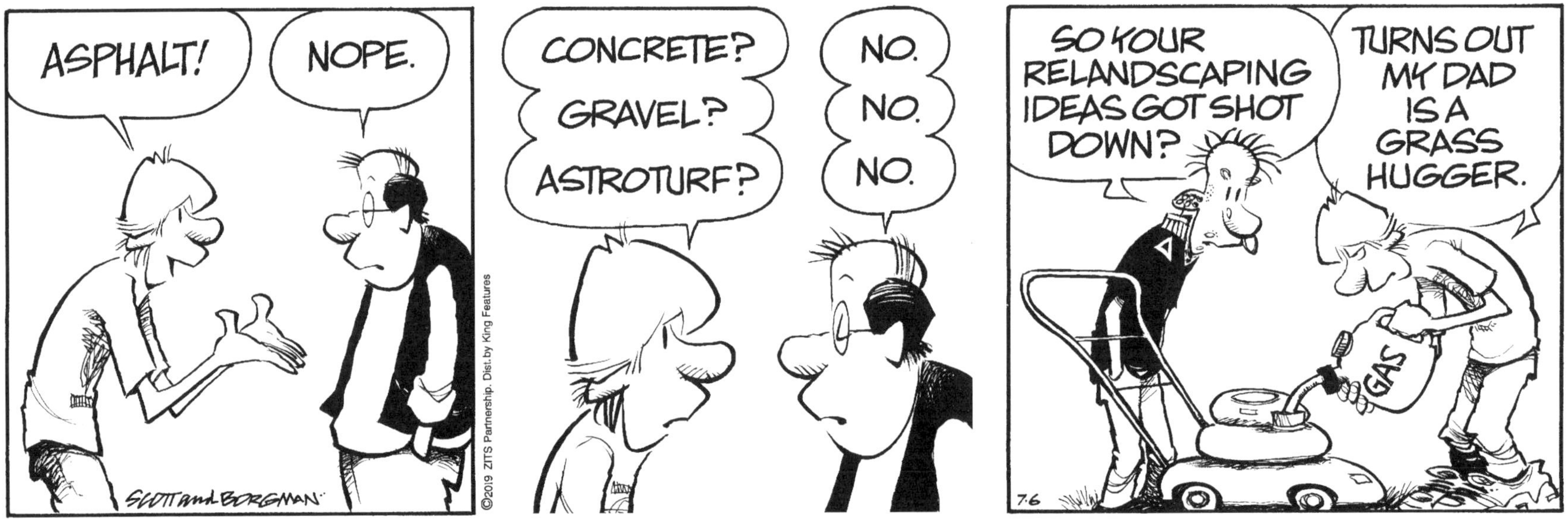
ASPHALT!
NOPE.
SCOTT and BORGMAN
©2019 ZITS Partnership. Dist. by King Features
CONCRETE?
GRAVEL?
ASTROTURF?
NO.
NO.
NO.
SO YOUR RELANDSCAPING IDEAS GOT SHOT DOWN?
TURNS OUT MY DAD IS A GRASS HUGGER.
GAS
7·6

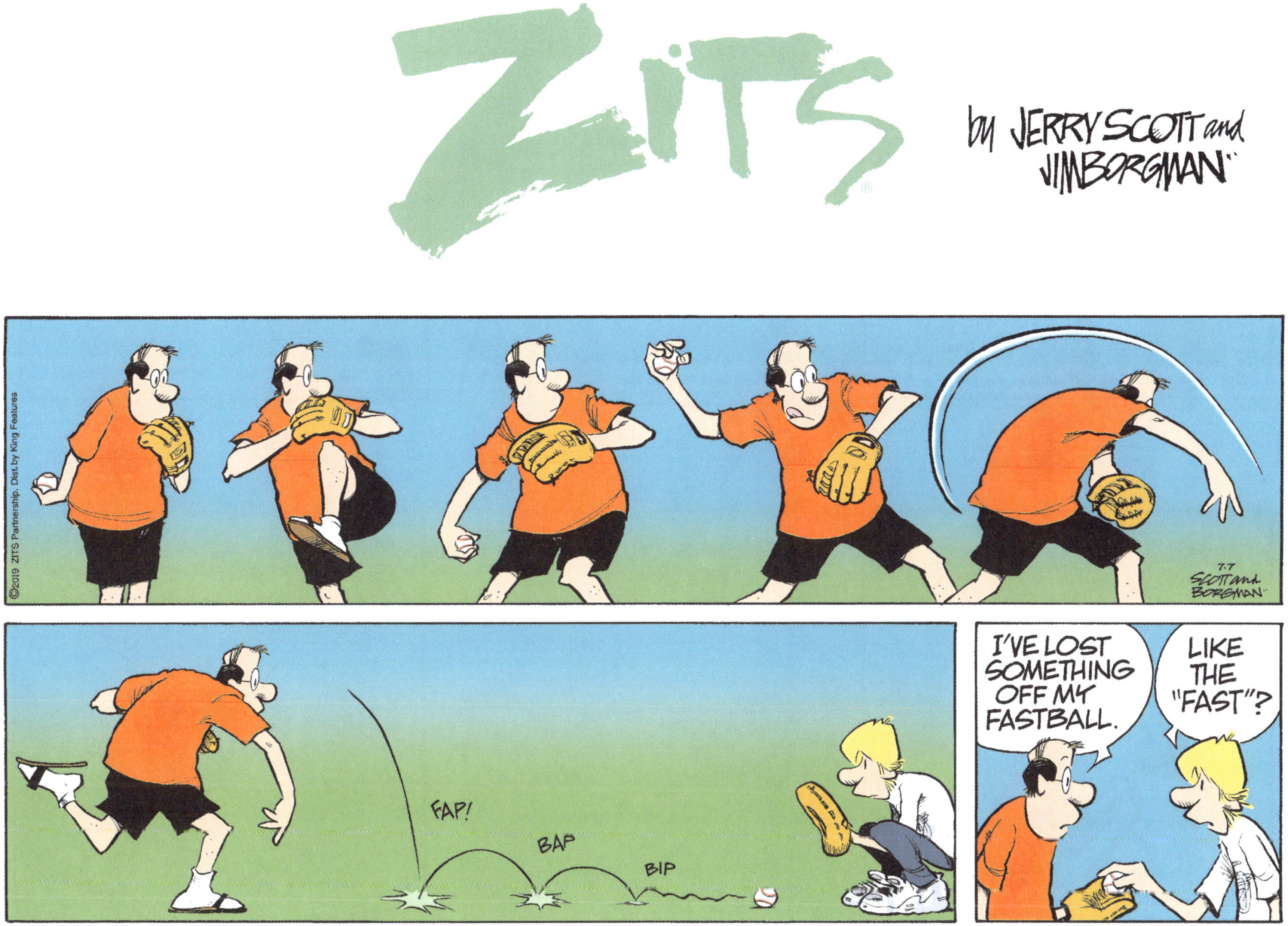
ZITS
by JERRY SCOTT and JIM BORGMAN
©2019 ZITS Partnership. Dist. by King Features
7-7 SCOTT and BORGMAN
FAP!
BAP
BIP
I'VE LOST SOMETHING OFF MY FASTBALL.
LIKE THE "FAST"?

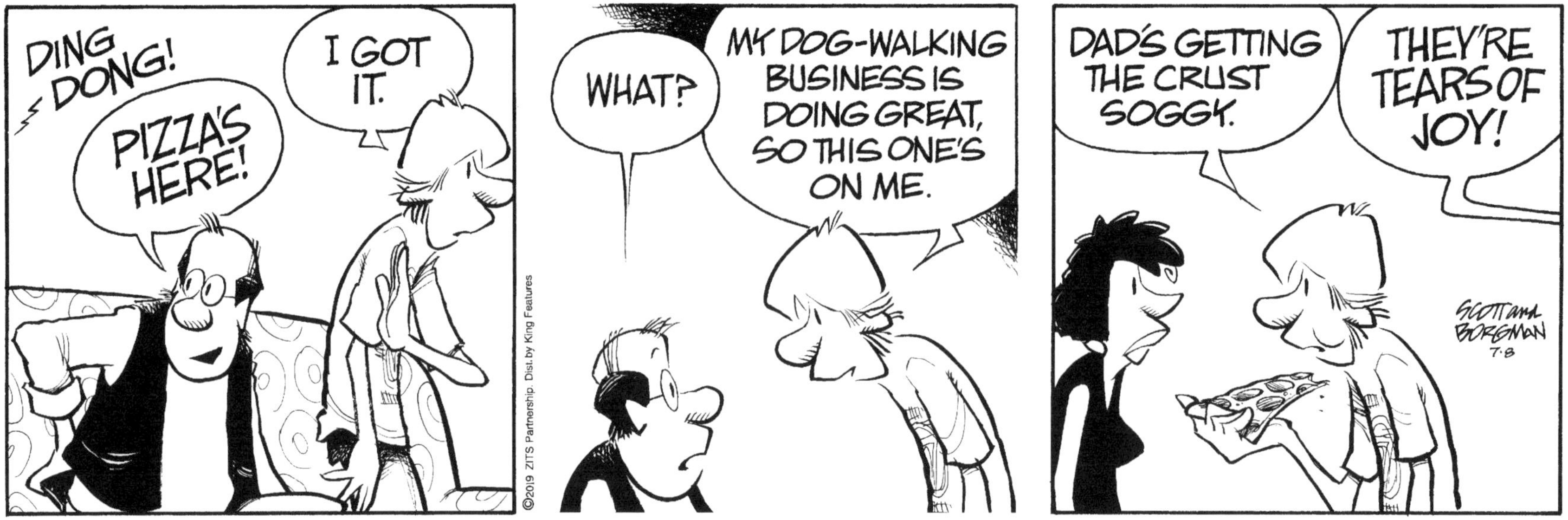
DING DONG!
PIZZA'S HERE!
I GOT IT.
©2019 ZITS Partnership. Dist. by King Features
WHAT?
MY DOG-WALKING BUSINESS IS DOING GREAT, SO THIS ONE'S ON ME.
DAD'S GETTING THE CRUST SOGGY.
THEY'RE TEARS OF JOY!
SCOTT and BORGMAN 7-8

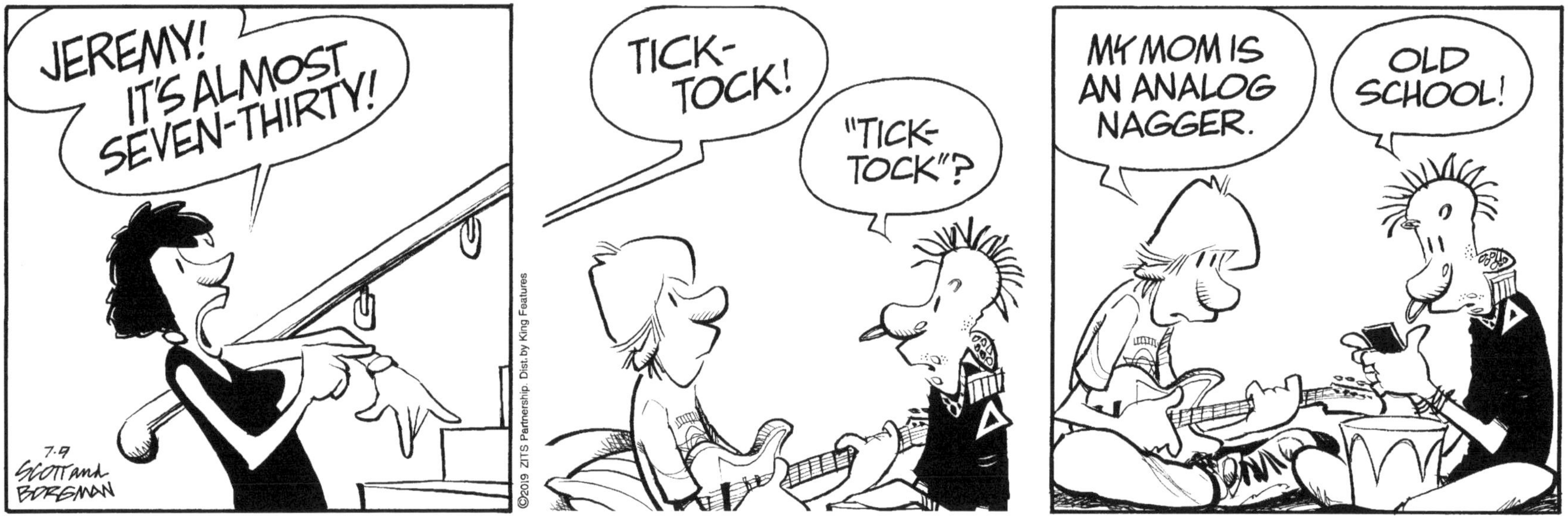
JEREMY! IT'S ALMOST SEVEN-THIRTY!
7-9 SCOTT and BORGMAN
©2019 ZITS Partnership. Dist. by King Features
TICK-TOCK!
"TICK-TOCK"?
MY MOM IS AN ANALOG NAGGER.
OLD SCHOOL!

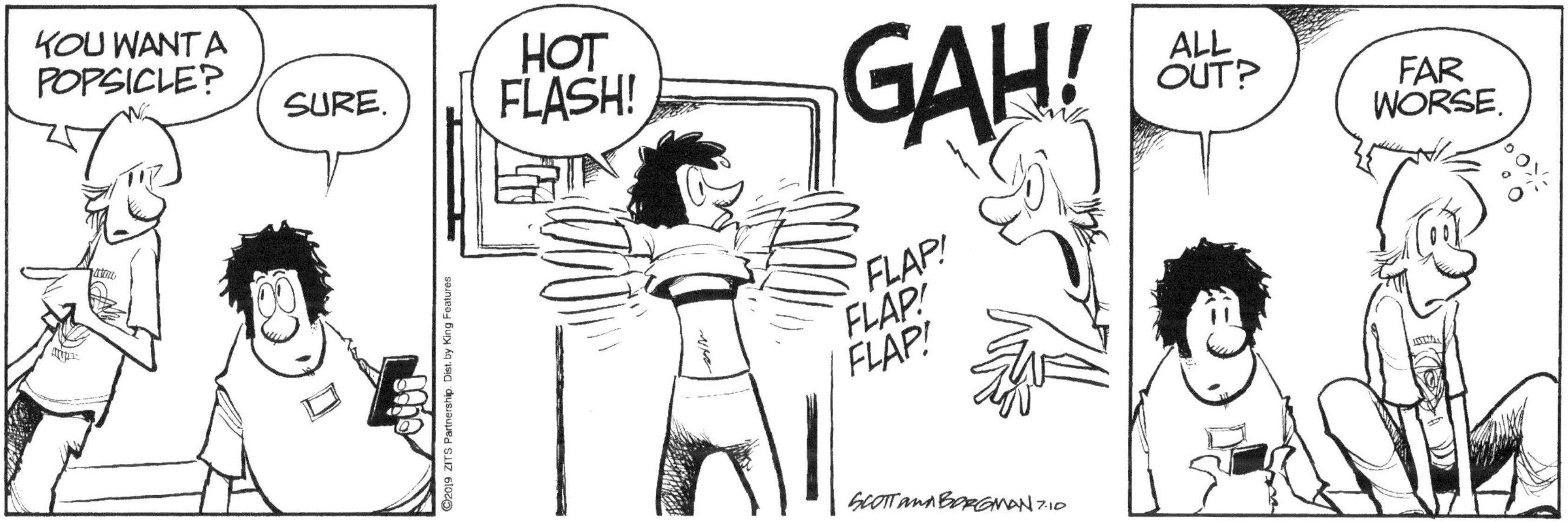
YOU WANT A POPSICLE?
SURE.
©2019 ZITS Partnership. Dist. by King Features
HOT FLASH!
FLAP! FLAP! FLAP!
GAH!
SCOTT and BORGMAN 7.10
ALL OUT?
FAR WORSE.

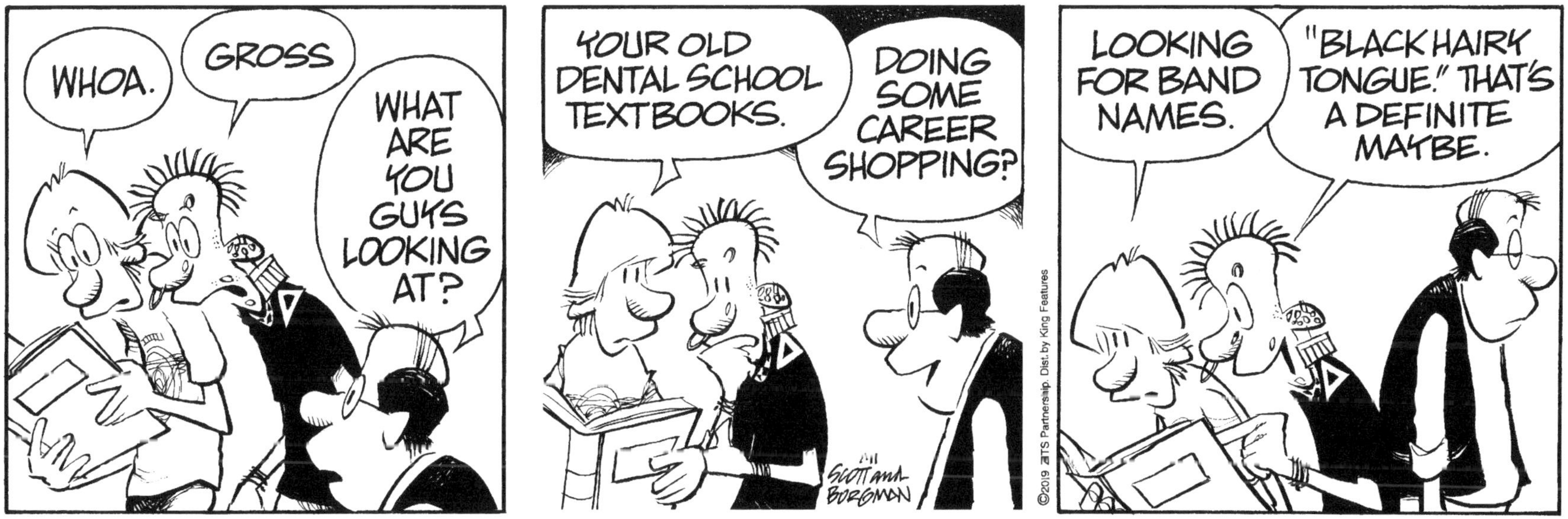
WHOA.
GROSS
WHAT ARE YOU GUYS LOOKING AT?
YOUR OLD DENTAL SCHOOL TEXTBOOKS.
DOING SOME CAREER SHOPPING?
SCOTT and BORGMAN
©2019 ZITS Partnership. Dist. by King Features
LOOKING FOR BAND NAMES.
"BLACK HAIRY TONGUE." THAT'S A DEFINITE MAYBE.

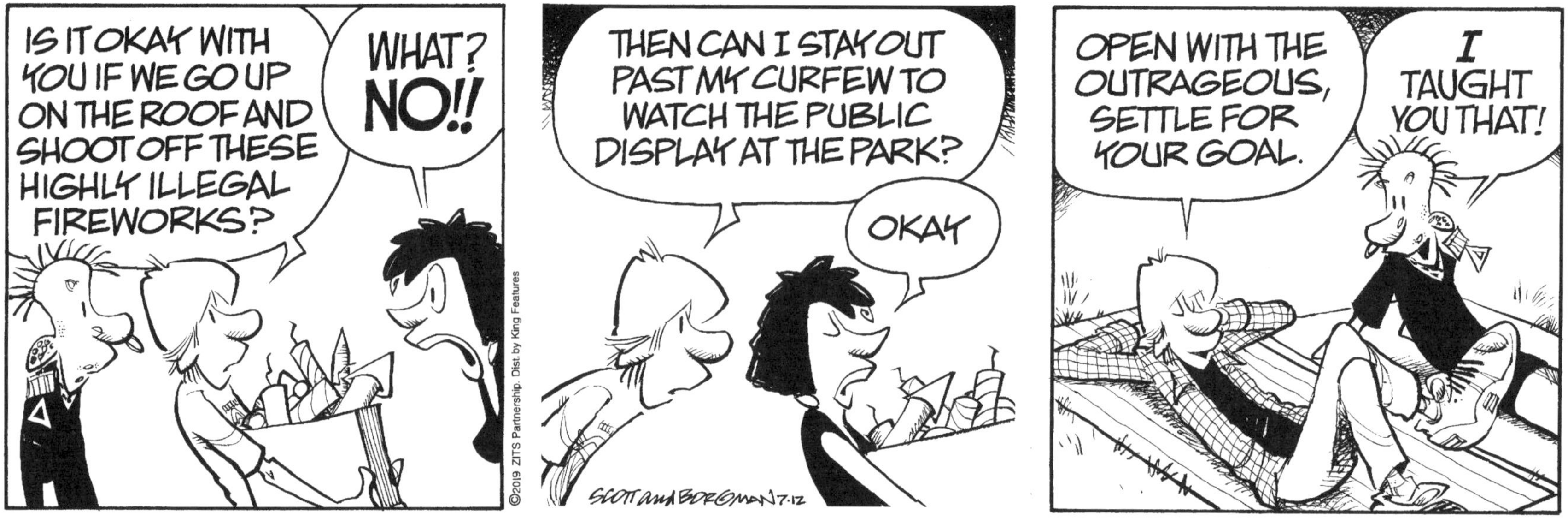
IS IT OKAY WITH YOU IF WE GO UP ON THE ROOF AND SHOOT OFF THESE HIGHLY ILLEGAL FIREWORKS?
WHAT? NO!!
©2019 ZITS Partnership. Dist. by King Features
THEN CAN I STAY OUT PAST MY CURFEW TO WATCH THE PUBLIC DISPLAY AT THE PARK?
OKAY
SCOTT AND BORGMAN 7.12
OPEN WITH THE OUTRAGEOUS, SETTLE FOR YOUR GOAL.
I TAUGHT YOU THAT!

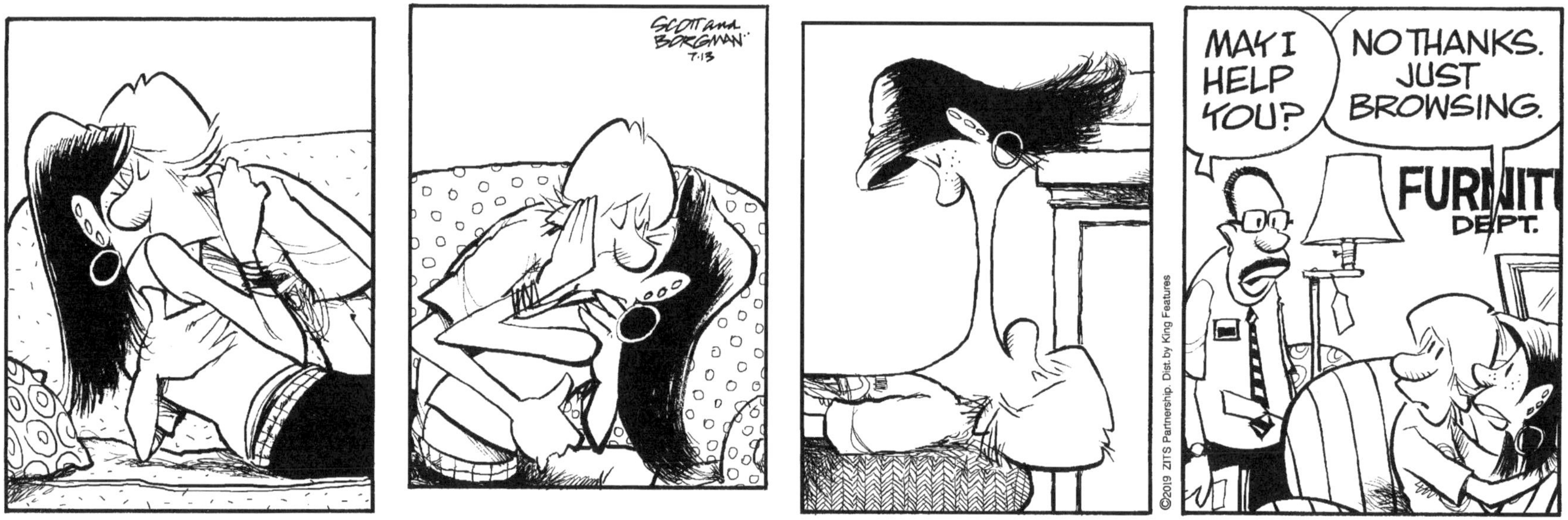
SCOTT AND BORGMAN 7.13
©2019 ZITS Partnership. Dist. by King Features
MAY I HELP YOU?
NO THANKS. JUST BROWSING.
FURNIT
DEPT.

ZITS

by JERRY SCOTT and JIM BORGMAN

HI, MOM. WHAT'S UP?
WELL...
...I'VE BEEN STRUGGLING WITH THE GAS COMPANY ALL DAY.
THEY SAY WE HAVE A FOUR-DOLLAR CREDIT, BUT I CAN'T FIND AN OVERPAYMENT.
I'VE LOOKED THROUGH RECEIPTS AND CANCELED CHECKS, MADE FIVE PHONE CALLS... I EVEN SPOKE TO A SUPERVISOR WHEN--
--JEREMY?
HEY! YOU ASKED ME A QUESTION!
YEAH, BUT I DIDN'T WANT AN ANSWER!
7·14
SCOTT and BORGMAN
©2019 ZITS Partnership. Dist. by King Features

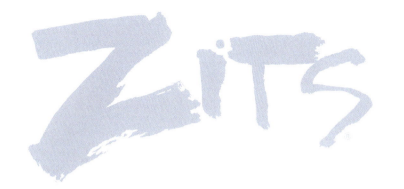

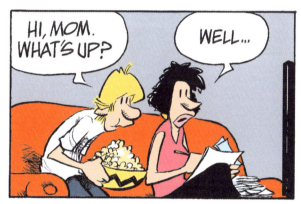

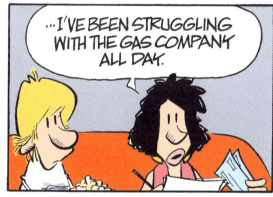

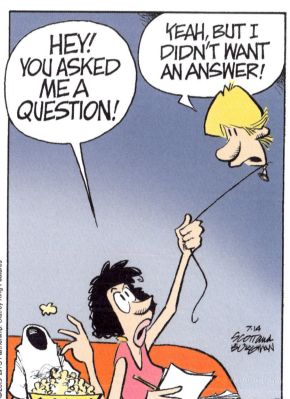

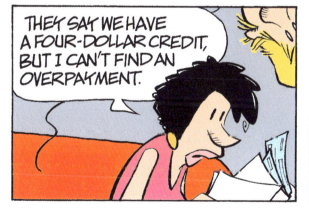

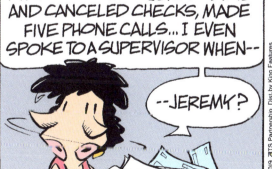

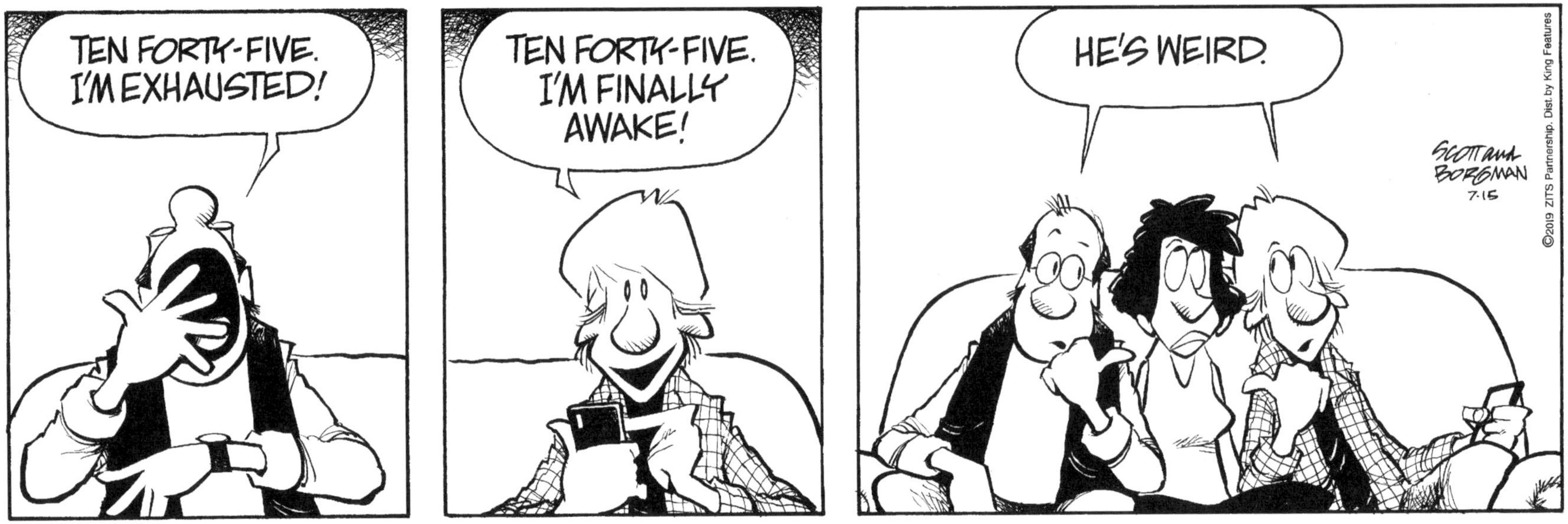
TEN FORTY-FIVE. I'M EXHAUSTED!
TEN FORTY-FIVE. I'M FINALLY AWAKE!
HE'S WEIRD.
SCOTT and BORGMAN 7·15
©2019 ZITS Partnership. Dist. by King Features

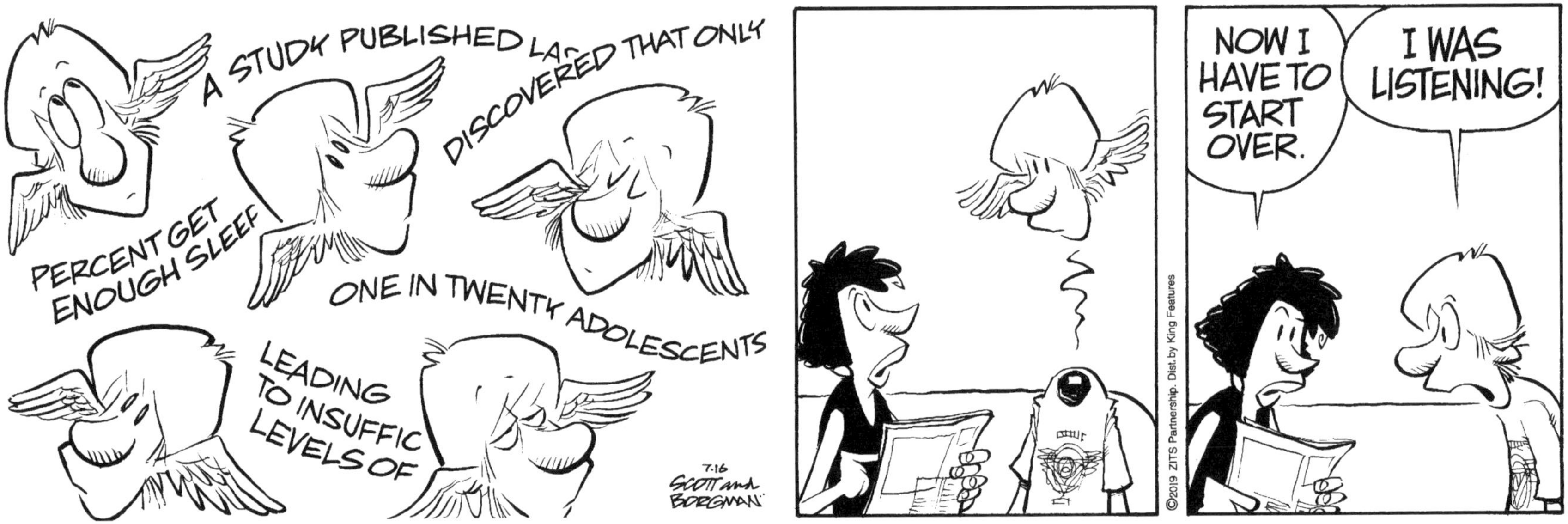
A STUDY PUBLISHED LA
DISCOVERED THAT ONLY
PERCENT GET ENOUGH SLEE
ONE IN TWENTY ADOLESCENTS
LEADING TO INSUFFIC LEVELS OF
7·16 SCOTT and BORGMAN
©2019 ZITS Partnership. Dist. by King Features
NOW I HAVE TO START OVER.
I WAS LISTENING!

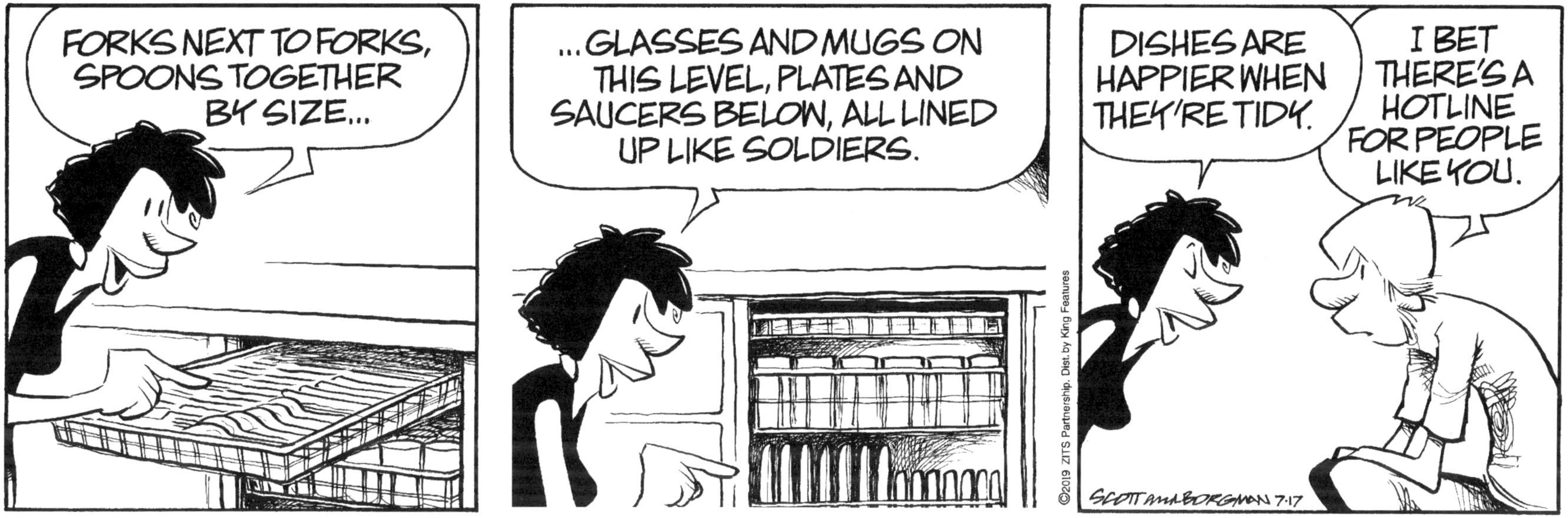
FORKS NEXT TO FORKS, SPOONS TOGETHER BY SIZE...
...GLASSES AND MUGS ON THIS LEVEL, PLATES AND SAUCERS BELOW, ALL LINED UP LIKE SOLDIERS.
DISHES ARE HAPPIER WHEN THEY'RE TIDY.
I BET THERE'S A HOTLINE FOR PEOPLE LIKE YOU.
©2019 ZITS Partnership. Dist. by King Features
SCOTT and BORGMAN 7.17

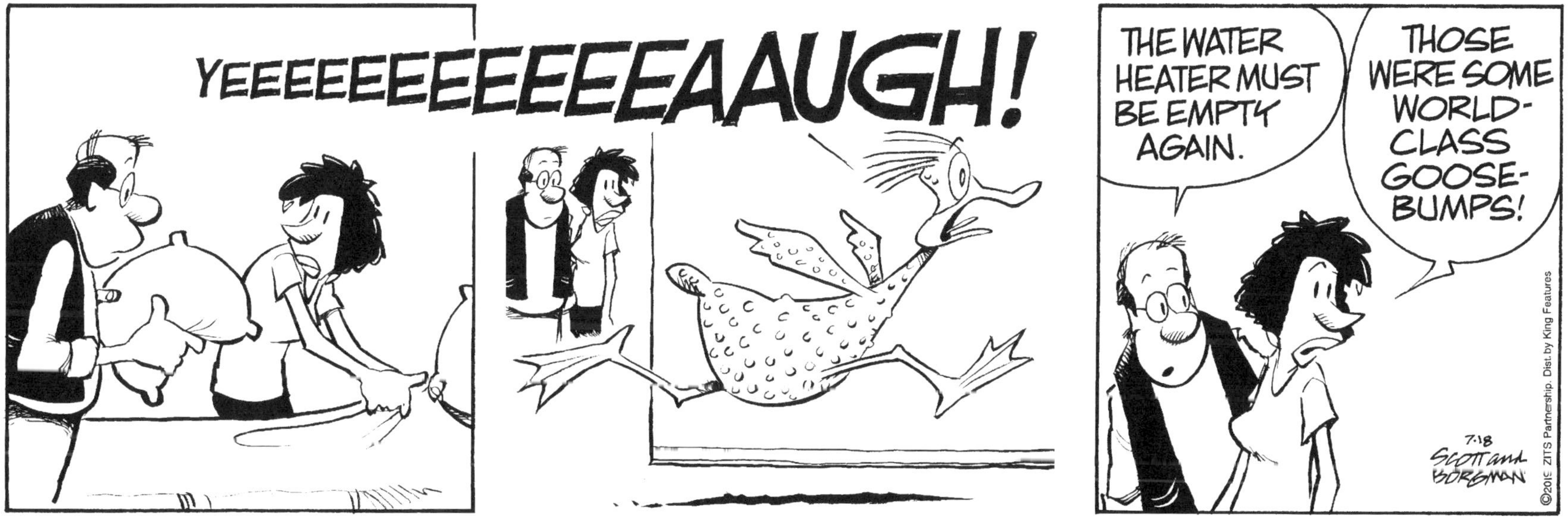
YEEEEEEEEEEEEEAAUGH!
THE WATER HEATER MUST BE EMPTY AGAIN.
THOSE WERE SOME WORLD-CLASS GOOSE-BUMPS!
7.18
SCOTT and BORGMAN
©2019 ZITS Partnership. Dist. by King Features

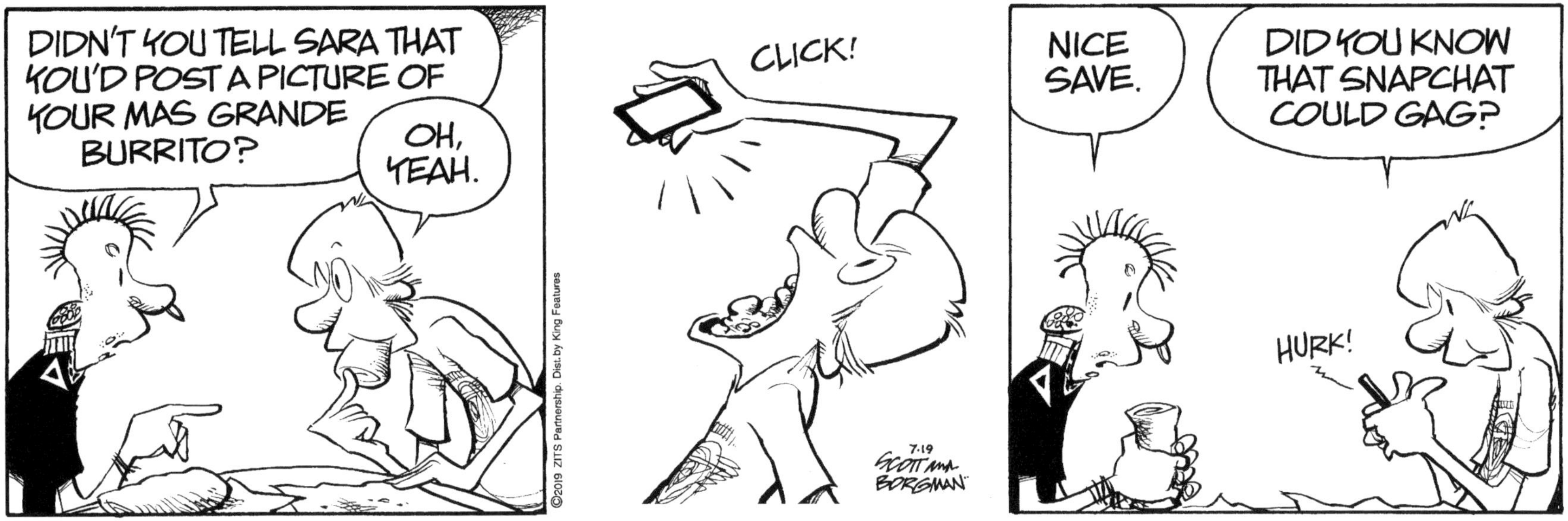
DIDN'T YOU TELL SARA THAT YOU'D POST A PICTURE OF YOUR MAS GRANDE BURRITO?
OH, YEAH.
CLICK!
NICE SAVE.
DID YOU KNOW THAT SNAPCHAT COULD GAG?
HURK!
©2019 ZITS Partnership. Dist. by King Features
7·19
SCOTT AND BORGMAN

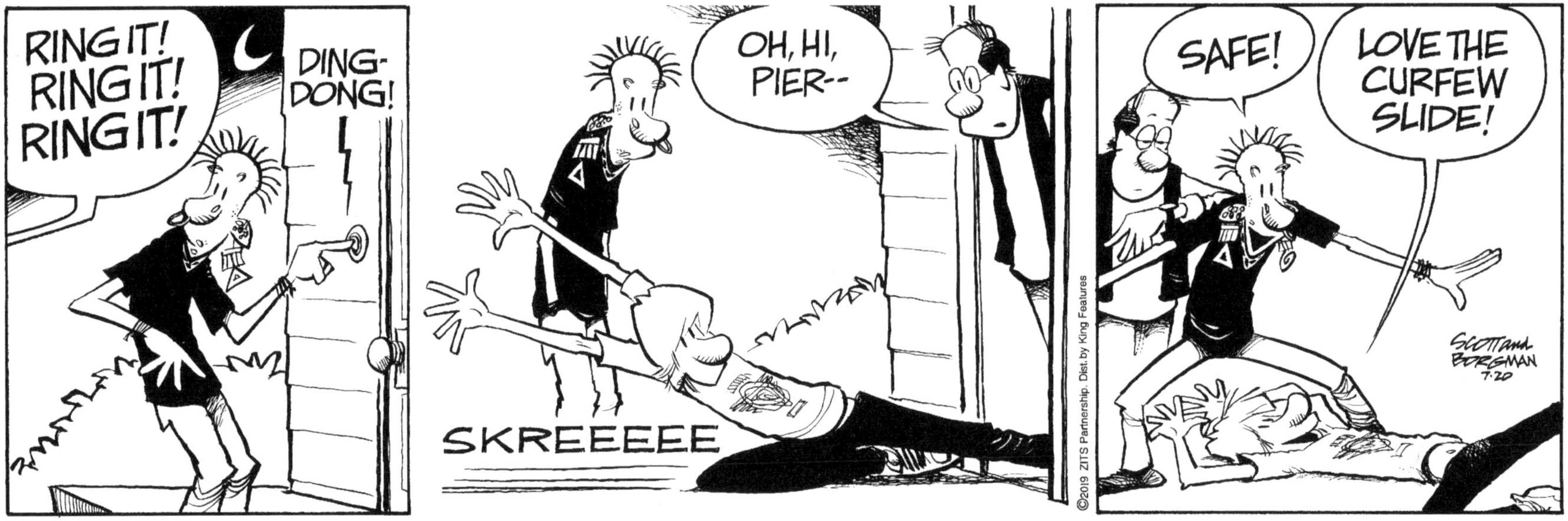
RING IT! RING IT! RING IT!
DING-DONG!
OH, HI, PIER--
SKREEEEEE
SAFE!
LOVE THE CURFEW SLIDE!
©2019 ZITS Partnership. Dist. by King Features
SCOTT AND BORGMAN 7·20

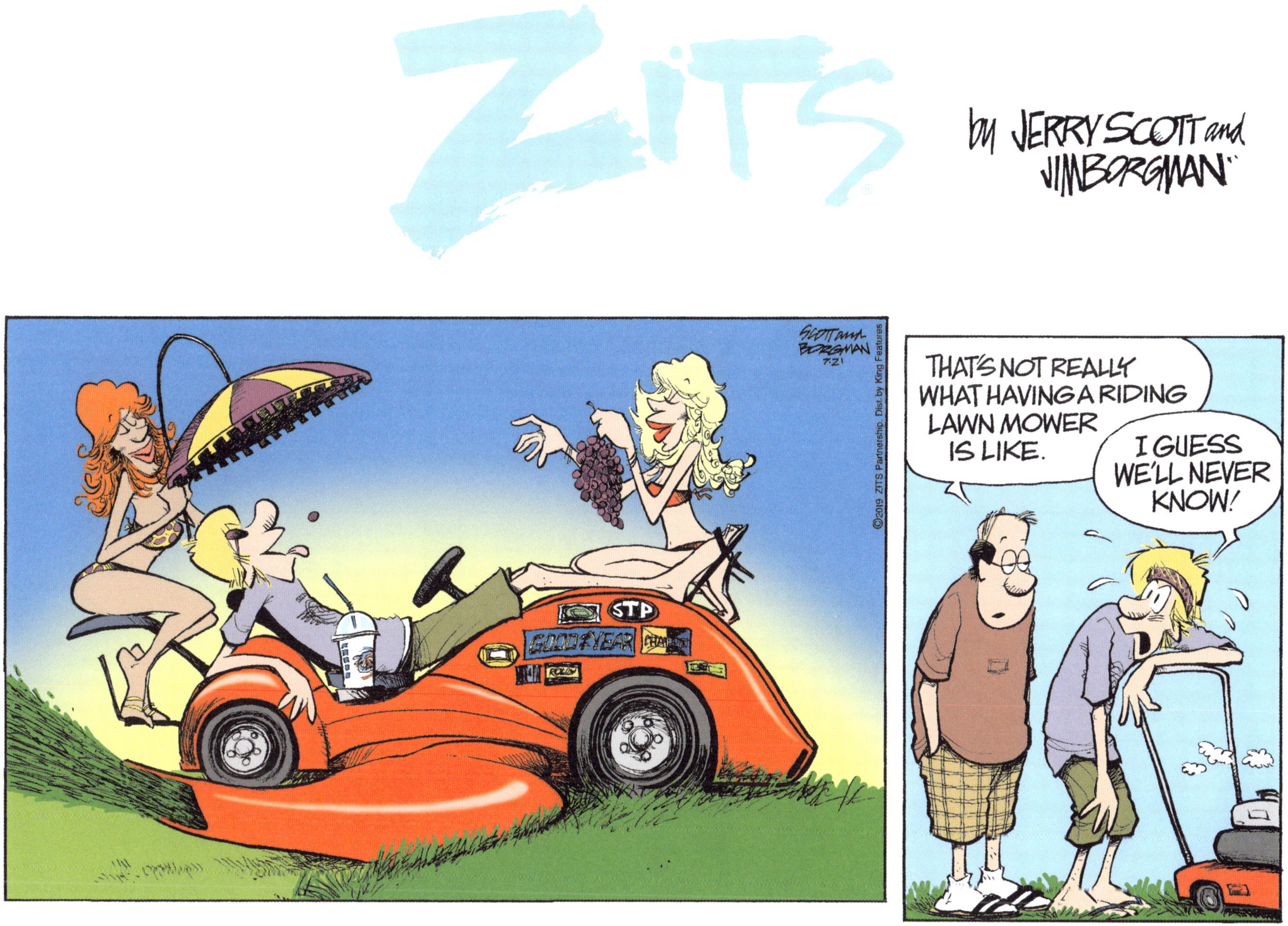
ZITS
by JERRY SCOTT and JIM BORGMAN
SCOTT and BORGMAN 7.21
©2019 ZITS Partnership. Dist. by King Features
STP
GOODYEAR
THAT'S NOT REALLY WHAT HAVING A RIDING LAWN MOWER IS LIKE.
I GUESS WE'LL NEVER KNOW!

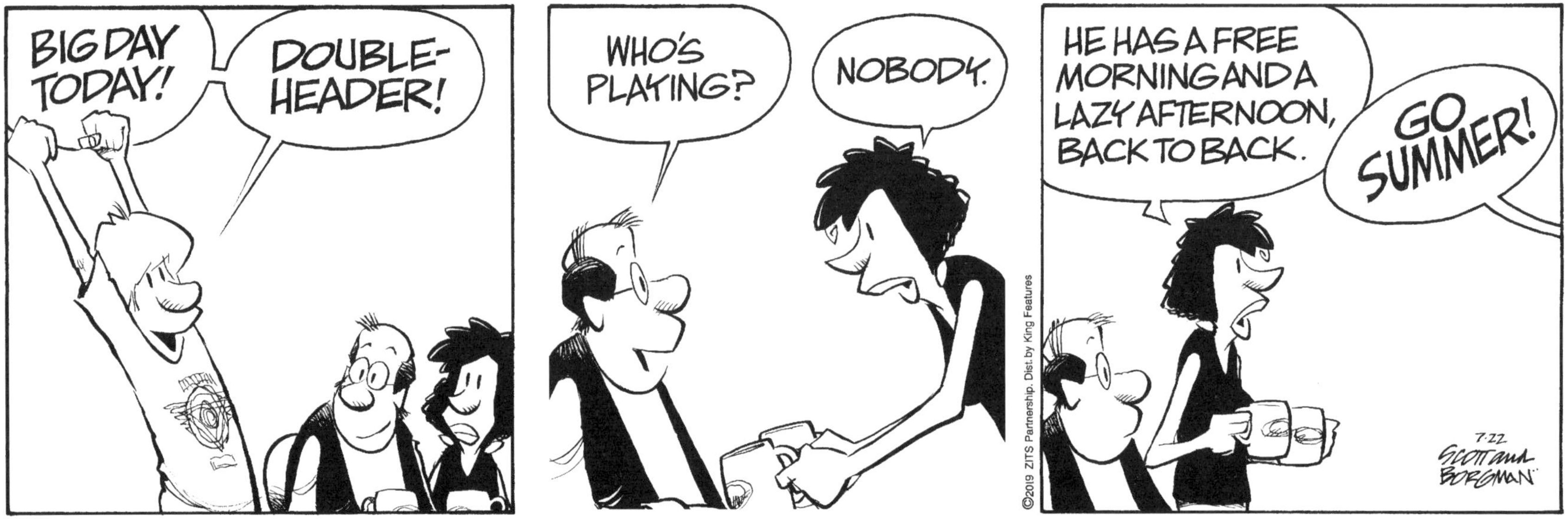
BIG DAY TODAY!
DOUBLE-HEADER!
WHO'S PLAYING?
NOBODY.
©2019 ZITS Partnership. Dist.by King Features
HE HAS A FREE MORNING AND A LAZY AFTERNOON, BACK TO BACK.
GO SUMMER!
7·22
SCOTT and BORGMAN

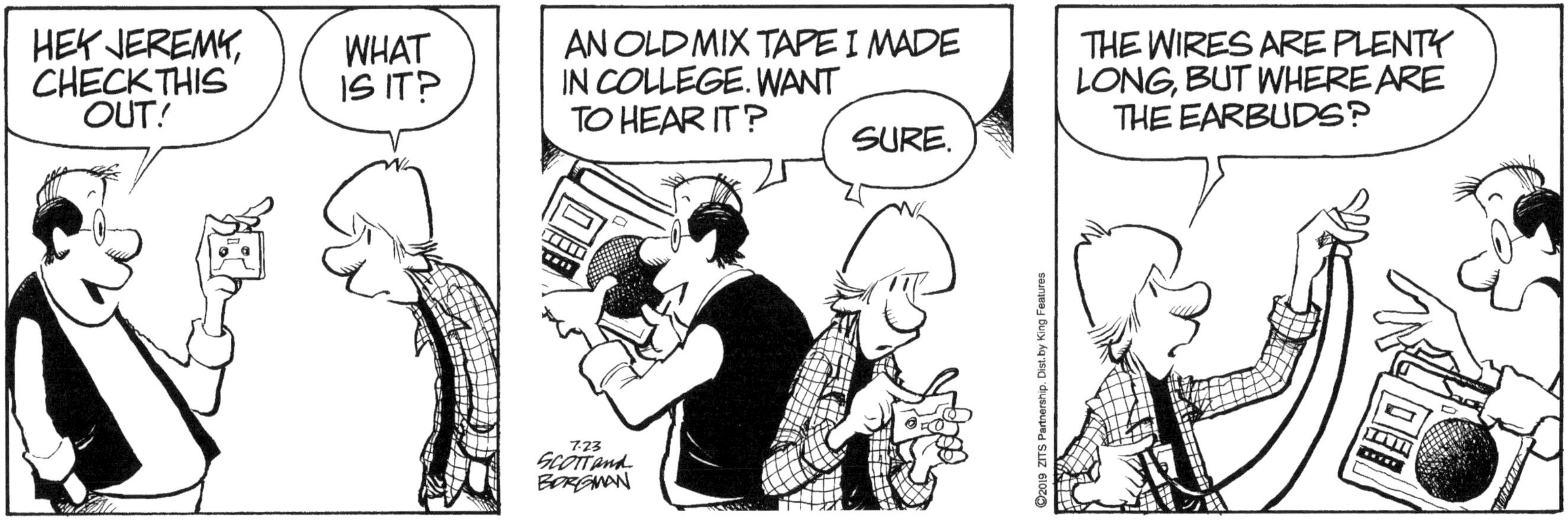
HEY JEREMY, CHECK THIS OUT!
WHAT IS IT?
AN OLD MIX TAPE I MADE IN COLLEGE. WANT TO HEAR IT?
SURE.
7·23
SCOTT and BORGMAN
©2019 ZITS Partnership. Dist.by King Features
THE WIRES ARE PLENTY LONG, BUT WHERE ARE THE EARBUDS?

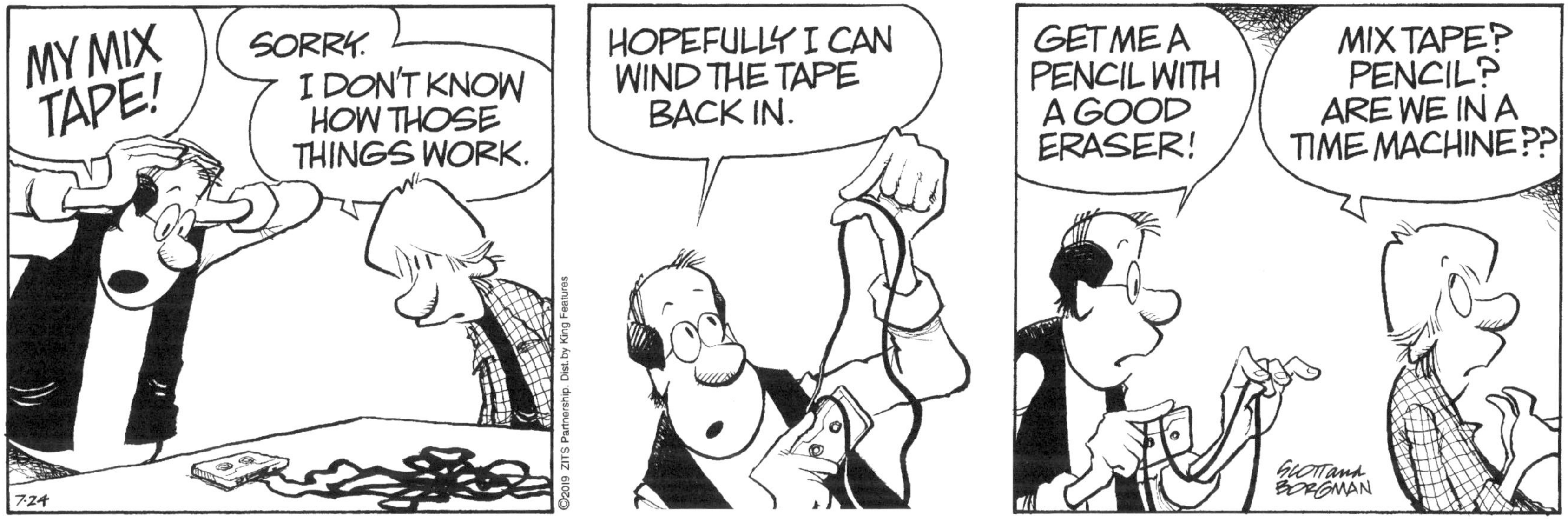
MY MIX TAPE!
SORRY. I DON'T KNOW HOW THOSE THINGS WORK.
7·24
©2019 ZITS Partnership. Dist. by King Features
HOPEFULLY I CAN WIND THE TAPE BACK IN.
GET ME A PENCIL WITH A GOOD ERASER!
MIX TAPE? PENCIL? ARE WE IN A TIME MACHINE??
SCOTT and BORGMAN

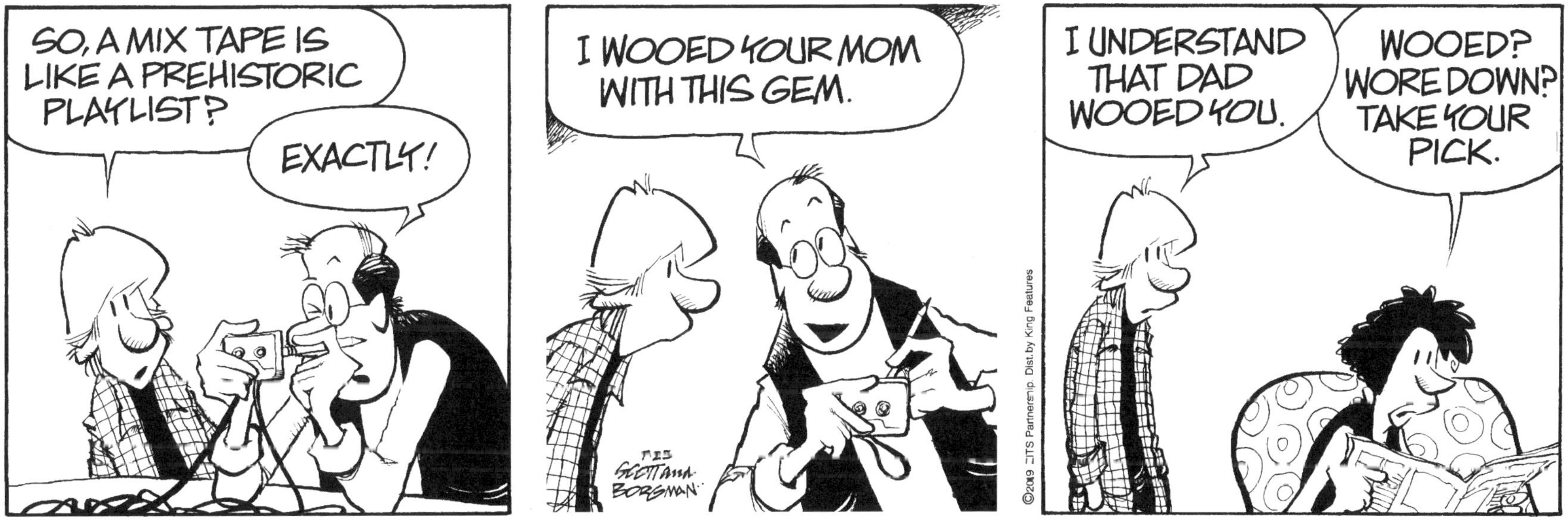
SO, A MIX TAPE IS LIKE A PREHISTORIC PLAYLIST?
EXACTLY!
I WOOED YOUR MOM WITH THIS GEM.
SCOTT and BORGMAN
I UNDERSTAND THAT DAD WOOED YOU.
WOOED? WORE DOWN? TAKE YOUR PICK.
©2019 ZITS Partnership. Dist. by King Features

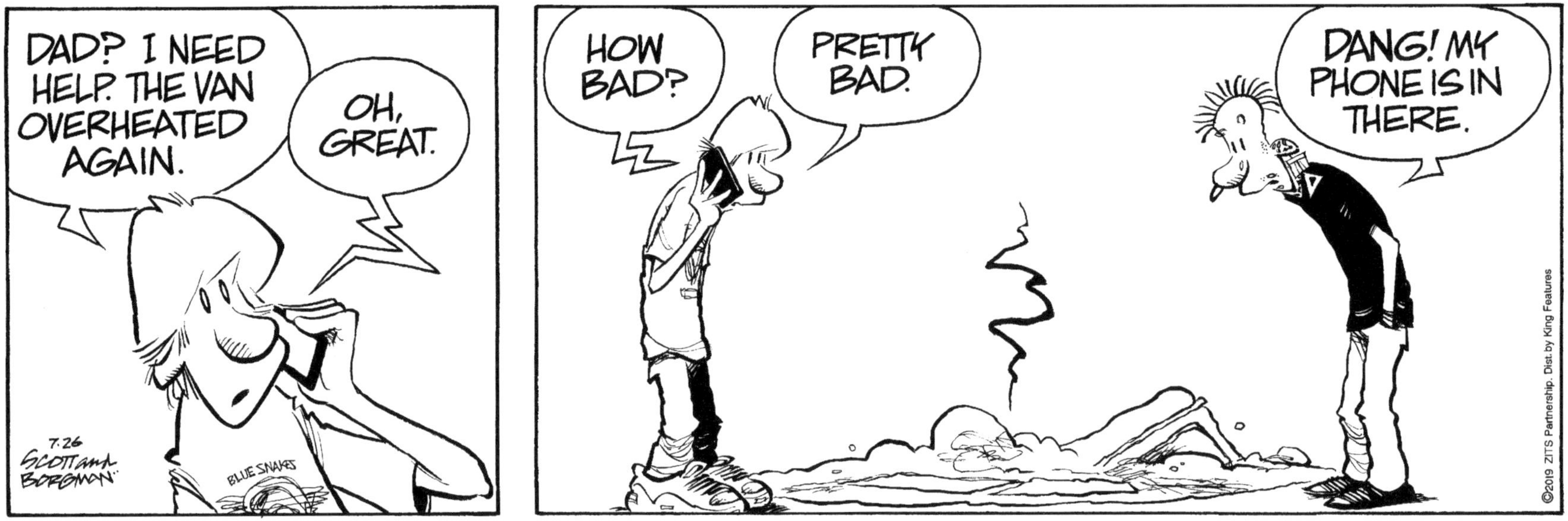
DAD? I NEED HELP. THE VAN OVERHEATED AGAIN.
OH, GREAT.
HOW BAD?
PRETTY BAD.
DANG! MY PHONE IS IN THERE.
BLUE SNAKES
©2019 ZITS Partnership. Dist. by King Features

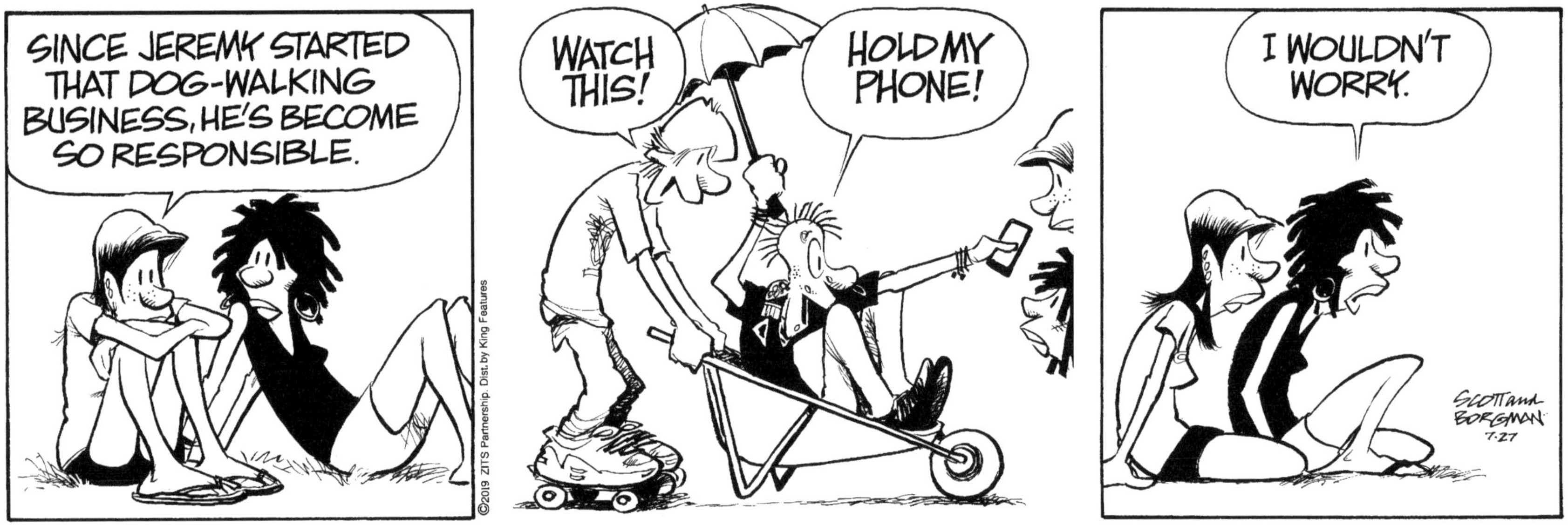
SINCE JEREMY STARTED THAT DOG-WALKING BUSINESS, HE'S BECOME SO RESPONSIBLE.
WATCH THIS!
HOLD MY PHONE!
I WOULDN'T WORRY.
©2019 ZITS Partnership. Dist. by King Features

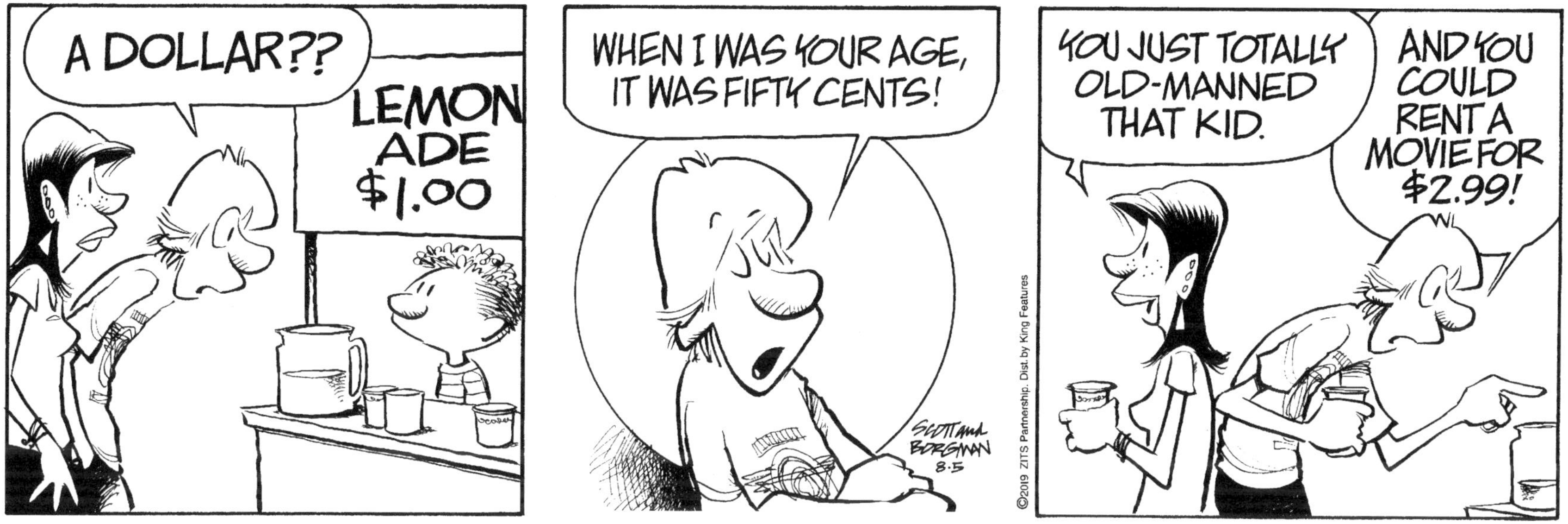
A DOLLAR??
LEMON ADE $1.00
WHEN I WAS YOUR AGE, IT WAS FIFTY CENTS!
SCOTT and BORGMAN 8·5
©2019 ZITS Partnership. Dist. by King Features
YOU JUST TOTALLY OLD-MANNED THAT KID.
AND YOU COULD RENT A MOVIE FOR $2.99!

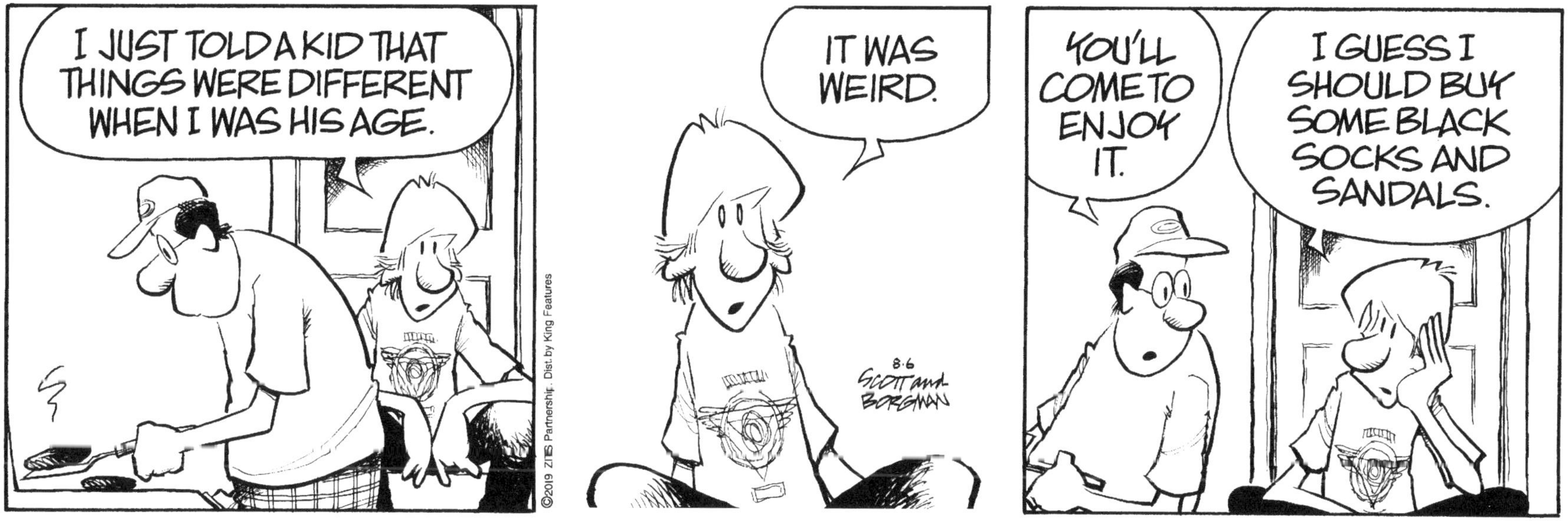
I JUST TOLD A KID THAT THINGS WERE DIFFERENT WHEN I WAS HIS AGE.
©2019 ZITS Partnership. Dist. by King Features
IT WAS WEIRD.
8·6 SCOTT and BORGMAN
YOU'LL COME TO ENJOY IT.
I GUESS I SHOULD BUY SOME BLACK SOCKS AND SANDALS.

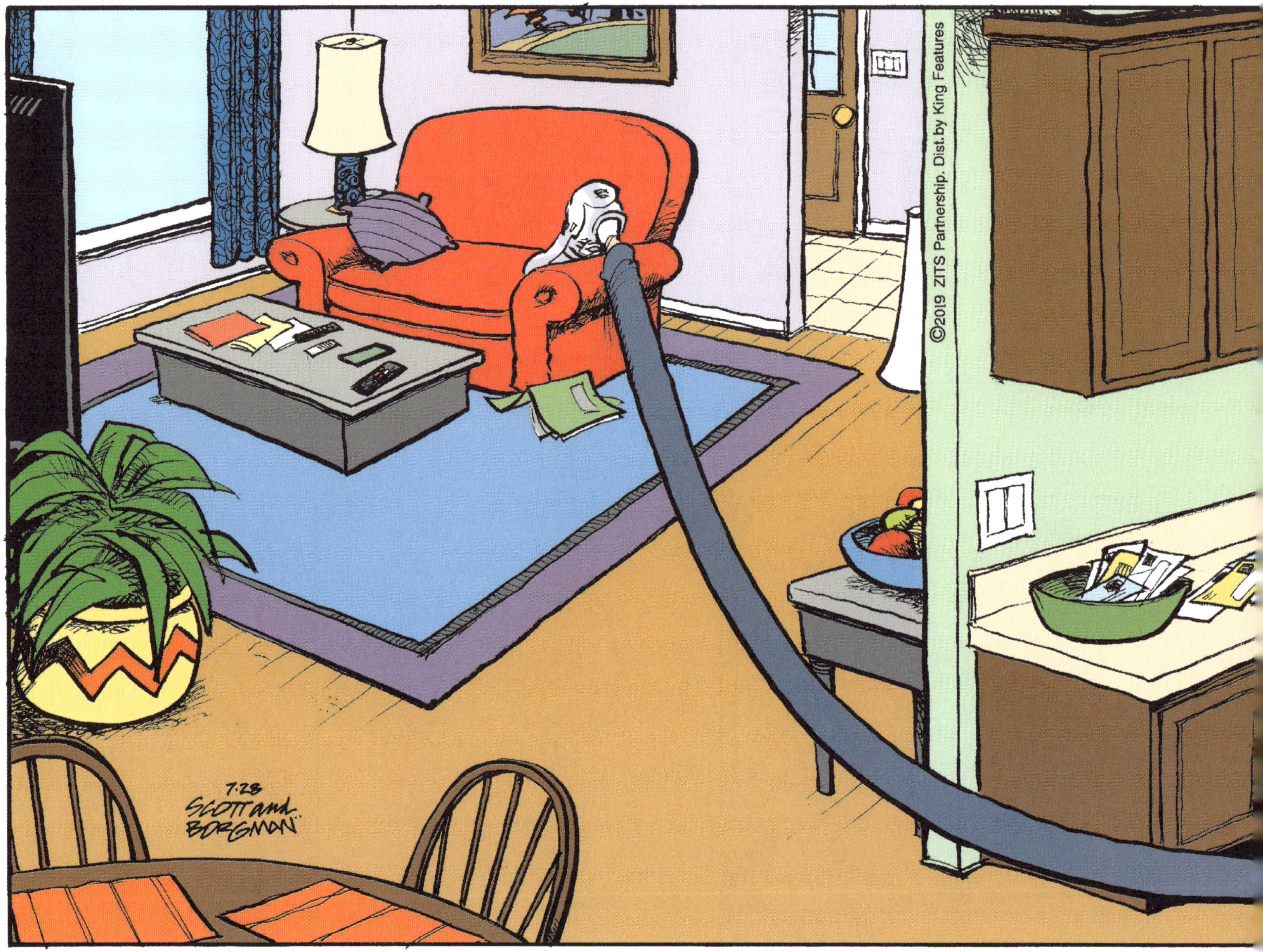
©2019 ZITS Partnership. Dist. by King Features
7·28
SCOTT and BORGMAN

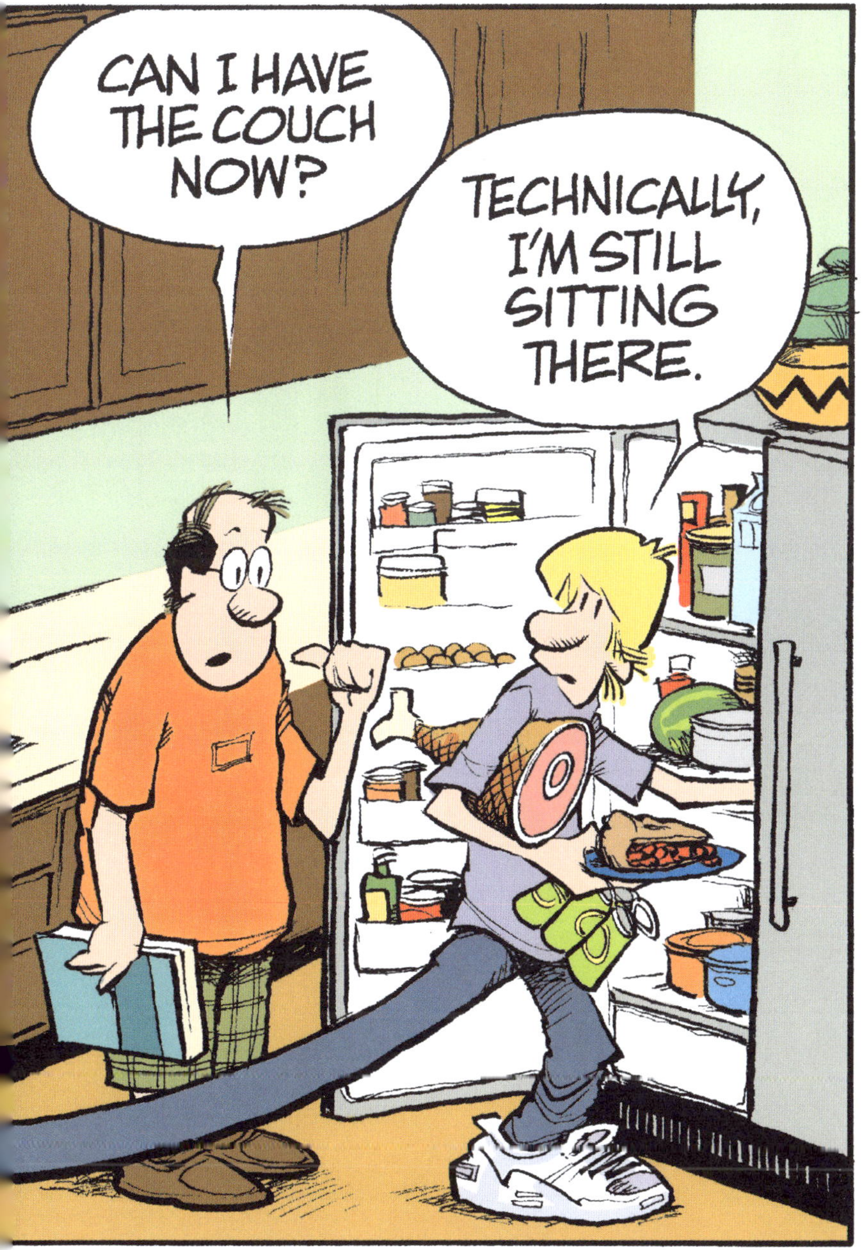
CAN I HAVE THE COUCH NOW?
TECHNICALLY, I'M STILL SITTING THERE.

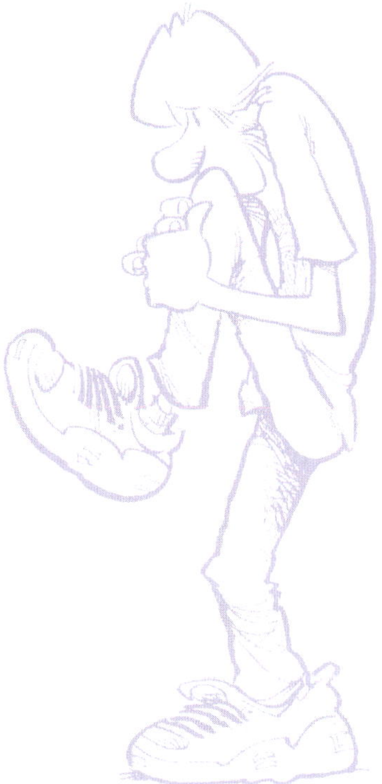

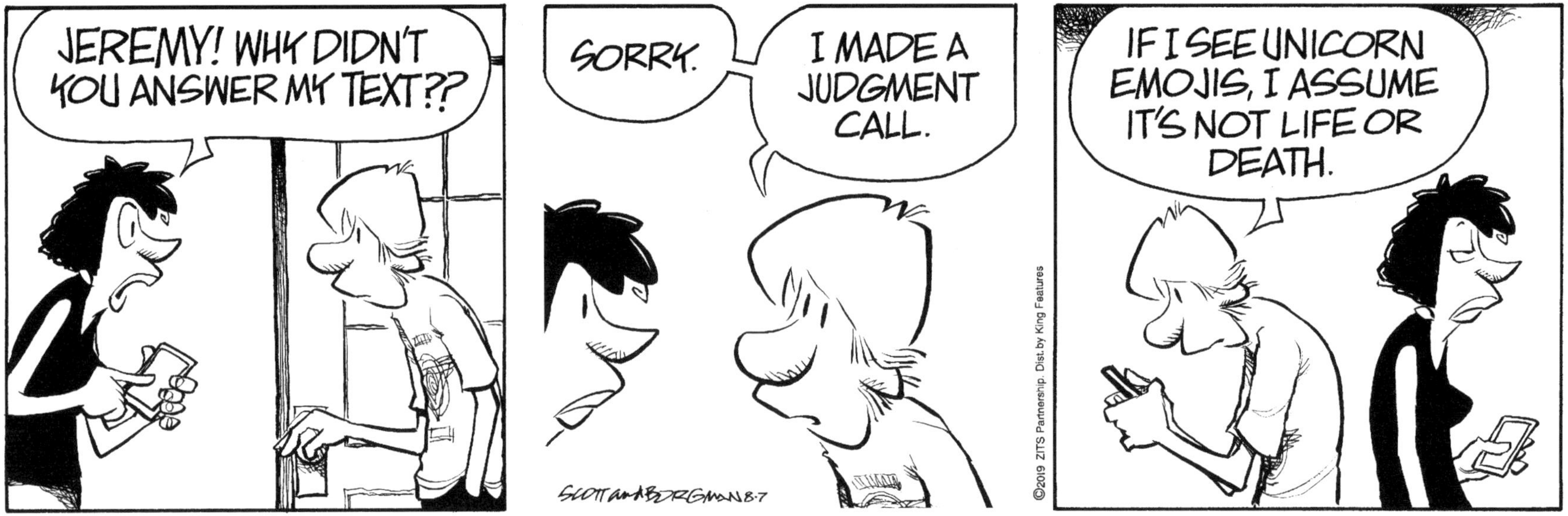
JEREMY! WHY DIDN'T YOU ANSWER MY TEXT??
SORRY.
I MADE A JUDGMENT CALL.
IF I SEE UNICORN EMOJIS, I ASSUME IT'S NOT LIFE OR DEATH.
SCOTT AND BORGMAN 8·7
©2019 ZITS Partnership. Dist. by King Features

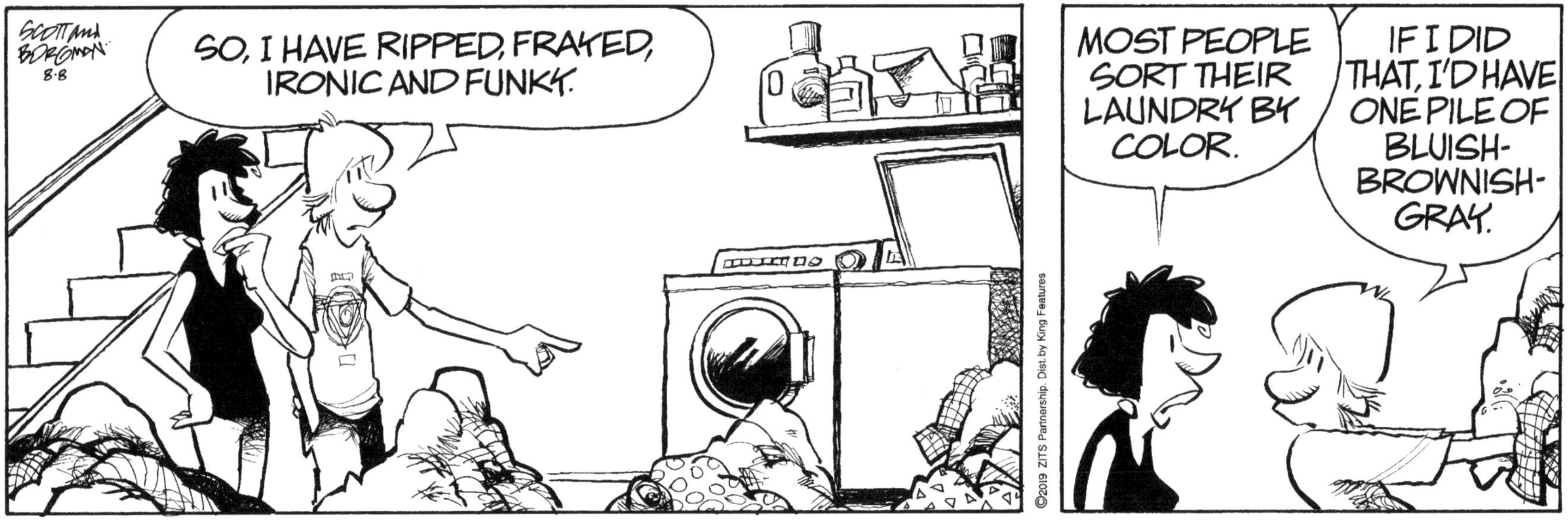
SCOTT AND BORGMAN 8·8
SO, I HAVE RIPPED, FRAYED, IRONIC AND FUNKY.
MOST PEOPLE SORT THEIR LAUNDRY BY COLOR.
IF I DID THAT, I'D HAVE ONE PILE OF BLUISH-BROWNISH-GRAY.
©2019 ZITS Partnership. Dist. by King Features

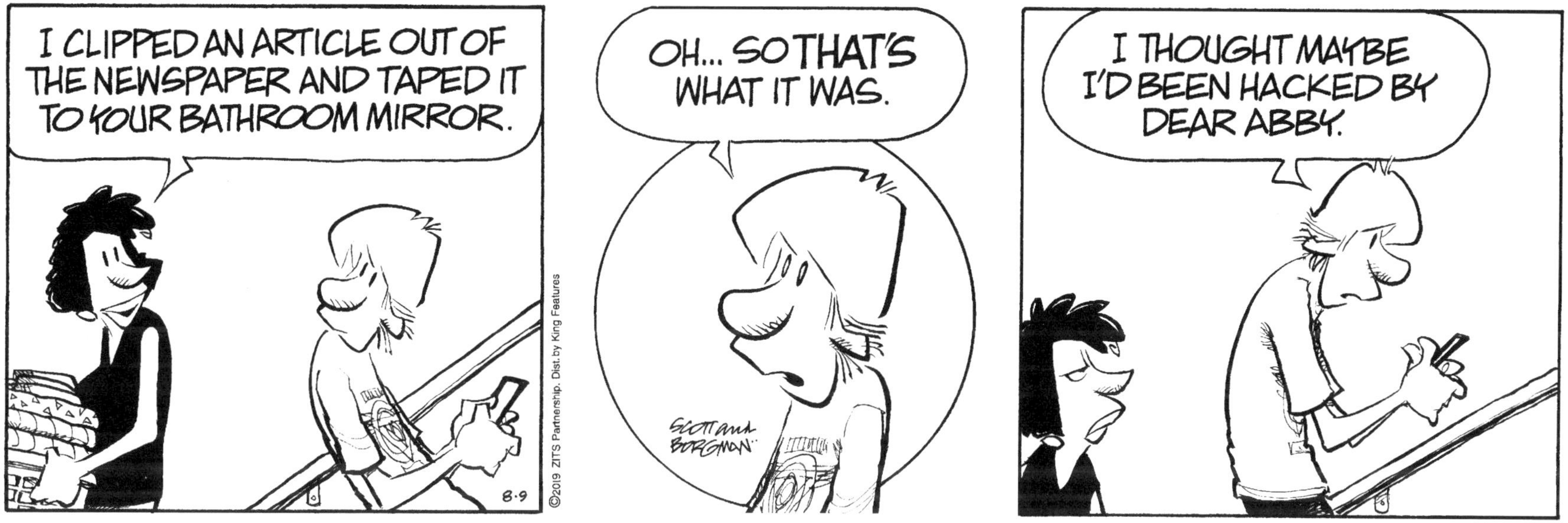
I CLIPPED AN ARTICLE OUT OF THE NEWSPAPER AND TAPED IT TO YOUR BATHROOM MIRROR.
8·9
©2019 ZITS Partnership. Dist. by King Features
OH... SO THAT'S WHAT IT WAS.
SCOTT AND BORGMAN
I THOUGHT MAYBE I'D BEEN HACKED BY DEAR ABBY.

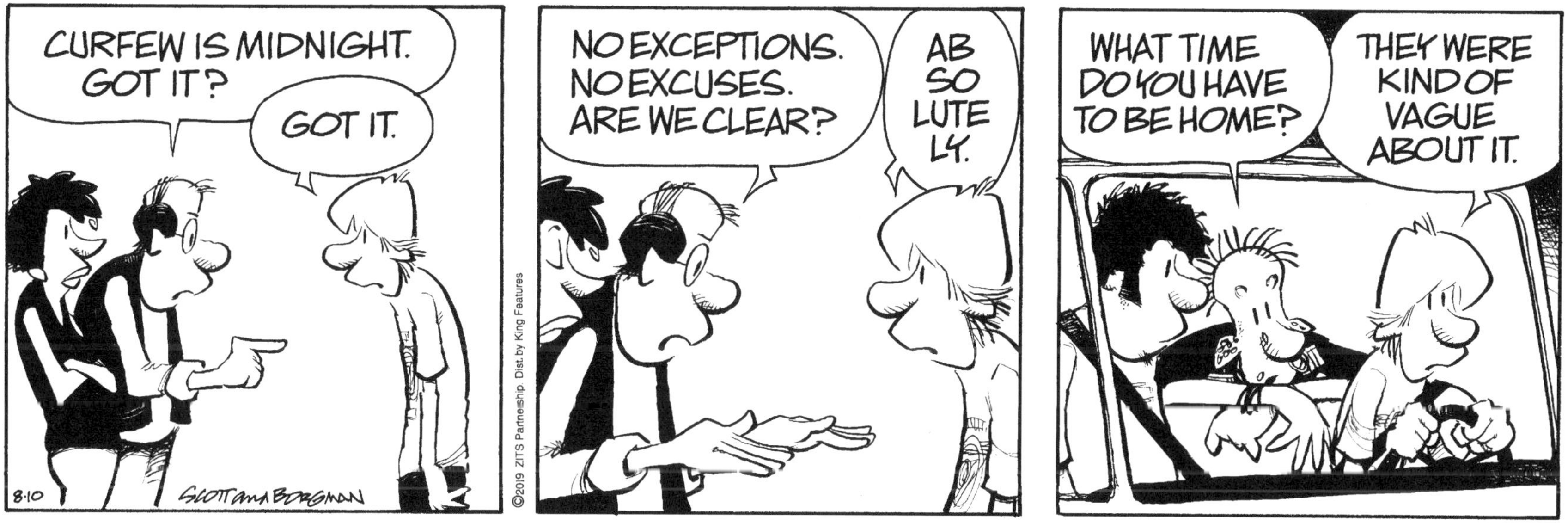
CURFEW IS MIDNIGHT. GOT IT?
GOT IT.
8·10
SCOTT AND BORGMAN
©2019 ZITS Partnership. Dist. by King Features
NO EXCEPTIONS. NO EXCUSES. ARE WE CLEAR?
AB SO LUTE LY.
WHAT TIME DO YOU HAVE TO BE HOME?
THEY WERE KIND OF VAGUE ABOUT IT.

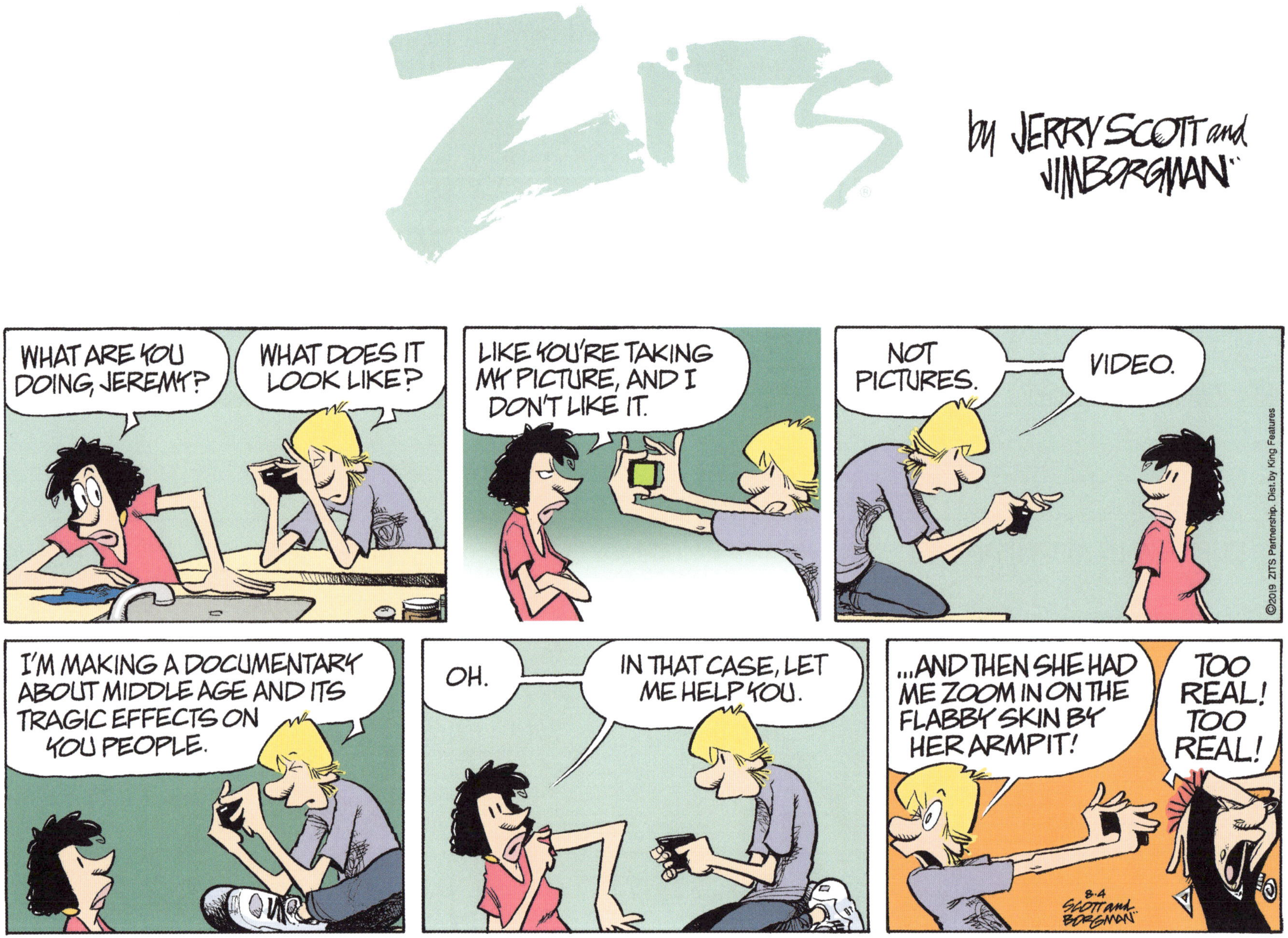
ZITS
by JERRY SCOTT and JIM BORGMAN
WHAT ARE YOU DOING, JEREMY?
WHAT DOES IT LOOK LIKE?
LIKE YOU'RE TAKING MY PICTURE, AND I DON'T LIKE IT.
NOT PICTURES.
VIDEO.
©2019 ZITS Partnership. Dist. by King Features
I'M MAKING A DOCUMENTARY ABOUT MIDDLE AGE AND ITS TRAGIC EFFECTS ON YOU PEOPLE.
OH.
IN THAT CASE, LET ME HELP YOU.
...AND THEN SHE HAD ME ZOOM IN ON THE FLABBY SKIN BY HER ARMPIT!
TOO REAL! TOO REAL!
8-4 SCOTT and BORGMAN

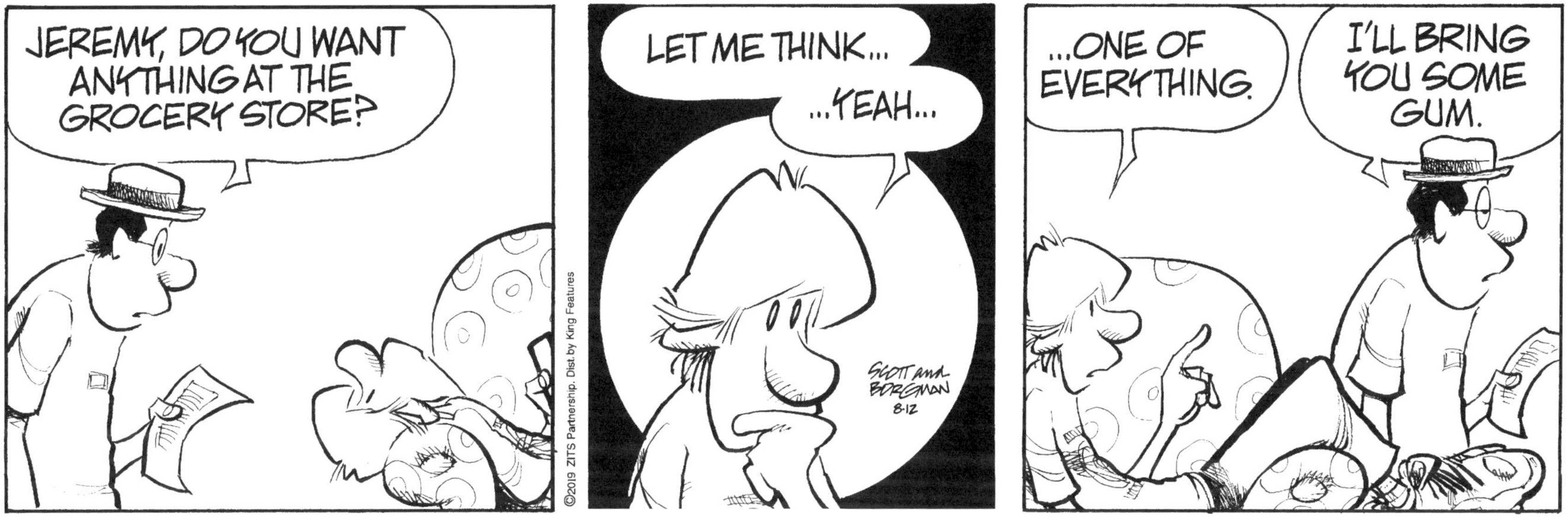
JEREMY, DO YOU WANT ANYTHING AT THE GROCERY STORE?
©2019 ZITS Partnership. Dist. by King Features
LET ME THINK...
...YEAH...
SCOTT AND BORGMAN 8-12
...ONE OF EVERYTHING.
I'LL BRING YOU SOME GUM.

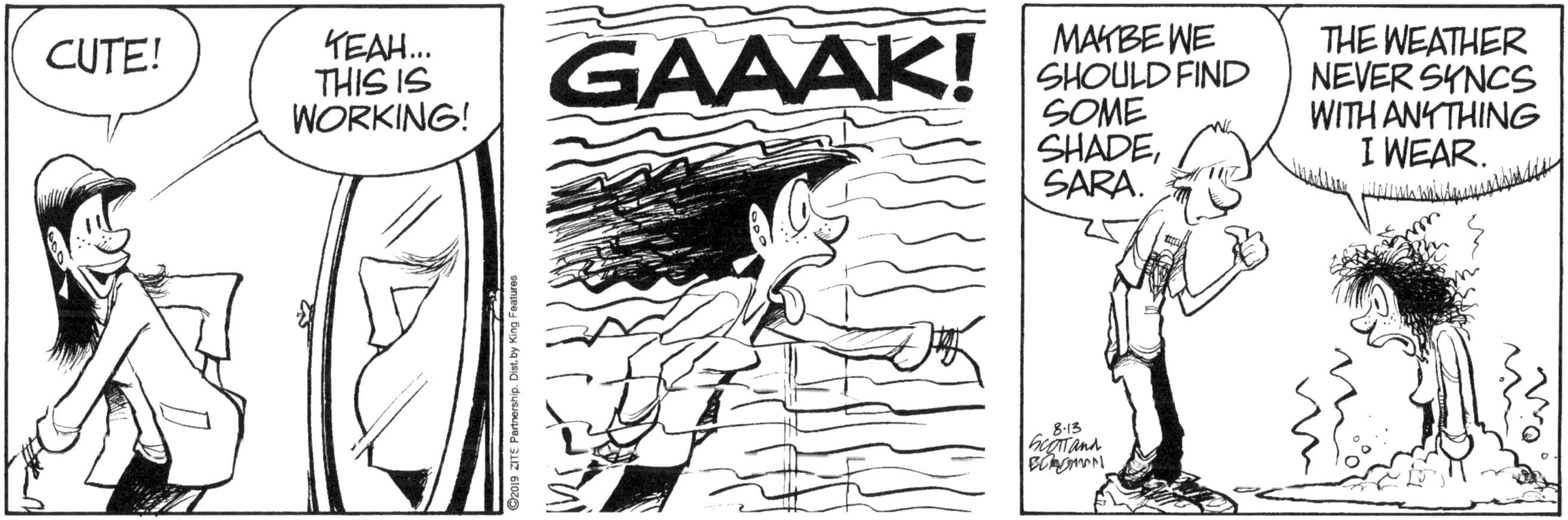
CUTE!
YEAH... THIS IS WORKING!
©2019 ZITS Partnership. Dist. by King Features
GAAAK!
MAYBE WE SHOULD FIND SOME SHADE, SARA.
THE WEATHER NEVER SYNCS WITH ANYTHING I WEAR.
8-13 SCOTT AND BORGMAN

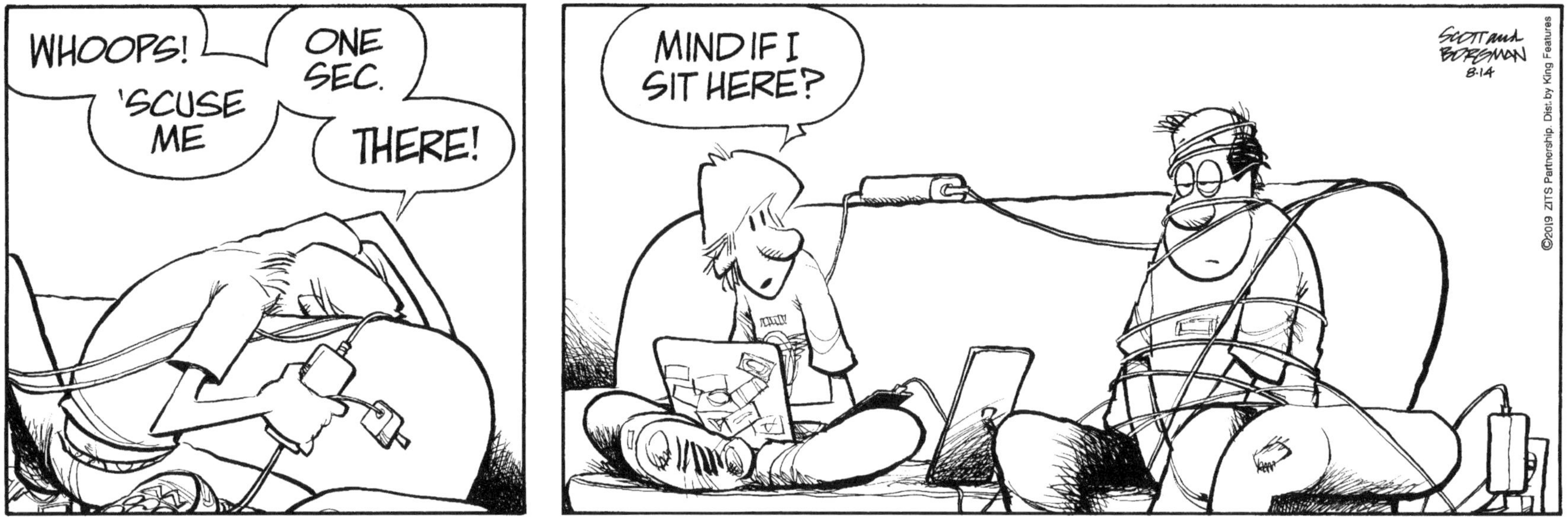
WHOOPS!
'SCUSE ME
ONE SEC.
THERE!
MIND IF I SIT HERE?
SCOTT AND BORGMAN 8·14
©2019 ZITS Partnership. Dist. by King Features

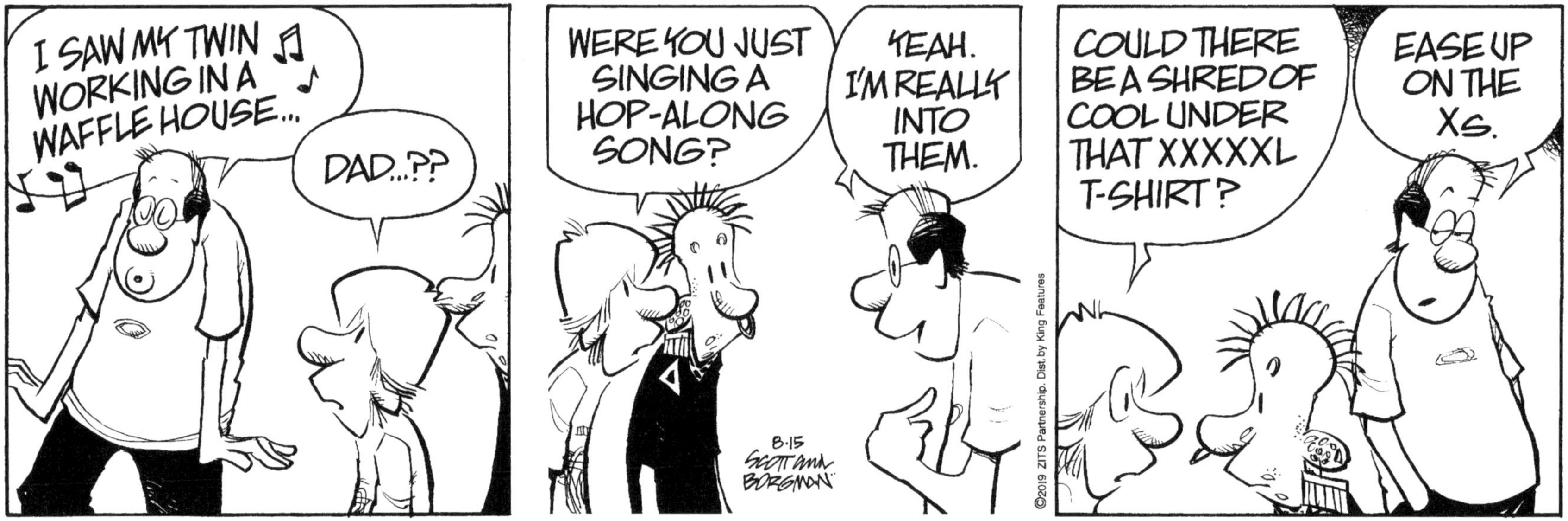
I SAW MY TWIN WORKING IN A WAFFLE HOUSE...
DAD...??
WERE YOU JUST SINGING A HOP-ALONG SONG?
YEAH. I'M REALLY INTO THEM.
8·15 SCOTT AND BORGMAN
©2019 ZITS Partnership. Dist. by King Features
COULD THERE BE A SHRED OF COOL UNDER THAT XXXXXL T-SHIRT?
EASE UP ON THE XS.

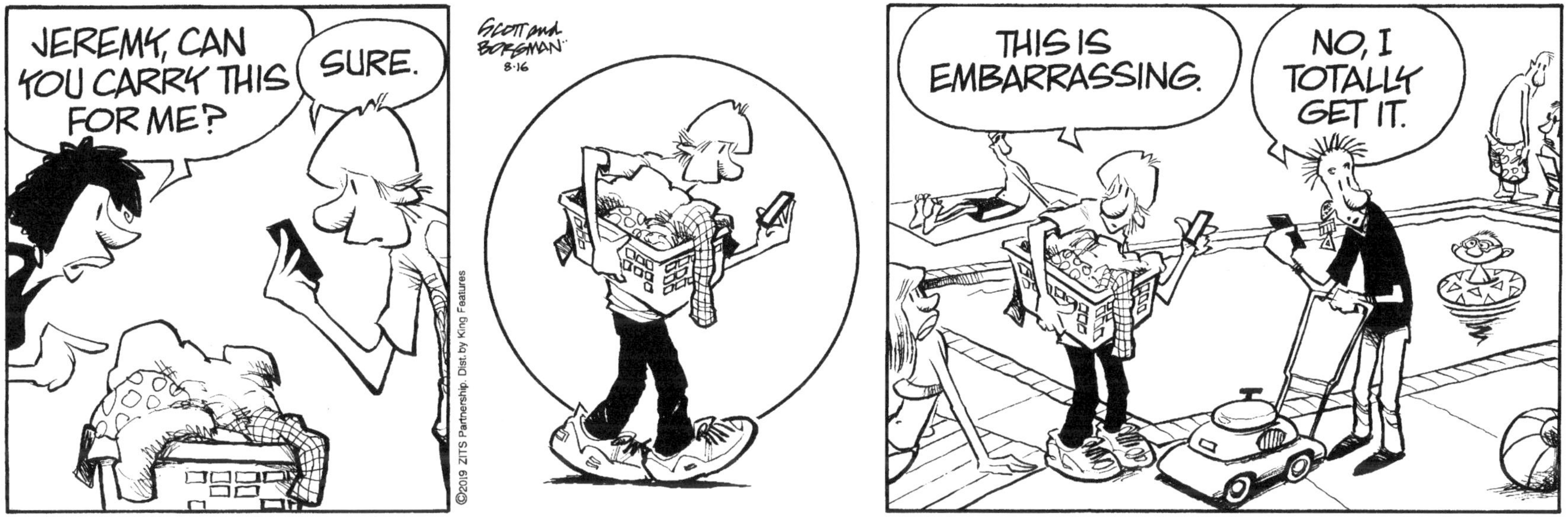
JEREMY, CAN YOU CARRY THIS FOR ME?
SURE.
SCOTT and BORGMAN 8·16
©2019 ZITS Partnership. Dist. by King Features
THIS IS EMBARRASSING.
NO, I TOTALLY GET IT.

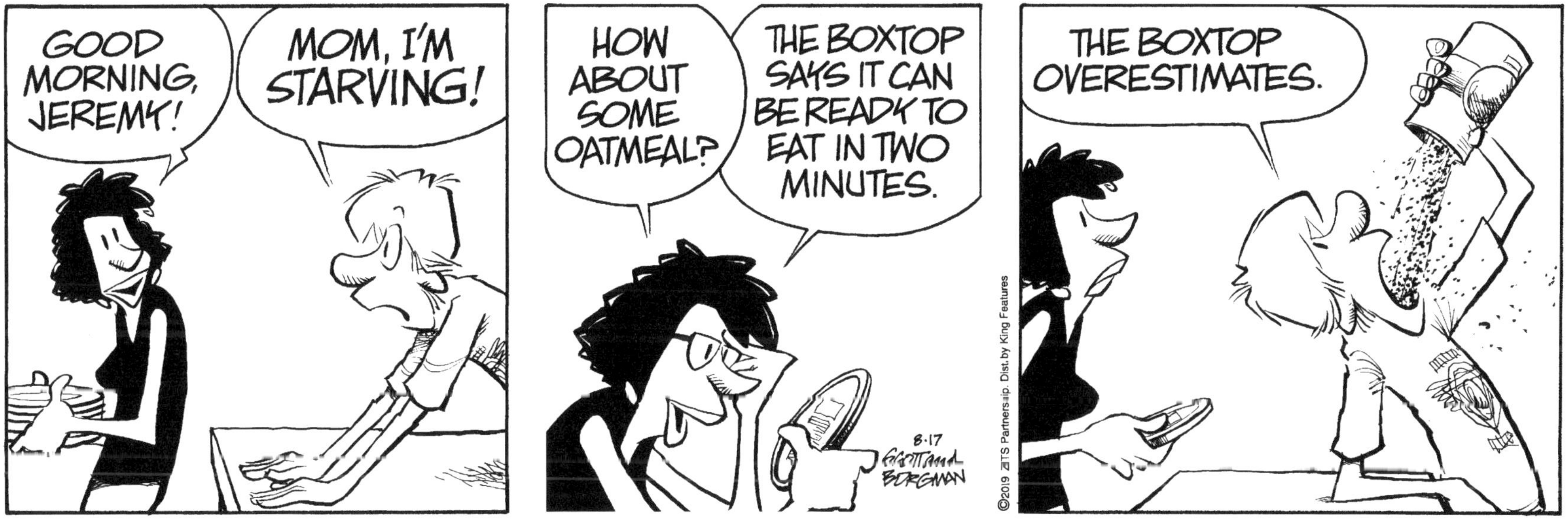
GOOD MORNING, JEREMY!
MOM, I'M STARVING!
HOW ABOUT SOME OATMEAL?
THE BOXTOP SAYS IT CAN BE READY TO EAT IN TWO MINUTES.
8·17 SCOTT and BORGMAN
©2019 ZITS Partnership. Dist. by King Features
THE BOXTOP OVERESTIMATES.

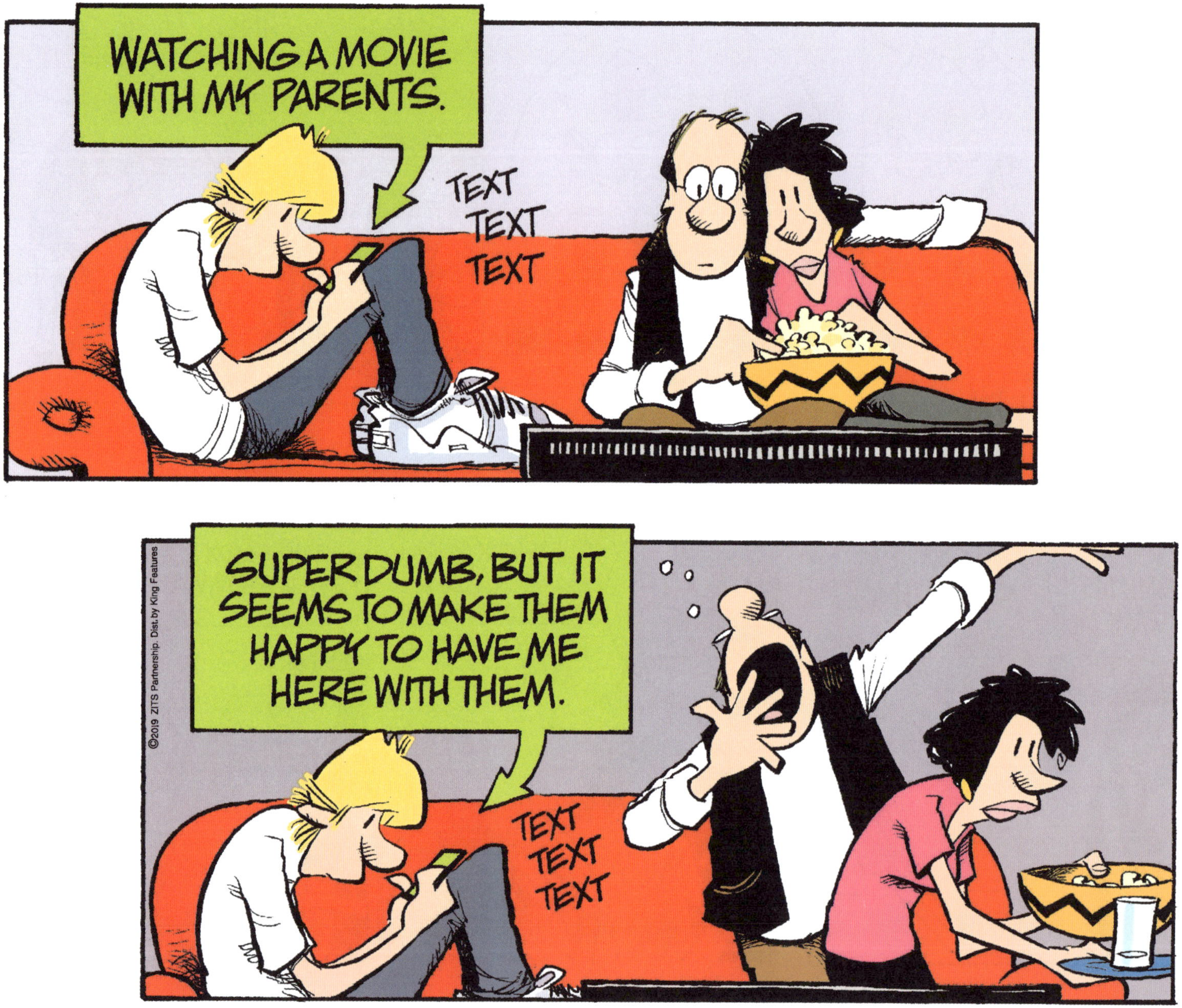
WATCHING A MOVIE WITH MY PARENTS.
TEXT TEXT TEXT
SUPER DUMB, BUT IT SEEMS TO MAKE THEM HAPPY TO HAVE ME HERE WITH THEM.
TEXT TEXT TEXT
©2019 ZITS Partnership. Dist. by King Features

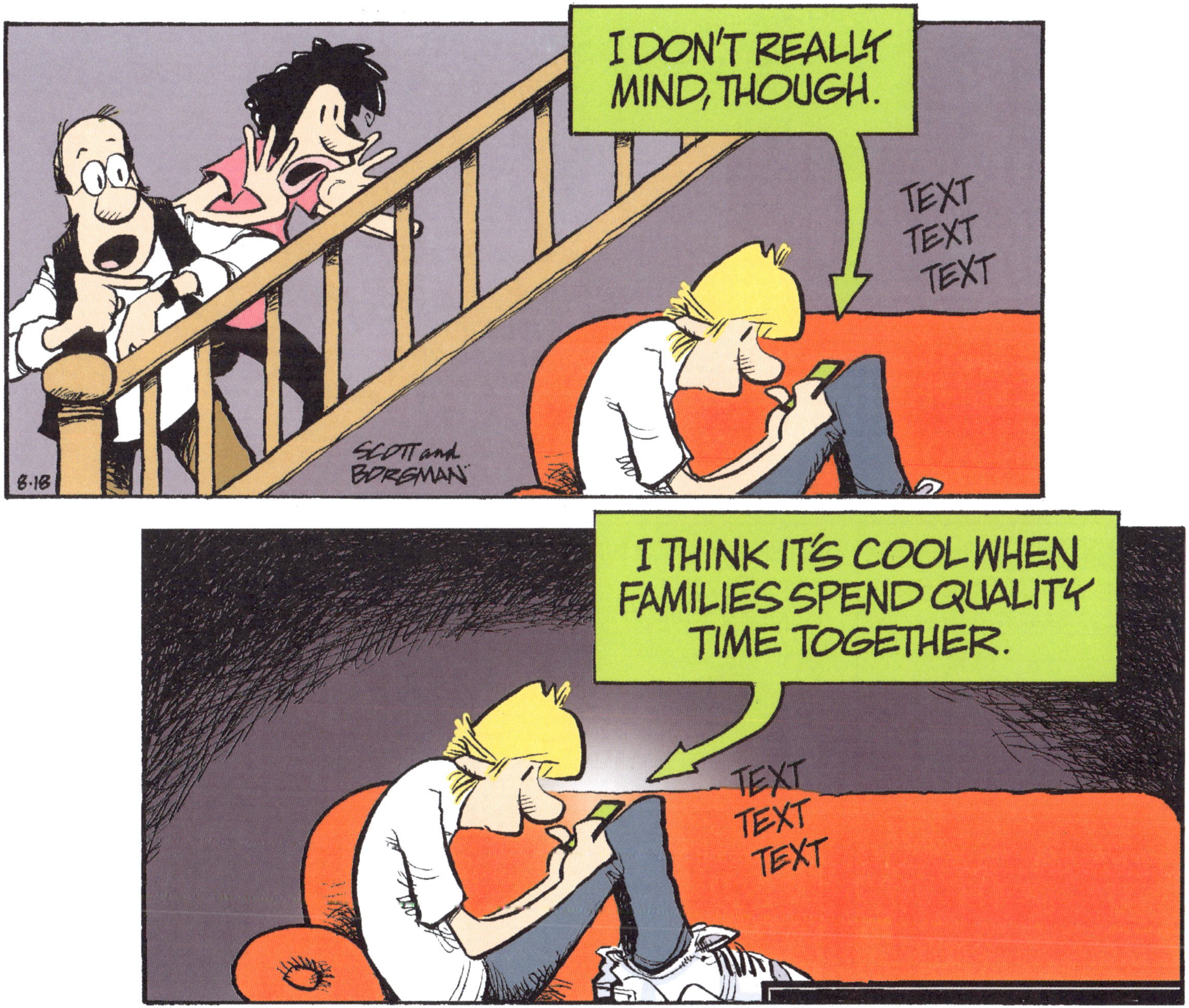
I DON'T REALLY MIND, THOUGH.
TEXT
TEXT
TEXT
SCOTT and BORGMAN
8·18
I THINK IT'S COOL WHEN FAMILIES SPEND QUALITY TIME TOGETHER.
TEXT
TEXT
TEXT

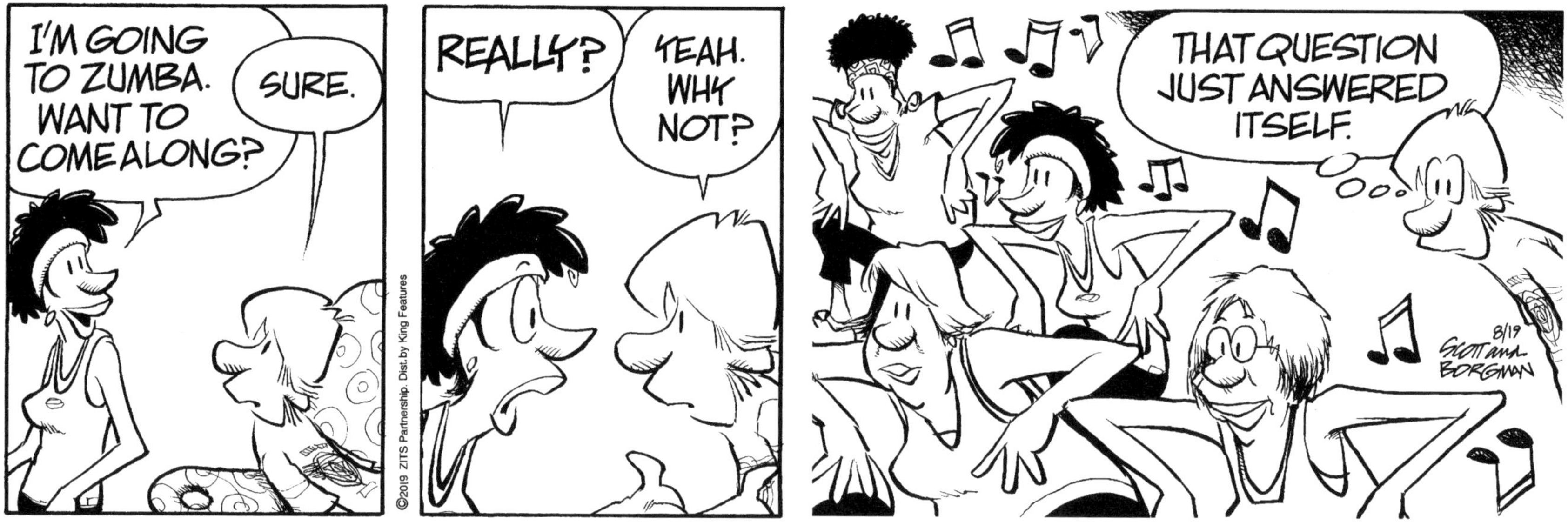
I'M GOING TO ZUMBA. WANT TO COME ALONG?
SURE.
©2019 ZITS Partnership. Dist. by King Features
REALLY?
YEAH. WHY NOT?
THAT QUESTION JUST ANSWERED ITSELF.
8/19
SCOTT and BORGMAN

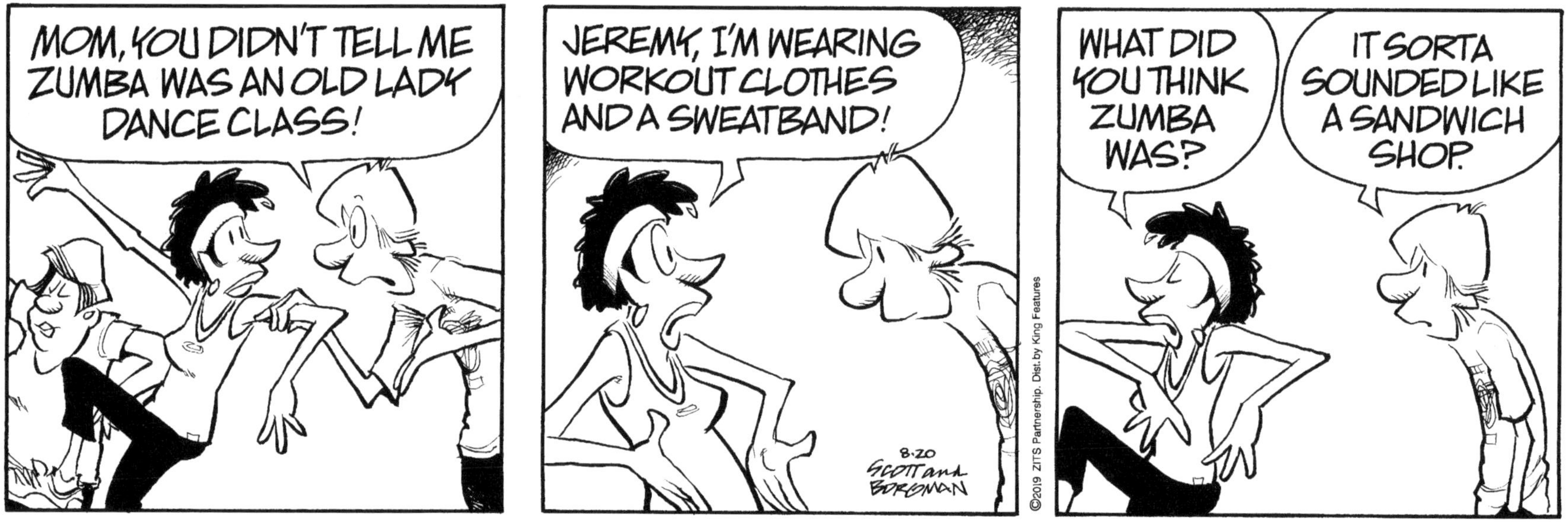
MOM, YOU DIDN'T TELL ME ZUMBA WAS AN OLD LADY DANCE CLASS!
JEREMY, I'M WEARING WORKOUT CLOTHES AND A SWEATBAND!
8.20
SCOTT and BORGMAN
©2019 ZITS Partnership. Dist. by King Features
WHAT DID YOU THINK ZUMBA WAS?
IT SORTA SOUNDED LIKE A SANDWICH SHOP.

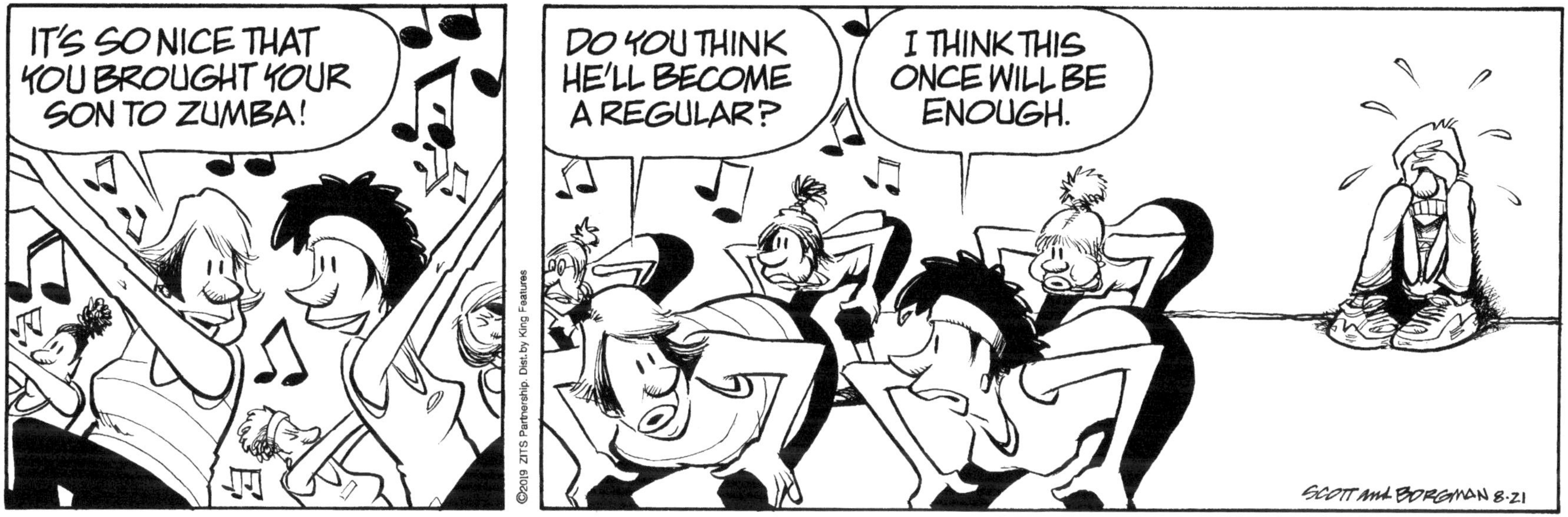
IT'S SO NICE THAT YOU BROUGHT YOUR SON TO ZUMBA!
DO YOU THINK HE'LL BECOME A REGULAR?
I THINK THIS ONCE WILL BE ENOUGH.
©2019 ZITS Partnership. Dist. by King Features
SCOTT AND BORGMAN 8-21

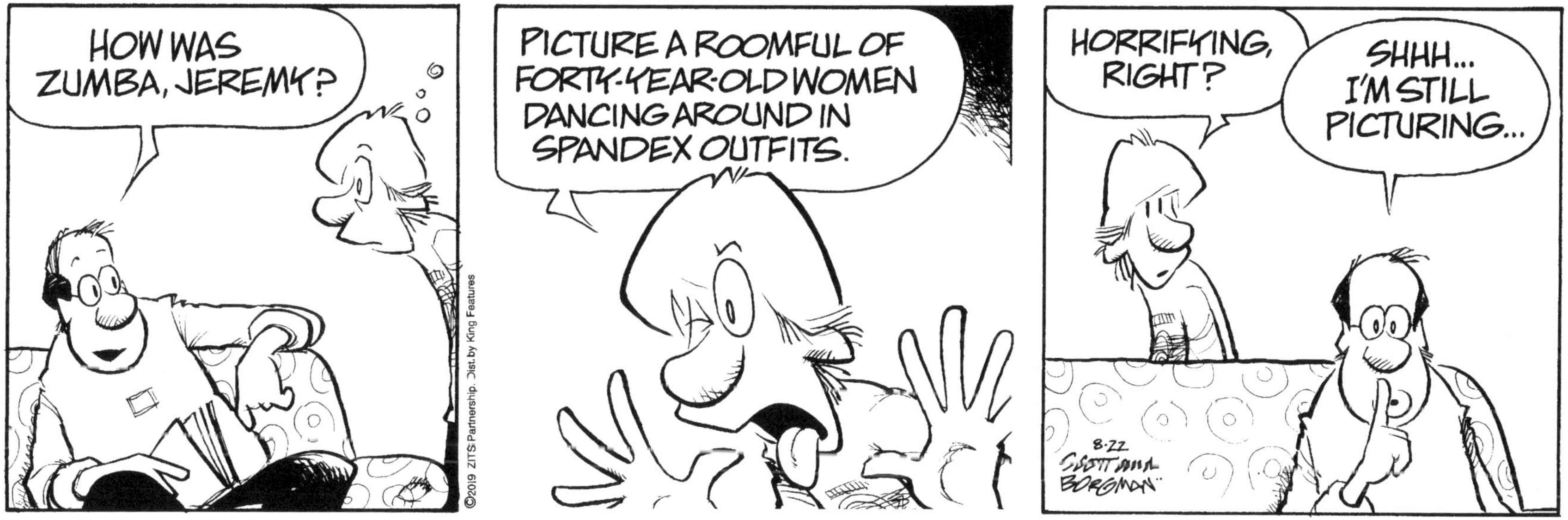
HOW WAS ZUMBA, JEREMY?
©2019 ZITS Partnership. Dist. by King Features
PICTURE A ROOMFUL OF FORTY-YEAR-OLD WOMEN DANCING AROUND IN SPANDEX OUTFITS.
HORRIFYING, RIGHT?
SHHH... I'M STILL PICTURING...
8-22 SCOTT AND BORGMAN

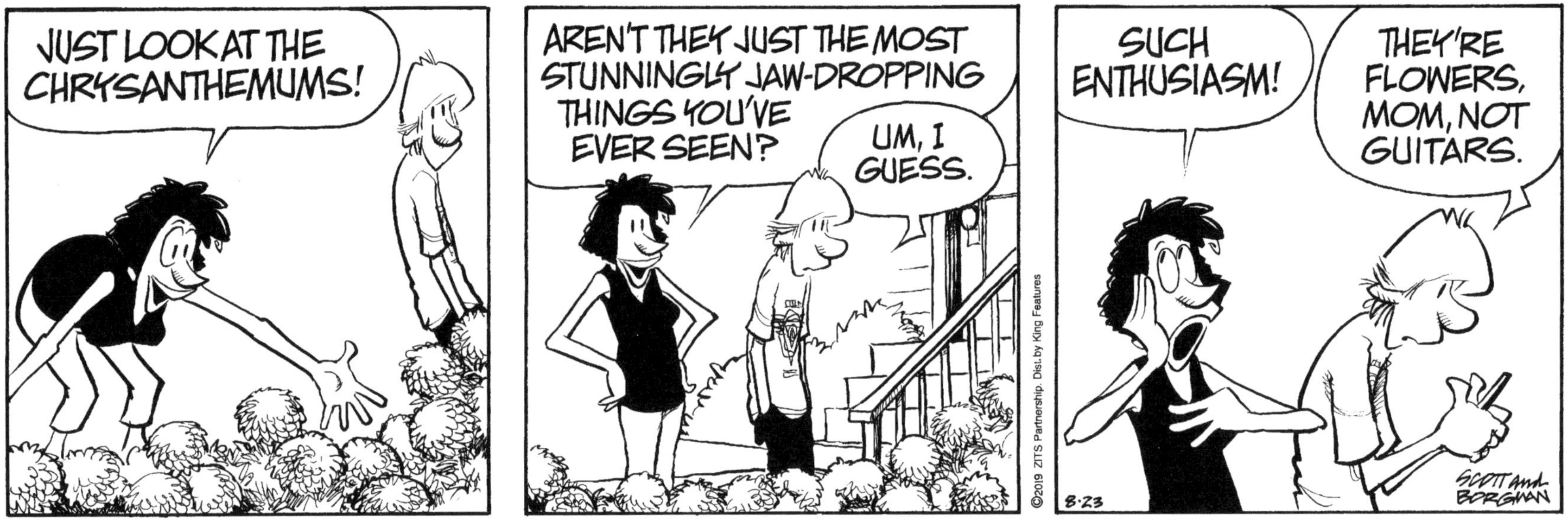
JUST LOOK AT THE CHRYSANTHEMUMS!
AREN'T THEY JUST THE MOST STUNNINGLY JAW-DROPPING THINGS YOU'VE EVER SEEN?
UM, I GUESS.
©2019 ZITS Partnership. Dist. by King Features
8·23
SUCH ENTHUSIASM!
THEY'RE FLOWERS, MOM, NOT GUITARS.
SCOTT AND BORGMAN

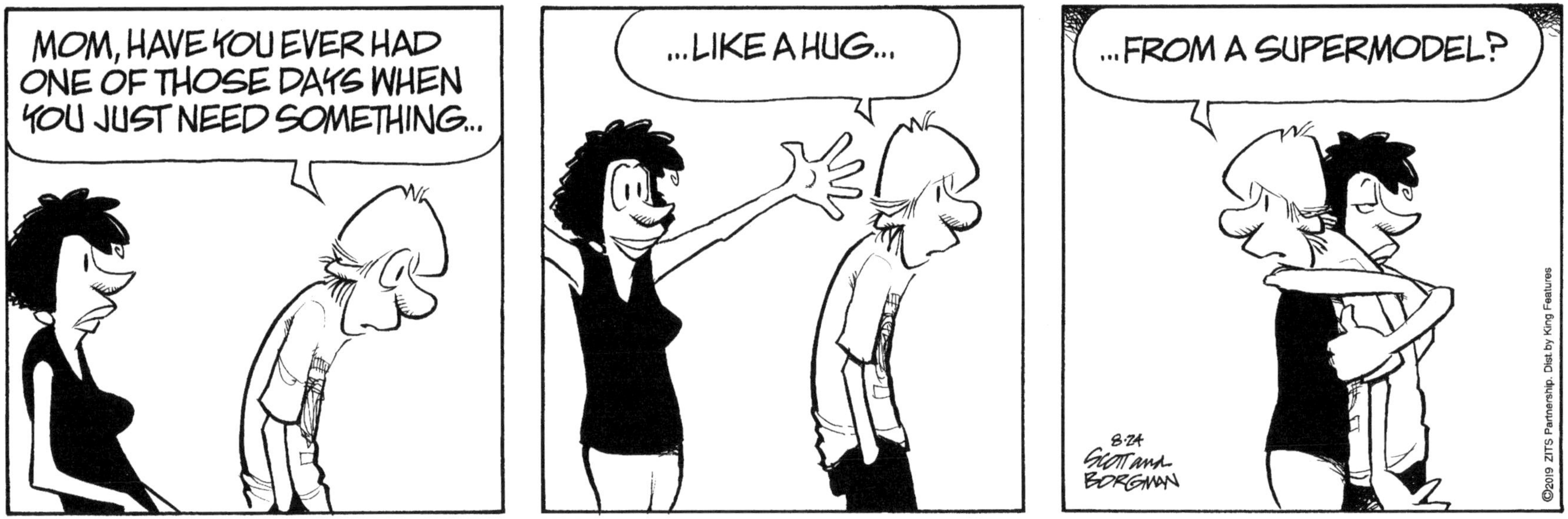
MOM, HAVE YOU EVER HAD ONE OF THOSE DAYS WHEN YOU JUST NEED SOMETHING...
...LIKE A HUG...
...FROM A SUPERMODEL?
8·24
SCOTT AND BORGMAN
©2019 ZITS Partnership. Dist. by King Features

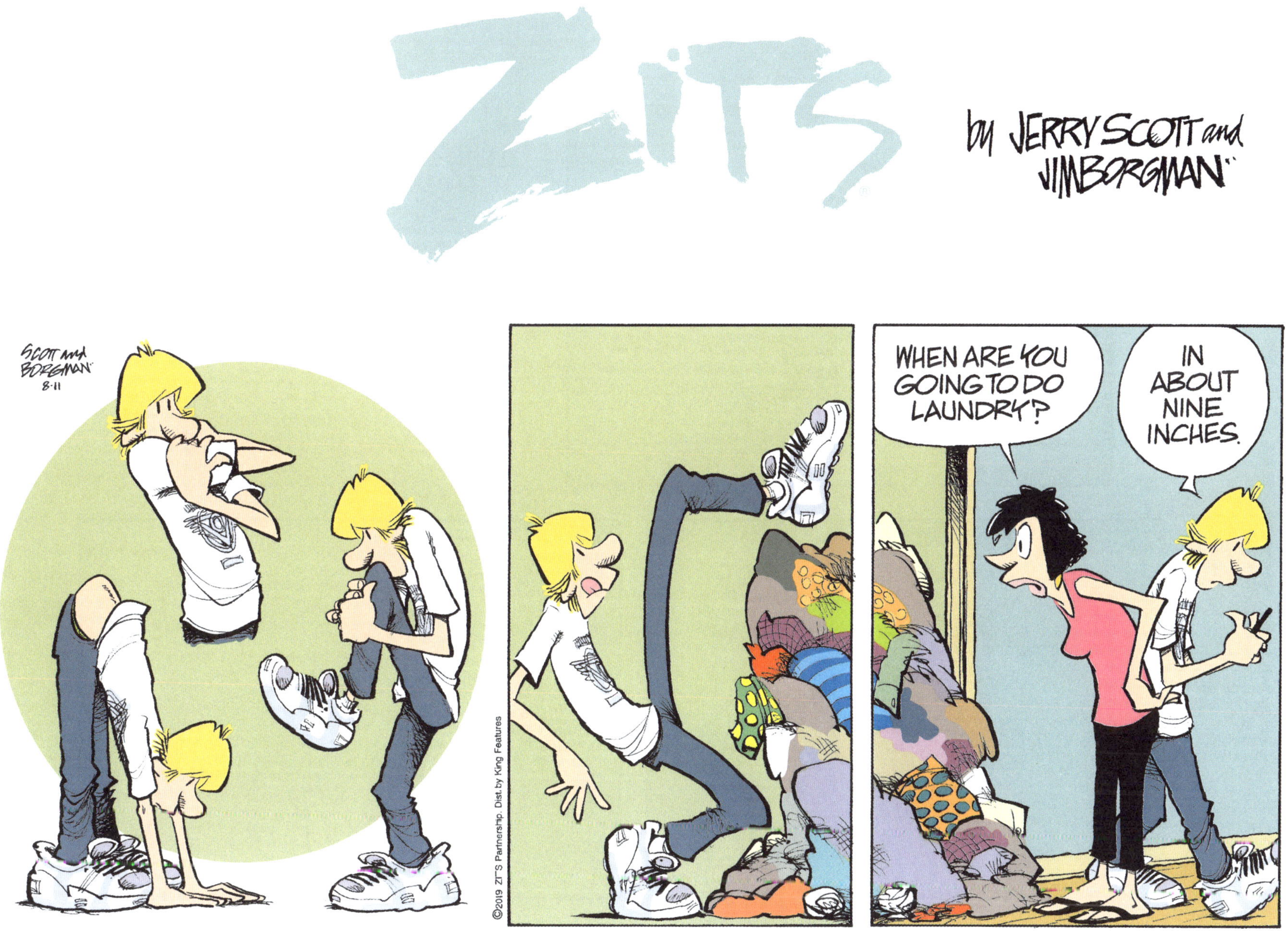
ZITS
by JERRY SCOTT and JIM BORGMAN
SCOTT AND BORGMAN 8-11
©2019 ZIT'S Partnership. Dist. by King Features
WHEN ARE YOU GOING TO DO LAUNDRY?
IN ABOUT NINE INCHES.

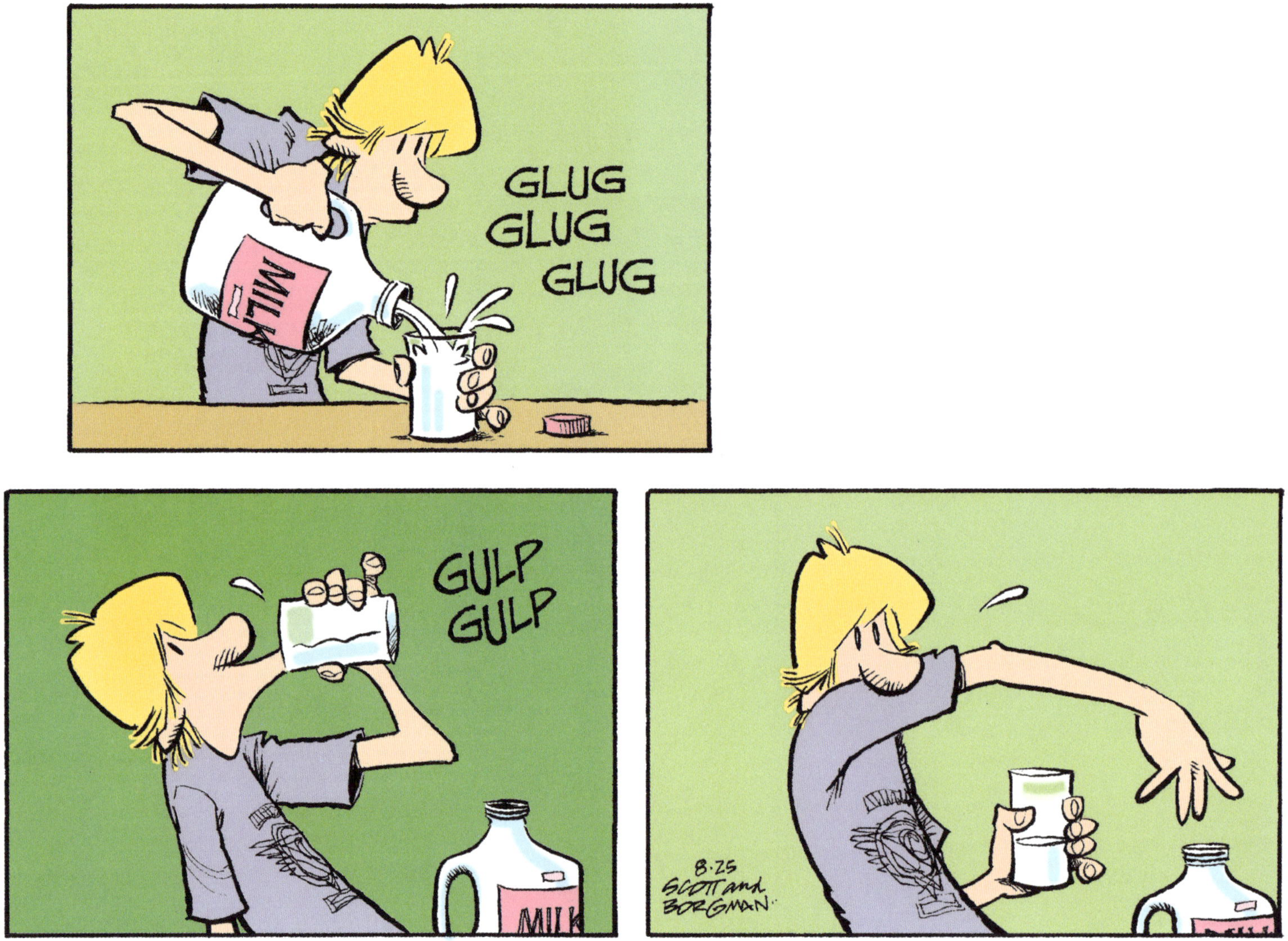
GLUG
GLUG
GLUG
MILK
GULP
GULP
MILK
8·25
SCOTT and
BORGMAN

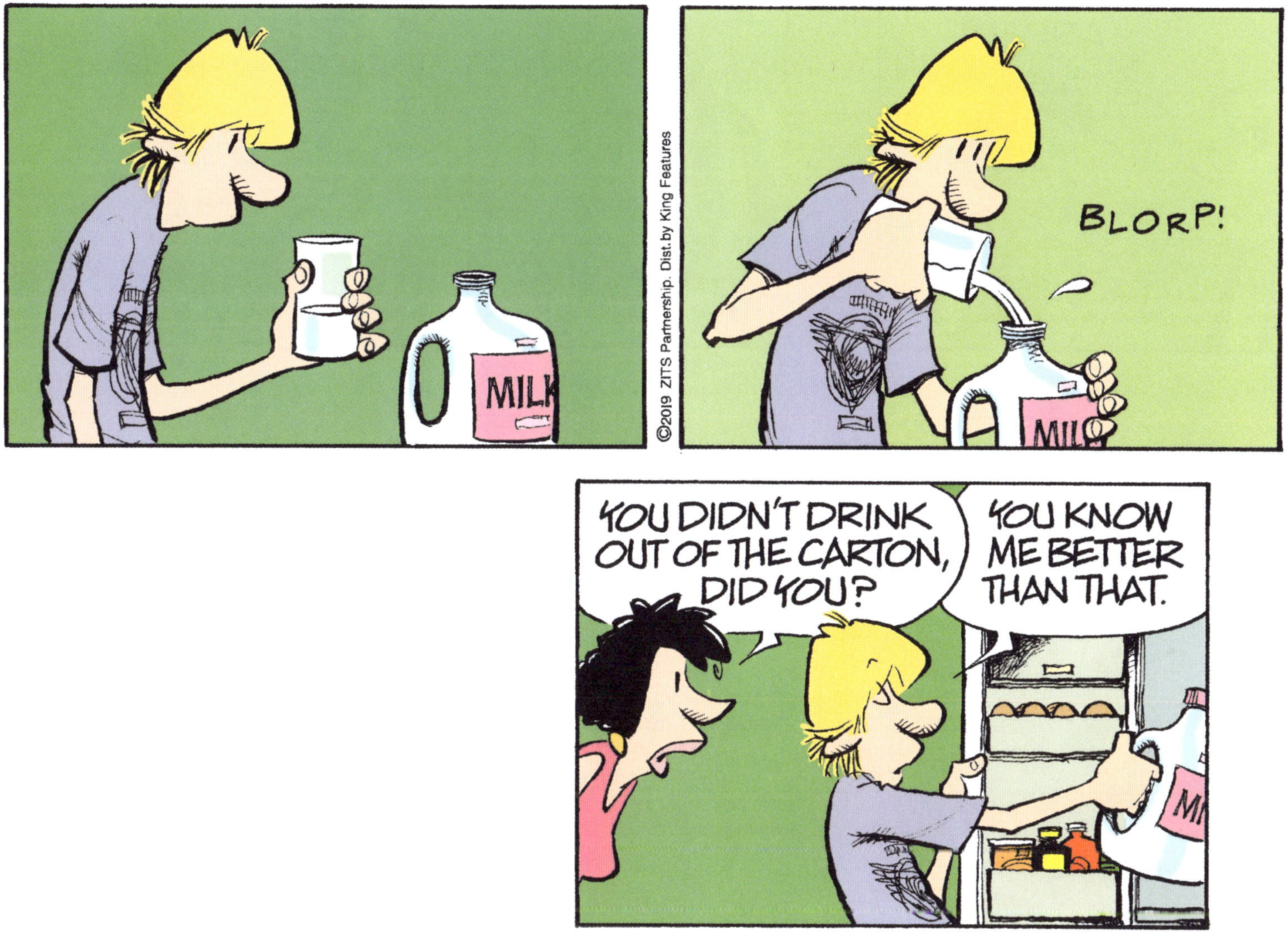
MILK
BLORP!
YOU DIDN'T DRINK OUT OF THE CARTON, DID YOU?
YOU KNOW ME BETTER THAN THAT.

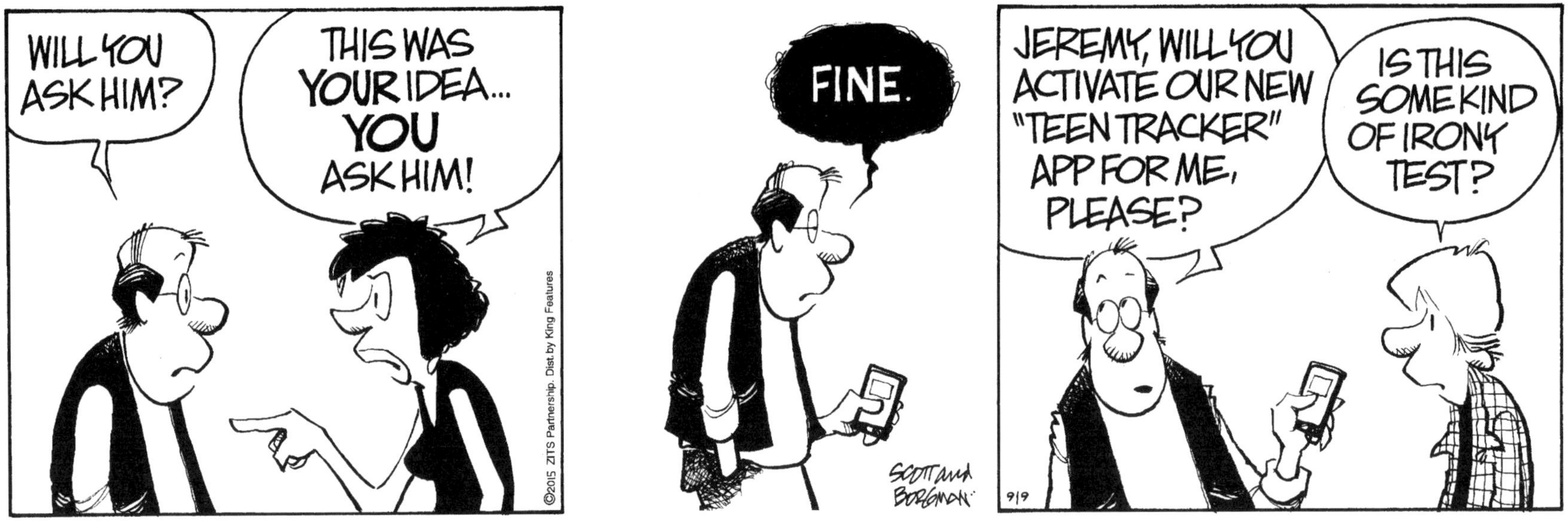
WILL YOU ASK HIM?
THIS WAS YOUR IDEA... YOU ASK HIM!
FINE.
JEREMY, WILL YOU ACTIVATE OUR NEW "TEEN TRACKER" APP FOR ME, PLEASE?
IS THIS SOME KIND OF IRONY TEST?
©2015 ZITS Partnership. Dist. by King Features
SCOTT and BORGMAN
9/9

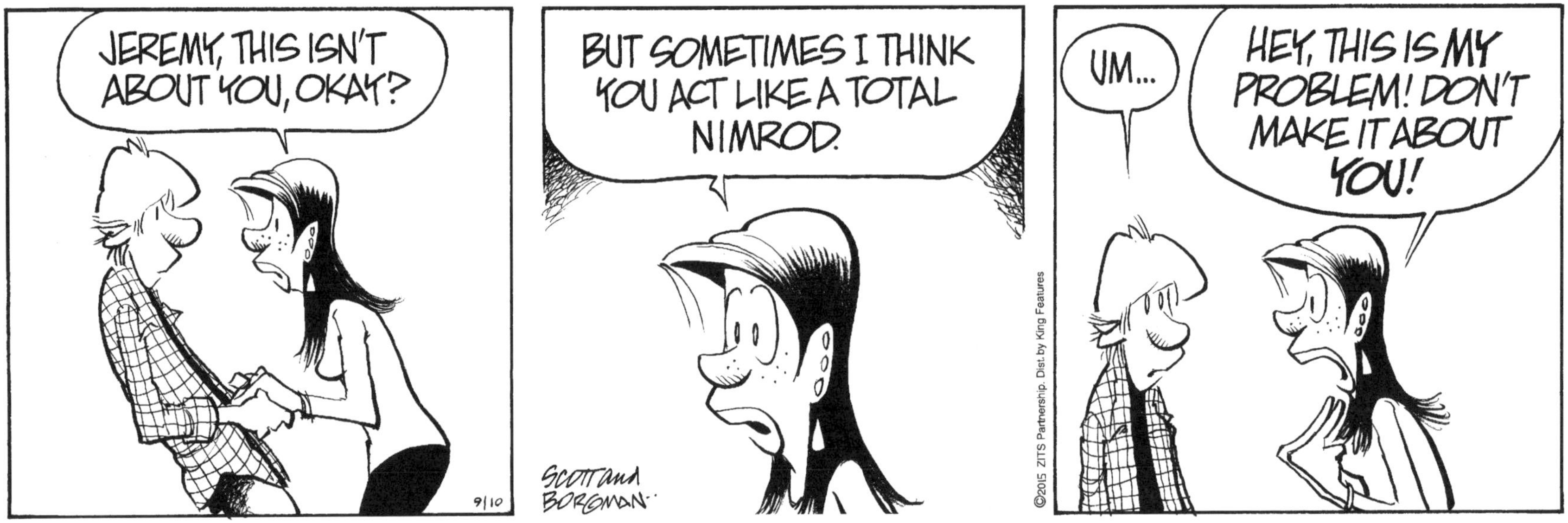
JEREMY, THIS ISN'T ABOUT YOU, OKAY?
9/10
BUT SOMETIMES I THINK YOU ACT LIKE A TOTAL NIMROD.
SCOTT and BORGMAN
UM...
HEY, THIS IS MY PROBLEM! DON'T MAKE IT ABOUT YOU!
©2015 ZITS Partnership. Dist. by King Features

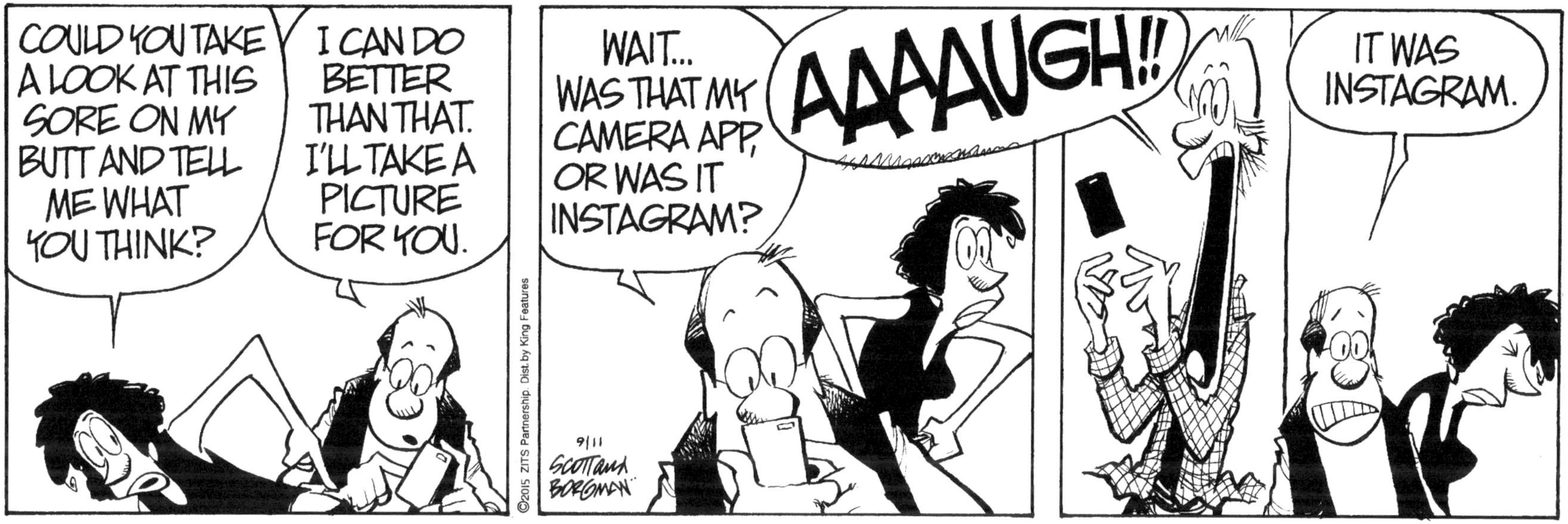
COULD YOU TAKE A LOOK AT THIS SORE ON MY BUTT AND TELL ME WHAT YOU THINK?
I CAN DO BETTER THAN THAT. I'LL TAKE A PICTURE FOR YOU.
WAIT... WAS THAT MY CAMERA APP, OR WAS IT INSTAGRAM?
AAAAUGH!!
IT WAS INSTAGRAM.
9/11
SCOTT and BORGMAN
©2015 ZITS Partnership. Dist. by King Features

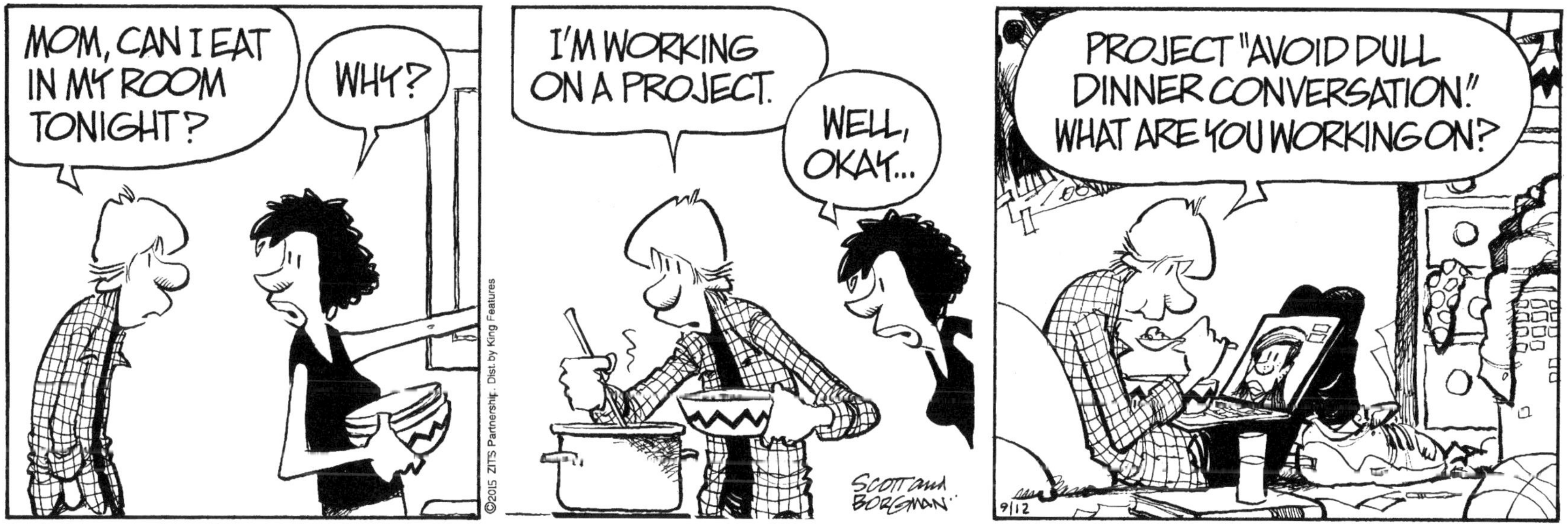
MOM, CAN I EAT IN MY ROOM TONIGHT?
WHY?
I'M WORKING ON A PROJECT.
WELL, OKAY...
PROJECT "AVOID DULL DINNER CONVERSATION." WHAT ARE YOU WORKING ON?
SCOTT and BORGMAN
9/12
©2015 ZITS Partnership. Dist. by King Features

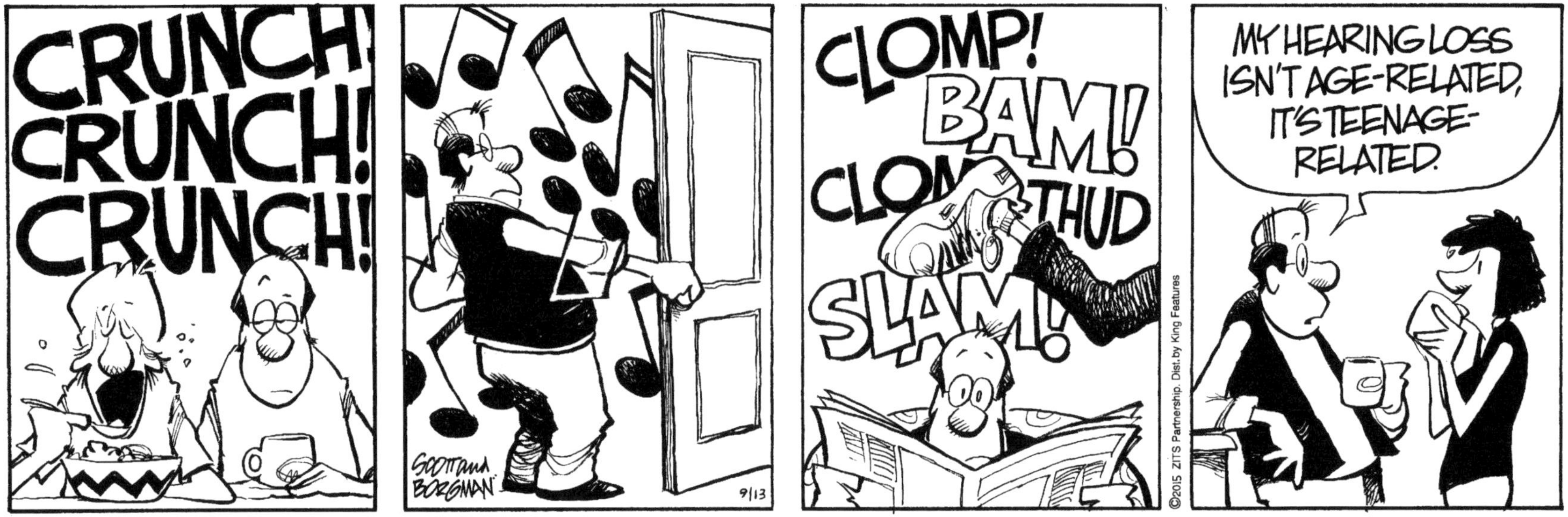
CRUNCH! CRUNCH! CRUNCH!
SCOTT and BORGMAN
9/13
CLOMP! BAM! CLOMP THUD SLAM!
©2015 ZITS Partnership. Dist. by King Features
MY HEARING LOSS ISN'T AGE-RELATED, IT'S TEENAGE-RELATED.

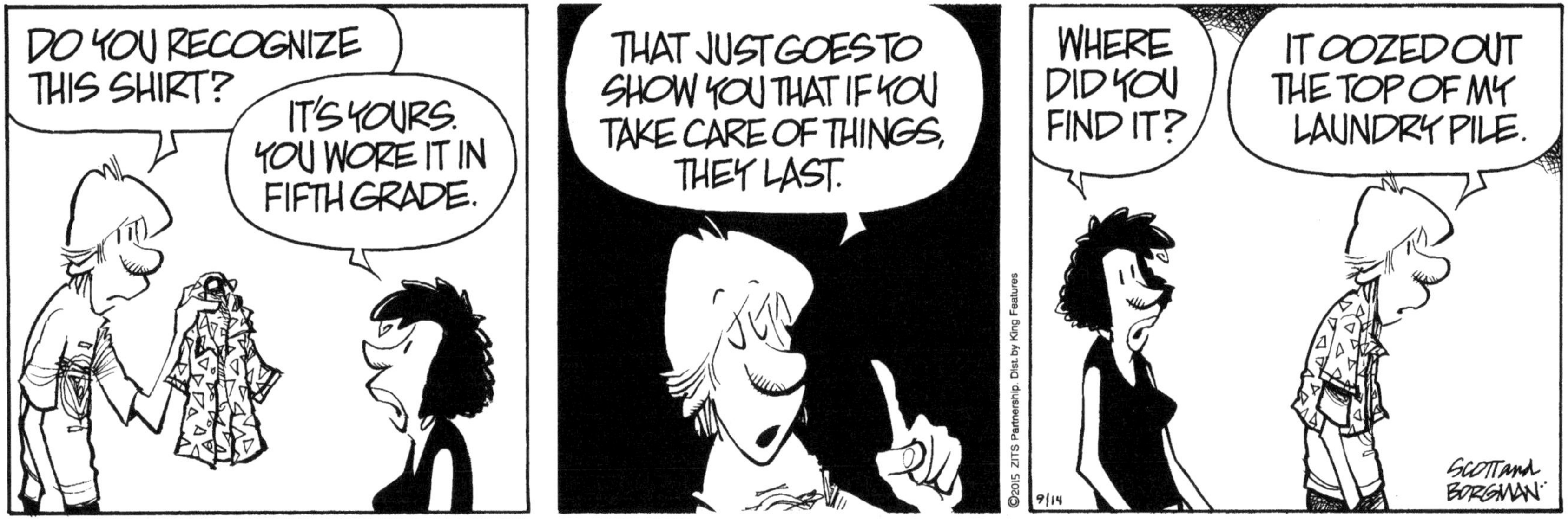
DO YOU RECOGNIZE THIS SHIRT?
IT'S YOURS. YOU WORE IT IN FIFTH GRADE.
THAT JUST GOES TO SHOW YOU THAT IF YOU TAKE CARE OF THINGS, THEY LAST.
©2015 ZITS Partnership. Dist. by King Features
9/14
WHERE DID YOU FIND IT?
IT OOZED OUT THE TOP OF MY LAUNDRY PILE.
SCOTT and BORGMAN

ZITS

by JERRY SCOTT and JIM BORGMAN

JAB!
POKE!
JAB!
JAB!
OW!
DINNER-TIME.
DID YOU FIND JEREMY?
AFTER SOME POKING AROUND.

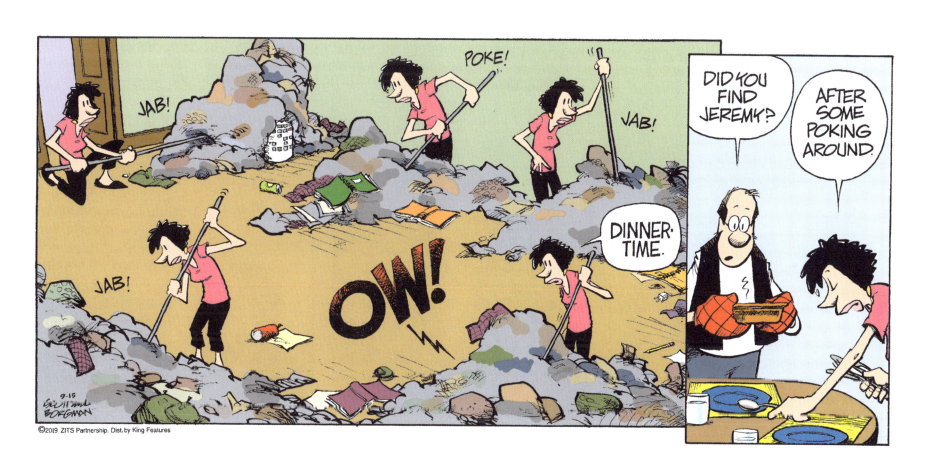

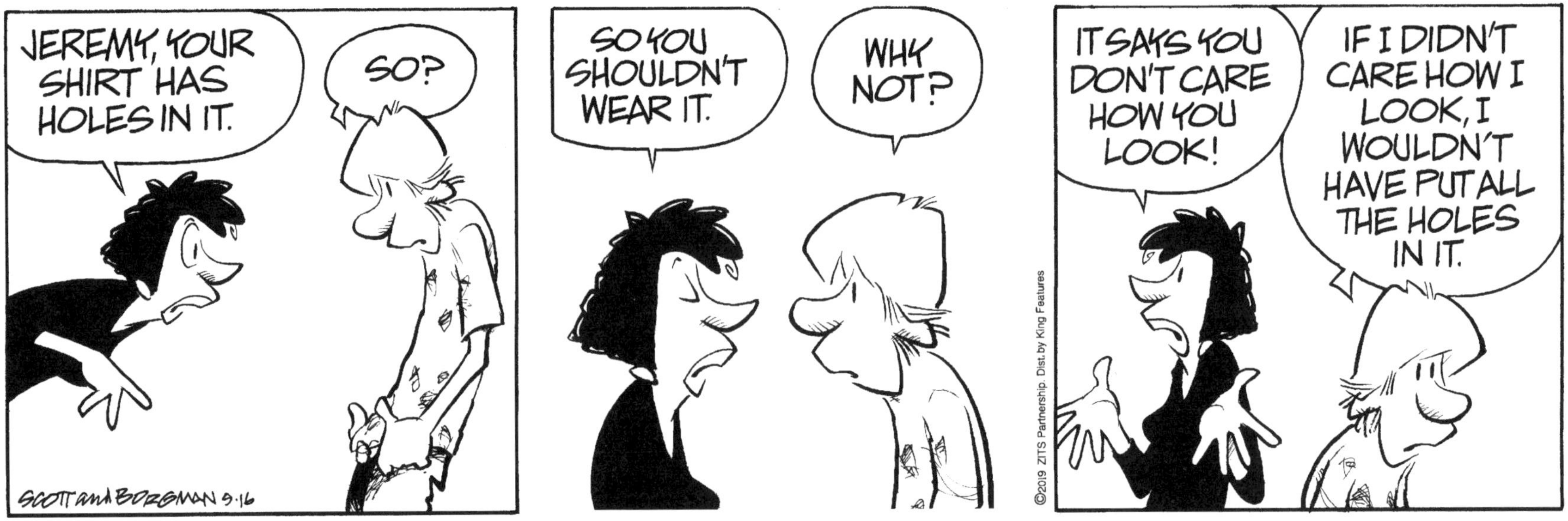
JEREMY, YOUR SHIRT HAS HOLES IN IT.
SO?
SO YOU SHOULDN'T WEAR IT.
WHY NOT?
IT SAYS YOU DON'T CARE HOW YOU LOOK!
IF I DIDN'T CARE HOW I LOOK, I WOULDN'T HAVE PUT ALL THE HOLES IN IT.
©2019 ZITS Partnership. Dist. by King Features

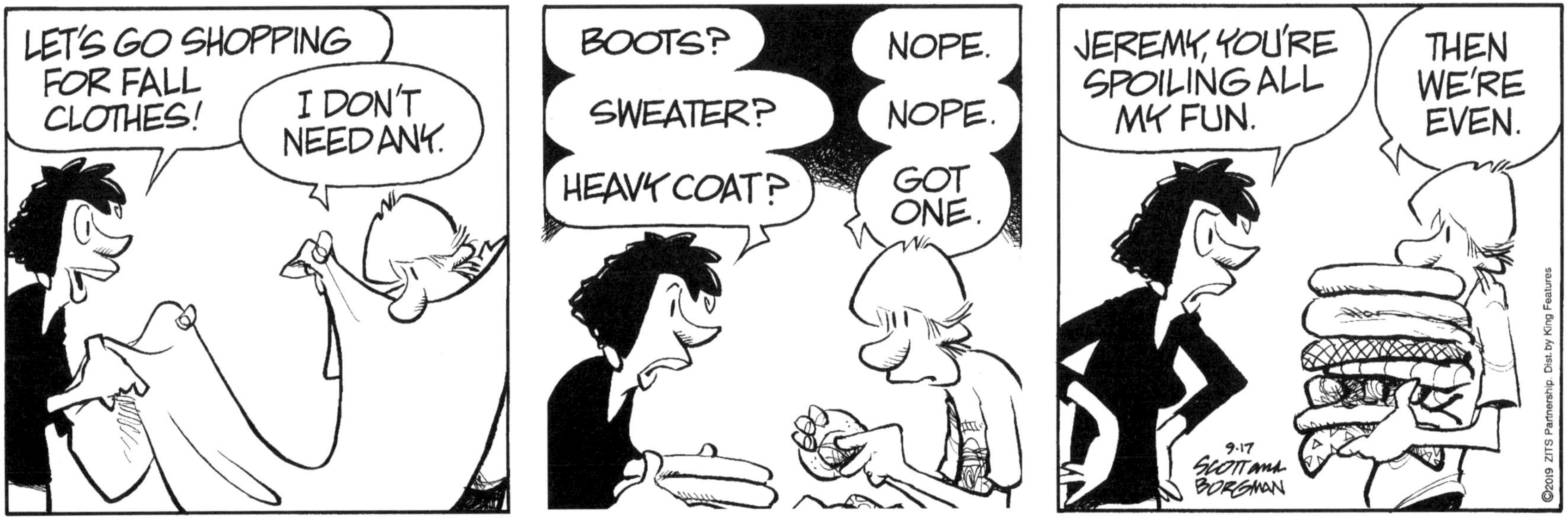
LET'S GO SHOPPING FOR FALL CLOTHES!
I DON'T NEED ANY.
BOOTS?
NOPE.
SWEATER?
NOPE.
HEAVY COAT?
GOT ONE.
JEREMY, YOU'RE SPOILING ALL MY FUN.
THEN WE'RE EVEN.
©2019 ZITS Partnership. Dist. by King Features

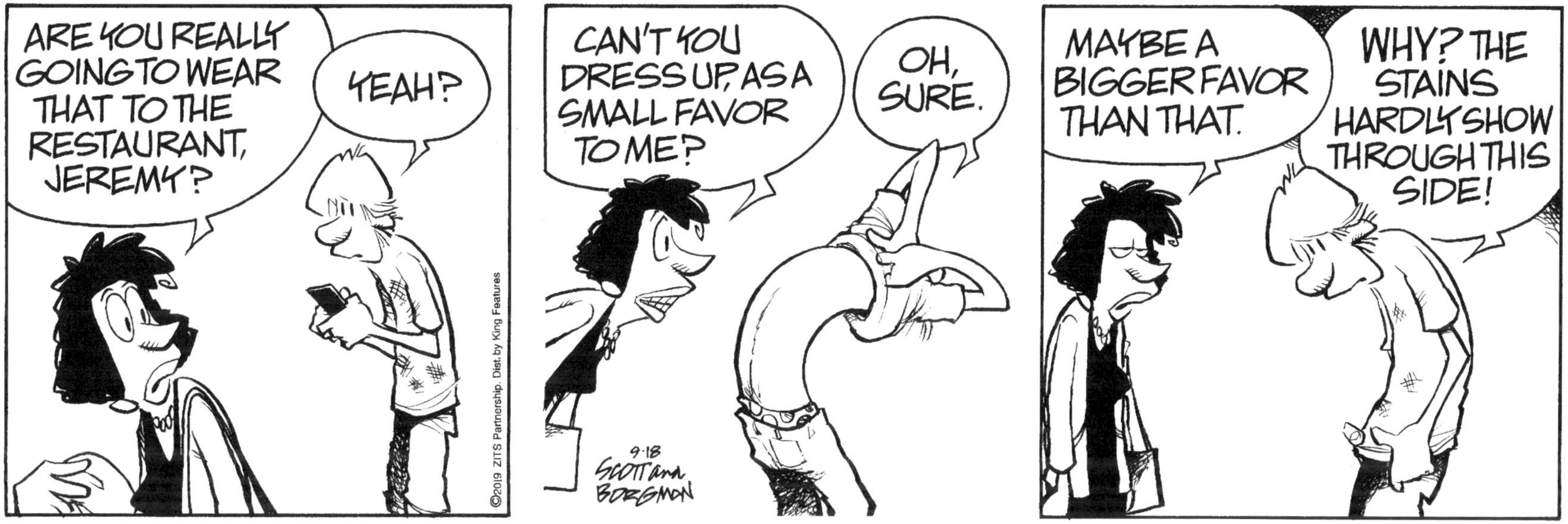
ARE YOU REALLY GOING TO WEAR THAT TO THE RESTAURANT, JEREMY?
YEAH?
©2019 ZITS Partnership. Dist. by King Features
CAN'T YOU DRESS UP, AS A SMALL FAVOR TO ME?
OH, SURE.
9·18 SCOTT and BORGMAN
MAYBE A BIGGER FAVOR THAN THAT.
WHY? THE STAINS HARDLY SHOW THROUGH THIS SIDE!

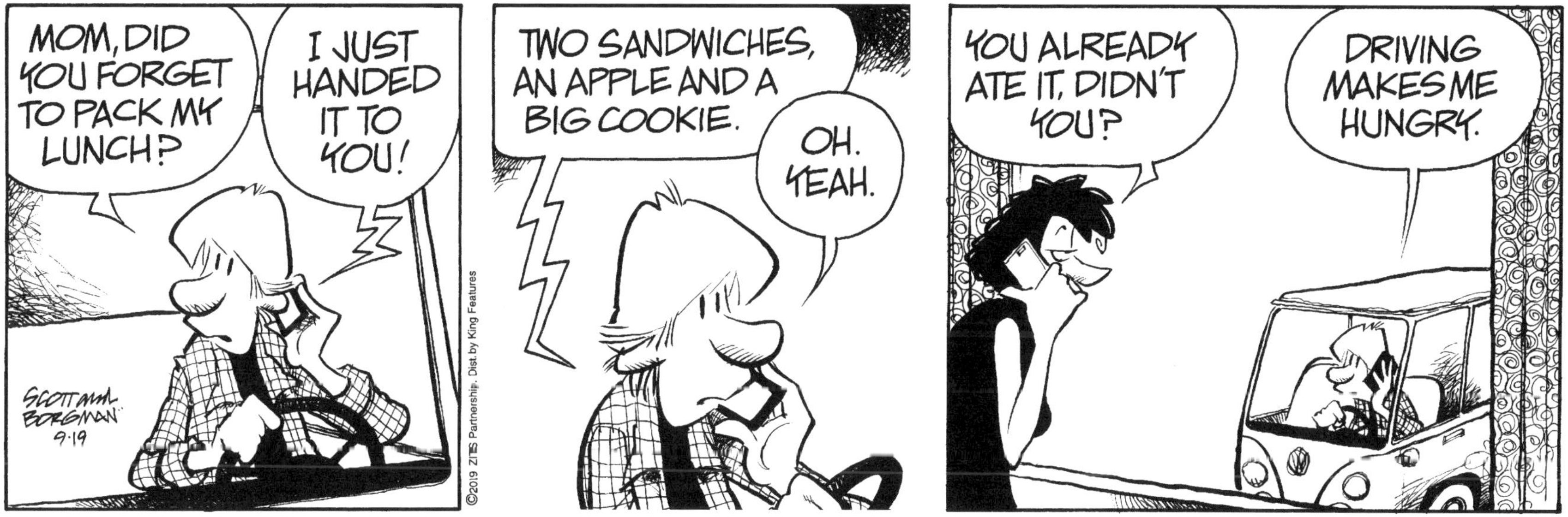
MOM, DID YOU FORGET TO PACK MY LUNCH?
I JUST HANDED IT TO YOU!
SCOTT and BORGMAN 9·19
©2019 ZITS Partnership. Dist. by King Features
TWO SANDWICHES, AN APPLE AND A BIG COOKIE.
OH. YEAH.
YOU ALREADY ATE IT, DIDN'T YOU?
DRIVING MAKES ME HUNGRY.

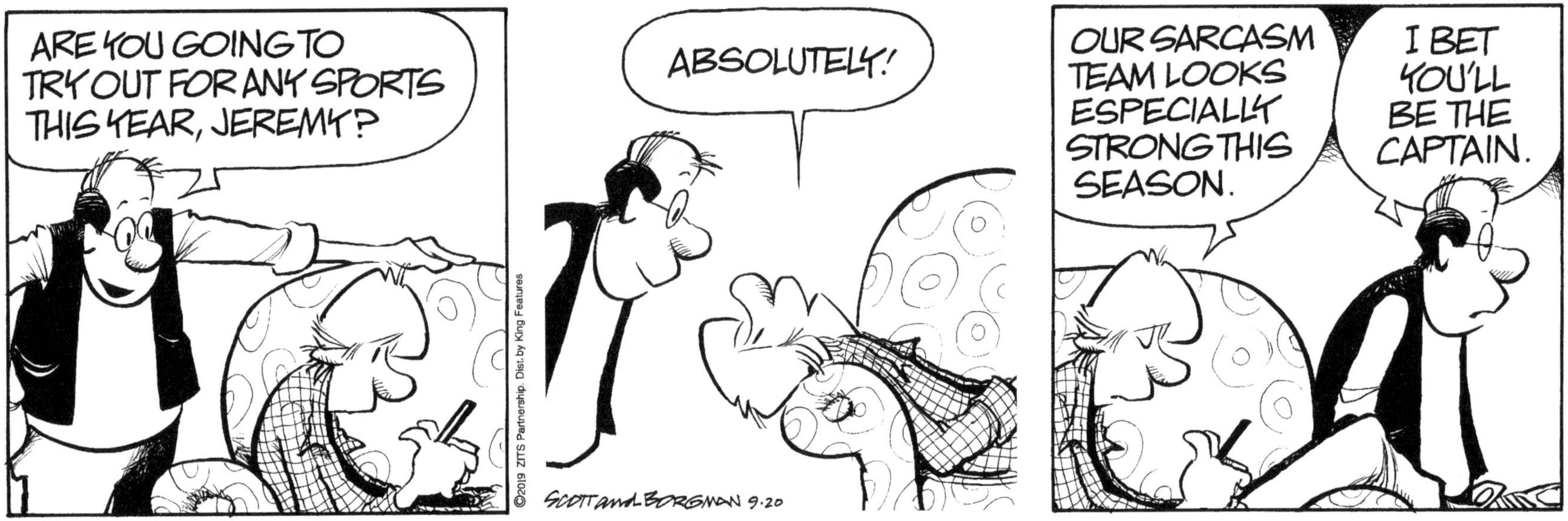
ARE YOU GOING TO TRY OUT FOR ANY SPORTS THIS YEAR, JEREMY?
ABSOLUTELY!
OUR SARCASM TEAM LOOKS ESPECIALLY STRONG THIS SEASON.
I BET YOU'LL BE THE CAPTAIN.
©2019 ZITS Partnership. Dist. by King Features
SCOTT and BORGMAN 9.20

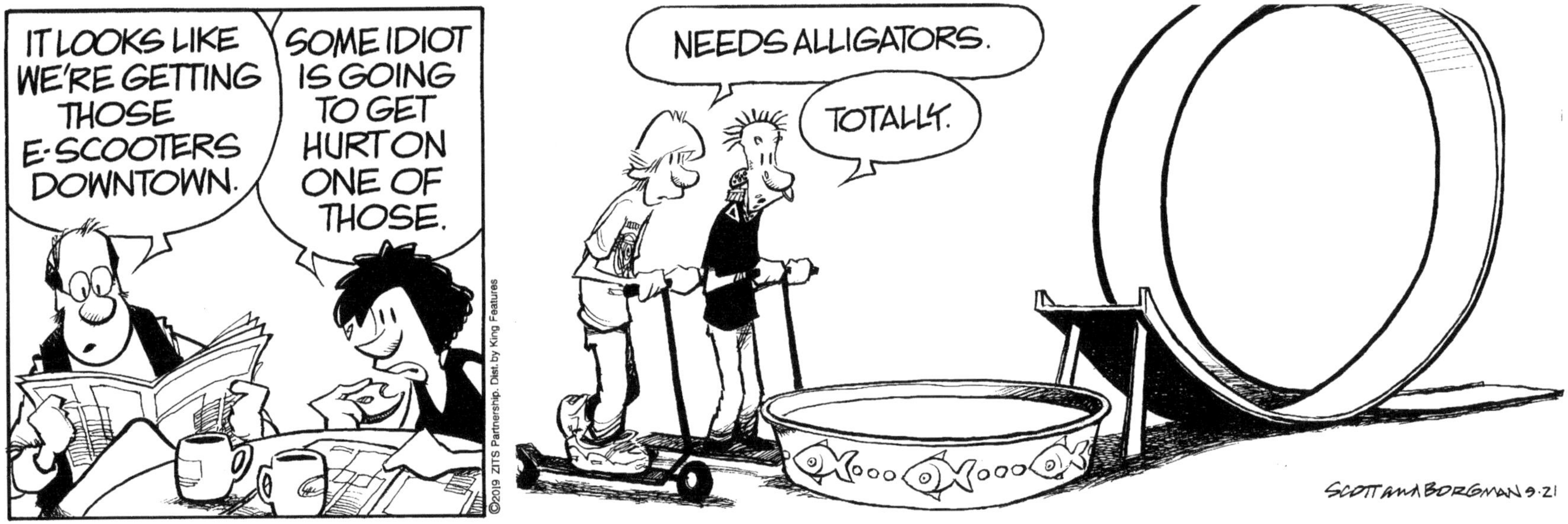
IT LOOKS LIKE WE'RE GETTING THOSE E-SCOOTERS DOWNTOWN.
SOME IDIOT IS GOING TO GET HURT ON ONE OF THOSE.
NEEDS ALLIGATORS.
TOTALLY.
©2019 ZITS Partnership. Dist. by King Features
SCOTT and BORGMAN 9.21

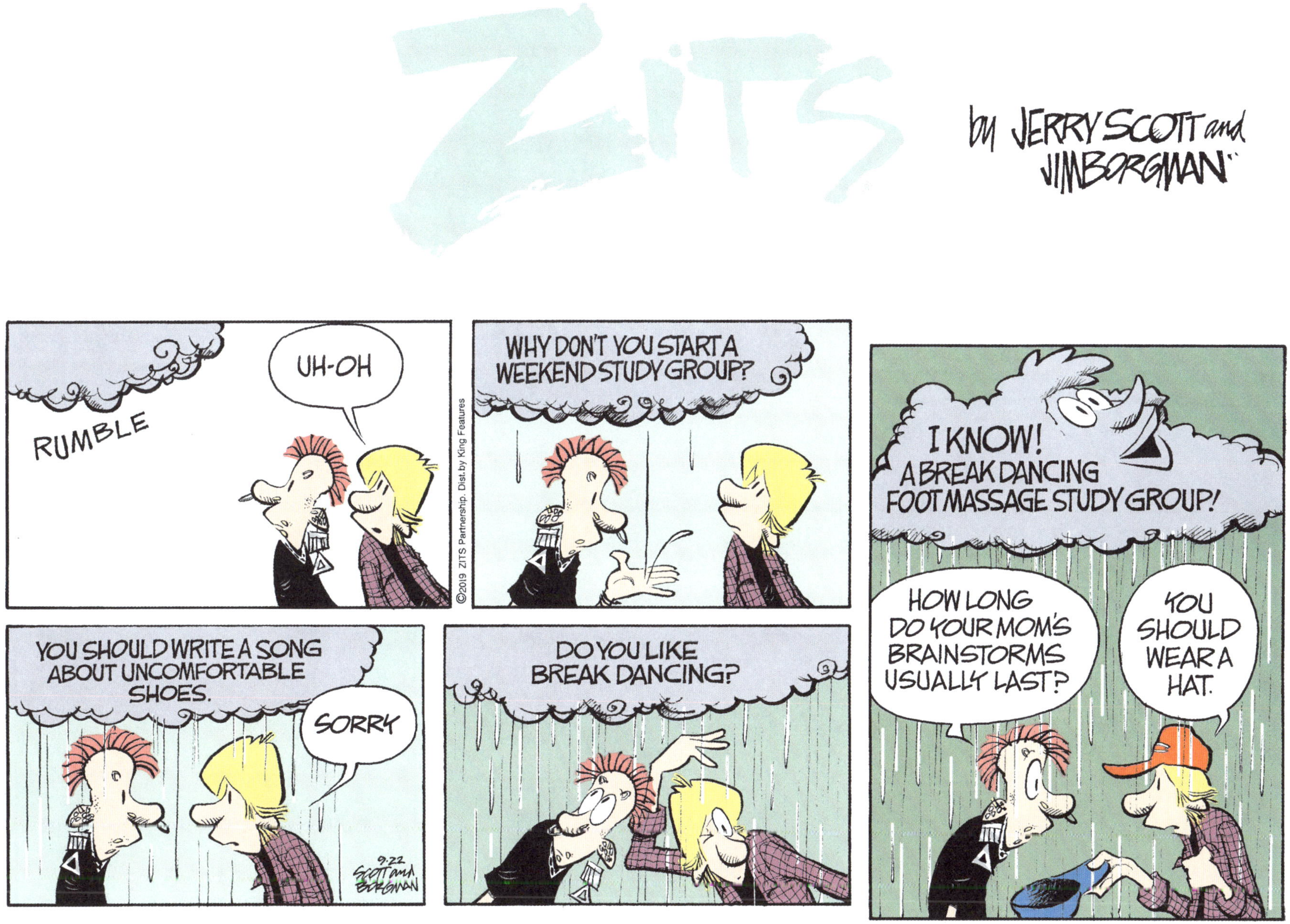
ZITS
by JERRY SCOTT and JIM BORGMAN
RUMBLE
UH-OH
©2019 ZITS Partnership. Dist. by King Features
WHY DON'T YOU START A WEEKEND STUDY GROUP?
YOU SHOULD WRITE A SONG ABOUT UNCOMFORTABLE SHOES.
SORRY
9·22 SCOTT AND BORGMAN
DO YOU LIKE BREAK DANCING?
I KNOW! A BREAK DANCING FOOT MASSAGE STUDY GROUP!
HOW LONG DO YOUR MOM'S BRAINSTORMS USUALLY LAST?
YOU SHOULD WEAR A HAT.

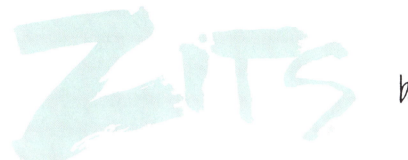

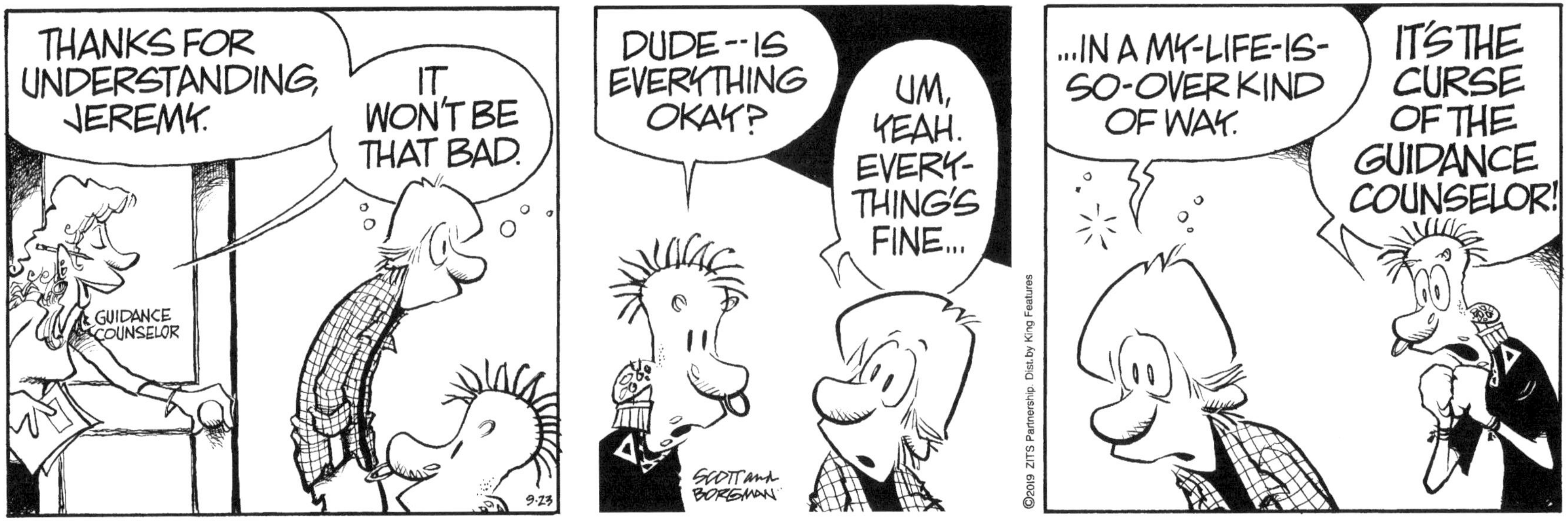
THANKS FOR UNDERSTANDING, JEREMY.
IT WON'T BE THAT BAD.
GUIDANCE COUNSELOR
9·23
DUDE--IS EVERYTHING OKAY?
UM, YEAH. EVERY-THING'S FINE...
SCOTT and BORGMAN
©2019 ZITS Partnership. Dist. by King Features
...IN A MY-LIFE-IS-SO-OVER KIND OF WAY.
IT'S THE CURSE OF THE GUIDANCE COUNSELOR!

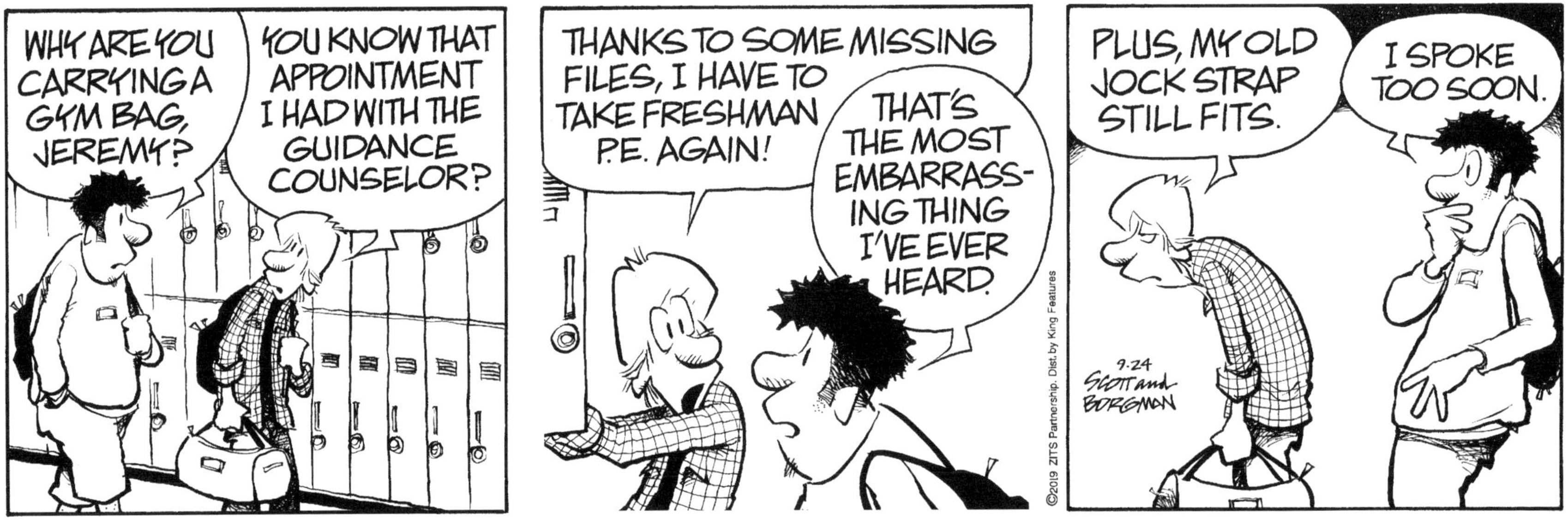
WHY ARE YOU CARRYING A GYM BAG, JEREMY?
YOU KNOW THAT APPOINTMENT I HAD WITH THE GUIDANCE COUNSELOR?
THANKS TO SOME MISSING FILES, I HAVE TO TAKE FRESHMAN P.E. AGAIN!
THAT'S THE MOST EMBARRASS-ING THING I'VE EVER HEARD.
©2019 ZITS Partnership. Dist. by King Features
PLUS, MY OLD JOCK STRAP STILL FITS.
I SPOKE TOO SOON.
9·24
SCOTT and BORGMAN

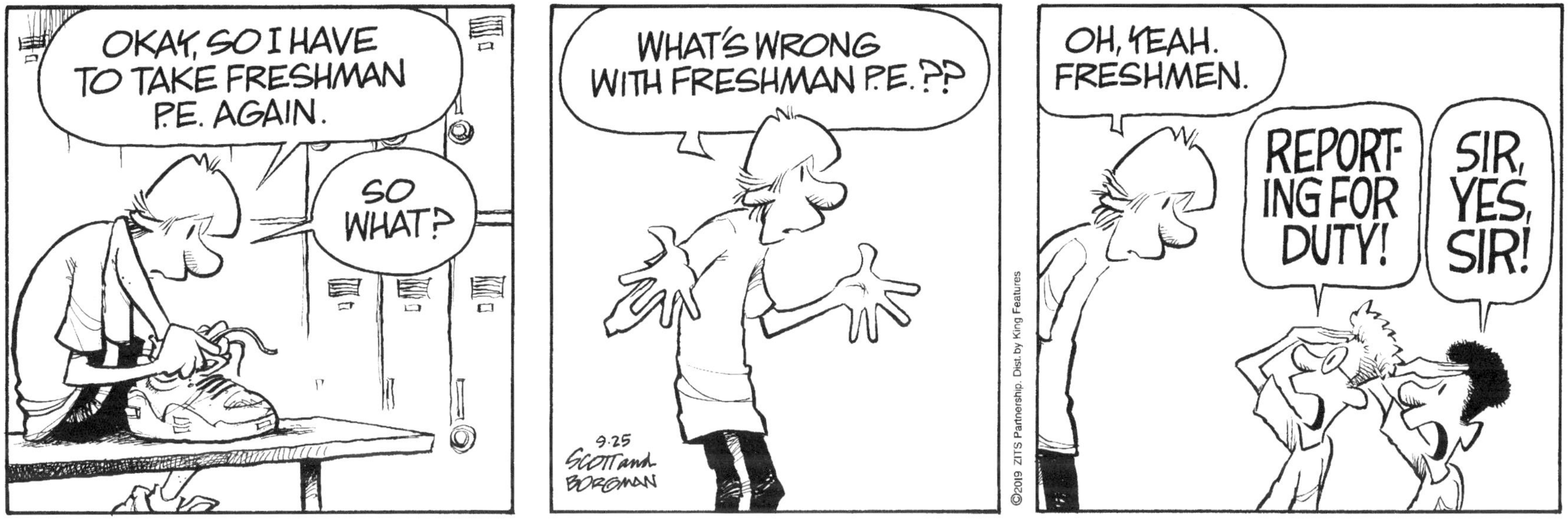
OKAY, SO I HAVE TO TAKE FRESHMAN P.E. AGAIN.
SO WHAT?
WHAT'S WRONG WITH FRESHMAN P.E.??
9-25
SCOTT and BORGMAN
OH, YEAH. FRESHMEN.
REPORT-ING FOR DUTY!
SIR, YES, SIR!
©2019 ZITS Partnership. Dist. by King Features

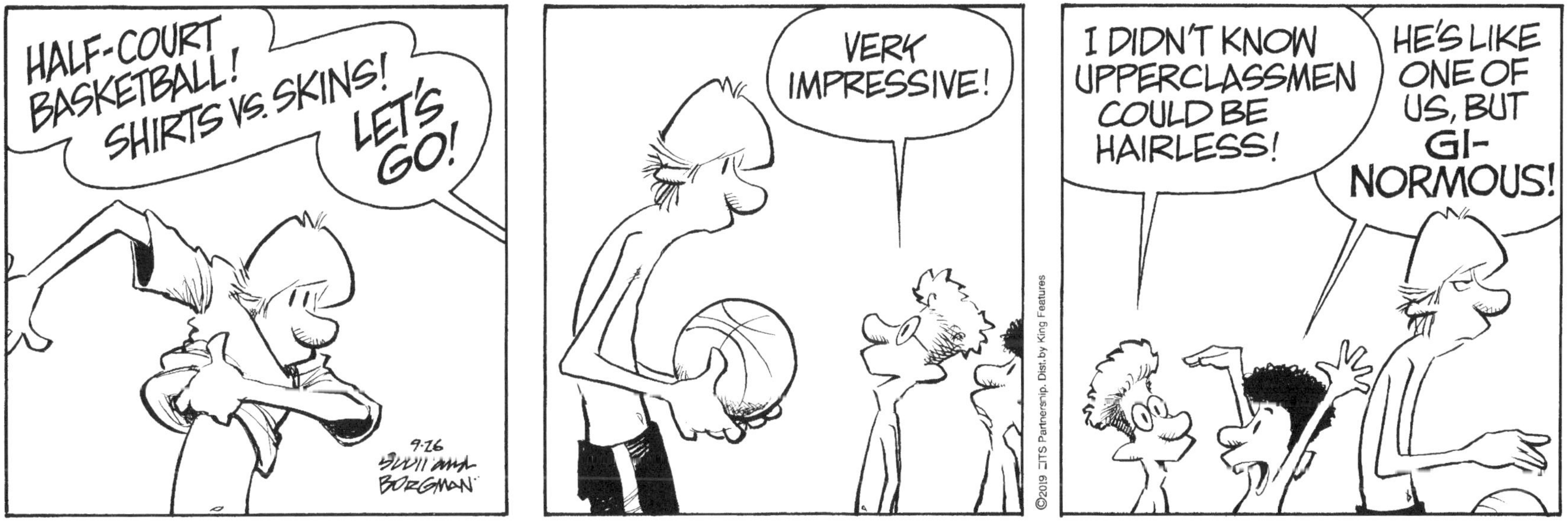
HALF-COURT BASKETBALL! SHIRTS VS. SKINS!
LET'S GO!
9-26
BORGMAN
VERY IMPRESSIVE!
©2019 ZITS Partnership. Dist. by King Features
I DIDN'T KNOW UPPERCLASSMEN COULD BE HAIRLESS!
HE'S LIKE ONE OF US, BUT GI-NORMOUS!

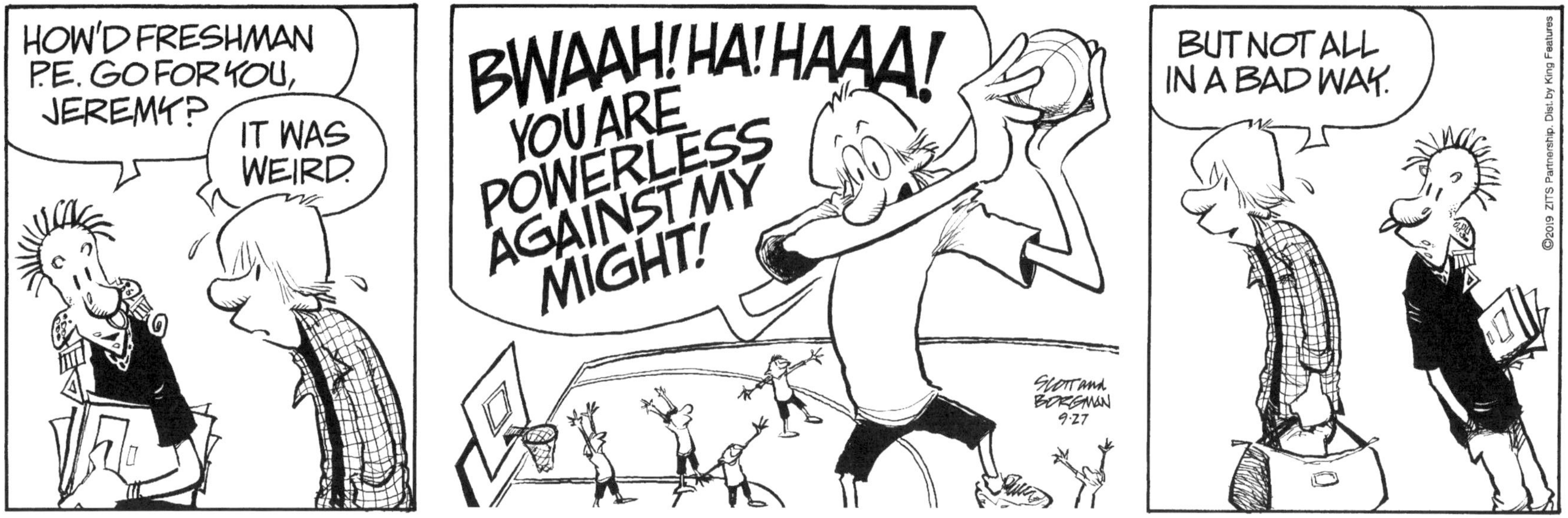
HOW'D FRESHMAN P.E. GO FOR YOU, JEREMY?
IT WAS WEIRD.
BWAAH! HA! HAAA! YOU ARE POWERLESS AGAINST MY MIGHT!
SCOTT AND BORGMAN 9·27
BUT NOT ALL IN A BAD WAY.
©2019 ZITS Partnership. Dist. by King Features

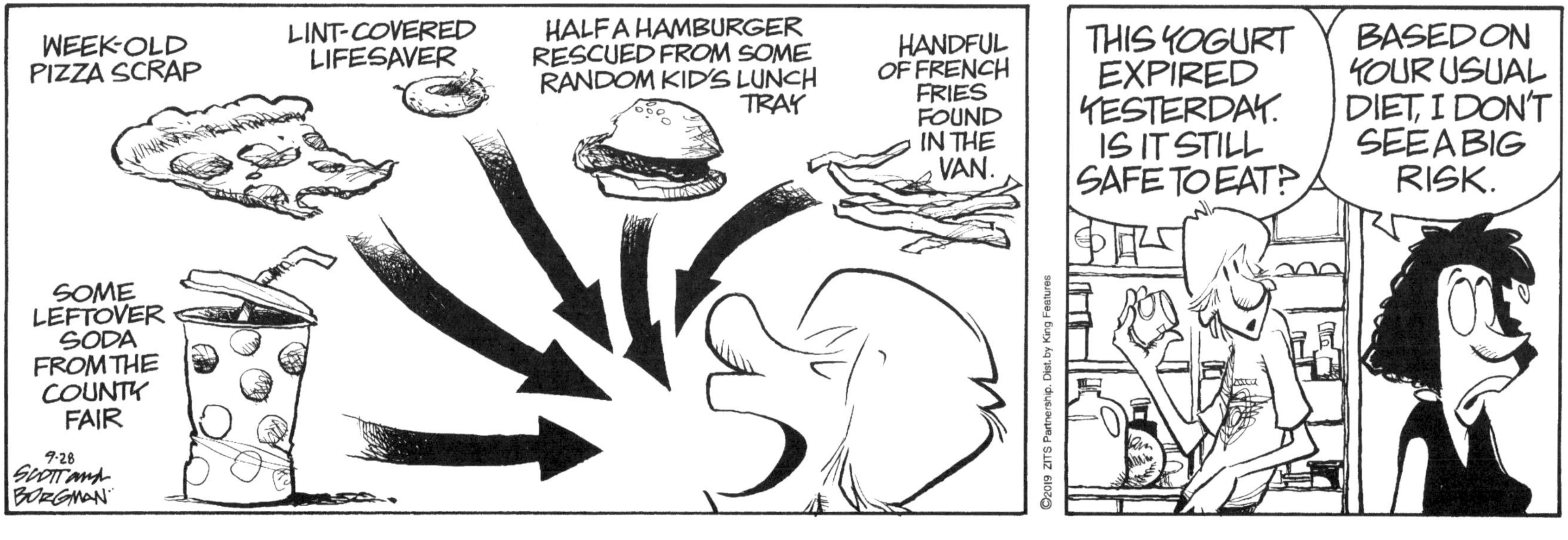
WEEK-OLD PIZZA SCRAP
LINT-COVERED LIFESAVER
HALF A HAMBURGER RESCUED FROM SOME RANDOM KID'S LUNCH TRAY
HANDFUL OF FRENCH FRIES FOUND IN THE VAN.
SOME LEFTOVER SODA FROM THE COUNTY FAIR
9·28 SCOTT AND BORGMAN
©2019 ZITS Partnership. Dist. by King Features
THIS YOGURT EXPIRED YESTERDAY. IS IT STILL SAFE TO EAT?
BASED ON YOUR USUAL DIET, I DON'T SEE A BIG RISK.

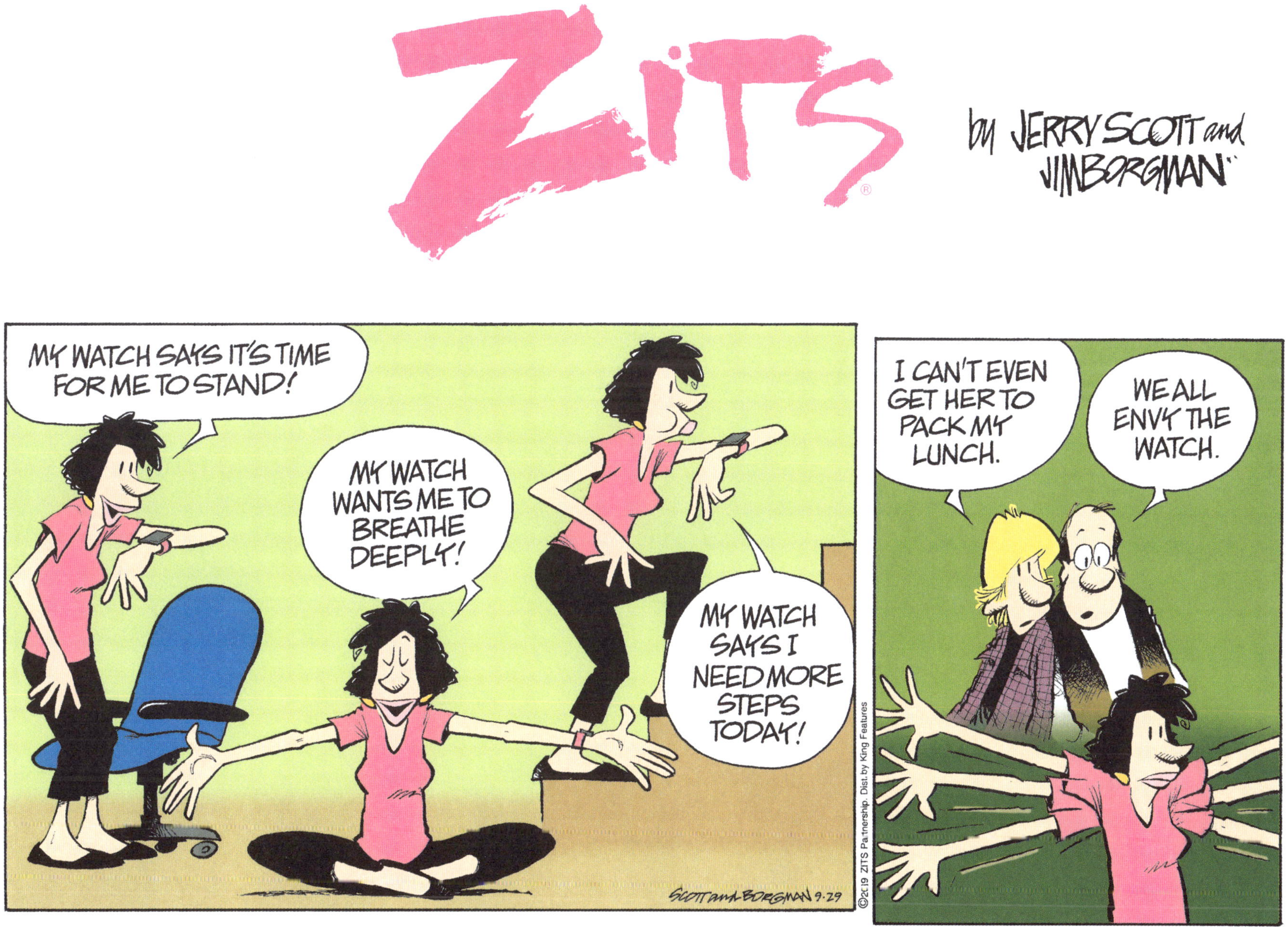
ZITS®
by JERRY SCOTT and JIM BORGMAN
MY WATCH SAYS IT'S TIME FOR ME TO STAND!
MY WATCH WANTS ME TO BREATHE DEEPLY!
MY WATCH SAYS I NEED MORE STEPS TODAY!
SCOTT and BORGMAN 9-29
©2019 ZITS Partnership. Dist. by King Features
I CAN'T EVEN GET HER TO PACK MY LUNCH.
WE ALL ENVY THE WATCH.

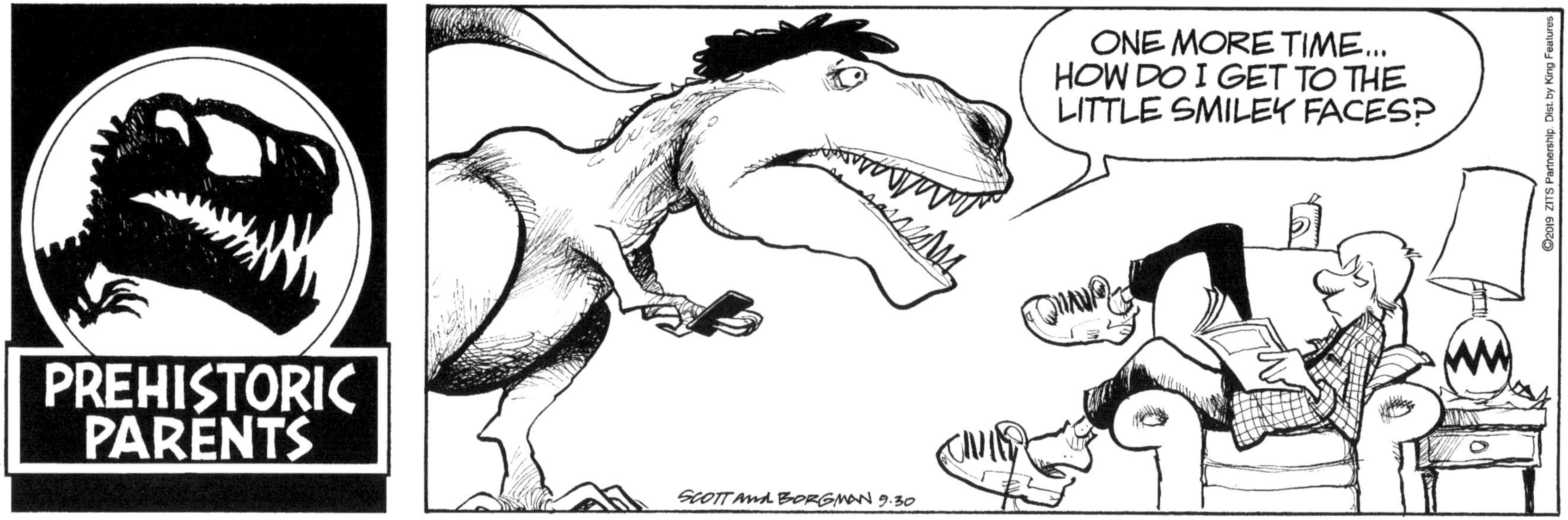
PREHISTORIC PARENTS
ONE MORE TIME... HOW DO I GET TO THE LITTLE SMILEY FACES?
SCOTT AND BORGMAN 9.30
©2019 ZITS Partnership. Dist. by King Features

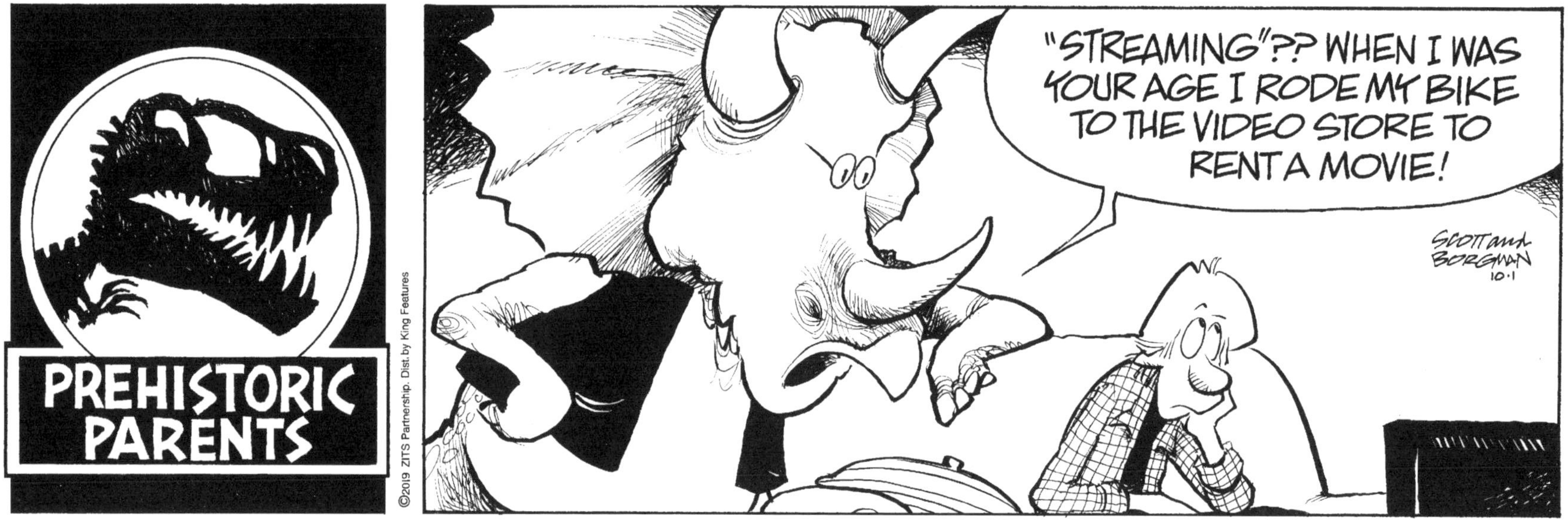
PREHISTORIC PARENTS
"STREAMING"?? WHEN I WAS YOUR AGE I RODE MY BIKE TO THE VIDEO STORE TO RENT A MOVIE!
SCOTT AND BORGMAN 10.1
©2019 ZITS Partnership. Dist. by King Features

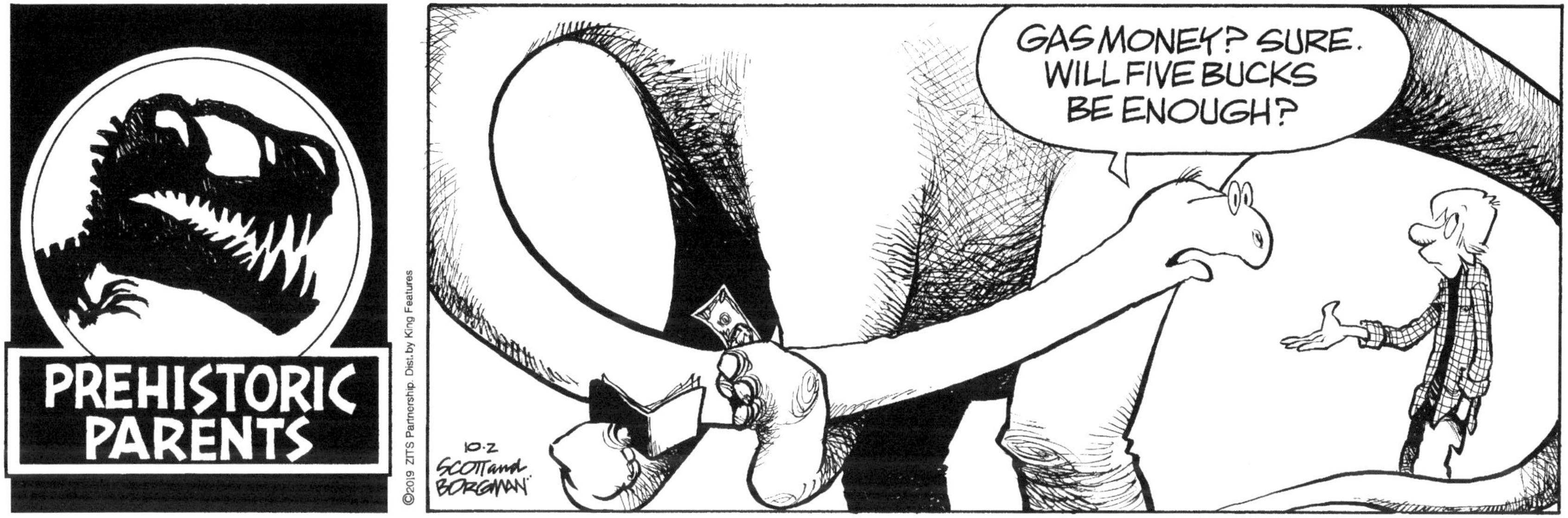
PREHISTORIC PARENTS
©2019 ZITS Partnership. Dist. by King Features
GAS MONEY? SURE. WILL FIVE BUCKS BE ENOUGH?
10.2 SCOTT and BORGMAN

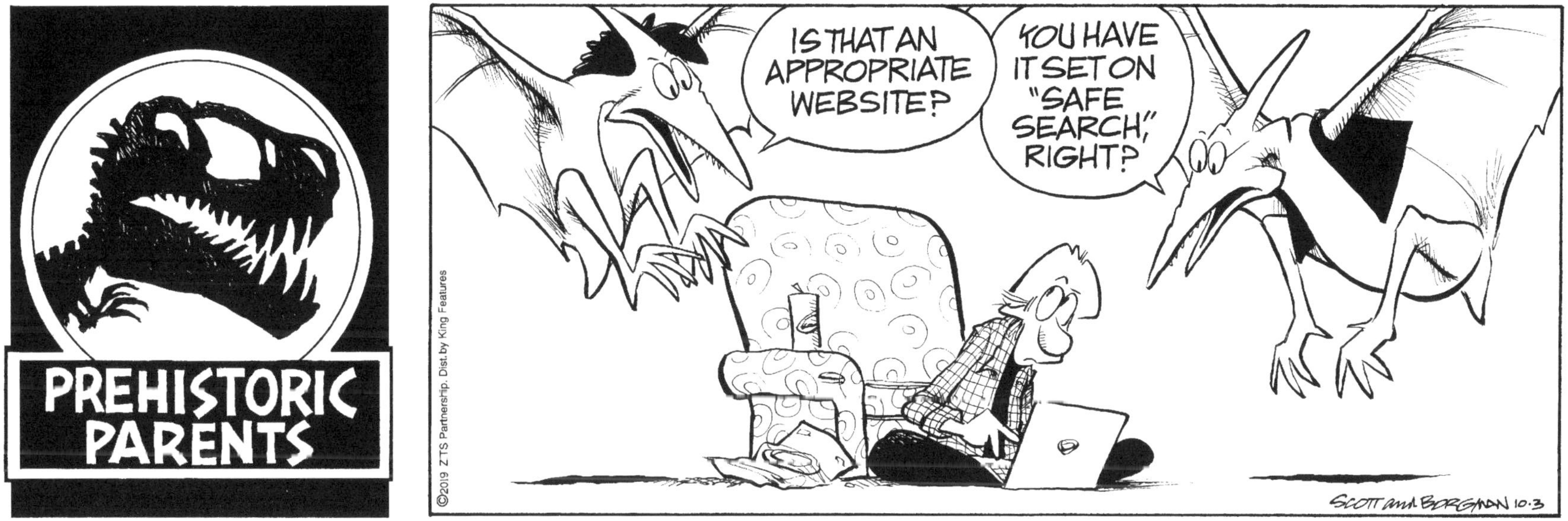
PREHISTORIC PARENTS
©2019 ZITS Partnership. Dist. by King Features
IS THAT AN APPROPRIATE WEBSITE?
YOU HAVE IT SET ON "SAFE SEARCH," RIGHT?
SCOTT and BORGMAN 10.3

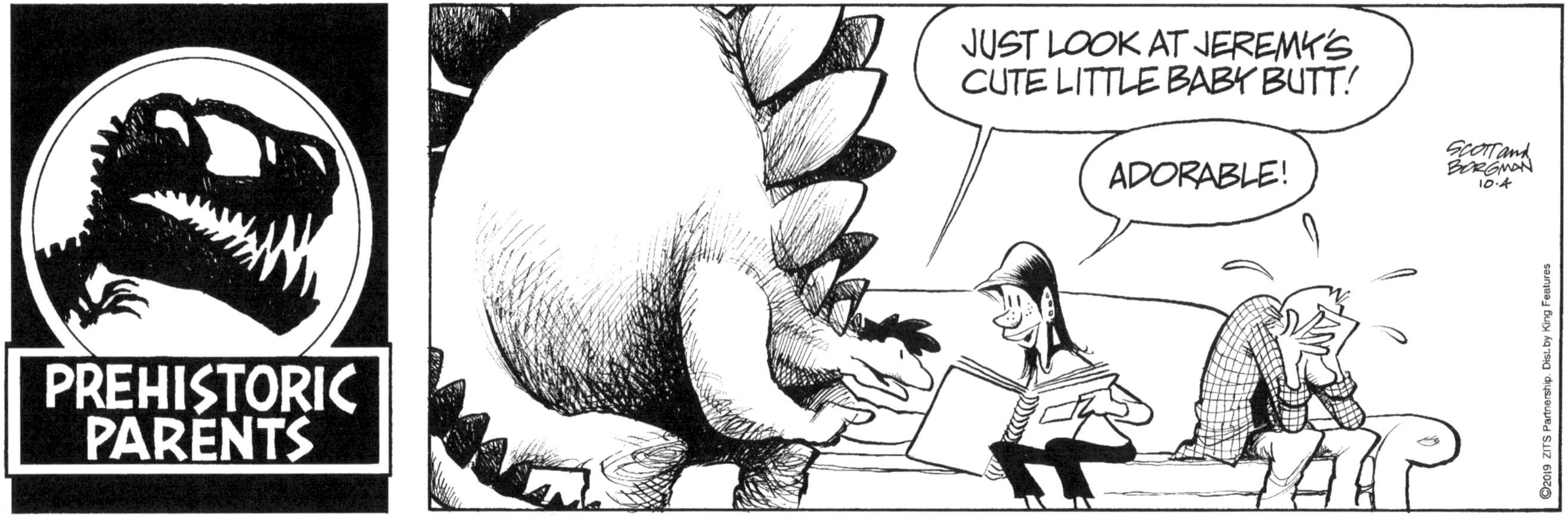
PREHISTORIC PARENTS
JUST LOOK AT JEREMY'S CUTE LITTLE BABY BUTT!
ADORABLE!
SCOTT and BORGMAN 10·4
©2019 ZITS Partnership. Dist. by King Features

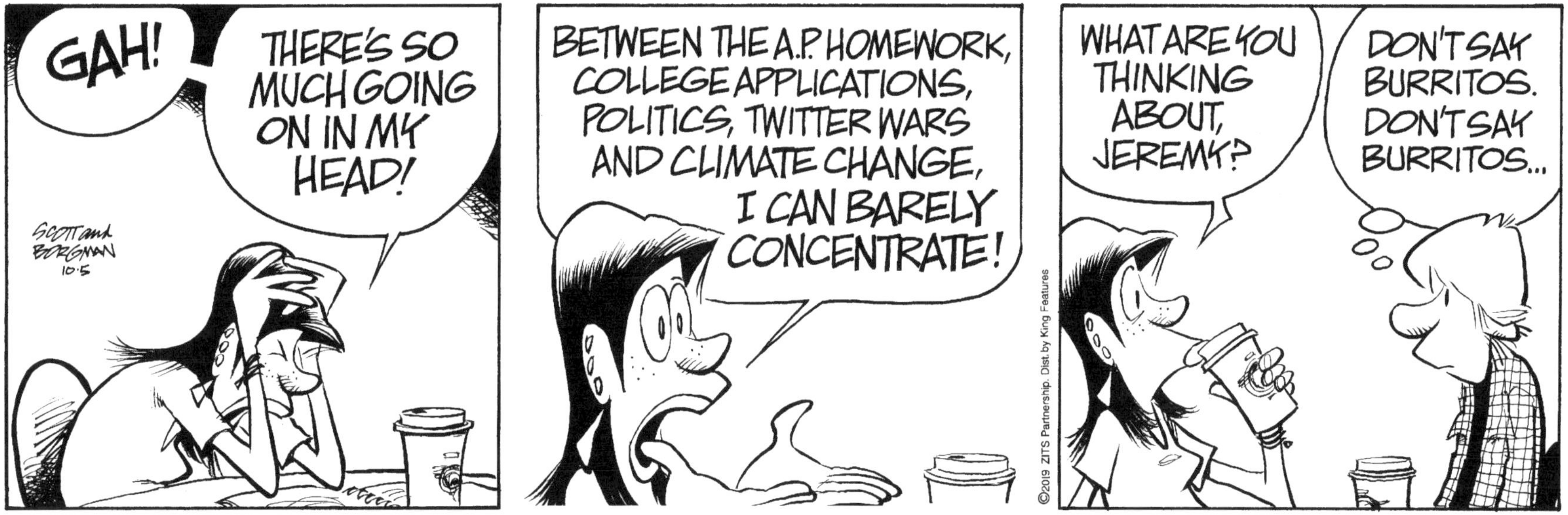
GAH!
THERE'S SO MUCH GOING ON IN MY HEAD!
SCOTT and BORGMAN 10·5
BETWEEN THE A.P. HOMEWORK, COLLEGE APPLICATIONS, POLITICS, TWITTER WARS AND CLIMATE CHANGE, I CAN BARELY CONCENTRATE!
©2019 ZITS Partnership. Dist. by King Features
WHAT ARE YOU THINKING ABOUT, JEREMY?
DON'T SAY BURRITOS. DON'T SAY BURRITOS...

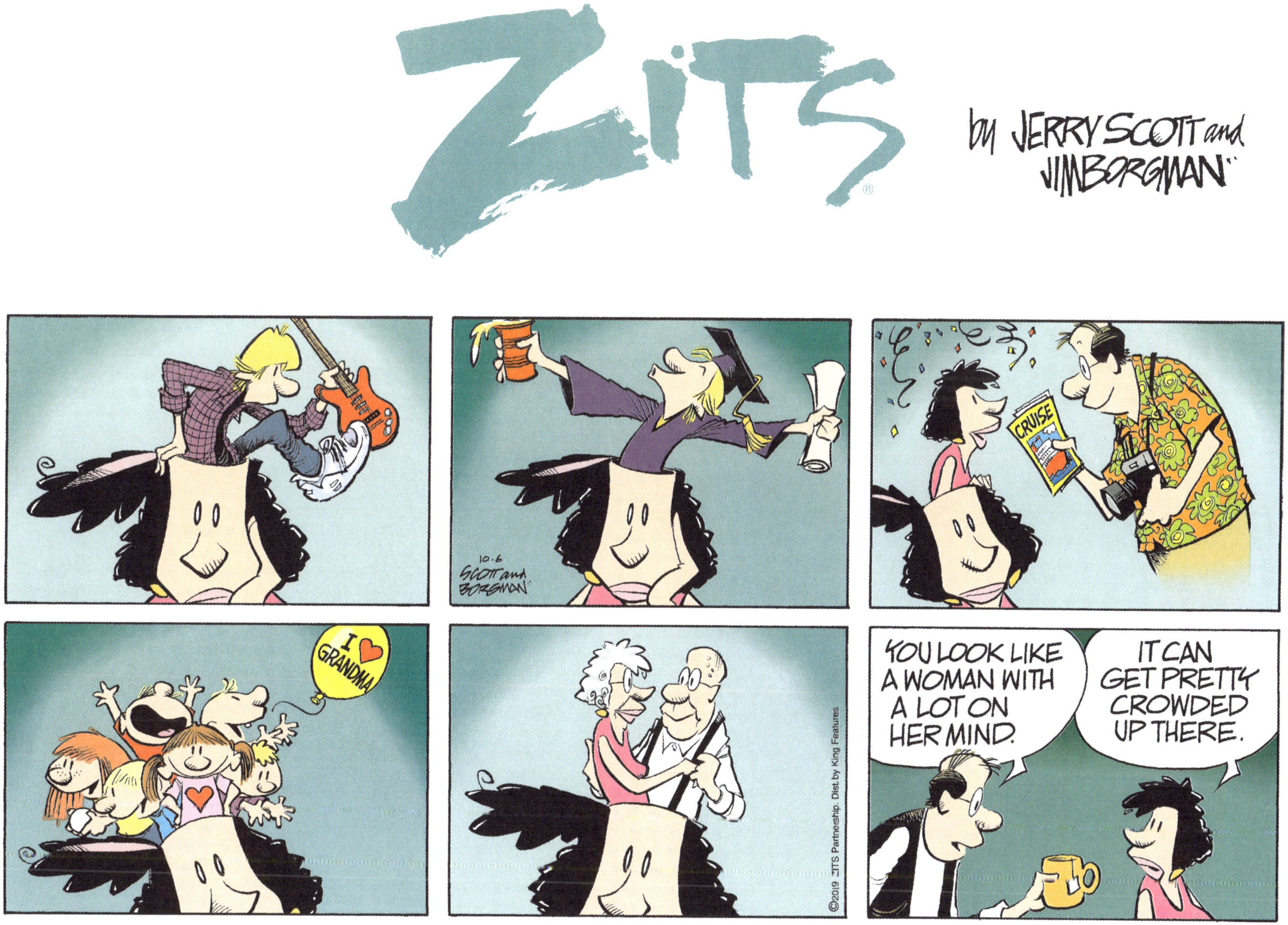
ZITS
by JERRY SCOTT and JIM BORGMAN
10-6
SCOTT and BORGMAN
CRUISE
I ♥ GRANDMA
©2019 ZITS Partnership. Dist. by King Features
YOU LOOK LIKE A WOMAN WITH A LOT ON HER MIND.
IT CAN GET PRETTY CROWDED UP THERE.

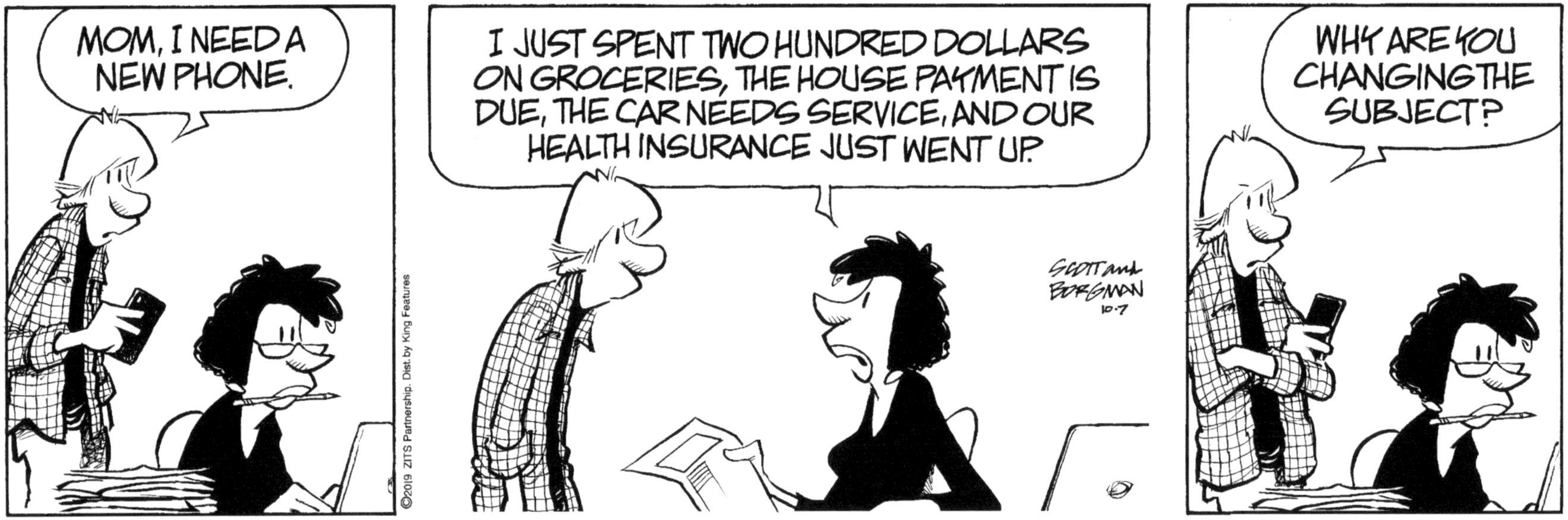
MOM, I NEED A NEW PHONE.
I JUST SPENT TWO HUNDRED DOLLARS ON GROCERIES, THE HOUSE PAYMENT IS DUE, THE CAR NEEDS SERVICE, AND OUR HEALTH INSURANCE JUST WENT UP.
WHY ARE YOU CHANGING THE SUBJECT?
©2019 ZITS Partnership. Dist. by King Features

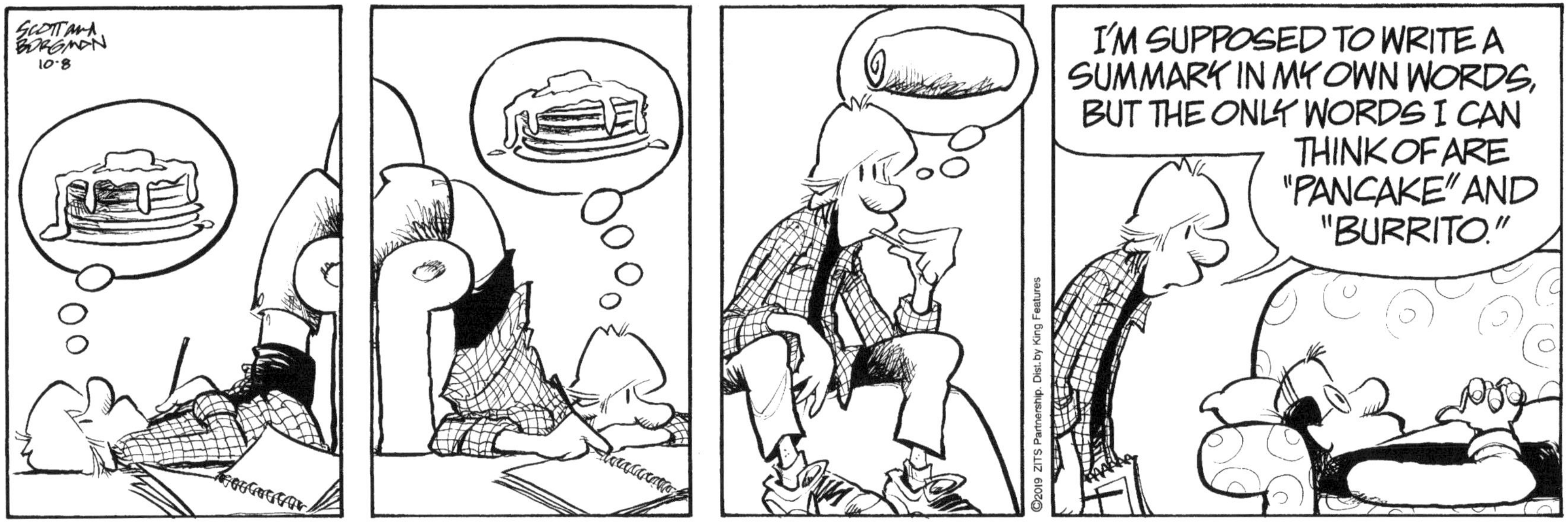
I'M SUPPOSED TO WRITE A SUMMARY IN MY OWN WORDS, BUT THE ONLY WORDS I CAN THINK OF ARE "PANCAKE" AND "BURRITO."
©2019 ZITS Partnership. Dist. by King Features

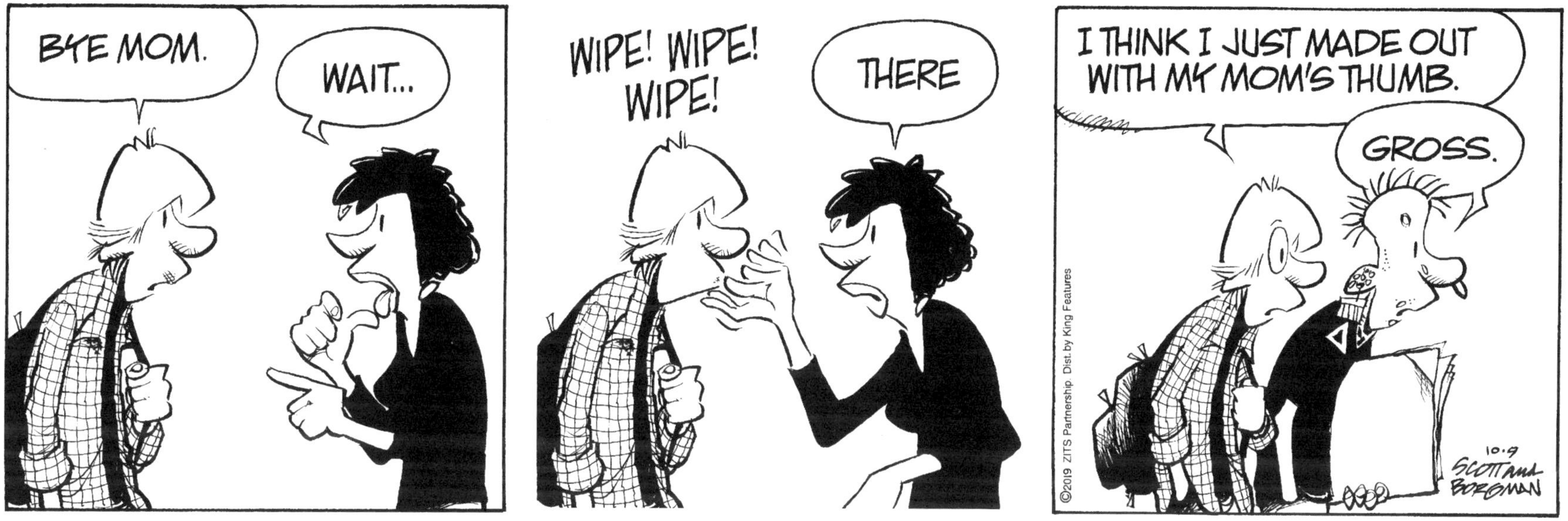
BYE MOM.
WAIT...
WIPE! WIPE! WIPE!
THERE
I THINK I JUST MADE OUT WITH MY MOM'S THUMB.
GROSS.
©2019 ZITS Partnership. Dist. by King Features
10.9
SCOTT and BORGMAN

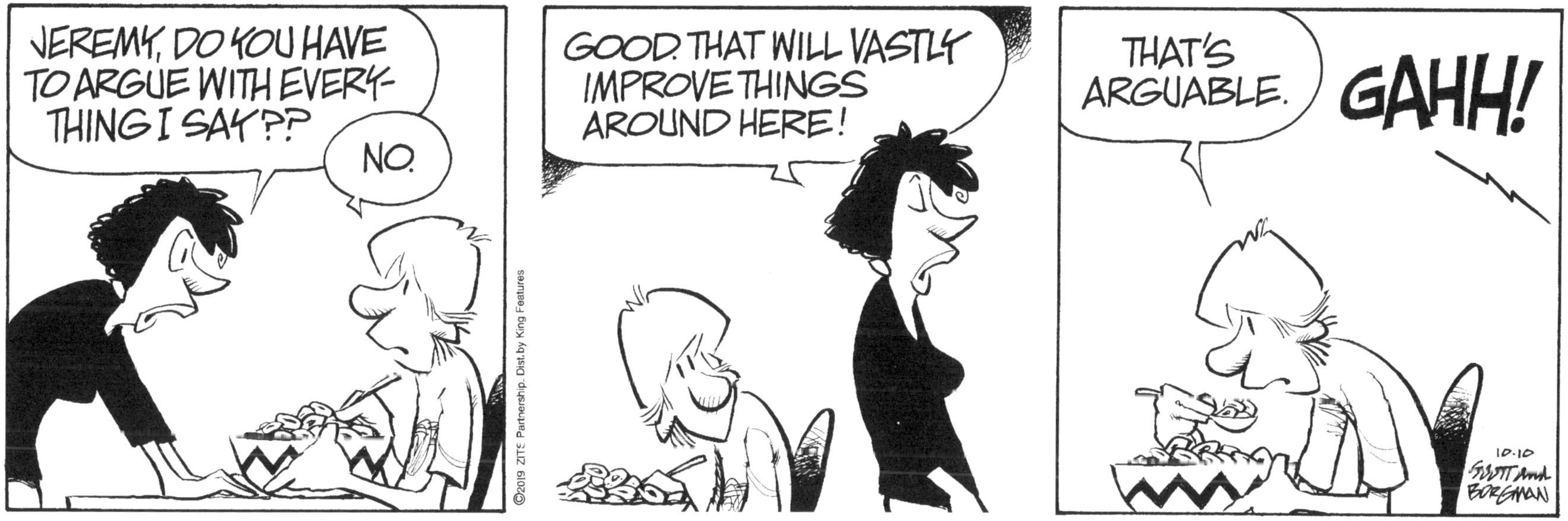
JEREMY, DO YOU HAVE TO ARGUE WITH EVERYTHING I SAY??
NO.
©2019 ZITS Partnership. Dist. by King Features
GOOD. THAT WILL VASTLY IMPROVE THINGS AROUND HERE!
THAT'S ARGUABLE.
GAHH!
10.10
SCOTT and BORGMAN

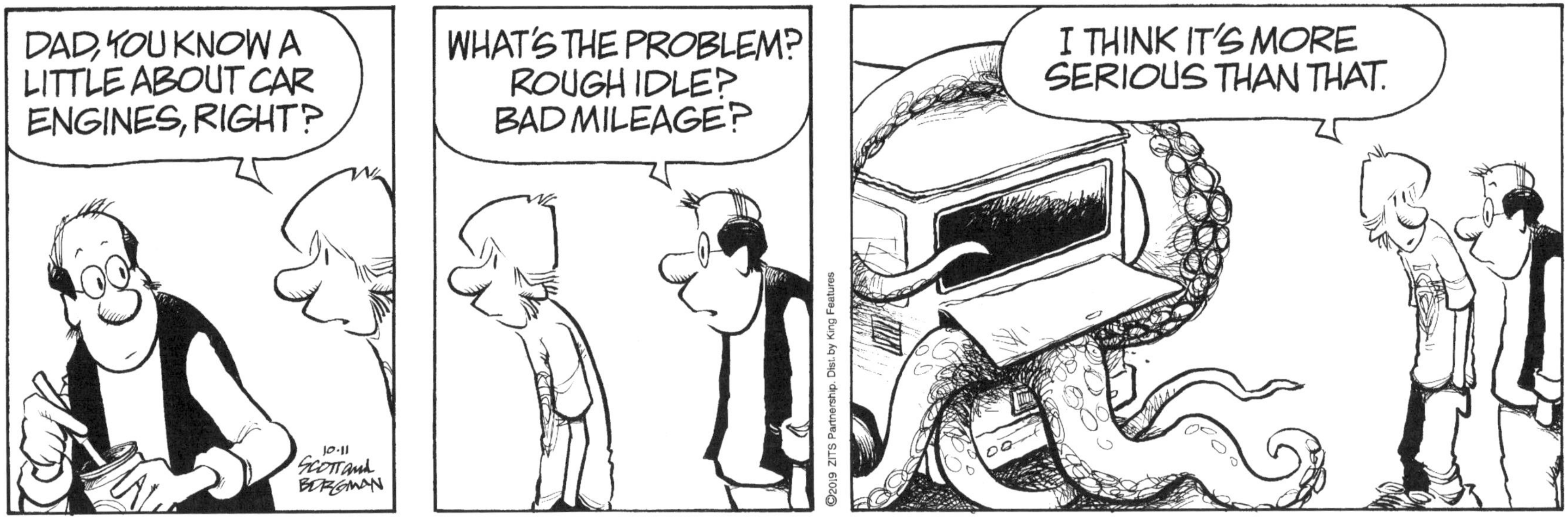
DAD, YOU KNOW A LITTLE ABOUT CAR ENGINES, RIGHT?
10-11 SCOTT and BORGMAN
WHAT'S THE PROBLEM? ROUGH IDLE? BAD MILEAGE?
©2019 ZITS Partnership. Dist. by King Features
I THINK IT'S MORE SERIOUS THAN THAT.

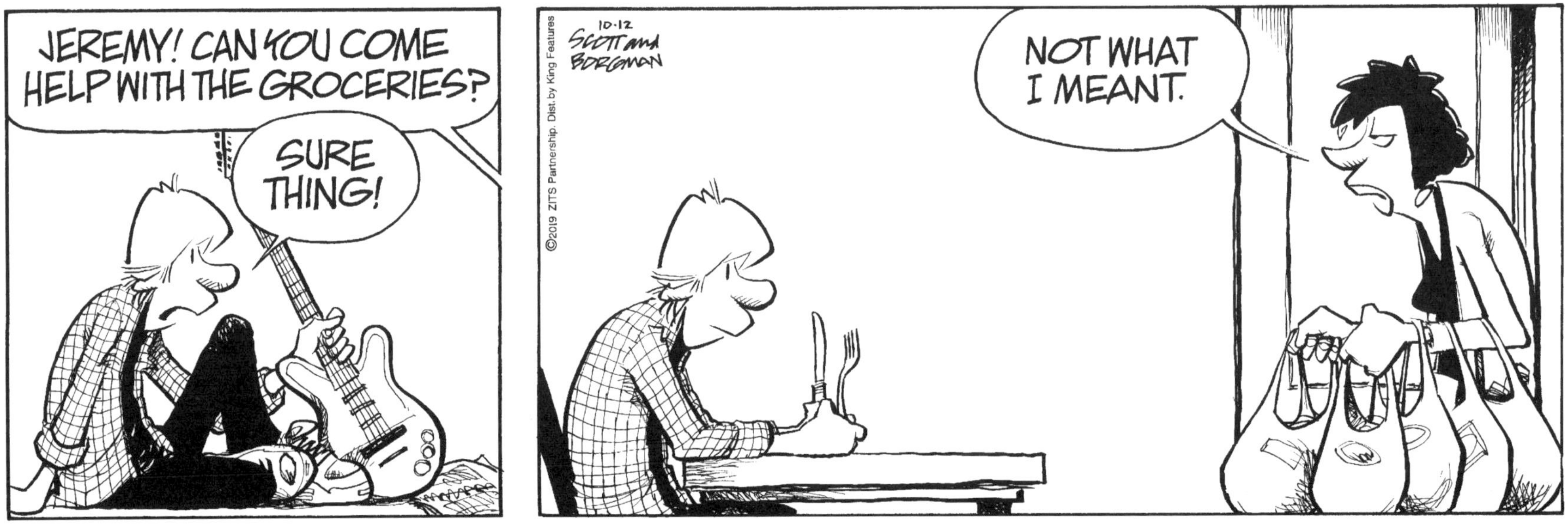
JEREMY! CAN YOU COME HELP WITH THE GROCERIES?
SURE THING!
©2019 ZITS Partnership. Dist. by King Features
10-12 SCOTT and BORGMAN
NOT WHAT I MEANT.

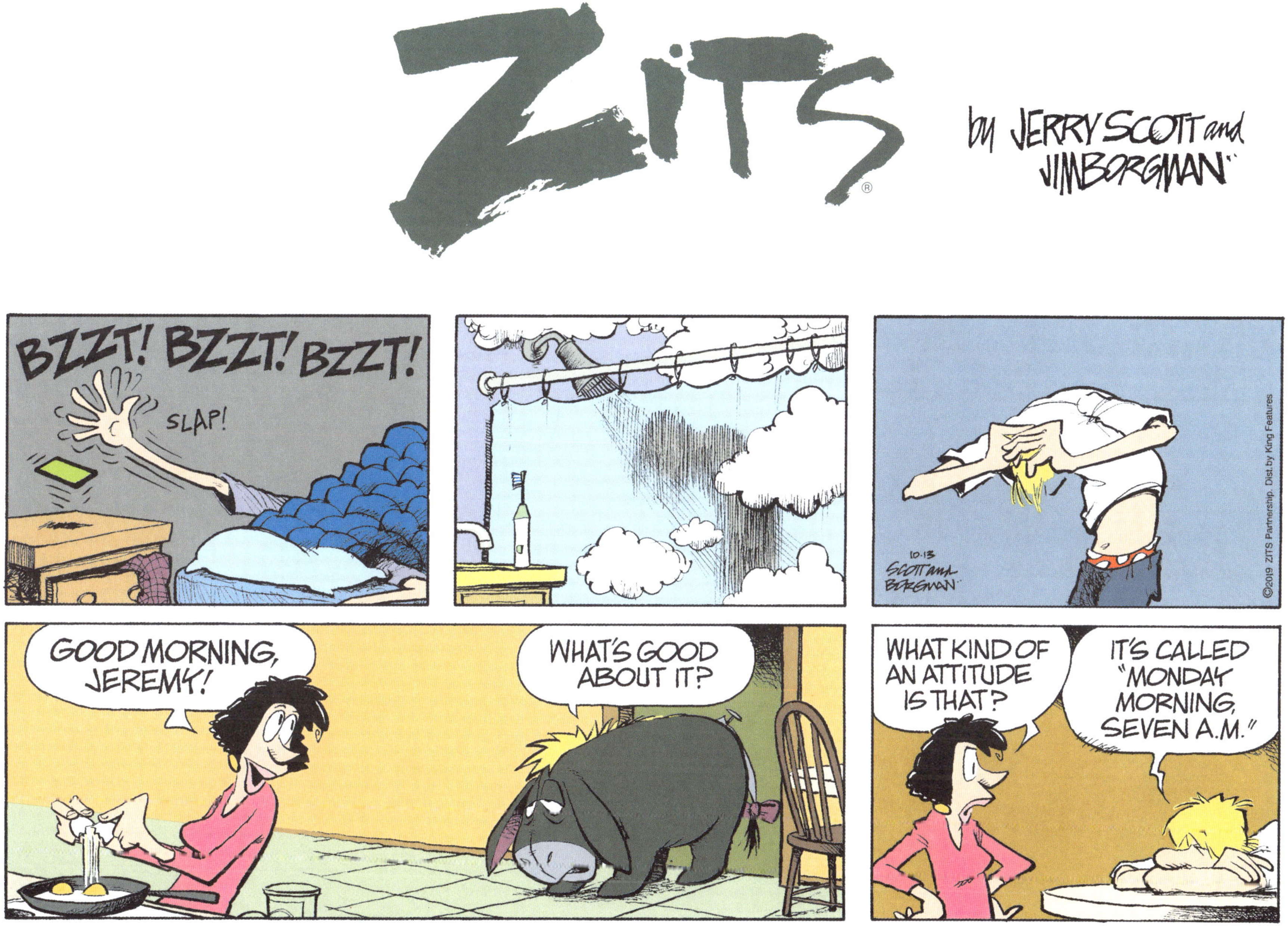
ZITS®
by JERRY SCOTT and JIM BORGMAN
BZZT! BZZT! BZZT!
SLAP!
10-13
SCOTT AND BORGMAN
©2019 ZITS Partnership. Dist. by King Features
GOOD MORNING, JEREMY!
WHAT'S GOOD ABOUT IT?
WHAT KIND OF AN ATTITUDE IS THAT?
IT'S CALLED "MONDAY MORNING, SEVEN A.M."

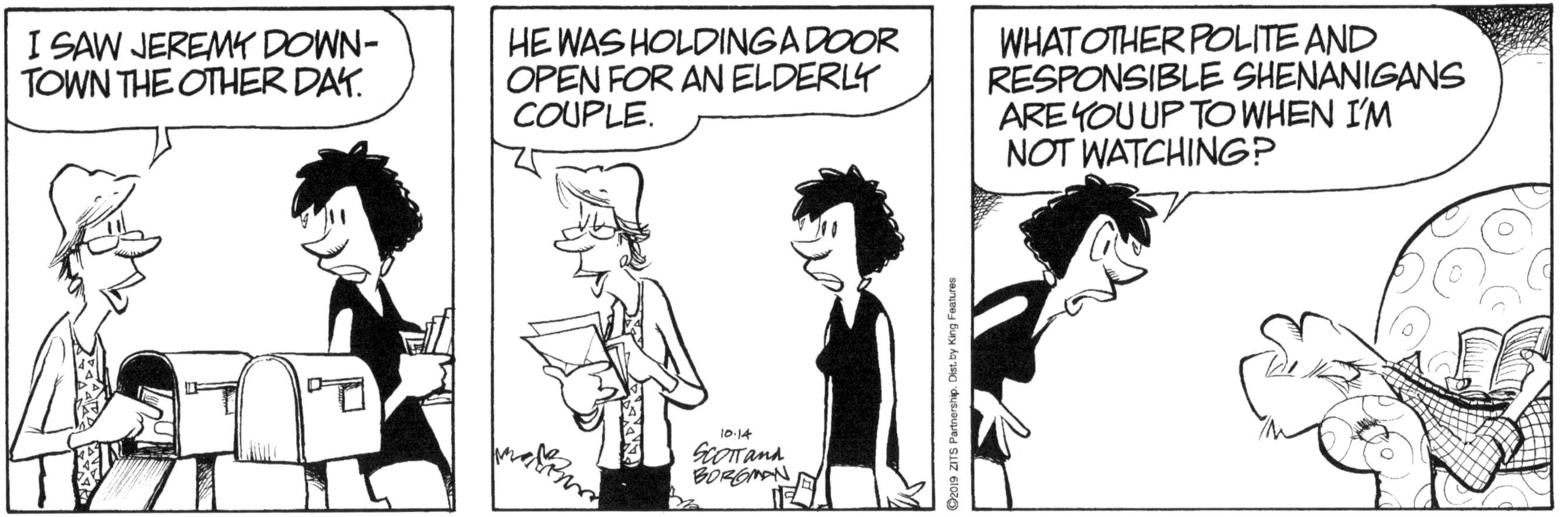
I SAW JEREMY DOWN-TOWN THE OTHER DAY.
HE WAS HOLDING A DOOR OPEN FOR AN ELDERLY COUPLE.
10.14 SCOTT and BORGMAN
©2019 ZITS Partnership. Dist. by King Features
WHAT OTHER POLITE AND RESPONSIBLE SHENANIGANS ARE YOU UP TO WHEN I'M NOT WATCHING?

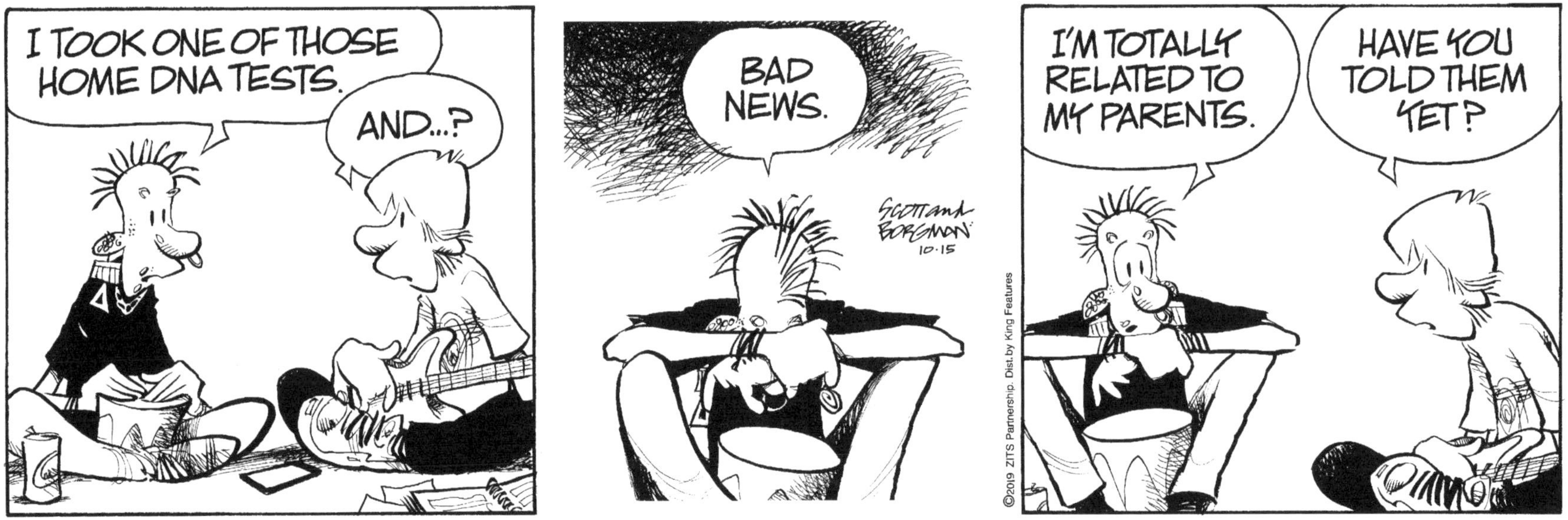
I TOOK ONE OF THOSE HOME DNA TESTS.
AND...?
BAD NEWS.
SCOTT and BORGMAN 10.15
©2019 ZITS Partnership. Dist. by King Features
I'M TOTALLY RELATED TO MY PARENTS.
HAVE YOU TOLD THEM YET?

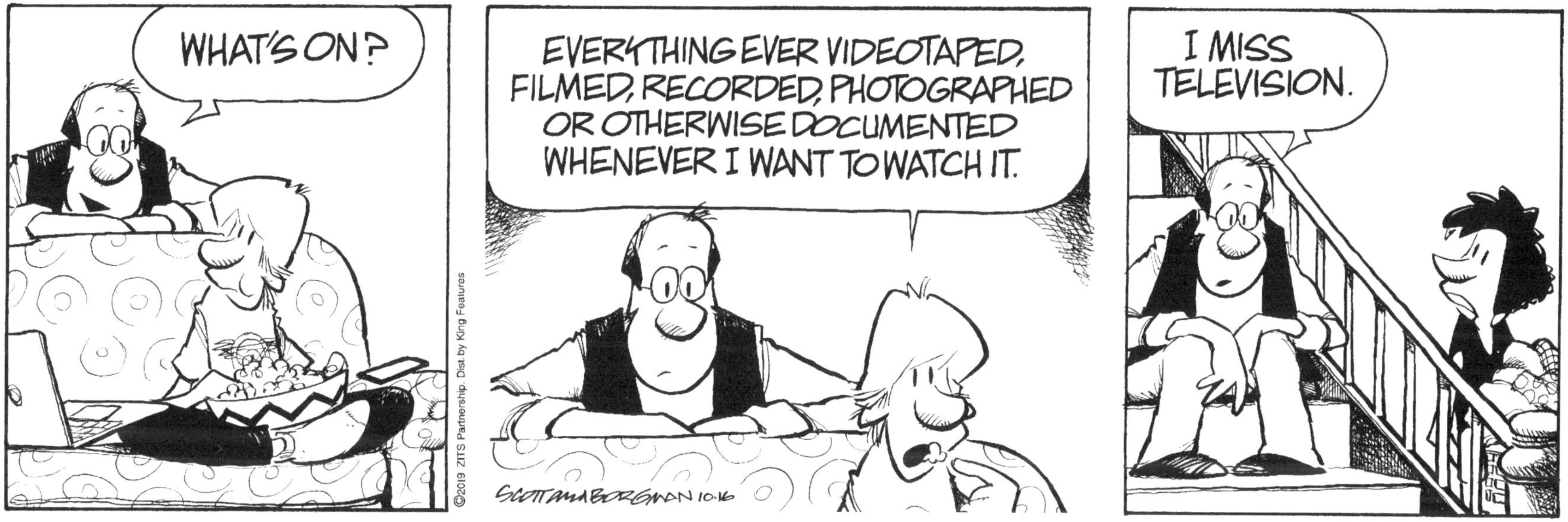
WHAT'S ON?
EVERYTHING EVER VIDEOTAPED, FILMED, RECORDED, PHOTOGRAPHED OR OTHERWISE DOCUMENTED WHENEVER I WANT TO WATCH IT.
I MISS TELEVISION.
©2019 ZITS Partnership. Dist. by King Features
SCOTT AND BORGMAN 10·16

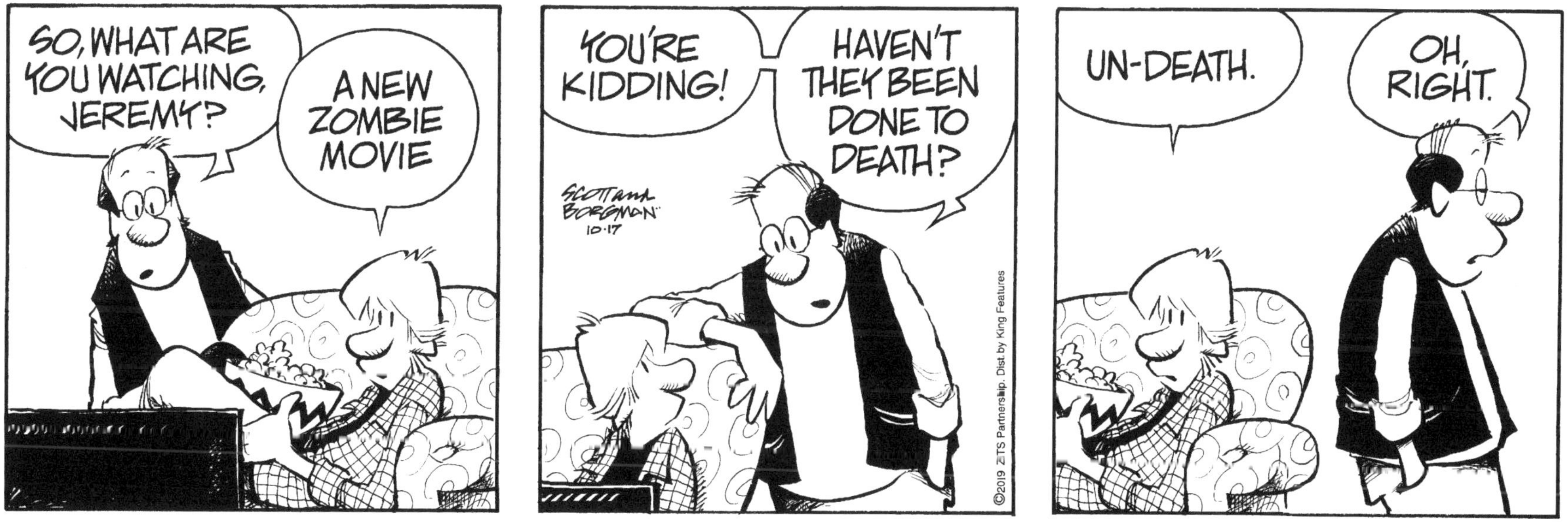
SO, WHAT ARE YOU WATCHING, JEREMY?
A NEW ZOMBIE MOVIE
YOU'RE KIDDING!
HAVEN'T THEY BEEN DONE TO DEATH?
UN-DEATH.
OH, RIGHT.
SCOTT AND BORGMAN 10·17
©2019 ZITS Partnership. Dist. by King Features

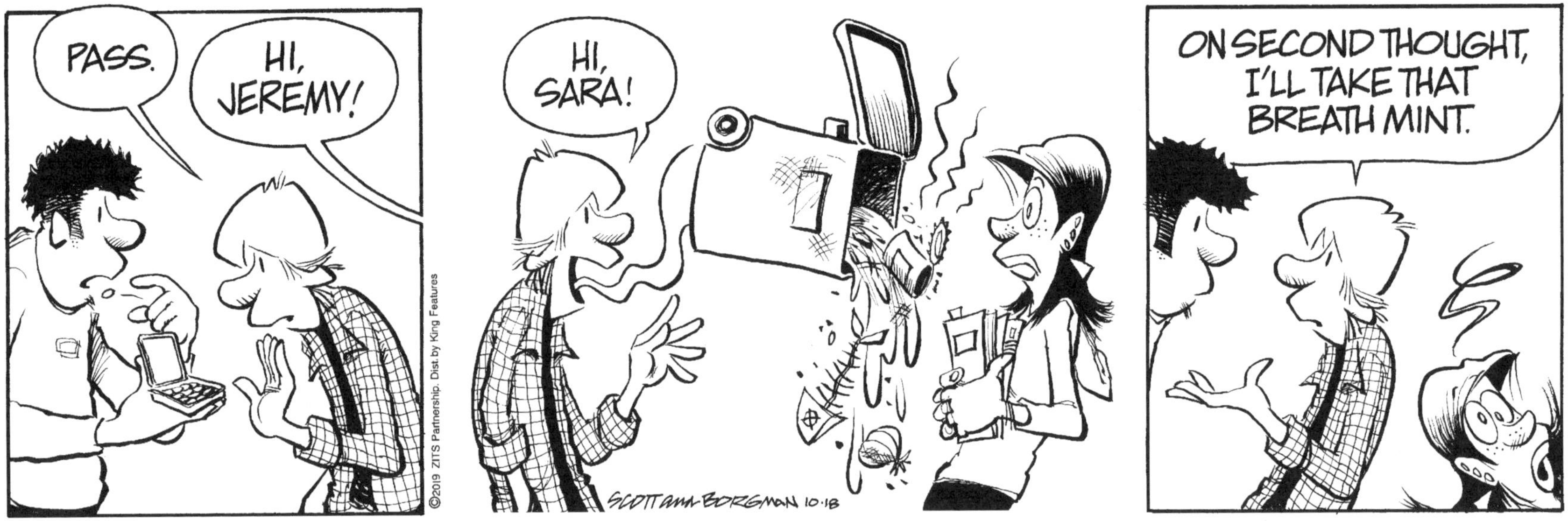
PASS.
HI, JEREMY!
HI, SARA!
ON SECOND THOUGHT, I'LL TAKE THAT BREATH MINT.
©2019 ZITS Partnership. Dist. by King Features
SCOTT and BORGMAN 10·18

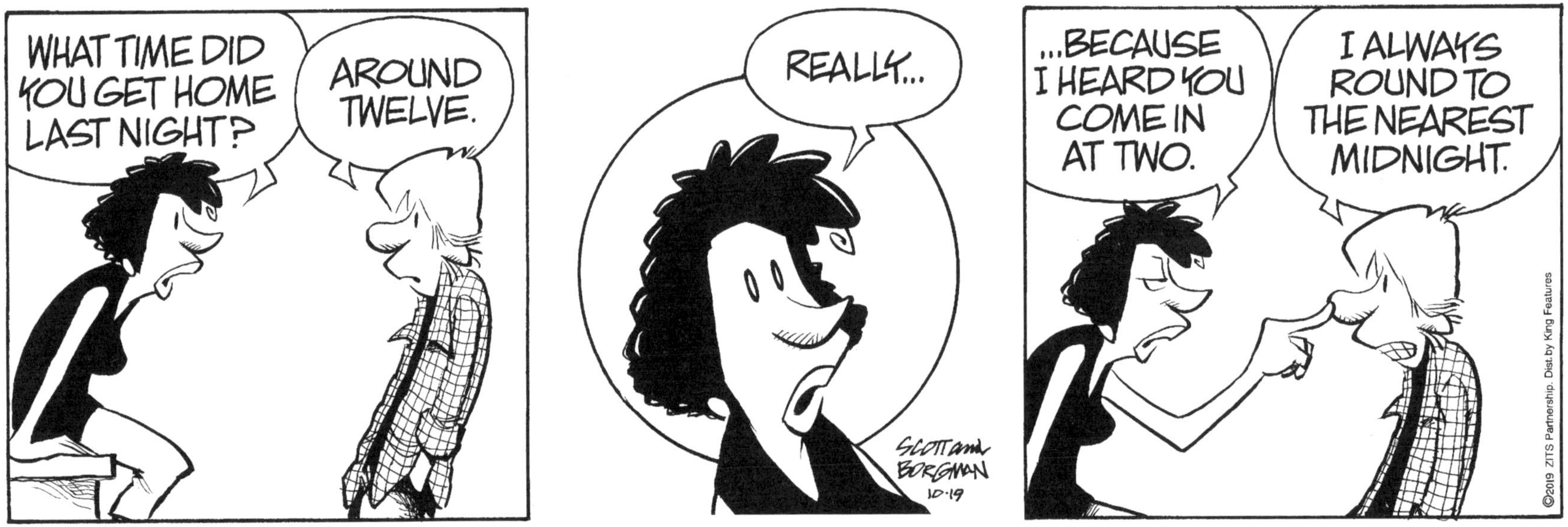
WHAT TIME DID YOU GET HOME LAST NIGHT?
AROUND TWELVE.
REALLY...
...BECAUSE I HEARD YOU COME IN AT TWO.
I ALWAYS ROUND TO THE NEAREST MIDNIGHT.
SCOTT and BORGMAN 10·19
©2019 ZITS Partnership. Dist. by King Features

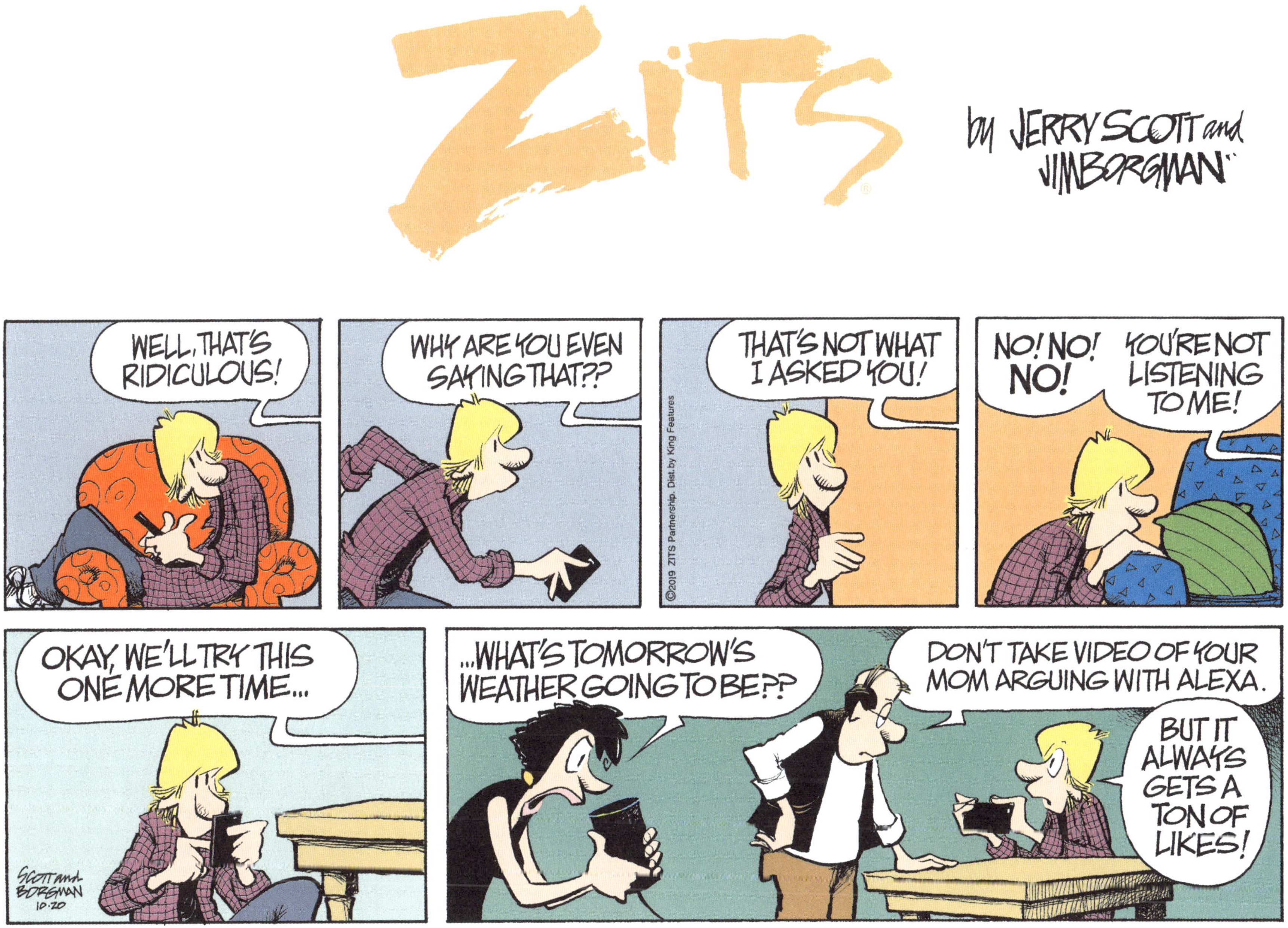
ZITS
by JERRY SCOTT and JIM BORGMAN
WELL, THAT'S RIDICULOUS!
WHY ARE YOU EVEN SAYING THAT??
©2019 ZITS Partnership. Dist. by King Features
THAT'S NOT WHAT I ASKED YOU!
NO! NO! NO!
YOU'RE NOT LISTENING TO ME!
OKAY, WE'LL TRY THIS ONE MORE TIME...
SCOTT and BORGMAN 10-20
...WHAT'S TOMORROW'S WEATHER GOING TO BE??
DON'T TAKE VIDEO OF YOUR MOM ARGUING WITH ALEXA.
BUT IT ALWAYS GETS A TON OF LIKES!

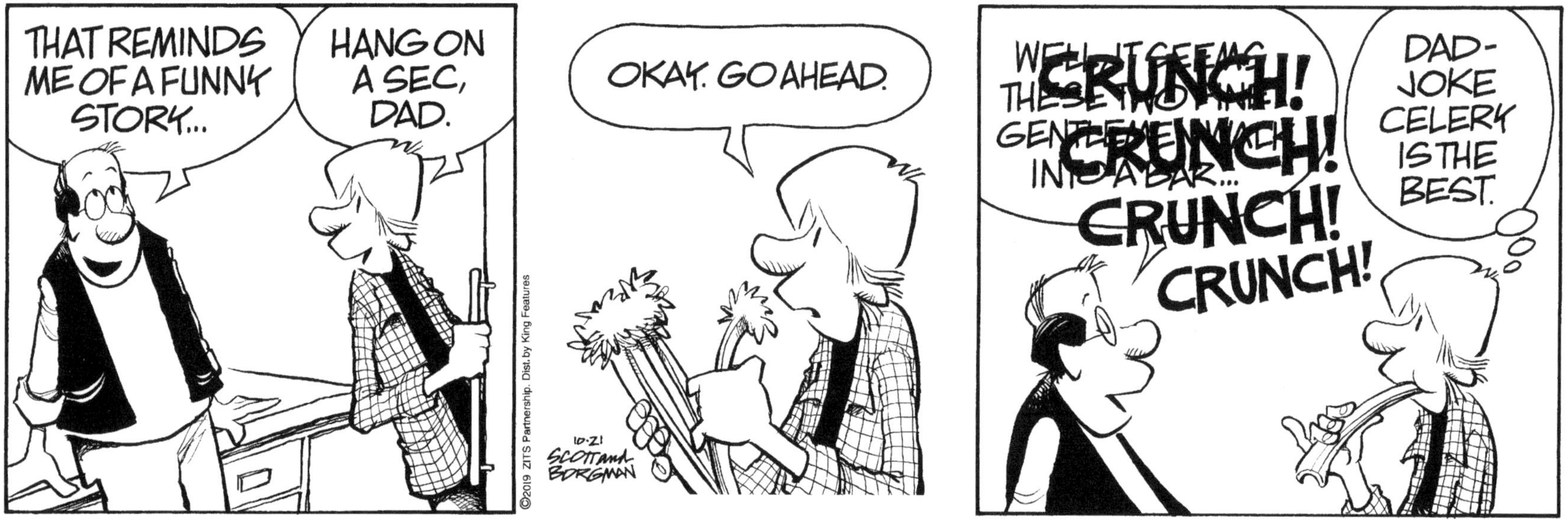
THAT REMINDS ME OF A FUNNY STORY...
HANG ON A SEC, DAD.
©2019 ZITS Partnership. Dist. by King Features
OKAY. GO AHEAD.
10·21 SCOTT and BORGMAN
CRUNCH!
CRUNCH!
CRUNCH!
CRUNCH!
DAD-JOKE CELERY IS THE BEST.

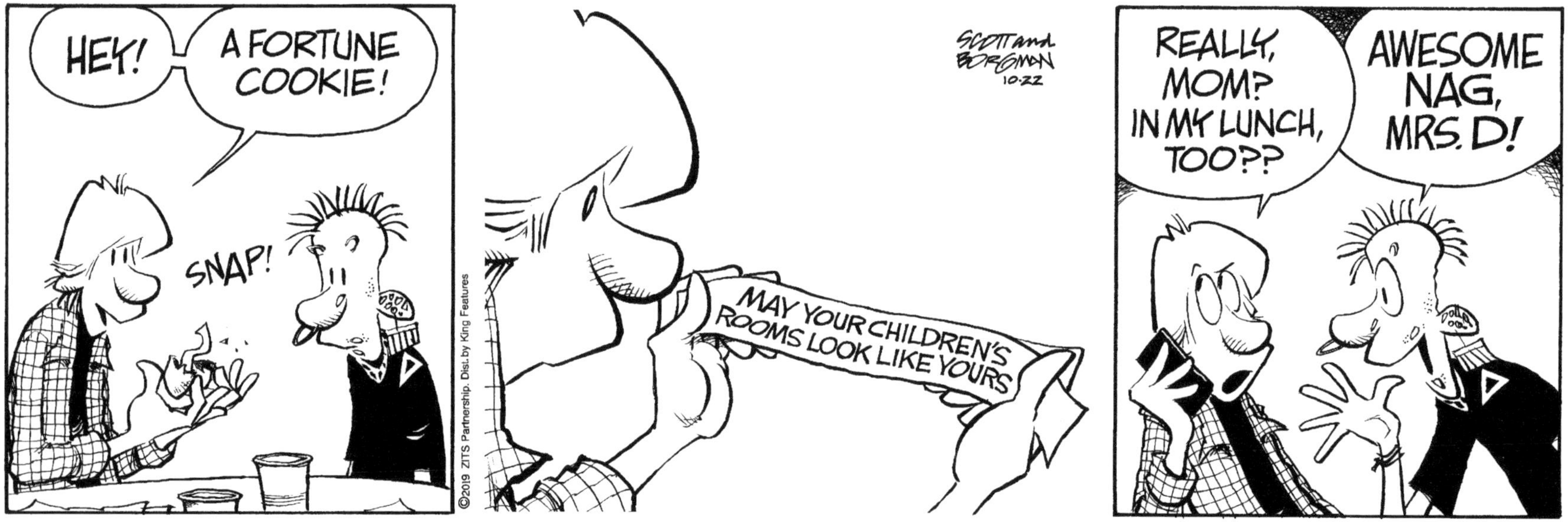
HEY!
A FORTUNE COOKIE!
SNAP!
©2019 ZITS Partnership. Dist. by King Features
MAY YOUR CHILDREN'S ROOMS LOOK LIKE YOURS
SCOTT and BORGMAN 10·22
REALLY, MOM? IN MY LUNCH, TOO??
AWESOME NAG, MRS. D!

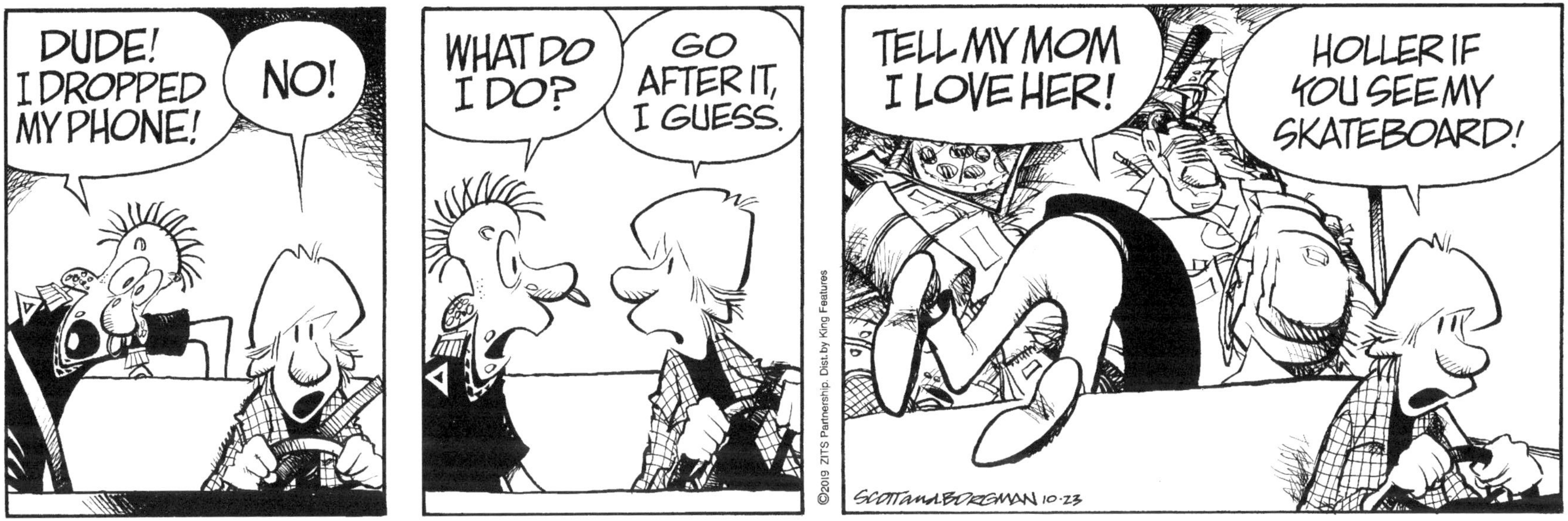
DUDE! I DROPPED MY PHONE!
NO!
WHAT DO I DO?
GO AFTER IT, I GUESS.
TELL MY MOM I LOVE HER!
HOLLER IF YOU SEE MY SKATEBOARD!
©2019 ZITS Partnership. Dist. by King Features
SCOTT and BORGMAN 10·23

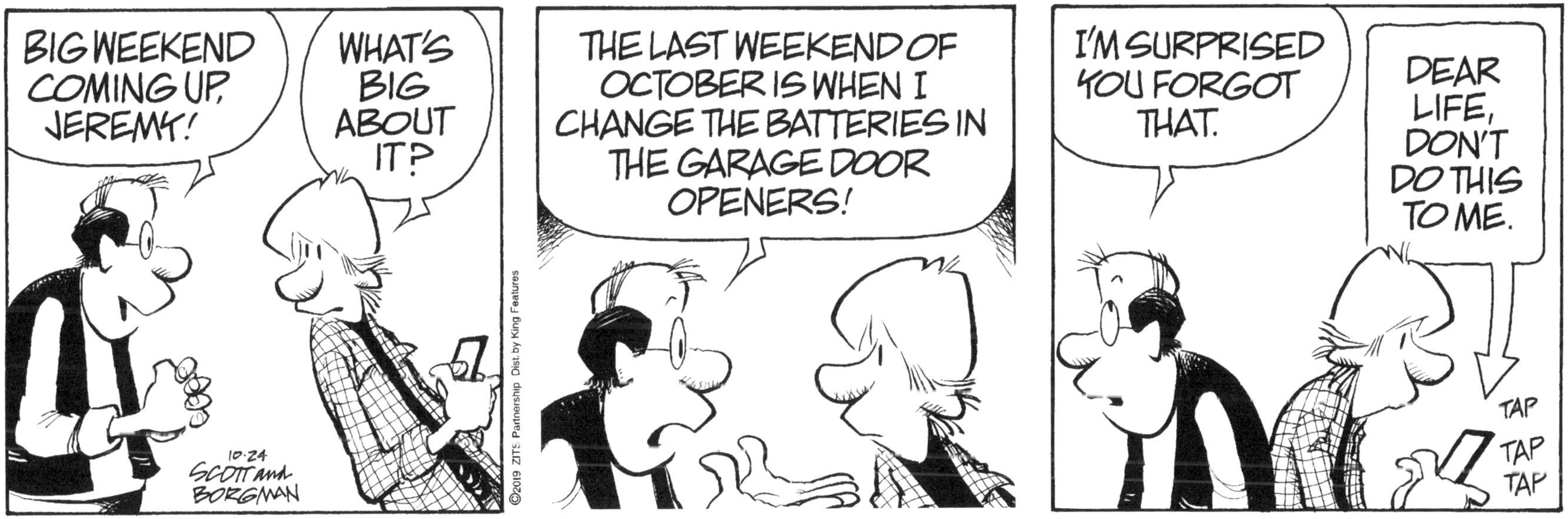
BIG WEEKEND COMING UP, JEREMY!
WHAT'S BIG ABOUT IT?
10·24 SCOTT and BORGMAN
©2019 ZITS Partnership. Dist. by King Features
THE LAST WEEKEND OF OCTOBER IS WHEN I CHANGE THE BATTERIES IN THE GARAGE DOOR OPENERS!
I'M SURPRISED YOU FORGOT THAT.
DEAR LIFE, DON'T DO THIS TO ME.
TAP
TAP
TAP

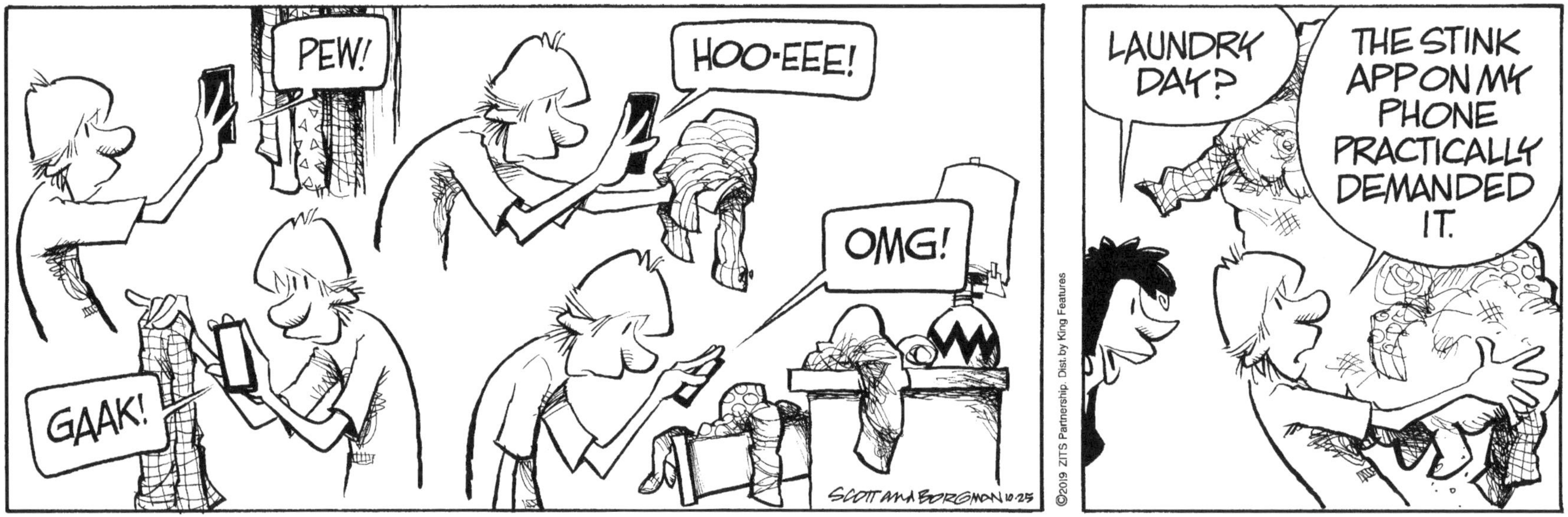
PEW!
GAAK!
HOO-EEE!
OMG!
SCOTT and BORGMAN 10-25
LAUNDRY DAY?
THE STINK APP ON MY PHONE PRACTICALLY DEMANDED IT.
©2019 ZITS Partnership. Dist. by King Features

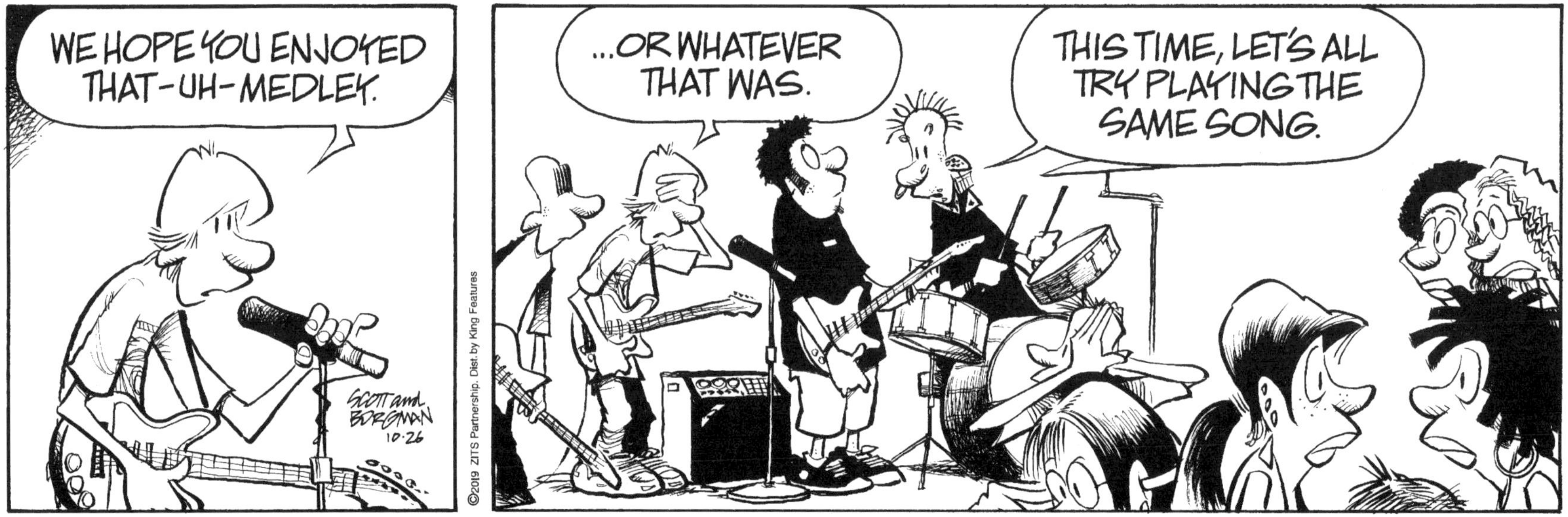
WE HOPE YOU ENJOYED THAT-UH-MEDLEY.
SCOTT and BORGMAN 10-26
©2019 ZITS Partnership. Dist. by King Features
...OR WHATEVER THAT WAS.
THIS TIME, LET'S ALL TRY PLAYING THE SAME SONG.

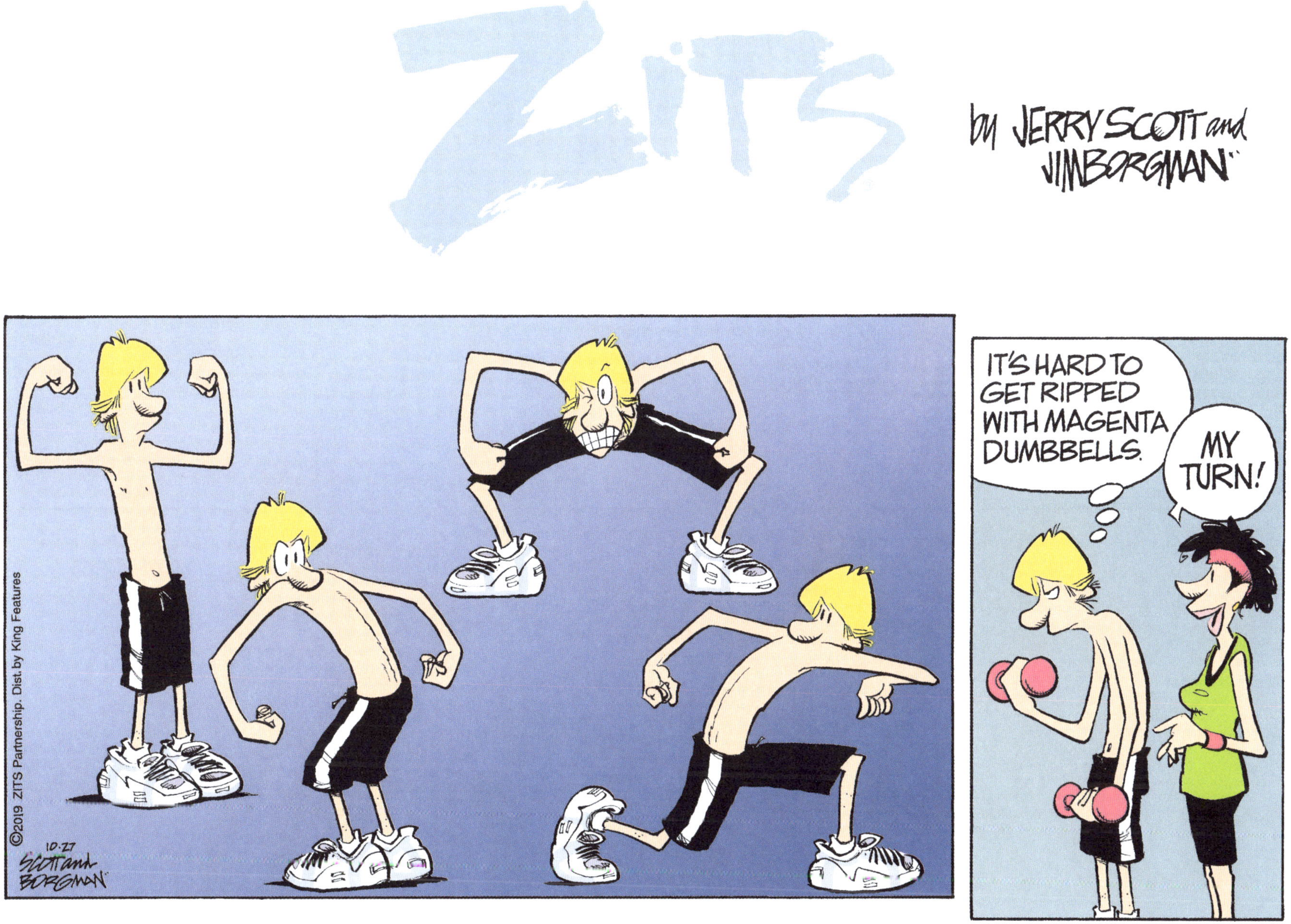
ZITS
by JERRY SCOTT and JIM BORGMAN
©2019 ZITS Partnership. Dist. by King Features
10-27 SCOTT and BORGMAN
IT'S HARD TO GET RIPPED WITH MAGENTA DUMBBELLS.
MY TURN!

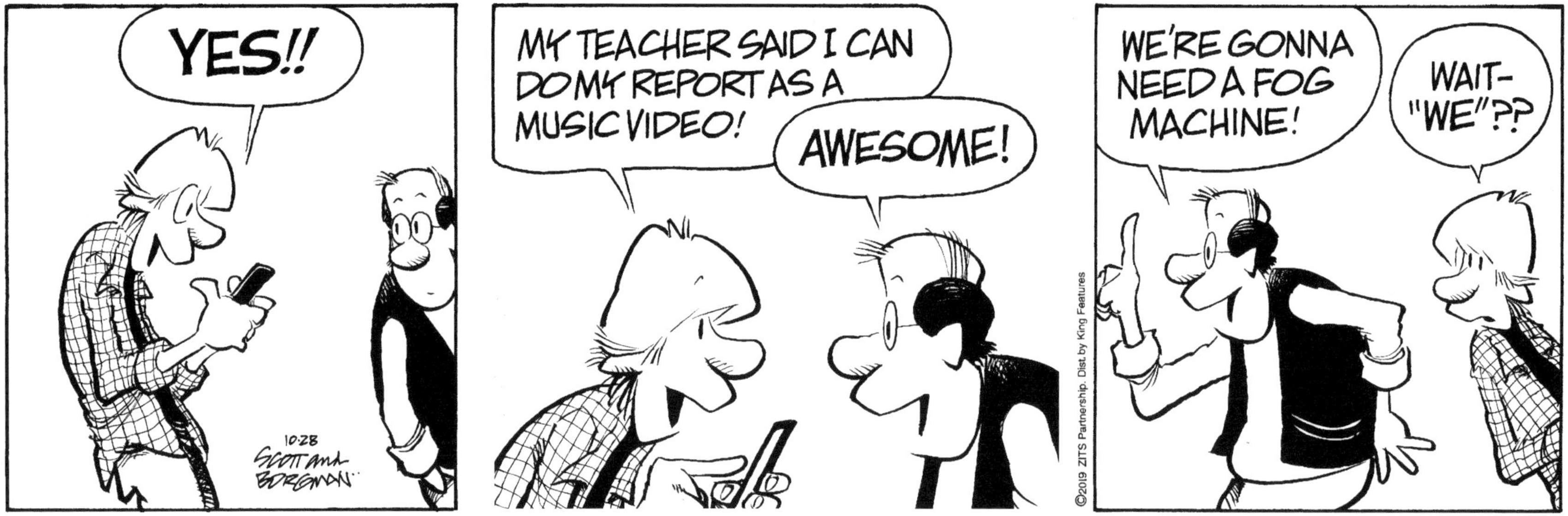
YES!!
10·28 SCOTT and BORGMAN
MY TEACHER SAID I CAN DO MY REPORT AS A MUSIC VIDEO!
AWESOME!
©2019 ZITS Partnership. Dist. by King Features
WE'RE GONNA NEED A FOG MACHINE!
WAIT- "WE"??

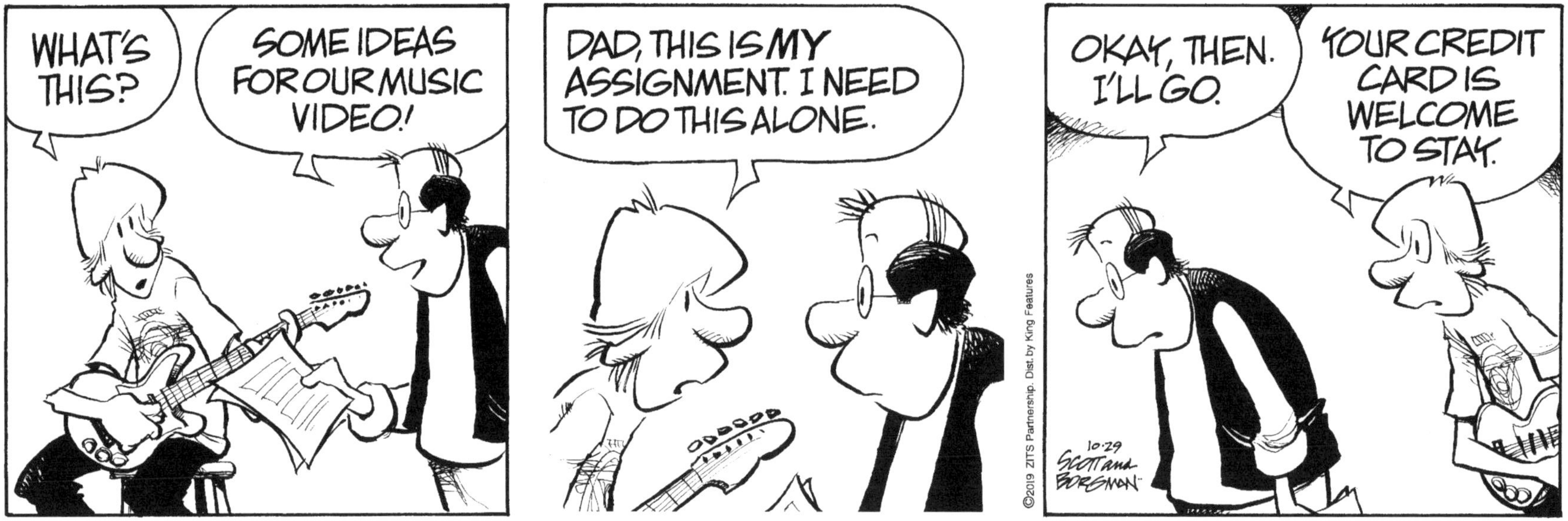
WHAT'S THIS?
SOME IDEAS FOR OUR MUSIC VIDEO!
DAD, THIS IS MY ASSIGNMENT. I NEED TO DO THIS ALONE.
©2019 ZITS Partnership. Dist. by King Features
OKAY, THEN. I'LL GO.
YOUR CREDIT CARD IS WELCOME TO STAY.
10·29 SCOTT and BORGMAN

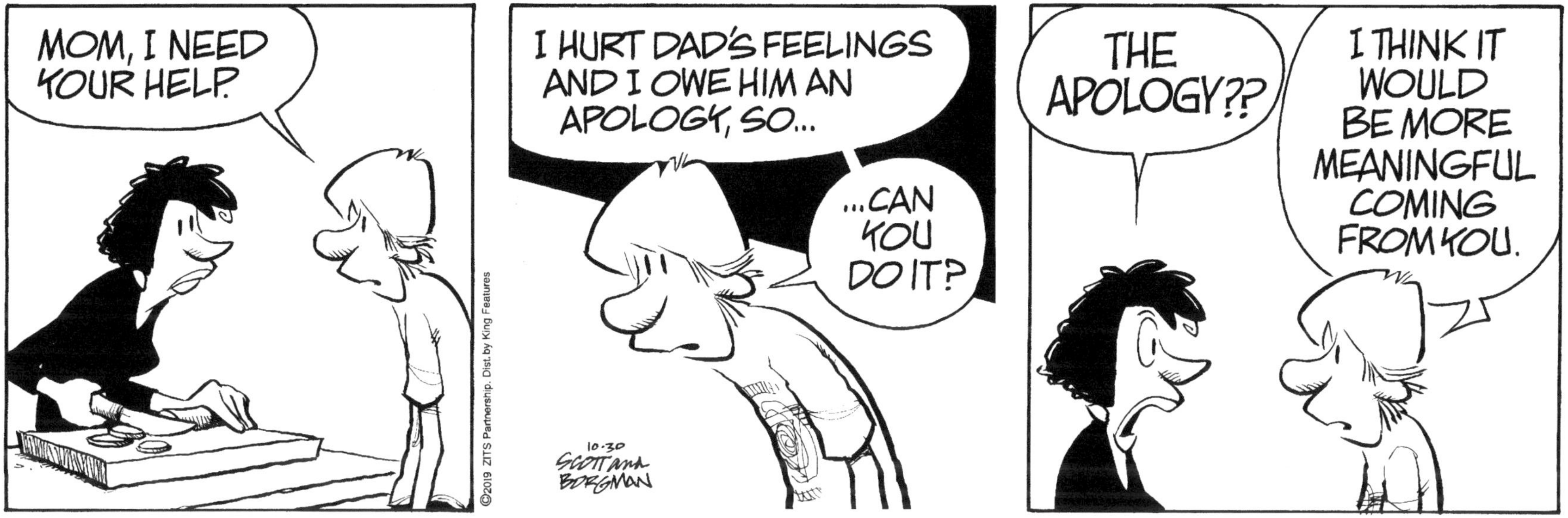
MOM, I NEED YOUR HELP.
I HURT DAD'S FEELINGS AND I OWE HIM AN APOLOGY, SO...
...CAN YOU DO IT?
THE APOLOGY??
I THINK IT WOULD BE MORE MEANINGFUL COMING FROM YOU.
©2019 ZITS Partnership. Dist. by King Features
10-30

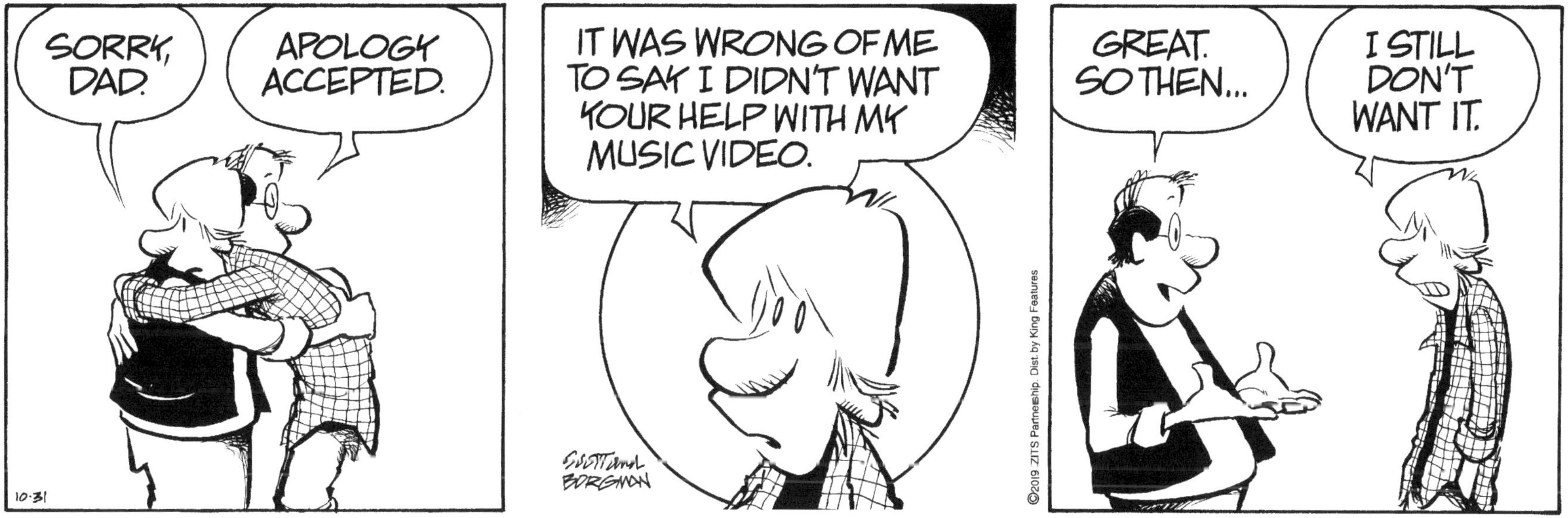
SORRY, DAD.
APOLOGY ACCEPTED.
IT WAS WRONG OF ME TO SAY I DIDN'T WANT YOUR HELP WITH MY MUSIC VIDEO.
GREAT. SO THEN...
I STILL DON'T WANT IT.
10-31
©2019 ZITS Partnership. Dist. by King Features

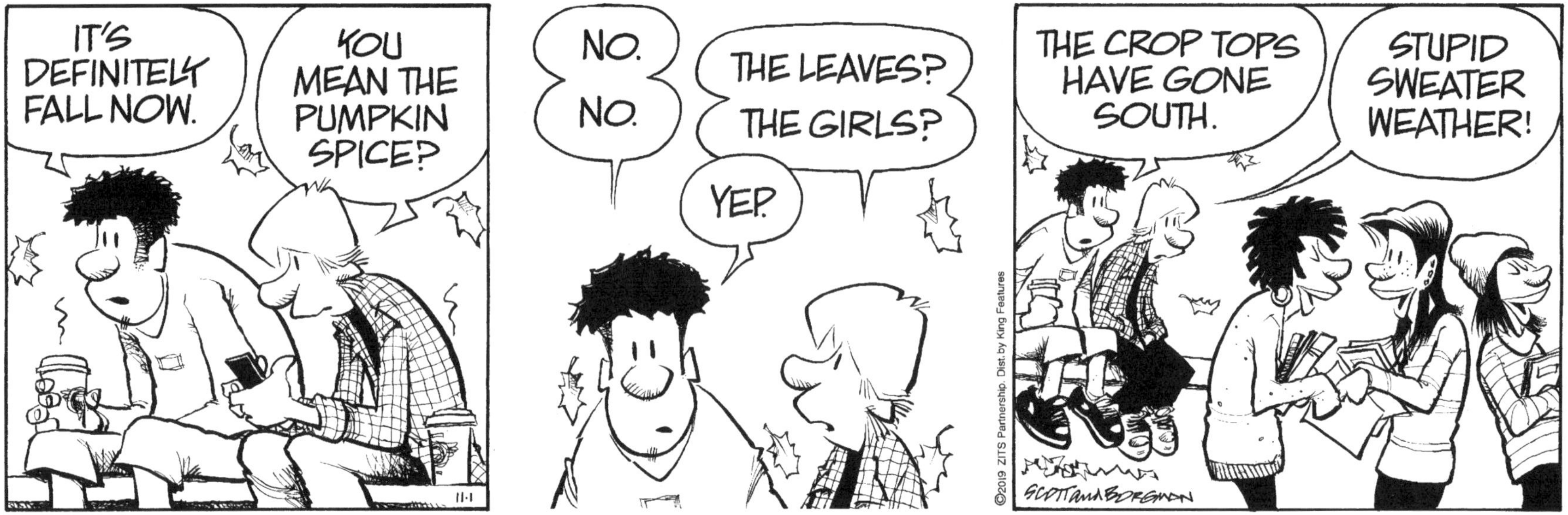
IT'S DEFINITELY FALL NOW.
YOU MEAN THE PUMPKIN SPICE?
NO.
NO.
THE LEAVES?
THE GIRLS?
YEP.
THE CROP TOPS HAVE GONE SOUTH.
STUPID SWEATER WEATHER!
©2019 ZITS Partnership. Dist. by King Features

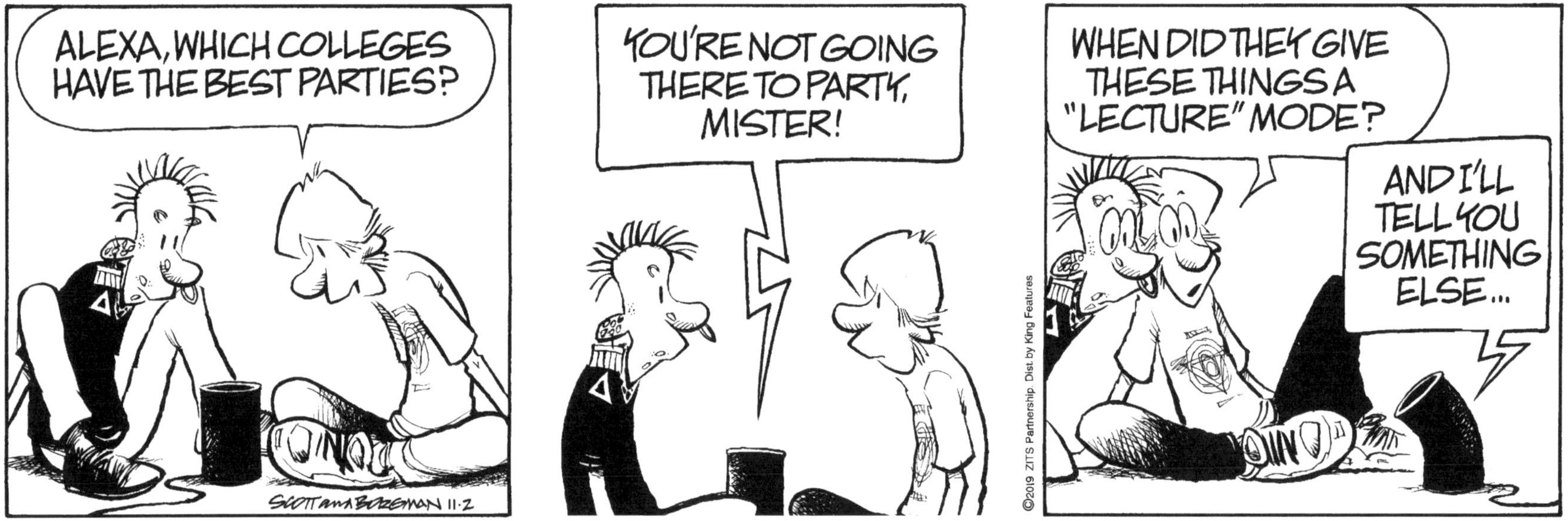
ALEXA, WHICH COLLEGES HAVE THE BEST PARTIES?
YOU'RE NOT GOING THERE TO PARTY, MISTER!
WHEN DID THEY GIVE THESE THINGS A "LECTURE" MODE?
AND I'LL TELL YOU SOMETHING ELSE...
©2019 ZITS Partnership. Dist. by King Features

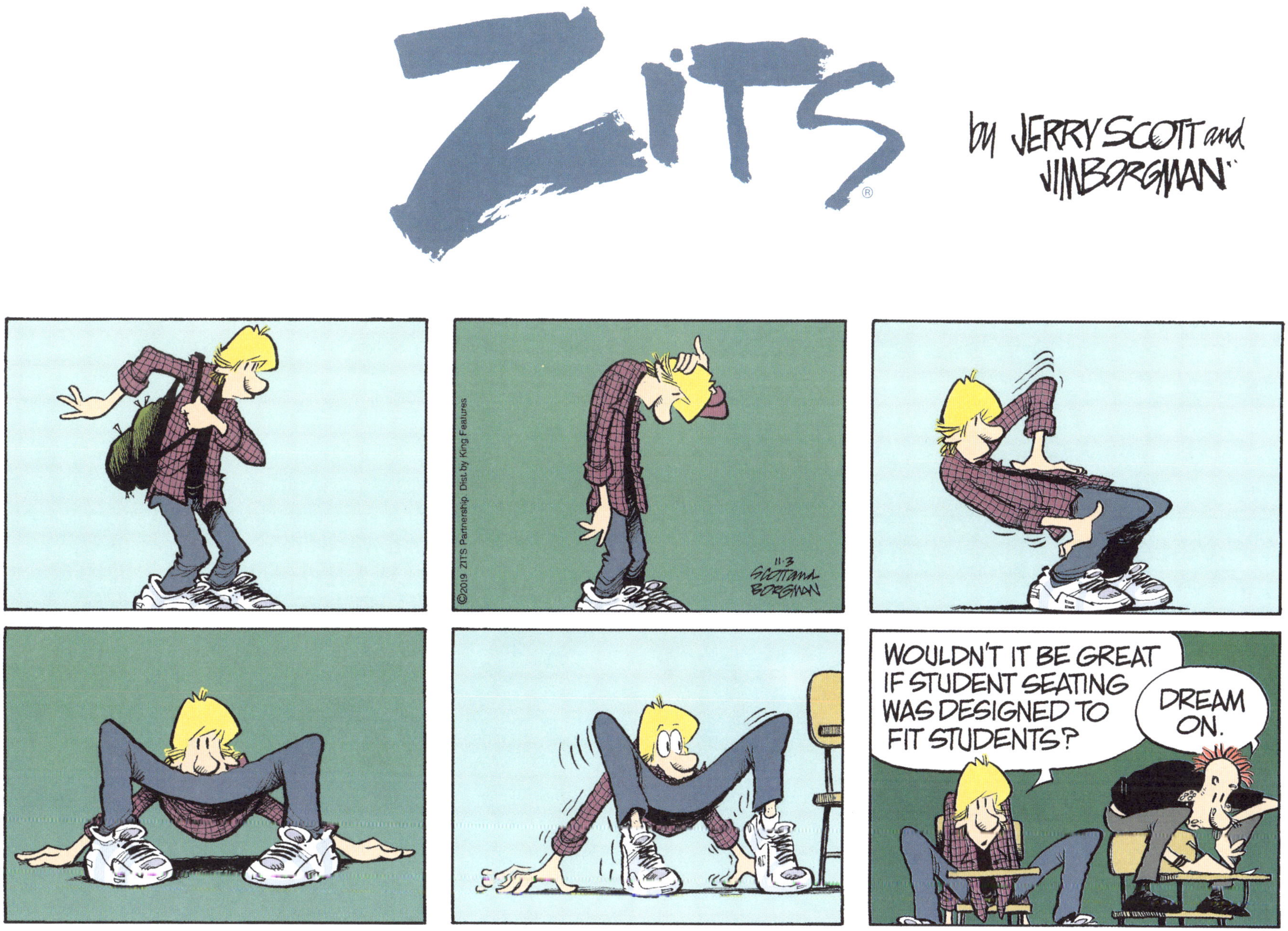
ZITS
by JERRY SCOTT and JIM BORGMAN
©2019 ZITS Partnership. Dist. by King Features
11·3 SCOTT and BORGMAN
WOULDN'T IT BE GREAT IF STUDENT SEATING WAS DESIGNED TO FIT STUDENTS?
DREAM ON.

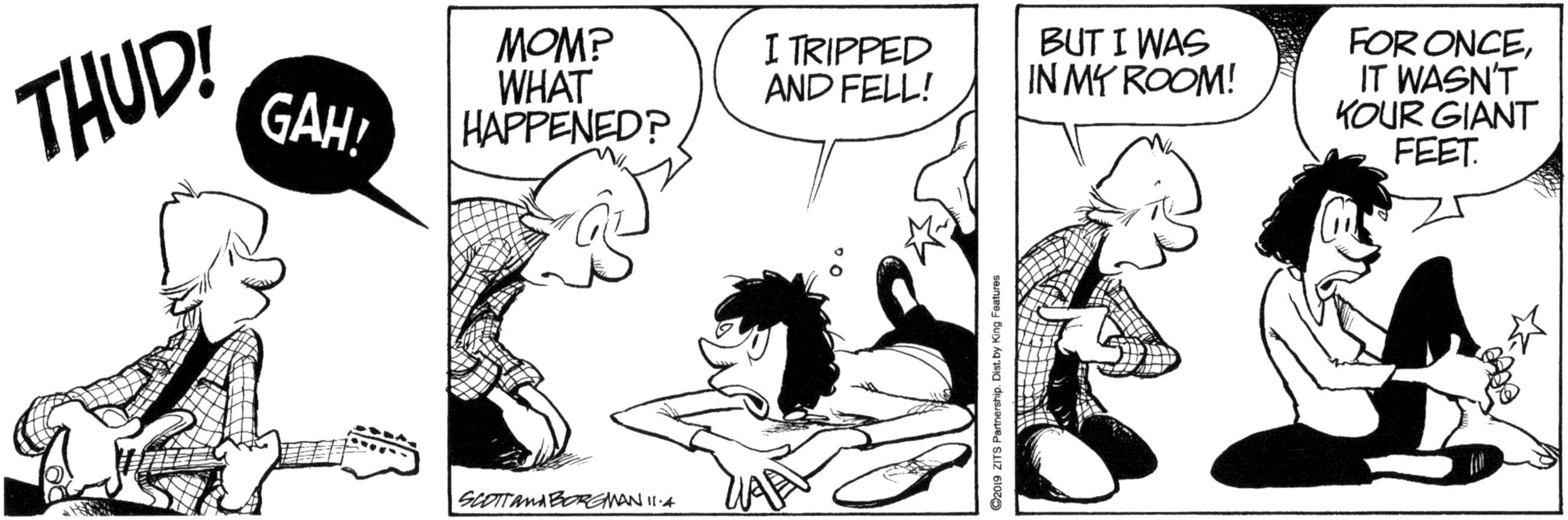
THUD!
GAH!
MOM? WHAT HAPPENED?
I TRIPPED AND FELL!
SCOTT and BORGMAN 11·4
©2019 ZITS Partnership. Dist. by King Features
BUT I WAS IN MY ROOM!
FOR ONCE, IT WASN'T YOUR GIANT FEET.

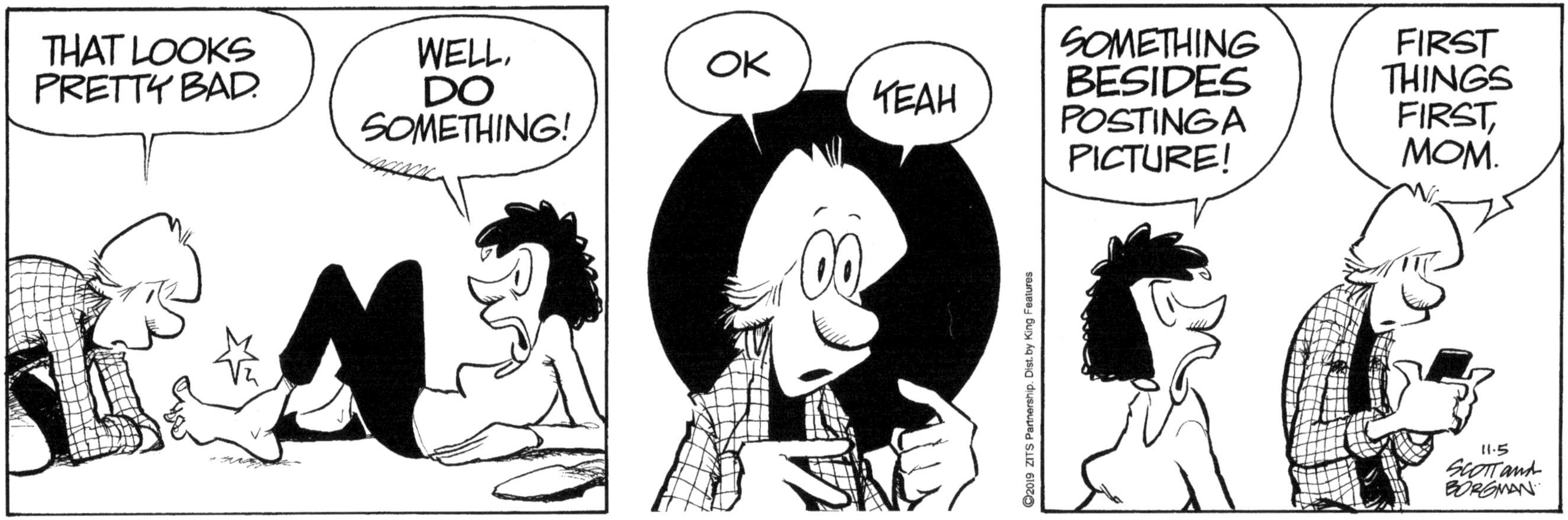
THAT LOOKS PRETTY BAD.
WELL, DO SOMETHING!
OK
YEAH
©2019 ZITS Partnership. Dist. by King Features
SOMETHING BESIDES POSTING A PICTURE!
FIRST THINGS FIRST, MOM.
11·5 SCOTT and BORGMAN

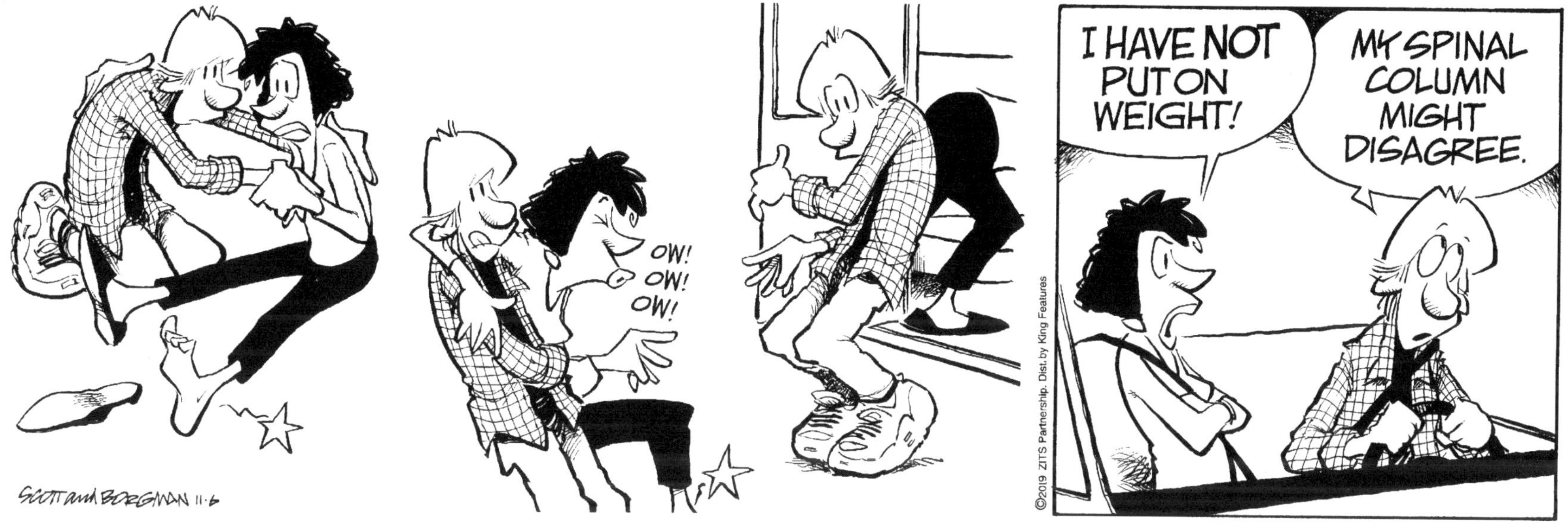

OW! OW! OW!
I HAVE NOT PUT ON WEIGHT!
MY SPINAL COLUMN MIGHT DISAGREE.
©2019 ZITS Partnership. Dist. by King Features

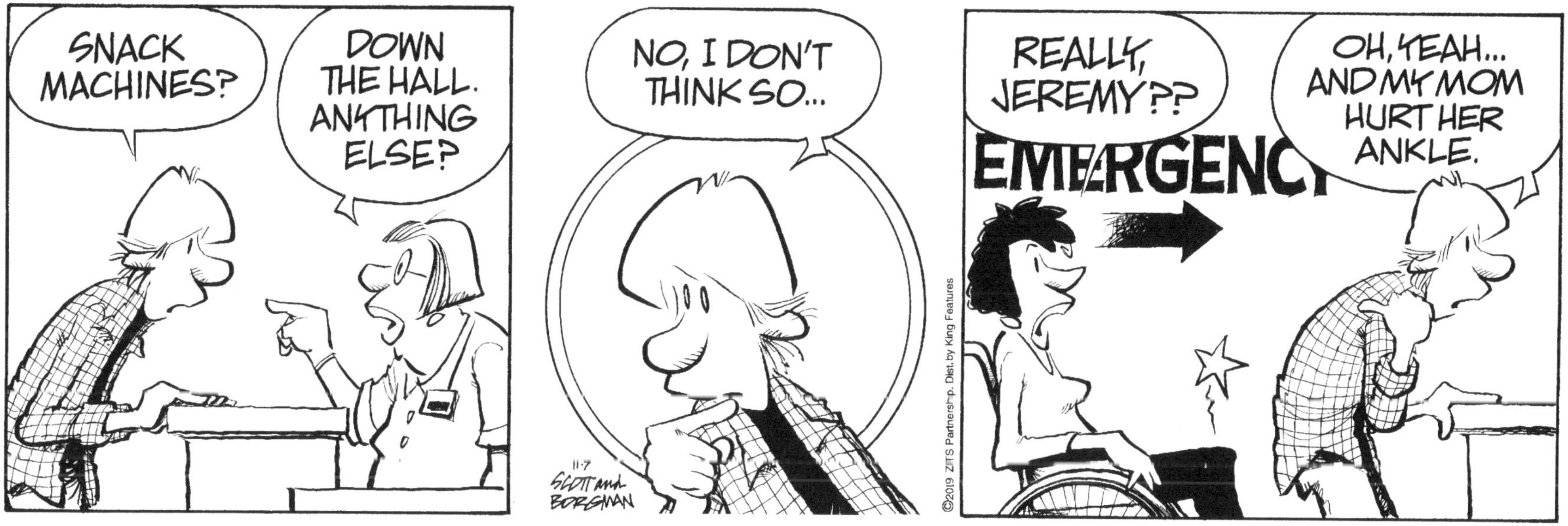

SNACK MACHINES?
DOWN THE HALL. ANYTHING ELSE?
NO, I DON'T THINK SO...
REALLY, JEREMY??
OH, YEAH... AND MY MOM HURT HER ANKLE.
EMERGENCY
©2019 ZITS Partnership. Dist. by King Features

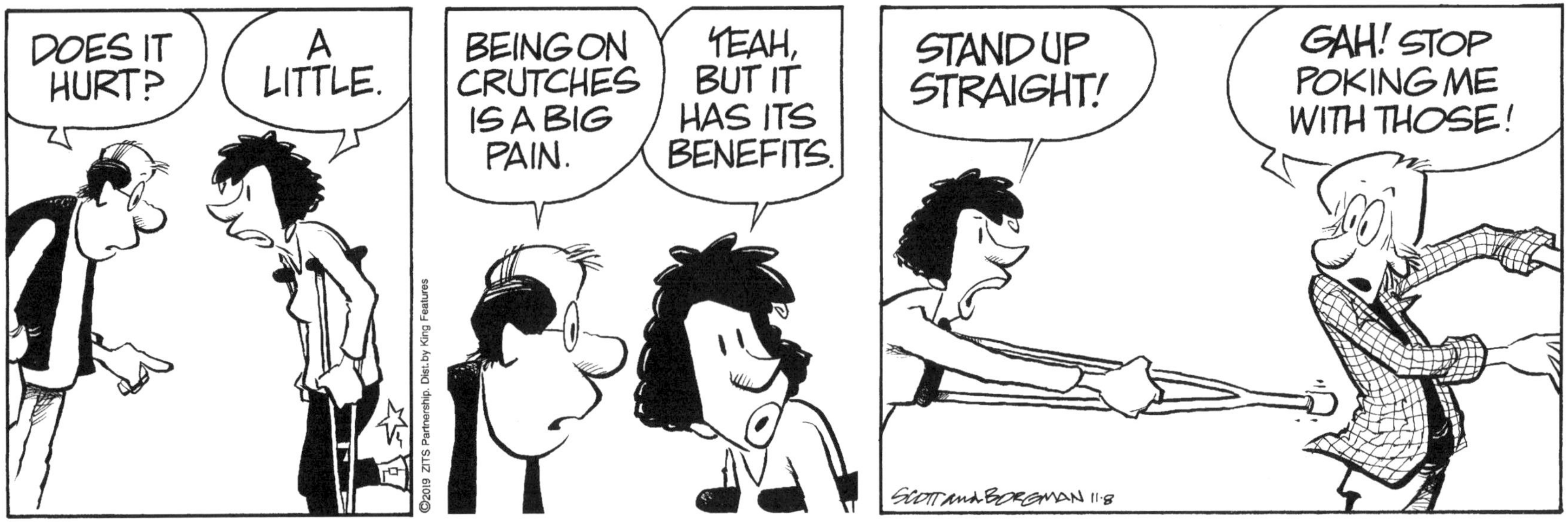
DOES IT HURT?
A LITTLE.
©2019 ZITS Partnership. Dist. by King Features
BEING ON CRUTCHES IS A BIG PAIN.
YEAH, BUT IT HAS ITS BENEFITS.
STAND UP STRAIGHT!
GAH! STOP POKING ME WITH THOSE!
SCOTT and BORGMAN 11·8

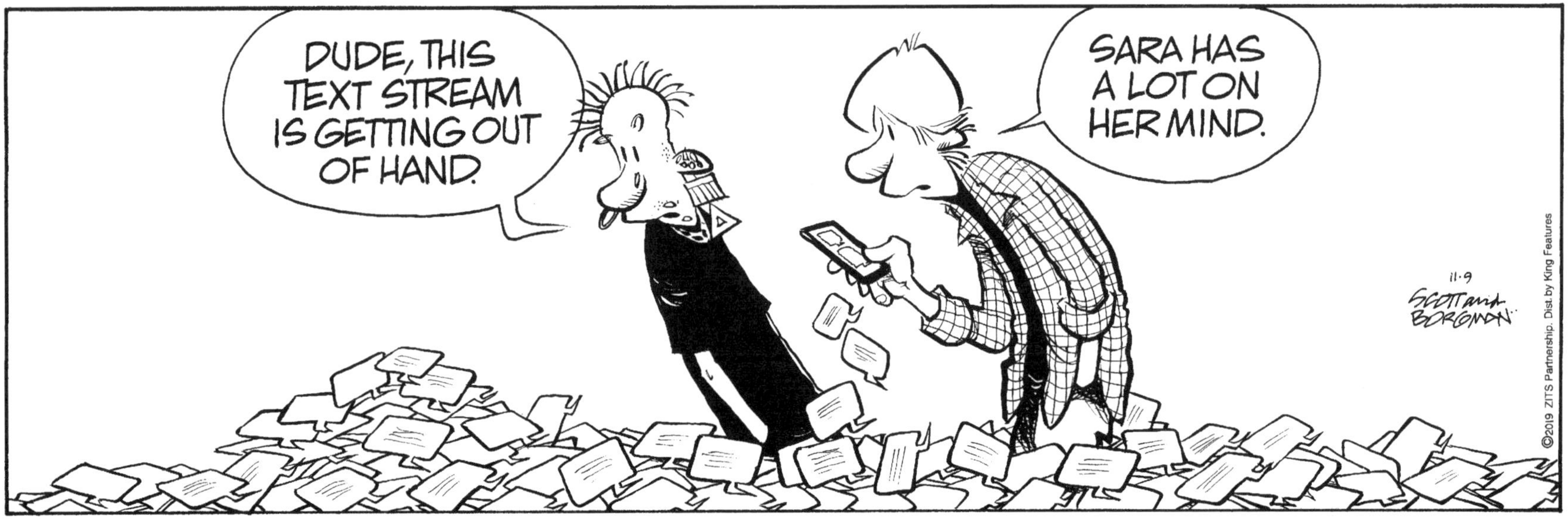
DUDE, THIS TEXT STREAM IS GETTING OUT OF HAND.
SARA HAS A LOT ON HER MIND.
11·9 SCOTT and BORGMAN
©2019 ZITS Partnership. Dist. by King Features

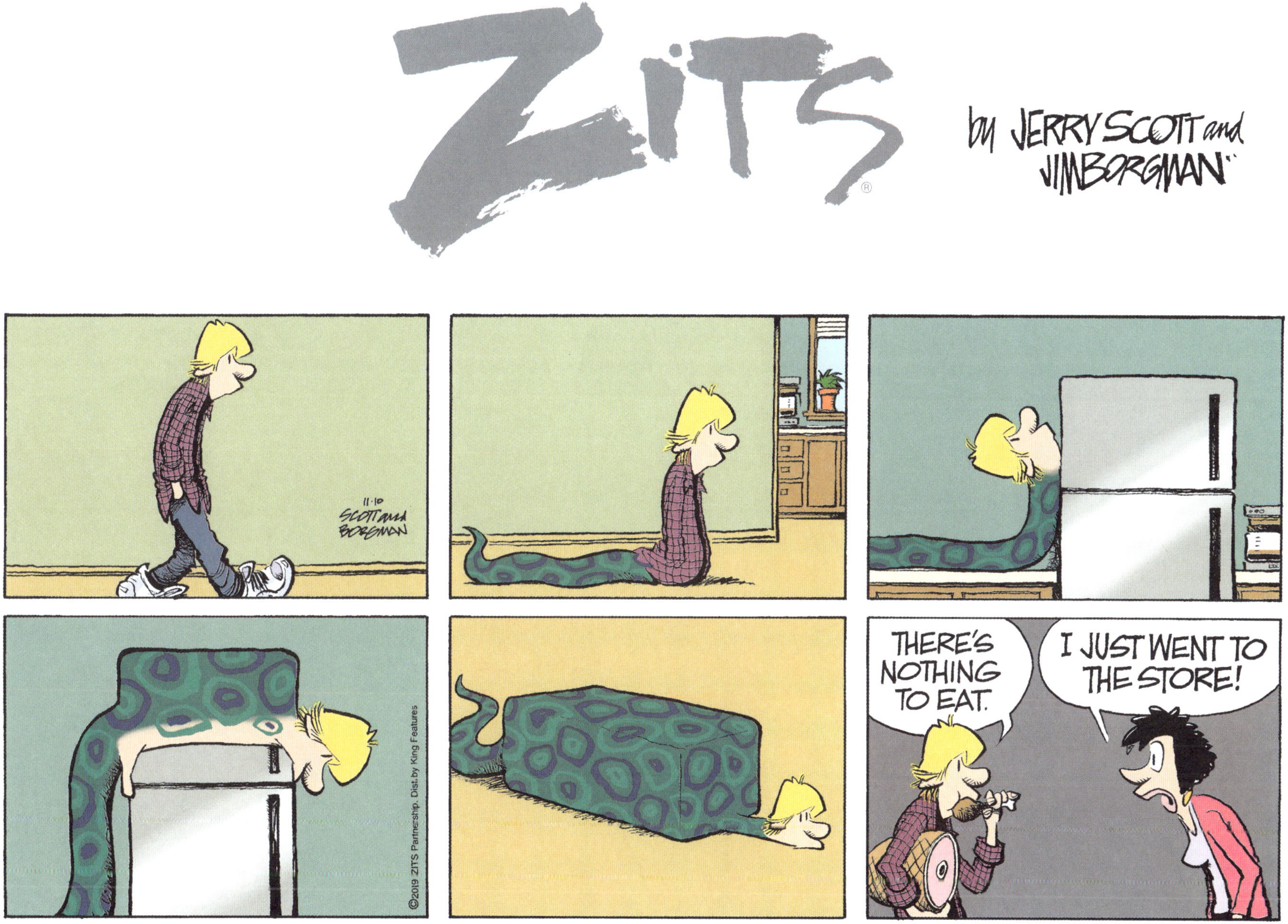
ZITS
by JERRY SCOTT and JIM BORGMAN
11-10 SCOTT and BORGMAN
©2019 ZITS Partnership. Dist. by King Features
THERE'S NOTHING TO EAT.
I JUST WENT TO THE STORE!

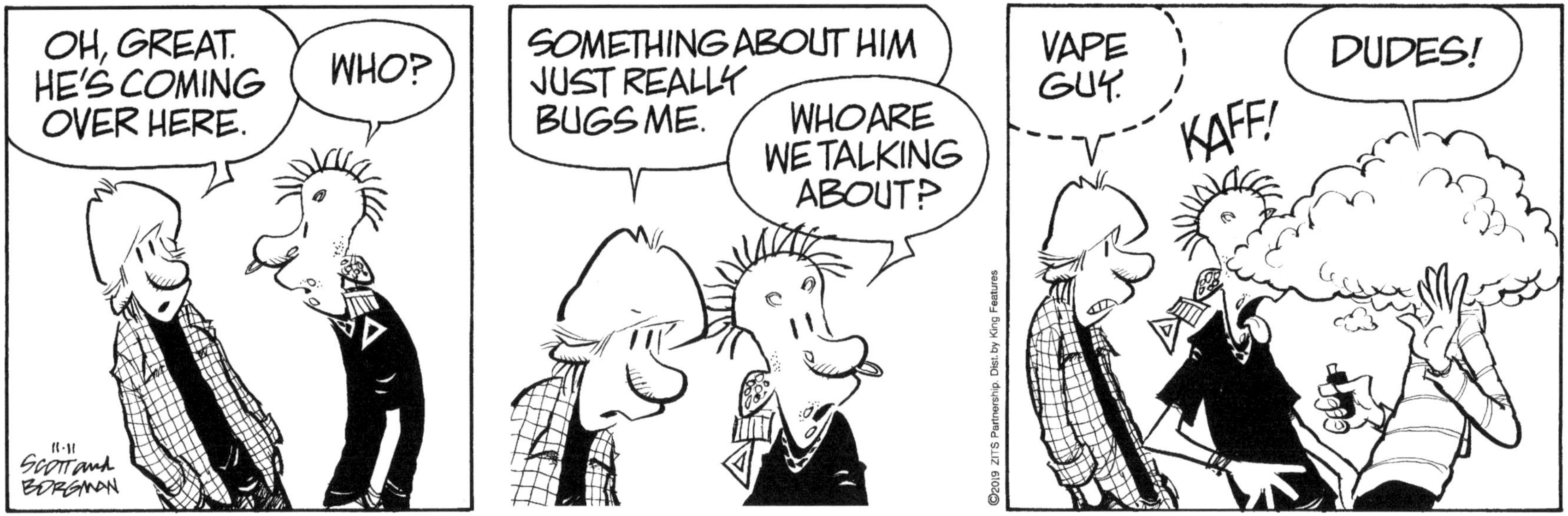
OH, GREAT. HE'S COMING OVER HERE.
WHO?
11-11 SCOTT and BORGMAN
SOMETHING ABOUT HIM JUST REALLY BUGS ME.
WHO ARE WE TALKING ABOUT?
©2019 ZITS Partnership. Dist. by King Features
VAPE GUY.
KAFF!
DUDES!

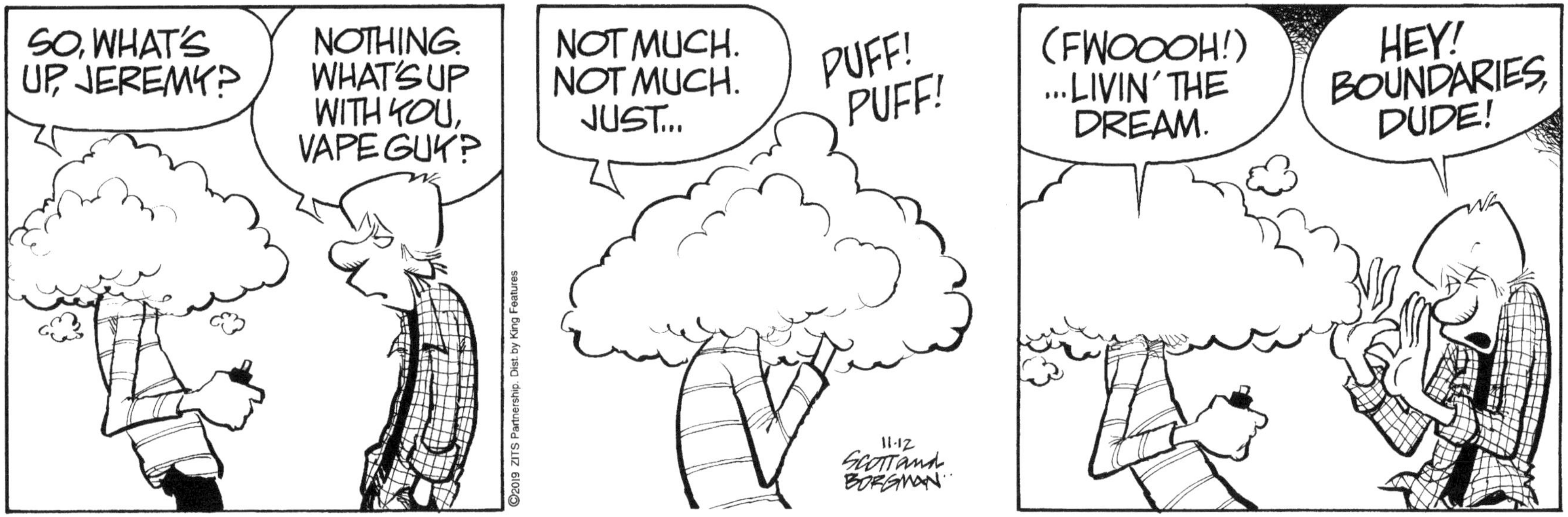
SO, WHAT'S UP, JEREMY?
NOTHING. WHAT'S UP WITH YOU, VAPE GUY?
©2019 ZITS Partnership. Dist. by King Features
NOT MUCH. NOT MUCH. JUST...
PUFF! PUFF!
11-12 SCOTT and BORGMAN
(FWOOOH!) ...LIVIN' THE DREAM.
HEY! BOUNDARIES, DUDE!

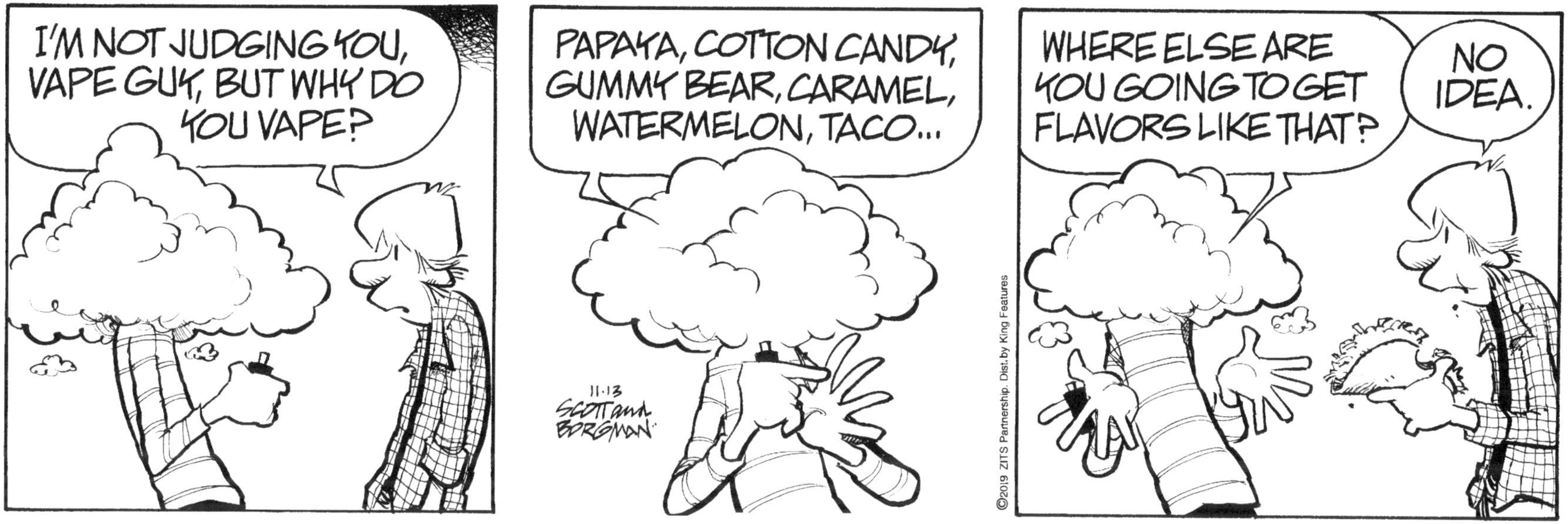
I'M NOT JUDGING YOU, VAPE GUY, BUT WHY DO YOU VAPE?
PAPAYA, COTTON CANDY, GUMMY BEAR, CARAMEL, WATERMELON, TACO...
11·13
SCOTT and BORGMAN
WHERE ELSE ARE YOU GOING TO GET FLAVORS LIKE THAT?
NO IDEA.
©2019 ZITS Partnership. Dist. by King Features

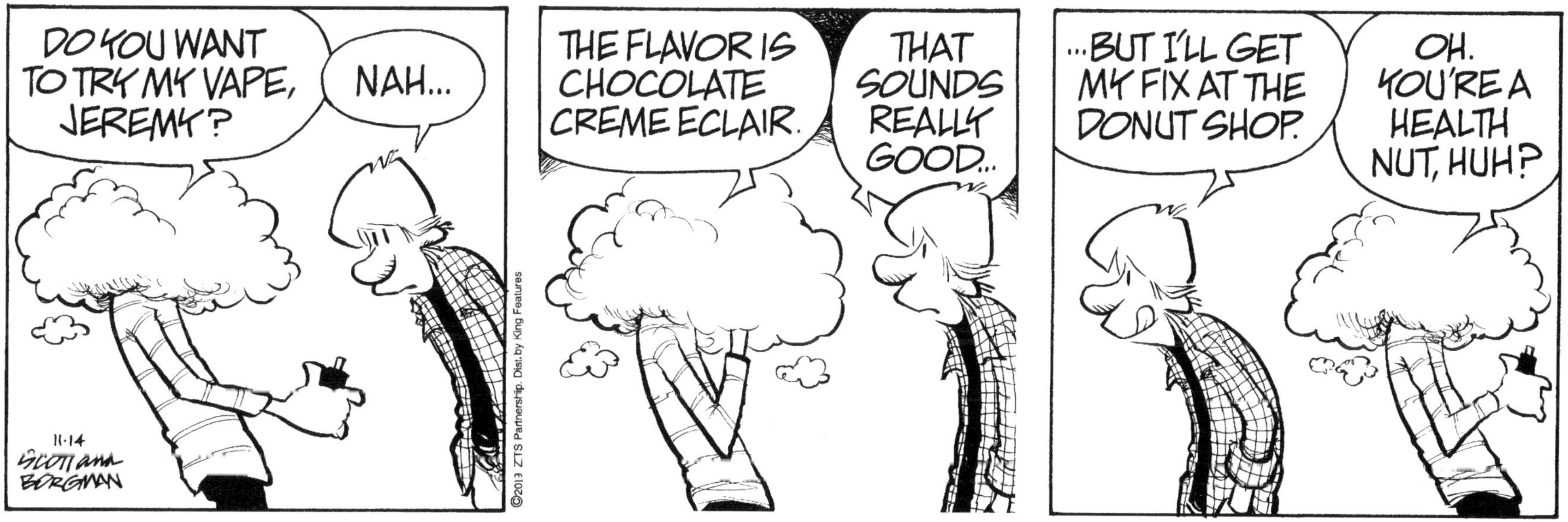
DO YOU WANT TO TRY MY VAPE, JEREMY?
NAH...
11·14
SCOTT and BORGMAN
©2013 ZITS Partnership. Dist. by King Features
THE FLAVOR IS CHOCOLATE CREME ECLAIR.
THAT SOUNDS REALLY GOOD...
...BUT I'LL GET MY FIX AT THE DONUT SHOP.
OH. YOU'RE A HEALTH NUT, HUH?

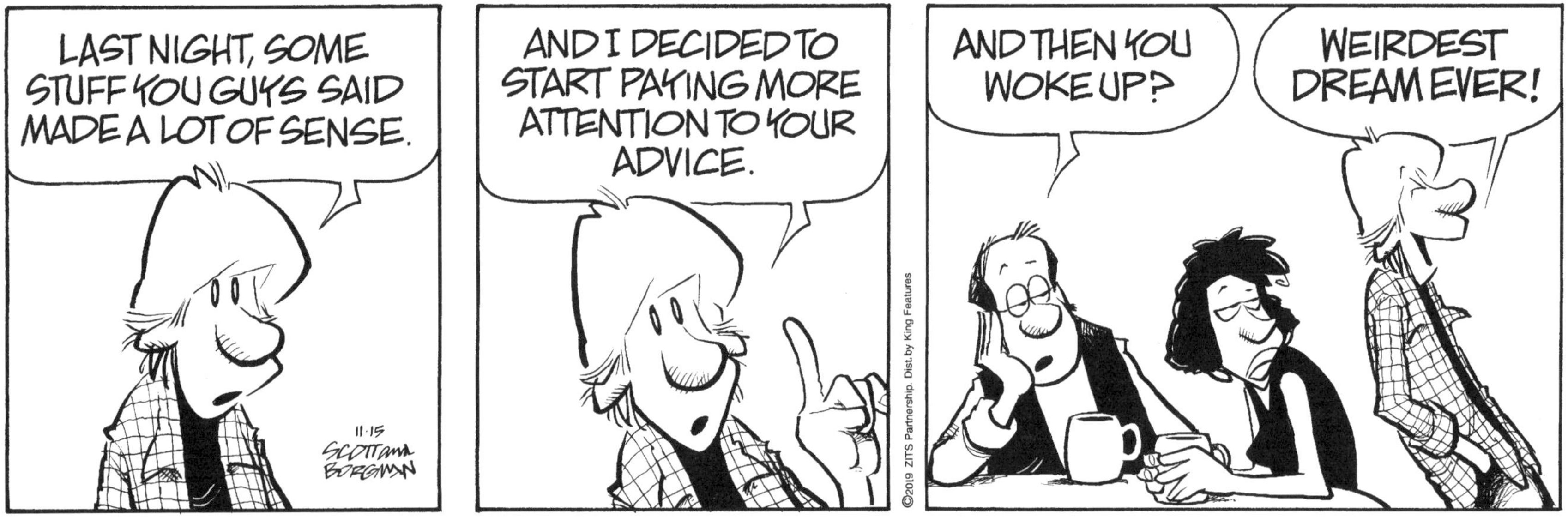
LAST NIGHT, SOME STUFF YOU GUYS SAID MADE A LOT OF SENSE.
11·15 SCOTT and BORGMAN
AND I DECIDED TO START PAYING MORE ATTENTION TO YOUR ADVICE.
©2019 ZITS Partnership. Dist. by King Features
AND THEN YOU WOKE UP?
WEIRDEST DREAM EVER!

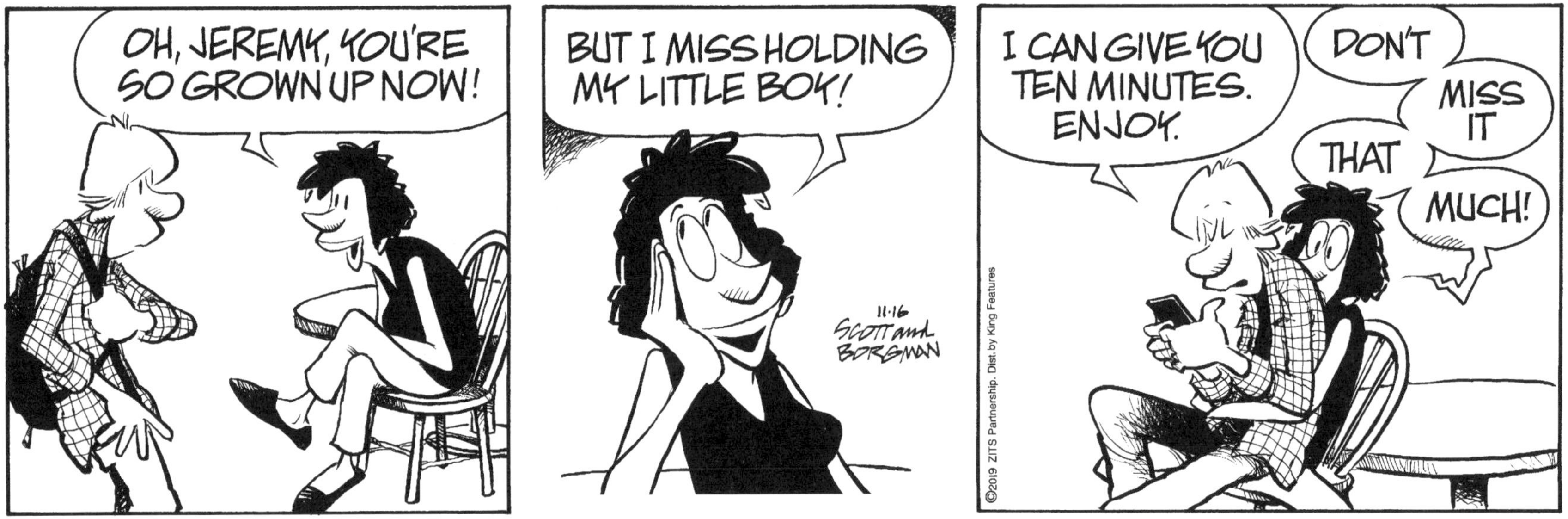
OH, JEREMY, YOU'RE SO GROWN UP NOW!
BUT I MISS HOLDING MY LITTLE BOY!
11·16 SCOTT and BORGMAN
©2019 ZITS Partnership. Dist. by King Features
I CAN GIVE YOU TEN MINUTES. ENJOY.
DON'T
MISS IT
THAT
MUCH!

ZITS®

by JERRY SCOTT and JIM BORGMAN

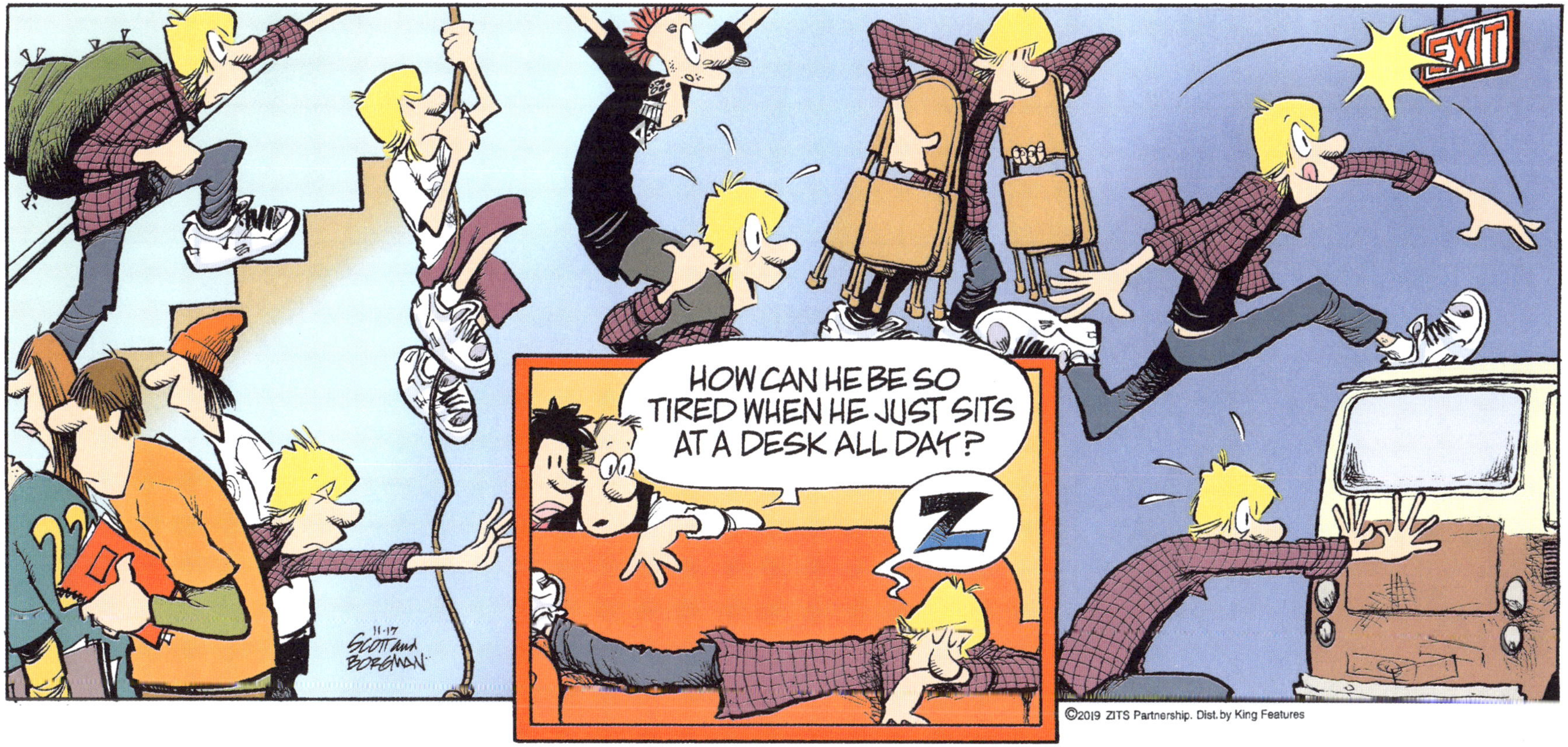
EXIT
11-17 SCOTT and BORGMAN
HOW CAN HE BE SO TIRED WHEN HE JUST SITS AT A DESK ALL DAY?
Z
©2019 ZITS Partnership. Dist. by King Features

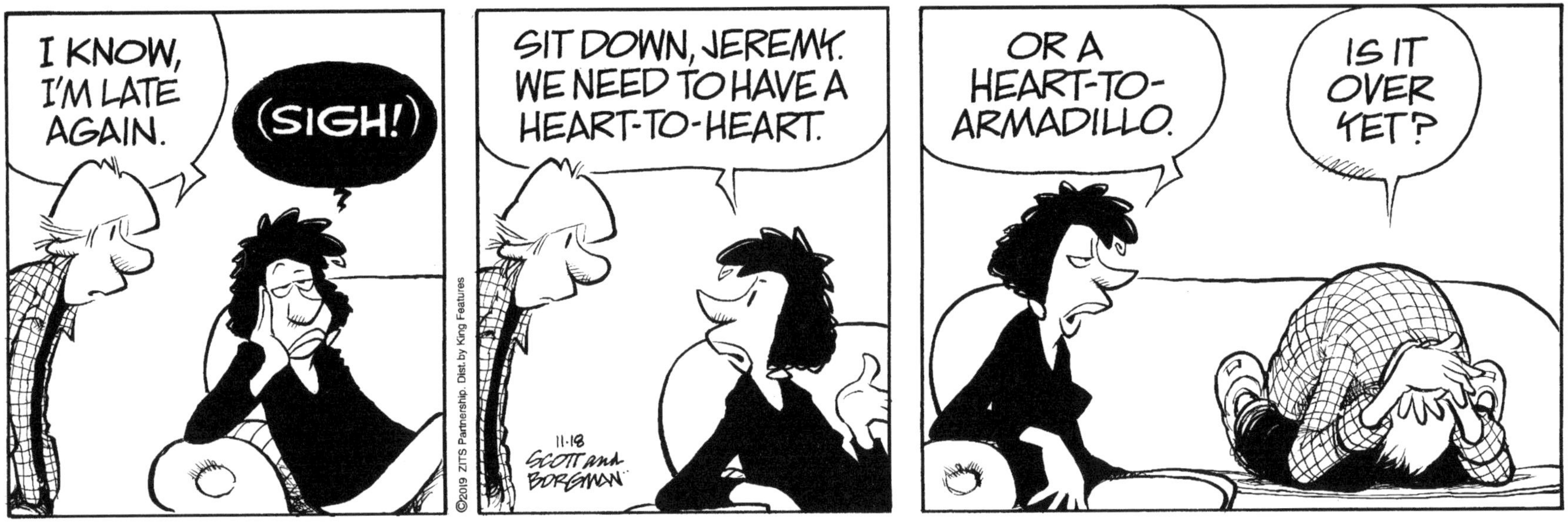
I KNOW, I'M LATE AGAIN.
(SIGH!)
SIT DOWN, JEREMY. WE NEED TO HAVE A HEART-TO-HEART.
OR A HEART-TO-ARMADILLO.
IS IT OVER YET?
©2019 ZITS Partnership. Dist. by King Features
11·18 SCOTT and BORGMAN

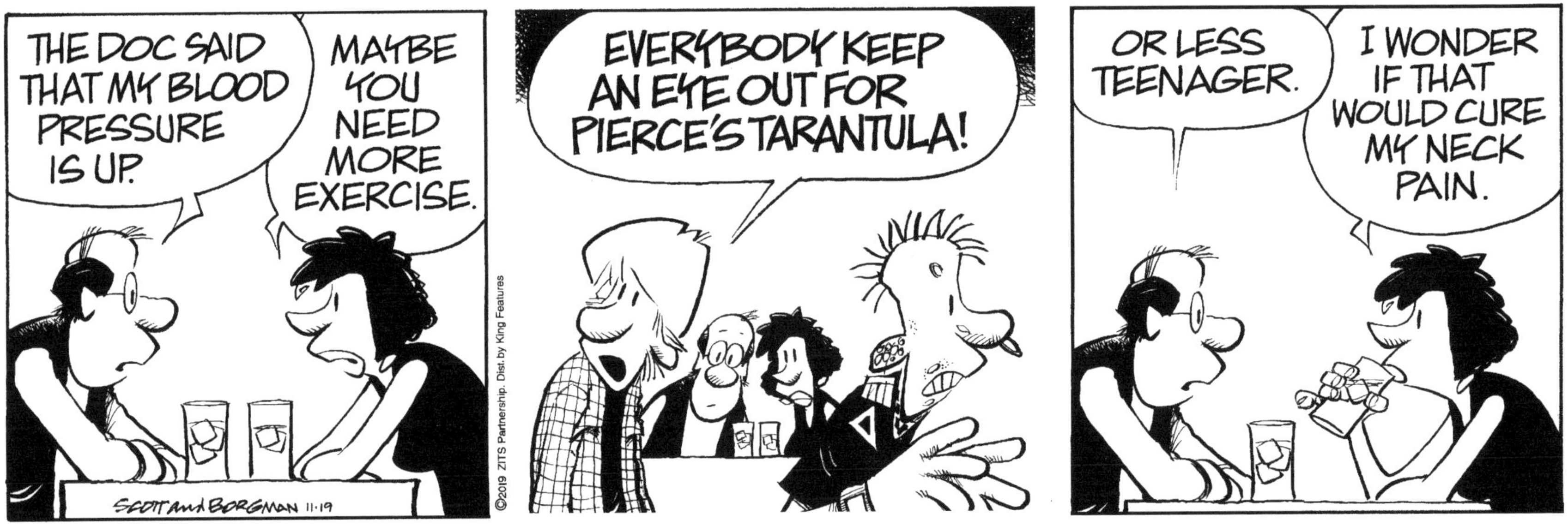
THE DOC SAID THAT MY BLOOD PRESSURE IS UP.
MAYBE YOU NEED MORE EXERCISE.
EVERYBODY KEEP AN EYE OUT FOR PIERCE'S TARANTULA!
OR LESS TEENAGER.
I WONDER IF THAT WOULD CURE MY NECK PAIN.
©2019 ZITS Partnership. Dist. by King Features
SCOTT and BORGMAN 11·19

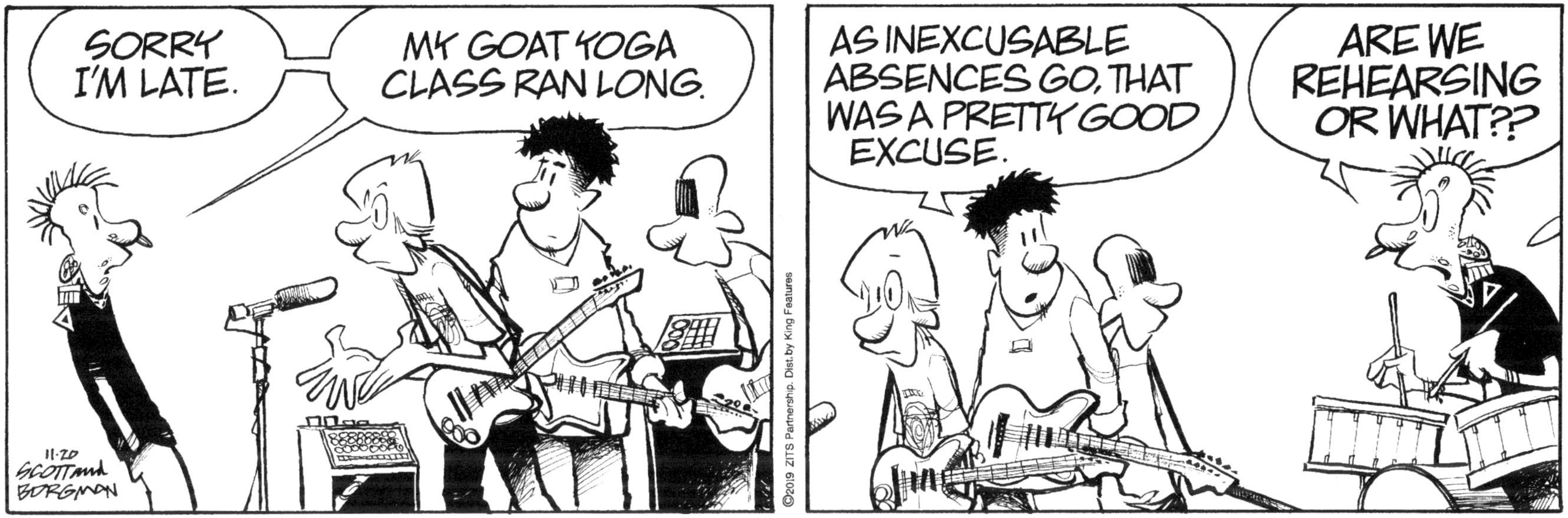
SORRY I'M LATE.
MY GOAT YOGA CLASS RAN LONG.
AS INEXCUSABLE ABSENCES GO, THAT WAS A PRETTY GOOD EXCUSE.
ARE WE REHEARSING OR WHAT??
11-20
SCOTT and BORGMAN
©2019 ZITS Partnership. Dist. by King Features

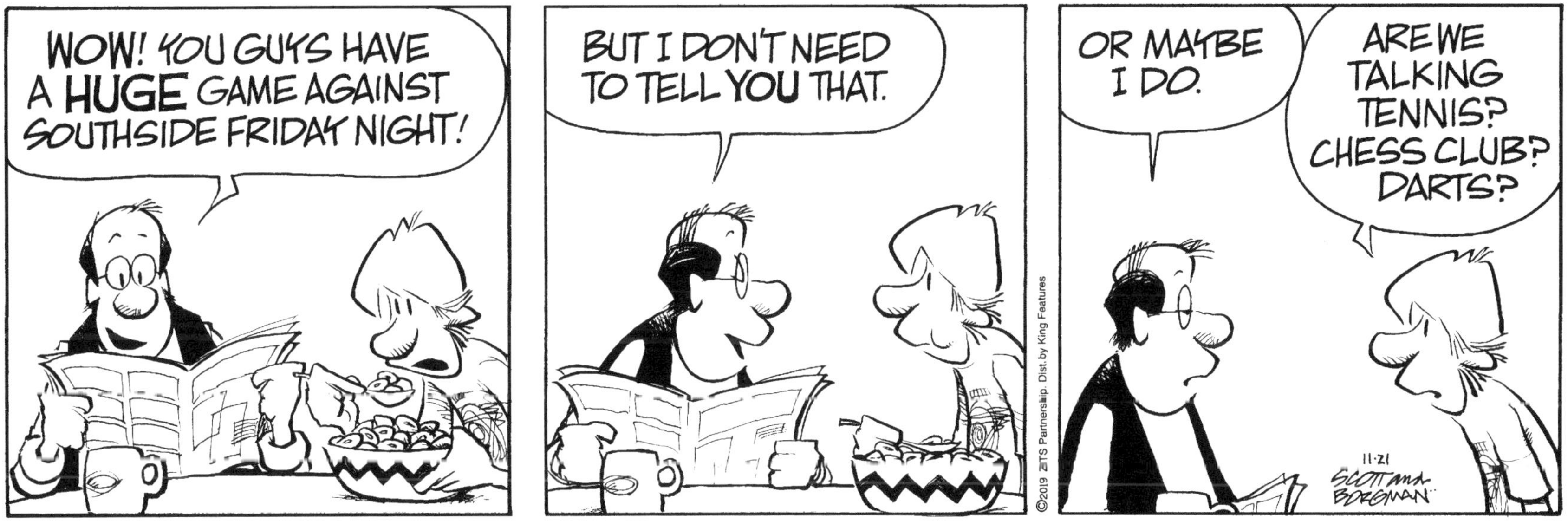
WOW! YOU GUYS HAVE A **HUGE** GAME AGAINST SOUTHSIDE FRIDAY NIGHT!
BUT I DON'T NEED TO TELL **YOU** THAT.
OR MAYBE I DO.
ARE WE TALKING TENNIS? CHESS CLUB? DARTS?
11-21
SCOTT and BORGMAN
©2019 ZITS Partnership. Dist. by King Features

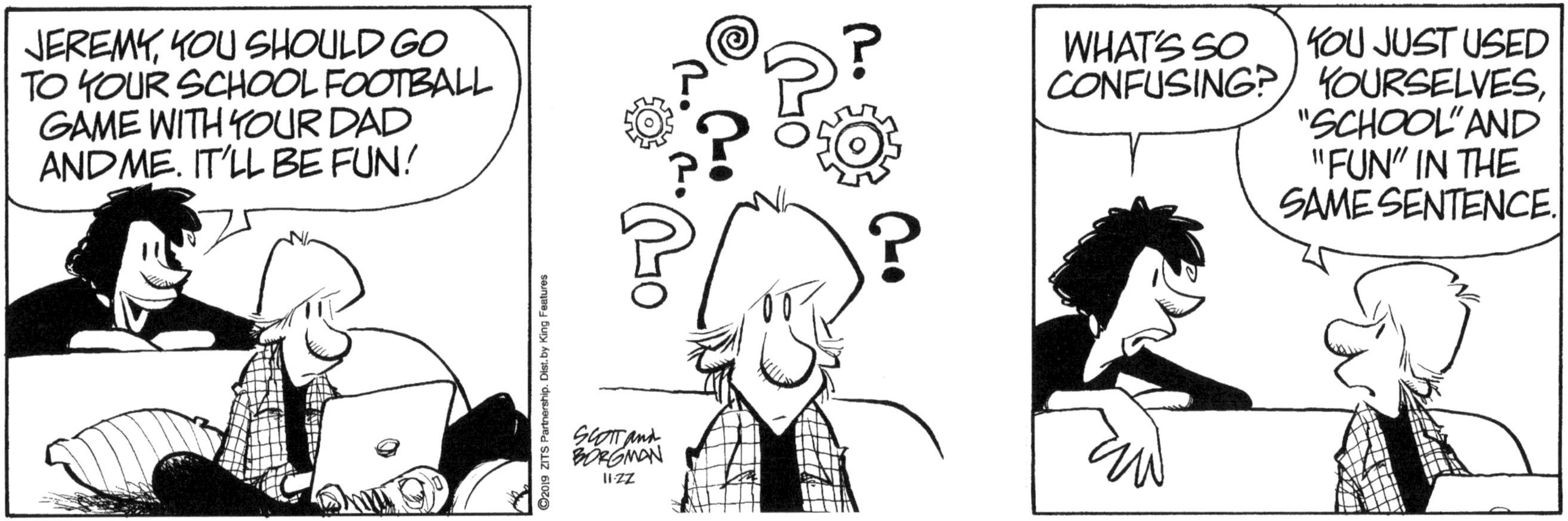
JEREMY, YOU SHOULD GO TO YOUR SCHOOL FOOTBALL GAME WITH YOUR DAD AND ME. IT'LL BE FUN!
©2019 ZITS Partnership. Dist. by King Features
SCOTT and BORGMAN 11-22
WHAT'S SO CONFUSING?
YOU JUST USED YOURSELVES, "SCHOOL" AND "FUN" IN THE SAME SENTENCE.

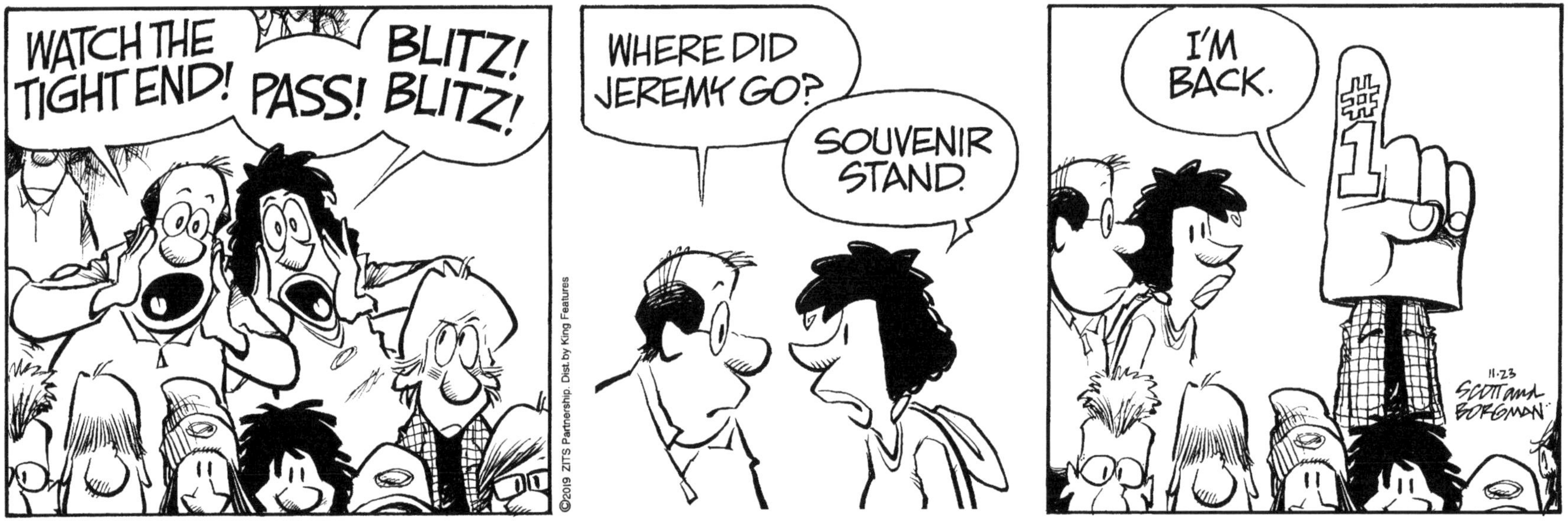
WATCH THE TIGHT END!
PASS!
BLITZ! BLITZ!
©2019 ZITS Partnership. Dist. by King Features
WHERE DID JEREMY GO?
SOUVENIR STAND.
I'M BACK.
#1
11-23 SCOTT and BORGMAN

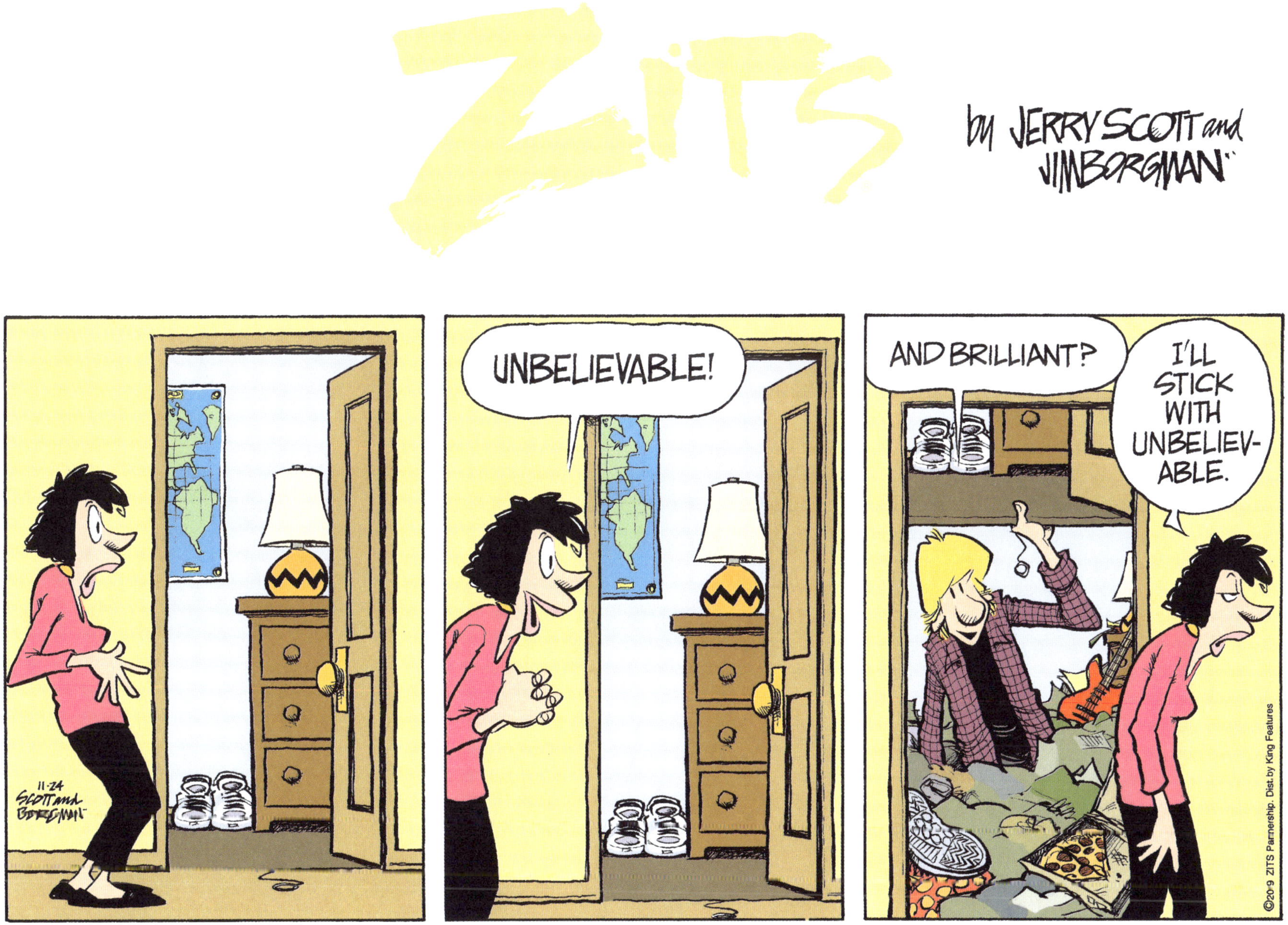
ZITS
by JERRY SCOTT and JIM BORGMAN
11-24 SCOTT and BORGMAN
UNBELIEVABLE!
AND BRILLIANT?
I'LL STICK WITH UNBELIEV-ABLE.
©2019 ZITS Partnership. Dist. by King Features

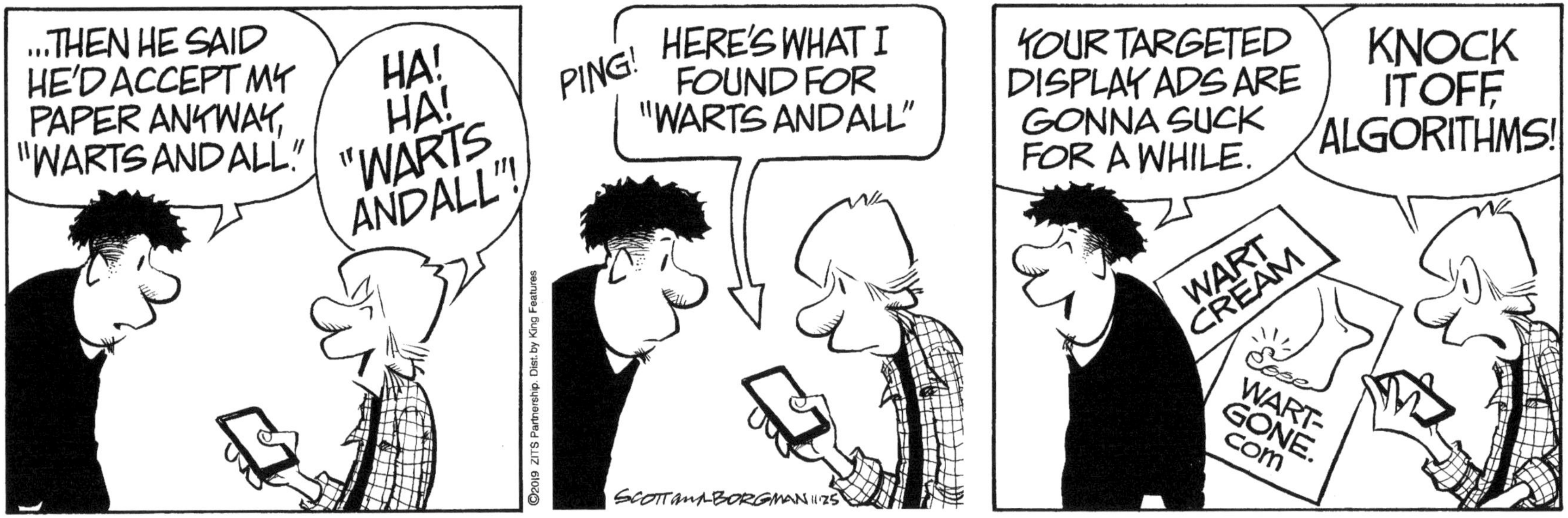
...THEN HE SAID HE'D ACCEPT MY PAPER ANYWAY, "WARTS AND ALL."
HA! HA! "WARTS AND ALL"!
©2019 ZITS Partnership. Dist. by King Features
PING!
HERE'S WHAT I FOUND FOR "WARTS AND ALL"
SCOTT and BORGMAN 11.25
YOUR TARGETED DISPLAY ADS ARE GONNA SUCK FOR A WHILE.
KNOCK IT OFF, ALGORITHMS!
WART CREAM
WART-GONE.com

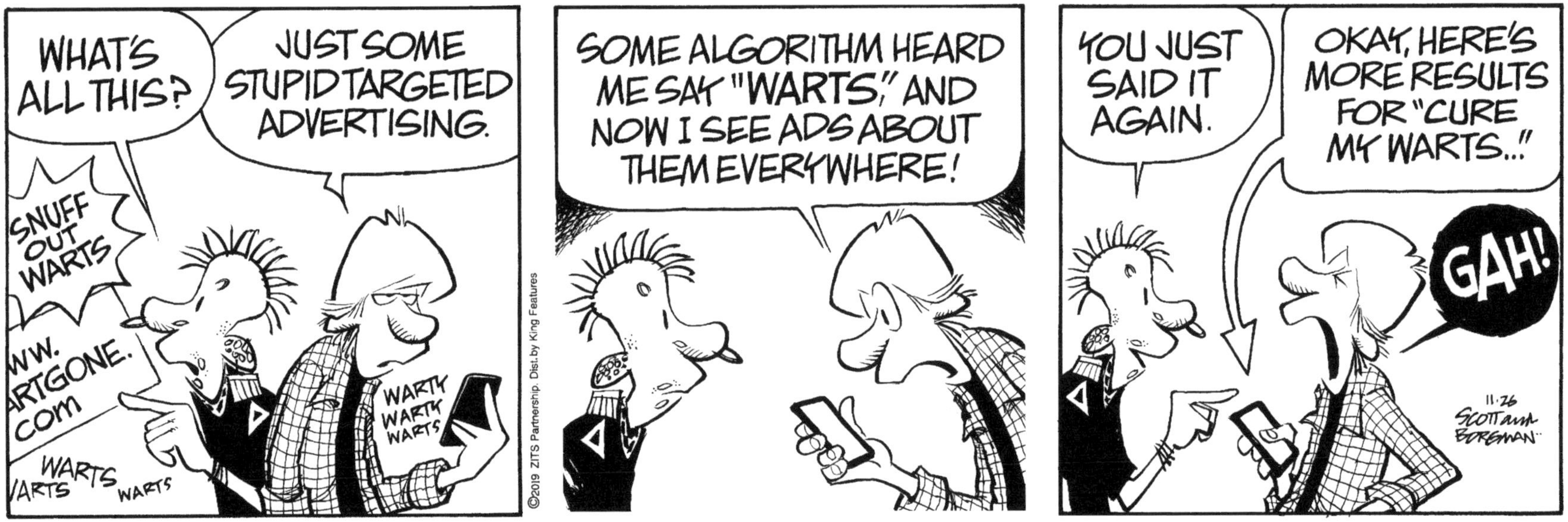
WHAT'S ALL THIS?
JUST SOME STUPID TARGETED ADVERTISING.
SNUFF OUT WARTS
WW. ARTGONE. com
WARTS WARTS WARTS
ARTS WARTS WARTS
©2019 ZITS Partnership. Dist. by King Features
SOME ALGORITHM HEARD ME SAY "WARTS," AND NOW I SEE ADS ABOUT THEM EVERYWHERE!
YOU JUST SAID IT AGAIN.
OKAY, HERE'S MORE RESULTS FOR "CURE MY WARTS..."
GAH!
11.26 SCOTT and BORGMAN

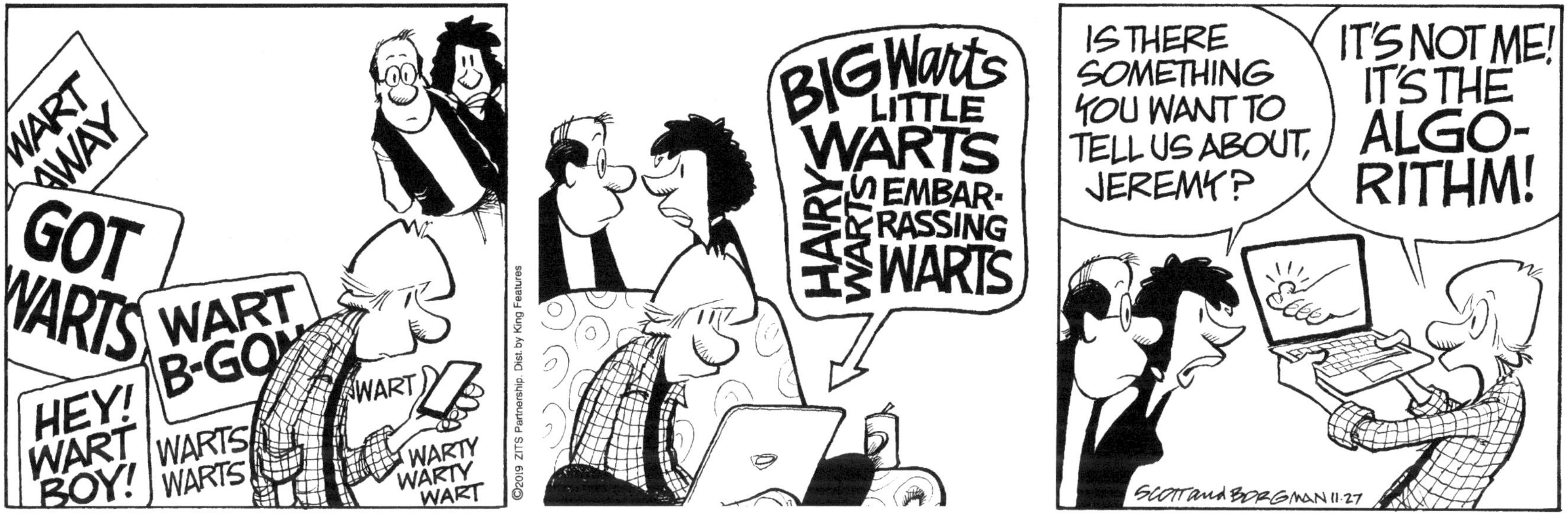
WART AWAY
GOT WARTS
WART B-GO
HEY! WART BOY!
WARTS WARTS
WART
WARTY WARTY WART
©2019 ZITS Partnership. Dist. by King Features
BIG Warts
LITTLE WARTS
HAIRY WARTS
EMBARRASSING WARTS
IS THERE SOMETHING YOU WANT TO TELL US ABOUT, JEREMY?
IT'S NOT ME! IT'S THE ALGORITHM!
SCOTT and BORGMAN 11-27

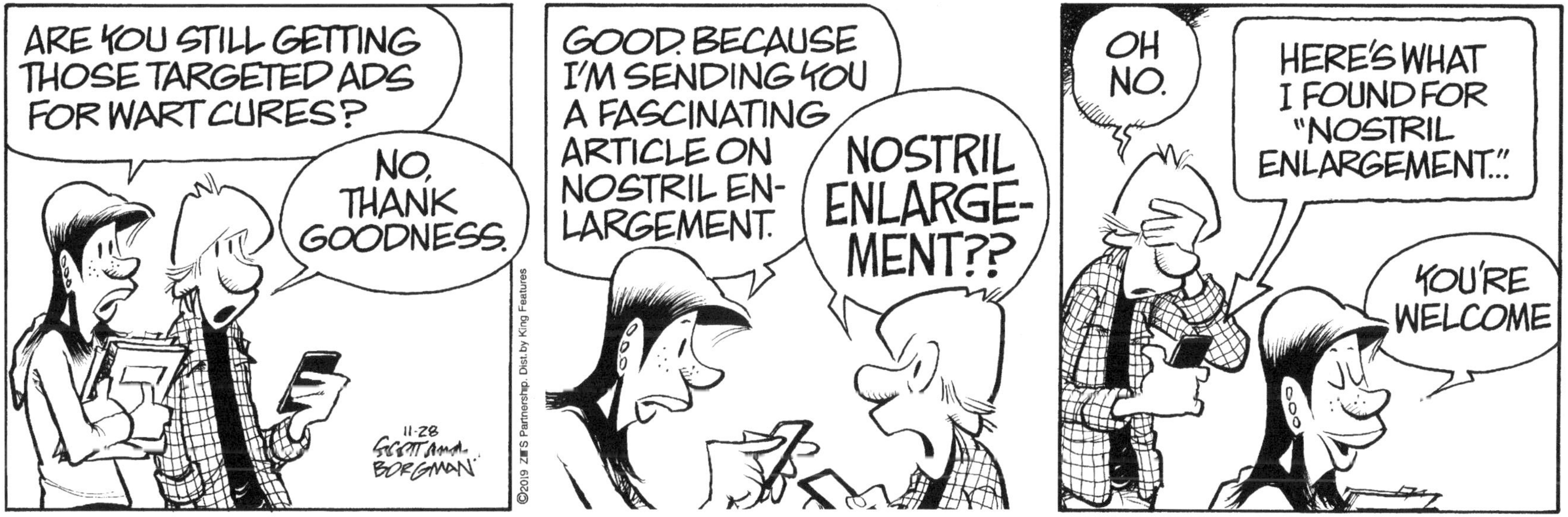
ARE YOU STILL GETTING THOSE TARGETED ADS FOR WART CURES?
NO, THANK GOODNESS.
11-28 SCOTT and BORGMAN
©2019 ZITS Partnership. Dist. by King Features
GOOD. BECAUSE I'M SENDING YOU A FASCINATING ARTICLE ON NOSTRIL ENLARGEMENT.
NOSTRIL ENLARGEMENT??
OH NO.
HERE'S WHAT I FOUND FOR "NOSTRIL ENLARGEMENT."
YOU'RE WELCOME

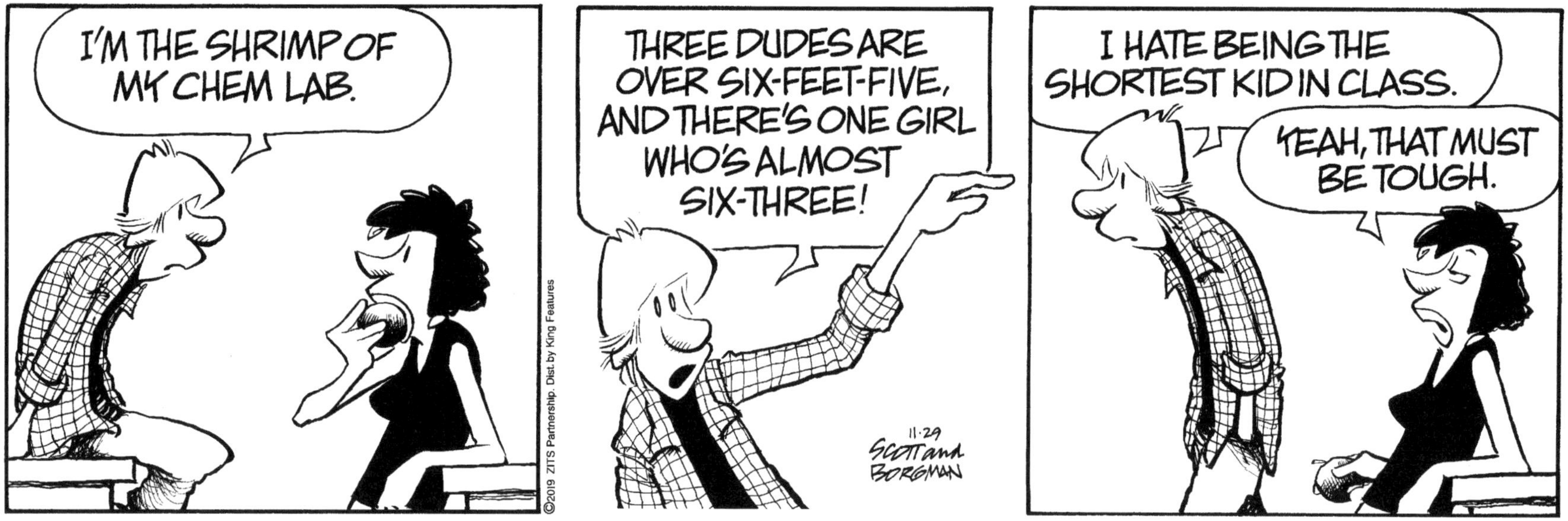
I'M THE SHRIMP OF MY CHEM LAB.
THREE DUDES ARE OVER SIX-FEET-FIVE, AND THERE'S ONE GIRL WHO'S ALMOST SIX-THREE!
I HATE BEING THE SHORTEST KID IN CLASS.
YEAH, THAT MUST BE TOUGH.
©2019 ZITS Partnership. Dist. by King Features
11·29 SCOTT and BORGMAN

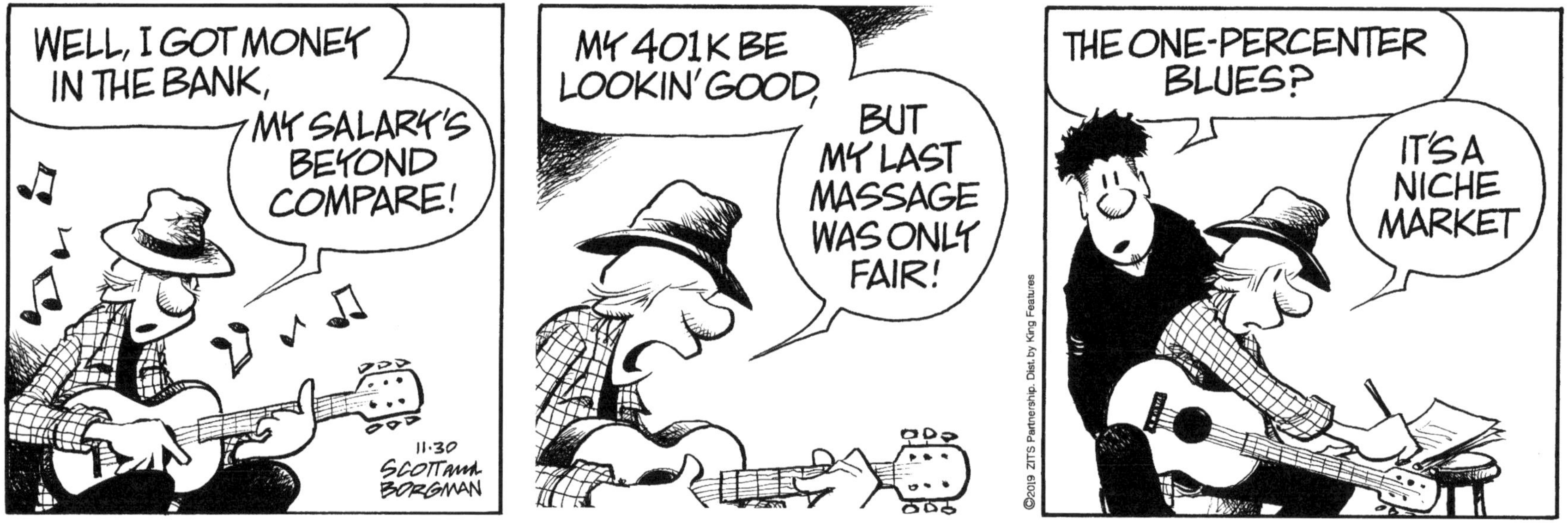
WELL, I GOT MONEY IN THE BANK,
MY SALARY'S BEYOND COMPARE!
11·30 SCOTT and BORGMAN
MY 401K BE LOOKIN' GOOD,
BUT MY LAST MASSAGE WAS ONLY FAIR!
THE ONE-PERCENTER BLUES?
IT'S A NICHE MARKET
©2019 ZITS Partnership. Dist. by King Features

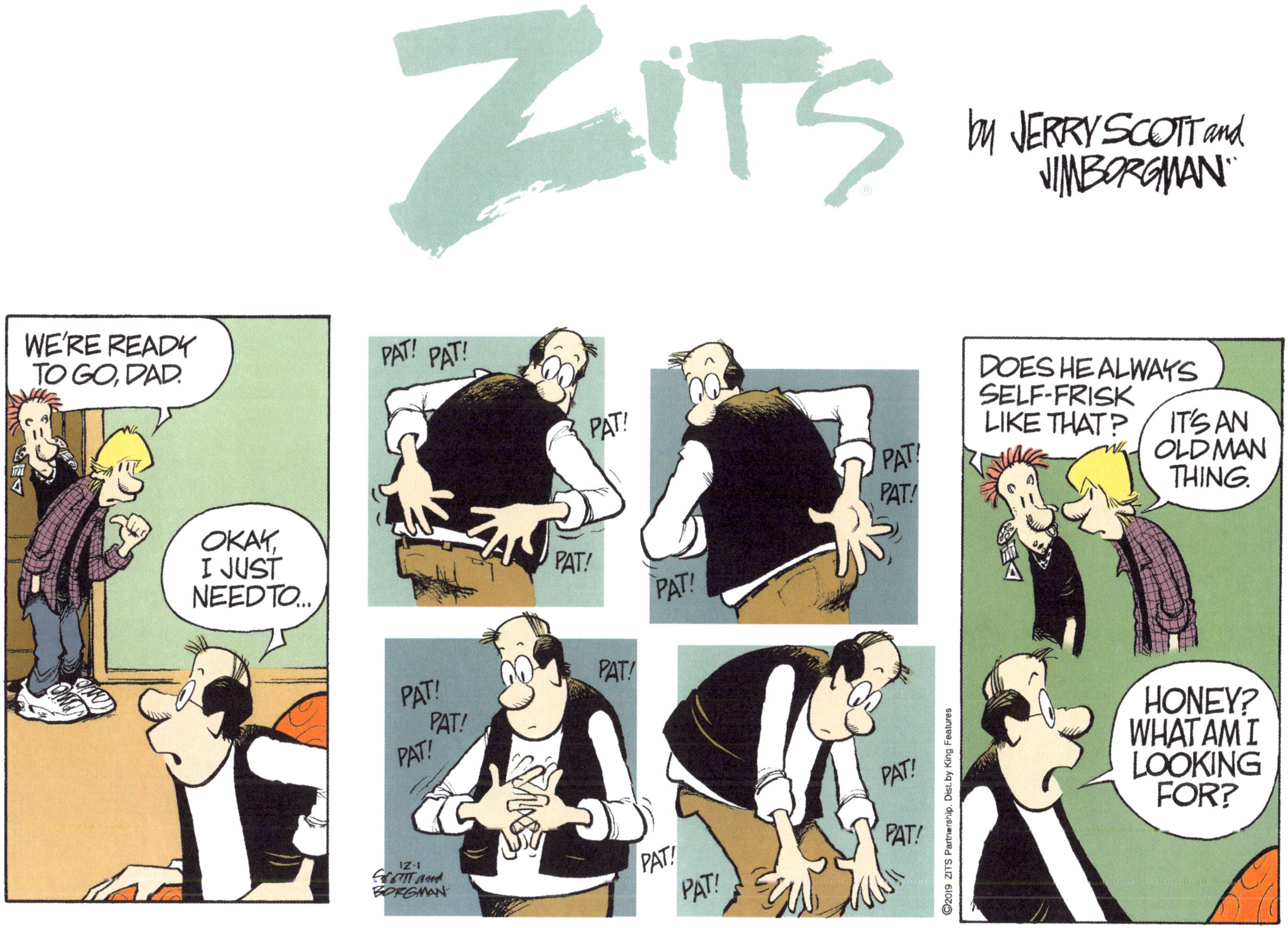
ZITS
by JERRY SCOTT and JIM BORGMAN
WE'RE READY TO GO, DAD.
OKAY, I JUST NEED TO...
PAT! PAT!
PAT!
PAT!
PAT!
PAT!
PAT!
PAT!
PAT!
PAT!
PAT!
PAT!
PAT!
PAT!
PAT!
DOES HE ALWAYS SELF-FRISK LIKE THAT?
IT'S AN OLD MAN THING.
HONEY? WHAT AM I LOOKING FOR?
12-1 SCOTT and BORGMAN
©2019 ZITS Partnership. Dist. by King Features

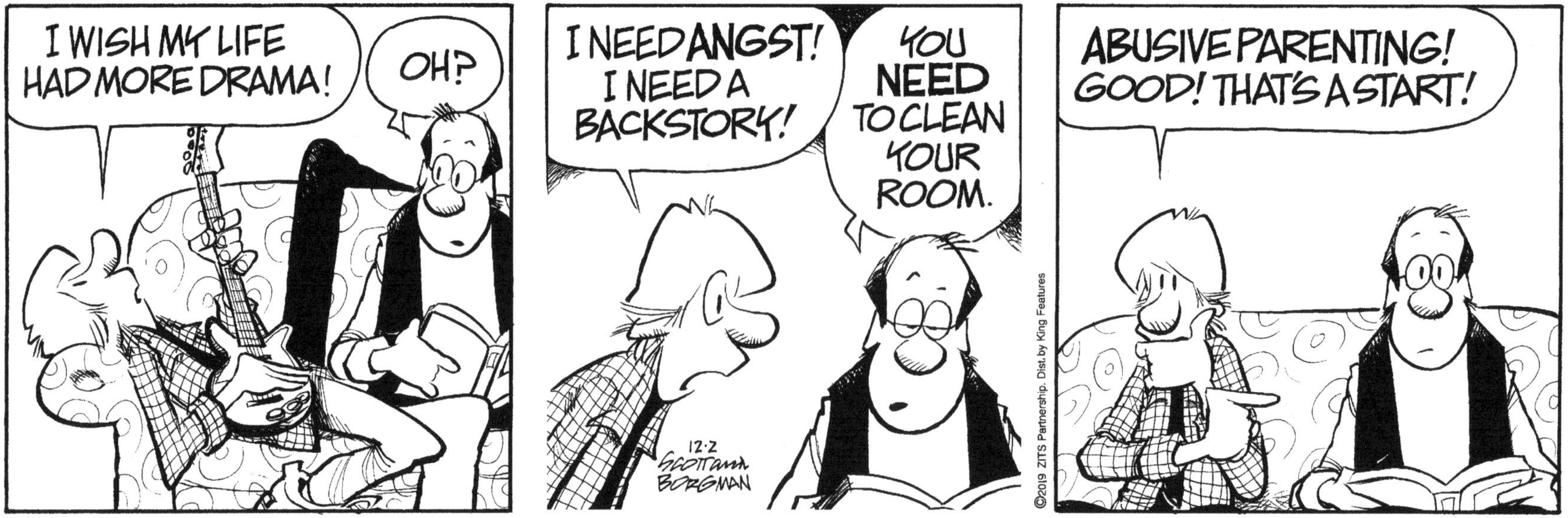

I WISH MY LIFE HAD MORE DRAMA!
OH?
I NEED ANGST! I NEED A BACKSTORY!
YOU NEED TO CLEAN YOUR ROOM.
12·2 SCOTT and BORGMAN
©2019 ZITS Partnership. Dist. by King Features
ABUSIVE PARENTING! GOOD! THAT'S A START!

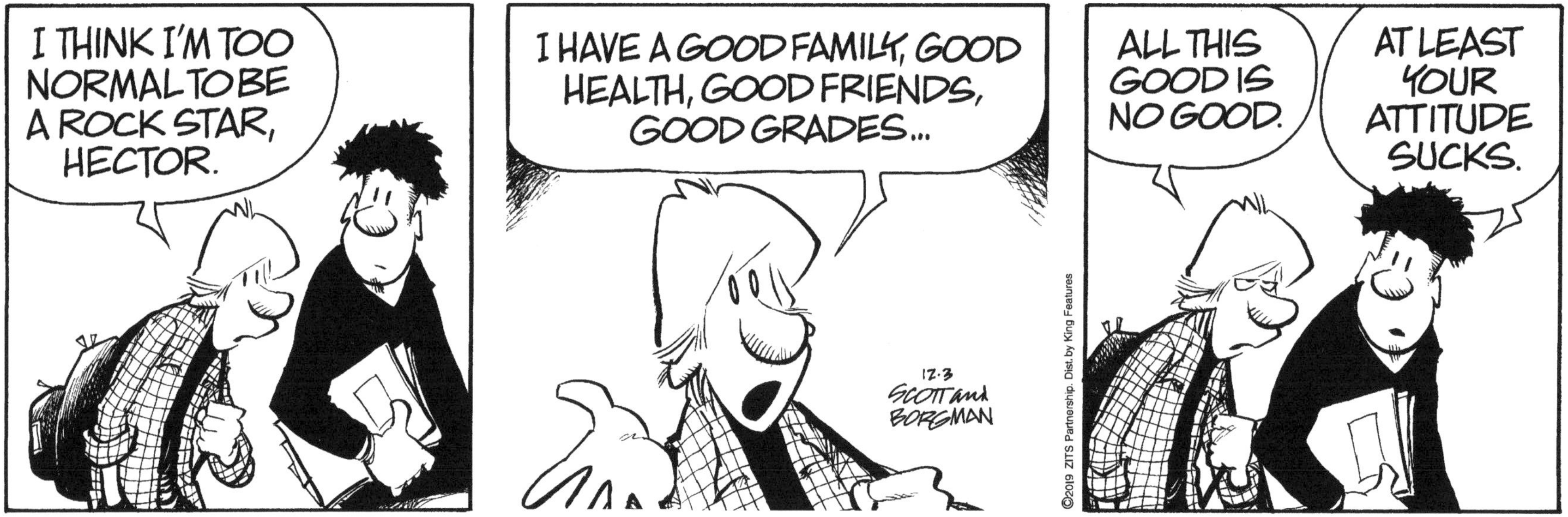

I THINK I'M TOO NORMAL TO BE A ROCK STAR, HECTOR.
I HAVE A GOOD FAMILY, GOOD HEALTH, GOOD FRIENDS, GOOD GRADES...
12·3 SCOTT and BORGMAN
©2019 ZITS Partnership. Dist. by King Features
ALL THIS GOOD IS NO GOOD.
AT LEAST YOUR ATTITUDE SUCKS.

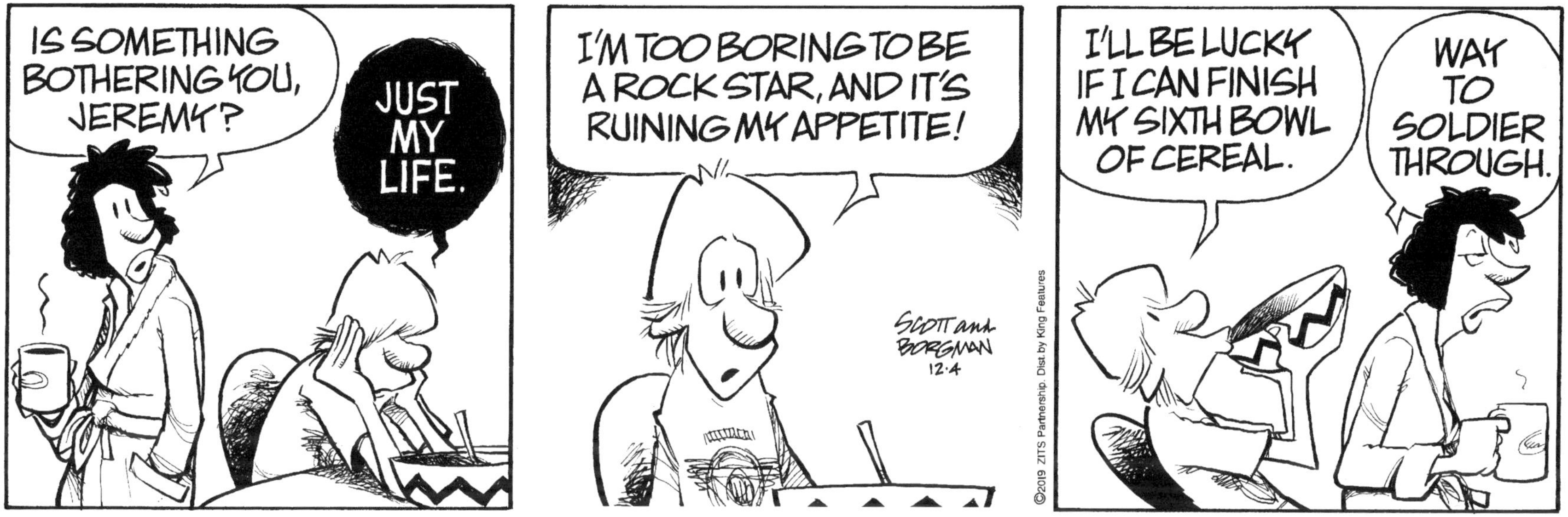
IS SOMETHING BOTHERING YOU, JEREMY?
JUST MY LIFE.
I'M TOO BORING TO BE A ROCK STAR, AND IT'S RUINING MY APPETITE!
SCOTT and BORGMAN 12·4
I'LL BE LUCKY IF I CAN FINISH MY SIXTH BOWL OF CEREAL.
WAY TO SOLDIER THROUGH.
©2019 ZITS Partnership. Dist. by King Features

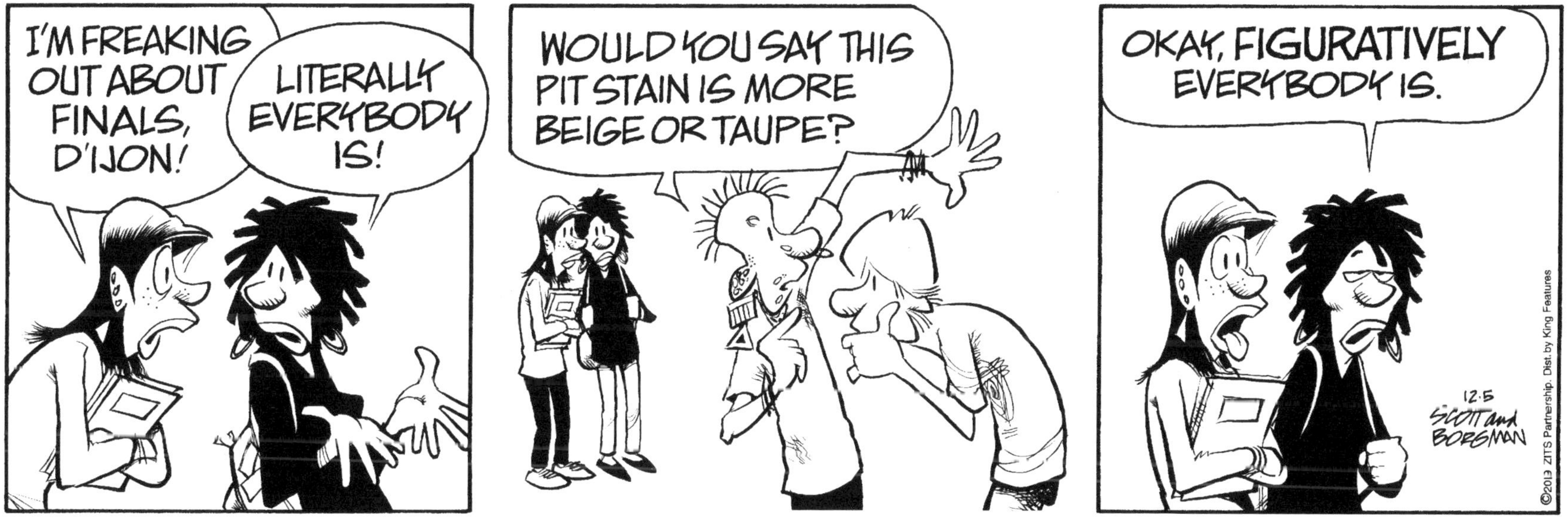
I'M FREAKING OUT ABOUT FINALS, D'IJON!
LITERALLY EVERYBODY IS!
WOULD YOU SAY THIS PIT STAIN IS MORE BEIGE OR TAUPE?
OKAY, FIGURATIVELY EVERYBODY IS.
12·5 SCOTT and BORGMAN
©2013 ZITS Partnership. Dist. by King Features

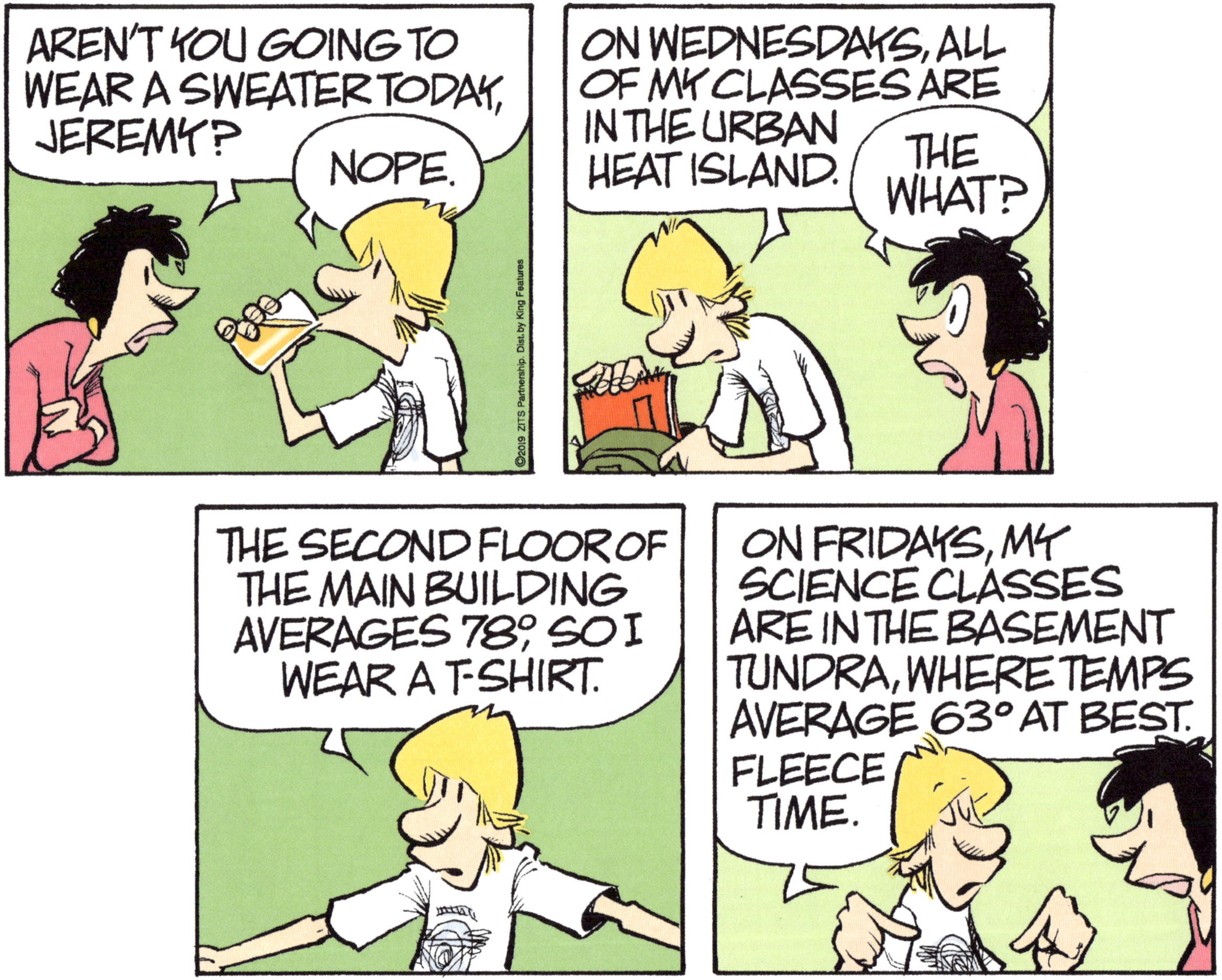
AREN'T YOU GOING TO WEAR A SWEATER TODAY, JEREMY?
NOPE.
©2019 ZITS Partnership. Dist. by King Features
ON WEDNESDAYS, ALL OF MY CLASSES ARE IN THE URBAN HEAT ISLAND.
THE WHAT?
THE SECOND FLOOR OF THE MAIN BUILDING AVERAGES 78°, SO I WEAR A T-SHIRT.
ON FRIDAYS, MY SCIENCE CLASSES ARE IN THE BASEMENT TUNDRA, WHERE TEMPS AVERAGE 63° AT BEST. FLEECE TIME.

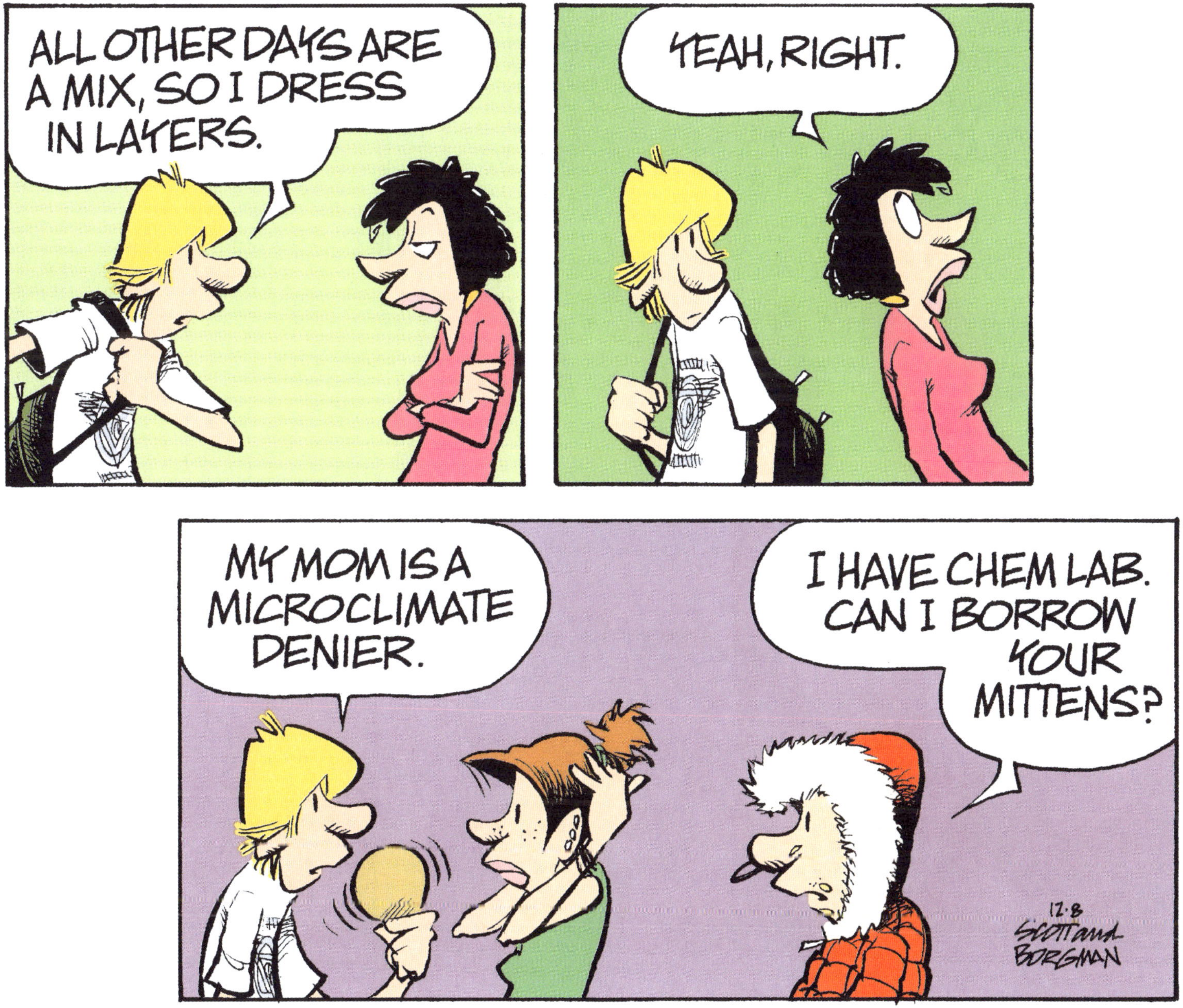
ALL OTHER DAYS ARE A MIX, SO I DRESS IN LAYERS.
YEAH, RIGHT.
MY MOM IS A MICROCLIMATE DENIER.
I HAVE CHEM LAB. CAN I BORROW YOUR MITTENS?
12·8 SCOTT and BORGMAN

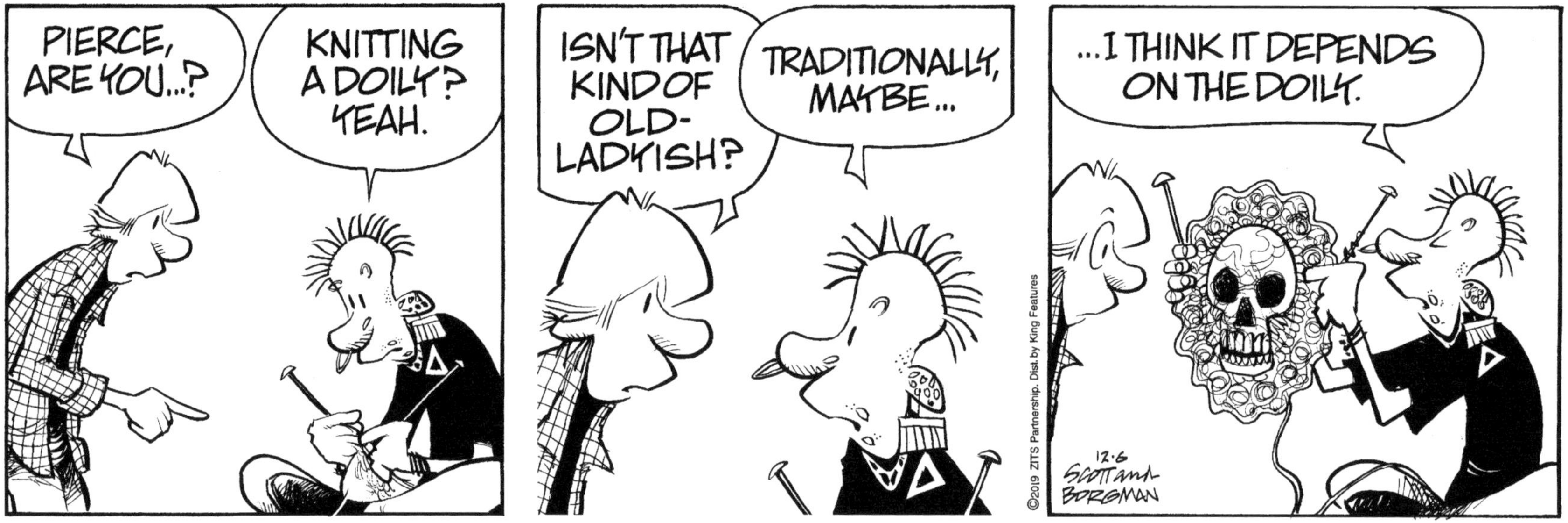
PIERCE, ARE YOU...?
KNITTING A DOILY? YEAH.
ISN'T THAT KIND OF OLD-LADYISH?
TRADITIONALLY, MAYBE...
...I THINK IT DEPENDS ON THE DOILY.
©2019 ZITS Partnership. Dist. by King Features
12·6 SCOTT and BORGMAN

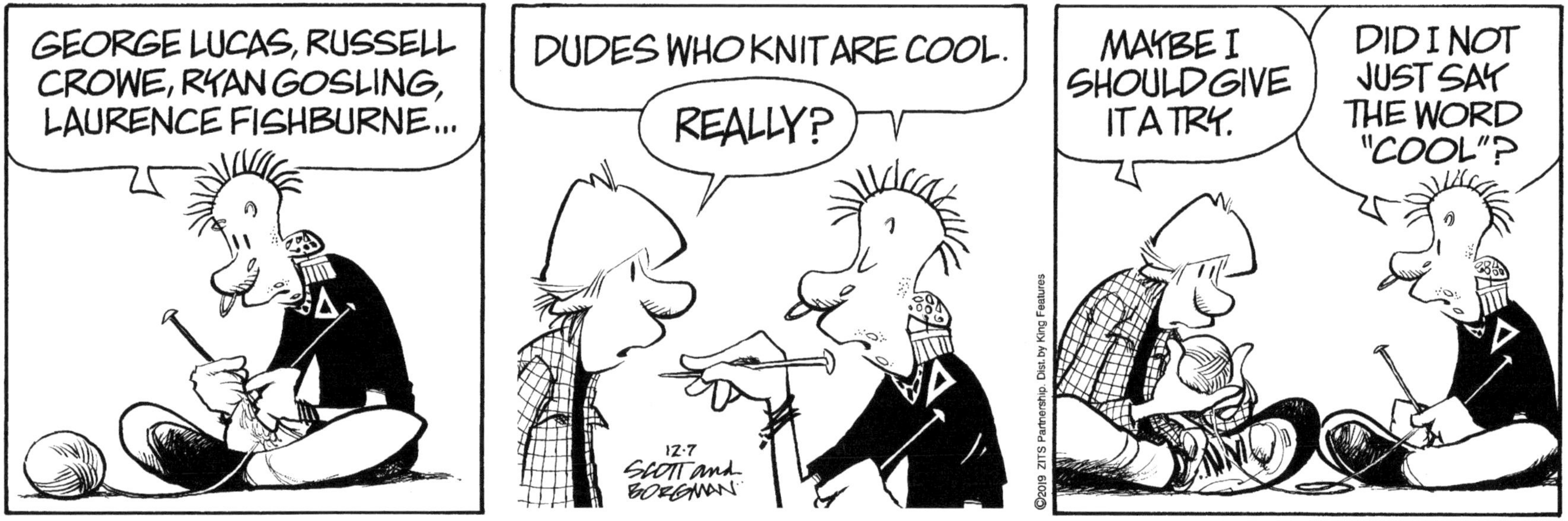
GEORGE LUCAS, RUSSELL CROWE, RYAN GOSLING, LAURENCE FISHBURNE...
DUDES WHO KNIT ARE COOL.
REALLY?
12·7 SCOTT and BORGMAN
©2019 ZITS Partnership. Dist. by King Features
MAYBE I SHOULD GIVE IT A TRY.
DID I NOT JUST SAY THE WORD "COOL"?

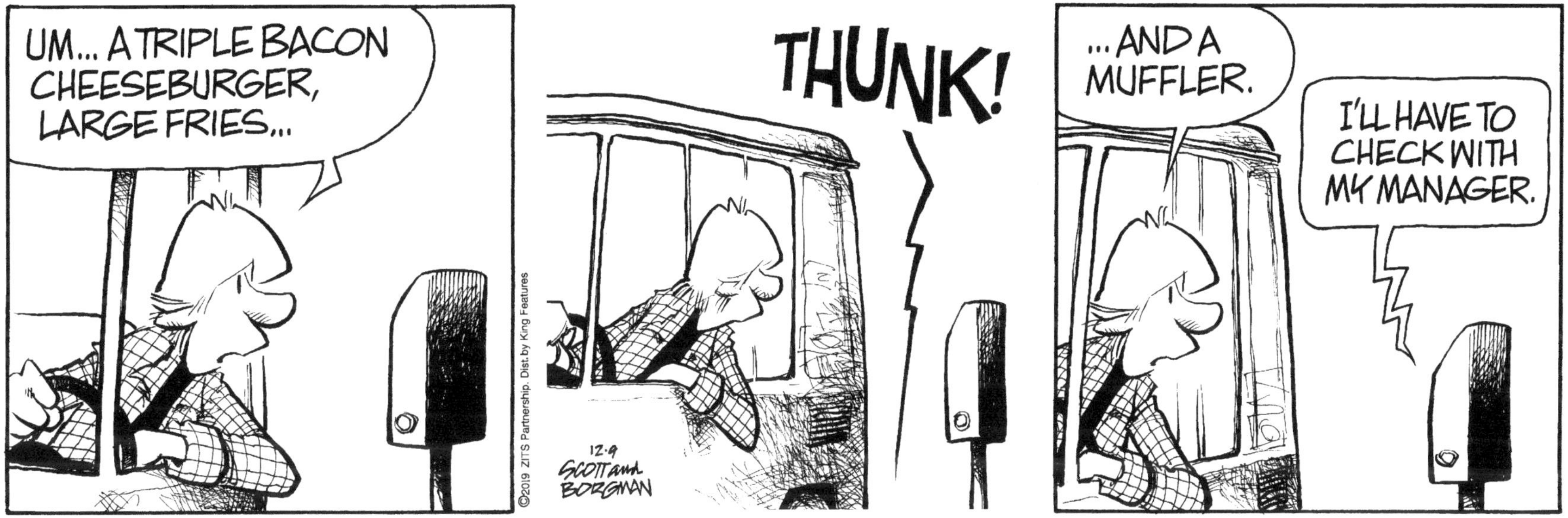
UM... A TRIPLE BACON CHEESEBURGER, LARGE FRIES...
THUNK!
...AND A MUFFLER.
I'LL HAVE TO CHECK WITH MY MANAGER.
©2019 ZITS Partnership. Dist. by King Features
12·9 SCOTT and BORGMAN

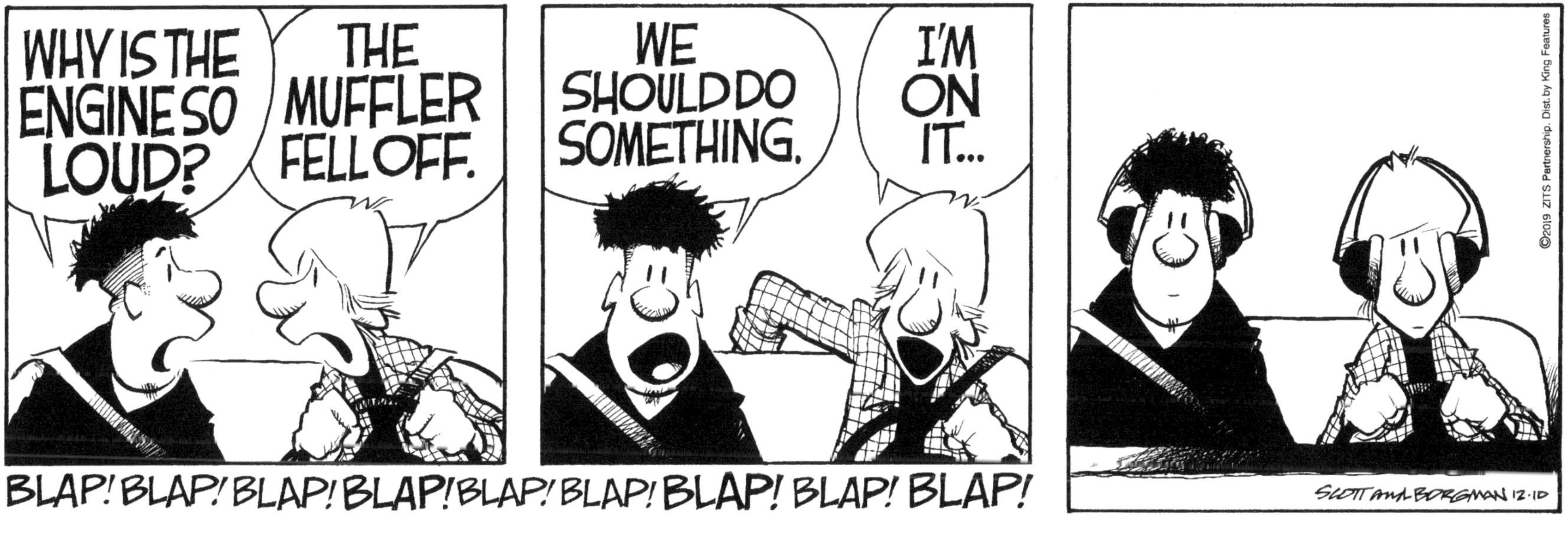
WHY IS THE ENGINE SO LOUD?
THE MUFFLER FELL OFF.
WE SHOULD DO SOMETHING.
I'M ON IT...
BLAP! BLAP! BLAP! BLAP! BLAP! BLAP! BLAP! BLAP! BLAP!
©2019 ZITS Partnership. Dist. by King Features
SCOTT and BORGMAN 12·10

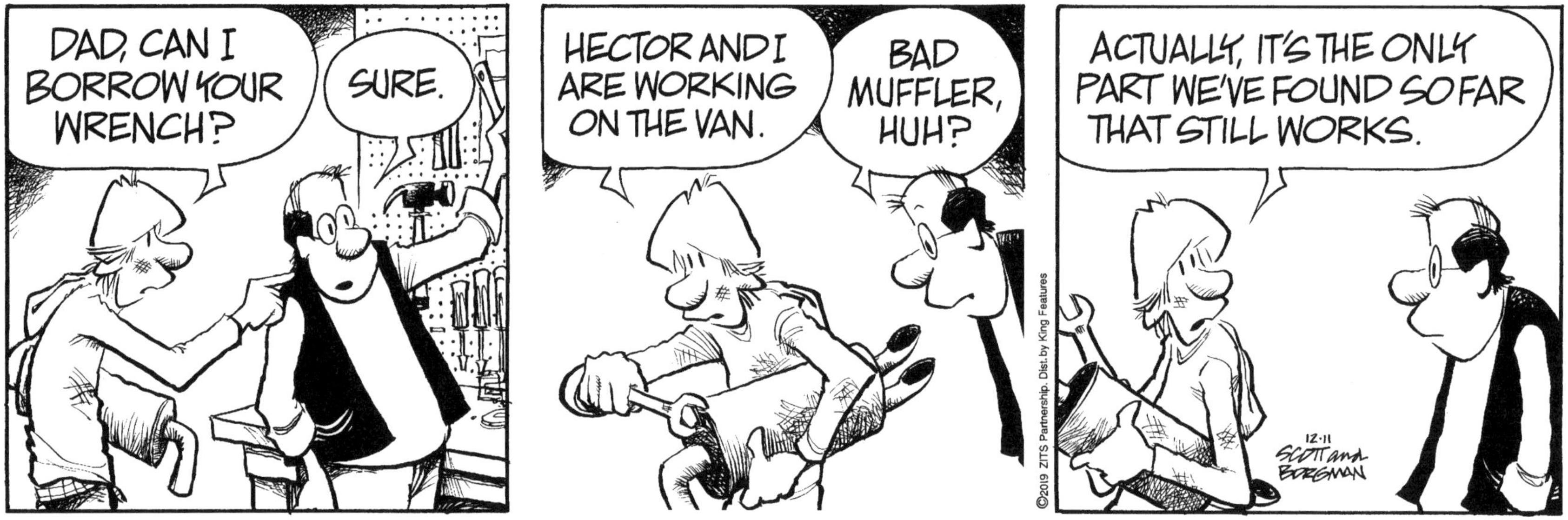
DAD, CAN I BORROW YOUR WRENCH?
SURE.
HECTOR AND I ARE WORKING ON THE VAN.
BAD MUFFLER, HUH?
©2019 ZITS Partnership. Dist. by King Features
ACTUALLY, IT'S THE ONLY PART WE'VE FOUND SO FAR THAT STILL WORKS.
12·11
SCOTT and BORGMAN

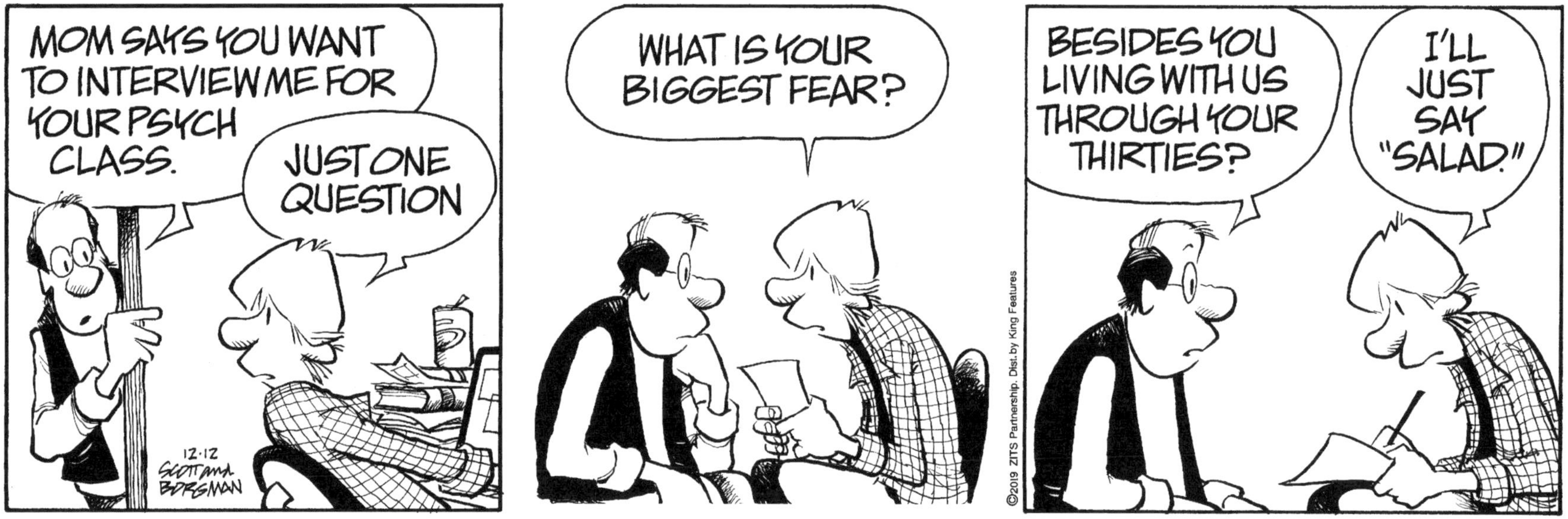
MOM SAYS YOU WANT TO INTERVIEW ME FOR YOUR PSYCH CLASS.
JUST ONE QUESTION
12·12
SCOTT and BORGMAN
WHAT IS YOUR BIGGEST FEAR?
©2019 ZITS Partnership. Dist. by King Features
BESIDES YOU LIVING WITH US THROUGH YOUR THIRTIES?
I'LL JUST SAY "SALAD."

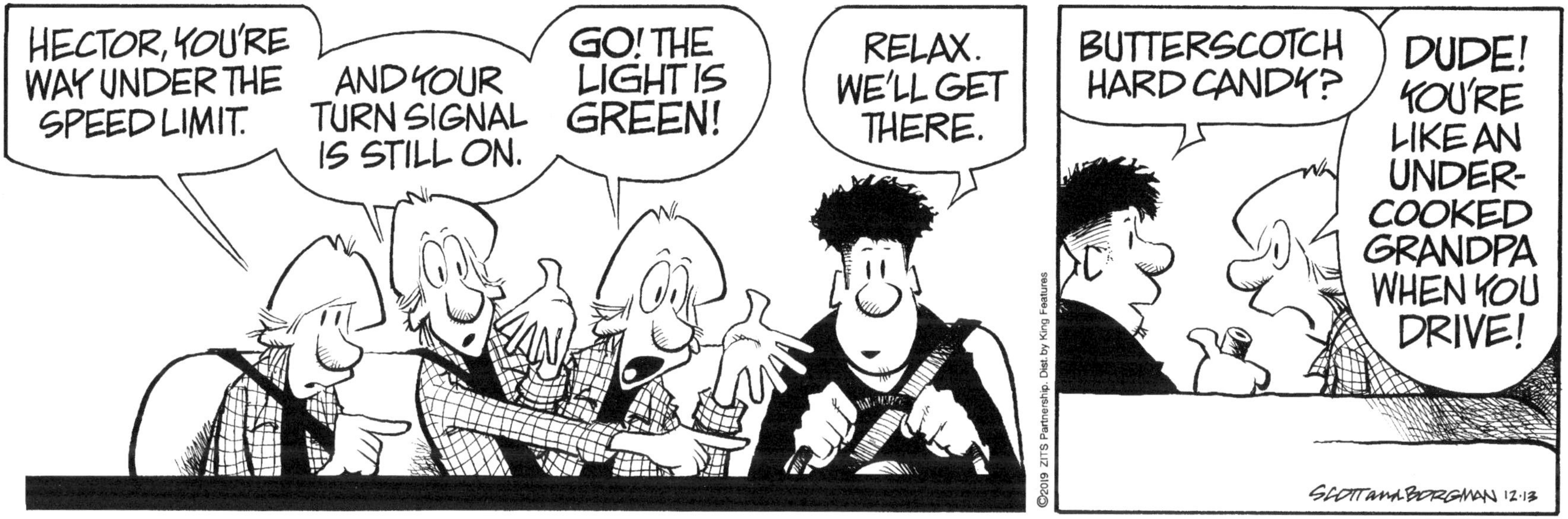
HECTOR, YOU'RE WAY UNDER THE SPEED LIMIT.
AND YOUR TURN SIGNAL IS STILL ON.
GO! THE LIGHT IS GREEN!
RELAX. WE'LL GET THERE.
BUTTERSCOTCH HARD CANDY?
DUDE! YOU'RE LIKE AN UNDER-COOKED GRANDPA WHEN YOU DRIVE!
SCOTT AND BORGMAN 12·13
©2019 ZITS Partnership. Dist. by King Features

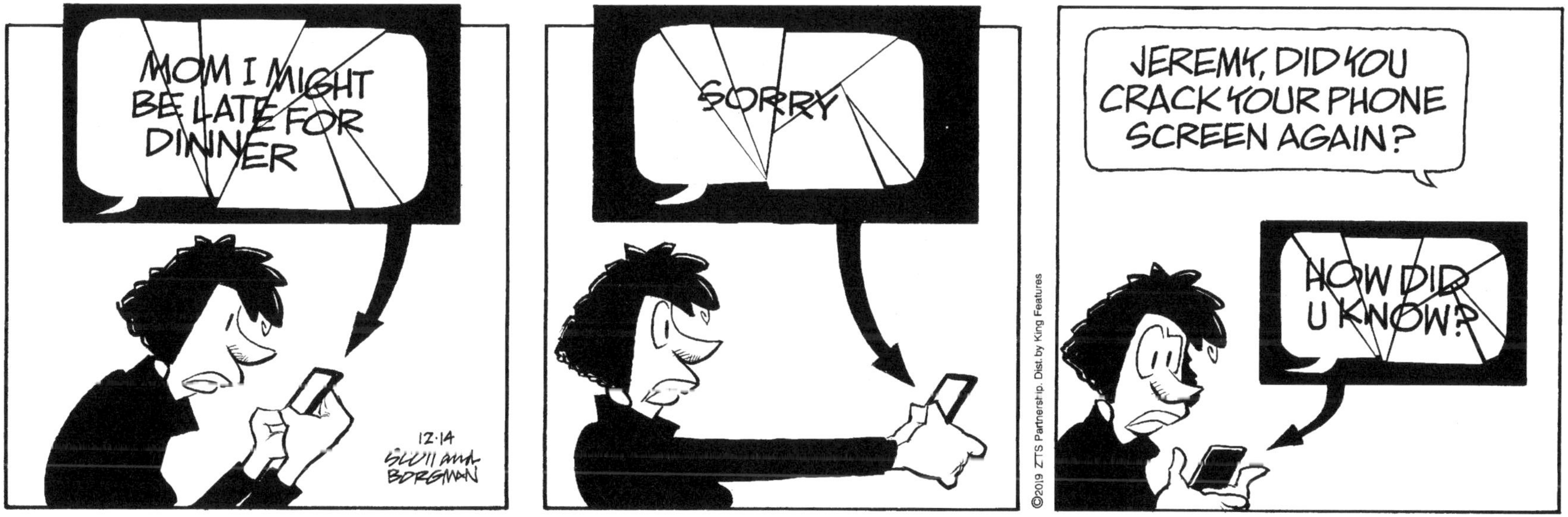
MOM I MIGHT BE LATE FOR DINNER
12·14 SCOTT AND BORGMAN
SORRY
JEREMY, DID YOU CRACK YOUR PHONE SCREEN AGAIN?
HOW DID U KNOW?
©2019 ZITS Partnership. Dist. by King Features

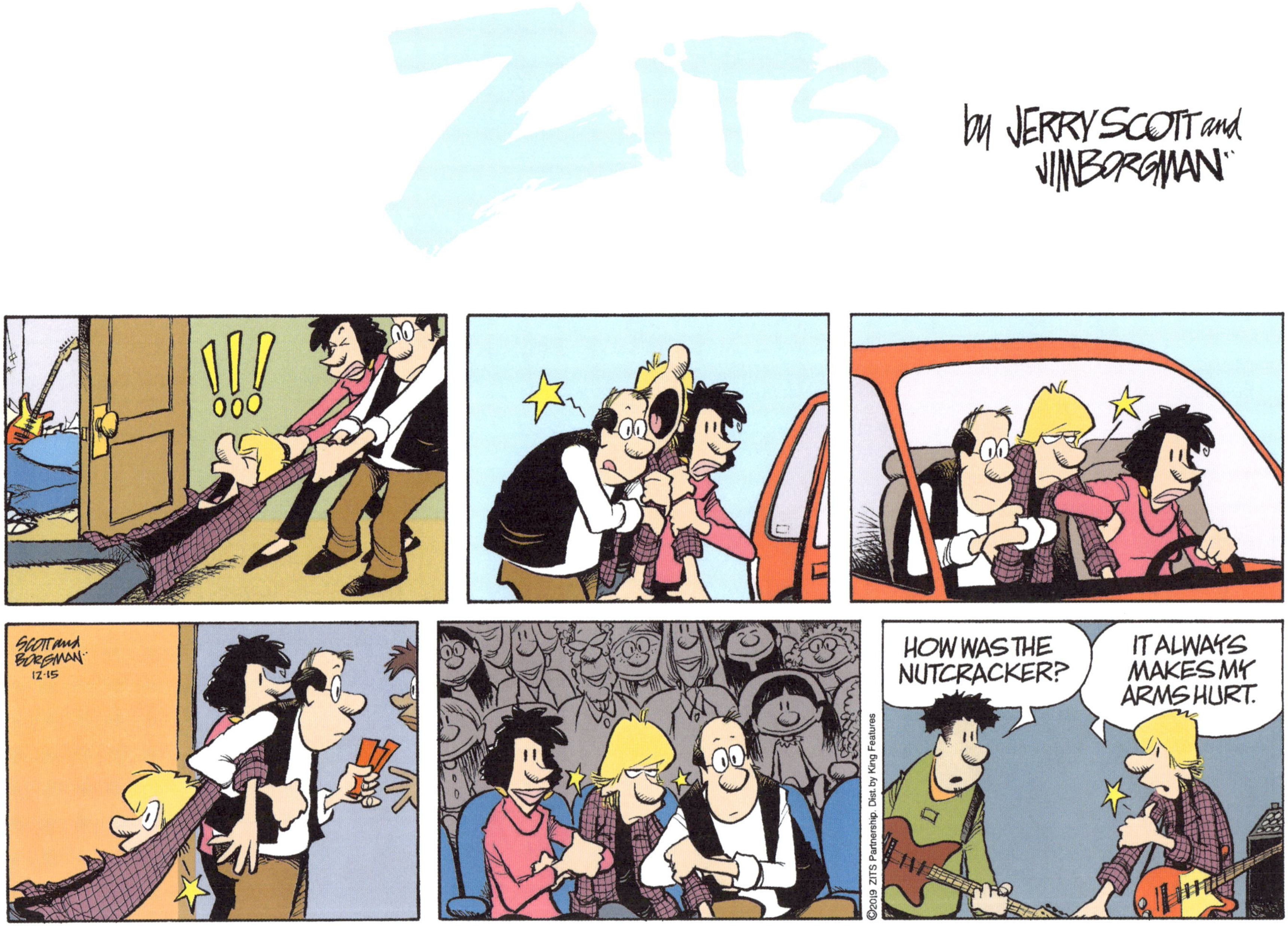
ZITS
by JERRY SCOTT and JIM BORGMAN
!!!
SCOTT and BORGMAN 12-15
©2019 ZITS Partnership. Dist. by King Features
HOW WAS THE NUTCRACKER?
IT ALWAYS MAKES MY ARMS HURT.

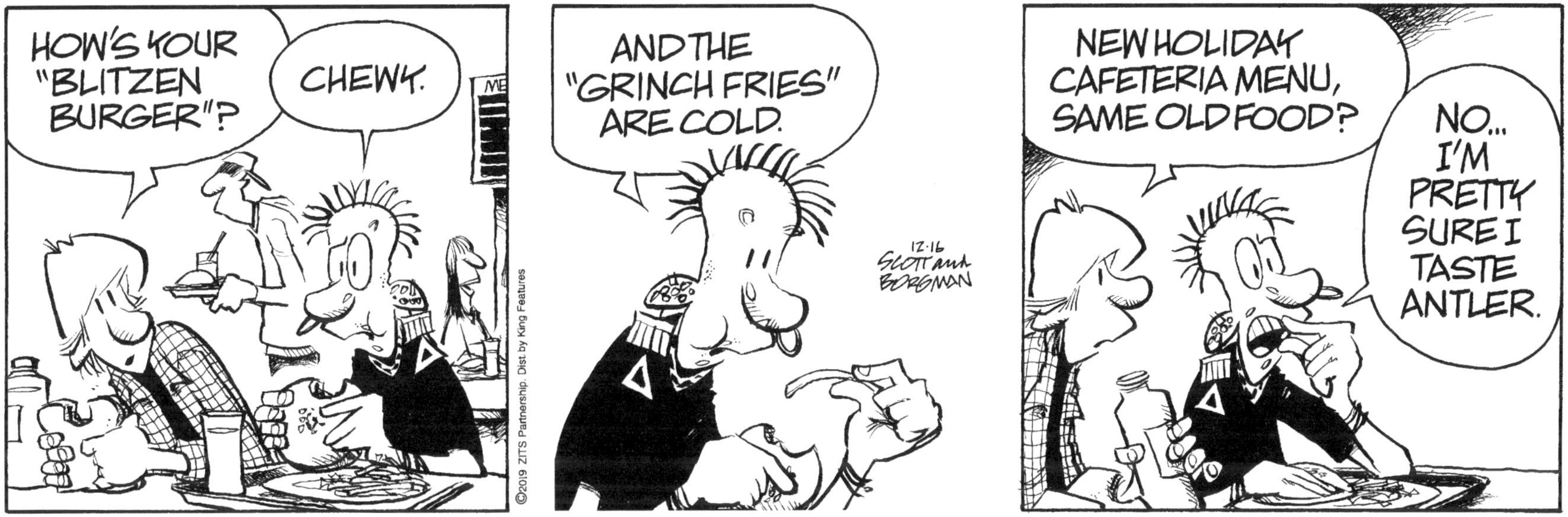
HOW'S YOUR "BLITZEN BURGER"?
CHEWY.
©2019 ZITS Partnership. Dist. by King Features
AND THE "GRINCH FRIES" ARE COLD.
12·16 SCOTT and BORGMAN
NEW HOLIDAY CAFETERIA MENU, SAME OLD FOOD?
NO... I'M PRETTY SURE I TASTE ANTLER.

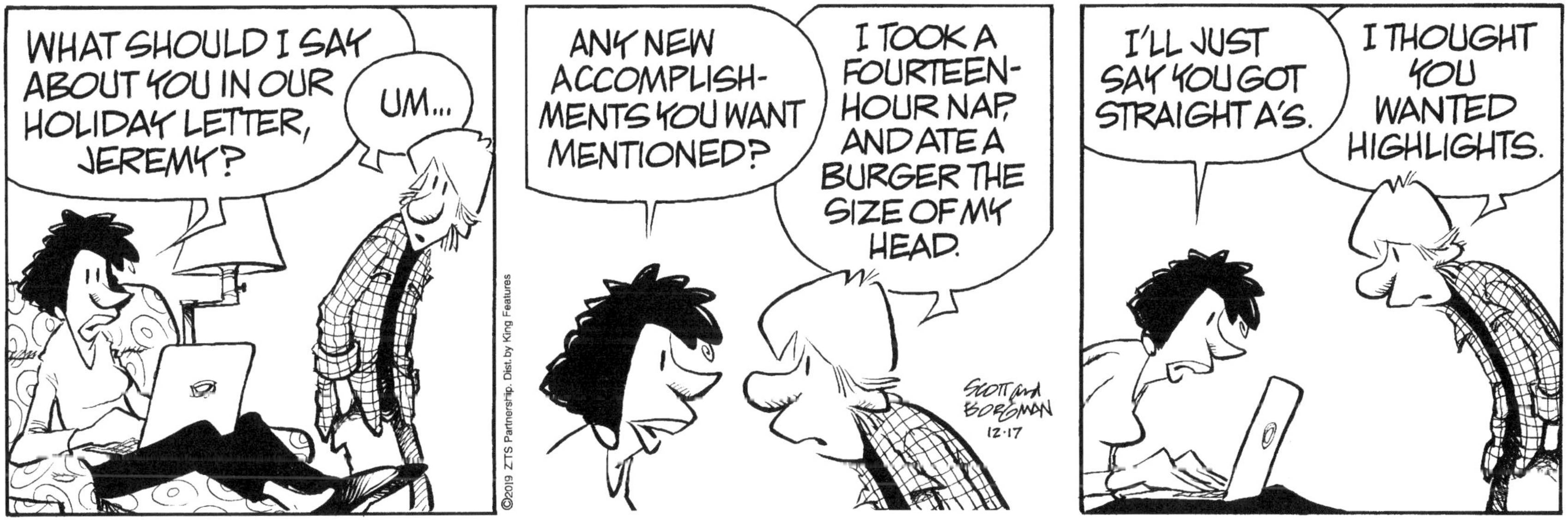
WHAT SHOULD I SAY ABOUT YOU IN OUR HOLIDAY LETTER, JEREMY?
UM...
©2019 ZITS Partnership. Dist. by King Features
ANY NEW ACCOMPLISH-MENTS YOU WANT MENTIONED?
I TOOK A FOURTEEN-HOUR NAP, AND ATE A BURGER THE SIZE OF MY HEAD.
SCOTT and BORGMAN 12·17
I'LL JUST SAY YOU GOT STRAIGHT A'S.
I THOUGHT YOU WANTED HIGHLIGHTS.

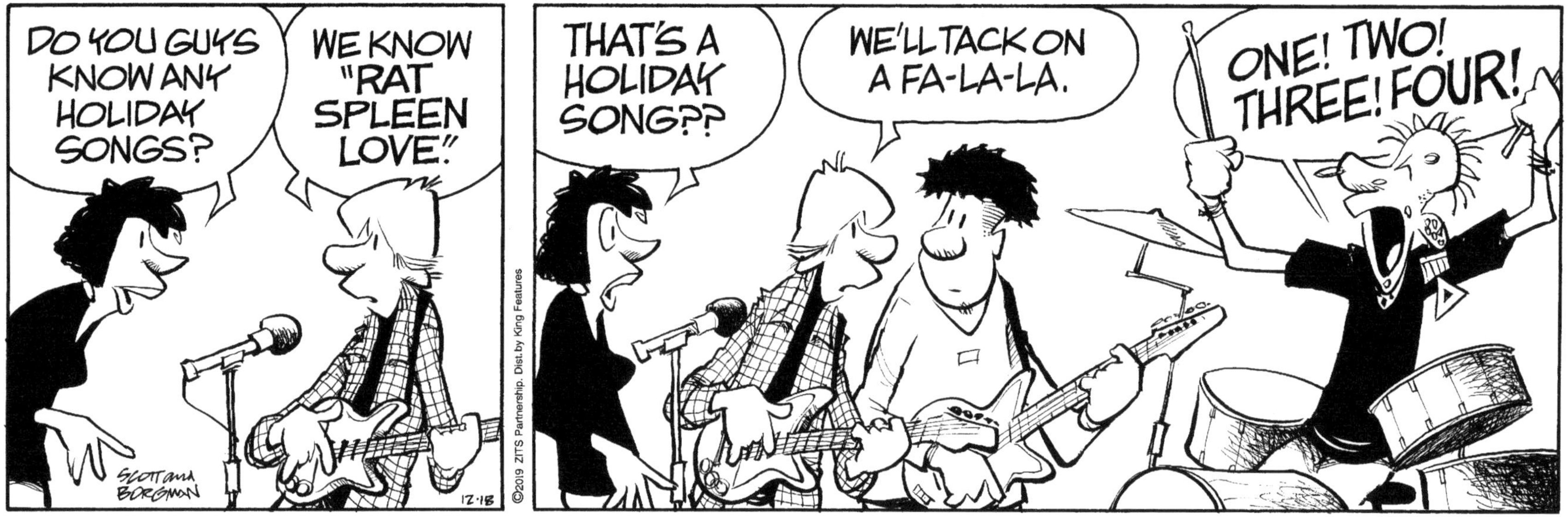
DO YOU GUYS KNOW ANY HOLIDAY SONGS?
WE KNOW "RAT SPLEEN LOVE."
SCOTT AND BORGMAN
12·18
©2019 ZITS Partnership. Dist. by King Features
THAT'S A HOLIDAY SONG??
WE'LL TACK ON A FA-LA-LA.
ONE! TWO! THREE! FOUR!

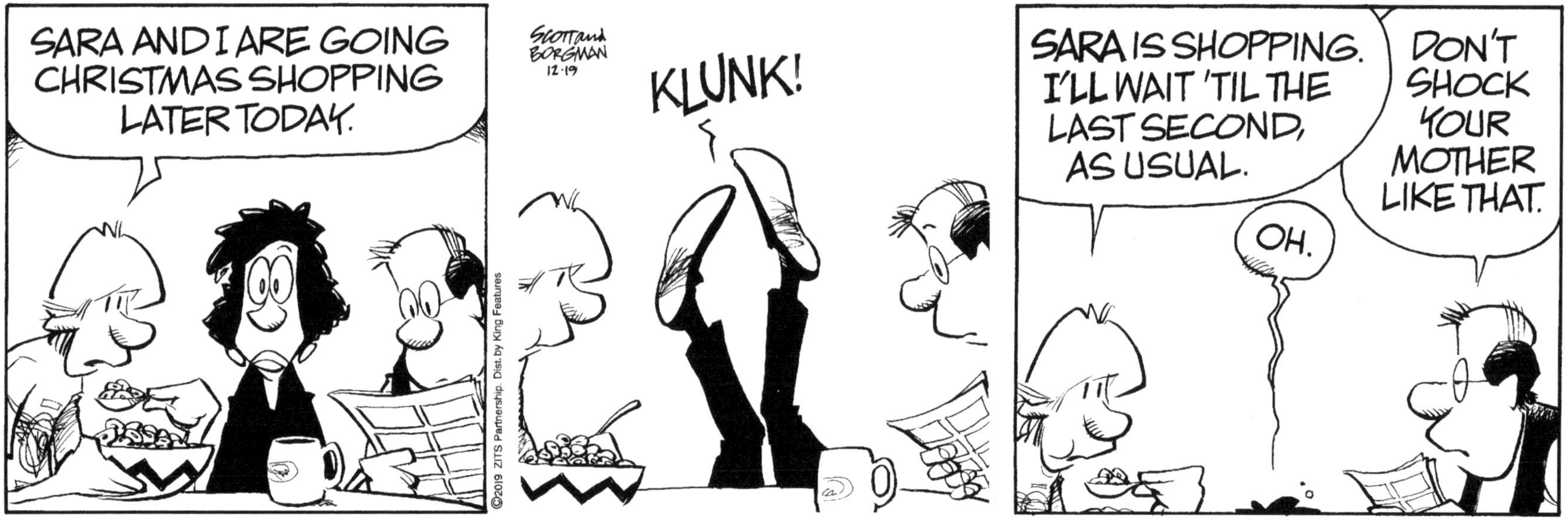
SARA AND I ARE GOING CHRISTMAS SHOPPING LATER TODAY.
©2019 ZITS Partnership. Dist. by King Features
SCOTT AND BORGMAN
12·19
KLUNK!
SARA IS SHOPPING. I'LL WAIT 'TIL THE LAST SECOND, AS USUAL.
OH.
DON'T SHOCK YOUR MOTHER LIKE THAT.

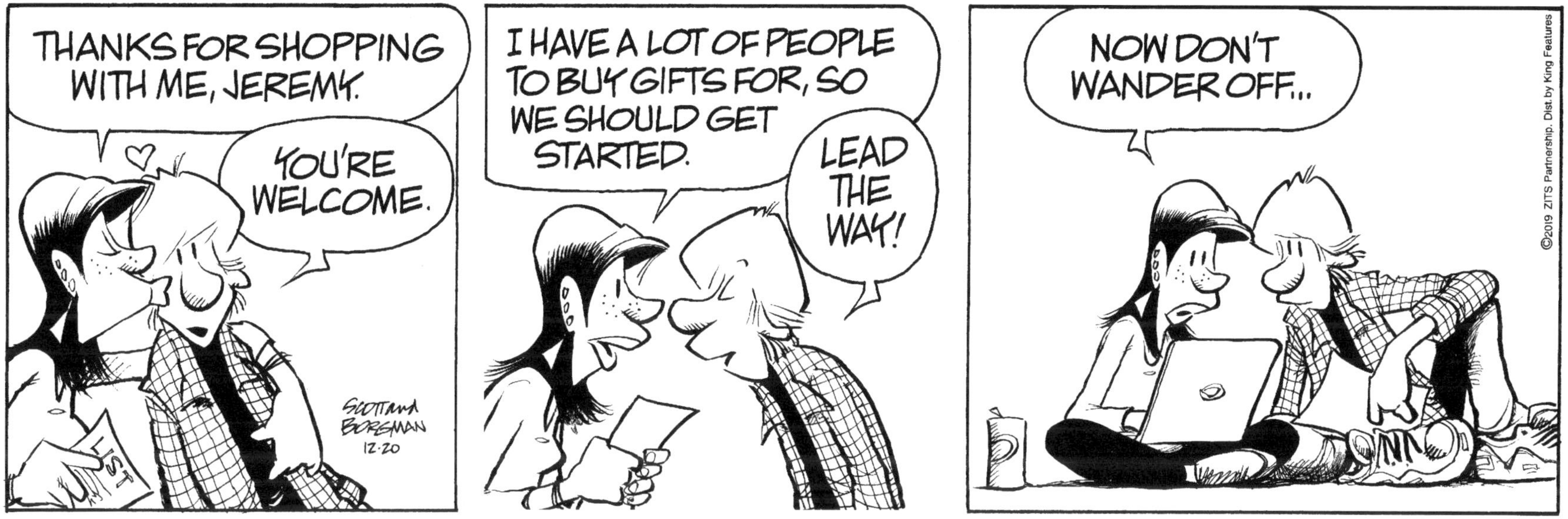
THANKS FOR SHOPPING WITH ME, JEREMY.
YOU'RE WELCOME.
SCOTT AND BORGMAN 12·20
I HAVE A LOT OF PEOPLE TO BUY GIFTS FOR, SO WE SHOULD GET STARTED.
LEAD THE WAY!
NOW DON'T WANDER OFF...
©2019 ZITS Partnership. Dist. by King Features

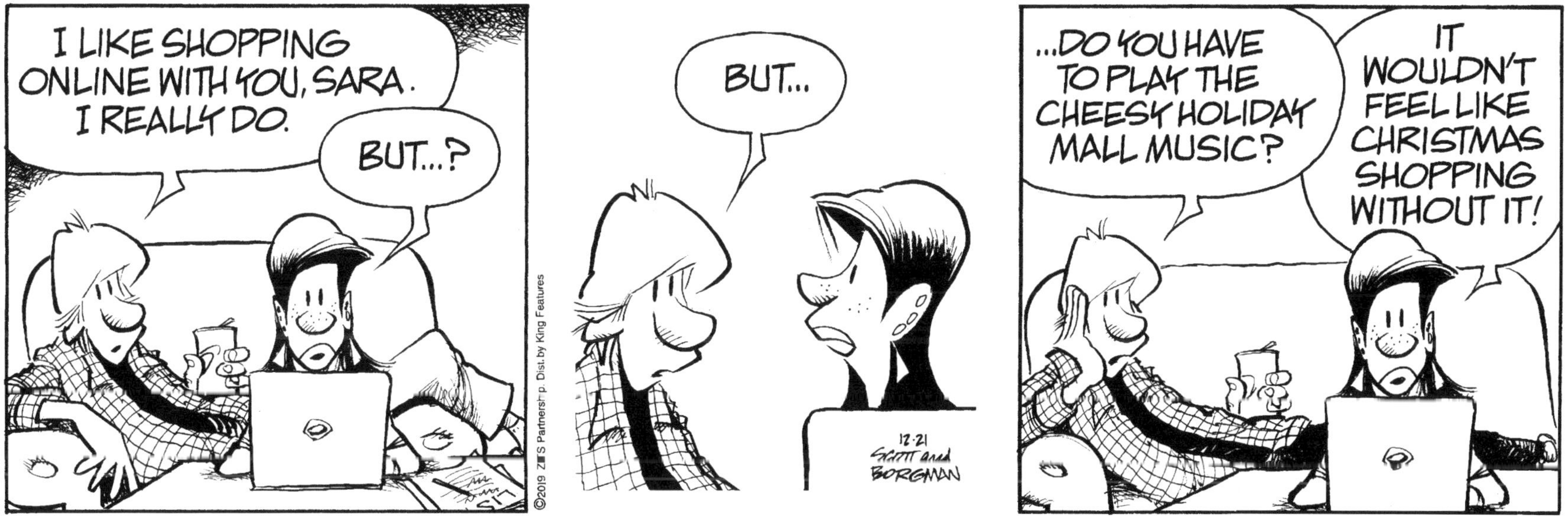
I LIKE SHOPPING ONLINE WITH YOU, SARA. I REALLY DO.
BUT...?
BUT...
12·21 SCOTT AND BORGMAN
...DO YOU HAVE TO PLAY THE CHEESY HOLIDAY MALL MUSIC?
IT WOULDN'T FEEL LIKE CHRISTMAS SHOPPING WITHOUT IT!

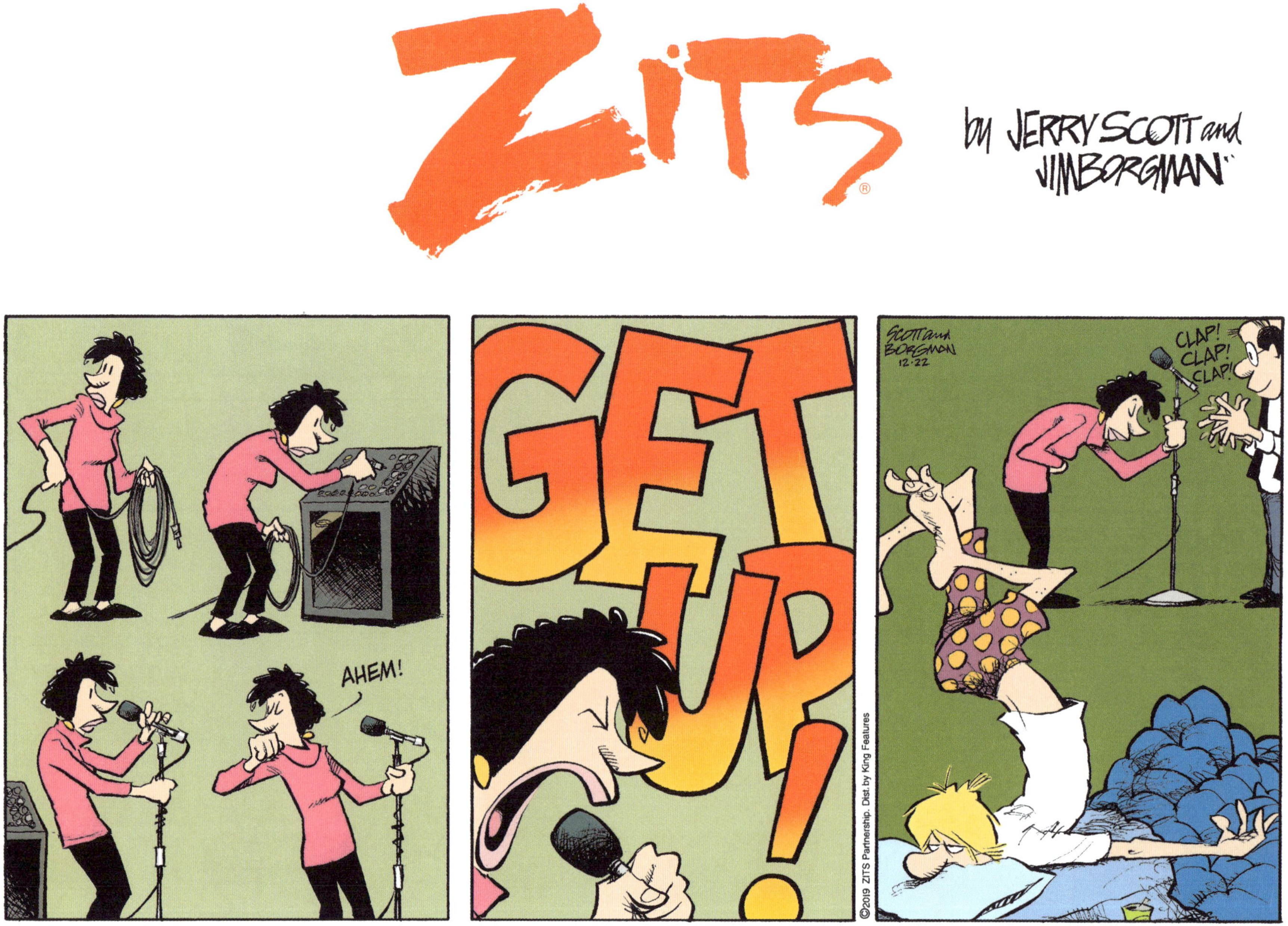
ZITS
by JERRY SCOTT and JIM BORGMAN
SCOTT and BORGMAN 12-22
AHEM!
GET UP!
©2019 ZITS Partnership. Dist. by King Features
CLAP! CLAP! CLAP!

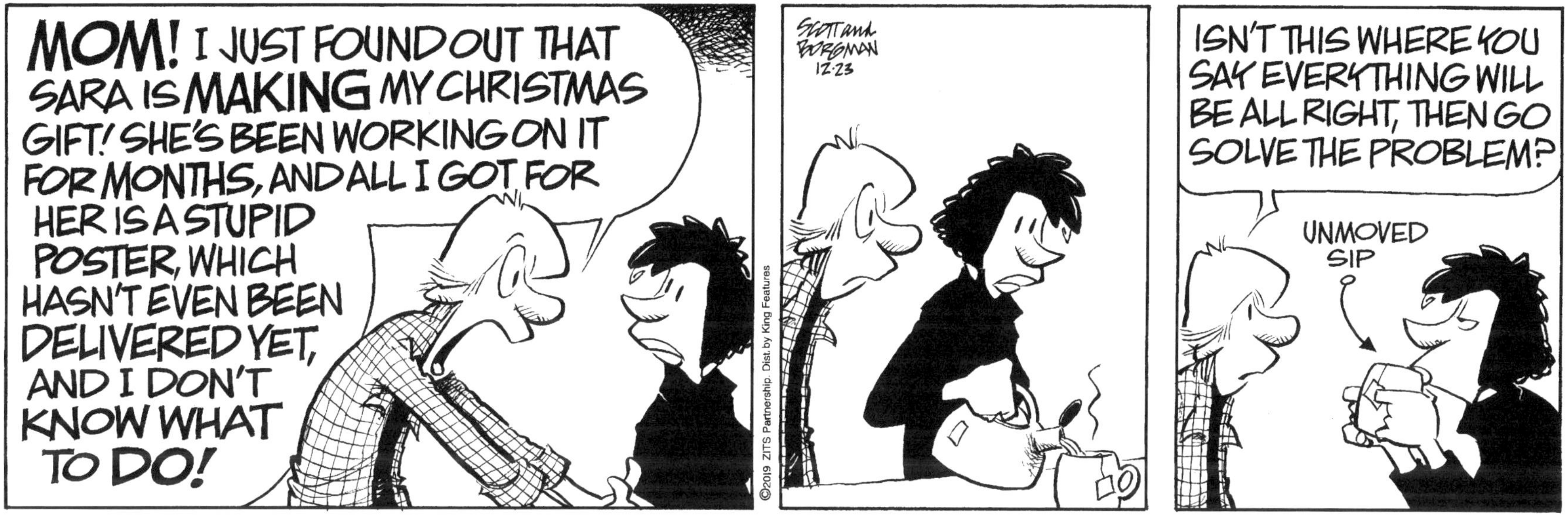
MOM! I JUST FOUND OUT THAT SARA IS MAKING MY CHRISTMAS GIFT! SHE'S BEEN WORKING ON IT FOR MONTHS, AND ALL I GOT FOR HER IS A STUPID POSTER, WHICH HASN'T EVEN BEEN DELIVERED YET, AND I DON'T KNOW WHAT TO DO!
©2019 ZITS Partnership. Dist. by King Features
SCOTT and BORGMAN 12·23
ISN'T THIS WHERE YOU SAY EVERYTHING WILL BE ALL RIGHT, THEN GO SOLVE THE PROBLEM?
UNMOVED SIP

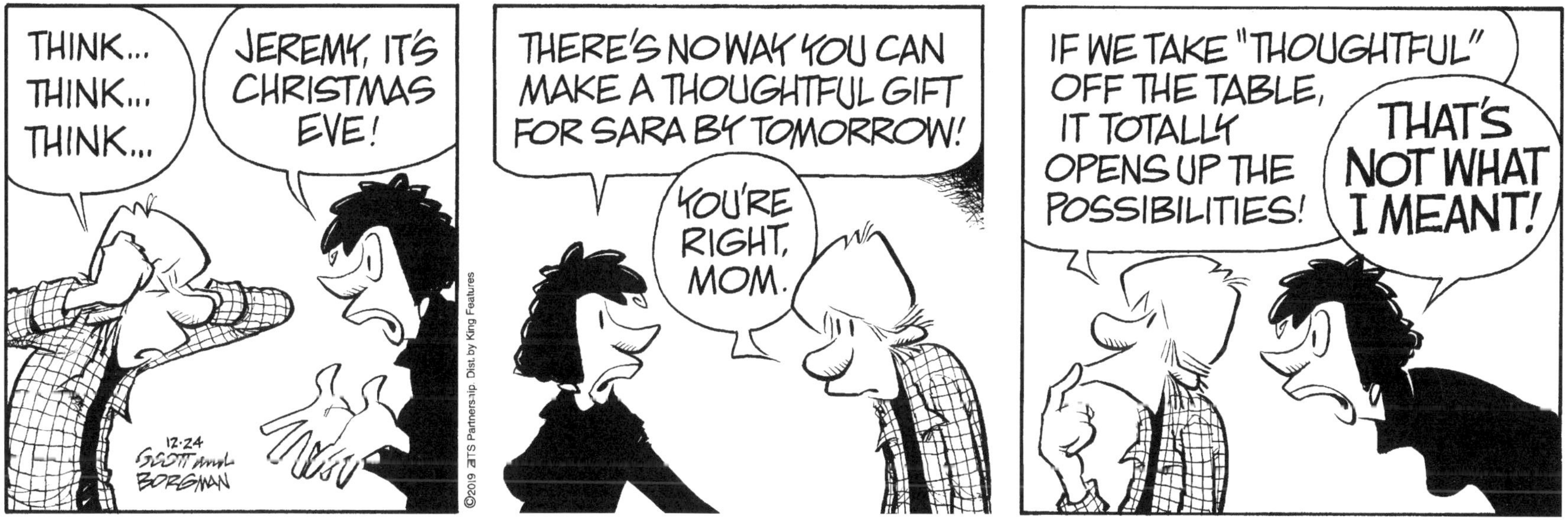
THINK... THINK... THINK...
JEREMY, IT'S CHRISTMAS EVE!
12·24 SCOTT and BORGMAN
©2019 ZITS Partnership. Dist. by King Features
THERE'S NO WAY YOU CAN MAKE A THOUGHTFUL GIFT FOR SARA BY TOMORROW!
YOU'RE RIGHT, MOM.
IF WE TAKE "THOUGHTFUL" OFF THE TABLE, IT TOTALLY OPENS UP THE POSSIBILITIES!
THAT'S NOT WHAT I MEANT!

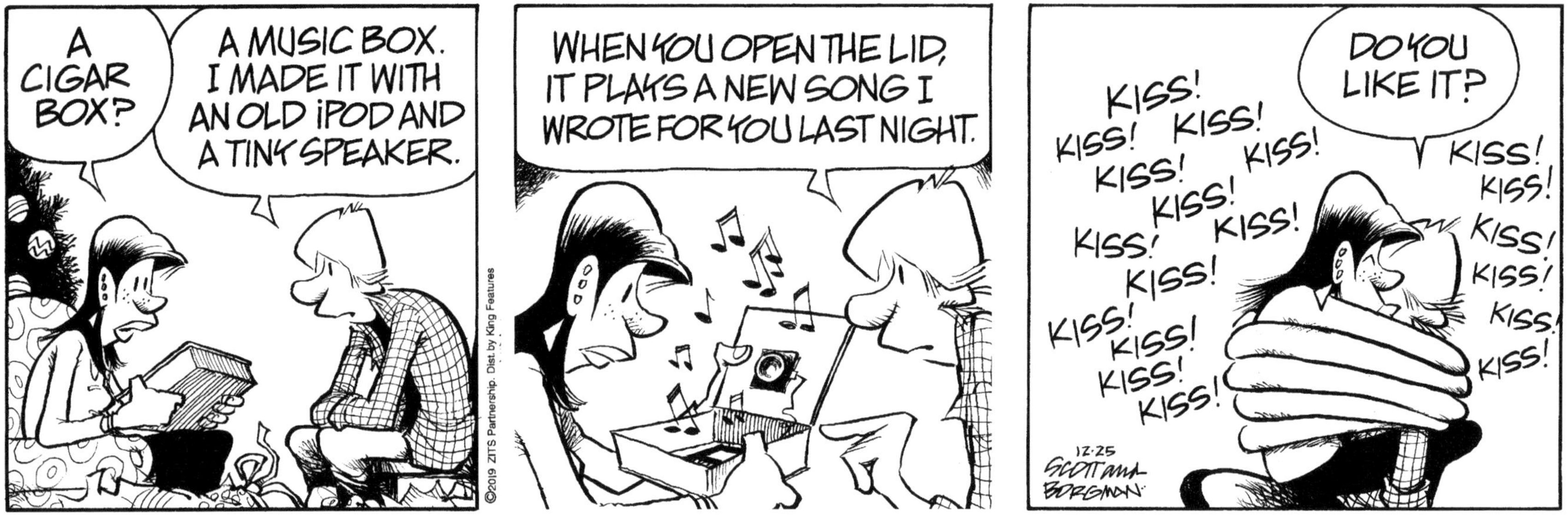

A CIGAR BOX?
A MUSIC BOX. I MADE IT WITH AN OLD iPOD AND A TINY SPEAKER.
©2019 ZITS Partnership. Dist. by King Features
WHEN YOU OPEN THE LID, IT PLAYS A NEW SONG I WROTE FOR YOU LAST NIGHT.
KISS! KISS! KISS! KISS! KISS! KISS! KISS! KISS! KISS! KISS! KISS! KISS! KISS!
DO YOU LIKE IT?
KISS! KISS! KISS! KISS! KISS! KISS! KISS!
12·25 SCOTT AND BORGMAN

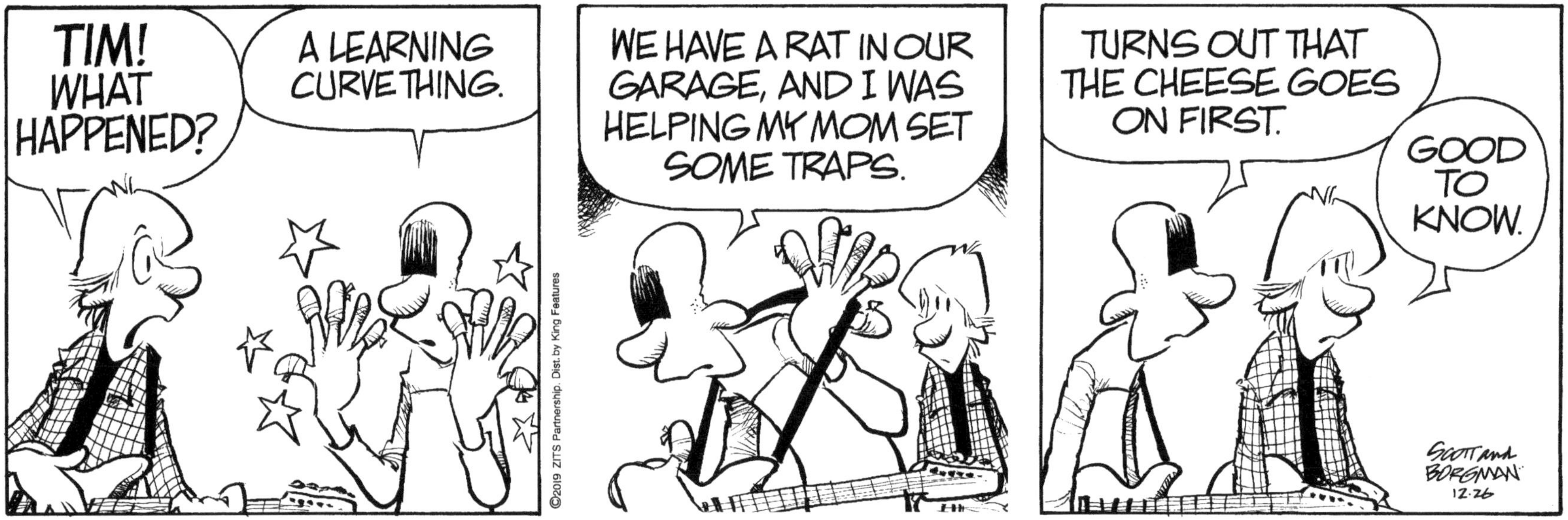

TIM! WHAT HAPPENED?
A LEARNING CURVE THING.
©2019 ZITS Partnership. Dist. by King Features
WE HAVE A RAT IN OUR GARAGE, AND I WAS HELPING MY MOM SET SOME TRAPS.
TURNS OUT THAT THE CHEESE GOES ON FIRST.
GOOD TO KNOW.
SCOTT AND BORGMAN 12·26

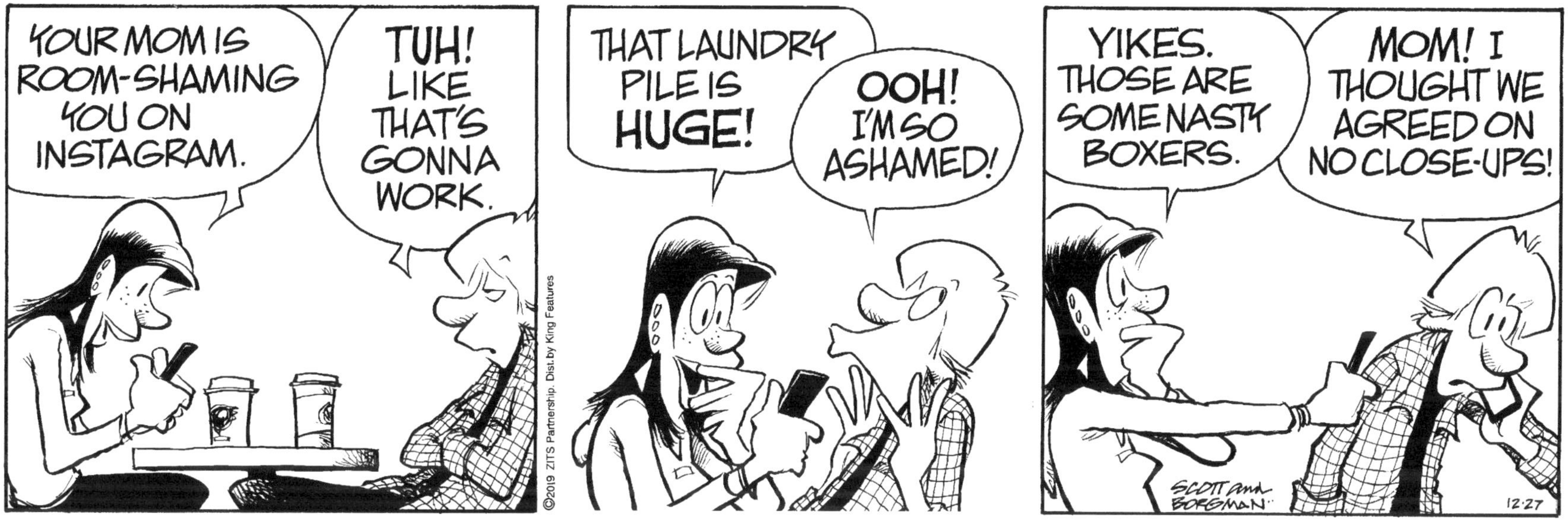
YOUR MOM IS ROOM-SHAMING YOU ON INSTAGRAM.
TUH! LIKE THAT'S GONNA WORK.
©2019 ZITS Partnership. Dist. by King Features
THAT LAUNDRY PILE IS HUGE!
OOH! I'M SO ASHAMED!
YIKES. THOSE ARE SOME NASTY BOXERS.
MOM! I THOUGHT WE AGREED ON NO CLOSE-UPS!
SCOTT AND BORGMAN
12·27

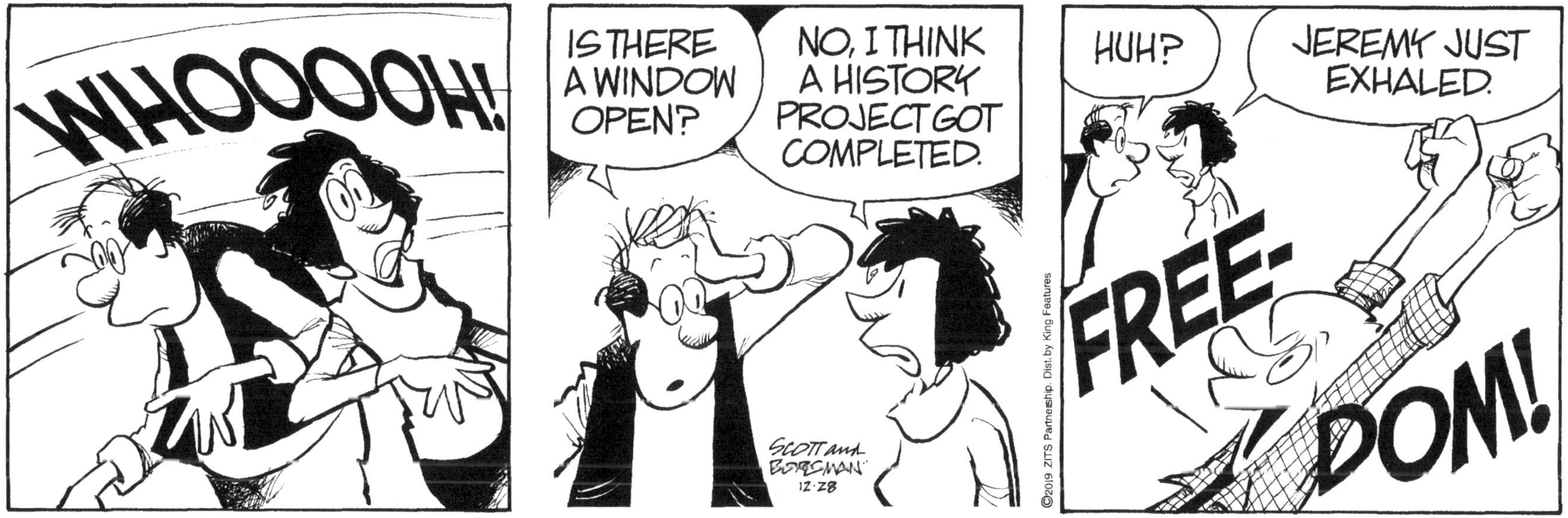
WHOOOOOH!
IS THERE A WINDOW OPEN?
NO, I THINK A HISTORY PROJECT GOT COMPLETED.
SCOTT AND BORGMAN
12·28
©2019 ZITS Partnership. Dist. by King Features
HUH?
JEREMY JUST EXHALED.
FREE-
DOM!

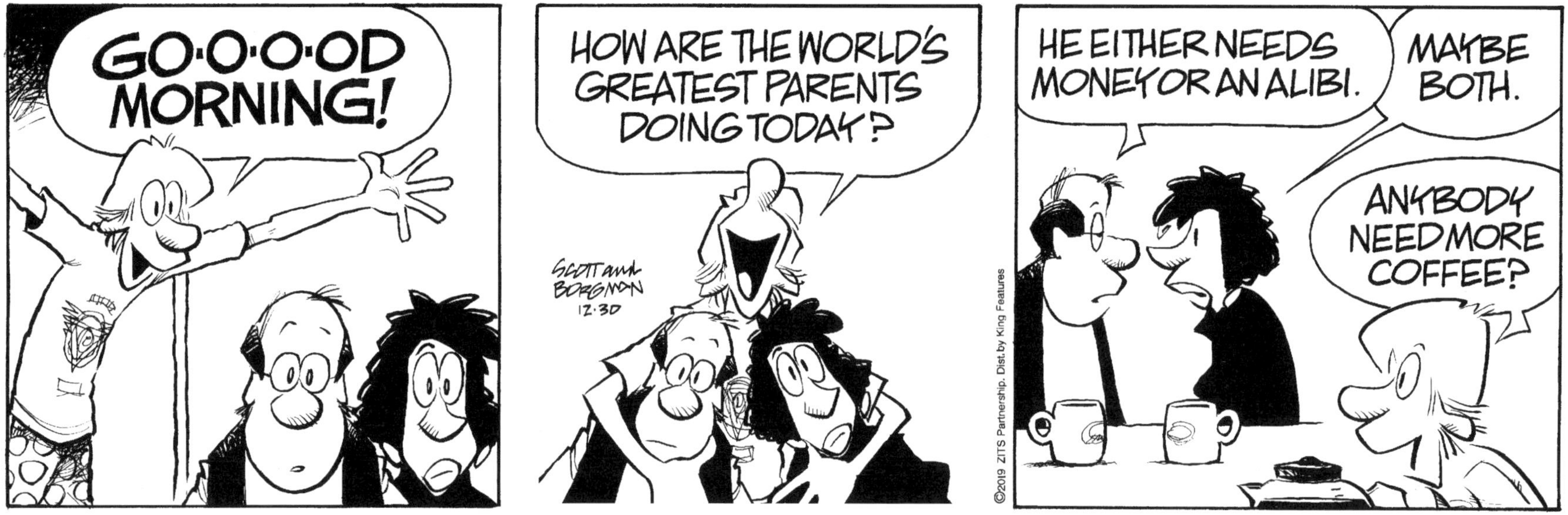
GO·O·O·OD MORNING!
HOW ARE THE WORLD'S GREATEST PARENTS DOING TODAY?
SCOTT AND BORGMAN 12·30
HE EITHER NEEDS MONEY OR AN ALIBI.
MAYBE BOTH.
ANYBODY NEED MORE COFFEE?
©2019 ZITS Partnership. Dist. by King Features

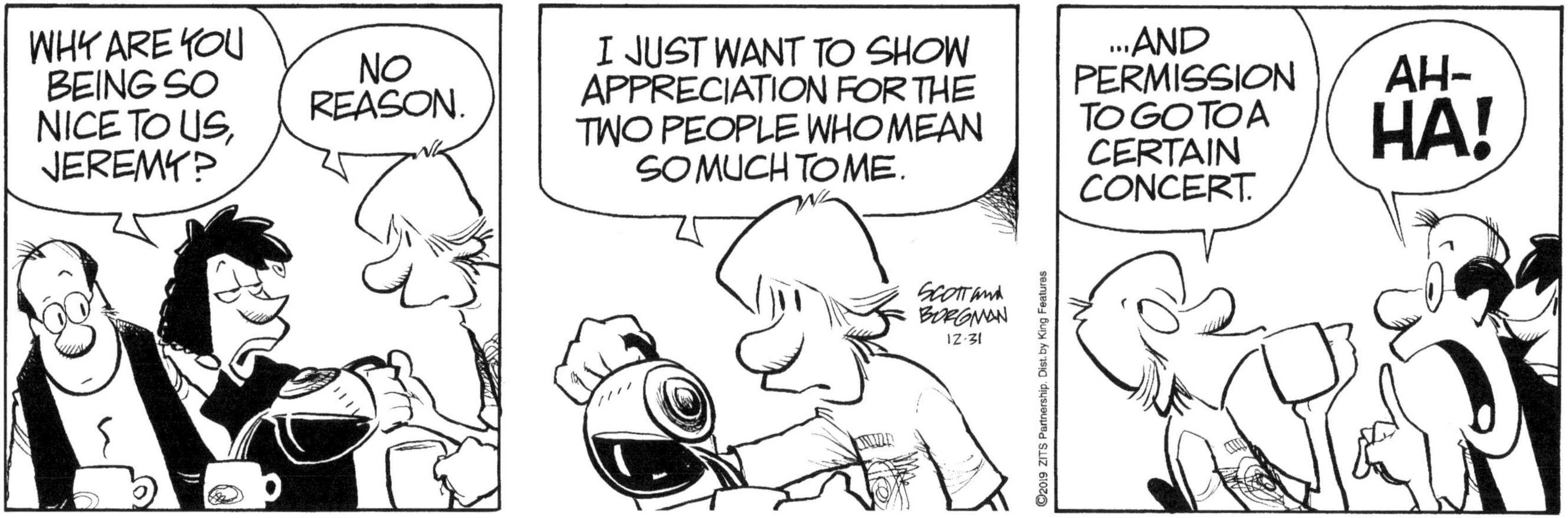
WHY ARE YOU BEING SO NICE TO US, JEREMY?
NO REASON.
I JUST WANT TO SHOW APPRECIATION FOR THE TWO PEOPLE WHO MEAN SO MUCH TO ME.
SCOTT AND BORGMAN 12·31
©2019 ZITS Partnership. Dist. by King Features
...AND PERMISSION TO GO TO A CERTAIN CONCERT.
AH-HA!

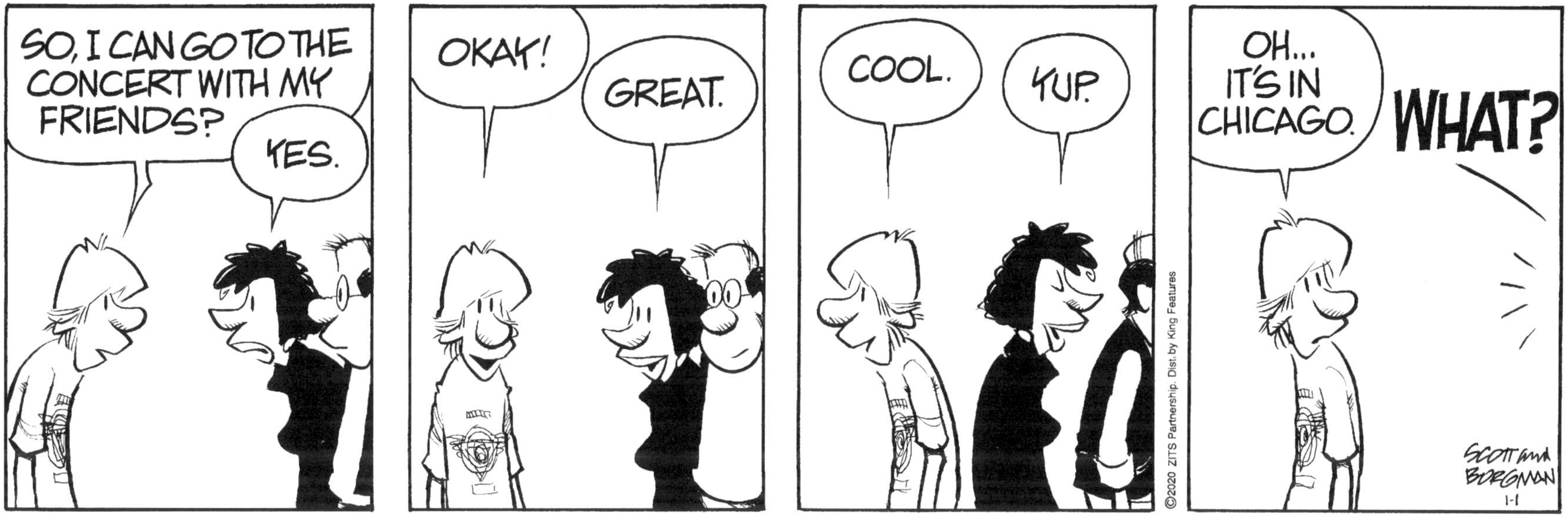
SO, I CAN GO TO THE CONCERT WITH MY FRIENDS?
YES.
OKAY!
GREAT.
COOL.
YUP.
OH... IT'S IN CHICAGO.
WHAT?
©2020 ZITS Partnership. Dist. by King Features
SCOTT and BORGMAN 1-1

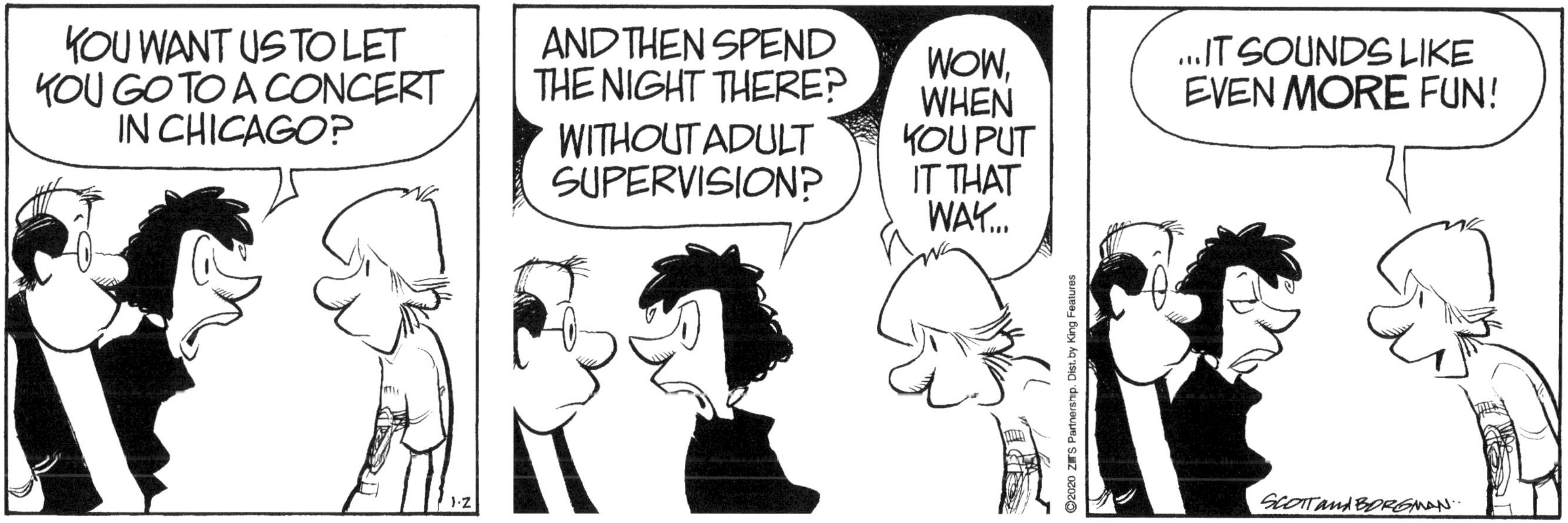
YOU WANT US TO LET YOU GO TO A CONCERT IN CHICAGO?
1-2
AND THEN SPEND THE NIGHT THERE?
WITHOUT ADULT SUPERVISION?
WOW, WHEN YOU PUT IT THAT WAY...
©2020 ZITS Partnership. Dist. by King Features
...IT SOUNDS LIKE EVEN MORE FUN!
SCOTT and BORGMAN

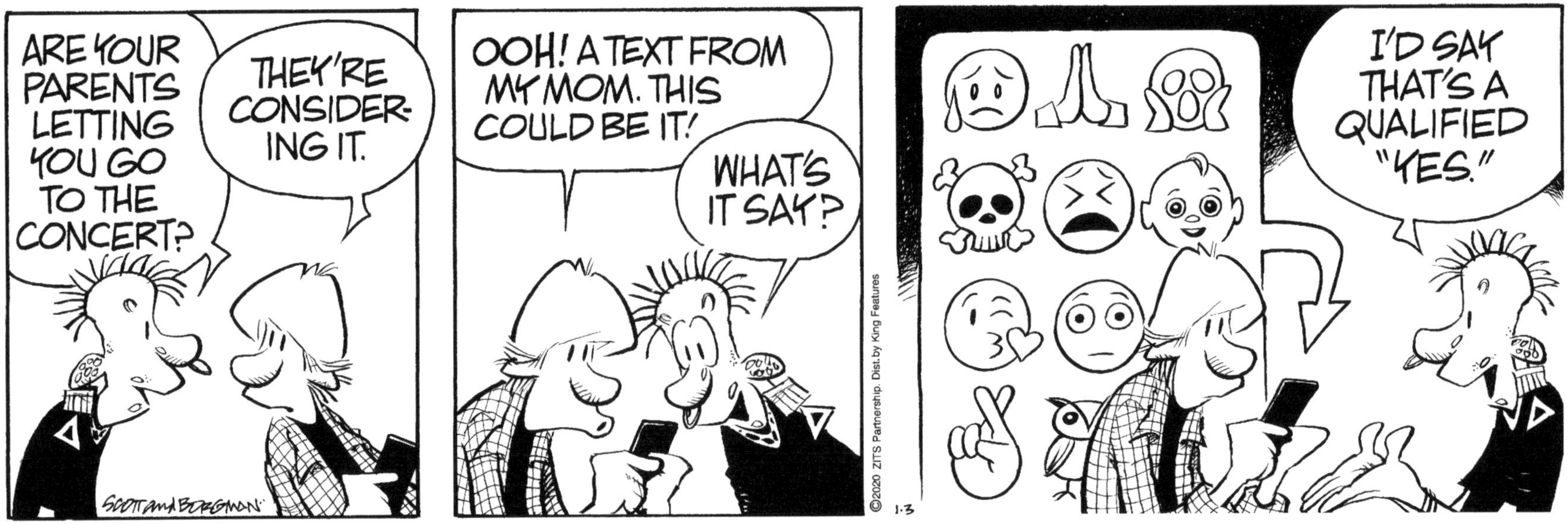
ARE YOUR PARENTS LETTING YOU GO TO THE CONCERT?
THEY'RE CONSIDER-ING IT.
SCOTT and BORGMAN
OOH! A TEXT FROM MY MOM. THIS COULD BE IT!
WHAT'S IT SAY?
©2020 ZITS Partnership. Dist. by King Features
1·3
I'D SAY THAT'S A QUALIFIED "YES."

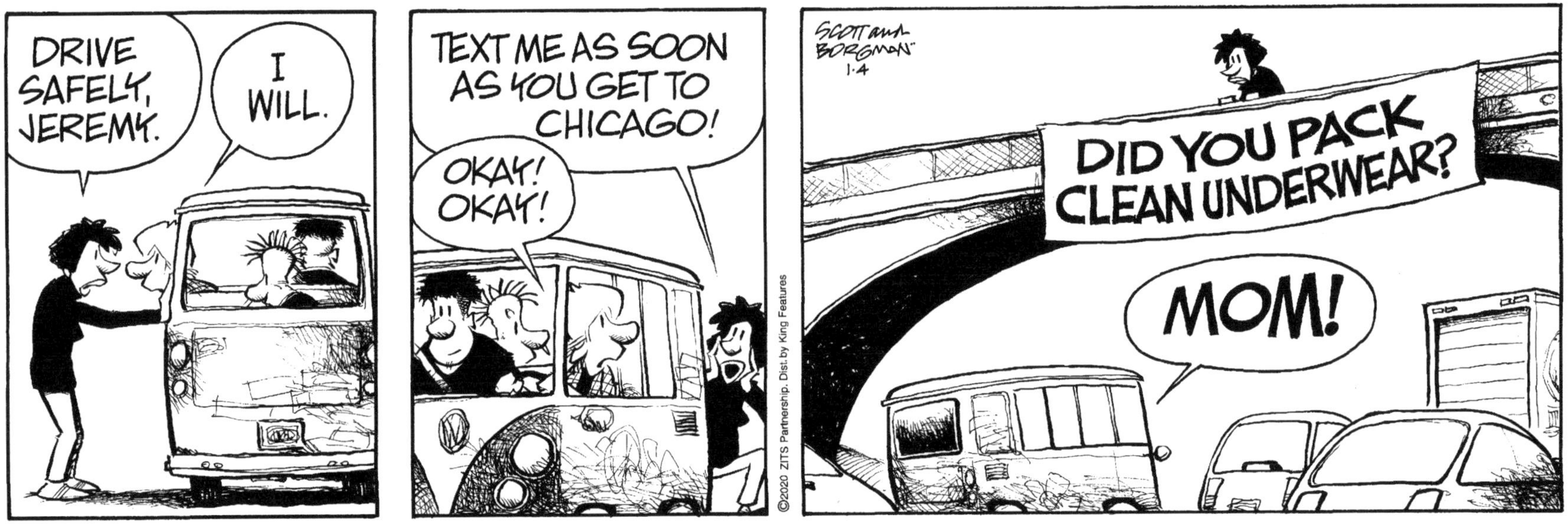
DRIVE SAFELY, JEREMY.
I WILL.
TEXT ME AS SOON AS YOU GET TO CHICAGO!
OKAY! OKAY!
©2020 ZITS Partnership. Dist. by King Features
SCOTT and BORGMAN
1·4
DID YOU PACK CLEAN UNDERWEAR?
MOM!

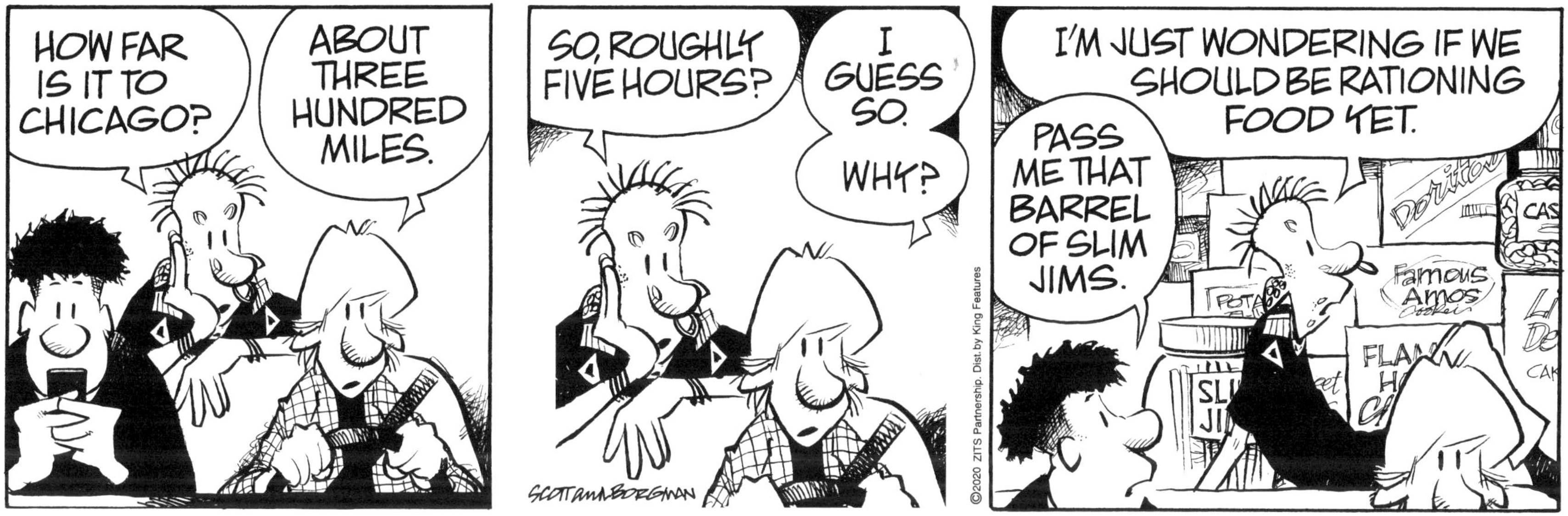
HOW FAR IS IT TO CHICAGO?
ABOUT THREE HUNDRED MILES.
SO, ROUGHLY FIVE HOURS?
I GUESS SO.
WHY?
I'M JUST WONDERING IF WE SHOULD BE RATIONING FOOD YET.
PASS ME THAT BARREL OF SLIM JIMS.
Famous Amos
©2020 ZITS Partnership. Dist.by King Features

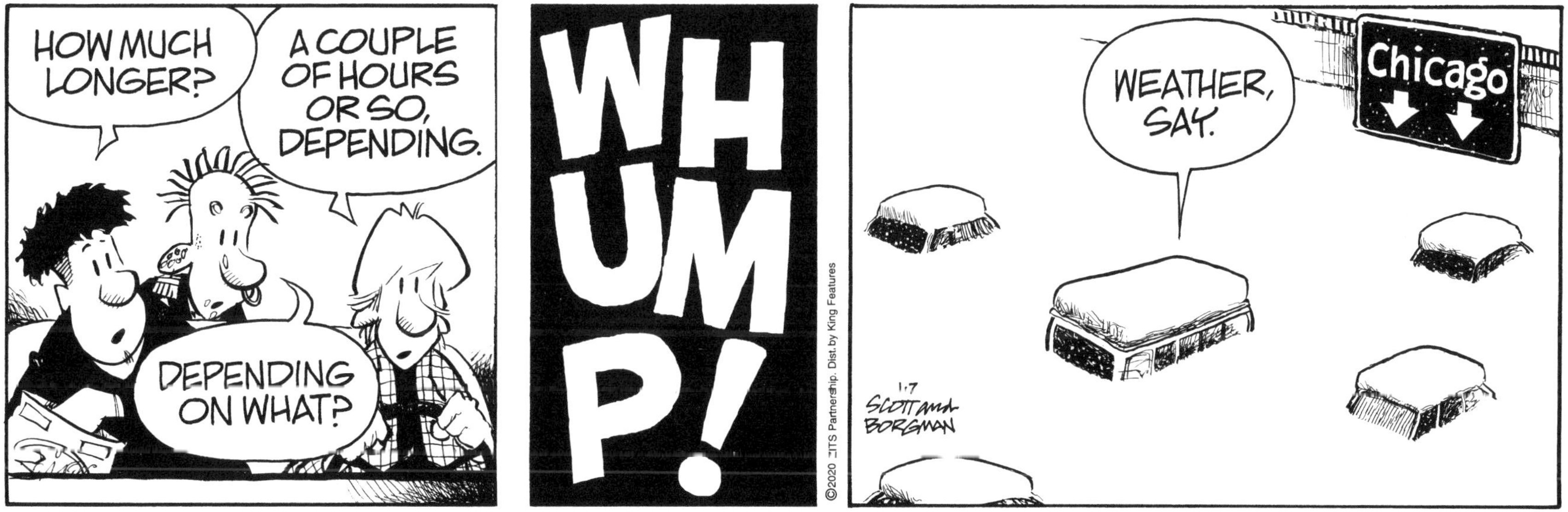
HOW MUCH LONGER?
A COUPLE OF HOURS OR SO, DEPENDING.
DEPENDING ON WHAT?
WHUMP!
WEATHER, SAY.
Chicago
©2020 ZITS Partnership. Dist.by King Features

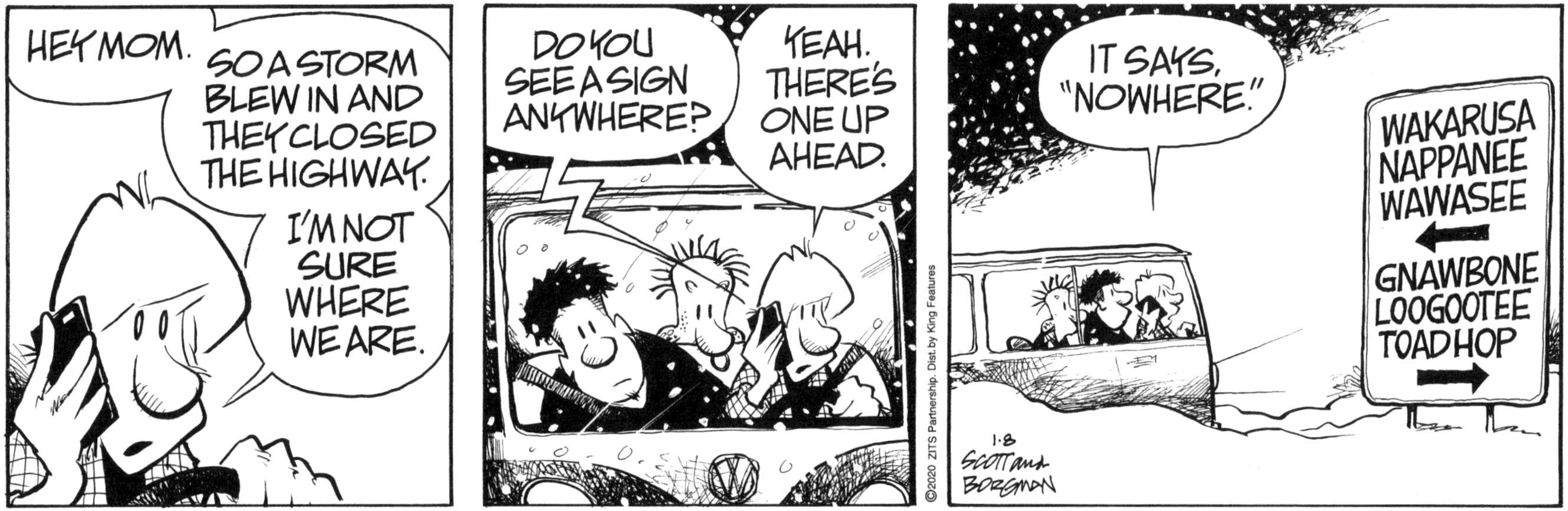
HEY MOM.
SO A STORM BLEW IN AND THEY CLOSED THE HIGHWAY.
I'M NOT SURE WHERE WE ARE.
DO YOU SEE A SIGN ANYWHERE?
YEAH. THERE'S ONE UP AHEAD.
©2020 ZITS Partnership. Dist. by King Features
IT SAYS, "NOWHERE."
WAKARUSA
NAPPANEE
WAWASEE
GNAWBONE
LOOGOOTEE
TOADHOP
1·8
SCOTT and BORGMAN

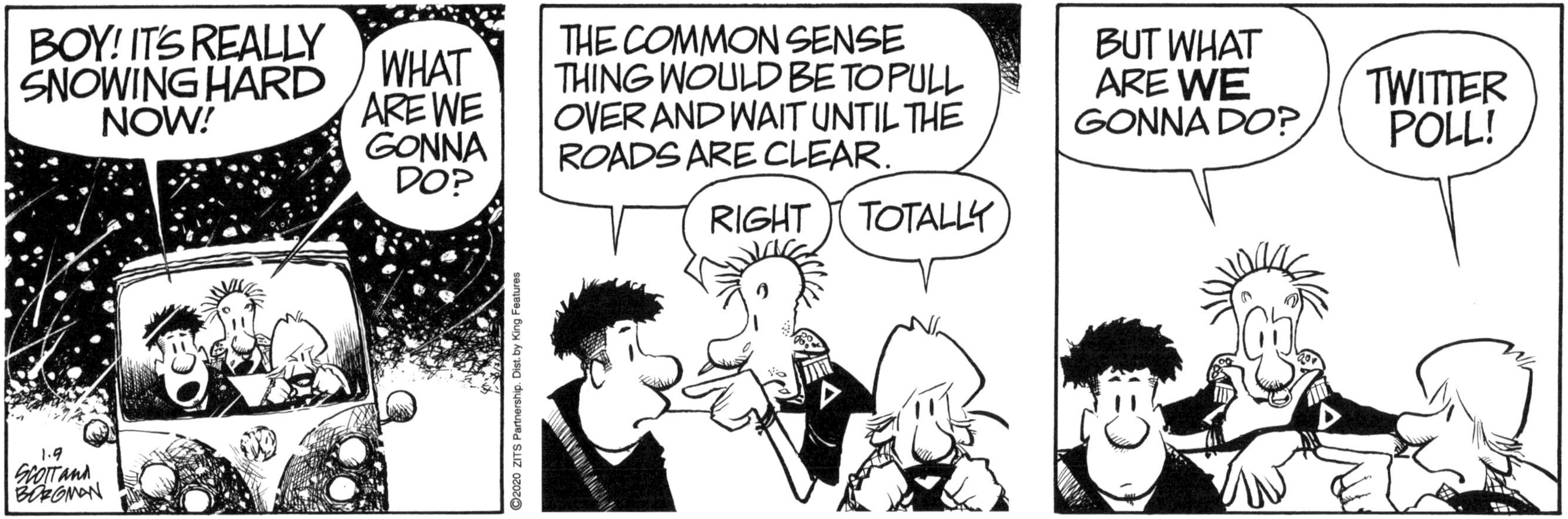
BOY! IT'S REALLY SNOWING HARD NOW!
WHAT ARE WE GONNA DO?
1·9
SCOTT and BORGMAN
©2020 ZITS Partnership. Dist. by King Features
THE COMMON SENSE THING WOULD BE TO PULL OVER AND WAIT UNTIL THE ROADS ARE CLEAR.
RIGHT
TOTALLY
BUT WHAT ARE **WE** GONNA DO?
TWITTER POLL!

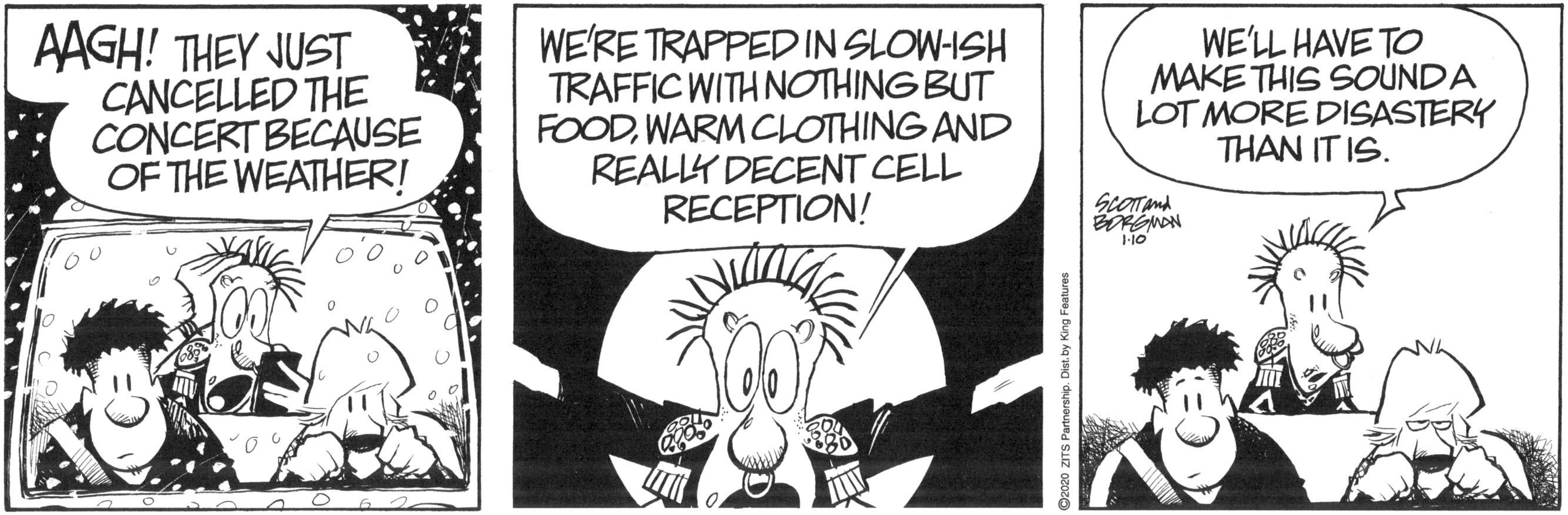
AAGH! THEY JUST CANCELLED THE CONCERT BECAUSE OF THE WEATHER!
WE'RE TRAPPED IN SLOW-ISH TRAFFIC WITH NOTHING BUT FOOD, WARM CLOTHING AND REALLY DECENT CELL RECEPTION!
WE'LL HAVE TO MAKE THIS SOUND A LOT MORE DISASTERY THAN IT IS.
SCOTT and BORGMAN 1·10
©2020 ZITS Partnership. Dist. by King Features

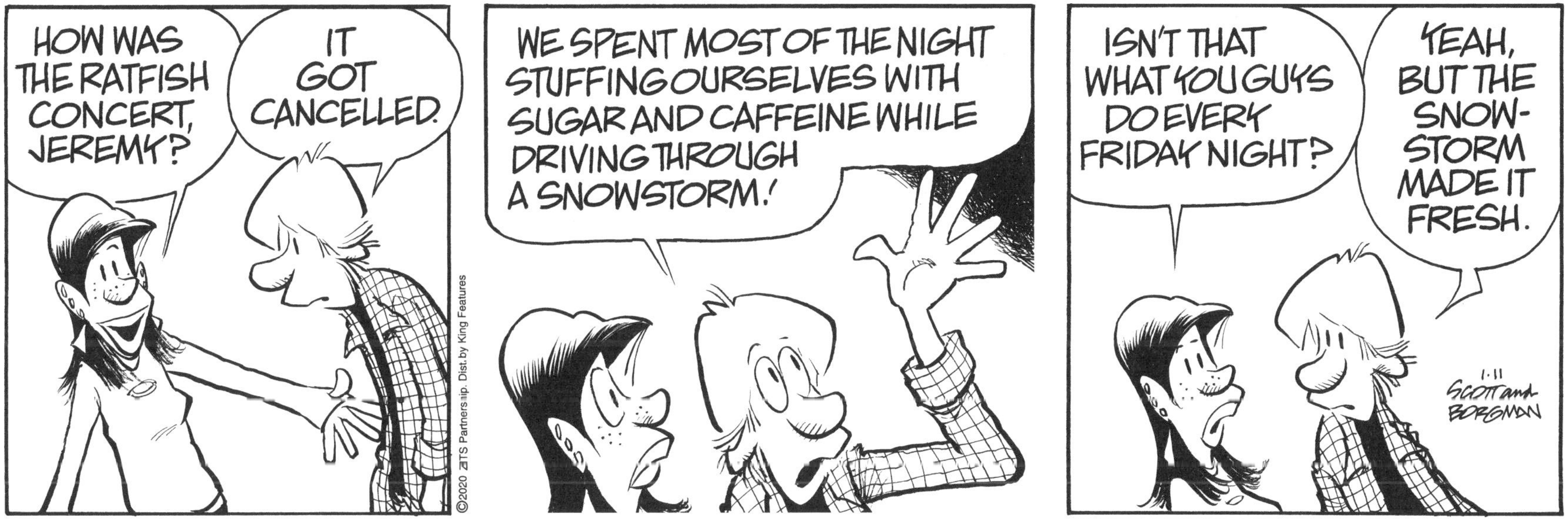
HOW WAS THE RATFISH CONCERT, JEREMY?
IT GOT CANCELLED.
©2020 ZITS Partnership. Dist. by King Features
WE SPENT MOST OF THE NIGHT STUFFING OURSELVES WITH SUGAR AND CAFFEINE WHILE DRIVING THROUGH A SNOWSTORM!
ISN'T THAT WHAT YOU GUYS DO EVERY FRIDAY NIGHT?
YEAH, BUT THE SNOW-STORM MADE IT FRESH.
1·11 SCOTT and BORGMAN

Zits® is syndicated internationally by King Features Syndicate, Inc.
For information, write King Features Syndicate, Inc., 300 West Fifty-Seventh Street, New York, New York 10019.

Zits®: *Undivided Inattention* copyright © 2021 by Zits Partnership. All rights reserved. Printed in China.
No part of this book may be used or reproduced in any manner whatsoever without
written permission except in the case of reprints in the context of reviews.

Andrews McMeel Publishing
a division of Andrews McMeel Universal
1130 Walnut Street, Kansas City, Missouri 64106
www.andrewsmcmeel.com

21 22 23 24 25 SDB 10 9 8 7 6 5 4 3 2 1

ISBN: 978-1-5248-6069-1

Library of Congress Control Number: 2021934836

Editor: Lucas Wetzel
Designer/Art Director: Holly Swayne
Production Manager: Chuck Harper
Production Editor: Emma Wheatley

ATTENTION: SCHOOLS AND BUSINESSES
Andrews McMeel books are available at quantity discounts with bulk purchase for educational, business, or sales promotional use.
For information, please e-mail the Andrews McMeel Publishing Special Sales Department:
specialsales@amuniversal.com.

zitscomics.com • facebook.com/zitscomics • instagram.com/zitsguys